THE CENTURY HISTORICAL SERIES
William E. Lingelbach, Editor

EUROPE IN THE
TWENTIETH CENTURY

EUROPE *in the* TWENTIETH CENTURY

Walter Phelps Hall, Ph.D.

DODGE PROFESSOR OF HISTORY, EMERITUS
PRINCETON UNIVERSITY

APPLETON-CENTURY-CROFTS, INC.

New York

PREFACE

This book is designed for a one-semester course in recent European history. It is an attempt to strike a happy medium between texts which begin in 1914 with the First World War and those bulkier volumes which treat more extensively the background of this century and its early years.

Unless the student has a fair appreciation of the pride that men of 1900 took in the peace, prosperity, and hope of progress that characterized their age, and of their faith in the permanence of these conditions, he has no yardstick by which to measure the uncertainties of our present time of troubles.

To provide for these needs this book was organized. The first three chapters describe the peacefulness, growing prosperity, and optimism that existed in Europe in the early nineteen-hundreds, and then show how the two interlocking ideologies of nationalism and imperialism brought the world to the brink of war in 1914. These chapters are followed by the second half of the fourth revised edition of *The Course of Europe Since Waterloo*, published in January, 1957, carrying the European story down to the present, with an added paragraph or two to bring it up to date. The continued popular demand for that book, as evinced by four editions, owes much to the lively and dramatic style of presenting historical data of my original collaborator, the late William Stearns Davis of the University of Minnesota.

W. P. H.

v

CONTENTS

vii

CONTENTS

LIST OF MAPS

LIST OF ILLUSTRATIONS

Chapter 1

PEACE, PROGRESS, AND PROSPERITY

THE YEAR IS 1900. Three events mark the new century. In China an international army under a German general marches on Pekin. In the army are Japanese soldiers and American marines. In South Africa a much larger army marches on Pretoria, capital of the South African Republic. It is a British army, commanded by a famous soldier, Lord Roberts. In Leipzig, Germany, a propaganda sheet rolls off the press. It is called *Iskra*—The Spark. The editors are Russian conspirators. Among them is Vladimir Ulianov, known to the world as Lenin.

These three events foreshadowed the shape of things to come. The German general, Von Waldersee, captured Pekin with ease. The Boxers, superstitious Chinese peasants who defended it, found their magic incantations useless against bullet and shell. Few then could have pictured a reborn China contesting the control of Korea with an American army, wresting the northern and choicer part of Indo-China from the French Republic, ultimately becoming powerful enough to drive France out of Southeastern Asia altogether and to infiltrate into British Malaya. All this in half a century!

War in South Africa was to last until 1902. The Boer farmers who fought Britain were not numerous, at most but 40,000 men and boys capable of bearing arms. It took some 250,000 British troops to beat them down. Seemingly the British victory was complete. Few then could have seen the coming of a day when the defeated would become the victors; and an Afrikander nation would be born, claiming all South Africa for its own, forging a national language out of a local dialect, and a tradition of national glory out of sturdy resistance to all-powerful Britain.

Iskra, The Spark, was not sold on newsstands. Printed on the thinnest of paper, it was smuggled in small bundles across the Russian frontier from Germany. Copies were dropped on factory floors, pasted at night on the walls of houses, thrown, also at night, from theater galleries onto onlookers below. The process was called "sowing."

Lenin was the sower. None then foresaw the coming day when this fast-aging Russian fugitive, hiding in a German slum, would become the hero of a world-shaking revolution. Yet in seventeen short years his name

1

would be familiar to millions, and a few years later, after death, both glorified and sanctified, all the way east from Winston Churchill's "Iron Curtain" to the shores of the Pacific.

For the nonce, however, these fires burned underground, or beyond the boundaries of civilization, over the rim of the world. Europe, and America as well, did not regard Africa or even Asia as "civilized" regions. Africans or Asians were not progressive; they were not Christians; and in the words of that famous missionary hymn, From Greenland's Icy Mountains: "They call us to deliver their land from error's chain."

It was not so in the West, in Europe, where lived superior white folk who prided themselves on the peace, progress, and prosperity which they enjoyed—and merited. Yet scarcely threescore years passed before peace was a mockery, progress a mirage, and hunger rampant. This swift, devastating twist in the fate of nations is the subject of this book.

Peace

There had been no war in Europe, if we exclude the rugged Balkans, since 1870, and hopes ran high that there would never be another. Among "civilized" countries coöperation was the order of the day. One traveled freely throughout Europe, except for Turkey and Russia, without passport or visa. Currencies were everywhere interchangeable at fixed ratios, copyright and patent laws standardized. Arbitration of international disputes was a growing practice. In 1902 the King of England arbitrated one between Chile and the Argentine; in 1903 England and the United States arbitrated another in regard to the Alaska-Canadian boundary; and in 1909 France and Germany agreed to arbitrate conflicting interests in Morocco.

Pacifism was growing. In Sweden Alfred Nobel gave the greater part of his fortune to endow the search for peace among nations; in America Andrew Carnegie endowed the Carnegie Foundation for International Peace and built the Peace Palace at the Hague. The world's most famous man of letters, Leo Tolstoy, treated pacifism and Christianity as almost interchangeable. And in 1910 Norman Angell published his *Great Illusion* to prove that in the long run no country could profit from war.

Europe was, to be sure, divided by two great military alliances, the Triple Alliance of Germany, Austria, and Italy, and the Dual Alliance of Russia and France. But these alliances were defensive in character and were approximately equal in striking power, the Triple Alliance having the choicer location in the heart of Europe, the Dual Alliance neatly combining French gold with Russian manpower. Thus the balance of power was preserved, a thin reed but better than none.

These alliances, unfortunately, were sustained by large standing armies. But world opinion was becoming more and more aware of the danger

Ewing Galloway

THE "PEACE PALACE" AT THE HAGUE, NETHERLANDS

lurking in that fact, and international conferences to limit armaments attracted much attention. One held in 1899 at the Hague was attended by twenty-six nations, and another in 1907 brought delegates from forty-four countries. These peace conferences were for the most part a failure; but nonetheless there was a widespread belief that there would be more of them, and that ultimately war would be outlawed as well as outmoded.

This happy state of affairs, it was thought, would result from the extraordinary progress taking place in all forms of human activity. A truly international spirit was something more than a figment of the imagination. International finance, international socialism, and international culture, evinced by international studies, travel, exchange professorships, music festivals, and Olympic Games, would tend to banish war. If man could do so much, in so short a time, toward conquering his environment and improving his social and political institutions, and become wealthier while doing so, surely war, inevitably, would cease to plague him.

Progress

The early twentieth century was optimistic concerning progress. How could it be otherwise in view of recent scientific and technological advances? Never had there been a time when man knew so much; never had there been a time when he was so inventive. Within less than a hundred years he had invented the locomotive, the steamship, the camera, the telegraph, the telephone, the sewing machine, the bicycle, the phonograph, the cinematograph, electric lighting, and the automobile. And now, within the first decade of the new century, the wireless and the airplane.

In medicine, for instance, and in the general understanding and control of public health striking advances were recorded. Although the industrial cities in Europe grew rapidly in population and became yearly more congested, the death rate in many of them decreased during the hundred years after Waterloo by more than fifty per cent. Typhus fever in Western Europe during the same period was eliminated and other terrifying diseases brought under control.

In bacteriology the advance was noteworthy. The bacilli of malaria, of tuberculosis, and of diphtheria were discovered and studied, their final defeat plotted. Proper treatment began for pneumonia. Biological chemistry brought new light to bear on the digestive functions, and the complexities of human metabolism were, for the first time, partially understood—physiology was becoming a new science. German research taught us how to understand neurology, and in German laboratories the germ of syphilis was isolated and a cure found for that dread disease.

Noteworthy progress was made in politics, education, labor legislation, and growing international goodwill. In politics one could point to the map of Europe and show how it had been simplified and made more intelligible. Thanks to Cavour, that "geographic expression," Italy, had been made a nation; thanks to Bismarck, the thirty-nine Germanies of 1815 had become one nation. By 1914 every country in Europe, Russia excepted, had some kind of constitution. Almost every adult male had a vote in England, France, and Germany, and before the World War of 1914-19 women could vote in Denmark and Norway. Democracy was forging ahead.

In all that had to do with political and constitutional progress Britain led the world. And to analyze what took place there one cannot do better than study the significance of the Parliamentary election of December, 1905.

The membership of the new House of Commons chosen then was divided as follows:

397 Liberals,
 53 Laborites, 29 of them members of a new political party, the remainder not willing at first to accept the whip (discipline) of the Labor Party but before long to adhere to it.
 83 Irish Nationalists,
157 Conservatives, for the time being called "Unionists," since they had formed a union with anti-Gladstonian Liberals.

For some ten years the Conservatives (Unionists) had controlled the British government. Now a Parliamentary upheaval had given the Liberals a handsome majority over all.

The Liberal party which took over the reins of government in January, 1906, would have shocked that great exemplar of nineteenth-century liberalism, W. E. Gladstone. No longer did it adhere to the traditional liberal philosophy, the less government the better (laissez faire). Even before Gladstone died left-wingers in his party were changing fast. And those left-wingers now controlled the party, committed to a policy of governmental intervention on behalf of low-income groups whose share in the general prosperity of the time was so pitifully low.

New ideas were making headway. Some of them were due to the influence of Henry George, an American, whose book, *Progress and Poverty,* met with a warm reception in England. George was no Socialist but a radical who attacked "landlordism," rampant in Britain where the ownership of land, both agricultural and urban, was monopolized by a handful. Other ideas concerning social reform like the above were held by many Liberals and by most of the Labor men, separately organized but pressing steadily on the government in a more radical direction. The membership of the Labor party came overwhelmingly from the trade unions, of which there were some 1250 enrolling over 2,000,000 men. Hitherto few had been interested in politics: but now a legal decision (Taff Vale), handed down by the highest law court in Britain, made unions financially responsible for damages to property resulting from picketing during strikes. This led many workmen to change their minds and to vote "labor."

When the new Parliament met, the Prime Minister said that the government would introduce measures looking toward " a greater equalization of wealth." "Property," declared the Chancellor of the Exchequer, "must be associated in the minds of the people with the ideas of reason and of justice." Whereupon the liberals, spurred on by the Laborites, enacted a whole series of laws which, from the laissez-faire philosophy of the preceding century, were almost revolutionary.

Thus, for instance, the Trades' Dispute Bill and the Workingmen's Compensation Act, both passed in 1906. The first virtually repealed the Taff Vale decision, since it forbade any suit brought against a union for peaceful picketing; the second forced most employers to take out insurance to pay for accidents and occupational diseases. Two years later came the Children's Act which, among other things, provided for free medical attendance at birth; and this same year (1908), the Old-Age Pension Act was enacted with the proviso that the state must provide small pensions for needy persons. Then, in 1909, came the Trades' Board Act, which put a floor under wages in the "sweated industries"; and in that same year the Housing Act was passed which gave the local government board authority to clear slum areas. Also in 1909 came the celebrated

Lloyd George budget involving new principles of taxation. This in turn produced the Parliament Act of 1911, of which more later. And finally, in 1912, we meet the National Insurance Act against sickness and unemployment, with one third of the premium paid by the employer, one third by the state, and the remaining third by the wage earner.

Of these three statutes the more significant are: Old-Age Pensions; the Lloyd George budget; and the Parliament Act.

Old-age pensions brought a complete about-face in England as to the theory and practice of laissez faire; they also were very expensive. To pay for them Lloyd George, Chancellor of the Exchequer, introduced the most radical budget in English history. It imposed a supertax on top of the normal income tax, to be paid by everyone with an annual income of over £5,000; and it adopted part of Henry George's program by taxing unutilized agricultural land, and by a tax of twenty per cent on the rise in value of urban property.

The budget could not be said to raise the added funds exclusively from the wealthy since it called for increases in tobacco and liquor taxes. Nevertheless it was heavily loaded against landowners, as such, and carried with it the implication of far-reaching social changes. Placing their emphasis on this, the House of Lords refused to accept it. Whereupon a general election was held, the first of two in 1910, and the Liberals, triumphant, passed the budget a second time, and the Lords accepted it. British precedents made it mandatory that they should.

The victorious coalition of Liberals, Labor men, and Irish Nationalists now thought the time ripe to clip the wings of the House of Lords by passing the Parliament Act through the Commons. Rejected by their Lordships, they held a second election in 1910. Again the coalition gained a majority in the Commons. Once more the Parliament bill was passed by it. Fearing lest worst betide the Lords if they refused, this time (1911) the bill passed both houses of Parliament and became a statute of the realm.

Politically this was the greatest victory of political democracy in Britain since the Reform Bill of 1832, as the veto power of the Lords was now limited to two years, and during that time it was no longer necessary to hold a general election to give evidence of popular support to any measure.

In France the picture was somewhat more confused owing to the multiplicity of political parties and splinter groups. What was known as "the Republican bloc" was in power during the early years of the twentieth century, composed of centrist and left-of-center parties busily engaged in stamping out monarchial sentiment in the army; in wresting the control of education from Catholic monastic orders; and in making an end to the concordat, or treaty, made by the Emperor Napoleon a hundred years earlier, whereby France was recognized as a Catholic country and the salaries of the clergy paid for by the State.

All this was done in the name of democracy by a popularly elected legislature, supposedly acting in the name of a republic which the army was sworn to defend and which the Pope counseled good Catholics to accept. But the French Republic, we must needs remember, was little more than two decades old, and many Frenchmen were more loyal to monarchial tradition than to Republican ideals. Particularly was this true among army officers and aristocratic families who made use of religion as a cloak beneath which to agitate for the return of the monarchy. This led to the suspicion that anti-republicanism was fostered in monastic schools and that the Church in general was lukewarm in its loyalty to Republican France.

Labor legislation took a somewhat less radical color in France than in Britain, partly because Frenchmen enjoyed a more equitable division of wealth than in Britain, partly because of the outbreak in France of what was called syndicalism, involving as it did extensive sabotage in factories. This led in turn to more conservative policies, the power of the syndicalists being stamped out by summoning them to the colors, thus defeating strikes.

Germans were progressive in everything that had to do with technology, physical well-being, and education. For this they owed nothing directly to democracy; but they owed a great deal to past traditions of frugality, to the intervention of the Roman Catholic Church, and to the competition between that organization and the Social Democratic party for the votes of workingmen.

The heart of German industrial life lay in the Rhine Valley and in West Germany. Here the Catholic Church had its major strength, as was also true of the German Socialists. The Church was openly in politics, determined to retain its grip on schools paid for by the State, resolute also, in accordance with Papal Encyclicals, in insisting that Christianity and social welfare went hand in hand. The Socialists objected to Church schools but agreed with the Church in regard to labor legislation. Between them they brought heavy and successful pressure on the government to ensure it.

Every adult male in Germany had a vote, and to that extent democracy prevailed. But by his vote all that he could accomplish, directly, was to secure seats in the Reichstag, the lower chamber in the legislature which had little power. The government was headed by the chancellor, who was not responsible to the Reichstag; it could not dismiss him; it had no power over him. The chancellor was responsible only to the Bundesrath, the upper chamber of the legislature which in turn was controlled by Prussia; and the King of Prussia, by the German constitution, was Emperor of Germany. The Emperor (Kaiser) appointed the chancellor.

Nevertheless the chancellor always found it to his advantage to have a majority behind him in the Reichstag since all appropriations for new taxes had to be approved by that body.

In the election of 1903 the Centre Party (Roman Catholic) elected to the Reichstag 103 members and was the largest party of all, the second largest being that of the Social Democrats with 79 members. By the election of 1912 the figures were reversed; in that year the Socialists won 110 seats, the Centre coming in second with 90 seats. In both the last elections before the war, these two parties, if combined, would have had a majority over all.

There was no alliance between the two parties, and if there had been it could only have affected, indirectly, the course of German policy. The Centre party was not revolutionary; it supported capitalism and was loyal to the Kaiser. The Social Democratic Party opposed the Kaiser, was revolutionary in theory but not in practice. Furthermore, many who voted for it were not even socialists. They had no other way of showing their dislike of the Kaiser but to vote Social Democratic.

A unique feature of the German Empire, before the world was engulfed in war, 1914-18, was the autonomy enjoyed by German cities. Many of them were very old municipalities originally surrounded by fortified walls. As they expanded these walls were torn down and their place taken by parks. Beyond the parks were open spaces, not left to the mercy of land speculators but taken over by the cities which built garden homes and apartments on them. Almost every German city of any size had its own municipal opera house, and very frequently city breweries to provide cheap and abundant beer. The German workman received a slightly smaller wage than his British counterpart, but this disadvantage was more than offset by the greater comfort of his surroundings.

In Russia, as the century opened, there was no check whatsoever on the despotic tyranny of the Czar, and of political democracy there was no trace. Below the surface, however, there was agitation for change which broke out in 1905-6 in a violent revolution.

Western Europe and the United States were delighted. Here was proof that democracy and liberal institutions were seeping eastward, and that soon all Europe would be blessed by some kind of constitutional government with guarantees of individual liberty.

The immediate cause of the Russian revolution was the defeat of Russian armies in 1904 in Manchuria in Eastern Asia. The Czar was blamed for the defeat; and at the same time the absence of his armies in Asia made the time propitious for an uprising at home.

The revolution began in January, 1905, with the march of St. Petersburg factory operatives on the Winter Palace. They bore with them a petition to the Czar asking for a constituent assembly to draw up a constitution, also for "freedom of speech, press and conscience; the immediate release of political prisoners; free public education; full equality before the law; abolition of indirect taxes in favor of a progressive income tax; guarantees for unions and coöperatives; collective bargaining; the eight-hour day and a minimum wage." [1]

As the marchers drew near the Winter Palace they were greeted with a hail of bullets. The news spread like a forest fire. The country was infuriated. Houses of the nobility went up in flames; unpopular officials were assassinated; strikes broke out in Russian cities and traffic was paralyzed on Russian railways.

In October, 1905, the Czar yielded, and authorized the election by universal suffrage of a Duma (Parliament). There was universal rejoicing, particularly by the progressive middle class, when it was revealed that their party, that of the Constitutional Democrats, won the greater number of seats. The "Cadets," as they were called, had high hopes of creating a liberal form of government on the general model of that found in Britain.

They were grievously to be disappointed. The Czar had no intention of giving the Duma any real power except the right of approving or disapproving such legislation as he thought desirable; and when the Duma proved recalcitrant he dissolved it, calling for the election of a second Duma with a restrictive franchise. Leading Cadets slipped out of Russia to Finland, there to take an oath of loyalty to one another and the freedom sought for. They were arrested, some of them jailed, others disenfranchised.

The second Duma proved more amenable but not sufficiently so to the reactionary advisers of the Czar. And so there emerged a third Duma and finally a fourth, which was permitted to survive purely as a debating society. By 1907 the revolution was over.

Several reasons explain why. One important one was the device whereby the wrath of the proletariat was diverted from the misdeeds of the government to furious hatred of the Russian Jew. There were several million Jews, for the most part herded in ghettos. Rumors were circulated accusing these Jews of atrocious crimes, including the killing of small Gentile children to obtain blood for sacramental use. Cut-throat gangs (The Black Hundreds) were organized and paid by the government to attack the Jews who, finding no protection from the authorities, fled by the thousands to America.

Another cause for the revolution's failure was a large loan advanced the Czar's government by French bankers. Fearing lest loans already made to construct Russian railways be repudiated by revolution, they did their best to crush this one, and not unsuccessfully. And still another cause for failure was the enormous area covered by the Russian empire, and the lack of any central focal point from which to conduct successful

[1] A. Shub, *Labor in the Soviet Orbit*, 1956, page 7.

fighting. In the French Revolution of the eighteenth century Paris was
the nerve center of France, and that city once thoroughly under the control of the revolutionary forces the revolution could go on from victory
unto victory. But with great Russian cities like Odessa, Moscow, and St.
Petersburg separated from one another by thousands of miles and poor
communication, revolutionary cadres were at a disadvantage.

In this abortive revolution of 1905-7 the well-disciplined Bolsheviki of
Lenin played a very minor role. As the all-or-nothing faction in the Social
Democratic party they refused to coöperate with the Mensheviki faction
of Socialists willing to accept a half-loaf for the time being when nothing
else was available. Lenin would not hear of anything less drastic than
open civil war and favored starting one at Moscow. To him any thought
of compromise was abhorrent. Constitutional Democrats, the Cadets,
were "vermin." Ten more years and a much greater war than the one in
Manchuria must first take place before history would hear from Lenin.

No sooner did this Russian revolution in favor of constitutional government and democracy collapse than another, comparable to it in some
ways, broke out in the Ottoman Empire. In 1908 Turkish army officers,
known as "Young Turks," seized Constantinople and proclaimed the
revolution.

Again, as in the case of Russia, the West was electrified by the news.
Was not Sultan Abdul Hamid II, symbol of despotism and treachery over
all the world, now shorn of power, and Turkey at last to enjoy a constitution, a Parliament, and guarantees of civil liberty?

It did not work out that way. Too many minority groups were displeased. If Turkey was to be modernized along Western lines, the Young
Turks thought it desirable to have a common language—Turkish. But this
offended the Arabs in the Empire who could not talk Turkish and who
found that they were forbidden to make speeches in Arabic in the new
Parliament. Greeks were unhappy because they discovered that a common law code for all Turkey meant that they had lost their old right of
having their own courts. Albanians now found to their chagrin that they
were expected to pay taxes and to refrain from carrying rifles, unheard-of
reforms in the old days when Albanians were honored by successive
Sultans as fierce Moslem warriors, useful in intimidating Christians on
their flank in European Turkey. And finally Bulgars, Greeks, and Serbs
living in Macedonia, a Turkish province, were informed that since Turkey
was now a modern state they were subject to conscription, a service from
which as Christians they hitherto had been exempt.

And so this Young Turk revolution of union and progress got off to a
poor start. How it resulted in three little wars (1911-13) will be described
in a later chapter. As far as political progress went, there was none of it
in Eastern Europe. But Western ideas concerning democracy and constitutional government continued to infiltrate into that region.

Wealth

As the nineteenth century slid into the twentieth, Europe was wealthier than at any time in her past history. A full pocketbook led to optimism and contentment, and added much to the prevailing notion that wars on any considerable scale were things of the past.

Particularly notable was the increase in economic wealth. In almost every industry new inventions enlarged the volume of production. The cost of steel dropped steadily after Bessemer converters came into use, and dropped still more after the open-hearth process of manufacture was developed. Cheap steel led to the invention and perfection of many new machines, from hydraulic cranes to Otis elevators. In agriculture the use of new fertilizers grew apace, and the breeding of live stock on scientific lines developed with rapidity—hens laid more eggs and cows gave more milk in 1914 than in 1814. Coal tar, as a source for dyes, cheapened and improved textiles. Hydroelectric power had already displaced steam in certain industries; Diesel and gasoline engines no longer were toys. The world looked forward to a new and peculiarly promising Industrial Revolution.

Improvements in distribution did not lag far behind. One by one came the great transcontinental railroads: the Union Pacific in the United States, following hard upon the close of the Civil War; the Canadian Pacific, opening up the wheat lands of the Prairie Provinces; the Trans-Caucasian, already by 1888 reaching the fabled city of Samarkand; the Trans-Siberian, begun in 1890 and diverting in part the trade routes of the Orient; the Berlin-Byzantium-Bagdad Intercontinental, in process of construction; the Cape-to-Cairo inspiration of Cecil Rhodes, already stretching from Egypt to the Sudan and from Cape Town to the Zambesi.

Just as noteworthy were improved transportation facilities within Europe. At the Simplon and St. Gotthard passes, railway tunnels pierced the Alps. From the Ukraine wheat now reached Europe overland through Germany and Austria. Light railways, such as Belgium specialized in, were laid down near commercial centers, and interior canalization also, in which Germany excelled, was developed. In consequence, freight rates dropped, and the volume of commerce grew in proportion.

In ocean transportation the advance was even more marked. The eighteen-eighties saw steel supplanting iron in the construction of ships —nearly as substantial an improvement over the iron ships of the sixties as the latter were over their wooden predecessors. The turbine engine, although invented, had not as yet made clear its usefulness; but on the other hand, the triple expansion engine of the end of the century had enormously economized ship space, while the installation of twin screws and of watertight compartments diminished largely the danger of disaster in mid-ocean. On all the seven seas the tramp cargo carriers of England,

Norway, and Germany competed fiercely with each other; while on the Atlantic, the phenomenal success of the Hamburg-American Line, rapidly rising to first place among the steamship companies of the world, gave constant proof of marine progress undreamed of fifty years before.

Increased production, without new markets, then meant overproduction, and new markets were speedily forthcoming. To a great extent, Europe and the Ámericas provided them, but not solely. Asia proved to be a quick absorber of the surplus production of Europe and, somewhat less so, Africa. As early as the sixties, Karl Marx had noted the extent to which machine-made cotton cloth had depressed the hand loom weaving of India. Now Germany, as well as England, was discovering in India an ever-increasing market for her manufactured goods before the twentieth century was even under way. Guns, munitions of war, clocks, cloth, sewing machines, hardware, steel rails, linoleum, an endless list of articles from European workshops began to flood the undeveloped continents. Peasants in Syria began to clamor for the red-tiled roofing of France; the cheap agricultural implements of Germany found a ready market in distant Java as well as in the nearer Balkans. On the banks of the Irrawaddy English cutlery was sold, and black maidens of Nyasaland clothed themselves in Lancashire cottons.

Nor did the cargo boats return empty. Tea and coffee, raw silk, tobacco, ivory, tin, peanuts, gold, diamonds, rubber, spices—all of these commodities entered Europe in ever-increasing volume. By 1914, many luxuries of 1814 had become daily necessities.

England was recognized as the wealthiest country in the world, its foremost manufacturer, banker, and trader. The rich inheritance of British capital invested overseas continued to increase until by 1914 and the First World War it stood close to £4,000,000,000. Railroads in Canada, Argentina, and even the United States, rubber plantations in Malaya, coffee plantations in Kenya, tea plantations in India and Ceylon, diamond and gold mines in South Africa, cotton and tobacco firms in Egypt, business concessions and enterprises in China, account in part for it. England was preëminently "the creditor nation." All the world was in her debt. And to add still further to these economic glories, her citizens owned the finest and the largest merchant fleet in all recorded history.

In second place, and rapidly catching up with England, came Germany. The steel industry in Britain kept growing, but in Germany it bounded upward at a faster rate. German steel production, insignificant when the Empire was founded in 1870, by 1900 was running neck and neck with that of Britain, and by 1914 was well in the lead. Even in shipping the Germans were able to compete with Britain; the largest passenger liner in the world flew the German flag, and for a short time the Germans captured the blue ribbon of the Atlantic. In chemistry with its numerous ramifications from coal tar derivatives to fertilizers, Germans were far ahead. In textiles, however, the British kept a safe lead, and the sum total of the British export trade continued to exceed that of Germany. But the margin was close. In 1900 British exports amounted to £291,000,000, German exports to £237,000,000. In 1913 British exports totaled £525,-000,000, German exports £509,000,000.

Hitherto Britain had had it all her own way in trade and commerce; no competitor was in sight on the Continent. The British, proud of the traditions of their firms, had not tried hard to push their wares. But now the thoroughgoing and meticulous Germans were coördinating factories, railroads, steamships, and finance to challenge England. Mr. Smith of Birmingham had the curious sensation that his competitor was not simply Herr Schmidt of Essen but the entire German nation. The Germans were turning out commodities more cheaply than the British. Occasionally they were inferior in quality; but their sale in places like South America and Russia was facilitated by commercial travellers who spoke Spanish or Russian as the case might be, and who studied the whims and fancies of their customers. South Americans were fond of color; and German firms packed their goods in colored tissue paper. Russians wanted long-term credits; they were granted them.

The ubiquitous Germans even invaded the British home market. A German engineering firm built new waterworks for the city of Glasgow; its bid was the lowest. Foreign goods sold in Britain were compelled to bear the mark of their origin. Soon it was discovered that even cricket bats bore these words, "Made in Germany." These proofs of Teutonic prowess worried Britain somewhat.

As the world grew wealthier, so did France. The French had specialized since the days of Louis XIV, and earlier, in the manufacture of fine rather than bulky wares, and they continued to do so. They made the best wines, the best gloves and chinaware, the finest silk cloth, and other goods which commanded high prices in a luxury-loving world. Wedding-dresses for the daughters of the wealthy in both hemispheres were made of French silk, and bachelor dinners specialized in French champagne. Paris, no longer the pivot wheel of European politics as in the days of Napoleon III, still remained the foyer of European fashion, and the wealthier Chicago, Bremen, and Manchester became, the more money there was available for Parisian luxuries.

The French specialized in luxuries for others, but were noted for their own frugality, choosing to invest their money in loans to Russia, Turkey, and other countries who would pay good interest. And there was much money to loan, for in the decades between the Franco-Prussian War and the First World War the national wealth of France increased fifty per cent! That wealth was widely distributed, a fact which made for general material comfort. The land policy of the French Revolution still held and peasant proprietorship continued. Industrial establishments were small, ordinarily employing but very few workmen; but there were many such establishments and petty capitalists were numerous. In fact, almost every one was a petty capitalist with some property. More than 8,000,000 French citizens held title to real estate in France. With a population of under 40,000,000, there were over 14,000,000 individual savings-bank accounts; the Bank of France had over 30,000 stockholders, a great many of whom only owned a few shares apiece. The national debt was high, but so widely scattered among Frenchmen that French credit was of the best and the government was able to borrow at three per cent at a time when five per cent was considered only a fair yield. When the Pennsylvania Railroad, in the prewar days, floated a bond issue in France, there was no trouble in getting the money provided the bonds were printed in sufficiently small denominations. Hence rose the American practice of selling "baby bonds," an idea worked out first of all to satisfy French investors who collectively possessed much but who individually insisted on having bonds in denominations of less than $1,000.

Little wonder that the observant American, Barret Wendell, wrote of France in 1900: "This country is prosperous above all countries. Nowhere else will you receive a more general impression of solid, substantial well-being."

This economic upswing was felt in most of Europe. French loans and cheap labor enabled Russia to increase its railway mileage from 22,000 miles in 1895 to 50,000 in 1913. In processing iron Russia surged ahead so rapidly that by 1914 she produced more than France. Russian cities were growing. St. Petersburg by 1914 had over 2,000,000 inhabitants, and Moscow was only slightly behind.

Meanwhile Italy, specializing in silk and cotton textiles, doubled and trebled her exports, and the smaller countries, too, shared in the general prosperity. Coöperative farming in Denmark resulted in that country becoming England's major source of butter and eggs. Sweden and Finland with their huge forests met the ever-increasing demand for more lumber. Through the Netherlands funnelled the rich products of the Dutch East Indies. And Switzerland, vacation paradise for all Europe, rejoiced in the prosperity of her neighbors.

The world, indeed, was a pleasant place for entrepreneur and capitalist, intent on new enterprises or eager to enlarge old ones; for those skilled artisans who belonged to trade unions and whose standard of living had risen steadily; for the majority of public officials and lawyers; for those who possessed private property and for those who ministered to their wants; for many scholars and scientists modestly endowed; and for those clergymen, writers, and publicists with faith rooted firmly in orderly evolution, regarding this if not the best of all possible worlds at least as one growing steadily better.

Chapter 2

THE MENACE OF NATIONALISM

In 1900 all seemed well on the surface. Then, in 1914, peace, progress, and prosperity vanished in the backwash of war. Two interlocking ideologies, nationalism and imperialism, in large measure account for this debacle.

Nationalism might roughly be defined as the desire of people having a common tradition and background, speaking the same language, occupying contiguous territory, and professing in general the same religion, to control their own destiny, to have their own government, and to be free from alien and more powerful neighbors.

As such, nationalism has long been a characteristic of European history, predating Napoleon and the French Revolution which made him. As far back as Shakespeare's day, men were proud of being Englishmen, and Frenchmen died for France, or at least for the Valois and Bourbon families. Even earlier yet, a kind of nationalism flourished in the sense of local pride or regionalism. Bruges, Geneva, Venice, like the city-states of Greece, thought well of themselves; and it must be remembered that the Crusaders fought not only as Christians but also as Burgundians, Germans, Englishmen.

Nevertheless, prior to the French Revolution, nationalism differed from its corresponding phenomena in modern times in at least three ways: national loyalties tended to be personal rather than territorial (that is, attached to some leader, feudal chief, or family rather than to a country or region); they were more cultural than political in character; and, until the French Revolution, they did not carry with them the totalitarian idea of a nation in arms.

Englishmen, for instance, in 1688 were as apt to debate their loyalty to King James or King William as they were to discuss the welfare of the English people. In Italy, in Dante's day, people were for pope or emperor or city—only Dante seemed to be for Italy. In the Middle Ages it was Saracen against Christian rather than German against French, and down to the sixteenth century, both religion and education transcended nationalistic lines. Protestantism, it is true, weakened such international ties as the Roman Catholic Church had afforded and gave a decided stimulus to

15

nationalism as we know it; but after all a great tradition of common culture remained. Latin and Greek were common denominators for the
educated of all countries. Although there were no airplanes or radios to
connect nations, the educated all over Europe were accustomed to think
alike, for they were brought up on the same books—Virgil, Homer, Plato,
Aristotle, Plutarch, and the Christian Scriptures.

In the eighteenth century there was a good deal of what has been
called cultural nationalism, such, for instance, as English pride in Sir
Isaac Newton as mathematician and scientist and in Pope as poet. Frenchmen glorified Molière and Voltaire, Germans rejoiced in Mozart and
Goethe, and Spaniards honored Cervantes. But Voltaire did not write
patriotic essays, Mozart patriotic songs, nor Pope patriotic poetry.
Goethe's fatherland was neither the first, second, nor third Reich but
wherever the good and the beautiful were to be found; Voltaire's fatherland was where a man was comfortable. Neither Frenchman nor German
bothered his head about inherent qualities of grandeur connected with
Gallic or Teutonic traditions.

And finally there was the concept of the nation in arms. Robert the
Bruce fought for an independent Scotland and William Tell for a free
Switzerland, but neither conceived of such a thing as compulsory universal military service—the nation in arms of the French Revolution. Fighting in times past had been done generally by mercenary troops, or at most
by volunteers. It remained for the French to give birth to the idea that
old and young alike were obligated to dash to the ramparts (or trenches),
there to fight for a "nation." The French Revolution popularized this
doctrine; Bonaparte utilized it; the Germans copied Bonaparte and improved upon him in theory and in practice.

From Waterloo to the present, the onward march of nationalism has
continued unabated. In 1800 there was no German, Italian, or Russian
nationalism in the modern sense of that term, yet within fifty years it
spread to those lands and to many others such as Hungary and Belgium.
The seemingly impossible was accomplished. There were no natural boundaries to Poland or to Finland; but that did not stay the progress, except
temporarily, of Polish and Finnish nationalism. Any historic tradition of
unity among Greeks, Irish, and Rumanians was so far in the background
as to be quite shadowy; but that fact did not make them immune to
nationalistic fever. By 1914 nationalism swept on from Ireland in the
northwest to Turkey in the southeast, and after the World War of
1914-18 its speed accelerated. Its ever-growing momentum throughout
the last century and a half is one of the most striking facts of modern
history.

For the first two-thirds of the nineteenth century, nationalism served
a useful purpose. In Germany it brought an end to centuries of discord;
in Italy it freed the Italian peninsula from the heavy hand of Austrian

despotism; in the Balkans it lifted the Turkish yoke from Serbia, Greece, Rumania, and Bulgaria. For the most part, at that time, nationalism was concerned with *liberating* various nationalities from alien control and fusing them together as national states.

Later on, however, and particularly in the early twentieth century, self-glorification and inordinate pride in nationalistic achievement led certain powerful countries, such as Russia, Germany, and Britain, to suppress minority activities within their borders. Thus the Russians tried to stamp out nationalism in Finland; Russians and Germans alike bore down despotically on the Poles; the Germans behaved badly toward Alsatians who continued to speak French, thus antagonizing France; and smoldering antagonism between British and Irish brought their respective nationalities to the brink of war in 1913.

The more extreme German and Russian nationalists professed unbridled ambitions. In Germany they were known as "Pan-Germans," advocating the bringing together of all Germanic peoples under the aegis of the German Empire, the annexing to it of the 10,000,000 South Germans living in Austria; the majority of the Swiss; the Danes; and also the Netherlanders, with their rich possessions in the East Indies. Nor were the Russians far behind. Their slogan was "Pan-Slavism," the liberation of all Slavic peoples from German, Austrian, Hungarian, and Turkish misrule. This once accomplished, there were various ideas as to the future of these Slavs, varying all the way from a federation under Russian hegemony to political unity under the direct rule of the Czar. Ideas like the above were widely disseminated in both countries and boded no good to the world.

Polish Resistance to German and Russian Rule

In 1900 some 21,000,000 Poles lived in East Central Europe. About 3,800,000 were in Germany, 5,000,000 in Austria-Hungary, some 12,000,000 in Russia. Juridically speaking, there was no longer a Poland. Three times during the eighteenth century Russia, Austria, and Prussia had partitioned this unhappy land. As a country it ceased to exist politically at the third partition in 1795. But as a nation it was, and still is, very much alive. Despite these calamities, or perhaps because of them, the Poles clung to their nationalism with passionate devotion. They might not have a country; but they had a language, a past tradition of greatness, a literature, and a devotion to the Roman Church as strong as that of the Irish. Staunchly and abidingly they refused to lose their identity.

In the nineteenth century they had risen in rebellion, had tried to fight the Muscovite armies, had been crushed, their young men sent to Siberia. The Russia of the Czars reduced Poland to a mere satrapy; but fortunately for the Poles the Russians were so slovenly in their administration that the Poles eked out some small liberties by bribing their Russian overlords.

The Poles in Germany were in harder case. The Russians were at least fellow Slavs, but the Germans were Protestant and Teutonic and determined to root out Polish nationalism.

One way to do this was by expropriating land held by Poles and settling German farmers on it. But German farmers could not be cajoled into quitting comfortable holdings elsewhere in Germany to settle in an uncongenial "enemy's country," where police protection was often needful. The Poles clung desperately to their habits and language, and their unwelcome guests had to become Slavized in order to secure the least companionship.

Against the tenacious use of the native vernacular, the Prussian government fought yet again with its trusty subalterns—the schoolmasters. In 1872 German was made the sole language in the elementary schools, except that religion could still be taught (by the Catholic clergy) in Polish; but as soon as the children learned a little German they were transferred to German religion classes. Inasmuch as religion and patriotism had now, for the Poles, become practically inseparable, the resentment was widespread and intense. The clergy, in fact, branded the new mandates as an indirect and clumsy way for teaching Protestantism. The lot of every German-speaking priest soon became unhappy.

Finally, in 1906, came the famous school strike in Posen and West Prussia. Some 60,000 pupils, of course at parental instigation, refused to answer questions on the catechism in German or to learn German hymns. The vernacular press condemned the attempt to teach religion in the language of the conquerors as "A tyranny over the conscience, in which only the devil in the gorge of hell and the Prussian government could find satisfaction." Children met their unlucky teachers of religion with Polish songs or curses, and strewed the roadside with the tatters of their German catechisms. The Prussian government struck back by refusing promotion to recalcitrant children, fining and sometimes imprisoning the parents who encouraged them, and (most effective coercion of all) appointing extra teachers on the school staffs in the malcontent villages. These additional instructors were sustained directly by the local taxes. This broke the strike. It ended in 1907.

During the three decades before the First World War, the Prussian Poles were fighting tooth and nail to preserve their language. The government police were constantly suppressing all Polish outdoor meetings and permitting Polish indoor meetings only under the strictest surveillance. Polish theatrical performances were frequently prohibited; and Polish pleadings were forbidden in the courts, even in strictly Slavic districts. No Pole was admitted to the judgeships, the postal service, the enormous state railway service, or to any other part of the great army of civil officials. To Germans, Poland had been a country but now was one no longer.

Slavic and Rumanian Nationalism in Austria-Hungary

South of Germany and southwest of Russia was the Dual Monarchy of Austria-Hungary. Within its borders were nine different nationalities: Germans, Magyars (Hungarians), Czechs, Poles, Ruthenians (of Little Russia), Rumanians, Croats, Slovenes, and Italians. Top dog were the Germans in Austria and the Magyars in Hungary, disliking one another but determined to keep their ramshackle empire together because they must. Only by so doing could they keep down the bottom dog—the more disparate nationalities within their borders. As long as they acted together they separated the North Slavs (Poles, Czechs, and Ruthenians) from South Slavs (Croats and Slovenes); as long as they did so they could keep open their exits to the sea. Trieste, Austria's one seaport, was situated in a veritable nest of Slovenes and Italians. Fiume, Hungary's one seaport, and its immediate hinterland, was inhabited by Italians, Slovenes, and Croats. Once German-Magyar unity was lost the Germans in Austria and the Magyars in Hungary would be landlocked.

The Slavic peoples in Austria-Hungary, multiplying like rabbits, restless and eager to escape Austrian and Magyar domination, angrily were demanding national autonomy if not freedom, as were Rumanians living in Eastern Hungary. By the time the First World War broke the entire Dual Monarchy was alive with insurgent demonstrations, the Czechs demanding the restoration of their ancient kingdom of Bohemia; the Croats equally vociferous in calling for the restoration of the ancient privileges of the Kingdom of Croatia; Rumanians desirous of joining their blood brothers in Rumania; and many Serbs looking longingly at independent Serbia across the Danube.

Over this hodgepodge and mélange of different nationalities presided Emperor Francis Joseph. In 1914 he was eighty-four years old and the greater part of his long rein had been spent in propping up the impossible. Sooner or later intransigent nationalism promised to bring his empire crashing to the ground.

Alsace-Lorraine after Annexation to Germany in 1871

There were danger signals also along the Rhine. Fronting it was Alsace, one of the two French provinces annexed by Germany in 1871. "Let the memory of Alsace and Lorraine be engraved on your hearts forever" was said to be Gambetta's charge to his countrymen after the Franco-Prussian War; and in Paris the statutes representing Alsace and Lorraine annually were draped in black. The French did not forget.

Old wounds heal slowly, but they do heal. Given time and fair treatment the men of Alsace and Lorraine would gradually in a few generations have ceased to mourn. But they were not so treated. If Alsace-
Lorraine had been made as autonomous in the Reich as Bavaria all might
have been well. Bismarck, however, had no intention of having another
Roman Catholic state with votes in the powerful Bundesrath, and so the
two provinces were simply made a *Reichsland,* an imperial dependency
under the tutelage of Prussia, and for decades kept under the thumb of
the military. Scarcely, indeed, had the French flag been lowered, before
the teaching of the French language in elementary schools was forbidden.
In that Strasbourg where the Marseillaise had been first flung to the
breeze, French could not be studied save as a "foreign tongue," like
English or Italian. The French rulers had never suppressed the common
use of a mongrel type of German in the Alsatian villages. Now, by natural
reaction, many a German-speaking Alsatian began to pride himself on
chattering a very bad French.

But the German military conscription stirred the greatest anguish.
While their slain French comrades were hardly cold, Alsatian youths
were made to don the Prussian spiked helmet. Vain were protests. In
1871 a deputation expostulated with Bismarck. He told them that conscription was a school for loyalty. "Get the king's coat on a man's back and
you have made both a good soldier and a good 'burgher' [for Germany]
out of him." "Yes," retorted the leader of the deputation, "but you must
get the coat on first—and *that* you can never do!" Twelve thousand Alsatian youths fled to France and entered the French army; the rest entered
the German service so sullenly as to impair their value as soldiers.

The conquerors adhered to the policy of "thorough" with all their
native tenacity. French rule had been lax, somewhat inefficient, but
usually tender of local susceptibilities. Now came a swarm of Prussian
officials, keyed up to more than their wonted rigidity. Down to 1879, the
provinces were ruled by a military dictator sent down from Berlin. After
that, they formed a *Reichsland,* with the emperor naming the governor-
general and a very powerful council, but with some form of local self-
government; an extremely weak elective Diet, and enough popular bal-
loting to register ineffective protests against one ministerial ordinance
after another. A really humane and enlightened governor, Baron von
Manteuffel, who won much personal good-will, was appointed; but he
was thwarted by his lesser officials, who could only bully and tyrannize,
and he was compelled to enforce an impossible policy. In 1885 he died,
having accomplished little.

After Manteuffel, the carpet-bagging German officials induced Berlin
to attempt another regime of "proper severity." Kindness had failed;
police dragooning was therefore again in order. Alsatian societies of all
varieties were dissolved. Natives were forbidden to receive passports to

cross the frontier, even in order to visit near relatives in France. Arrests were made for every possible cause. An Alsatian had tattooed upon his body *"Vive la France!"* When he appeared in a public bath he was seized by the police. The natives retaliated by that passive resistance which is always so exasperating to an autocratic government.

The Reichsland under William II: Continued Bitterness until 1914

William II's advent brought a little relaxation of the police regime, but his speeches were adamantine. "We would rather," said he in an oration, "sacrifice our eighteen army corps and our 42,000,000 [Prussian] inhabitants in the battlefield than yield one stone which my father and [his generals] have gained."

A complete lack of humor, as well as of tactfulness, made the German administration at times a laughing-stock. In 1895 there was a peasant at the village of Detwiller near Saverne. He raised a fine white cock with a lordly red crest, whereupon he dyed the bird's tail blue—making the creature a veritable emblem of the Tricolor. The imperial police pounced on the sedition-teaching fowl. The owner refused to slaughter him; at which the police saber ended the feathered traitor and avenged the Fatherland. The affair was soon in the Paris papers. Its effect completely offset certain well-meant efforts of the Emperor to cultivate "good relations" with France, at the celebration of the opening of the Kiel Canal.

From this time onward, matters did not improve. One petty persecution or collision followed another. The French journals in the two provinces were suppressed under every possible pretext. Passport regulations again made it extremely difficult for a Frenchman to visit Strasbourg. A historical play requiring the display of the Tricolor was presented in that city. The police permitted only the use of the *Dutch* flag, wherein the red, white, and blue stripes ran horizontally instead of vertically. Sarah Bernhardt desired to play in Strasbourg. She was refused permission unless she would also play in Berlin; the famous actress swallowed her pride and consented, but she retaliated by using her enormous international influence to create hostility everywhere for Germany, even in America. And so the open sore remained unhealed.

Finally, in 1911, the German authorities reverted again to "benevolence." The Reichsland was given a constitution with considerable autonomy, somewhat on a par with other imperial states, although the governor-general was still sent down from Berlin. But the newly elected Landtag showed its feeling by at once cutting down the governor's salary and by refusing the annual allowance for the Emperor's hunting trips to Alsace. The "All-Highest" was extremely angry and on a visit to Strasbourg in

1912 flung an open warning to the mayor: "Listen! Up to now you have
only known the good side of me. You might be able to learn the other
side . . . If this situation lasts we will suppress your constitution and annex
you to Prussia."

WILLIAM II, EMPEROR OF GERMANY AND KING OF PRUSSIA
(1859-1941)

Followed then in short order the notorious Zabern (Saverne) incident.
A garrison lieutenant, annoyed by jeering school boys, harangued his
soldiers, calling Alsatians dirty names. They were immediately reprinted
both in the local papers and by the French press. A civilian crowd gathered in front of the barracks. The colonel in command sent a subaltern
ordering the crowd to disperse. He was disobeyed. Whereupon the military swept through the street, arresting all and sundry, among them three
high judges and the state prosecuting attorney.

The commandant at Zabern was now arrested for violating the law forbidding soldiers to interfere in civilian matters. He was promptly acquitted. The governor of Alsace resigned in protest at this decision. Almost
immediately Lieutenant Baron Von Forstner was in the headlines again.
He fell into public altercation with a lame shoemaker. The latter made
unflattering remarks. Forstner ordered two soldiers to hold the cripple
while he slashed him with his sabre. Once more there was sensational
news emanating from Alsace. Forstner was courtmartialed, sentenced to

one year in custody, and on appeal to a higher court acquitted altogether on the ground of self-defense.

The French public, historically sensitive to insults hurled at French citizens, anywhere and anytime, were peculiarly aroused by these events. Once more nationalistic fervor swept the boulevards of Paris. Hatred of the conquering Germans of 1870-1 swelled again in French hearts. The military alliance of France with Russia of 1896 became more popular than ever. To Frenchmen it did more than guarantee France against German aggression; it offered hope of the return some time of Alsace-Lorraine to France.

Russian nationalism versus German nationalism; Italian and Slavic nationalism versus Austria and Hungary; French nationalism versus German: here was good seed ground for the dragon-teeth of the Argonauts and starting future wars.

Nationalistic Conflicts in the British Empire: Irish Agitation for Home Rule: The Boer War

Even Britain, supposedly taught a lesson by the American Revolution, and long mellowed by political experience, was not immune to nationalistic conflicts. She was confronted with one near at hand in Ireland and with another in distant South Africa.

The title, "United Kingdom of Great Britain and Ireland" was a misnomer. Ever since the days of the first Elizabeth, Ireland had been a source of disaffection. Scotland had settled down peacefully in the early eighteenth century in the United Kingdom, the Scots having made a good bargain and, what is important psychologically, having won victories in the field over British armies. But always the Irish, when they fought, were defeated. They hated the conquerors, and were treated by them sometimes cruelly, more frequently with contempt, and occasionally with condescending kindness.

Twice in the nineteenth century Gladstone, Liberal Prime Minister, had done his best to gain Parliamentary approval for an Irish Home Rule Bill, setting up a Parliament at Dublin, granting to it autonomy in internal affairs. Both bills were defeated. The English had no confidence in the financial integrity of any popularly elected Parliament at Dublin; they did not trust the loyalty of Roman Catholic Irishmen in control of an island that lay athwart their sea lanes; and furthermore, somewhat more than half of the inhabitants of Ireland's most prosperous province, Ulster, were Protestants, who legally were British citizens and as such were determined to remain.

The Liberal Party, having failed twice to obtain Home Rule for Ireland, lost interest in "the most distressful Country," until it needed the votes of the Irish Nationalists at Westminster to pass the Parliament Act

of 1911. The help was given. The Irish got their reward, a third Home
Rule Bill introduced in Parliament in 1912.

Once again it was Ulster that raised the greatest hue and cry against
the bill. Ulster had been Oliver Cromwell's major contribution to Anglo-
Irish discord; he it was who dispossessed Irish peasants in Ulster, exiled
them to the West Indies, settled their land with hard-bitten Presbyterians
from Scotland, the Scotch-Irish who played such an important role in
American history. These were the men who founded the Orange lodges
to keep Ulster a British garrison, safe for the Protestant religion and the
Union Jack.

The Protestant majority in all Ulster was slim, only fifty-five per cent;
but that fifty-five per cent was wealthy, determined, powerful, and led
by one of the ablest men of the British bar, Sir Edward Carson, who from
the beginning had refused all compromise and who held that even the
British Parliament itself had no right to exclude Ulster from union with
Britain without a direct mandate to that effect.

Now there had been a Parliamentary election on the Lloyd George
budget in 1910, and another the same year on the Parliament Act. The
Liberals, therefore, could fairly claim that they had a mandate to govern
the country. Were they to hold a third Parliamentary election within three
years on the noisy demand of the Conservatives, they would create a
precedent whereby at any time it would be necessary to hold a plebiscite
on almost any issue not specifically voted upon at an earlier election.
Therefore they continued to ignore Carson and his friends and to press
the passage of the bill.

As they did so, Carson changed the theater of his agitation from
Parliament to Ulster. Thousands there took the oath upon the open Bible
and the Union Jack, swore solemnly to resist by force any effort to detach
them from their own country. They went further; they donned uniforms,
engaged in military drill and gun-running. Armed to the teeth, they
paraded up and down the countryside, prepared to prevent the enforcement of an act of the British Parliament. Yet this was only hypothetical
treason; the law was not yet on the statute books.

From England there came much sympathy and encouragement, both
from within the House of Commons and without. All the social bitterness
that smoldered in the hearts of upper-class Englishmen as they surveyed
the Liberal-Labor victories of the last few years now took fire. They did
not believe that there was any majority in the United Kingdom, outside
of Ireland, for Home Rule, and possibly they were right. At any rate, they
were most determined to help Ulster fight the good fight of British patriotism. The cabinet thereupon hastily devised a compromise. Every county
in Ulster (there were nine) was to vote separately as to whether it desired
inclusion in the new Ireland. If it rejected union it was to stay outside of it
for six years, that is, until two Parliamentary elections were held. But

Carson would have none of this. "No six-years' suspension of death for Ulster," he cried. Shortly thereafter, the government ordered a detachment of the British army in Ireland north to protect his Majesty's stores. The officers resigned rather than risk firing upon Ulstermen whose sole wish was to stay British. Again the government hesitated, as every Tory newspaper and every Tory drawing-room roared approval.

Meanwhile, as Ulster drilled and marched, the Roman Catholic Irish to the south did likewise. Civil war threatened to engulf Ireland in this summer of 1914. Only one thing stayed its coming—the hurricane of *world* war. To meet that emergency an Irish compromise hastily was arranged. The third Home Rule Bill became statute law. Simultaneously its execution was postponed indefinitely.

In South Africa Britain confronted another problem involving nationalism. Two old British colonies were located there, Cape Colony and Natal. North of them were two Boer republics, the Transvaal or South African Republic, and the Orange Free State. The inhabitants of the two republics were of Dutch descent. They spoke a kind of Dutch dialect, called Afrikaans, and disliked their British neighbors. They had reason to do so. Early in the nineteenth century they, and not the British, had occupied Cape Colony. When it was annexed to England after the Napoleonic wars they had trekked into the wilderness to live their own lives as they saw fit. In 1852 their independence had been recognized by Britain; in 1877 the British had annexed the Transvaal; and in 1880 the Boer farmers there had revolted, defeating the redcoats at Majuba Hill. Followed then complicated and unclear settlements. Did or did not the British renounce the suzerainty they claimed over the Transvaal? The point was never settled. Instead, in 1899 came war.

Its cause was the discovery of gold in the Western Transvaal, a great reef of gold to which miners rushed from over all the world. A British financier and Empire builder, Cecil Rhodes, was interested financially in the gold mines and became the recognized spokesman of the miners. Their number was increasing very rapidly and soon threatened to exceed that of the adult Boers. The latter, fearing lest they be swamped by this inrush of aliens, were strict in their naturalization laws. The miners, on the other hand, clamored for the franchise. They wanted schools, sewers, a water system, and street lighting in the city of Johannesburg, center of their industry: but the Boers, rural folk, would not pay for these improvements, and they alone had the vote in the Transvaal.

The debate grew hotter. Cecil Rhodes was premier of the British Cape Colony. He connived with a Dr. Jameson for an armed raid across the border which would seize Johannesburg and, presumably, hoist the Union Jack over that city. But the raid was nipped in the bud and the raiders captured.

The British government disowned this act of Rhodes's, and he lost his premiership; but it kept on insisting on a lowered franchise. The Boers offered to enlarge their citizenship if the British officially would abandon claims of suzerainty. Neither side would yield. Money raised by taxing the mines was spent by the Boers in buying guns and ammunition, and the British began concentrating troops in South Africa. This led to a Boer ultimatum and in 1899 to war.

It was a hard-fought war; and more than two years passed before the Boers, who called themselves Afrikanders, surrendered. With peace came magnanimity. Self-rule was restored by the British and large sums given to restock the farms of their late enemies. And the two Boer republics were federated in 1909 in the Union of South Africa, a self-governing Dominion in the British Commonwealth.

The British congratulated themselves, and most of the world congratulated Britain, on thus solving the problem of two nationalities in South Africa. But the gripping power of nationalism was underestimated. In the new Dominion the men of Afrikander blood and background exceeded those of British descent. The Afrikanders had long memories; and memories of defeat are more poignant than those of victory. The Union of South Africa was listed as a British Dominion—as was Ireland, for a time. But what is listed in books does not necessarily coincide with what is deep in human hearts. Afrikander nationalism was destined to grow and not wane, and by mid-century to become second to none in chauvinistic arrogance.

Chapter 3

EUROPEAN IMPERIALISM
IN AFRICA AND ASIA

WHEN THE nineteenth century dawned, a number of ports on the African littoral flew European flags and Dutch farmers had pushed north a few miles from Capetown. Aside from Egyptian antiquities scarcely anything was known of the Dark Continent. Almost the same could be said of Asia. Parts of the Indian peninsula had been absorbed into the British Empire and Siberia had been claimed by the Muscovite. But that was all: Persia, Afghanistan, Tibet, Siam, China, and Japan were *terra incognita* to Europeans. A hundred years later everything was different. By 1914 almost all Africa had been explored and partitioned among European countries, except the rough highlands of Abyssinia. And most of Asia was under European dominance. Independence of a sort remained to China; but alien people held her ports and dictated her economic policy. Japan alone of the Asiatic countries had succeeded in freeing herself from the meddling interference of the white man.

The process by which this was done is called "imperialism," and it came to a culmination in the very decade of the First World War. The causes were various. Anyone interpreting history from the standpoint of economics would point to three: (1) pressure from an increased population; (2) need of raw materials; (3) the necessity of finding new markets. Increase in population in Europe was unprecedented and alarming. In Russia it jumped from 38,000,000 to 111,000,000 between 1800 and 1900; in Germany from 21,000,000 to 56,000,000; in Italy from 18,000,000 to 32,000,000; in Great Britain from 16,000,000 to 41,000,000; and for all of Europe there was an increase in this century alone of 250 per cent—this despite emigration to the Americas and elsewhere. Here was one reason why Europe sought control over other lands. Furthermore, raw materials were in increasing demand as the Industrial Revolution spread. Iron and coal Europe had in abundance, but of the big four—cotton, rubber, oil, and copper—there was only oil and the latter in Russia and the Balkans alone. And finally there was the problem of marketing the finished goods. England produced more cotton cloth than she could sell in Europe, as did the Germans with their hardware and cutlery, and the French with their kid gloves and fine wines. If the blacks of Africa and the yellow folk of Asia could only be persuaded to wear English cloth, to shave with German razors, and to drink French wine, so much the better for the countries with surpluses of those and other commodities to dispose of.

But there were other causes of imperialism, among them nationalistic ambition. To interpret French imperialism, for instance, simply in terms of economics is fanciful. Modern French imperialism was under way early in the century, long before the Industrial Revolution created a demand for new markets; and furthermore, such goods as France did produce for international trade were articles of luxury for which neither then nor now was there any large demand in Africa, the principal area of French expansion. The Russians also did not penetrate the trans-Caucasian region north of Persia and Afghanistan primarily for economic reasons. There was no booty to be gained there commensurate with the expense; the land, aside from the oases, was desiccated and unfertile; and at the time when Russia absorbed these particular Asiatic uplands there was neither middle class nor Industrial Revolution worthy of the name in the country of the Czar. France and Russia were drawn into imperialistic enterprises, more than for any other reason, by the simple desire to dominate and to master more and more territory. Frenchmen and Russians found reflected glory for themselves in contemplating their own national glory. The English also felt this urge and so later did the Germans. The ego of many a little English boy expanded as he contemplated the red splotches in his geography, and as we near the era of the First World War there is equal evidence of Teutonic satisfaction in the conquest of a newly-won empire overseas. The economic motive is by no means to be dismissed, but alongside of it there evidently was another one, not so easy to define but none the less real. Perhaps we might call it, in psychological parlance, the power complex—sheer love of power.

Upon the surface it might seem as though the economic motivation was the more basic. For instance, the American Civil War and cotton. The blockade of the South caused the price of cotton to rise to famine heights. That made European capital flow into Egypt. When cotton prices fell Egypt became bankrupt. Her ruler, under pressure, placed Egyptian finance under the control of France and England. A native revolt against this alien intervention followed. Arabi Bey, who led it, menaced the Suez Canal. A British army seized the canal and occupied Egypt. From the viewpoint of the economic historian this sequence of events speaks for itself.

The Chinese used opium, brought in British ships from India. Disputes arose. Out of them came a minor war. Chinese ability to fight was inadequate. The British won. Certain seaports in China were opened to the British, the American, and the French trader. In them exterritoriality was granted—a system whereby separate law courts were granted to white men living in these ports. Thus began the disintegration of Chinese independence. Here was imperialism—its taproot trade and commerce!

On the uplands of Kenya in East Africa the climate was healthy for Europeans, the soil excellent for coffee culture. Masai warriors armed with spears could not withstand the rifles of the white man. The Masai were driven to the hinterland, placed on reservations. They may no longer herd their cattle in the Kenya Highlands, expropriated for the exclusive use of the white coffee growers.

Extend this argument many times and a strong case can be made to prove that desire for gain lured the European powers into imperialistic adventures in Asia and Africa.

The argument is strengthened by theories of imperialism acceptable to Marxian and left-wing economists, pacifists, and many humanitarians. Of these there are two, the underconsumption theory and that of finance capitalism: the first associated with the writings of Karl Marx, in which there is little concerning imperialism; and the second fathered by Lenin, who regarded imperialism as of utmost importance and whose findings became official Communist dogma on that subject.

The older theory went somewhat as follows: As the period of what is known as high capitalism, circa 1875-85, drew near, the production of commodities became so plentiful that there was no longer a home market for them. In consequence, capital flowed overseas. But surpluses kept piling up and markets overseas were limited. Manufacturing countries competed with one another for them. Competition became more and more acute. Land was annexed in Africa; spheres of influence and protectorates were set up in Asia. Sooner or later the continuing unmarketed surplus must result in international war, inevitably brought about by fierce competition for dwindling markets.

The theory is plausible, and there was a substratum of truth in it. Nevertheless it is open to valid objections. It was based on the Marxian assumption that the proletariat would sink to mere existence level and would grow in numbers, as little capitalists and small businessmen lost status and dropped down into it; that the richer capitalists would fight it out among themselves and grow richer. But the facts did not correspond with the presumptions. The proletariat did not become poorer. Thanks to the trade unions and other causes, the lot of the poor improved and the consumption of goods by them was not held to a minimum. Many small businesses did fail; but the men who conducted them frequently became salaried employees of corporations, and by so doing often improved their financial status. Nor did the wealth of those who managed industrial enterprises snowball upwards. Owing to heavy taxes laid upon them to finance armaments and to pay for the extension of social services like old-age pensions, the very rich were relatively less wealthy in 1914

than in 1900. Meanwhile the number of shareholders in industrial concerns increased enormously. The world was a more comfortable place for
more people in 1914 than in 1900. The dismal predictions of Marx that
disaster was close at hand because of the inner contradictions of capitalism, as *The Communist Manifesto* proclaimed, needed revision.

One was provided by Lenin in his book, *Imperialism, The Last Stage
of Capitalism*. Like the theory of underconsumption it asserted as a universal truth that private property and capitalism were near the end of
their tether; but it differed from it by discovering a new culprit. This
was monopoly finance. The basis for the new argument was that capitalism produced monopolies, and the presumption that went along with it
was that "the state is necessarily the organ of the predominant type of
economic organization." [1]

This theory of Lenin is supported by some facts, at some times, and
to some extent. It is also contradicted by some facts, and cannot be sub-
stantiated as universal truth as Marx-Leninism asserts.

Thus, for instance, let us look at the South African War, 1899-1902. In
so far as the Jameson raid may be regarded as its cause the Marx-Lenin
theory is applicable. Wealthy international capitalists wished to mo-
nopolize the gold found in the South African Republic, and Cecil Rhodes,
her Majesty's Prime Minister of Cape Colony, was one of them.

But this argument in support of Lenin's theory, strong as it appears,
is not altogether watertight. Rhodes was a very rich man; but he never
used his riches except for political ends. Above everything else his heart
was set on obtaining the vast uplands north of the Limpopo River, now
known as Rhodesia, for the British Empire. To secure a charter for his
South African Company, and to organize settlements there for British
immigrants, took money, much money. Rhodes was frequently careless in
the way he made it. There were, however, other issues involved in the
Jameson raid which had nothing to do with the pocketbooks of the capitalists. President Kruger of the South African Republic had no intention
of accepting the Limpopo River as his country's permanent boundary.
He also was believed to be in touch with German agents, eager as he was
to prevent the British Empire acquiring the desired uplands. The Jameson
raid would not simply make rich men richer; it also might be the means
of thwarting Kruger.

Apply Lenin's theory now to two other instances of imperialism, one
in Asia, the other in Africa.

In the valley of the Yalu River, on the frontier between Manchuria
and Korea, an apparently innocent lumber company was cutting timber
shortly before the Russo-Japanese War of 1904-5. The lumbering was
done by Russian soldiers dressed as civilians. Russian officers directed
operations. In theory they were building roads to transport lumber and

[1] Lionel Robbins, *The Economic Causes of War*, p. 34.

warehouses in which to store it. But the roads, as it was afterwards proved, were for transporting soldiers and the warehouses were for barracks. Finance capitalism had nothing to do with this so-called commercial company. It never was anything but a blind behind which political and military maneuvers took place.

Underwood & Underwood

CECIL RHODES (1853-1902)

Turn now to the Italian conquest of Tripoli in 1911. Italy was a poor country, and there was no surplus investment capital in Italy urging the government into this profitless venture. But in this same year, 1911, the French were spreading westward from Algeria into Morocco, and as an offset to this French imperialism the publicity-seeking Italians thought the time ripe to stage a little war of their own in Africa. It would look well, however, if there appeared other reasons for so doing than political prestige. Therefore the Banco di Roma was ordered to produce evidence that Italian commercial rights in Tripoli had been set at naught by the Turkish authorities. The bank produced the evidence on demand, the pretence was provided, and with a great deal of flag waving Italian troops, *ready to disembark long before the evidence was manufactured,* landed in Africa. Prestige and politics were the reason, not finance capitalism.

These illustrations are advanced to prove the weakness of the official Communist dogma that investment bankers *always* are responsible for shoving their countries into wars. Just as often it has been ambitious politicians who have compelled bankers to support their risky adventures. "Bankers in general seem to have been more peacefully inclined, and to have been more favorably disposed than their governments to international coöperation and to reconciliation and to settlement of differences by friendly negotiation in a spirit of mutual compromise." [2] As a German diplomat is said to have remarked at a time of tension between Germany and France: "As soon as you mention Morocco the bankers all go on strike, every man jack of them."

The Partition of Africa

The precipitate rush to partition Africa was caused as much by the international anarchy of the time and sheer love of political power as by economic factors. Thus in Egypt the French were much more involved financially than the British in 1882. But the French withdrew from joint action with Britain in that year, because, it was rumored, of fear of their old enemy, Germany. And from that time on until 1904 they did whatever they could to embarrass the British authorities in Egypt, despite the fact that their presence there was good insurance for French investments.

Egypt during this period was only indirectly under British governance. Juridically it remained a part of Turkey, and Britain did not even declare a protectorate over it until world war broke. Yet in the last analysis it was under one man's rule, that of Cromer, merely her Majesty's counsel-general. All that this quiet gentleman did was to give the Khedive advice. But it was always followed, since British troops were stationed in Cairo. Cromer brought Egypt out of bankruptcy into solvency, yet at the same time cut taxes and raised the standard of living. In doing this he was assisted by the Egyptian Civil Service which he created. Only graduates of Oxford, Cambridge, and Trinity College of Dublin were admitted to this body. The members were not indifferent to money, but essentially were not interested in accumulating it. They had a more potent stimulus, that of personal power exercised over ignorant and helpless Egyptian peasants. This was a matter of political tradition. An English gentleman of tradition, all for the love of noblesse oblige, felt it more an honor to serve his country in a hot and humid land than to be a London banker. He preferred political power to financial gain.

As a variation of this political theme one might cite the highly nationalistic French. Conscious that population statistics proved that France was

[2] J. Viner, *International Economics*, p. 85.

PARTITION OF AFRICA

MEDITERRANEAN SEA

STRAIT OF GIBRALTAR
Algiers
MADEIRA IS. (PORT.)
Fez
MOROCCO
ALGERIA
TUNIS
LIBYA (IT.)
SUEZ CANAL
CANARY IS. (SP.)
LIBYAN DESERT
Cairo
EGYPT
RIO DE ORO (SP.)
TROPIC OF CANCER
S A H A R A
NIGER R.
RED SEA
NILE
SENEGAL
ANGLO-EGYPTIAN SUDAN
ERITREA (IT.)
FR. SOMALILAND
GAMBIA (BR.)
PORT. GUINEA
S U D A N
NIGERIA (BR.)
BR. SOMALIL'D
SIERRA LEONE (BR.)
LIBERIA (IND.)
ASHANTI (BR.)
TOGO (GER.)
FERNANDO PO I. (SP.)
KAMERUN (GER.)
FRENCH CONGO
ETHIOPIA (IND.)
ITALIAN SOMALILAND
EQUATOR
ST. THOMAS I. (PORT.)
UGANDA (BR.)
LAKE VICTORIA
BRITISH EAST AFRICA
Mombasa
FRENCH CONGO
CONGO R.
BELGIAN CONGO
LAKE TANGANYIKA
GERMAN EAST AFRICA
ASCENSION I. (BR.)
LAKE NYASSA
ATLANTIC
OCEAN
ST. HELENA I. (BR.)
ANGOLA (PORT.)
RHODESIA (BR.)
MOZAMBIQUE (PORT.)
MADAGASCAR (FR.)
BRITISH CENTRAL AFRICA

BRITISH
FRENCH
GERMAN
ITALIAN
BELGIAN
SPANISH
PORTUGUESE
INDEPENDENT

GERMAN SOUTHWEST AFRICA
BECHUANALAND (BR.)
TROPIC OF CAPRICORN
TRANSVAAL (BR.)
ORANGE FREE STATE (BR.)
NATAL (BR.)
CAPE COLONY (BR.)
Cape Town
INDIAN OCEAN

TRM

33

steadily falling behind Germany in the number of her citizens, the French sought to annex African territory, that they might transform black Senegalese into good French soldiers, useful in defending the Rhine frontier against a potential enemy. Also, the highly nationalistic and successful Germans, noting that the British were firmly entrenched at either end of the continent, thought to spread German power east and west across Africa, using the colonies they had already established on either side of Africa to achieve that end. And this, in turn, met with opposition from the no less nationalistic British, determined at all hazards to maintain their traditional role of maritime supremacy. They knew from past experience that colonies meant shipping, and that shipping called for a navy to defend it.

The British and the Germans compounded their colonial differences in Africa as early as 1890. They agreed to a line from the East African coast straight across Lake Victoria Nyanza, thus dividing the lake between them. To the north was British East Africa; to the south, German East Africa, which included within it the eastern shores of Lake Tanganyika. Across that lake and all the way to the Atlantic was the Congo Free State, administered, presumably in the interests of civilization, by the king of Belgium. Britain did not want the expanding German Empire to possess it and suggested that Portugal should do so. Since Portugal was an ancient ally of Britain, that suggestion met with disapproval. Consequently the great rain forests of the Congo were left to the tender mercies of Leopold, King of the Belgians, whose early promise as a humanitarian and enemy of slavery was so belied by his atrocious treatment of the helpless blacks as to become a world scandal.

In the first decade of the twentieth century, as Anglo-German friction in Africa diminished, Anglo-French friction became more marked. The major contest between the two countries related to the upper Nile valley. The French were much closer to it than the British, since French Equatorial Africa was west of the upper Nile. On the other hand, the water of the upper Nile was of instant importance to Egypt, under British dominance. Between the sources of the Nile and Egypt lay the Sudan. It had been abandoned by Egypt in the eighteen-eighties by British advice. With the passage of the years this region, never prosperous, sank further into the abyss of poverty, the population declining from an estimated 5,000,000 to approximately 1,000,000. Now, however, in 1898 an Anglo-Egyptian army reconquered the Sudan just as Captain Marchand of the French army planted the Tricolor at Fashoda on the upper Nile, roughly half the way between Khartum and the Albert Nyanza Lake.

To this act Britain immediately took exception. General Kitchener, commander of the Anglo-Egyptian army, immediately steamed south from Khartum to Fashoda. The French asserted that the Sudan had been abandoned, was no man's land, that he had arrived first at Fashoda. But

Kitchener was adamant, and he had the greater force. The French must evacuate Fashoda. The French withdrew. There was nothing else they could do. Thus did the upper Nile valley become posted for the future by the British Empire.

How out of this ugly situation evolved the Franco-British entente of 1904 is described in the next chapter. The background is given here to illustrate how competitive and dangerous nationalism was augmented by these scrambles for African land, a fact not without grim significance in leading to war.

The story of European imperialism in Africa is relatively simple compared with the same phenomena in Asia. Africa was close at hand, scantily populated, and without resistant power; and climate rather than indigenous races stood in the way of European penetration. Asia, on the contrary, was far distant, densely populated, the home of ancient cultures too deeply rooted to be swept aside by any superficial victories which the West might win. Although European guns might breach Asiatic walls and European vigor open Asiatic markets, it was not possible in China and Japan, or even in India, to do much more than secure a good military foothold. In Asia as in Africa, imperialism was rampant; but in the former continent the Europeans walked more warily, and particularly in the Far East, where they contented themselves for the most part with economic concessions, spheres of influence, and a few seaports, making, apart from Russia, no considerable effort to carry their flag inland.

In Asia two powers not engaged in African imperialism played an important imperialist role—Russia and Japan.

Russian and British Rivalry in Asia

Ever since the Russo-Turkish War of 1877 in which Britain had assisted Turkey there had been growing enmity between Russia and Britain, highlighted by Russian expansion in Central Asia, where a great railroad had been constructed linking the oases north of Afghanistan with Russia. Suppose that railroad were extended south to Cabul, capital of Afghanistan? If that were done a Russian army might pour down the Khyber Pass to India—all the historic invasions of India had followed that route. Against the Russian Bear the British must protect their Indian empire. West of Afghanistan lay Persia, the buffer state between the two imperial empires of Russia and England. But in northern Persia Russian influence was omnipresent, and Persia to the south fronted on the blue waters of the Persian Gulf, and a Russian fleet there could interrupt free passage of British ships India bound through the Suez. North of India was Tibet, ill disposed to Britain, with a Russian tutor employed for the Lama. Britain needed to be on guard.

Britain's Indian interests were in the capable and fearless hands of George Nathaniel Curzon, Viceroy, who checked all three dangers. He organized a new Indian province, the Northwestern, to extend India's military sway farther toward the Khyber; he dispatched a British man-of-war to prevent a Russian coaling station at Bunder Abbas at the mouth of the Persian Gulf; he entered that body of water with the most considerable naval force it had ever witnessed to overawe sheiks and tribesmen; and he sent a military expedition into Tibet to compel the Lama to sign a treaty and agree that no foreign country could have diplomatic representatives at Lhasa without British consent. It was clearly evident that, at that time, the British Lion could and would fight.

The Russian Bear, however, counted on easier gains elsewhere, and in Eastern Asia. By posing as China's friend in 1860, at a time when French and British soldiers were occupying Pekin, China awarded Russia the vast region that lay between the Amur River and the Pacific Ocean, with the magnificent harbor of Vladivostok at its southern tip. For a long while it had been a Russian dream to reach open sea, and now at last she had an ocean outlet opposite northern Japan, suitable also as a terminus for a Trans-Siberian railway.

Between Russia's new port and Siberia lay the rich Chinese province of Manchuria with the Liaotung peninsula projecting far into the Yellow Sea, commanding the approach to Pekin. Good luck would put that, too, within the Bear's grasp; but greed, arrogance, and a fighting Japan would soon rob him of this new conquest.

Japan and China

The story now turns to Japan. How that secluded Asiatic land early asserted its independence of European controls and sloughed off such traces of subordination to European imperialism as exterritoriality and a fixed customs tariff is a matter of nineteenth-century history, not twentieth. Suffice it to recall that Japan in a very few decades jumped clear out of feudalism into modernity, able to cope with the West in all material matters such as railways, telegraph lines, and military and naval self-sufficiency, and prepared by 1894 to give a decisive drubbing to the somnolent Chinese dragon.

What took place in that year stepped up the process by which China found herself chained to the chariot wheels of European imperialism; it led also to the Russo-Japanese War of 1904-5 which in turn brought even further limitations on Chinese freedom, made Japan an imperialist country in her own right, and aided mightily in sowing the seeds of virulent anti-foreign nationalism throughout Asia.

Now it so happened in the nineties of the last century modern Japan and ancient China fell to quarreling over Korea. War followed. Europe and America looked for a speedy Chinese victory. Had not that clever Chinese statesman, Li Hung Chang, dubbed the Bismarck of the East, created an army which wore uniforms and carried rifles; had he not built a navy with second-class battleships, far stronger on paper than Nippon's fleet of light cruisers? On the other hand, few folk knew anything of Japan's progress. To most people Japan was still the funny little country immortalized by Gilbert and Sullivan in *The Mikado.*

Western onlookers of this war were soon undeceived. China's modernization was but a screen behind which flourished nepotism and corruption. The bullets for the Chinese rifles were duds; the shells for the Chinese navy were filled with sand. There were no pitched battles. Through Korea to the banks of the Yalu marched the triumphant Japanese, then onward, unopposed, all the way across Southern Manchuria to the Liaotung Peninsula.

Whereupon China agreed to the Treaty of Shimonoseki which ended the war. By its terms the Liaotung Peninsula was ceded to Japan, also Formosa and the Pescadores Islands. China recognized also that Korea was independent.

The fruits of victory, however, were immediately snatched away. Russia had her own ambitions in Northeastern China and objected to the presence of the Japanese in the Liaotung Peninsula. The French and the Russians, allied together and intervened. They were joined by the Germans. In a joint note the three European powers forbade Japan's making any annexations on the Asiatic mainland. Japan had to yield; there was nothing else she could do.

China and the European Powers (1894-1904)

China's weakness in the war with Japan was a notice to all and sundry that the Celestial Empire was ripe for the plucking. All of the great European powers now fell upon China without resistance, until Italy, too, suggested that she deserved a Chinese port, a demand too much for even China to swallow.

First in the competition for Chinese loot was France. No sooner had the Treaty of Shimonoseki been signed than the French asked for and obtained an enlargement of their territory in Indo-China. Then came Russia, a country which had been expanding its territory since the seventeenth century clear across Siberia to Alaska, sold later to the United States. The Russians were too far to the north for their own comfort, since the Amur River was their boundary, and they had coveted very much the land immediately north of Korea between the Amur and the Pacific. This they obtained from China in 1860 and had named it the Maritime Provinces, with the capital at Vladivostok. Even so they were not content. They claimed the island of Sakhalin, north of Japan, and secured title to it by a treaty with the Mikado in 1875. Continuing to press forward, they made an agreement in 1884 to train the Korean army in return for which they were to receive a Korean port. Confronted, however, with protests from both Japan and England, Russia withdrew from this project, only to bide her time.

It came with the defeat of China by Japan. Li Hung Chang, in despair at the extent of Japanese demands in 1894 turned to Russia for help and received it—at a price. The Czar was willing to force Japan's withdrawal from the Liaotung Peninsula if China in return would grant permission for the construction of a railway across Manchuria. A few years before Russia had commenced the Trans-Siberian Railway which was to extend all the way to Vladivostok. Its construction was expensive, and if the line was to be kept within Russian boundaries it must swing far to the north around Manchuria and then head for Vladivostok to the south. But if a railway could be built directly across the Manchurian plain the cost would be less and the economic possibilities greater. China now granted a charter for such a railway; it was to be called the Chinese Eastern and (ostensibly) was to be a joint Sino-Russian enterprise. At the end of thirty-six years China was to have the option of buying the road. If this option was not taken up at the end of eighty years the road was to revert to her free of charge. It looked like a pretty good bargain for China, but there were jokers concealed in the Sino-Russian treaty in regard to the use of land on either side of the line and the military protection which the road must have.

It was now the turn of Germany. That country being one of the three powers to force Japan back, claimed a Chinese port as her reward. When it was not forthcoming the Germans took advantage of the murder of two German priests by brigands and occupied Kiaochow Bay on the Shantung peninsula. Result: In 1898 the port of Tsingtao on this bay was leased with its hinterland to Germany for ninety-nine years, and to Germany was promised the future economic development of all Shantung mines and railways.

Followed then Russia again and finally England. The former country got a twenty-five year lease of the Liaotung Peninsula with permission to build a railroad south to it from the Russian-controlled Chinese Eastern; the latter, alarmed at Russian success (for this meant that Port Arthur at the tip of Liaotung would be a Russian port), secured a lease of Weihaiwei on the southern shores of the Gulf of Pechili, across from Port Arthur, a lease which was to be coterminous with the Russian occupation of the more northern port. This British action in turn stirred the French, who demanded and obtained a ninety-nine year lease of 200 square miles or more of Chinese land; whereupon the British, not to be outdone, got even more land opposite Hongkong on a lease of equal length.

One result of these nibblings of Chinese territory was greatly to strengthen the hand of Tz'ŭ Hsi, the old dowager Empress, who, emerging from seclusion, took over the reins of government; another was the rapid growth of bands of "Boxers" (Fists of Righteous Harmony). The Boxers were reactionary patriots who hated missionaries and all Western ideas. They took to the warpath, burned bridges, killed missionaries, tore up the railway which ran from Taku on the Gulf of Pechili to Peking. They got control of China's capital, besieged the legations in their compounds, and killed the German ambassador. Whereupon an international army exacted a humiliating peace in accordance with which large indemnities were to be paid, and armed guards of all the treaty powers were to be stationed permanently in Peking.

This Boxer revolt was not displeasing to Russia; it afforded her a good excuse for moving large bodies of troops into Manchuria on the plea that they were necessary to preserve order. All the countries protested, including China, and Russia promised to withdraw her soldiers, something she had no intention of doing. The Russian lease of the Liaotung was for twenty-five years only; but the Russians fortified Port Arthur very heavily and in addition built at Dalny huge docks to make that place a commercial entrepot, and between 1900 and 1904 Manchuria, a territory of China, became to all intents and purposes a Russian protectorate, with Russia in control of the two great trunk railways which bisected it, the Chinese Eastern running east and west, and the Southern Manchurian running from Harbin on the former railway straight south to Port Arthur and Dalny.

The Russo-Japanese War (1904-5)

The ominous encroachments of the Russian Bear on Chinese land did not go unnoticed in Tokyo. Japan stepped cautiously. She tried to come to terms with Russia. Let us, she said in effect, divide Manchuria and Korea into two spheres of influence, Russia to take Manchuria; and Japan, Korea. The Russians delayed their answer. Their Trans-Siberian railway was not completed and Japan felt that was the reason why Russia would give no answer. If Japan had to fight she might better do so before the completed railway made it possible for the Muscovites to inundate Manchuria with their troops.

Therefore in February, 1904, Japan struck hard. The Czar's navy in Pacific waters was divided between Port Arthur, Chemulpo in Korea, and Vladivostok. At the first two ports it was rendered *hors de combat* by surprise torpedo attacks; at Vladivostok it was blockaded. The sea was clear of Russians. Soon it was black with Japanese transport. Once again the enemy was driven back across the Yalu, this time a Russian not a Chinese enemy. A wedge was driven in between the Russian forces in Port Arthur and those farther north. Short and snappy were the victories

THE TREATY OF PORTSMOUTH (1905)

Theodore Roosevelt with Russian and Japanese representatives

won by the Japanese. The Russians retreated along the line of their railway and dug themselves in at Port Arthur. On both fronts the Japanese
attacked with fury. Port Arthur held out for almost eleven months. So
strong was that fortress, and so well stocked with food and munitions,
that it would not even then have fallen had the Russian general in command been as determined and as courageous as his men.

Even so Japan had not won the war. From the Baltic to the Sea of
Japan slowly advanced the Russian navy. On paper it looked like a goodly
armament; but in the Straits of Tsushima near Korea it proved a paper
fleet. The Russians could not shoot; they could not navigate; and Admiral
Togo of the Rising Sun was a complete victor.

And yet the Japanese had not won the war. The Russian armies in the
north grew larger daily and the Russian purse was long. Graft and drunk-

enness if not treachery, however, were rife in the Czar's army, and this most distant war was highly unpopular at home. Therefore Russia accepted the invitation of President Theodore Roosevelt to discuss peace terms which were drawn up in the United States and embodied in the treaty of Portsmouth (1905).

That treaty was Japan's revenge for 1894. It gave to Japan all those treaty rights in Manchuria and Liaotung of which Russia had become possessed; it recognized Korea as independent but under predominant Japanese interests; it ceded to Japan the southern half of Sakhalin; but no indemnity was paid by Russia, much to the distress of the victorious Japanese whose economic resources had been strained to the uttermost.

The repercussions of the Russo-Japanese War were profound. For the first time in modern history an Asiatic country had won a clean-cut military victory over a Western power, and the news of this event was quick to percolate not only through the Far East but also in the bazaars of crowded Indian cities, in Afghan defiles, and even on the upland plateaux of Persia. What one Oriental country had done might not another accomplish? Everywhere in Asia the stirrings of nationalistic pride were felt, even in China. As for Japan, the capitalization of her victory was immediate. Into Korea her merchants and entrepreneurs poured rapidly, and it was not long before the country in which she was recognized as having especial interests came thoroughly under the thumb of a Japanese resident-general (1907) and soon afterward was annexed to Japan (1910). Manchuria, meanwhile, more informally but none the less realistically was divided between the former enemies, Russia taking the more northern part and Japan confining herself for the time being to southern Manchuria, the Liaotung Peninsula, and the railway leading to it from its junction with the Chinese Eastern, this north and south railway (rechristened the Southern Manchurian) becoming a great commercial enterprise, owning docks, warehouses, land, and hotels. And holding a majority of the stock was the Japanese government!

China, 1905-14

As Japan advanced from glory unto glory China went through troubled times. She was far from being mistress in her own house. At Canton, Shanghai, Tientsin, Hankow, and other treaty ports European settlements to all practical purposes became little foreign enclaves in Chinese territory, even in Hankow, hundreds of miles up the Yangtse. Huge sums of money, borrowed for railways, telegraphs, and war indemnities, were owed to Europeans. Interest rates ran from five to seven per cent, and for security not only the Chinese customs but also internal taxes were pledged. Nor could China borrow money where she pleased and spend it as she saw fit. The valley of the Yangtse, for instance, was recognized

ASIA
1914

ARCTIC OCEAN

NOVA ZEMBLA

KARA SEA

NORTH SEA

Berlin

Vienna

Warsaw

Stockholm

BALTIC SEA

Petrograd

Moscow

R U S S I A N

MTNS.

Obdorsk

YENISEI R.

Surgut

Tobolsk

B-
Krasno-
yarsk

E U R O P E

VOLGA R.

URAL

Kurgan

Ishim

Omsk

Tomsk

Kustani

IRTISH R.

Semipalatinsk

Urulsk

URAL R.

Guriev

Kobdo

LAKE BALKHASH

Constantinople

BLACK SEA

Sinope

Siwas

Batum

CASPIAN SEA

Baku

ARAL LAKE

Khiva

Tashkend

Aksu

EASTERN TURKESTAN

Smyrna

TURKEY

Tabriz

Mery

Bokhara

Kokand

Kashgar

CYPRUS

Beirut

Antioch

Mosul

Alex-
andria

Khotan

Yarkand

KUEN LUN MTNS.

Cairo

Jerusalem

Babylon

Bagdad

Teheran

Ispahan

PERSIA

Herat

AFGHANISTAN

Kabul

Peshawar

TIBET

Gartok

Lassa

Akabad

ARABIA

Koweit

Shiraz

Kerman

Kbelat

BALUCHISTAN

INDUS R.

HIMALAYA MTNS.

NEPAL

BHU-
TAN

AFRICA

RED SEA

Medina

Mecca

PERSIAN GULF

GULF OF OMAN

Maskat

OMAN

Oman

Delhi

Jodhpur

Lucknow

GANGES R.

Benares

I N D I A

Calcutta

Nagpur

Puri

Sana

Makalla

Aden

ARABIAN SEA

Bombay

Haidarabad

BAY OF BENGAL

Panjim
(PORT.)

Mysore

Madras

Calicut

Pondicherry

LACCADIVE IS.

CEYLON

I N D I A N

MALDIVE IS.

Colombo

O C E A N

1000 MILES

60°E

80°E

NEW SIBERIA IS.

ARCTIC CIRCLE

STANOVOI MTNS.

Abadirsk

Oliutersk

BERING SEA

COMMANDORSKI IS.

ALEUTIAN IS.

40 N

LENA R.

Verkhoyansk

E M P I R E

Okhotsk

Icha

Petropavlovsk

Yakutsk

SEA OF OKHOTSK

SAKHALIN

KURIL IS.

Vitemsk

LAKE BAIKAL

AMUR R.

Khabarovsk

Vladivostok

YESSO

Chita

Irkutsk

Aigun

MANCHURIA

Harbin

Sendai

HONDO

OF JAPAN

Urga

KHINGAM MTS.

Mukden

CHOSEN

Wonsan

Seoul

JAPAN SEA

Tokyo

Osaka

MONGOLIA

DESERT OF GOBI

INNER MONGOLIA

GREAT WALL

Peking

Pt. Arthur

Fusan

Kiauchau

YELLOW SEA

KIUSHU

Nagasaki

TROPIC OF CANCER

BONIN IS.

20 N

Suchau

Ninghia

HOANG R.

Lanchau

Singau

Honan

Tientsin

C H I N A

Shanghai

EAST CHINA SEA

Ningpo

Wenchau

RIUKIU IS.

LADRONE IS.

Paoning

YANGTZE R.

Hankan

Changsha

Fuchau

E M P I R E

PACIFIC OCEAN

GUAM

Yunnan

Amoy

Canton

FORMOSA

Shunning

SI R.

Macao

Hong Kong

BURMA

Mandalay

Hanoi

HAINAN

LUZON

Manila

PHILIPPINE ISLANDS

Hue

FRENCH INDO-CHINA

SOUTH CHINA SEA

CEBU

MINDANAO

KAISER WILHELM LAND

Rangoon

SIAM

Bangkok

Saigon

SULU SEA

EQUATOR

0

NEW GUINEA

ANDAMAN IS.

PAPUA

NICOBAR IS.

MALAY PENINSULA

STRAITS SETTLEMENTS

BR. N. BORNEO

SARAWAK

CELEBES SEA

MOLUCCA IS.

TORRES STRAIT

CORAL SEA

ST. OF MALACCA

Singapore

BORNEO

CELEBES

BANDA SEA

ARAFURA SEA

Padang

SUMATRA

JAVA SEA

Batavia

JAVA

TIMOR

AUSTRALIA

100 E

120 E

140 E

TRM

as a British sphere of influence. Conversely Britain held aloof from Manchuria, the Russian sphere, from Shantung, the German sphere, and from
Southeast China, allotted by informal understanding to French enterprise.

These humiliating concessions roused the wrath of patriotic Chinese,
particularly those south of the Yangtse River. A scapegoat was found in
the Manchu dynasty, and revolutionary clubs and societies were organized for the purpose of ousting the Manchus and establishing a Chinese
republic. Chief among the conspirators was Dr. Sun Yat-sen, a much
traveled physician who had been educated in Hawaii and was as much
at home in London and St. Louis as in Canton. The revolutionary movement which he headed was utterly unlike the Boxer movement of 1900;
for that had aimed at restoring Chinese independence by ignoring the
West. Dr. Sun was a modern of the moderns; he aimed at Chinese independence by copying the West as Japan had done. In 1911 the revolution
suddenly broke, spread like wild-fire, and in January, 1912, Dr. Sun found
himself at Nanking, President of the Chinese Republic.

That republic was not to last long; Sun Yat-sen and his radical inno-
vators had not counted sufficiently upon the inherent conservatism of the
Chinese, and they had won the victory too easily. Within four years, their
republic was to be snuffed out.

When it had been proclaimed the imperial troops in North China
under the able Yuan Shi-kai were still undefeated, and it was doubtful
if a victory could be won over them. Dr. Sun did not welcome the con-
tinuance of civil war, and so he resigned in favor of Yuan Shi-kai who
accepted the provisional presidency without any republican convictions
whatever. The Chinese masses were not ready for a republic and their
leaders had no first-hand experience with constitutional procedure. Consequently, the forces of privilege and reaction soon were able to bowl
them over.

When the provisional Parliament refused to confirm his nominees for
office and rejected a foreign loan which he had negotiated, Yuan Shi-kai
took the law into his own hands. Thereupon the southern representatives
in Parliament started civil war against Yuan. The latter crushed the rebels
in a few weeks and proclaimed himself permanent president of China—
this even before a constitution had been adopted. Meanwhile the members of the Kuomintang, Dr. Sun's revolutionary society which had
started the original revolt, were ousted from the Chinese Parliament.

China remained a republic in form, even after this event, but in practice she rapidly succumbed to a dictatorship under Yuan Shi-kai. Finally,
in 1915, even the form of a republic was abolished, and Yuan, yielding
reluctantly to popular will (so he said) reëstablished the empire, an act
which almost instantly led to a recurrence of Chinese civil war.

India: Reaction against British Rule

In India reaction against alien imperialism was far less strong than in China. True, there was an Indian Nationalist Congress; but until well into the twentieth century its purpose was religious rather than political, focused on purifying ancient Hindu beliefs. Only very gradually did it turn to political agitation and accuse the British of imperialistic exploitation.

Its charges on the economic level were not well sustained. That large payments were made to Britain by India was a fact; but the major part of them were for interest paid to British firms for building railways, irrigation ditches, reservoirs, and so forth; and also for pensions to Indian civil service officials, retiring after years of useful service in enforcing law, order, and justice in a land of divergent and frequently quarreling nationalities. Their pay was high; but what they did was worth the money. The annual budget of India also provided for an army of 225,000, one-third of whom were British soldiers. On the other hand India contributed nothing for the support of the royal navy.

On the governmental level, however, India had just cause for complaint. The Indian civil service was recruited exclusively in Britain. Indians might receive appointment; but the examinations were held in London and could only be taken by men within the ages of twenty-one and twenty-four. Furthermore, these examinations were of such a character as to limit success in them to the classically trained graduates of the British public schools and universities. If an occasional Indian passed he never rose to the higher ranks of the administrative hierarchy. Even the lesser services such as education, forestry, and engineering were generally monopolized by the British. "According to a calculation made in 1904, out of 1,370 appointments with a salary of £800 and upward, 1,263 were held by Europeans, 15 by Eurasians, and 92 by natives of India." [3]

This situation was unjust. No matter how efficiently the government might function it was government by an outsider; leading inevitably to class distinctions on racial lines, breeding pride and arrogance on one hand, jealousy and hate on the other. The British at one time had thought to reform it. But before 1900 there had been little open pressure from Indian opinion; why act in advance of it?

Finally, in 1908 came the Morley-Minto reforms, named after John Morley, secretary of state for India, and Lord Minto, British Viceroy. They were not revolutionary. Provision was made for a Council of Notables to advise the government of India—this by way of offset to the Indian Nationalist Congress. To the executive council of the Viceroy an Indian was now to be appointed. To the legislative council a few

[3] *Encyclopaedia Britannica*, eleventh edition, XIV, s86.

Indians were to be elected, but they were not to have a majority, even in this house of little power. In addition the right of interpellation was granted.

To the Indian moderates these reforms were not ungenerous; but other Indians were quick to attack them, and the understandable but untactful removal of India's capital from Calcutta to Delhi aroused the hostility of the Indian Hindus, for Delhi was in the mountain country and the site of India's capital under the great Moslem rulers of the past. Anti-British agitation spread rapidly and Lord Minto, unfortunately, took the quick and speedy way of suppressing it; he deported the agitators without jury trial.

Indian nationalism was rising; probably it was inevitable. The victory of the Japanese army in Manchuria was one cause; were not the British white men, like the Russians? The spread of British education with its emphasis on English literature and history was another cause, carrying with it a passionate devotion to liberty. The Indians were quick to draw analogies between contemporary India and England in the days of King John and Oliver Cromwell. And yet a third cause would seem to be the wave of unrest in all dependent and semi-dependent lands under European overlordship. Young Egypt, Young Turkey, Young Persia, Young India—nationalistic reactions against imperialism were making headway fast.

Influence of the Missionaries

Concurrent with the imperialism of the great powers but not identical with it was the work of the Christian missionary. In 1900 the Christian churches, both Catholic and Protestant were pushing forward so rapidly in the foreign field that optimists confidently spoke of the evangelization of the world in one generation. Few would subscribe to that cheerful view in the mid-twentieth century. What happened?

Not since the days of Xavier and Marquette had the Roman Church shown such enthusiasm for missionary work in distant lands. It was carried forward by the old established orders, Franciscan, Dominican, and Jesuit, and by new orders, such as that of the "White Fathers"; and by 1900 a million converts in China and more than twice as many in Africa attested to its success. The Protestant churches before the nineteenth century had spent little time or labor in missionary work. Suddenly their interest, too, was aroused. German, Danish, Swedish, British, and American missionaries vied with their Roman Catholic brethren in bringing the message of salvation to those who "bowed down to wood and stone."

The influence of the missionaries was not simply to be measured in terms of converts. They did more than translate the gospel into the vernacular and preach it; they founded schools where sanitation and agriculture as well as the three R's were taught; they set up hospitals; they were the transmitters of European ways of living, and to some extent European ways of thinking. The results were not always salutary. The Chinese resented being told that chastity was a higher virtue than obedience to parents, and African bushmen found Pauline theology difficult to grasp. Yet the missionaries did good work in innumerable ways, in ending illiteracy, in elevating the status of women, in persuading the Chinese not to bind the feet of little girls, in helping to raise the status of Hindu widows, in showing Egyptian peasants how to avoid ophthalmia, in proving to African tribesmen that twin babies were not sired by the devil. The missionaries, it is true, sometimes played a double role and aided their respective governments in ways not altogether sanctioned by the Christian religion. But it was not always their fault if the authorities back home protected them by armed intervention and demanded reparation for their death at the hand of infuriated mobs. Any one inclined to cavil at their work would do well to read *The Edge of the Primeval Forest*, or how that celebrated German musician and theologian, Albert Schweitzer, gave up the amenities of cultural society to aid his fellow men.

Yet, as the years passed, the prospects of Christianity, in any evangelical sense, tended to fade. Christian missionaries, for the most part, have been white men. And in a world where blacks, browns, and yellows are in revolt against all and every form of dominance exercised by the whites, the Christian missionary operates under a terrific handicap. As seen through the eyes of African and Asiatic nationalists all foreigners had become suspect. The missionary was not the agent of imperialism and frequently opposed imperialism in practice. But his coming to Africa and Asia synchronized with the coming of imperialism, a fact that made Christianity appear the religion of the white man, and as such unwanted.

Chapter 4

THE DIPLOMATIC BACKGROUND OF
THE FIRST WORLD WAR

THE IMPERIALISTIC adventures of the European Powers comprise a part only of the story of international politics in the decades preceding World War I (1914-18). The conflicting ambitions and mutual jealousies thereby engendered contributed their share to the amassing of armaments, the growth of tension between the powers, and their final and fatal alignment into two hostile camps; but it was not imperialism alone which did this. Smoldering nationalism throughout Europe; a longing for lost provinces on the part of France; an eagerness on the part of Italy to extend her influence; a determination on the part of England to continue mistress of the seas; Russian Pan-Slavism thrusting intermittently toward Constantinople, toward India, toward the Pacific; German uneasiness lest the Germanic folk be caught unawares by hostile armies on either flank; Pan-Germanism arrayed against Pan-Slavism; and, above all, the yeastlike budding of fervent nationalism among the various nationalities in the Balkans bursting forth in full bloom in the Balkan Wars of 1912-13—these were the imponderables which weighed quite as much with European diplomats as the planting of the flag overseas, the winning of African colonies, the earmarking of Asiatic spheres of influence. To these diplomats and to their handling of international crises in the generation before the war, this chapter is devoted.

The Bismarck Era

The story goes back to the victorious Bismarck of 1871. France for the time being lay helpless and he wanted her to remain so. Without allies the Gallic foe could not hope to cross swords with him again, and for precaution's sake he deemed it wise that Germany not France secure allies. Therefore in 1873 he organized the *Dreikaiserbund,* or Three Emperors' League—Austria, Russia, and Germany being the signatories.

This *Dreikaiserbund* was no hard and fast military alliance; there were no mutual pledges given or taken for armed assistance. All that the three emperors agreed to do was to assist one another in maintaining the status quo and to consult should it be endangered. The *Dreikaiserbund* came to grief as a result of the Congress of Berlin. After its sessions Russia felt convinced that her old traditional friendship with Prussia had been betrayed by Bismarck. The Chancellor of Germany insisted that he only played the honest broker, but Russia believed herself double-crossed. What she saw was the double-eagle of Austria-Hungary in Bosnia and herself defrauded of Balkan gains. Her annexation of Bessarabia and her territorial gains east of the Black Sea hardly seemed compensation for the annulment of the Treaty of San Stefano. From this time forward Russia never again quite trusted Germany.

Bismarck may not have been responsible for Russia's failure to gain more in 1878, but he knew that Berlin had been the place where Russia's defeat had been recorded and that he had presided over the congress held there. Immediately, therefore, he sought to repair his diplomatic fences by tying up as closely with Austria as that country would permit. If he had to make a choice between Austria and Russia, he preferred the former country. Her frontier marched more closely with that of Germany; her armies held the bastions of the Carpathian Mountains from whence they could debouch upon advancing Russians; and furthermore, within Austria-Hungary were over 10,000,000 Germans who might yet be incorporated into a greater Reich.

Consequently Bismarck betook himself to Vienna. What he hoped to obtain was a hard and fast military alliance whereby Austria and Germany would bind themselves to resist with all their forces a renovated French army attacking Germany or a Russian army attacking Austria; what he did obtain was an agreement concerning Russia alone. In case of war provoked by Russia upon either signatory the other agreed to march to the defense of its ally. This was the celebrated Dual Alliance between Austria and Germany, signed in 1879 and destined to become the nucleus of a most intricate network of alliances and counter-alliances between various European states.

The Austro-German alliance worried the Czar. He began to think more kindly of his old ally, Germany, and Bismarck with an eye toward placating Russia (a characteristic of his diplomacy throughout a long lifetime) cheerfully consented in 1881 to a renewal of the *Dreikaiserbund*. The terms were more specific than those of the old agreement. All three emperors agreed to remain neutral in case one of their three countries was attacked by a fourth. In the event of Turkey in Europe being divided they were to agree in advance upon the spoils. Austria was to be permitted to annex Bosnia outright, provided she raised no objection to the union of Bulgaria with Eastern Rumelia.

The second *Dreikaiserbund* was to be wrecked, as was the first, by a renewal of Austro-Russian jealousy concerning the Balkans. This time it was Bulgaria which caused the trouble. That country (1885-87) objected vigorously to the tutelage of Russia, drove Russian officers out of her army, annexed Eastern Rumelia to Bulgaria without Russian permission. The Czar, infuriated, took steps to punish Bulgaria, Austria objecting. Bismarck cared nothing about the Balkans; what he wanted above everything else was to prevent his two allies from quarreling. Fortunately for him, a very definite stand was made unnecessary by England and Italy joining Austria in a Mediterranean agreement (1887), preserving the status quo in that sea and in the Near East.

Russia was now thoroughly angry at Austria and more suspicious than ever of Germany whom, despite professions of friendship, she suspected of conniving at her Balkan defeat. Therefore she would have no more to do with the *Dreikaiserbund*.

Bismarck's years of service were now nearly over, but before retiring he made one more desperate and successful effort to insure the eastern marches of his fatherland against Muscovite invasion. In 1887 he made a curious treaty with Russia. He called it a "reinsurance treaty" and it was to run for three years. Its provisos were three: (a) Germany and Russia to be neutral if either country became involved in war; (b) the above not to apply to a war "against Austria or France resulting from an attack upon one of these two Powers by one of the contracting powers"; (c) Germany "to recognize rights historically acquired by Russia in the Balkans."

A curious treaty this! Did it mean that Bismarck was double-crossing his ally, Austria? Technically, of course, the answer was in the negative. He was still pledged to assist Austria by force of arms if Russia attacked her; only in case of Austria attacking Russia was Germany to remain neutral. On the other hand, it was difficult to draw a line between offensive and defensive war. Suppose Russia should mobilize her huge strength against Austria in order to prod the latter country into fighting. Who then could be said to have started the war? Bismarck was skating on thin ice by this treaty; but all of his life he had kept some line to Russia open and he did not want to tempt the Czar into a possible French alliance, always a nightmare to him.

Meanwhile, to the dual alliance with Austria-Hungary there came in 1882 an accession of strength—or of weakness—Italy. That nation had been consumed with anger at the French occupation of Tunis one year earlier. Bismarck was largely responsible for that Gallic advance, since he had suggested after the Franco-Prussian War that the French seek compensation in Africa for the loss of Alsace-Lorraine. Then when Britain annexed Cyprus after the Congress of Berlin, Disraeli had added his advice to that of Bismarck and suggested Tunis as a proper field for French exploitation. But Tunis was less than a hundred miles from Sicily and the European population there was largely Italian in blood. Nobody had offered Italy anything after the Berlin Congress and the Italians were bitter at this French coup. Therefore they came knocking at the Berlin gate seeking allies.

Bismarck did not trust the Italians and he was not anxious to have them included in his alliance system. If a refusal, however, meant that the Italians might sign up with another group, that was another matter. Thereupon Bismarck suggested to the Italians that they approach Austria first, for owing to the inclusion of many Italians within the boundaries of Austria there had been friction between the two countries. Austria proved willing to admit Italy to the Austro-German fold, for she did not want a potential foe at her back door should she engage in war with Russia, and Bismarck was willing to have still another guarantee against France. Consequently, in 1882 the Dual Alliance between Germany and Austria was supplemented by the new Triple Alliance of Germany, Austria, and Italy.

With Italy in the bag, with Rumania part way in (that country had an alliance with Austria but not with Germany), and with his Russian reinsurance treaty, Bismarck left Germany in a secure position at the date of his retirement (1890).

William II Ruins the Work of Bismarck

She was not to stay there. One of the first acts of the melodramatic young Kaiser after forcing Bismarck's resignation was to wreak havoc with the latter's diplomacy by refusing to renew the reinsurance treaty in 1890. This act inevitably drove France and Russia together. In some respects the alliance between these two countries, the new dual alliance, was not natural. Republican France had never forgotten Alsace-Lorraine, but to autocratic Russia it made no difference who ruled those two provinces; vice versa, the Balkan jealousies of Austria and Russia in the Balkans did not interest Paris. Both France and Russia held grievances against England, the former in Egypt and the Upper Nile, the latter on the Afghan border. But it is doubtful if these alone would have brought France and Russia into an alliance. It was Germany in conjunction with England that cemented it. In the nineties there was a goodly possibility that England might become a fourth partner in the Triple Alliance, leaving France and Russia isolated and alone. In 1890 Germany and England signed a treaty liquidating certain colonial disputes, England assuming a protectorate over Zanzibar, Germany annexing Helgoland, and more agreements might follow. St. Petersburg and Paris took alarm. The Russians needed French money, the French, Russian warpower. And so in 1894 they became allied, "If France is attacked by Germany, or by Italy supported by Germany," the treaty read, "Russia shall employ all her available forces to attack Germany. If Russia is attacked by Germany or by Austria supported by Germany, France shall employ all her available forces to fight Germany." And lest there be any doubt as to just what that meant, the commitments were made quite specific. According to clause three: "The forces to be employed against Germany will be, on the part of France, 1,300,000 men, on the part of Russia 700,000 to 800,000. These forces will engage with all their might, so that Germany has to fight both on the East and West."

Thus were the rival camps established, the new dual alliance against Bismarck's Triple Alliance. The bad dreams of the Iron Chancellor had come to pass: Germany had potential foes on either flank.

There was as yet no immediate danger of war. All the alliances were said to be defensive and the two rival camps balanced off neatly against one another. The triplice had, to be sure, the advantage of interior lines, if it came to a fight; but on the other hand the nationalistic divergencies of the Austro-Hungarian peoples were a drawback and the potential manpower of Russia was enormous.

Possibly there might not have been any international war at all had it not been for Anglo-German rivalry and misunderstanding. For many decades the Germans and the British had been drifting apart. The British thought the Germans were a misguided folk who had not shown the intelligence to plan their national development along British constitutional lines. They had not forgotten that Bismarck carried through his increase in the Prussian army without pretense of popular consent, and they remembered the annexation of Schleswig-Holstein without British consent and the fact that Queen Alexandra, wife of Edward VII, was a Danish princess. They also viewed with disfavor the German tariff system, the embryonic German navy, the Teutonic demands for colonies, and the commencement of German competition overseas in steel and iron products. Always, too, the hardness of tone and vulgarity of manners of the new Germany jarred the sensibilities of the British.

Germans, on the other hand, chafed under what they considered British patronage. The complacent universality and self-assured superiority of their island neighbors in their opinion was without justification. The Germans regarded Britain as a retired robber turned pious, desirous of spending his declining years in luxury without anyone inquiring into the sources of his wealth. Von Treitschke, Germany's great historian, taught the German youth that the day of England's greatness was past and most Germans believed him.

Nevertheless, despite these facts there seemed more reasons for Britain allying herself with Germany than with any other country—if an alliance became necessary for national safety and if reliance no longer could be put on "splendid isolation," England's great tradition. To begin with there were as yet no such specific grounds for disagreement between England and Germany as existed between the latter country and France, or England and France, or England and Russia. The open sore of Alsace-Lorraine still remained unhealed. The Third Republic and the British Empire clashed at many points in Siam, in Egypt, in Oceania, north of the Gulf of Guinea, and along the headwaters of the Nile. The British Lion and the Russian Bear growled at one another across half a dozen Asiatic frontiers and the Trans-Caucasian Railway had brought Russian Cossacks within striking distance of the Khyber Pass. Furthermore, the Trans-Siberian Railway threatened to bring all North China under Russian influence, a thought most distasteful to British diplomats.

Consequently, the British toyed in the eighteen-nineties with the idea of a German-British alliance and so, too, did German statesmen. In fact, one might well have eventuated had it not been for three factors: (a) the personality of the Kaiser, (b) the belief of German diplomats that Britain ultimately would have to join the triplice, thus making it a quadruple alliance, and (c) the South African war of 1899-1902.

Kaiser William II never was able to view objectively the homeland of his mother, the British princess Victoria, favored daughter of the old British queen. This nervous, neurotic, yet frequently brilliant ruler of Germany blamed his mother for the withered arm with which he was born, hated her violently, and, through her, England. Great predecessors of his on the Prussian throne had become famous for their armies; why should he not be enrolled among the famous of Valhalla as the founder of German sea power? British newspapers mocked at his country and at him and he resented it—yet curiously enough, with all his Anglophobia there was mixed much admiration for England and what he would say about that country never could be predicted. If he had only kept silent . . . but that was one thing William II could not do. He was determined that "the old peacock," his uncle, Edward VII, should be put in his place; he always wanted to show off before the British who became alarmed that one possessed of such unquestionable power should be so irresponsible.

The German diplomats, meanwhile, overplayed their cards. They had an idea that England would come to them cap in hand and that they only had to wait long enough and England would beg to be admitted to the Triple Alliance. Now many influential British statesmen were quite willing to make a defensive treaty with Germany alone, the two countries to stand shoulder to shoulder if attacked; but they were unwilling to commit their country to any Austro-German policy in the Balkans, which might be necessary if they joined hands with Italy and Austria. Consequently, there was a great deal of smoke and but very little fire in regard to the projected alliance.

Then, too, there was the South African problem which culminated in the Boer War. The Germans were accustomed to consider the Boers as racial cousins who might form the nucleus of a potentially Teutonic nation in South Africa. German Southwest Africa was only separated

from the Transvaal by the thinly populated Bechuanaland; and furthermore the Transvaal abutted on Portuguese East Africa, through which
ran the railway from Pretoria. Suppose that Delagoa Bay were some day
to fall to Germany, or perhaps Bechuanaland? German influence was felt
at Pretoria and the Germans were keenly alive to the advantages which
might accrue to themselves if the two Boer republics remained independent long enough. When the Jameson Raid occurred in 1895 the
Kaiser was wildly excited and insisted upon telegraphing his congratula-
tions to Kruger, a fact which added to his unpopularity in Britain.

The advent of the South African war found German public opinion
heavily Anglophobe, and when the British illegally stopped a German
merchant ship bound for Delagoa Bay, relations between the two countries
became very strained. Germany preserved neutrality throughout the war,
and the Kaiser discouraged the Russians when they suggested a continental front against England; but this did not discourage the German
press from attacking England. Chamberlain, England's spokesman, did,
it is true, continue to hold out the olive branch to Germany, suggesting
an Anglo-Saxon alliance of Germany, England, and the United States;
but his appeal fell upon deaf ears. The Colonial Secretary was not a
tactful man. Somewhat later in the war, in defending the conduct of the
British troops, he implied that their behavior was at least more exemplary
than that of the Prussians in 1870-71, and as he did so the newspapers of
Germany took up the challenge in no peaceful strain. Echoes of the Boer
War were to continue for a good many years and as late as 1908 the
Kaiser added greatly to his unpopularity in England by an interview
granted to the London *Daily Telegraph* wherein he boasted that the
plans of campaign used by the British armies in South Africa had been
drawn up by his imperial self.

The growing animosity, however, between England and Germany did
not mean that the former country was prepared to enter the Franco-
Russian camp—not yet. The tradition of isolation was still strong in
England, even if the Boer War did make the British feel that they were
without friends on the Continent. And therefore Lord Lansdowne, foreign
secretary in the Balfour government (1902-1905) contented himself with
striking an alliance with Japan in 1902 whereby that distant Asiatic
empire exchanged mutual guarantees with Britain, the alliance to be
invoked in case either country got into a war in Far Eastern waters (1902).

Ultimately, Britain was to veer into alignment with France and Russia,
but her doing so was a long and slow process. She never got all the way
into the Franco-Russian tent, one foot, perhaps, being outside the flap
as late as 1914. When the World War broke, the alignment of Powers
quite properly was called the Triple Alliance and the Triple Entente, but
even the word "entente" is a little too strong to imply Anglo-Russian
relations. France and Russia were very closely allied but England was

allied with neither. The truth then was that she was on something more than good terms with Russia and under very definite obligations to France.

The Entente Cordiale

The story of how that came about relates more properly to France than to England. In the former country at the turn of the century was one of Europe's cleverest diplomats, Delcassé. He had been a bitter enemy of England, and at the time of Kitchener's bloodless victory at Fashoda on the Upper Nile over Captain Marchand, Delcassé raged. But the Frenchman was a realist; he knew that overseas it was impossible to defy Britain. Why not therefore come to terms with her and extend the French colonial empire in those regions (if there were any such) to which the British laid no claims? What Delcassé had his eye on was Morocco; if the British would but give him a free hand there he felt it quite worth while to surrender French claims in the Upper Nile valley (unenforceable anyway) and in Egypt where they possessed a nuisance value only. Other outstanding rivalries in the colonial world might be compounded also, fishing disputes off the Newfoundland coast, islands in Oceania, the island of Madagascar, boundary lines and frontiers still in dispute between France and England in tropical Africa north of the Gulf of Guinea, and also in Siam, which little country was most unfortunately situated, indeed, with British Burma on the west and French Indo-China on the east.

Cautiously, Delcassé approached Lansdowne; would his lordship be agreeable to a general colonial settlement? The French suggested terms, the British counterterms, and a protracted bargain in colonial frontiers was under way. The result was almost a diplomatic revolution. Britain abandoned at this time (1904) not only her traditional anti-French policy in respect to colonial expansion but also the time-honored policy of abstention from continental commitments sponsored by Canning, Palmerston, and Salisbury, and only slightly compromised by her participation in the Crimean War. It proved the beginning of what was to England an insurance policy against an unpredictable Kaiser and an aggressive Germany; and what was to Germany the commencement of a policy of encirclement initiated by the jealous British who sought to surround Germany with an iron ring.

The Anglo-French accord looked harmless. In the more important of the treaties now signed, France acknowledged the priority of Britain's position in Egypt, the British in return recognizing that French interests in Morocco were more important than their own. But the Germans suspected secret clauses and were justified in so doing, clauses which stated that if England in the future decided to change the status quo as to

Egypt, France would support her in so doing, and that if France found it necessary to change the status quo in Morocco, Britain would support her, in the latter eventuality provision being made for Spanish annexations in Morocco, since England did not want a powerful France opposite Gibraltar.

The treaty said nothing about Italy; it did not need to, since four years earlier (1900) France had made a bargain with Italy which provided for Italian compensation in Tripoli should France decide to push westward from Algeria to Morocco. The treaty said nothing about Germany; but after all why should she be invited to share in the exploitation of Morocco; did not that region lie adjacent to French territory (Algeria), and was there not much more French money invested in Morocco than there was German?

Nevertheless, Morocco was supposed to be independent; there were German merchants there; and somewhat earlier when ambiguous Anglo-German negotiations were afoot there had been British suggestions that England would not oppose Germany gaining a foothold in Morocco. The German foreign office was indignant at this disregard of German colonial ambitions and brought pressure to bear on a very reluctant Kaiser to land at Tangier and to make a provocative speech in which he congratulated the Sultan of Morocco upon retaining his independence and assured him of German friendship.

With one of those flares of real insight which occasionally came to him the German ruler scented trouble, and he found it. The French were furious at this German intervention and the British, although more calm, aligned themselves with the French. Delcassé talked too much and too belligerently, and the French, not eager for war, dismissed him. The Germans, however, not content with getting rid of Delcassé, demanded that an international conference be held to decide Morocco's future.

The proposal was an unfortunate one for Germany, since the conference of 1906 which met at Algeciras proved a great setback for her. England supported France, as of course did Russia. But Italy supported France, too, since owing to her treaty of 1900 with that country, Tripoli was earmarked for Italy if France gained control over Morocco. The Italians now had their feet in both camps and the Germans realized as never before what an insecure hold they had on Italy. Spain also joined the anti-German group, owing to the promise of enlarged territory opposite Gibraltar, and even the United States threw the weight of her influence against Germany.

Two questions were in the foreground at Algeciras—finance and police. The finances of Morocco were as hopelessly muddled as those of Egypt in 1878, and since French bankers had loaned most of the money borrowed by the Sultan, France demanded a Bank of Morocco under a French president. This French claim was not sustained; nevertheless, the French won an indirect victory, since the international bank that was established was largely controlled by the Bank of France, the Bank of England, the Bank of Spain, and the German Imperial Bank, and the French knew that the Spaniards and the English were on their side.

But how was order to be maintained in Morocco, particularly in the seaports and along the frontier? The Germans demanded a share in policing this unruly country and they did not succeed in obtaining it. In this lay their major defeat. The conference voted that France, assisted by Spain, should officer the police, and to give an international appearance to this decision a Swiss inspector-general was appointed. Thus ended 1906. The Kaiser's intuition of the preceding year had been a good one.

In 1907 Germany was to receive a further shock in the announcement of an Anglo-Russian treaty. Like the Anglo-French treaties of 1904, it looked innocent enough, but the Germans wondered what might be behind it.

Russo-German relations since the non-renewal of Bismarck's reinsurance treaty had been unstable. When Russia and Japan fought it out in Manchuria, the Kaiser had been violently pro-Russian. To his heated imagination it was a war of East against West, of Asiatic paganism against Christian culture. He bombarded the Czar with advice as to how the war might be won; he took an active part in assisting the coaling of the Russian fleet bound to Asiatic waters; and he sent the draft of a projected treaty of alliance between Germany and Russia to the Czar for approval. Shortly after in 1905 he met the Czar off the coast of Finland and persuaded that weak monarch to sign the treaty of Björko, definitely committing himself to an alliance with Germany. The Russian foreign office was horrified; France had not been consulted. When that country resolutely refused to enter into any alliance in which Germany was a partner as long as Alsace-Lorraine remained German, the Czar backed out of the Björko treaty with what grace he could. A year later, at Algeciras, Russia voted with France against Germany, and the Kaiser and everybody else who knew anything about it realized that Björko was meaningless.

Meanwhile, Anglo-Russian relations during this same period were more unfriendly than in several decades. The Anglo-Japanese treaty of 1902 angered the Russians and prevented any hope they might have of allies in their Far Eastern adventure; and an accidental firing upon British trawlers in the North Sea by Russian warships made British public opinion even more Russophobe than it had ever been in more recent years.

It had been sufficiently so before. During the Boer War the Russians steadily encroached on the independence of Persia and endeavored as well to obtain a coaling station adjacent to the Persian Gulf over the waters of which, according to Lord Curzon, Britain exercised a kind of Monroe Doctrine. In Tibet and in Afghanistan there were Russian intrigues afoot, and any rapprochement between England and Russia seemed as remote in 1905 as one between England and France in 1904.

Nevertheless, that rapprochement took place. The treaty of 1907 between England and Russia related, it is true, entirely to Asia. By it the paramount interest of Britain in Afghanistan was recognized, Tibet was guaranteed as a no man's land, and Persia was divided by the two signatories into three zones. The first of these, the northern and most important, containing the cities of Tabriz and Teheran, went to Russia. Then came an intermediate zone in which neither Britain nor Russia claimed influence. The third zone, to the south and east, was given to Britain. These zones in theory simply marked off spheres of economic influence. Persia's independence solemnly was recognized, as was customary in treaties of this ilk.

The treaty was a blow to the Germans. England now was the friend of both Russia and France; Russia, although not anti-German, was the foe of Austria, Germany's sole dependable ally in the Balkans; Russia also was the close ally of France, still hostile to Germany because of Alsace-Lorraine. The Germans were worried and felt more need than ever of Austria.

Because of this fact Germany felt it very necessary to take a firm stand at the next international crisis which arose in the Balkans in 1908. Behind it lay the somewhat unsavory machinations of the Russian foreign secretary, Isvolski, and the Austrian foreign minister, Aerenthal. These two men concocted a secret agreement at Buchlau whereby the straits which connected the Black Sea with the Mediterranean should become open for Russian warships in return for which the Austrians should be permitted to annex Bosnia and Herzegovina, which they had been administering since 1878 in the name of the concert of Europe. A first-class diplomatic crisis now occurred when Aerenthal suddenly annexed Bosnia, despite the fact that England and France were apparently unwilling to permit the opening of the straits. Neither France nor England was disposed to back Russia in this abrupt tearing-up of the Treaty of Berlin; the Young Turks had no intention of quietly permitting Russian warships to move back and forth in front of Constantinople; and the Serbs were enraged at not being consulted and considered that the annexation of Bosnia with its large Serbian population was a direct attack on their nationalistic aspirations. Why not then another international congress to review the work done in 1878? The English and the French were agreeable to that but not the Germans or the Austrians, who had no intention of attending another Algeciras. Germany and Austria would consent, they said, only if acknowledgment were given in advance that the Bosnian annexation was accepted. Russia now was in an uncomfortable dilemma; the Serbs were pressing hard for Russian help, and French and British aid was lacking. The Kaiser saw his opportunity and brought diplomatic pressure to bear on St. Petersburg to recognize the annexation. Russia was in no condition for war; she was too exhausted after her conflict with Japan. Therefore Russia yielded: She did not get the straits but Austria did obtain Bosnia. As a distinguished historian puts it: "The weakness of Russia was revealed to the world, the Straits remained closed, the minister's prestige at home and abroad was shattered, the central empires were triumphant, the Western powers dismayed."

The German victory in the Balkans was more than counterbalanced by renewed friction with England. In the background of Anglo-German relations there always lay the naval situation, a dangerous ground for disagreement after the Germans began building rapidly in the first decade of the twentieth century. A naval race between the two countries, however, could scarcely be said to have existed until the British virtually started one by laying down in 1905 the *Dreadnought*, the first super-battleship. Whereupon the Germans followed suit. As both powers then began to construct this new type of huge battleship, Britain's superiority in naval vessels showed a relative decline since the pre-dreadnought type, in which she possessed a tremendous preponderance, became less and less important.

In England the Liberals were in office pledged to expensive social reform. They had no zest for more battleships and they hoped to set an example by only authorizing two dreadnoughts for the year 1908. A new German navy law at this same date paid no attention to this British naval move: the German law authorized four capital ships a year from 1908 to 1911, and not until after that was the rate of increase halved to two yearly. This resulted in a hasty conference in Berlin between British and German representatives which ended in recrimination. Thereupon a naval panic swept through England in 1909. "We want eight and we won't wait" was the popular slogan, as England insisted on maintaining the two-power standard, the English navy to be on a par with any two other navies in the world.

In Germany there was a hot dispute concerning this naval rivalry. Bülow, the chancellor, was for concessions and for slowing down the German rate of construction to three capital ships a year. All he wanted, he claimed, was a "risk navy," in other words, one sufficiently powerful to make it very dangerous to attack Germany. Von Tirpitz, however, head of the German admiralty, was in favor of pushing construction ahead at top speed. The Kaiser flitted from one side to the other but tended more frequently to rest on Tirpitz's perch than on that of Bülow. The British now went in for superdreadnoughts and six of their eight ships authorized in 1908 were of this variety. The result of this was to make the Germans change their plans and build superdreadnoughts also, a fact which delayed their program so that by 1912 instead of the thirteen great ships which the British had prophesied, the Germans had but nine whereas at the same date the British possessed eighteen.

This naval rivalry lay in the background of the next international crisis which arose in 1911. It came about as the result of the fast-moving Moroccan situation. Scarcely had the ink become dry on the agreement of Algeciras than the French began to strengthen their hold upon Morocco. In order to punish mutinous tribesmen near the Algerian frontier, they occupied villages in eastern Morocco; in order to quell anti-European riots at Casablanca on the Atlantic, they despatched thither an army of several thousand. Aggressive acts like the above brought about the downfall of Sultan Abdul-Aziz, a Francophil, and the elevation of his brother Mulay Hafid, a Francophobe. But Mulay Hafid now leaned like his brother upon the French for support, for they had money. The bankers at Paris paid his debts in return for new concessions, and then fresh revolts broke out, this time directed against Mulay Hafid. The capital, Fez, was said to be endangered and to protect that city the French occupied it with an army early in 1911.

How long were the French to stay in Fez? The Quai d'Orsay really could not say; evacuation would take place when order was restored. The Germans grew uneasy as the weeks passed; they recalled the British occupation of Alexandria and Cairo and came to the conclusion that the end of Moroccan independence was not far away. Should that happen the Germans felt that some colonial pickings elsewhere might as well be gathered by the Fatherland. They began a number of conferences with the French ambassador at Berlin for a quid pro quo, but the French seemed unwilling to make definite offers. The Germans then tried to force the issue. They sent a small gunboat, the *Panther,* to the Atlantic coast of Morocco and stationed it off the seaport of Agadir to protect, they said, certain German merchants, who were in danger there.

Whether this was political blackmail or not it at least hastened the willingness of the French to negotiate. The German demand was for the French Congo in return for a free hand in Morocco. The French were horrified that Germany should expect so much, and the latter country was said to have countered by offering to throw her colony of Togo into the bargain. Then came the intervention of England. That country, not having been consulted, was indignant and demanded an explanation of the *Panther's* spring. Before the German reply reached England, Lloyd George, the radical chancellor of the exchequer, made an inflammatory speech in which, in indirect fashion, he hinted at war. His words were rather strong for pre-War diplomacy, and Germany was deeply insulted when her own bad manners were imitated.

During August, 1911, peace hung in the balance. The English seemed quite willing to fight but nobody else was. The financial condition of Germany was none too pleasant; Russia warned France that she probably would not participate in a war unless France made concessions in Central Africa, and in France herself, the pacifist Caillaux was temporarily in power. In consequence France ceded Germany more than 100,000 square miles in the French Congo adjacent to the German colony of Kamerun and of very little value. Germany recognized France's right to a protectorate over Morocco. This ended the crisis of 1911, a very strange one, indeed, and only to be explained as far as England is concerned by her constant worry about Germany's fleet and her maritime ambitions. For Agadir, it must be remembered, was not inland but on the Atlantic.

One result of this crisis was a great speeding-up of the German naval program. This disturbed the British who sent their secretary of state for war, Lord Haldane, to see if something could not be done to stay the hand of the German admiralty. The Germans were not of one accord in regard to their shipbuilding program. Von Bethmann-Hollweg, the chancellor, thought it very undesirable to endanger Anglo-German relations further by still greater naval appropriations, and at times it seemed as though he had the ear of the Kaiser. But Admiral Tirpitz persuaded his Imperial Majesty that a further increase in the German fleet was imperative.

The German program primarily was directed at an enormous increase in personnel which called for four-fifths of the entire navy being permanently in commission. It meant also new battleships and new cruisers, a total by 1920 of forty-one battleships, twenty battle cruisers, and forty small cruisers. That program the Germans intimated they might modify or withdraw if a satisfactory political agreement could be had; which meant, from their point of view, an ironclad promise of neutrality on the part of England in case Germany became involved in a Continental war. This Haldane could not offer, nor would the British cabinet hear of it. The British would promise not to join in any unprovoked attack on Germany, but that was as far as they would go.

So the Haldane mission proved a fiasco with most serious results. Great Britain could and did build up her fleet against Germany's, but, expensive as that proved to be, it was not the gravest result of the Haldane failure. There was another card that Britain played at this time: she entered into a naval agreement with France. That country agreed to concentrate her fleet in the Mediterranean, there to guard British interests (by implication) while Britain moved her larger ships from the Mediterranean to the Channel and the North Sea to guard (by implication) French ports on the Channel and on the Atlantic. Accompanying this change in the location of their respective fighting craft there was an exchange of letters between Sir Edward Grey and Cambon, French ambassador at London. The letters expressly stated that this agreement in the stationing of the warships was not to be interpreted as a restriction of the freedom of either government, that it was not to bind them to come to each other's military assistance. If, however, either government had reason to suspect an unprovoked attack by a third power, then consultation in common was to be taken by England and France for the purpose of preventing aggression and preserving peace.

This was the closest that England ever came to making an alliance with France. From the point of view of the French, these letters bound England to come to France's aid if attacked by Germany. Some Englishmen were to agree to this later, some to differ.

Three Little Wars

We turn now to the Mediterranean and to the Balkan Peninsula where three little wars, of 1911, 1912, and 1913 respectively, were destined to become three little curtain raisers for the world tragedy of 1914-18.

The first of these wars was fought in 1911 by Italy against Turkey. The Italians saw their chance in 1911 and took it. In the midst of all the excitement of that year of Agadir, it seemed relatively unimportant that Italy should occupy Tripoli. There was nothing to prevent her doing so, since long ago she had secured France's blessing and that carried with it England's tacit consent. Germany and Austria were her allies and could not well object. There was, of course, Turkey, and Tripoli was a part of the Ottoman Empire. But that ancient vestige of an empire was in sorry plight with a revolution on its hands, and consequently Italy did not expect much if any resistance to her ultimatum that Tripoli be handed over to her.

The Turks, however, showed fight. Their scanty troops in Tripoli retreated to the interior oases from whence they could harass the invaders, and what was more important, Turkey refused to sue for peace. What were the Italians to do? They occupied the Turkish island of Rhodes and the Dodecanese archipelago; they bombarded the forts at the entrance of the Dardanelles: but the Turks did nothing except expel Italians from the Turkish empire and close the Dardanelles to the shipping of all nations. The mobilization of both fleet and army was proving very expensive to the Italians and the war might have dragged on indefinitely had not the whole Near Eastern Question been reopened by it. The Bulgars, Greeks, Serbs, and the men of Montenegro now saw their chance. Clever diplomacy, very largely Greek and Russian in its origin, healed for the time being ancient jealousies among these Balkan peoples and they prepared to take the warpath against the Ottomans.

Turkey, then, confronted with the likelihood of another war, and this time against the Balkan States, made peace with Italy. In the autumn of 1912 the treaty was signed. Tripoli was yielded informally to Italy, and the Italians agreed to withdraw from the islands which they had captured, once Tripoli was completely pacified. The Italians still occupied in 1941 those islands; their promise to withdraw was but a polite gesture, for they could always claim that any little riot anywhere in Tripoli was evidence that pacification had not been completed.

As the Italian-Turkish War drew to a close a new one commenced, this time between Turkey and the Balkan States. It was brief and decisive as far as its military features are concerned, and was followed in 1913 by a second war in the same area, also brief and decisive. These two Balkan wars form an integral part of the history of the Eastern Question; they also are intimately correlated with the diplomacy antecedent to the World War of 1914-18. Their diplomatic aspects will be treated in this chapter; their military history is in the second chapter on the Eastern Question.

There were a number of factors which helped bring about the united front of the Balkan States against Turkey.

Among them were: (a) the success of Austria in annexing Bosnia, which created fear in Bulgaria and Greece as well as in Serbia, lest it be but the forerunner of an Austrian thrust down into Macedonia, thus bringing an end to the territorial ambitions of all the Balkan States; (b) the recent success of the Albanians in resisting the Turks, which indicated that the strength of the Turkish army had been overestimated; (c) the encouragement of Russian diplomats who were striving hard to bring about Balkan unity; and (d) the Italian attack on Tripoli which not only gave renewed evidence of the weakness of Turkey but also demonstrated that the European concert was either unable or unwilling to prevent local wars. In consequence there followed a series of Balkan alliances and understandings binding Bulgaria, Montenegro, Serbia, and Greece together and a formal demand of these four allies upon Turkey for drastic reforms in Macedonia.

The concert of Europe now swung into action. The Austrian and Russian ambassadors (the latter presumably with tongue in cheek) handed in at each of the Balkan capitals a solemn warning that the six Great Powers would attend themselves to Macedonian reforms and if, despite their wishes, "war did break out they would not admit at the end of the conflict any modification of the territorial status quo of European Turkey."

One hour after the delivery of this note the Montenegrin representative at Constantinople asked for his passports and on his way home stated at Bucharest: "Montenegro wants territorial increase and will not give back whatever conquests she makes." Almost simultaneously the first Balkan war began—Serbia, Bulgaria, Montenegro, and Greece against Turkey.

These two wars in the Balkans, 1912-13, were to hasten and in part to cause the European holocaust of 1914-18. That, of course, had many roots—Alsace-Lorraine, Morocco, Anglo-German commercial and industrial and naval rivalry—but no single one was more important than the conflicting aims and ambitions of Austria and Russia in the Balkan Peninsula, the former country determined that come what might, Serbia should not succeed in becoming "the little Piedmont of the South Slavs," drawing into her fold the restive Slovenes and Croats of Austria-Hungary and the rebel Serbs of Bosnia, the latter country equally resolved that the Slavic folk of southeastern Europe should realize their nationalistic ambitions and that, too, with the aid and assistance of Russia. Since this was so; since Germany was tied to Austria, France to Russia, and England partially tied to France, it was evident that new and severe international crises were imminent if there should be any violent change in the territorial status quo in the Balkans.

Both Balkan wars were to result in such changes. In the first one the Bulgars, Serbs, and Greeks won amazing victories over Turkey. In fewer days than it took Moltke to burst the bubble of the Second Empire in 1870, the Balkan allies overwhelmed the Turks. Within one month the Bulgars routed the main Turkish armies twice and drove close to the defenses of Constantinople. Meanwhile, the Serbs struck south, forced the Turks out of Usküb, surrounded them at Monastir, and took 40,000 prisoners. And as they did so the triumphant Greeks not only pounced upon the Turkish islands in the Aegean, but pushing north and east captured Salonika at the mouth of the Vardar River. Turkey in Europe now practically had disappeared except for Constantinople and a few isolated fortresses, two of which in Albania were besieged by Montenegrins.

The Turk had been almost expelled from Europe. The four Balkan allies had won a smashing victory. If they avoided dissensions among themselves, and the Western Powers played them fair, their triumph meant nothing but good for the world. The Sick Man of Europe had been nearly relegated to Asia, where alone he belonged. The Macedonian problem seemed settled. Montenegro, Serbia, Bulgaria, and Greece had all received extensions of boundary which they sorely needed. The first Balkan war had appeared to justify itself by promising blessings to mankind.

This happiness was not to be; the allies had been the victims of the very magnitude of their victory. They had hoped to win a few square miles apiece and to force a Christian governor on Macedonia, after a hard, wavering war. Instead they had almost exterminated Turkey in Europe! But they did not find themselves at liberty, after their victory, to distribute their spoils according to the division compacts which they had made before commencing the joint campaign. Now, one of the prime objects of the war had been to get some kind of a fair outlet for Serbia, preferably upon salt water. The Serbs, soon after their first successes, had struck into Albania, forced their way over the mountains, and for a few proud, hopeful days their flag had floated at Durazzo beside the blue Adriatic.

Both Austria and Italy were determined that it should be hauled down; they were prepared to act in defense of an Albanian nationalist movement which Serbia was anxious to crush in the bud; they objected to a clear belt of South Slav territory reaching from the Danube to the Adriatic, for both Italy and Austria were Adriatic powers and it was not to their interest to have a Slav state perched on the eastern shores of that sea. And as a corollary Montenegro should be forced to relinquish Scutari, the Albanian fortress, on which she had set her heart. Since the Turks were now gone, an independent "Principality of Albania," they argued, should be set up under the protection of the powers, who were to provide it with a respectable sovereign.

The situation, therefore, was as follows. Bulgaria had seized most of Thrace, and by its location neither Greece nor Serbia could have that territory. But the Bulgars were also intensely interested in getting a great part of Macedonia. Here were the "unredeemed" lands of their people, and it was largely for them that King Ferdinand's armies had rushed to war. By the compacts made before the struggle began, Bulgaria was certainly to be given a great extension in Macedonia. Serbia and Greece could not deny this letter of the bond. But they could argue, with much moral emphasis, that conditions had utterly changed. *They* had expected (Greece indeed less than Serbia) to get their reward in Albania. From Albania they had been excluded by the fiat of the Great Powers. Was it just that, with Serbia denied nearly all her expected gains and Greece also part of them, Bulgaria should continue to exact her pound of flesh in Macedonia? The net result of that would have been to give Bulgaria the most of *both* Thrace and Macedonia and her allies very little new land anywhere. Obviously, here was a case which could be very dangerous if handled by the ungentle methods of Balkan diplomacy.

The European chancellories were highly exercised over this situation and urged immediate termination of the war. The Turks were agreeable, and in May, 1913, the Treaty of London ostensibly brought it to an end. Turkey ceded to the Balkan States not only all of her territory in Europe a short distance beyond Constantinople but also the island of Crete. But no proviso was drawn in this treaty as to how the spoils of war should be divided. Italy and Austria stood firm in regard to Albania, the Bulgars firm in regard to Macedonia, and none could foretell the outcome.

This situation led to the second Balkan war (June-July, 1913) in which Bulgaria fought alone against her former allies, Greece and Serbia, and a new foe, Rumania.

That war came about as follows: it was very much to the interest of Russia that her Balkan protégés should not fall to fighting among each other, and the Czar offered to arbitrate the division of land won by the first Balkan war. It was very much to the interests of Austria (the constant enemy of Serbia) that the reverse should take place and it pleased Austria highly when the Bulgars proved very truculent, threatening to seize by force Macedonian land occupied by Serbs and Greeks. The latter formed a military alliance against Bulgarian attack and just in time. Without warning the Bulgars treacherously hurled themselves on the Serbs and Greeks, only to be badly beaten, the Greeks pursuing them over the mountains into their homeland. As this happened Rumania invaded Bulgaria from the north and Turkey struck at her erstwhile foe, now helpless. The Bulgars surrendered at discretion; there was nothing else for them to do.

There followed a peace treaty, that of Bucharest (1913). Bulgaria was all but expelled from Macedonia; she lost land to Rumania on the northeast, and even most of her gains in Thrace. Rumania gained at the expense of Bulgaria 2,687 square miles and 286,000 inhabitants. Serbs and Greeks had triumphed and they did so handsomely, Serbia nearly doubling her territory, annexing 15,000 square miles in Macedonia and about 1,500,000 people, Greece gaining 18,000 square miles and an added population of about 1,700,000.

The second Balkan war was now over. In a certain sense both conflicts might be regarded as frontier wars occurring in an out-of-the-way corner of Europe, and the fact that they were concluded without any of the six Great Powers taking up arms seemed to the optimistic a hopeful sign. Europe had passed through crisis after crisis in the twentieth century successfully, two in Morocco in 1905 and 1911, and two in the Balkans in 1908, and again in 1912-13. Surely this must augur well for the future; surely those prophets of gloom who had shaken their heads at the very mention of the Balkans ever since 1878 and the Treaty of Berlin must acknowledge themselves mistaken. The errors of that treaty were now largely liquidated; the Turks had practically been expelled from Europe; Balkan nationalism had received due recognition; Bulgaria had been treated roughly, it is true, but so condign had been the punishment meted out to her that it might be many decades before she could dispute the mastery of Macedonia with Greece and Serbia.

On the other side of the ledger there were, of course, imponderables. How strong a force, for instance, was Pan-Germanism with its drive toward southeastern Europe; how strong Russian Pan-Slavism thrusting in that same direction; could a conflict between them be avoided? The defeat of Turkey was to some extent a blow at German prestige and the victory of Serbia an even greater one to Austria, Germany's ally. Austria, with Italy's help, had kept Serbia landlocked, away from the Adriatic; but she had been unable to prevent the aggrandizement of her troublesome neighbor who had never become reconciled to the Austrian annexation of Bosnia in 1908. Now, even more than before, Serbia could be counted Austria's implacable foe.

One more year of peace remained to Europe and during it the powers which were the more conciliatory were England and Germany. Neither country wanted war, and both made gestures of peace toward one another while exercising a moderating influence on the two chief trouble-makers, Russia and Austria. Anglo-German disputes of long standing concerning the building of the Berlin-Bagdad Railway were amicably settled, and finally so by a curious irony of fate in July, 1914. Russia was wildly indignant at the appointment of a German general to re-organize the Turkish army but found England unwilling to protest. The Austrians, their jails in Bosnia and Croatia overflowing with rebellious South Slavs, thought seriously of trying to annex Serbia outright, but Germany restrained them.

The French, the Austrians, and the Russians, however, all vied with one another in heating troubled waters to the boiling point. France increased her loans to Russia for military service, elected Poincaré, an intense nationalist from Lorraine, to the presidency, and started to raise the term of service of the French conscripts to three years, thereby setting the pace for Germany to follow and that, too, rapidly, for the increase in the German army occurred as France debated the issue. Meanwhile, as we have seen, Austria delivered an ultimatum to Serbia in 1913 to evacuate in eight days a part of Albania which that country had occupied in order "to preserve order." Sazonov, Russian foreign minister, journeyed among the small countries of southeastern Europe, holding forth promises of territorial enlargement at Austria's expense, and early in 1914 the Russian government held a Crown Council at which the forcing of the Straits by a military coup was seriously debated. "In the summer of 1914 peace was at the mercy of an accident."

Summer, 1914

Then, on June 28, 1914, came the assassination of the heir to the Austrian throne, the Archduke Francis Ferdinand, and within five weeks Europe was plunged into the maelstrom of World War.

The murder took place in Sarajevo, capital of Bosnia, the murderer a youthful Bosnian student who was a member of the Black Hand, a secret society of Serbian terrorists. The deed aroused the horror of the whole civilized world, and sympathy for Austria was both deep and widespread in Entente countries as well as in those of the Triple Alliance.

Nearly a month passed before Austria took public action, time spent ostensibly in ferreting out the instigators of the crime, time more largely devoted in bringing about an agreement between Tisza, Prime Minister of Hungary, and Berchtold, the Dual Monarchy's foreign secretary, for

EUROPE
1914

the Magyar statesman was for caution, whereas the Austrian whose ideas prevailed was for condign punishment of Serbia and immediate aggression against that country.

On July 23, an Austrian ultimatum was delivered at Belgrade which, in addition to demanding apologies and pledges to refrain from anti-Austrian propaganda in the future, stipulated that Austrian representatives should participate in Serbian trials and that Serbia remove from her employ "all officers and functionaries guilty of propaganda against the Austro-Hungarian Monarchy whose names and deeds the Austro-Hungarian Monarchy reserve to themselves the right of communicating to the Royal Government." Forty-eight hours was given for the reply.

The Serbian reply was submissive in tone but in substance only partially so; to some of the Austrian demands it yielded and to none did it give a pointblank refusal. Nevertheless, within half an hour after the receipt of the Serbian reply the Austrian ambassador had left Belgrade, bag and baggage.

Austria and Russia now started to mobilize. On July 28, Austria declared war on Serbia; on August 1, Germany, realizing that Russia was mobilizing against her as well as Austria, declared war on the country of the Czar; on August 3, on the refusal of the French to give guarantees of neutrality, she declared war on France; on August 4, her troops invaded Belgium; and on August 4, England declared war on Germany.

How did it happen that Europe, having successfully weathered crisis after crisis in the twentieth century, succumbed to this one; what country, what government, or, indeed, what individual should be held the more largely accountable? The first question is difficult to answer; the second is impossible. Possibly in the last analysis the reason why this particular crisis became unsurmountable was because it came so quickly, without premonition. That atonement must be made by Serbia for the Archduke's murder was generally agreed, but only the general tenor of the ultimatum delivered by Austria was known by Germany, and the text was not available until it was too late to make changes. Equally unpredictable was the immediate rush of Russia to Serbia's aid. In consequence there were only a few days granted to men of good will to fight for peace. Fear paralyzed action during this last week of July, and the militarists had their way.

Nor can any single power justly be accused of bringing on the World War, or any group of powers. Beyond doubt and beyond cavil it became clear afterwards that the Serbian government was guilty of knowing in advance that there was a plot against the Archduke which it made no effort to prevent; but Serbia was not one of the European Powers. How the latter reacted to the crisis we shall now describe, since the picture may be seen better if we paint it country by country rather than day by day.

The responsibility of Austria was heavy in that she used the death of Francis Ferdinand as an excuse for destroying Serbian independence. The Austrians neither expected nor wanted their ultimatum to be accepted and they drew it up with confident hope of its rejection. They were determined, a priori, to make war on Serbia. Furthermore, the Austrians, secure in their knowledge that they could depend on Germany, refused to listen to any warnings from Russia, from England, or even from their own ally. The Germans raised very pertinent objections to what the Austrians were doing, as we shall see later, but to them the Austrians apparently were completely deaf; to the many telegrams coming from Berlin they returned the vaguest replies, and even those that they did make were frequently so belated as to be worthless. Austria may justly be accused of dragging her own ally and all of Europe into the abyss.

So also, however, does Russia stand accused; the case against her is quite as black as that against Austria. In regard to Russia there are dark surmises; there are also demonstrated facts. As an illustration of the former, let us take the activities of the Russian ambassador at Belgrade who died as the war began. He was a notorious Austrophobe and on intimate terms with various Serbian officials who were privy to the plot which killed the Archduke. Was the ambassador conversant with it also? We can prove nothing. What we can prove is that Russia first began mobilization on a big scale and that the Russians lied about it to the Germans. Sazonov, the Russian foreign minister, first suggested that mobilization be partial only and directed simply against Austria-Hungary. He was persuaded by the military men that partial mobilization was impractical, and the Czar signed an order for general mobilization on July 29. True, he shortly after cancelled this order but, owing to the pressure of the general staff, renewed it the following day. When the Bolshevists came to power in 1917 they placed on trial a number of high officials of the Czar's government, and the Russian chief of staff testified that the German ambassador at St. Petersburg protested to him against Russia adopting general mobilization in July, 1914, only to be told by the chief of staff on his honor as a gentleman that there was no truth in the rumor. "And all the time I had the order for general mobilization in my pocket," said the chief of staff.

Mobilization, it must be remembered, was considered generally by military men as tantamount to war. The Franco-Russian armies, as far as numbers went, were decidedly superior to those of the Triple Alliance. Once give Russia all the time she wanted to mobilize, and victory presumably would be hers.

Both Germany and France were less responsible for initiating the war in 1914. The old accusation against the Germans, the "Potsdam Plot," has been proved pure myth. In accordance with it the Kaiser is said to have summoned to Potsdam in July his principal military, naval, and civilian advisers together with certain key men in the world of business and finance and to have asked them if they were ready for war. They all reported that they were prepared except the financiers who asked for more time. This was given them and to allay suspicions the Kaiser went on a yachting trip to Norway. The only truth in the story is that the Kaiser took his cruise; most of the men named as participating in this plot were known to have been elsewhere. As a matter of fact it would have been decidedly better if there had been a crown council at Potsdam; in that case Germany would not have treated the entire crisis with such cavalier indifference as she did during its earlier stages. With almost criminal negligence the Germans told the Austrians to go ahead and that Germany would support them. This was the German "blank cheque" to Austria.

But on behalf of Germany it must be remembered that she tried during the last week of peace to prevent Austria from cashing that cheque. The Kaiser was pleased with the submissive character of the Serbs' reply to the Austrian ultimatum and considered it both unnecessary and unwise for Austria to proceed further. Even after Austria's declaration of war on Serbia the Kaiser urged his ally to be content with the occupation of the capital of Serbia across the Danube and to make no further conquests. "Halt in Belgrade" was the advice from Berlin.

The Austrians, however, paid no attention to these admonitions coming from Berlin, not even at the very end of July when it was almost inevitable that all Europe would be involved in disaster unless Austria was willing to delay. The German ambassador at London wired Berlin that England might become involved unless Austria's hand was stayed and Berlin relayed the warning to Vienna. And still later Berlin added: "We must earnestly and emphatically urge upon the consideration of the Vienna cabinet the adoption of mediation. . . ." The Germans now were seeking to undo the harm their careless promise of assistance had caused; but their Austrian allies refused to listen. No ultimatum from Berlin to Vienna, threatening nonsupport unless the Austrians did thus and so, was ever sent. The German chancellor was worried, but not so the German General Staff, which looked forward happily to a war for which it was well prepared.

What of France? Her responsibility for the war is less susceptible of proof than that of Germany, but possibly it may have been as great. Did the French give a blank cheque to Russia and, unlike their German neighbor, fail to protest its cashing? There is not a scintilla of documentary evidence to prove this, but there is circumstantial evidence to indicate its possibility, perhaps even probability. As far as we can judge France did very little to stop the war. A long telegram, somewhat ambiguously worded, was sent to Russia from Paris on July 30 which stated that it would be "opportune" for Russia not immediately to take steps which would give Germany a pretext for "a total or partial mobilization." In no sense of the word, however, could this message be considered a veto on Russian mobilization or even, for that matter, a solemn warning. Poincaré, the French president, does not seem to have been disturbed by the course of events and Isvolski, at that time Russian ambassador at Paris, even gloated over the situation, claiming afterward that he had brought on the war.

Isvolski's words, however, need to be discounted heavily; his previous career had not heightened his reputation for truthfulness. On the other hand, Poincaré was visiting St. Petersburg at the time of the assassination and the French president at that time had lauded the Franco-Russian alliance. Furthermore, the French ambassador at the Czar's court in his memoirs let slip a most interesting account of how the Russians informed him of their mobilization and how it made him *sursauter* (jump) with excitement since he knew this meant war. But the Frenchman warned his informant that he, Paléologue, was only the political representative of the French government and that any information concerning military matter should be reported not to himself but to the French military attaché.

To England a fairly clean bill of health may be given, up to at least Germany's declaration of war against Russia. Sir Edward Grey, foreign minister, did his best to preserve peace by suggesting first, direct mediation between Russia and Austria, and secondly, a conference of the ambassadors of Germany, Italy, France, with himself in London. The first of these proposals was unwelcome to the French who were willing enough to have mediation between Serbia and Austria but not between Russia and Austria, since they were afraid that would weaken the Triple Entente; and the second was vetoed by Germany who felt that a conference consisting of France, England, Italy, and Germany would result in a three-to-one adverse vote since the Germans had no confidence in the good faith of the Italians. Beyond this Sir Edward Grey did little; but on the other hand, what could he have done? It has been suggested that he might have stopped the war by a direct threat to involve England in it on the side of France and Russia unless Germany bridled Austria; that he might have informed the French that England would not fight unless the Russians ceased to mobilize; that he might have made a direct appeal to Austria, based on England's ancient friendship with that country. Whether any of these three lines of action would have borne fruit it is impossible to say. Sir Edward was but one member of the British cabinet and the others were only partly informed on foreign affairs. The members of the cabinet were aware of the exchange of letters between Grey and the French ambassador which had taken place two years earlier (see p. 61) but this was not true of the House of Commons, ultimate source of authority in Great Britain in which were many pacifists. Sir Edward, therefore, was no free agent.

From the first of August, however, the date of the German declaration of war against Russia, the foreign policy of England was more open to question. Was that country in honor bound to France in case of war? The French were quite certain that she was and the French ambassador at London asked Grey if England was willing to erase the word "honor" from the dictionary when he refused to commit himself. Then, on August 2, the English recognized limited liability, at any rate when they guaranteed the French coast against naval attack from Germany—the result of the exchange of letters. But beyond this was England obligated to stand by France? Nobody knew, least of all the Germans, who were very curious to discover and besought Sir Edward again and again for information but without result.

On August 4, British qualms were laid at rest by the invasion of Belgium. Here again Sir Edward refused to state in advance what England's position would be and the Germans had to guess at it. They took a chance and lost; but of course they might have gone through Belgium anyway in their desire quickly to dispose of the French.

England certainly was under treaty obligation (as was Germany) not herself to violate Belgian neutrality; but whether she was under obligation to fight other countries to prevent it is open to question. Such, presumably, had not been the belief of Gladstone when, during the Franco-Prussian War he had made supplementary treaties with France and Prussia agreeing to war against France should France violate Belgium and vice versa. England, it was noted, made no protest against the violation of Luxembourg's neutrality, yet her obligation to prevent such an act was similar to her obligation to Belgium. It is of course possible to argue that Britain interpreted her Belgian obligations purely in terms of self-interest. Belgium was on the seacoast and Luxembourg was not. In the days of Philip II of Spain, in those of Louis XIV of France, and in those of Napoleon Bonaparte she fought to prevent the Low Countries from falling completely into the maw of any great European power. Self-interest now indicated that she do likewise; that is evident. None the less, in so doing, England did support, and ultimately help to rescue, a small nation which, innocent of all warmongering, was in no way responsible for the world conflict.

Chapter 5

THE FIRST WORLD WAR (1914-16)

GERMANY WAS the foremost military power in Europe. In peace time the Kaiser had in the neighborhood of 800,000 troops actually with the colors; but owing to her reserves Germany was able to put under arms nearly 5,000,000 men and still leave a sufficient number of civilians for necessary industries, transportation, and agriculture. Her ally, Austria, was more poorly organized. At the outset she was not able to mobilize more than 2,000,000, although as time passed her large population enabled her to conscript larger numbers.

Russia, on paper, was the most important foe of the central empires. The Czar was reputed to have 1,500,000 Russians in barracks, even in days of peace. At mobilization this total was lifted to 5,000,000, and behind these were indefinite further millions if arms and officers could be found.

France, with a population two-thirds that of Germany, maintained a peace army approximately equal to that of her rival, and on paper slightly larger. Owing to rigorous conscription, trained reserves were large, and the Third Republic faced the crisis with rather more than 3,700,000 soldiers; but behind them was only two-thirds the manpower east of the Rhine.

As for the British Empire, if the continental system of conscription had been enforced, King George could have mobilized 4,000,000 or more troops. As it was, England, still clinging to her old professional army, had perhaps 250,000 regular troops in it, 160,000 of whom had been allocated for an expeditionary force.

Finally, Turkey and Italy had respectively 200,000 and 300,000 peacetime troops, and about 1,000,000 and 1,500,000 more subject to mobilization.

It thus became evident that battles in this war were apt to be unimportant unless hundreds of thousands were involved. Repeatedly in the First World War the fighting swayed continuously along enormous fronts with nearly 2,000,000 men at each other's throats. In the forty-seven days of the Argonne battle the Americans alone had over 1,000,000 engaged. By the time the war ended the British Empire had over 5,000,000 men in her armies and the United States nearly 4,000,000. And as they did so the Continental powers, except Russia, exhausted every resource to replace their war losses. The upkeep of all these soldiers required civilian armies as well as military. The railroad workers, the metal workers, the miners of coal and iron, the sailors on transports, the workers in factories were as essential as machine gunners in the trenches. Food problems became as important as those of high strategy. Economic waste was incalculable. "War" had once involved at most the hiring of a few thousand mercenaries and the devastation of a few counties. "War" now involved throwing to the winds the principles of sound finance, floating bond issue after bond issue, multiplying bank notes, spending on every conceivable object from heavy artillery to foreign press propaganda.

Everywhere it was assumed that when the war was over the foe would do the paying; everywhere, also, the working class was kept from striking by constant increase in pay as well as by promises of "a new day" after victory. The war affected the home of nearly every man and woman and the diet of nearly every child. It was to cost over seven million lives and was to spread poverty, disease, and starvation throughout most of Europe.

For the first time in history war became three-dimensional: from the air, on the land, below the surface of the sea. The airplane made its debut for scouting purposes, and as the war advanced certain other new factors came into play. In 1914 the submarine was an experiment, regarded by some as a dangerous toy, by others as an irresistible craft. In practice it proved neither. Once having learned to deal with it, warships were fairly safe from its attacks; but from 1915 on it became a matchless destroyer of commerce. The automobile and the auto truck now made their debut in war, and after two years came the armored caterpillar car, the tank, a moving fort which crossed trenches, crushed barbed wire, and drove a highway for advancing infantry. And also there was poison gas, at first sent drifting upon the wind and then later flung at great range in artillery bombs.

The Schlieffen Plan and the First Marne

The older Moltke had died in 1891, having devoted the last twenty years of his life to rendering his war machine increasingly effective, and after him Count von Schlieffen, as chief of general staff, had continued endless preparation for the next war. Under his direction a meticulously detailed plan had been made ready for the invasion of France by way of Belgium. Within forty days after the declaration of war the French armies were to be enveloped, then annihilated, and the German host was to pour into Paris. Meanwhile, the Germans would stand on the defensive in the east with about one-fourth of their troops, but the moment the French had been rendered impotent the superb German railroad system would shift most of the Kaiser's divisions to the Vistula. Deprived of her ally, feeble in her industrial development, demoralized by Czarist misrule, Russia would sue for peace. England was discounted. She might, possibly, enter the war and land 100,000 troops in France; but it was thought they would arrive too late to save Paris. After France was done for, and with Russia crying for mercy, then Germany would negotiate with the mistress of the seas, or fight her, as the occasion might warrant.

The Germans dashed to the war like salmon to the sea. For forty-three years their war machine had been perfected for this vital moment; all was ready, not merely guns and ammunition but enough field glasses for every officer, and any quantity of proclamations urging Poles to rise against their Russian oppressors, for use when the German armies turned against Warsaw. The troops left Berlin assured victors with "Pleasure trip to Paris" chalked upon their transport cars. Widely circulated was the alleged saying of the Kaiser, "By Christmas we will be home."

Belgium's turn came quickly. On the morning of August 4 the Germans swarmed across the border by horse, automobile, bicycle, and on foot. All had their weapons ready, the chauffeurs driving with one hand, a cocked revolver in the other. By night the good folk of Liége were awakened by a cannonade, the German field batteries exchanging their first salvos with the forts around the city.

The violation of Belgian neutrality was no surprise, not even to the Belgians. Their engineers had built seemingly impregnable forts around Liége, Namur, and Antwerp. Liége would halt invaders from Germany, Namur those from France, and Antwerp would be a haven of refuge for the Belgian army if overwhelmed in the field. But the German experts remembered the dictum of Clausewitz, "the pit of the stomach of the French monarchy is between Paris and Brussels." The best available military road into France lay across Liége province—therefore they would take it.

The Germans came on with the speed of the wind. Liége withstood them a few days, but the mobile howitzers of the German army pounded the Belgian forts into powder, and by the twentieth of August the invader was before Namur. Five days later this Belgian stronghold was in ruins and France lay open.

The French, meanwhile, instead of rushing to the aid of the Belgians, attacked the Germans in Alsace, captured a few villages and for a short time the city of Mulhouse. And now they were forced to confront the Teutonic tide at its crest, with only the help of some 70,000 British regulars thrown across the Channel. But the British "Tommies" and their French allies at least did not repeat the mistake of 1870; they were not surrounded. For ten sweating, bloody days they fought a rearguard action, frequently half-starved, and nearly dead with fatigue and loss of sleep. On came the Germans, too fast perhaps for their own good. By the fifth of September the First German Army under Kluck was at Meaux, fourteen miles from Paris. The French government was transferred to Bordeaux. Paris seemed doomed.

Then came the counterthrust, the first battle of the Marne. It began with a French attack on Kluck's right wing, so fierce that he was compelled to deplete his left wing to reinforce his right. By so doing, he left a gap between his left wing and the Second German Army, and into that gap drove the French and the well-nigh exhausted "old contemptibles" of England. There was now a wedge between the First and Second German Armies, and both were forced to retreat. Such, in major outline, was the turning point in the first Marne, a sanguinary battle which really stretched almost all the way from Paris to the eastern frontier. For the Germans it must be said that the Schlieffen plan never was carried out, since Kluck's army had been shorn of several divisions withdrawn for the German armies facing Russia. For the Allies, for the first time since the war started, came a taste of victory. They now pursued the enemy but could not catch him. Safe behind the Aisne River, the Germans dug themselves in.

Before the end of September the main conflict shifted to the north— to French Flanders and to Picardy. Hither dashed the British army, and as many French divisions as well, in a race to the sea, striving to crowd around the German right flank and to squeeze the Germans out of western Belgium. In this the Allies failed, and again the German artillery and superior organization stemmed retreat. King Albert, with the Belgian field army, was holding out hopefully behind the forts of Antwerp; but when the Germans fell upon him there were no troops available to help except a few brigades of British marines, and Antwerp fell. The Belgian field army retreated to the mouth of the little River Yser, to a tiny strip of Belgian land which it was to hold as long as the war lasted. The French and British meanwhile came up in time to cover the Channel ports, and as they did so the Germans tried to blast their way across the northern seacoast of France. Ypres, an old Flemish city, stood in their way. Its defense fell mainly on the British. For days the situation remained indescribably dubious as thousands fought in a mud-sea. By bulldog courage the British held on until the exhausted Germans quit. Early in November the first battle of Ypres ("Wipers," the Tommies called it) came to an end and the great deadlock on the western front began.

The War in the East

Meanwhile, across the seven thousand and more miles from Kurland to Kamchatka, millions leaped to arms at the behest of the great white Czar.

The danger to France was recognized at Petrograd, and an instant effort was made to divert Germany's attention. By the middle of August a Russian army forced the frontier and was in full advance on Königsberg. A second army struck northward from Russian Poland into East Prussia. At the very moment when the Germans rejoiced over their victories in Belgium there was a rush of terrified refugees into Berlin. The Cossacks were devastating East Prussia and alarmists were saying that the German soldiers must retreat to the line of the Vistula.

The Kaiser then summoned Hindenburg, a retired general, known to have made a close study of the system of marshes and barriers created by the Masurian lakes on the eastern frontier. While seated at a café in Hanover, he received a telegram appointing him commander-in-chief in East Prussia. His chief of staff was a younger general, Eric Ludendorff, who had already won fame before Liége. The two leaders had been placed in a partnership which was to influence the whole course of the war.

Hindenburg had inferior numbers, but he trusted to lakes and swamps to prevent the two Russian armies from joining. Within a few days after his appointment he sprung his trap. Caught in the treacherous lake district, entangled in swamps and forests, the Russians were assailed furiously on their flanks. By the end of August one army had been practically destroyed in the four-day battle of Tannenberg in which Hindenburg took 70,000 prisoners; and the other escaped only by precipitate retreat. Germany rang with the praises of Hindenburg and Ludendorff, who henceforth became the trusted heroes of the Empire.

But if Prussia flung back the Muscovites, not so with Austria. Late in August the Austrians undertook to invade Serbia and were repulsed ignominiously. And now, even as Hindenburg closed in on the Russians, two of the Czar's best commanders entered Galicia. They met with feeble resistance; Lemberg and a great part of Austrian Poland passed under the Czar's power; and in Petrograd the Russian victories caused rejoicings that effaced the mourning over Tannenberg.

Thus began the long tragedy of the campaigns on the eastern front, costing more in human loss and agony than even the wars of gods and titans in Picardy and Champagne; for here there was no long deadlock along a stabilized war zone, and enormous armies, sweeping backward and forward over wide regions, carried all the work of the devil with them.

After Tannenberg the Germans did their best to relieve the pressure on Austria by a drive on Warsaw. The Russians put up a skilful and stubborn defensive. Twice the Germans penetrated deep into Poland, but twice Russian valor and winter mud forced them back. The year 1914 closed with the Germans holding about one-quarter of Russian Poland, but with the Russians themselves holding nearly all of Galicia. They were pressing through the passes in the Carpathian Mountains and threatening the plains of Hungary; they were dangerously close to Cracow, the stronghold and key position at the western end of Austrian Poland; and they were blockading and starving out a large Hapsburg army, in a great entrenched camp around Przemysl. Germany thus defeated Russia, and Russia, Austria.

Nevertheless, by December, 1914, Russia was in dangerous plight. Nearly all the ammunition accumulated in the arsenals had been shot away, and the munition plants were inadequate for replacement. There was a growing shortage of all the tens of thousands of things which modern warfare requires and which only a great industrial country can provide. As early as October, 1914, the general at the head of the Czar's artillery is alleged to have gone weeping to the war minister: Russia, he said, would have to make peace owing to shortage of ammunition. Never before had the lack of sea doors counted so terribly against what was apparently a mighty empire. The Baltic was closed by the German fleet. Only a trickle of supplies could come in via the White Sea, frozen half the year, or via Vladivostok and the Trans-Siberian. The Black Sea route was closed by the hostility of Turkey. If, however, the water gates at Constantinople could only be opened, then Russia would be brought in contact with her allies once again; munitions would flow into Russia, and from that country would come surplus grain needed in the West. We turn now to efforts to open them.

Gallipoli

When the war clouds broke there were two German warships in the Mediterranean. The Allies assumed that they would run for shelter into the Austrian Adriatic, but instead they made for the Dardanelles. Not by accident had they steamed toward Constantinople. The Young Turk rulers had already given secret pledges to Berlin, and late in October, without any declaration of war, a combined German-Turkish fleet bombarded Odessa. The Czar replied by declaring war on Turkey, an action followed by France and England. Vast prospects were thus opened, thanks to the supposed influence of the Sultan, of an extension of the war to the east; and in Berlin there was now cheerful talk of the invasion of Egypt and even of India.

Around Turkey soon raged unlimited warfare. During the winter of 1914-15 there was fierce fighting in the Armenian mountains along the Caucasus frontiers. A Turkish attack on the Suez Canal ignominiously failed, and the British declared a direct protectorate over Egypt; but the Straits of Constantinople were, of course, now sealed to Russo-British commerce. The munition situation in Russia was already giving great anxiety in London, while on the other hand the food situation in England

From LET THERE BE SCULPTURE *by Jacob Epstein (published by G. P. Putnam's Sons, New York, 1940).*

LORD JOHN FISHER, FIRST LORD OF THE ADMIRALTY (1841-1920)

was growing uncomfortable, and the release of the great South Russian crop would assist enormously. Would not the defeat of Germany be hastened if the Dardanelles and the Bosporus were in Allied hands?

The Turkish forts at the Dardanelles were considered fairly formidable, but Liége, Namur, and Antwerp had not proved too difficult for the new artillery. In London the civilian head of the British admiralty was Winston Churchill, full of driving energy and high imagination. The British war office was under Lord Kitchener, highly honored for his victories in the Sudan, and Boer War. Kitchener was alive to the desirability of opening the Straits, but he already had promised the French heavy British reinforcements in Picardy, where there were great hopes of breaking the German front as soon as spring opened. He had no surplus troops available. Nevertheless, he let Churchill work out the problem of a British naval attack, although a land force would be needed in any case, if only to hold Constantinople after the navy had conquered it.

No enterprise that actually failed ever came nearer to justification. Its success would have convinced all the wavering Balkan kingdoms that the Allies were bound to triumph. The capture of Constantinople might have averted the agony of the Russian Revolution, might have rendered American intervention in the war unnecessary, and by ending the struggle two years earlier might have rendered a great service to Germany herself. All this hung on the razor-edge of fate during the spring and summer of 1915.

To reduce seacoast batteries by naval bombardment had hitherto been considered impractical, but the guns of the British battleships were powerful. Churchill was overwhelmingly convinced of the desirability of forcing the Straits, and although his naval experts in London questioned, they did not veto the enterprise. The older battleships of the British navy could be used, and their loss would not weaken the dreadnoughts holding the North Sea against Germany.

Turkish forces at the Straits were weak. As late as February, 1915, when the naval attack began, they numbered only 20,000, and were ill-organized, and widely scattered; and the forts were but poorly supplied with ammunition. There were 36,000 French and British troops available, and these once flung ashore, the defenders would have been demoralized and the fall of the forts well-nigh certain. But Kitchener neither sent his soldiers in time nor warned Churchill that if the British navy failed the British army could do nothing. There were orders and counterorders to the forces on the transports. There were intrigues with Greece (then neutral) to get a Greek army corps to strike a blow at its old foe, the Turk. On February 19, the British ships aided by a French squadron, attacked the outer forts of the Dardanelles and silenced them. Mine sweepers penetrated far up the waterway. In Constantinople panic reigned, and the Sultan's harem packed for a hasty trip to Asia.

The first progress was not followed up promptly. Not until March 18 did the Franco-British fleet at length attack the inner forts, the key to Constantinople. The bombardment proved less successful than was hoped; the batteries were not permanently silenced. Late in the day, two British and one French battleship struck mines in an area supposed to have been swept clear, and were sunk. Nevertheless, it was assumed everywhere that the naval attack would be renewed, and there is now competent evidence that the Turks were nearly at the end of their heavy ammunition.

But the British fleet had lost two battleships. It had been contrary to all naval axioms for ships to contend with forts. The technical heads of the admiralty had discovered that Kitchener was now willing to try to force the Dardanelles by a land attack, and were only too happy to pass the task on to the British army.

The Turkish forces were still few in number, and British troops had already been sent to the Dardanelles under Sir Ian Hamilton. But he found on arriving before the Straits that the transports had been so carelessly loaded that nearly everything needed for landing a great force and for fighting hard battles had been buried at the bottom of his transports. His ships therefore sailed away ingloriously to the nearest adequate harbor, Alexandria, to reorganize their cargoes; and the Turks had ample warning of what was coming.

A month earlier the Turks on the Gallipoli Peninsula, covering the Dardanelles, could have been defeated by a swift attack; in March they were more numerous but still outnumbered by the British. But by April, when the attack came, the Turks were equal in numbers and under the command of an experienced German, Liman von Sanders.

Despite underwater entanglements of barbed wire and shores lined with machine guns, the British threw themselves ashore near the tip of the peninsula. Their losses were terrible (nearly 19,000 in the first two weeks' fighting), but they made good their landing. To penetrate inland to the heights of Krithia was another matter, and soon the British and the Turks were looking at each other across two lines of trenches in a deadlock as complete as that in France. Hamilton nevertheless clung on, awaiting reinforcements without which nothing could be done.

Meanwhile, in London, owing to a cabinet crisis, Churchill ceased to be civilian head of the admiralty, and all projects for another naval attack lapsed. Kitchener ordered more troops to the Dardanelles, but they made haste slowly. At length, late in July, Hamilton had forces that three months earlier might have brushed the Turks aside like gossamer. But now, although he commanded 120,000, Sanders had approximately as many. The British, thanks to their command of the sea, were able to make a surprise landing at a new and unguarded point. A wholly new force was landed at Suvla Bay, up the peninsula to the north where (if success attended) the Turkish strongholds on the Straits could be over-whelmed from the rear. But it was now too late; the Turks were ready. Sanders had arrived at the scene of action together with his able lieu-tenant, Kemal Bey (later dictator of the post-War Turkish republic). The magnificent valor of the English, Australian, and New Zealand troops wore itself out against the stubborn and skilful resistance of the rein-forced enemy. By August the great attack had spent itself with none of the key positions taken. Hamilton had lost about 30,000 men in a single week and the entire campaign collapsed. Altogether the British lost at Gallipoli over 100,000 killed or wounded. The prestige of the great empire was shaken by this policy of "too little and too late."

Japan and Italy Enter the War

Meanwhile, two new allies joined the Belgians, the French, and the British. They were Japan and Italy, the former declaring war on Germany in August, 1914, the latter declaring war on Austria in May, 1915.

Concerning the entrance of Japan, little need be said. The statement of Count Okuma, head of the Japanese government, may be discounted. According to him,

not only in the Far East, but everywhere else that may be necessary, Japan is ready to lay down her life for the principles that the foremost nations will die for. It is to be in line with these nations that she is at that time opposing and fighting what she believes to be opposed to these principles. Japan's relation to the present conflict is as a defender of the things which make for higher civilization and a more lasting peace.

The real reason was quite different. Japan saw a golden opportunity to avenge herself on Germany for past wrongs and to seize the German colony of Kiauchow. It was true that Japan was bound to England by treaty, but only in case of an unprovoked attack upon either England or Japan in India or eastern Asia. Germany was making no attack there, and as Winston Churchill afterwards acknowledged, "no clauses in the Anglo-Japanese treaty entitled us to invoke the aid of Japan."

The case with Italy was much more complicated. That country was a member of the Triple Alliance; she also, as we may recall, had signed treaties with both England and France, thus having a foot in both camps. That she was entitled to remain neutral was juristically clear, since Austria had not consulted Italy in the critical June and July of 1914 in regard to her Serbian policy, thus breaking the terms of the Austro-Italian alliance. This in itself, however, scarcely justified Italy in deserting her old allies and siding with their foes; for Italy in this war simply put herself up at auction and sold herself to the highest bidder.

It was a long-drawn-out auction, lasting for months. The Germans were willing to offer Italy a good deal of Austrian territory for Italy's neutrality, and the Austrians reluctantly agreed to the cession of the South Tyrol, occupied mainly by Italians. But the Allies offered far more for Italy's active participation on their side—not only the South Tyrol but the city of Trieste, a large part of the Istrian Peninsula and of Dalmatia, Avlona in Albania, islands in the Aegean seized by Italy in her war with Turkey, and compensation in Africa if England and France annexed territory there after the war. This bargain was ratified by the Treaty of London (April, 1915), and in view of its terms it is interesting to note what Woodrow Wilson told the Italian Chamber of Deputies on his visit to Rome in 1919. "Then back of it all, and through it all," said the President of the United States, "running like the golden thread that wove it together, was our knowledge that the people of Italy had gone into this war for the same exalted principle of right and justice that moved our own people."

Italy thus projected herself into the conflict, but a great disappointment awaited her optimists. For political and sentimental reasons her campaign was directed against Trieste. Therefore her general, Cadorna, was destined to throw away his men, ultimately by hundreds of thousands, on the Austrian positions along the Isonzo and in struggling to capture the Carso plateau which commanded Trieste. All through 1915 the Italians continued this warfare, spending themselves against rock and ice with but trifling advance.

Russian Defeat, Bulgarian Entry, and Serbian Collapse (1915)

During the winter of 1914-15 the German military came to a new decision: they would stay on the defensive on the west and strike at the east on the blood-soaked plains of Poland. The German drive there in 1915 was under the command of one of William II's ablest field commanders, Mackensen, and it speaks well for the ability of the Russian generals that, despite a ruinous lack of ammunition, they were able to call back their troops involved in the Carpathian passes and to conduct an orderly and stubbornly contested retirement. No soldiers ever endured more ruthless punishment than did those of Nicholas II, last Czar of the Russias. During the first three months they fired more shells per day than their factories put out per month. They had plenty of men but no rifles to put into their hands, and only by the use of the bayonet could they halt the German advance. By September, 1915, the Russians had lost all they had gained and were driven back far beyond their own frontiers.

The Central Powers now turned their attention to the southeast. Throughout 1915 Bulgaria had been listening to offers from both sides, and had the Allies won instead of lost the Gallipoli campaign, Bulgaria would probably have yielded to their wooing. The Allies were hampered, however, by the auction held at Sophia; they had less to offer Bulgaria than the Central Powers. There was nothing, indeed, very tempting that they could offer, except Turkish territory which Bulgaria did not care for, and possibly a port on the Aegean, provided Greece might be willing to cede one in return for promises of Turkish land in Asia Minor.

What Bulgaria did want, and want very much, was Macedonian territory annexed by Serbia in 1913. Since Serbia was an ally of France and England, this land could not be decently ceded to Bulgaria without Serbian approval, and this the Serbs stanchly refused to give.

No such difficulty confronted the Germans. They were quite willing that Bulgaria should annex the Serbian conquests of 1913 in Macedonia. The Bulgars liked the German offer, and in the summer of 1915 it seemed as though Germany was winning the war. Therefore, they allied themselves with the Central Powers and agreed to hit at Serbia from the east as the Austro-Germans struck that unfortunate country from the north.

This meant the collapse of Serbia. The victorious Mackensen, in command of the Austro-German army, overran North Serbia in October, 1915, and the Bulgars almost simultaneously occupied their chosen districts in Macedonia. The Serbs, fighting bravely, retreated to Montenegro and northern Albania; but rapidly they were driven out of these mountain fastnesses. By the end of February, 1916, all that was left of the Serbian army was encamped on the Greek island of Corfu, safe for the time being because the Allies controlled the seas.

The Western Front (1915-16): Verdun

Along the western front, meanwhile, approximately four million men were deadlocked. Thousands of cannon and tens of thousands of machine guns sustained these hosts. Air combats were incessant.

At long intervals would come battles, offensives designed to master large sections of the hostile lines. These contests were usually quite alike: intense artillery fire, the rush of infantry over earthworks and barbed-wire entanglements partly destroyed by the guns, the counter-fire of the enemy, trenches won, the rush of the enemies' reserves, counter-attack, bombs, and bayonets. Then the offense would spend itself and the section of the front where it took place would settle down to standardized petty slaughter. Almost every such offense succeeded—that is, if pushed resolutely it could win a few lines of trench. Almost every such offense was defeated—never coming to a genuine breakthrough so that the enemy could be chased back into the open country. And all this went on continuously for nearly four years until new weapons and new warriors brought a return to something like a war of maneuver.

Both the French and the British tried their best in 1915 to break

through, the former in the Artois district and in Champagne, the latter
at Neuve Chapelle and at Loos. The results were disappointing. It proved
possible to demolish the German front-line trenches with comparative
ease, and even to capture parts of the second line. But behind this there
was always a third, bristling and formidable. Before the artillery could
be moved forward to destroy this barrier, the Germans were always able
to hurry forward reserves and to concentrate their own batteries on the

chief points of danger. These inner trench lines simply could not be
stormed.

Then, as 1916 opened, the Germans in turn tried to recover the offensive on the western front. Germany had her own iron and coal; she was
also managing by desperate economies to get along with her own cereals;
nevertheless, the pressure of the British sea blockade, like the finger on
the wrestler's windpipe, was stifling the economic life of the Central
Powers. There was an especial absence of butter, lard, and all forms of
fat. Want of copper, rubber, cotton, and lubricating oils threatened. By

the end of 1915 Germany was already undergoing privation. British sea power was throttling her; what counterstroke was possible?

One possible form was the submarine, and another was a telling blow by land. Russia had been driven back about as far as it was safe to drive her. She must be left for the time being to her own miseries. Troops could be released from the eastern front for another offense against France; and if France could possibly be driven out of the war a reckoning might then be had with England. The Germans did not however, undertake a breakthrough on the main western front; they had learned the lesson of the Allies' failures of 1915. They resolved rather to win a startling success on a limited front; namely, by the capture of Verdun, the greatest of the barrier fortresses on the eastern frontier of the Third Republic.

Verdun had, indeed, been a pivotal position in the French military scheme since the beginning of the war. It was not an ordinary fortress but a vast entrenched camp, held by 175,000 men, and would never succumb to a mere park of siege-guns as did Liége and Namur. The Germans proposed to attack on a grand scale, using nineteen divisions. Preparations conducted with meticulous Prussian care were put through as secretly as possible and the French had only vague rumors as to where the blow would fall.

The attack began with a bombardment, up to that time the most severe recorded in history. It was maintained incessantly for nine hours, during which time the French trench system seemed annihilated and "the craters made by the huge shells gave all the country-side an appearance like the surface of the moon." The German infantry then went forward. But there were still Frenchmen alive in the midst of the chaos and their artillery in the rear had not been silenced. Both sides fed into the furnace of this incessant battle men, guns, and ammunition without stint, and around Verdun raged the fiercest and most sanguinary struggle of the entire war.

The great General Staff could not now break off its undertaking if it would. To relinquish the attack on Verdun meant a confession to the world of a great defeat. Every trench-line, salient, and petty hillock along the front of twenty-two miles became the scene of titanic conflict. Certain forts and important positions were taken and retaken, until their soil was drenched with blood. The famous cry of the French privates as this contest blazed hotter, *"They shall not pass!"* was more than a battle-cry; it was the expression of an inflexible will. The spirit of the defense was summed up in a scribbling found upon a wooden casing of a bomb-proof shelter in the French firing-line, near the center of the battle:

> *Mon corps à la terre,*
> *Mon âme à Dieu,*
> *Mon coeur à France.*

Against this spirit, although the German Staff flung its armed men into the conflict as recklessly as it might fling coal into the furnace, victory was impossible. By sacrifices that threatened to cripple their war-machine, the Teutons, nevertheless, pressed the attack through April and May, for the prestige of Prussian militarism was at stake before its own people. By June the Germans were slowly working their way toward the inner defenses, but the French commanders were now simply sparring for time. They knew that Britain was about to make an unprecedented counterthrust. On July 1, 1916, began the Battle of the Somme, and the German lines in Picardy were in deadly peril.

The Somme

The British now came to the help of their ally. A larger part of the front was taken over from the French, and behind that sector there was an accumulation of guns and ammunition, calculated to outrival the German concentration at Verdun. The results were imposing; the country was ready for the major British offensive of 1916.

It began with the British raining shells, not on a narrow sector as at Verdun, but over a wide front, and it continued for six days. Then, on July 1, the British assaulted twenty miles of trenches just north of the Somme River while the French struck along the ten miles directly south. The artillery fire was withering, but the destruction wrought was incomplete. Much barbed wire was cut; but many machine-gun nests were still in action, and the German artillery in the rear had not been silenced. At the northern end of the battle line the British met with a stone-wall resistance and their assault there failed. On the south they made gains of one or two miles deep on a front of about seven miles. The French, under the skilful direction of Marshal Foch, met with somewhat greater success and with smaller losses—but nowhere was there a breakthrough in sight. So ended the first day of the Somme. But it was only the beginning. Haig and his men kept it up. The battle of the Somme was continued well into November, sometimes conducted fitfully, sometimes with rekindled fury. By the end of that time a wedge had been driven into the German lines along a front of over forty miles. The Allies had captured 350 guns and 65,000 prisoners, and the whole German loss was around 600,000. But the British losses had been about 450,000, the French 200,000. Technically, the Somme was an Allied victory, but it had brought no decision, and it was not able to avert one more great disaster to the Allies in the east—the overrunning of Rumania.

Russia and Rumania (1916)

Russia had been beaten in 1915, but not to her knees. In the winter of 1915-16 there was a revival of patriotic enthusiasm. The troops had kept their courage and morale, and the Czar had able generals. The result was that for the last time the war machine which Peter the Great had originally fathered went forward to new campaigns with some enthusiasm.

The Central Empires had considered the Muscovites so completely defeated that in May and June, 1916, the Austrians started an offensive from the Trentino against the Italians. But no sooner had it got under way than the Russians struck once more and the danger to Italy was averted. The troops of Francis Joseph had to be hurried back to Galicia, and even these would never have sufficed to prevent the undoing of Austria had not sixteen divisions of German veterans been withdrawn from the western front to hold back the Slavic deluge.

On June 4, 1916, all the replenished Russian cannon thundered and a few hours later their infantry charged. The brunt of the attack fell upon the Austrian armies commanded by the Archduke Joseph Ferdinand, and he, like so many Hapsburg commanders, let himself be caught unprepared. Many of his troops were Czechs with no zeal for the Vienna rulers, and they surrendered in droves. Within a few days the Russians had advanced fifty miles and had taken 70,000 prisoners. Bukovina was again overrun and the Russians seemed on the point of taking Galicia. Then German help arrived, "like lime to strengthen wet sand," and Austria was saved.

It is difficult to visualize "these dim, weird battles of the east" when, with imperfect equipment and by sheer reckless energy and disregard of sacrifices, the Russians strove to force a decision by means of a million men at constant grips with nearly as many Germans and Magyars. By August this Russian attack had spent itself; the ammunition accumulated during the winter was nearly exhausted; and within the czardom there were signs of demoralization. But the Russian successes were taken by the unfortunate Rumanians as merely an earnest of a still fiercer winter campaign, and late in August, 1916, the Rumanians forsook their neutrality and entered the war on the Allies' side.

The Rumanians, like the Bulgars and the Italians, sold themselves to the highest bidder. The Central Powers were quite willing to offer Bessarabia, Russian territory in which Rumanians were numerous; and the Allies were quite agreeable to giving away Transylvania, Hungarian territory in which Rumanians were in the majority. Of the two regions, Transylvania was by far the more valuable. But the Rumanians wanted more from the Allies; they sought the province of Bukovina, north of the Carpathians and a part of Austria; they demanded also the Banat of Temesvar, across the Danube from Belgrade in Hungary, occupied in part by Serbs as well as by Rumanians. Since the Serbs likewise desired the Banat, the Allies were unwilling to pledge it to Rumania, but they finally did so and Bukovina as well. Hungary, meanwhile, despite suggestions from Berlin, resolutely refused to cede any Hungarian land to the Rumanians, and the latter chose the side of the Allies, since their bid in the international auction was highest, and since Russian arms (temporarily) were victorious in the early part of 1916.

For a moment there was panic in Vienna and Budapest, and jumpy nerves in Berlin. For a fortnight the Rumanians advanced. Then the Germans struck hard. From the south, Mackensen, the conqueror of Serbia, drove into the delta lands of the Danube, the Dobruja, with a mixed host of Germans, Bulgars, and Turks, and the invasion of Transylvania was met by a German army after the Rumanians were fairly involved in the Carpathian passes. The invading columns were caught and routed. By gallant exertion most of the Rumanian units fought their way home again, but they were unable to save Bucharest and the national capital had to be shifted to Jassy in Moldavia. The northern third of Rumania was saved, temporarily, from the victors; but nothing could take away the effects of this new defeat of the Allies. The Central Powers, by this last success, reduced their eastern front enormously; they had access to the Black Sea; they had won in Rumania wide grain lands and great oil wells which promised to ease their famine in food and fuel.

The War in Asia Minor and Mesopotamia: Kut-el-Amara and Bagdad (1916-17)

Only in one zone did the Allies make progress—the eastern frontier of Turkey. The Caucasus armies of Russia, routed a considerable Turkish army as early as January, 1915. A year later General Yudeitch, leading 170,000 Russians on one of the most remarkable winter marches on record, forced his way through snow-blocked passes, fought a three-day battle with the Turks, and flung them back on Erzerum, key to Armenia. Within a month almost all of Armenia was in his hands. But here again advance was halted. The British attack on Gallipoli failed and Turkish reinforcements could now be hurried over from the west. The Muscovites were at the end of their lines of communication and were ill-sustained from home; to penetrate farther into Kurdistan was impossible.

The British, however, were pushing the Turks hard from the South. No sooner had Turkey entered the war than they had seized Basra at the head of the Persian Gulf. In September they were in Kut-el-Amara, chief town along the river route to Bagdad. Pressing North they collided with a superior Turkish army. Driven back on Kut, their commander, General Townshend, was besieged by the Turks. An expedition was sent up the river to succor him, but it was held up by the winter rains and floods which turned the Tigris valley into swamps. Kut held out until April, 1916, when Townshend surrendered with 9,000 starving troops. It was now necessary for the British to take Bagdad or to lose face completely throughout all Asia. Heavy reinforcements, sorely needed in other fields, were therefore hurried to the miasmic, super-heated valleys of old Babylonia. The Bedouin desert tribes, who hated Turkish misrule, were carefully conciliated, and no mistake was made a second time in despising the foe. In February, 1917, Kut was retaken, and the next month a British cavalry column swung into Bagdad.

The capture of Bagdad restored throughout the East that British prestige which Kut and Gallipoli had shaken.

The War at Sea

Hardly had the first cannon thundered in Belgium before the influence of British sea power began to tell. Like a great bunker covering the German harbors, the physical length of Great Britain lay across the path of her foe to the outer ocean. German ships could find the Atlantic only through the vigilantly guarded Straits of Dover, or by a circuitous route to northward and westward, well through the North Sea. The British "Grand Fleet," the most powerful force of dreadnoughts in the world, mobilized far to the north at Scapa Flow, an island-locked area in the windy Orkneys. Here, for years, it maintained its chief base, unseen usually, but not unfelt.

The German battleships might, indeed, have crossed the North Sea and even possibly have thrown men ashore in the southern part of England, but (irrespective of their reception on land) the Grand Fleet would have been down upon their flanks at once. Never, in the whole war, did the Germans risk such an adventure. If they had tried to reach the Atlantic by way of Norway and the Shetlands, their foes would have been on them all the more quickly. As for the Channel passage, it was not held by a great force of battleships, but by sufficient lesser craft, sustained by mines, submarines, and coast batteries, so that any attempt to seize it would have been delayed until long after the arrival of the Grand Fleet. The result was that, most of the time, Tirpitz's costly creation, the German "High Seas Fleet" never saw the high seas at all, but lay in harbor watched by British spies.

Meantime, on the distant oceans, the scattered cruisers that Germany had stationed in remote corners of the world had been chased down. For three months, the *Emden* ranged the Indian Ocean, an effective commerce ravager, until she was destroyed by the more powerful Australian cruiser *Sydney*. More dramatic was the career of the German squadron under Admiral von Spee, who found himself, with two good armored cruisers (the *Scharnhorst* and the *Gneisenau*), and several lighter vessels, on the coast of China. Japan had declared war, and was closing in upon Kiauchow; but Spee would not let himself be caught in a hopeless blockade. As became a courageous seaman, he struck out boldly across the Pacific.

The British knew that he was approaching the coast of Chile, and sent thither Sir Christopher Cradock, with a light squadron. Reinforcements were on their way to Cradock, but when he discovered the Germans off Coronel, south of Chile, he knew it was the part of English seamen to fight, and he went down with his two largest ships. The third escaped to tell the tale and London acted instantly—British prestige on the seas was at stake. Two heavy battlecruisers, and other formidable craft, were sent, full speed, to the South Atlantic.

Spee rounded Cape Horn, and endeavored to work his way northeastward. On December 8, 1914, he approached the Falkland Islands, to raid what he imagined was an unprotected British colony, when, above the headlands, he saw the tripod masts of the battlecruisers. The German admiral fled instantly towards the open sea, but his case was hopeless. The battlecruisers chased him with superior speed, then sank his ships with superior gun power. One of his light cruisers (the *Dresden*) got away but was later destroyed off Juan Fernandez in the Pacific ("Robinson Crusoe's" island). Spee himself, refusing to strike his flag, perished in the icy waters of the South Atlantic.

Jutland

On May 31, 1916, in the North Sea not far from the Danish coast came the one great naval engagement of the war—the battle of Jutland. Admiral Scheer, in command of the German "High Seas Fleet," tired of inaction and tempted by the presence in home waters of large numbers of submarines, came out from behind his mine fields sending ahead on scouting duty a squadron under Admiral Hipper, the nucleus of which were five swift battle cruisers. The British, aware that the Germans were out, steamed forth to meet them. Their "Grand Fleet" under Admiral Jellicoe was at Scapa Flow in the far north, but Admiral Beatty, with a formidable squadron of battle cruisers was at Rosyth near Edinburgh. Both fleets sailed to meet the Germans, but it was Beatty who first came in contact with them.

It was a haphazard meeting. The smoke from a Danish trader drew Beatty eastward and Hipper to the west as their two fleets joined in action early in the afternoon. In this first encounter the Germans were victorious, two large British battle cruisers being blown up and a third seriously crippled, while their foe suffered no major casualty. Nevertheless, Beatty presumably would have won the day as his heavier and relatively slower battleships swung into action, had he not suddenly found himself confronted with the main German fleet under Scheer toward which Hipper skilfully had maneuvered.

Thereupon Beatty fled north, notifying Jellicoe of his discovery. Jellicoe instantly steamed south to join Beatty who was pursued by the Germans, and about six P.M. the two main fleets met. Scheer was ignorant of Jellicoe's presence and the superiority of the British metal and speed was assured. Almost before the German admiral realized it, the shells of his enemy began to drop around him. It was now the turn of the Germans to run for safety, one of their larger ships being wounded unto death and several others being thoroughly mauled. Jellicoe, however, was cautious in pursuit. When daylight came the Germans were no longer to be seen. Skilfully, they had worked their way through the British fleet and had withdrawn to the safety of their mine fields. Britain remained the mistress of the seas.

Chapter 6

THE FIRST WORLD WAR (1917-18)

AFTER TWO and a half years there had been no decision. Except on the high seas, the Central Powers had been the more successful; but the Allies clung on doggedly and their superiority in man power and matériel sooner or later presaged triumph. In 1917 unforeseen events occurred, but fortunately enough for the Allies they counterbalanced each other; one, the entry of the United States into the war, a portent of disaster for the Germans; the other, the withdrawal of Russia from the conflict, a body blow to Allied hopes.

Public opinion in America, on the whole, sided with the Allies, a fact accounted for by sympathy for Belgium, historic friendship for France, "cultural ties" with England, and, as the war continued, by the fact that the Allies bought profusely in the United States. Certainly America did not want to see her best customers become bankrupt. On the other hand, German-Americans were numerous in the United States and so, too, Irish-Americans, traditional haters of England; those facts, together with the stretching of the laws of blockade in which England engaged, tended to neutralize pro-Ally sentiment.

The United States, however, no sooner began vigorously to contest British interference with American commerce than she faced the submarine issue. On February 4, 1915, in retaliation, it was alleged, for the British blockade on foodstuffs, a "war-zone" order appeared from Berlin: German submarines were ordered to sink enemy merchantmen, especially in the waters around the British Isles, even if their crews and passengers could not be rescued; furthermore if neutral ships entered the "blockade waters," they "could not always be prevented from suffering from attacks meant for enemy ships."

The destruction of unarmed ships without first rescuing crews and passengers was contrary to accepted doctrines and international law, and President Wilson protested formally against the German war-order zone, saying that the United States would hold Germany to "strict accountability" for harm done to American lives and property. During two months nothing serious happened. Then, in March, 1915, an American citizen perished when the British merchantman *Falaba* was torpedoed by a submarine, and on May 1 the American ship *Gulflight* was torpedoed off the Scilly Isles with the loss of eleven lives. On the same day there was published in several American newspapers a formal notice warning United States citizens against traversing the war zone in ships of Britain or her allies. Within a week following came the submarining of the *Lusitania,* a British merchantman, unarmed but carrying ammunition. Upon this occasion 128 American citizens were drowned.

What would President Wilson do? He had urged his countrymen to be neutral "in both thought and deed"; he was a believer in international pacifism; and he was not particularly interested or conversant with foreign affairs. Some have thought that it was inevitable for the United States to favor the Allies because of the huge loans and credits obtained by the Allied governments in the United States with the tacit approval of the American government, and that the submarine issue raised by the sinking of the *Lusitania* was secondary in importance. This, however, remains a mere surmise. The fact remained that the Germans had violated important rights by sinking without warning an unarmed merchantship and that American lives had been lost. Clearly, action of some sort by the American President was in order.

Most German-Americans, Irish-Americans, and pacifist-Americans urged at this time, and continued to urge, that American citizens were not justified in running the risk of embroiling their country in war by insisting on their legal rights to travel on Allied merchantmen. They could either stay at home, or if business called them they could travel on such occasional liners as were entitled to fly the American flag or on ships of neutral nations—Dutch, Spanish, Danish. A compromise course of action, suggested but not followed, was for the United States to distinguish between Allied merchantmen carrying munitions and those that did not. On the former Americans should travel at their own risk; on the latter they would receive the full support of their government. The President, however, stiffly determined to stand by his original position. In his note to Germany he demanded disavowal and reparation for the sinking of the *Lusitania;* and he furthermore asserted that the United States "would omit neither word nor deed" in asserting her full rights under international law.

The Germans, on June 6, issued a formal order to U-boat commanders not to sink large passenger liners without warning; but nevertheless they had no mind to submit to Wilson's dictates and all through the summer of 1915, the sinkings by U-boats, with occasional peril to American lives, continued. As a climax, in August the British liner *Arabic* was torpedoed, and on board were Americans, of whom two perished. By this time, however, Bernstorff, German ambassador at Washington, convinced his home government that there might be limits to Wilson's patience. The submarine warfare, as then conducted, did not seem paying sufficient mili-

PRESIDENT WOODROW WILSON (1856-1924)

tary dividends to be worth braving American belligerency. The German government, therefore, gave pledge not to sink passenger liners without warning, provided they did not try to escape or resist capture.

The situation thus drifted until the spring of 1916. There were various submarine sinkings, but none sufficiently serious to cause a break. An obscure negotiation was conducted by the President's confidential agent, Colonel House, to get the Allies to enter into peace conversations with Germany; if Germany did not prove reasonable, America (the suggestion ran) would "probably" enter the war on the Allies' side. Nothing came of this, perhaps due to the word "probably." House also tells us that he got the British reluctantly to agree to take wheat off the list of contraband, provided the Germans in turn would abstain both from gas attacks and submarining merchantmen. And nothing came of this either, perhaps because of intimations to Berlin from Washington, relayed by the Austrian ambassador to the United States, who had the impression from former Secretary of State Bryan that there was no likelihood of the United States fighting over the submarine issue.

On March 24, 1916, the unarmed passenger steamer *Sussex* was sunk by a U-boat in the British Channel. Twenty-five of her passengers were Americans. On April 18, the United States reminded Germany of the *Arabic* pledge, recited how it had been broken, and warned Germany that diplomatic relations would be severed if a change of policy did not take place immediately. Severing diplomatic relationship would inevitably ere long have led to war, and Germany was not ready for that. Her U-boats were still few, and she expected to win the European contest by land battles. If her military chiefs had profound contempt for America, Bethmann-Hollweg, still clinging to office as imperial chancellor, realized something of what might come to pass. He had still strength enough in the empire's counsels to force a change of policy. A promise was given that merchant vessels "were not to be sunk without warning and without saving human lives," although the clause was added that if Britain persisted in her blockade Germany reserved "complete liberty of decision." For the time being, the crisis was ended.

During 1916, America went through the throes of a presidential election. Wilson's campaign managers capitalized the intense desire of a great part of the American people to keep if possible out of the European holocaust. *"He kept us out of war!"* was the campaign slogan with strong implications that if Wilson were reëlected he would continue the policy. In October, 1916, Bernstorff telegraphed to Berlin, begging that the U-boats conduct themselves moderately because "all Mr. Wilson's hopes of reëlection are based exclusively on the fact that, according to opinion over here, he has kept the United States out of the war."

In Germany, Wilson's reëlection was hailed as the triumph of the pacifist party in America. Meantime, the demand for "unlimited sub-marine warfare" against Britain was growing. Great numbers of U-boats had been built, and naval confidence in their efficacy was high. The food and fuel situation was causing intense hardship to German civilians. The army chiefs, the all-powerful circle around Ludendorff, accepted the assurance of the admirals that the U-boats, ruthlessly used, could speedily blockade England, create a worse food shortage than existed in Germany, and end the war abruptly in the Teutons' favor. Public sentiment strongly backed this opinion—if this policy angered America so much the better; by a sham neutrality she had grown rich selling munitions to Britain—and now let her iniquitous profits cease!

The United States Enters the War (April 6, 1917)

As 1916 approached its end, President Wilson, finding himself ever nearer the event he dreaded, sought peace by mediation. Germany fore-stalled him by capitalizing her Rumanian successes with a formal offer of peace to her enemies on December 12, but in very general terms. There was no renunciation of any claim upon Belgium; no repudiation of schemes of annexation clamored for by the Pan-German societies and the great Rhine industrialists.

The President, however, persisted. On December 18, he issued a formal appeal to both coalitions to state their war objects in order to see if any reconciliation were possible. The answers from *all* official spokesmen were such that, from every belligerent capital, immediately came the protest that the attitude of the foe made agreement impossible. Never-theless, behind the scenes the President's *alter ego* and "Père Joseph," Colonel House and Bernstorff were striving desperately to secure some basis for possible mediation. On January 22, Wilson addressed the United States Senate in a somewhat mysterious speech on the necessary condi-tions of a "League for Peace," to be established when hostilities should cease. The war, he declared, must first end in "peace without victory."

It was the last attempt to uphold his policy of neutrality which in-exorable events were rendering impossible. Already in late December, 1916, the German admiralty had drawn up a report that if "ruthless sub-marine warfare" were permitted England would be starved out and forced to capitulate. Such warfare, it held, was "the proper means of winning the war; moreover it is the only means to this end." Bethmann-Höllweg, German chancellor, had grave misgivings, but his objections were overruled. "We are counting on the chances of war with the United States," cried Hindenburg, "and have made all preparations to meet it. Things can not be worse than they are. The war must be brought to an end by the use of all means as soon as possible." The actual rulers of

Germany having thus spoken, a strictly secret order was issued in the Kaiser's name on January 9, 1917. "I order the unrestricted submarine warfare to be started with full energy on February 1."

On January 31, 1917, the German ambassador transmitted to the President of the United States the formal notice that, beginning the next day, in a wide ocean zone around Britain, France, and Italy, all navigation, that of neutrals included, would be "forcibly prevented." "All ships met within that zone will be sunk." A single American steamer a week was to be permitted to go to Falmouth, England, provided it was "painted with three vertical stripes, one meter wide, alternately white and red." Three days later Bernstorff received his passports and incontinently left Washington, while, simultaneously, Gerard was recalled from Berlin. In an address to Congress, Wilson, it is true, affected still to disbelieve that Germany would "pay no regard to the ancient friendship with America," but this hope died a few weeks afterward. On February 28, the war feeling was blown still hotter by the publication of a note sent in code on January 19 by Zimmermann, the imperial foreign minister, to the German minister to Mexico, proposing an alliance between that country and Germany, the latter country to finance Mexico and help her to "reconquer the lost territory in New Mexico, Texas and Arizona, taken from her by the United States."

The last stand of the pacifists in the United States Senate was to hold up by a Senatorial filibuster a bill authorizing the President to arm merchant vessels crossing the war zone; but the President, after denouncing "the little group of wilful men," armed the ships on his own authority. Followed then the Zimmermann note, seemingly a new evidence of German duplicity. On March 21 the President summoned Congress, and on April 2 he recommended it declare war. According to Wilson, Americans were to "fight for the ultimate peace of the world, and for the liberation of its peoples, the German peoples included. . . . The world must be made safe for democracy." The Congressional resolution, however, which declared war on April 6 spoke in somewhat less exalted language, reciting as grounds for action the wrongs committed on Americans by the German government.

The American entry came none too soon. On April 9, Rear-Admiral Sims of the American navy reached England to confer with Jellicoe, then first sea lord of the admiralty. The British admiral handed his American friend confidential tables showing that the U-boats had sunk of Allied and neutral shipping in February, 1917, 536,000 tons, in March 603,000 tons, and that the estimated figures for April would be in the neighborhood of 900,000 tons. Sims was astounded. "It looks," he said, "as though the Germans were winning the war."

Germany thought so, too. "Today England sees herself in a situation unparalleled in her history," announced Helfferich, imperial secretary of the interior. "Her food supplies across the sea disappear as a result of the blockade which our submarines are daily making more effective. We have considered, we have dared. Certain of the result, we will not allow it to be taken from us by anybody or by anything." Ludendorff, meanwhile, told Bernstorff in May, "We are going to end the business by the U-boat war inside of three months."

Fortunately the American navy was in better shape than the army, and able to help immediately. On May 4, six slim, gray destroyers glided up the Irish coast and entered Queenstown harbor. It was "the return of the Mayflower"—the first token that the United States was really in the war. By July 5 there were thirty-five American destroyers off the coast of Ireland. The American flotilla in British and French waters grew all too slowly for the anxious observers; but it grew and was of decisive use.

Prior to May, 1917, the Allied navies had fought against the submarines by means of destroyers and light patrol boats cruising wide areas of sea, and by nets and mine fields. By such means it had been possible to give heavy naval craft fairly good protection. But the merchant vessels had had to shift for themselves. Now, however, the British admiralty determined to try sending large fleets of merchantmen through the war zone under naval convoy; and it was to large extent owing to the increasing numbers of American naval craft in European waters that the convoy system became possible. Thanks to it and the devices which the naval escort could use (especially the "depth bomb") as soon as a U-boat periscope was sighted, the submarine campaign was first checked, then defeated.

The submarine danger was by no means ended; but it was held at bay. The first six destroyers at Queenstown multiplied presently into a great armada of American patrol boats; in 1918 an enormous barrier of mines was stretched across nearly the entire upper entrance to the North Sea. Without serious hindrance, vast quantities of supplies, and over 2,000,000 United States soldiers were conveyed to Europe. Months before the German chiefs called for an armistice, they knew that the "ruthless U-boat campaign" had recoiled upon their own heads; it was a failure. America was entering the war effectively and the sole hope of German victory lay in exploiting Russia and breaking the western military front before the new ally from overseas arrived in force.

But if the American navy was thus able from the outset to contribute to the Allied cause, the army was not. Volunteers could have been had in droves, but the government decided upon conscription, and machinery to enforce it had to be created. Training camps had to be constructed and civilians sent to them could not be converted into soldiers overnight. A very small expeditionary force could have been despatched to Europe immediately, but such an act would draft officers and potential non-coms out of the country at a time when they were needed desperately in the training camps. Therefore the American army did not contribute much to the cause of the Allies in 1917.

Fall of the Czardom (March, 1917)

Meanwhile, at Petrograd "dark influences" were at work. In 1916 the Czar removed his capable foreign minister, Sazonov, and in his place put the Czarina's protege, Stürmer, an arch-reactionary, suspected of being pro-German. The atmosphere was charged with intrigue, and anything seemed possible. Rasputin, "religious impostor and libertine," continued to lord it over the Czarina, and therefore over the Czar, his lodgings popularly known as "staff headquarters." The Czarina wrote constantly to her husband of "our friend," and on one occasion urged the Czar to comb his hair with Rasputin's comb in order to get strength to resist the demands of his ministers.

It proved impossible to prevent the Duma from assembling and in November, 1916, Miliukov, the liberal leader, handled Stürmer so roughly that the latter slunk out of office. Everywhere, in the army, in the navy, in the industries, in the railways, in finance, and in the food supply there was corruption. "If the German general staff," reported a commission to the Duma, "were allowed to direct our internal affairs and the conduct of the army it would do exactly what our government is doing."

But Stürmer had only been a figurehead for others more malevolent. There was Rasputin, whom the upper nobility hated, rightly fearing for the honor of their wives and daughters. They gave him a party, at which a group of princes too exalted even for the Czar to punish shot him dead. His body was flung under the ice of a canal and the slayers, not incorrectly, informed the police that they had killed a dog. But the Czarina mourned him passionately, and he had a saint's funeral.

Rasputin was a symbol, not a cause. Nicholas and his wife remained. The last Czarina had used all her influence from the commencement of the war to prevent her husband making liberal reforms. Her letters to Nicholas while he was pretending to command the army mingled personal pleadings with religious exhortations. "Don't laugh at silly old wifey; for she has trousers on unseen. Your faith has been tried and you remained firm as a rock. For that you will be blessed." She sent him holy images and ikons to strengthen his resistance to the liberals who were trying to reorganize Russia's broken war-machine. "We are living in the hardest times," she wrote late in 1916, "but God will help us through. Wifey is your staunch one, and stands as a rock behind you." And again, "Russia likes to feel the whip hand. How I wish I could pour my blood into your veins."

Thus Russia entered her year of crucifixion, 1917. The supporters of the government were growing fewer, and there was talk of deposing

Nicholas. As February advanced, the Speaker of the Duma waited on the Czar. It was time for plain speaking. Nicholas was informed that he could still save his throne if he would grant responsible ministerial government. If he did not do this, said the Speaker, there would be no further reports made by him to the Czar.

The First Revolution (March, 1917)

On Thursday, March 8, 1917, there was a gala performance in Petrograd at the Alexander Theater for the wealthy, while outside in the Russian cold long queues of women shivered before bakers' shops. In the Duma there was a perfunctory debate on the food supply and a few shops were looted. The next day the throngs in the streets were larger, angrier. Dense crowds seemed laughing, talking, always expectant. Cossacks patrolled the avenues but did not use their weapons. "You won't fire on us, brother," came from the crowds, "we want only bread." "No, we are hungry like yourselves," called back the soldiers. The city police, engaged in scuffles and arrested workingmen. On the tenth there were still greater crowds in the streets. Everybody was now asking, "What is about to happen?" The next day came street firing and some 200 were killed. A company of troops mutinied and refused to fire on the people. The Duma telegraphed a last appeal to the Czar at the front with the army. "Situation serious. Anarchy reigns in the capital. . . . It is absolutely necessary to invest someone who enjoys the confidence of the people with powers to form a new government. . . . Delay may be fatal." The Czar's ministers retaliated by ordering the Duma prorogued; but the deputies defied the order by refusing to disperse.

By dawn of March 12 the garrison of Petrograd had made up its collective mind; the troops would not obey the order to fire upon the city-folk. When certain regiments were ordered to send volleys into the crowd, they shot their own officers. Presently, many soldiers headed an unorganized mob moving straight on the public buildings, and especially on the prisons where political prisoners were held. The only government now left in Petrograd was the Duma, and it threw itself between the city and anarchy. In great haste it chose an executive committee of twelve to act in its name until a provisional government could be set up.

Nicholas had been near the front when the tempest broke at Petrograd. He started for the capital but revolting soldiers blocked the way. Two delegates from the Duma presently arrived and found the Emperor in his railroad carriage, "haggard, unwashed, and weary." The delegates informed him he must abdicate in favor of his son, with his brother Michael for regent. He demanded a sheet of paper, and drew up an abdication in favor of his brother the Grand Duke Michael. It was the last act of the czardom, for when the tidings reached Petrograd the city was in such a state that the Grand Duke, with obvious wisdom, declared that he could accept power only after it had been granted by a Constituent Assembly, elected by a plebiscite. So far as Russia had now any government at all, it was the provisional government headed by Prince Lvov, and composed of leaders among the liberal factions. The most advanced radical member was Kerensky, the new minister of justice—a "Social Revolutionary."

Simultaneous with this regime set up by the Duma, there was another power—the "Soviet (Council) of Workmen's and Soldiers' Deputies"— which desired passionately a republic, so far as it had any defined desires at all. For the moment, the "Soviet" (a roaring, gesticulating body) expressed faith in the provisional government. Nicholas II and his family faded out of view into captivity.

Russia seemed to have sloughed off the czardom without the miseries of the French Revolution and with relatively little bloodshed. The government seemed to be in the hands of moderate liberals, who would set up either a strictly limited monarchy, or, more probably, a democratic republic.

The fall of the czardom swept away those sanctions which hitherto had held together the empire. For the "Little Father," millions of peasants would fight and die; but for the provisional government there was no devotion—even though it did release political prisoners, restore autonomy to Finland, and introduce reforms. Prince Lvov and his colleagues who headed that government were convinced that a truly democratic regime could only be secured by first defeating the Prussian autocracy. But the nation had suffered terribly. The war had been the Czar's war. Now that the Czar was gone, let his war cease! The Russian people had no quarrel with the Germans. Constantinople, which had been pledged by the Allies, meant nothing to the Russian masses. Orders, issued by the Petrograd Soviet, destroyed discipline in the army, reduced officers to impotence, and practically placed the command with "Soldiers Councils"—fantastic debating clubs. Soon two slogans began to be heard in the camp, in the village, and in city soviets: (a) "self-determination," let every country decide its own future, and (b) "no annexations and no indemnities." By the middle of the summer the Russian war machine was a wreck; in the farming districts the peasants thought about one thing only—how to seize the land of the proprietors; and in the cities the workmen, sullen and discontented, spent much more time in exciting talk than in working in the factories.

And now in all the villages and the little wooden *izbas* one potent idea came home to the *muzhiks*—the chance to complete the emancipation of 1861. The former serfs and their children had never forgiven the decision to leave to their former owners a large part of the farm lands. Now was the opportunity to seize them. "It was here that they sought their annexations and indemnities!" All the peasants knew of the war was that it had sent off their sons to fight with pitchforks against machine guns and poison gas. The rural districts were soon everywhere in anarchy, the muzhiks seizing the estates of the helpless proprietors, just as all productive agriculture perishing amid rioting and confusion. From the demoralized army at the front, the soldiers (worried lest their neighbors at home take all the good land) deserted, literally, by hundreds of thousands.

In the cities, in the meantime, the workmen were for the most part socialists. They looked upon the revolution as their handiwork and they demanded drastic and immediate action toward the establishment of a socialist state. Particularly true was this of Lenin, leader of the more extreme socialists (the Bolsheviks), who had returned from exile in Switzerland in April through the kind assistance of the German authorities. Lenin was for instant peace. He had but one enemy—capitalism; he had no interest in the war, which he considered simply and solely as proof that international capitalism was in its death throes. The dawn of Messianic socialism had come and the end of the Russian bourgeois was at hand. Peace, bread, and land was his slogan, and this was the theme upon which he orated daily to the restless proletariat of Petrograd, spreading as he did so suspicion and hate of the provisional government.

As the army became more and more demoralized, and as discord grew at Petrograd, Miliukov, who had been provisional minister of foreign affairs, was forced to resign, since he had been committed to fight for Constantinople. The Duma had been elected by a very narrow franchise and carried no weight with the masses. Soon the virtual head of the government was Kerensky, hitherto counted a decided radical, but who, in any case, clearly realized the futility of trying to initiate a regime of democracy by opening the gates to the Hohenzollern.

Kerensky strove hard to combat the forces of disruption and anarchy; but he trusted too much to his eloquence and exerted no discipline over the army, where the soldiers were being taught by Bolshevik missionaries to distrust and hate their officers and to go back home and seize the old lords' acres.

The Overthrow of Kerensky: The Bolshevists Seize Power (November 7, 1917)

On July 14, the extremists tried to seize the government by force, but Kerensky had strength enough to stamp out the flames. Soon, however, the agitators were again at work; Russian industries became paralyzed; the peasants were not tilling the fields; and every wire and mail-bag brought to the distracted ministers new evidence of increasing demoralization.

In September, General Kornilov tried to force the provisional government to take round measures against the dissidents. A military coup was projected, with Kerensky himself apparently supporting the scheme. But very many around him were fearful that a bold strike would involve a return to the czardom. Kornilov was left unsupported and betrayed by men who had egged him forward. The coup failed, and this was the beginning of the end.

Kerensky was detested by the Bolshevists, and as October advanced his position grew weaker and weaker. He told the Western Powers that Russia was utterly weary and could play no active part in the war. The Bolshevists were now carrying on an active propaganda everywhere, promising universal peace and utopia. Although pledged to communism, their peace pledges pleased the peasants, who looked only for a chance to enjoy the seized lands. The crash at last came upon November 7, 1917, when the Petrograd garrison recognized the authority of the "Revolutionary Committee" of the Soviets. Kerensky issued vigorous proclamations, but found himself almost without armed supporters. Petrograd passed into the power of the Leninists with very little fighting. Kerensky fled, tried to return with the aid of a few Cossack squadrons too weak to recapture the city, and then disappeared completely. In Moscow the armed defenders of the provisional government were stronger; they yielded the Kremlin only after severe fighting, whereupon the revolutionists proclaimed: "The provisional government has been deposed. The power of the state is now in the hands of the Petrograd Soviet of Workers' and Soldiers' Deputies." And the Russian people were promised at once "the immediate offer of a democratic peace, the abolition of rights of landlordship, the workers' control of industry, and the establishment of a Soviet government."

Moves in Austria and Germany to Secure Peace (1917)

The war was now running into its third year, and another power besides Russia was becoming weary. At Vienna, the new Hapsburg emperor, the well-intentioned young Charles, was casting anxiously about him. The fate of Nicholas II afforded little lasting encouragement, even if it eased the military situation. The Vienna ministers knew that their ill-compacted government was cracking under the strain and was likely to fly asunder. "It is no good telling me," reported Czernin, Charles's foreign minister, "that the monarchical principle is too firmly rooted in Berlin and Vienna for the monarchy to be overthrown. This war has no precedent. If the monarchs do not make peace in the next few months, then the people will make peace over their heads; and then the waves of revolution will sweep away everything for which our sons are fighting today."

Charles even went so far as to negotiate with France, telling Paris that he would not sacrifice his country for the sake of a German victory, and that to get peace he would use his influence to support "the just claim of France in relation to Alsace-Lorraine." But the French promptly called attention to the claims of Italy; what concessions for her—not, of course, at Hohenzollern, but at Hapsburg expense? Charles could not bring himself to sign away Trieste and the Trentino.

Meanwhile, in Germany Matthias Erzberger, leader of the powerful Catholic Center party in the Reichstag, hitherto an advocate of wholesale annexations and exploitations, astonished a group of colleagues by telling them that "the war could not be won." His reversal of attitude caused a sensation in inner political circles; and speedily his opinions leaked out when he introduced resolutions before the Reichstag. "The Reichstag strives for a peace of understanding and the permanent reconciliation of the peoples. With such a peace, forced requisitions of territory and political, [or] economic oppressions are inconsistent."

Such resolutions the great General Staff that now ruled Germany met with unconcealed anger. Their particular rage was against Bethmann-Hollweg for having failed to maintain "the home front" against the enemy. The discredited chancellor now faded into private life. In his place the military autocrats set up a colorless Prussian official, Michaelis, who would at least do his masters' bidding. The Erzberger resolutions were passed by the Reichstag, but their effect was instantly destroyed by the announcement of the new chancellor that he accepted the proposition "as he understood it."

The French Offensive of 1917: The Pope Proposes Peace

In France, also, there was, presently, great discouragement. The war had come home to the republic as it had not to Britain, nor even to Germany. Nearly all the fighting on the western front had been on French soil. Several of the richest and most populous departments were in the clutches of the enemy, and the youth of the country seemed bleeding away. The situation was so desperate that the French decided to make one grand, furious assault on the Germans. There had been complete failure in 1915 and 1916 to accomplish this, both on the part of the Allies and on that of the Central Powers, but General Nivelle, successor to Joffre as commander-in-chief of the armies of France, was so buoyant and so optimistic that he persuaded not only his own government but that of Britain that it could be done.

Nivelle attacked in April on fifty miles of front in Champagne. He flung his main strength upon the Chemin des Dames, along the Aisne, which the Germans had been laboriously fortifying for two and half years. The first rush of the French attack enabled him to boast of taking

21,000 prisoners and 183 guns within four days; but his own losses had been appalling. The French infantry found that their artillery had failed to clear the ground properly—they were mowed down by machine guns, while they struggled with the unbroken barbed wire. Nivelle's casualties presently reached 107,000. The Germans were forced to cede valuable ground, but again no key positions were taken. There had been no breakthrough, and human energy could do no more. The Paris politicians were horrified at the profitless sacrifice; and on May 15, Nivelle was removed from command and replaced by the more steady Pétain. The new general had not merely to hold back the foe, but to restore the sorely shaken morale of the entire French army.

There had already been serious dissatisfaction among the French rank and file as to scanty leaves of absence, confusion in the medical service, and reports from home of how munition workers, exempted from military duty, were getting fat wages, while the women and children struggled to wrest a living from the farms of the peasant conscripts. Now, in addition to great military discouragement, there were serious mutinies. Certain divisions near Paris almost broke out into political revolution, and "defeatism"—advocacy of giving up the fight and compounding with Germany—spread.

The secret of the mutinies was, in fact, so well kept that not merely did the Germans fail to learn thereof, but even the British and Americans. Nevertheless, the main situation could not be concealed. Russia was falling from the war. France was temporarily unable to push any offensive. Italy was very tired. American troops were coming slowly. On Britain had to fall the main burden of any real pressure upon Germany during 1917.

Under such conditions, in August, Pope Benedict XV tried to mediate. A gesture during the summer to bring the warring elements together by means of a conference of socialist leaders at Stockholm had failed, partly because of the suspicion that German forces were controlling the undertaking; partly because the Allies distrusted any movement under the auspices of socialists. The attempt of the Vatican met with greater respect but no better fortune. In substance, the Pope called on the warring nations to forget their losses and wrongs and to make peace on the *status quo ante bellum*. Something ought to be done, the pontiff suggested, as to Armenia, Poland, and the Balkans, and occupied territory should generally be evacuated. This would have released Belgium, but would have left Alsace-Lorraine to Germany. There was much well-intentioned wisdom behind the note, but the Allied Powers were angered at the calm method with which the Pope treated both coalitions as equally innocent or culpable. The result, therefore, was foreordained. Berlin answered with apparent cordiality: they would be happy to negotiate along the suggested lines. But President Wilson was selected by the

Western Allies to be the chief spokesman. "The object of this war," he informed Pope Benedict, "was to deliver the free peoples of the world from the menace and actual power of a vast military establishment controlled by an irresponsible government which [had] secretly planned to dominate the world, and which was now in waging war stopping at no barrier of law or mercy."

Flanders and Caporetto

Despite the entrance of the United States into the war, the year 1917 was one of continued disaster for the Allies. The British were foiled in their offensives as well as the French. Twice the former tried to break through and twice they failed. Their first offensive came in Flanders, where, owing to unusual rain, the low terrain had been turned into a bog. A number of local successes were achieved, but that was all. The German grip on the Belgian coast and the coal fields around Lille had not been broken. Then, later in the year, the British made a surprise attack at Cambrai. This time there was no long artillery preparation; instead, four hundred tanks suddenly emerged from the haze of a November sunrise and went crashing through the German defenses, the infantry following. The use of tanks, begun at the Somme, was now vindicated; but unfortunately there were not nearly enough available, and a German counterattack won back most of the ground which the tanks had gained. Whereupon the western front settled down after this to another winter of local bombardments.

If the British were checked, the Italians were overwhelmed with disaster. An Austrian offensive at Caporetto, in the mountains north of the Adriatic, turned into an Italian rout. The front collapsed almost like magic. At certain points the disaffected troops greeted the enemy with white flags, while reserve battalions in the rear refused to march forward. The result was that the whole Italian front near Caporetto was broken and the Teutons poured in as through a sluice.

Despite heroic struggles, it became evident that the Italians had sustained not a defeat but a national disaster. The gains of twenty-nine months of war were gone instantly.

The crisis brought to the Italians aid which had been denied for their offensive. Six French and five British divisions were ordered entrained for cisalpine service. High French and British cabinet ministers and generals hastened to Italy, with moral support and counsel. All this, however, would have availed nothing, had the German-led forces of the Central Powers been in a position to exploit their advantage to the full.

Fortunately for Italy, this was not the case. The Germans, under whom were Magyar and Slovak troops, were delayed by the very extent of their victories, and the need of mopping up the conquered territory. They were not prepared for a headlong pursuit. Thus, the Italians, many of whose surviving troops were "disorganized, worn-out, sullen, and be-wildered," were given that short breathing time, during which a truly great people can pull itself together.

The knowledge that the country was in deadly peril, that preparations were being made to evacuate Venice, that if the Piave and Adige lines went, the Teutons might soon be in Milan, united the Italian nation. The clericals became patriotic; the pacifists and socialists became silent; a "spirit of desperate devotion ran from the Alps to Sicily." When the Austro-German attacks were renewed along the Piave and downward through the Alps, they were met with determination. A little more ground had to be ceded to the attackers, but the line of the Piave was not carried. The Teutons, for one moment, had seemed on the point of driving Italy out of the struggle with one great military thrust—but that moment had passed.

Nevertheless, the disaster at Caporetto seemed, for the moment, only to add one more misery to the Allies' winter. British and French troops, sorely needed on the western front, were in Venetia assisting Italy; Russian revolutionaries were negotiating a separate truce; and submarine warfare was constantly menacing England. In France the privations of the long war were bearing hard upon the civilian population. There was, in fact, general discouragement among the Allies. Many were wondering whether the war was not likely to end with a general social revolution. The new Bolshevik dynasts in Russia were sending wholesale promises to the "have nots" throughout the world, and certain high financial groups were reported to have taken alarm.

Lloyd George's and Wilson's Peace Programs: Brest Litovsk

Early in January, 1918, Lloyd George and Wilson made clear their war aims. The British premier chose studiously moderate language: Britain was not fighting to destroy Germany, or Austria-Hungary, or those parts of Turkey which were genuinely Turkish, but Belgium and Serbia must be restored and, of course, the occupied parts of France, Italy, and Rumania. The "legitimate claims" of the Italians for union with people of their own race and tongue were to be satisfied, and "genuine self-government" must be given the Austro-Hungarian nationalities. In that event, the Hapsburgs might continue at Vienna, although no longer as the "instruments of the military autocracy of Prussia." An independent Poland was "an urgent necessity," and the Turks, although they might keep Constantinople, ought to let Armenia, Syria, Mesopotamia, and Pales-tine enjoy "separate national conditions." As for Alsace-Lorraine, there must be a "reconsideration of the great wrong of 1871" done to France;

but concerning Russia, since her present rulers were negotiating separately with Germany, Britain could not be responsible for unhappy decisions.

These were carefully worded terms, skilfully calculated to drive a wedge between the allies of Germany and the Hohenzollerns, and to kindle all the dissident minorities, yet not to drive Germany to desperation. Wilson, a few days later, struck out somewhat more boldly. In a well-considered statement, Wilson summarized the American position in fourteen points. They came close to repeating the British terms in regard to territorial settlements on the continent: but they were somewhat more specific, and in addition called for freedom of the seas; removal of economic barriers; a treatment of colonial questions in accordance with the best interests of native peoples; and the creation of a League of Nations.

In Austria the olive branch of the Allies was welcome, but not so in Germany. Count Hertling, the new chancellor (replacing, in October, 1917, the feckless Michaelis), repudiated the idea that Alsace-Lorraine could possibly be ceded back to France; and concerning every other point he was vague and defiant. Russia must be left to the "return of order, peace, and conditions of her welfare," which the Teutonic allies were then arranging for her. The fate of Belgium could only be settled after elaborate negotiation, and the occupied parts of France were "valuable pawns in our hands." Poland was to be reconstituted, as Germany and Austria might agree among themselves—there was to be no outside interference —and so with nearly all the other points at issue.

At the dawn of 1918, it might have been possible for Germany to have driven a dangerous wedge between France and Britain and America by a conciliatory peace offer. The English-speaking powers would hardly have gone on making vast sacrifices solely to recover Strasbourg and Metz for a sister nation. But Hertling's speech cancelled any possible effect of Czernin's smoother platitudes, and almost convinced the most doubtful that Germany was playing for an absolute victory and a dictated peace. A few weeks earlier, William II, in an address to his armies, had promised that "we must bring peace to the world by battering in with the iron fist and shining sword the doors of those who will not have peace."

The confident tone of his Imperial Majesty was due to the collapse of the eastern front, where the Germans had good reason to feel resistance had vanished. In December, 1917, the Bolsheviks sent their commissars to negotiate with the representatives of the Teutonic empires at Brest Litovsk in Poland, where a protracted conference took place, lasting to the March of the subsequent year, when a Russo-German treaty was finally struck. The Bolsheviks had overwhelmed Russia with surprisingly little fighting and they believed that a similar revolt of the proletariat in Germany was about to send not merely the Kaiser and Junkers, but the whole Teutonic burgher class the way of the Czar. After that, the capitalistic strongholds in France, Britain, and America must speedily crumble, and next would follow the obliteration of obsolete and oppressive nationalistic boundaries, when all peoples of the earth were fused together in the Marxian earthly paradise. The Bolsheviks were confident that their industrial "comrades" in Germany would prevent any advantage being taken of their own military helplessness. "We did not overthrow the Czar," declaimed Trotsky, "in order to fall on our knees before the Kaiser, and beg for peace." Marvelously were he and his associates to be undeceived.

The victorious Germans asked Russia to recognize the independence of all the Baltic provinces, of Poland, of the Ukraine, that vast southwestern section of Russia in Europe, occupied by the Little Russians, and stretching south and southeast of Poland to the Black Sea. Over these extensive regions, destined for the German orbit, puppet governments were to be set up by the conquerors. The vista was now opened in Berlin of the control of the routes to the oil wells of Baku, to the cotton lands of Ferghana, to the very mountain passes leading to British India. Austria received minor pickings and Turkey recovered territory on the Caucasus. Austro-German financial groups were to exploit the Rumanian oil fields.

The Bolsheviks recoiled in disgust at the German proposals. Many favored rejection and the declaration of a revolutionary war. Lenin said Soviet Russia must accept or fight; to accept meant a chance to save the revolutionary regime; to fight meant defeat and conquest by the Central Powers. Trotsky favored refusing to make peace until compelled to do so by force. On February 9, the Central Powers signed at Brest a treaty with the Ukraine, and on the following day Trotsky made his famous "no peace, no war" declaration, to the effect that Soviet Russia would neither sign an annexationist peace nor go on with the war. The Germans therefore declared the armistice at an end and sent their troops forward toward Petrograd. Some of the Bolsheviks still wanted to fight; but Lenin, now supported by Trotsky, won a majority of the party leaders for peace. When the Bolsheviks agreed to sign, the Germans presented a revised text even more severe. There were more debates and Lenin said: "It is time to put an end to revolutionary phrases and get down to real work. If this is not done I resign from the government. . . . It is a question of signing the German terms now or signing the death warrant of the Soviet government three weeks later. . . ." Lenin carried the day and the Soviet delegates signed on March 3.

This Treaty of Brest Litovsk stripped Russia of approximately forty-four per cent of her population, twenty-seven per cent of her arable land, thirty-seven per cent of her average crops, twenty-six per cent of her railroads, thirty-three per cent of her manufactures, seventy-three per cent of her iron production, seventy-five per cent of her developed coal mines.

The Western Front, March, 1918

Russia was helpless; Italy was reeling; France, despite American economic relief, was bleeding white and very tired; Britain was carrying on gallantly, but without that dauntless confidence that had inspired her sacrifices of 1915-16. America was still three thousand miles across the Atlantic.

The U-boat war had proved a disappointment to its promoters, but the surrender of Russia had restored the prestige of the great General Staff. If civilian Germany went through the winter of 1917-18, once more shivering with the cold, hungering on turnip soup in lieu of meat and potatoes, with little children nursing on thin beer in lieu of milk, and with stripling youths and middle-aged men in broken health, drafted to the trenches by a pitiless conscription, it seemed, nevertheless, that the blessed end was in sight. Given time, the wheat fields of Ukrainia and the oil fields of Rumania would feed and warm the lands of the victors, and as for the military situation, conditions were still better.

It was known that the French army was dwindling in strength through the depletion of man power. The British were paying the penalty for the awful losses on the Somme and in Flanders; and the U-boat warfare was diverting an enormous number of men into the royal navy. Vast forces under the Union Jack had also to be maintained in Mesopotamia, Palestine (where Jerusalem had been taken from the Turks on December 10, 1917), and at Salonika. Besides all these, the danger of an invasion of England across the North Sea was reckoned with, 300,000 good troops being held in Britain to meet a very improbable catastrophe. As a result, Sir Douglas Haig commanded 180,000 less fighting men in March, 1918, than in March, 1917. The German high command knew all this. They knew that by spring barely 250,000 Americans had reached France, and that the great bulk of these troops were too untrained to send to the trenches. It was time to stake everything on one great blow on the western front that could undo the work at the Marne.

In view of these facts, Ludendorff hoped to win the war by a grand final offensive on the western front. He aimed it at Amiens, since if he could take that old Picard city he would sever direct communications between the British and the French. The latter he could fling backward in demoralization upon Paris; the former he could hustle in ever increasing rout to the Channel. Former offensives had failed because waged on too narrow a front; he would succeed now by breaking through on a wide one. He would use a method of offense tried out successfully against the Russians by which, instead of an intensive bombardment followed by a rush of infantry, the artillery hardly began its work before the infantry advanced in small detachments, infiltrating the enemy's positions, concealing their advance as much as possible, and using smoke screens and mustard gas to demoralize the foe. It was now or never for the Germans; they must strike and they must win before there were too many Americans in France, and before the food shortage got too bad in Germany.

Upon the extreme south of the British line on the 21st of March, 1918, the storm broke, and before that day was spent the Germans had penetrated deep into the British positions. The British reserves were exhausted and the onslaught not stayed. The following day, as the British divisions lost contact with one another, came worse disaster and a frantic retirement to the Somme. On the 23rd the attackers swept across that stream; and as the gaps between the British units grew wider and wider, the chance of stabilizing the line grew more and more faint. Ludendorff seemingly had accomplished the impossible—a breakthrough.

Almost, but not quite. Never fought men in a manner more worthy of their inheritance than that unbowed remnant of the British army. From the south the French hurried up veteran divisions to fill the gap and to cover Amiens. The Germans still made headway but no longer rapidly, and in a few days they halted. Nevertheless, on April 1, it was possible for Ludendorff to proclaim a magnificent success—90,000 prisoners and 1,300 guns.

Amiens was saved. But Ludendorff still had power for other blows. On April 9, the Germans struck again, this time further north. Once again there was almost a breakthrough, the British forced to retreat over old battlefields, drenched now with the blood of three and a half years.

Once more the German offensive ebbed away. There had been great territorial gains for Ludendorff; but he had not forced Haig's line or put the British army out of action. By the end of April, this Battle of the Lys, as it was called, was over. Ludendorff drew back to strike again.

May, 1918, nearly passed before another great German offensive came. Meantime, the ocean was sprinkled with convoys of liners bearing the man power of America. "The Allies are very weak," General Pershing had reported to Washington as early as December, 1917, "and we must come to their relief in this year, 1918. The year after may be too late." But during the winter the ocean convoys had been slow, and even the most hopeful of the commanders overestimated the period of training needful for the American troops before they could be sent to the battle-trenches. Nevertheless, in March, 84,900 were sent across and in April, 118,600. These numbers had seemed the reasonable limit, considering the shipping available; but with the whole war now on the razor-edge of fate, the British government drafted the liners from all its great trade routes, while the process of mobilizing and organizing in America was hastened to the uttermost. In May, 246,000 Americans were destined to cross the Atlantic, in June, 278,000, in July, 306,300. The government-controlled press of Germany denounced the figures published to hearten the Allies as gross fabrications and "Yankee bluff," but the General Staff, at least, began to realize that what it would do, it must do quickly.

Late in May, Ludendorff changed his objective. Abandoning the Channel ports, he aimed at Paris. His intelligence service told him that the line of the Chemin des Dames, along the Aisne, was held by only eight divisions, four French and four British, and that these were weary from fighting elsewhere and had been sent to this supposedly "quiet sector" to reorganize. Suddenly, on May 27, Ludendorff attacked with twenty-eight divisions on a thirty-five mile line. He won immediate results. A deep zone of territory was lost to the Allies, and that, too, in the area directly covering Paris.

The Germans reported 45,000 prisoners and 400 captured guns. They were well down to the Marne, almost to the region fought over in September, 1914. One more colossal effort—and France would be as Russia; then home to the Fatherland and glory.

The Second Marne

Ludendorff knew that the deep salient or pocket he had created by his third offensive must either be enlarged or abandoned, for it was fed by but one railroad and it was open to attack from both flanks. He had tried to enlarge it on the northwest and had failed. This time he would strike to the east of Reims, to widen it on the northeast, while at the same time he would strike to the south and west of Reims toward the Marne. When the Germans rushed on this, their fifth and last offensive, they found the foe ready. Their blow struck to the east of Reims met with complete discomfiture. Twenty-five picked German divisions were shattered by the French artillery and no appreciable progress was made. Slightly better fortune attended the German attack west of Reims in the Marne salient; some ground was gained; the Marne was crossed near Château-Thierry; progress on the military maps could be noted. But the salient in the Allies' lines, though deepened, had not been widened.

Foch's hour had come. Along the thirty-five mile western flank of the great Marne salient, after a night of thunderstorms and high winds which discouraged the German airmen, there emerged 321 Allied tanks out of the shelter of the concealing woods. Behind them, striking all the way from Château-Thierry to Soissons came Mangin's forces, thirty per cent American. The advance swept through the first German defenses before the Teutons so much as realized what was happening. When night fell the Allies had taken 16,000 prisoners and had gone far beyond winning a local success. They were closing the end of the German loop or pocket which had penetrated to the Marne. If they could only close it further, thirty German divisions would be trapped within. For the next few days the Germans struggled fiercely and at last escaped north to their old battlegrounds near the Aisne. They had lost the great gains of the first of June; they had lost something more precious, confidence in victory.

Three months and three days intervened between this British drive and the end of the war, an interval filled with incessant fighting. The initiative had completely passed into the hands of Foch, now general-issimo of all the Allied armies, and never once was Ludendorff able to make a serious counteroffensive. Foch struck now here, now there. The Belgians were again in action from that little strip of their fatherland near the Yser which they had held since 1914; the British were raining blows in Flanders and Picardy; the French were beating on the German lines along the Aisne and in Champagne; and the Americans, acting as a separate army, were putting through two major operations in the Meuse Valley.

The Final Franco-British-American Attacks

The German hosts on the western front had been fed by two trunklines of railroads—that through Liége and that through Sedan. The line through Liége was relatively safe, but by itself it was totally inadequate for maintaining the German army. The line through Sedan was within thirty miles of the Allied trenches near Verdun, but those miles included the Argonne Forest, a semi-wilderness of hills, woods, and ravines, ideal for defense, almost impossible for offense. Haig and Pétain (still in command of the French armies as coadjutor to Foch) undertook to force back the Germans across Flanders, Picardy, and Champagne by incessant attacks and pressure. They each had several American divisions in their armies, but the main American effort was elsewhere. Pershing undertook to cut through the Argonne to Sedan. When its trunk railroad was under the American guns, Ludendorff's armies must either flee in rout or capitulate.

Before cutting this railroad it was considered advisable that the Germans be driven out of the Saint-Mihiel salient near Verdun, and the task of doing so was assigned to the American army. Pershing fell upon this salient, using over half a million men. He won a relatively easy victory, since the Germans were preparing to abandon the salient anyway. Pershing then started forward on the main American offense, through the Argonne in the direction of Sedan.

The battle of the Argonne lasted forty-seven days. It was begun with 450,000 men, but as it raged other troops were thrown in until the whole number of Americans engaged was over 1,000,000. The American numerical preponderance was overwhelming and it must be remembered that the war-weary enemy was in retreat. Nevertheless, the German troops knew the terrain and the Americans did not. The forest country fought over had become an almost impenetrable tangle of fallen timber, an ideal place for nests of machine guns and for labyrinths of barbed wire. It

AMERICAN TROOPS IN ACTION ON THE WESTERN FRONT

was also cut by ravines so deep as to render tanks useless, and making it very hard for artillery to support the attackers. "It was a question of hard, slogging infantry fighting, and the American infantryman did slog hard," wrote a British general; by the middle of October "by grim, dogged effort he won his way through."

The German armies in France were caught, as it were, between enormous pincers, the Belgians and the British on one side, the Americans on the other, and the French in the center shoving their foe forward. Everywhere came the rat-tat-tat, of Foch on the retreating enemy who retired in good order, putting up everywhere a stiff rear-guard action. By the first of November the German forces were back where they had been in the summer of 1914.

Germany's Allies Surrender

As far back as September, Bulgaria had given evidence of cracking. An Allied army which had occupied Salonika after the Dardanelles defeat, forced that entire nation to remain mobilized. The Germans had handed over to Bulgaria a goodly share of the conquered Serbian lands but had exploited the supply of foodstuffs. At the very moment, furthermore, when German aid was needed most, German aid was withdrawn. Ludendorff required his men, his munitions, his money, elsewhere. Bulgaria, then, realizing that she had gambled unwisely, made peace quickly. The Bulgars agreed to demobilize their army, to evacuate all territory they had occupied, and to allow Allied armies free transit across Bulgaria to attack Turkey. The Serbs, now like raging lions, flung themselves on the small Austro-German detachments left in their country. They reëntered Nish, their ancient capital; and by the first of November they were again triumphantly in Belgrade, looking across the Danube where the first shots of the world contest had resounded fifty-one months earlier.

The collapse of Bulgaria was scarcely more rapid than that of Turkey. The Bedouin tribes of Arabia and Syria were now in full revolt against the Sultan. Jerusalem was occupied (Christmas, 1917), and during 1918 Allenby, the British commander, had pressed Liman von Sanders, the German general in command of the Turkish army, north from Nazareth to Damascus. The Sultan had hardly a single organized force to put in the field, if Allenby elected to advance across Anatolia to Stamboul. On October 25, he moved north again and took Aleppo, the great Turkish base in North Syria.

Syria was lost and Mesopotamia with it; Anatolia would soon be open and the Allies, moving across Bulgaria, would soon be pounding on the Tchalja lines behind Stamboul. Allah manifestly had spoken, and it was useless to strive against destiny. Turkish envoys, therefore, negotiated peace with the British admiral in the Aegean. The Turkish army was to be demobilized, the Turkish waterways opened; alliance with Germany was repudiated, and the whole fate of the Ottoman Empire was to be left for the final peace conference. On October 31 hostilities in the Near East ceased.

This general collapse of the allies of Austria and Germany in southeastern Europe was almost instantly followed by that of Austria. It was high time.

Czechs, Poles, Ruthenians, Slovaks, Slovenes, Croats, whom the lordly Germans and Magyars had trampled upon and despised, were turning now against the oppressor. "Self-determination" and "a world safe for democracy," supplied oil for fires of discontent already smoldering.

On October 16, the Hapsburg Empire underwent its death-bed repentance. The unfortunate Charles proclaimed his monarchy a "Federal State" in which each people could form its own government. But the Allies and the United States were now warning Vienna that there could be no peace unless the Czechs, Poles, and Yugo-Slavs were to be allowed to quit the empire outright if they so desired; and Hungary was also preparing to cut the last tie to Vienna, and set up as a completely independent government.

Austria's plight was Italy's opportunity. The Italian army, assisted by French and British units, drove in a wedge between the Austrian troops. The Austrians and the Magyars surrendered wholesale and prisoners were reckoned at more than 300,000. On November 3 Austria quit the war and a week later the Emperor Charles abdicated. German Austria became a republic; there was another republic in Hungary, a third in Czechoslovakia; Galicia was joining a revived republic of Poland; the Croats and the Slovenes were federating with the Bosnians and Serbs in the new kingdom of Yugoslavia; and Rumania had repudiated the forced Treaty of Bucharest and was seizing Transylvania. The Austrian monarchy (founded in 1272 by Rudolf of Hapsburg), that artificial but convenient makeshift and fiction which had dominated Central Europe for six hundred and forty years, was dead.

These happenings progressively heightened Germany's gloom. There was now no hope anywhere on the horizon. The army on the western front was retiring in good order and was in no immediate danger of encirclement; but even if it reached the Rhine safely there was no chance of ultimate victory. Consequently, Germany sued for peace by way of Washington. The President replied that there could be no peace unless the Allies had a representative government with which to deal, and the German militarists temporarily thought of renewing the war. But it was now known that Austria was done for and other men than Ludendorff were in charge of Germany's destinies.

The army did not finally yield, however, until socialistic revolts in the Fatherland made it inevitable that it must. The German Socialists had been wholeheartedly for the war at its commencement, only one of them, Liebknecht, voting against the first war credits. Late in 1915, however, fifteen other Socialists joined with Liebknecht, seceded from the Social Democratic party, and formed that of the Independent Socialists. They were a very weak faction and not until the treaty of Brest Litovsk in 1918 was there really any considerable revolutionary propaganda in Germany.

But as the German people became more and more hungry, revolutionary sentiment spread. And now, with Germany's allies falling away, and with Foch's legions likely to pour over the frontier any moment, a very small explosion could and did shatter the whole political structure. At Kiel the bluejackets, long disgruntled, hoisted the red flag of revolutionary socialism. This mutiny was no flash in the pan. By the 7th of November there were unkempt soviets claiming to be the government in Hamburg, Bremen, Hanover, Rostock, and lesser centers. The red flag was waving all over Germany; jails were broken open and hardened inmates released as an earnest of proletarian liberty.

Under such circumstances there was a revolution in Germany which complied completely with Wilson's demands that the Allies must deal with the representatives of the German people. The Germans not merely lost an emperor, they ceased to constitute a monarchy. On November 10 the Kaiser fled into Holland. On the same day Ebert, a journeyman saddler, accepted the chancellorship in the name of the Social Democrats, and straightway proclaimed the republic.

One day later came the armistice, the terms of which had been prepared at Paris by the Allied generals and admirals. The Germans were to surrender 5,000 cannon, 30,000 machine guns, 2,000 airplanes, and 5,000 locomotives. They were to evacuate immediately the "invaded countries" including Alsace-Lorraine, thereby automatically undoing the deed of 1871. They were to retire beyond the Rhine, and the Allied armies were to occupy not merely the western Rhinelands, but ample bridgeheads with wide radius opposite Mayence, Coblenz, and Cologne. All Allied prisoners were to be released immediately, all German mine fields to be swept; six battle cruisers, ten battleships, numerous smaller craft, and all submarines were to be interned in the ports of the victors; the remaining craft were to be disarmed and put under Allied supervision. In addition, the treaties of Brest Litovsk and Bucharest (with Rumania) were to be canceled.

At 5 A.M., at the first gray light of November 11, the German delegates, meeting Foch in his salon car, put their hands to the great surrender. Through the cold, foggy morning sometimes a shell burst, sometimes a great gun bellowed. It was said that most of the combatants were in a kind of stupor. They had fought so long, must they not fight on forever? Foch had telegraphed to his generals, "Hostilities will cease on the whole front on November 11, at eleven o'clock. The Allied troops will not, until further orders, go beyond the line reached at that hour." Suddenly, at one minute to eleven, the last "75" thundered on its carriage. The ensuing silence was more startling than even the terrible chorus of a barrage.

Presently, against the skyline, lifting themselves above the trenches, first cautiously, then bolder, were seen figures—staring, gesturing. They were Germans, gazing curiously. Americans, Frenchmen, Britons grew visible likewise. Machine-gunners unbuckled their belts, gave stiff salutes toward the opposing barbed wire, and next walked deliberately toward the rear. And then a sound "like the noise of a light wind" could be heard, whether the troops stood at Verdun or in Belgium. Across four hundred miles, millions of men were cheering from the Vosges to the sea.

Chapter 7

THE PEACE TREATIES AND THEIR
AFTERMATH (1919-23)

"THE ARMISTICE has been signed this morning. Everything for which America fought has been accomplished. It will now be our fortunate duty to assist by example, by sober, friendly counsel and by material aid in the establishment of a just democracy throughout the world."

Thus President Wilson to his countrymen, November 11, 1918. In a little more than two months he was to attend the opening session of the peace conference at Paris, there to do battle for long dreary months for those ideals which he cherished so dearly.

To what extent was this venture of the American President into the maelstrom of European diplomacy a success; to what extent a failure?

Any answer to that question calls for an analysis of the handicaps under which he labored. Among them six are outstanding: a disunited country behind him; an antagonistic House of Commons in Britain; territorial ambitions of the French; secret treaties struck by his allies before the close of the war; the impossibility of applying his principle of self-determination to the closely packed yet highly differentiated nationalities in Austria-Hungary; and Wilson's own temperament.

A new Congress had been elected in the United States in November, 1918. Wilson had asked for support and it had been denied him. The Republicans controlled both houses of Congress, and Republican leaders loudly proclaimed that Wilson did not represent his own country.

In Britain there had also been an election. The facile, evasive, and slippery Lloyd George had been endorsed even more emphatically by his electorate than Wilson had been repudiated by his. A short time before, Lloyd George had signed, together with Wilson, a document limiting the amount of money the Germans must pay in reparations. He was reëlected by repudiating his word, and by promising the British people that he would extract from the surrendered foe impossibly large sums. And behind Lloyd George now stood the most hardboiled House of Commons in British history.

Clemenceau detested Wilson and his emphasis on ideals. The Premier of France was the oldest and most experienced of the peacemakers. Twice he had seen Germans marching through Paris streets. There were many more million Germans in Europe than there were Frenchmen—far too many. The peace terms could not be too harsh for Clemenceau. He favored detaching the left bank of the Rhine altogether from Germany, the annexation of the Saar Valley and of German colonies to France.

The anti-Wilson forces confronted Wilson at Paris with a number of secret treaties they had made among themselves involving annexations. Among them was a treaty with Italy which guaranteed her lands occupied by German nationals. And another was a treaty between Britain and Japan giving Japan ownership of islands in the Pacific north of the equator. Those signing these treaties said their word was pledged. Wilson dug in behind the peace terms they had accepted. It was an impasse.

Then, too, it was impossible to unscramble the different nationalities in Austria-Hungary without injustice to large minorities. Geographically and economically the Danube valley was a natural unit; ethnographically it was a hodgepodge. It was impossible to draw the boundaries of a Czechoslovakia in order to give Czechs self-determination without denying it to Germans and Magyars. An enlarged Rumania which would guarantee self-determination to Rumanians automatically would deny it to Germans and South Slavs.

And finally there was Wilson's own temperament. Intent on broad objectives, he seemingly was oblivious to those minor courtesies which help to soften disagreements. In speaking in the Guild Hall in London, it never seems to have occurred to him to say a few gracious words in praise of British sacrifices in the war; during his long stay in France, it apparently never occurred to him to visit the battlefields, close as they were to Paris. Wilson was both prophet and statesman but not a good politician. Furthermore, such politics as he was familiar with were American, not European. He was lost in a strange environment. British journalists came to think of him as a man easily deceived by specious words; more fair, perhaps, would it be to regard him as a man who really was aware of what he was doing, and who sacrificed much—possibly too much —to gain acceptance for his life's dream, the League of Nations.

Under these circumstances, it is remarkable that the President was able to accomplish as much as he did. And unfortunate as the peace treaties turned out to be, it may well be argued that they would have been more so had it not been for Woodrow Wilson.

Always it must be remembered the Germans did not surrender unconditionally. Terms were granted them. They were fair terms, even if at times ambiguously stated. And their author had been Wilson. Before the armistice was drawn up, the Germans had agreed to lay down their arms on the guarantee that the peace to follow would be based on Wilson's fourteen points and his subsequent speeches and addresses.

Here were the pre-armistice terms, accepted by the British and the French as well as by the Germans. The British and the French did not like them; but when Wilson threatened to withdraw America's armies and to make a separate peace with Germany his allies accepted his proposals with two reservations. One of these related to "freedom of the seas," now deleted because of ambiguities. The other sharpened and defined what the Germans might be charged in way of reparations. In one of the President's speeches he had stated that they were responsible for the restoration of invaded territories. The revision was made to read, "responsible for damage done to the civilian population on land, sea and from the air." Obviously unless this change had been made Britain would have received nothing, since she had not been invaded, her direct civilian losses having come from submarine sinkings and air raids.

Wilson's Victories

The President's major victories at Paris were the curbing of French expansionists and the creation of the League of Nations. The French would have liked to have detached the Rhineland, that part of the German Empire west of the Rhine, from Germany altogether, and to have made of it a neutral buffer state. And in opposing this Wilson had the support of Lloyd George. The French then proposed the occupation of the Rhineland for thirty years, and at Wilson's insistence this was cut in half to fifteen years. The French then demanded the annexation of the Saar Valley with its overwhelming German population. Here once again Wilson opposed them, but accepted a compromise whereby France was given title to the coal mines of the Saar as compensation for the destruction of coal mines in France, and the Saar was put under the jurisdiction of the proposed League of Nations for fifteen years. At the conclusion of that time a plebiscite of the inhabitants was to decide whether they desired inclusion in the French Republic, or the continued rule of the League, or return to Germany. If the third option was taken proviso was made for the repurchase of the coal mines.

The greater part of the President's time and energy at the peace conference was devoted to the formation and acceptance of the League of Nations. The idea behind it was not new, and Wilson's league was of mixed Anglo-American parentage, the American League to enforce Peace, of which William Howard Taft had been president, and the British Society of Nations, whose head, Lord Phillimore, had drawn up a form of constitution which served as the original model. But Wilson was the principal advocate of the League at Paris, and he had worked hard and long over various drafts, and was responsible for the famous article X which guaranteed the signatories against external aggression.

Serious difficulties were encountered by Wilson. Some came from the

THE BEACON LIGHT.

[Lord ROBERT CECIL is taking a leading part in the campaign for making the objects of the League of Nations better understood.   The campaign opened on the anniversary of the Armistice.]

(*Punch,* Nov. 12, 1919.)

French, some from the Japanese, some from his own Americans. The French insisted on a league "with teeth," in other words with an international army, presumably against future German attacks, presumably also with a French general in command. The Japanese were equally determined that the League should include a specific affirmation of racial equality. American opinion, which was lukewarm, was certain to oppose both these ideas; and in addition it most certainly could not be won over to approval without specific recognition of the binding character of the Monroe Doctrine and without an escalator clause permitting members to resign. Final acceptance of Wilson's covenant, as he liked to call his league, did not come until late in the sessions of the conference, and not until after he had made a special trip back to America to plead for its approval there. And it was while he was so engaged that a number of compromises were made in the peace settlement by his alter ego, Colonel House.

The League of Nations, as finally drafted, provided for an assembly representing all countries with one vote each, and for a council of nine members, five permanent and four elected by the assembly to serve for one term each. Permanent seats were to be given to the United States, Great Britain, France, Italy, and Japan. The headquarters of the League were to be at Geneva, where a secretariat or permanent board of officials was to be located. Attached to the League was to be a World Court for the settlement of international judicial disputes and an international Labor Office, which it was hoped might standardize conditions of labor throughout the world. The Assembly of the League was to meet in Geneva once a year, the Council four times a year, but not necessarily in Geneva. The latter body also could be summoned any time if danger threatened world peace. All members of the League were obligated to submit disputes between them to arbitration or to the Council for review. Decisions, to be effective, had to be unanimous.

Wilson's Defeats

Wilson's major defeats at Paris were in regard to colonies, Japanese conquests in China, and the reparation settlement to be made with Germany.

In accordance with the pre-armistice agreement there was to be "an impartial treatment of the colonial question, having in mind the best interests of native peoples." (Number 5 of Wilson's accepted fourteen points.) There should be no trouble over this, said the British Prime Minister. German Southwest Africa has been conquered by the Union of South Africa, a democracy; German Samoa has been conquered by New Zealand, a democracy; German New Guinea has been conquered by Australia, a democracy. The best interests of the native peoples is best secured by annexing them to those countries whose democratic faith is the best guarantee of fair treatment. And needless to say this British demand for outright annexation was warmly seconded by France who had her eye on Togo and Kamerun, and by Japan firmly entrenched in German-owned islands north of the equator.

But Wilson had proclaimed in his speeches that there should be no annexations, and these proposed annexations were a repudiation of the pre-armistice terms. On the other hand he was opposed to the return of her colonies to Germany since such a course of action would be prejudicial to "the best interests of the native peoples."

Wilson's high hope was that his League of Nations might first be organized before anything was done about dependent possessions. His European allies, however, pressed for an immediate colonial settlement. The President then fathered an expedient which might have functioned well had there not been crippling amendments. This was the principle of the mandate or trusteeship, whereby the country having a mandate should hold it in trust for the League and report to it annually.

The idea looked good and was accepted. There were to be three classes of mandates. Class A consisted of those regions with a fair degree of cultural advancement which might look forward in the near future to independence. Here the control of the mandatory power was slight. Falling in this category were places like Syria, Palestine, and Iraq. Class B mandates were German colonies in central Africa where there was to be more detailed supervision, but none the less a fairly long list of guarantees, such as the prohibition of slavery, freedom of trade and equality of opportunity. Class C mandates were German colonies closely adjacent to the mandatory power, and to all intent and purpose incorporated in it, since its laws became immediately applicable to the mandate and guarantees protecting the natives were fewer in number than in Class B. For instance, in Class C mandates there was nothing said about "equality of opportunity." Virtually this was veiled annexation, the only difference being the pledged word of the mandatory power to make its annual report.

The acceptance of the mandate principle, although urged by Wilson, cannot be recorded as a Wilson victory. As things worked out, it was a Wilson defeat, since in drawing up the terms of the various mandates it proved possible to insert clauses *not* in the best interest of the native peoples. As an illustration the French inserted a clause in their mandate making it legal to conscript Negroes in Africa to fight not simply there but in Europe. This caught Wilson's eye and he would have none of it. The clause was stricken out and a more general statement made whereby, by a little twist here and a little twist there, the same thing could be done.

Wilson encountered a second defeat when dealing with Japan. The Japanese not only were in actual possession of the German islands north of the equator (Class C mandates); they also had seized the German-leased port of Tsingtao on the Shantung peninsula and were busily engaged in extending their sway beyond Kiaochow Bay. Meanwhile China had entered the war on the side of the Allies, and largely through American persuasion. Wilson, therefore, argued that Japan should return to China all concessions wrested from her by the Germans.

The Japanese, unable to obtain their coveted recognition of racial equality in the League of Nations, were determined not simply to retain German concessions in China but in addition those which they had forced an impotent Chinese government to yield to them in 1915. Trifling modifications of the latter were made by Japan. But on the main issue she remained adamant. Wilson yielded. If he had not done so, Japan made it clear that she would not become a member of the League.

A third defeat was the Italian settlement. The Italian frontier was not drawn in accordance with the pre-armistice guarantee "along clearly recognizable lines of nationality," but the reverse. Somewhere between 200,000 and 250,000 Germans in the Upper Tyrol were included in Italy. About fifty-two per cent of the people in the Istrian Peninsula, now given to Italy, were of non-Italian nationality, and seventy-five per cent, if not more, of the population of the annexed regions in Dalmatia on the east coast of the Adriatic were non-Italian.

The reason for this violation of Wilsonian principles is to be found in the "secret treaties" made between the Allies during the war; and the fact that they were not abrogated upon the acceptance of Wilson's fourteen points and subsequent addresses is (the one question of reparations aside) the strongest single argument against the treaty settlement as a whole.

For purely military reasons the Allies had in their hour of great peril paid high for Italian support. The French and British now claimed that they were in honor bound to keep their word to Italy. Wilson asserted that the acceptance of his principles cancelled the secret treaties made earlier. There certainly was much to be said for this point of view. Early in the war, before American troops embarked for Europe, the Allies might logically have expected Wilson to inquire into these treaties, but apparently he did not. Now that they were brought to light he denied their validity.

The American committee of experts on Italy's frontier could find no argument in favor of taking Upper Tyrol away from Austria, but it did discover plausible reasons for the Italian annexation of the Istrian Peninsula. Population strains were so mixed in the peninsula, they said, that it was impossible to tell very much about census statistics, and after all the Austrian government before the war had iniquitously imported Slovene laborers just for the purpose of swelling the anti-Italian total. As for Dalmatia and the eastern coast of the Adriatic Wilson's advisers gave contradictory counsel. His six experts were unanimous that it would be a violation of the pre-armistice terms if any of this Slavic-held land should go to Italy. On the other hand a number of his more politically-minded councillors argued that the cities on the coast had once been Venetian outposts and the Austrians for a long time had been playing dirty politics and oppressing those of Italian blood. Dalmatia, as a whole, was Italian in culture even if not in blood, and it was absurd to expect Italy to be content with a potential enemy directly opposite her on the eastern shores of the Adriatic.

Curiously enough, the President himself took no interest in the Tyrol question where his principles were so clearly defied. What enraged him was the Italian demand for Fiume on the eastern shores of the Adriatic, the former port of Hungary, a demand not based on the Treaty of London, which had left Fiume for the Yugoslavs, but founded on his own principle of self-determination. The Italians could not have it both ways, said President Wilson, gaining certain territory because of the secret treaty and yet other territory because they invoked his principles.

Meanwhile, the Italians who had walked out of the conference rather than lose Fiume hurried back to Paris in order to sign the Treaty of Versailles, since by so doing Italy obtained what she had bargained for in 1915.

The major defeat suffered by Wilson was the reparation settlement. What it legitimately called for was simple enough: an itemized bill for damages suffered by civilians as the result of German military attack from under the water, from invasion, and from the air. This was the letter of the bond, and this and no more was to be charged against the Germans.

Keynes, British financial expert, after a careful survey, estimated the total at somewhere between ten and eleven billion dollars. And as young John Foster Dulles, a lawyer attached to Wilson's staff, stated, the victors were precluded from demanding more, no matter how just such a demand might be, because they of their own accord had placed these limitations in the pre-armistice terms.

The issue was drawn. Lloyd George had assured the British electorate that his committee of bankers had said that the Germans could pay $100,000,000,000, and that in justice they should pay the entire cost of the war. Clemenceau supported Lloyd George. Woodrow Wilson refused to budge beyond the letter of the bond.

Enter then General Smuts, prime minister of the Union of South Africa, and author of a book on holism. Smuts was quite capable of making white seem black and the reverse. He won Wilson over to his side by this argument: It was no ordinary war that had been won. The Allied soldiers were mainly civilians who had been conscripted. If wounded they would receive pensions, and if killed their widows would be entitled to them. Pensions then were payments due people who were really civilians and only temporarily soldiers. They were therefore simply compensation for losses suffered by civilians which it was legitimate to charge against the Germans. This was a specious argument. Once admit pensions as damages done to civilians and it follows logically that the same argument could be made for taxes paid by civilians for carrying on the war. And in this case, if this were done, the Germans could be assessed for the entire cost of the war. And this the pre-armistice terms very clearly forbade.

One suspects that Wilson was dimly aware of the slippery character of Smuts' proposal, but he was thoroughly exhausted physically and had never shown much interest in purely economic matters. "Logic be damned," the President was quoted as saying, "I am going to sign for pensions." And so they were embedded in the peace treaty, the bill to be determined by an international reparations commission and presented to the Germans later.

Poland

There remained one other great controversy at the peace conference as regards Germany, and that was how to draw the boundaries of the resuscitated Poland. The settlement finally reached cannot well be included as a Wilson defeat or a Wilson victory, for the President in this particular fight was largely an onlooker, the two major contestants being Lloyd George and Clemenceau.

Traditional French foreign policy for centuries had been in favor of a strong Poland to exert pressure on Germany from the East. And now the French saw their chance: they demanded that the German city of Danzig on the Baltic at the mouth of the Vistula be given to Poland; and they also proposed that the Poles annex generous areas to the south and east of Danzig which, if consummated, would have reduced East Prussia to such minimal proportions that it would probably wither on the vine.

But Lloyd George would have none of this. He insisted that Danzig be placed under the jurisdiction of the League of Nations, that plebiscites be taken in those areas adjacent to that city which the French would hand over to Poland, and furthermore that a plebiscite be held in Upper Silesia, where it was believed that Germans were more numerous than Poles. The latter had been promised access to the sea; that meant the Vistula Valley, and certainly the right to export and import through Danzig, or else the pre-armistice terms would have been meaningless. But Danzig was close to a one-hundred-per-cent German town and the British Prime Minister would not consent to Poland having it.

His action in so doing made Lloyd George the standard bearer of Wilsonian principles and not the President, a situation not easy to explain. It may partly be accounted for by Wilson's distrust of Lloyd George; by worry over the League of Nations; by personal illness; and also by ill-informed American experts who assured him that Poles were far more numerous in the localities where plebiscites were taken than they after-

wards showed themselves to be. Wilson finally threw in the weight of
his influence behind Lloyd George; Danzig went to the League with
commercial rights in its guaranteed Poland; and the plebiscites all voted
for Germany rather than for Poland.

Austria-Hungary

Of the various problems which confronted the peacemakers, one of
the most complicated was what to do with the ramshackle empire of the
Hapsburgs. By the conclusion of the war both the Czechs and the South
Slavs had been promised independence, and to bring that about meant
the dissolution of Austria-Hungary. Wilson's fourteen points had merely
promised "free development" for the various nationalities within her
borders, and presumably the better part of wisdom would have been to
compel some form of federation for lands lying in the Danube valley.
But since the publication of the fourteen points the Czechs had fought
against the Germans and the South Slavs against the Austrians.

Furthermore, long before the last stages of the war Czech leaders had already organized an independent Czech government in Paris which had obtained recognition; and as early as April, 1918, Bosnians, Slovenes, and Serbs had met in Italy, and by the Pact of Rome had proclaimed an independent South Slav nation which was to become Yugoslavia. It was now too late to insist on mere federation.

New boundaries had to be drawn for the two enemy states, Austria and Hungary; and it is evident that both must lose a great deal of territory if justice was to be done to North Slavs, Czechs, Slovaks, Poles, Ruthenians, and Slovenes in the old Austria, and also to the Rumanians and South Slavs in Hungary. For the most part this was accomplished with a rough show of justice. Austria became a puny little country comparable to Switzerland in area. This, however, was inevitable since she lost Bohemia (home of the Czechs) and Galicia (home of the Austrian Poles and Ruthenians) as well as her southern provinces occupied by Slovenes. After all, most of the German-speaking people in the old Austria were still to be found in the new. Hungary also suffered the same fate. That too was necessary, since several million Magyars woke up to find themselves citizens of Czechoslovakia, Rumania, and Yugoslavia owing to the application of Wilsonian ideas of self-determination. Nevertheless, the great majority of Magyars still found homes for themselves within the shrunken borders of the new Hungary. That there were injustices in drawing the new boundaries will be apparent as we review the Danubian settlement; but it is desirable to remember that for the most part the principle of self-determination was followed. Violations of it were numerous but in most instances unavoidable.

Taking up one after another of the countries now carved wholly or in part out of the old Hapsburg lands, we come first to Czechoslovakia. An unfortunate name was given to it, one implying the union of Czechs and Slovaks. There was really no necessity of uniting them, except that the Slovaks, formerly under Hungarian rule, were scarcely strong enough to stand by themselves unless united with the Czechs, a much more numerous and advanced people formerly under Austrian rule. By placing both Czechs and Slovaks in one country, and by joining to them the old Hungarian province of Ruthenia, a queer-shaped state was evolved, looking somewhat like a tadpole with its head in Bohemia and its tail in Ruthenia.

Bohemia, if taken by itself, was an old country not manufactured out of whole cloth to please the Czechs. Its capital, Prague, had been a foyer of Christianity and culture at a time when the Teutonic tribes to the north were semi-nomadic barbarians, and at Prague had been established the first university in Central Europe. During the sixteenth century, however, Bohemia had fallen under Hapsburg sway, and in the

seventeenth and eighteenth centuries it had become more and more
Teutonized. During the last half of the nineteenth century, the submerged Czech nationality, perhaps always in the majority, had reasserted
itself, but even as late as 1914 the predominant class in Bohemia, certainly
in wealth and possibly in culture, had been South German, looking to
Vienna.

The Czechs in Bohemia outnumbered the Germans by possibly three
to one, and to a large extent it was impossible to give Bohemia or
Czechoslovakia any reasonable boundaries at all without including in

PARTITION
OF AUSTRIA-HUNGARY

GERMANS
CZECHO-SLOVAKS
ITALIANS
YUGOSLAVS
POLES
UKRANIANS
RUMANIANS
MAGYARS

them a large part of the 3,000,000 Germans in Bohemia, for the country,
topographically, was a flat pocket or plain surrounded by mountains, and
the majority of the Germans lived on or near the border. Nevertheless,
as the Americans on the Czechoslovak committee demonstrated, some
300,000 of these Germans in Egerland and in two other border districts
might have been permitted to join the Reich without serious strategic
injuries to the boundaries of the new country.

But it was not the Germans alone who were denied in this instance the
right of self-determination. If the boundaries of Czechoslovakia had been
drawn fairly on an ethnographical basis, instead of looking like a tadpole
the country more nearly would have resembled an hourglass. Only by
including thousands of Poles on the north and possibly 750,000 Magyars

on the south was it possible to make Czechoslovakia bulge out in the middle. Furthermore, for economic reasons it was considered essential that Czechoslovakia include land where these Magyars lived, since the only railway connection between Prague and eastern Czechoslovakia went through the old city of Pressburg on the Danube in Hungary and through parts of Slovakia where there were more Magyars than Slovaks.

The Magyars suffered even greater losses elsewhere. Rumania had, as we have seen (p. 90), been bribed into the war by Allied promises of (a) Bukovina, north of the Carpathians and formerly a part of Austria— in Bukovina thirty-four per cent of the population was Magyar; (b) Transylvania, or eastern Hungary—with a population largely Rumanian, but with a large Magyar and a lesser German minority; (c) the Banat of Temesvar, across the Danube, north of Belgrade, where Serbs, Rumanians, and Magyars were hopelessly mixed. All three regions were lost to Hungary, the Rumanians receiving Bukovina and Transylvania and dividing the Banat with Yugoslavia.

To do justice to both the Magyars and the Rumanians on the basis of self-determination was impossible. A large part of the Magyar folk in Transylvania, for instance, were located well toward the Carpathian Mountains and between them and their fellow Magyars was a solid section of Rumanians. Nevertheless, the peace conference might have been much more just in regard to Hungary's eastern and southern boundaries, for at least 500,000 Magyars on the western borders of Transylvania were included in the greater Rumania, while some 250,000 odd, on the borders of the Banat, were included in Yugoslavia, the excuse in the former case being that it was essential for Rumania to have possession of the only railroad running north and south through West Transylvania.

Arguments raised at the peace conference in regard to strategic boundaries, railroads, and economic necessity were numerous, and always the French insisted that the new nations must be *viable:* these were one-way arguments, never made in behalf of Austria and Hungary, enemy states, but ever appropriate to Italy, Yugoslavia, Rumania, and Czechoslovakia. Vienna, a city of 2,000,000, former commercial and banking entrepôt of the Danube Valley, now was left to starve in the center of a tiny country, largely mountainous, where almost every boundary was but an hour distant by train or automobile. Budapest at least had food supplies from the Hungarian plain, but the city itself was much too large for the purely agricultural population left within the truncated confines of the new Hungary.

Meanwhile, Germany was to recognize the independence of Austria, a neat way of preventing the Austrian Germans from pleading self-determination and joining forces with the Germans in the Fatherland.

Herein have been described the main provisos of the so-called peace settlement. By the Treaty of Versailles, made with Germany, that country lost relatively little territory. Alsace-Lorraine, three tiny enclaves on the Belgian border, measured more readily in hundreds of yards than in miles, a part of northern Schleswig given to the Danes after a plebiscite, the city of Memel on the northeastern boundary with surrounding territory to the League of Nations (Memel's population was about 20,000, mostly Germans, but Memel and, the whole region, about half the size of Rhode Island, contained possibly as many Lithuanians as Germans); the city of Danzig to the League of Nations (some 300,000 Germans here); but Danzig was at the mouth of the Vistula and was regarded as an essential port for Poland; the district of Posen to Poland (the greater part of the population unquestionably Polish); the Polish Corridor, and a large part of Upper Silesia, also to Poland. For most of these losses of territory there was real justification; at least their cession could not be called a failure to live up to the bargain whereby Germany ceased fighting.

For the economic settlement there was no justification. The demand that the Kaiser and high German officials be tried by Allied law courts was a vindictive absurdity, and quite as absurd was the celebrated clause in the treaty, Number 231, whereby Germany acknowledged on the part of herself and her allies entire responsibility for the losses suffered by the Allies during the war. The Germans were forced to sign this untrue and humiliating statement with a pistol pointed at their head, for the economic blockade of Germany still continued and Germans starved. No clause in the entire treaty gave Hitler more of a lever when the opportunity came to denounce "the dictate of Versailles."

Separate peace treaties also were signed with the other Central Powers, that of St. Germain with Austria, Trianon with Hungary, Neuilly with Bulgaria, Sèvres with Turkey. All of these four treaties violated the Wilsonian doctrine of self-determination to a greater or less degree. Much less important than the Treaty of Versailles, they none the less were a part of the peace settlement.

On the whole, the latter was unsatisfactory. No Talleyrand had represented Germany in Paris, and the Germans had been forced to sign on the dotted line. The American President, breathing forth idealism, had put his name to a treaty which in all that concerned economics was a breach of faith with the enemy. The Prime Minister of England, on the other hand, had been responsible more than any one else for the reparations muddle, although it must be acknowledged that the French were his close second. The treaty was so bad that General Smuts thought seriously of not signing. About all that could be said in its favor is that it might have been worse; it might have annexed the Rhineland to France; it might have divided Germany again at the River Main, as she was divided in 1866; and the treaties of St. Germain and Trianon might have given the Czechs a corridor across the Hungarian plain which they asked for, thus separating Austria from Hungary and joining Czechoslovakia with Yugoslavia. These absurdities were at least avoided. It is a wild exaggeration to speak of the settlement as a Carthaginian peace, as many writers have done. Carthage was demolished and its site sown with salt. In the last analysis, the defeated Germans had received much fairer treatment than they themselves had meted out to the defeated Russians at Brest Litovsk. The men of Versailles not only did not demolish Germany but left open two ways of mitigating the harshness of their terms. There was the Reparation Commission which might show sense in tuning down the economic settlement, and there was, of course, the League of Nations, to which the idealists clung, in despair mingled with rapture.

From 1919 to the Ruhr

The four years which succeeded 1919 were full of disaster for Europe. The peace treaties seemingly settled nothing and confusion became worse confounded. Worse than that; the economic burdens borne by the European peoples became heavier and more intolerable than they had been during the war.

The first country to repudiate the Treaty of Versailles was the United States. The reasons which motivated the United States Senate were not as admirable as they might have been. The senators did not oppose the Treaty because it was unjust and a repudiation of Wilsonian promises; what they objected to was the League, the only ray of light, and a dim one at that, in a world black with angry hate. Even so, Wilson could have secured ratification had he been willing to accept drastic amendments to the League. Upon his refusal, the Treaty was rejected by the Senate and the presidential election of 1920 confirmed its rejection, the United States choosing to make its own separate treaty with Germany.

The effect of so doing was profound. It meant that the United States would not be represented either at Geneva (a term now constantly to be used as a synonym for the League of Nations), or on the Reparations Committee which was to assess the final bill against the Germans. It also served notice on the French that their concessions at Paris in return for American and British guarantees of their eastern boundary lines were useless. Even if the Senate had approved the Versailles Treaty, it is improbable that it would have accepted the additional triangular treaty between France, England, and the United States in regard to that guarantee. Now it was evident that the latter was a worthless bit of paper; for with America dropping out, England no longer was under any obligation arising from that treaty.

France, indeed, in the hour of victory felt very uneasy. Three times within one hundred years her soil had been invaded by the Germans; suppose they should come again? For the time being the French had them in the gutter; Germany was convulsed with civil strife, without allies, and defended by an army reduced to 100,000. French troops, not German, kept the "Watch on Rhine." But suppose this situation changed? There were 20,000,000 Germans too many, so the French thought. France had wanted a league of nations equipped with an international army but had given in to the British and to the Americans; she had wanted to separate the Rhineland, which lay west of the river, from the Reich, or at least to occupy it for thirty years, and again she had yielded, cutting in half the period of occupancy; and now her third bulwark against a revived and powerful Germany—the Anglo-American guarantee was down. Under such circumstances she not only determined to keep the German foe in economic vassalage but to surround him with a chain of states bound to herself in defensive alliance.

The French found it easy at first to secure allies. A close alliance with Belgium was consummated very soon after the Versailles Treaty, and shortly after, both Czechoslovakia and Poland joined France in a military alliance, thus surrounding Germany on three sides by prospective foes.

Czechoslovakia owed a great deal to France. That country had recognized and equipped the Czechoslovakian national army, had offered Paris as a temporary headquarters for the Czechoslovakian government, and had supported through thick and thin the claims of Czechoslovakia at the peace conference, ever insisting that the new nation be made *viable*, have economic resources and a creditable transportation system, whether self-determination was violated or not. In vain had the "Sudeten-deutsch," as the Germans in the old Austrian province of Bohemia were known, begged for the recognition of that principle. They were told it was impossible to employ it, that they must rest content with the promise (never fulfilled) that the Republic of Czechoslovakia would be constituted on the Swiss model as a federative rather than as a unitary state.

Nationalistic minorities in this ward of France were clearly marked and from the beginning were troublesome. About two-thirds of the population was Czech or Slovak; but a great many Slovaks liked the Poles or the Magyars better than they did the Czechs. About one-quarter of the total population was German, bitterly opposed to Czechs and Slovaks alike. The remainder, approximately 1,500,000, consisted of Magyars, Jews, Poles, and Ukrainians, not easy to handle. Nevertheless, Czechoslovakia lay like a great bastion in Central Europe, and the French were delighted at the thought of a powerful Czechoslovakia threatening Germany on the south. The definite Franco-Czechoslovak alliance was not formally completed, it is true, until 1924, but from the beginning French advice, French money, and French military aid was placed freely at the disposal of this new state, the most important of all the smaller satellite nations that France hoped to attach to herself.

To the east of Germany lay Poland, another potential French ally. The Poles had been divided among themselves during the war as to how Poland might be resurrected. Some of them, among whom was the conspirator and revolutionary patriot Pilsudski, were bitterly opposed to Russia and thought it might best be accomplished through the instrumentality of Austria. Others thought the best hope lay in supporting Russia against Germany. Consequently, Poles fought on both sides in the World War. But after the victorious Austro-Germans set up a puppet state of Poland in the midst of the conflict, Pilsudski was disillusioned. Unwilling to support the Central Powers, he was thrown in prison, not to escape until after the armistice, after which he placed himself at the head of a temporary Polish government at Warsaw.

Meanwhile, a Polish army had been organized in France in 1918 and the Poles in it had fought on the western front for France. Other Poles were on the Italian front, some on the Italian side, some on the Austrian, and still other Polish troops were deep in the Ukraine. It was Pilsudski's task to get them all home, to draw up a constitution, to establish boundaries, to resurrect a nation.

In all these endeavors he received the staunch backing of France. She sent the Polish troops from the west through Germany as early as April, 1919; she assisted Pilsudski with money and munitions; she supported his demands at the peace conference fully and effectively, and if the French had not been opposed there by Britain, Poland would have dipped into former German territory even more than it actually did.

The Versailles Treaty practically determined the western boundaries of Poland, but toward the east Pilsudski's efforts practically were unchecked—except, that is, by British disapproval which the Polish chieftain ignored. He occupied Kiev in the heart of the Ukraine; he pounced upon Vilna, capital of Lithuania, to the northeast; he pressed on against the Russian Communists. The latter smote Pilsudski hip and thigh, and only through the timely arrival of a French military commission was he rescued from disaster in a battle before Moscow, which staved off communism from Poland and incidentally from Central Europe. The Treaty of Riga (1921) with Russia, which followed, extended the Polish boundaries well to the east, not so far as in 1772, the date of the first partition of Poland, but far enough to place some 4,000,000 Russians under Polish sovereignty.

Thanks also to French connivance, Pilsudski was able in 1923 to retain Vilna, in spite of the League of Nations. The French had been somewhat embarrassed when Poland and Czechoslovakia had almost come to blows over that small sector of Upper Silesia known as Teschen, for France wanted both Poles and Czechs as allies. That difficulty, however, was ironed out in 1920 by a division of Teschen between the two contestants, and now, thanks again to France, the Poles secured the better part of what was left of Upper Silesia.

The hot-headed Poles had tried to seize that rich district by a military coup in 1919 but were headed off since the great powers at Paris had provided for a plebiscite in Upper Silesia. Despite the fact that the Germans won the vote for the district as a whole, France insisted that it be divided, and in the final settlement of 1921 French aid was again given Poland. The award to that country of 53 coal mines out of 67, of 11 out of 16 zinc and lead mines, and of 21 out of 37 blast furnaces was, it is true, the award of the League of Nations. But behind the action of the League were French diplomacy and French pressure, for several months before Pilsudski had gone to Paris, there to conclude a strong military alliance with France.

To keep the Germans, however, in perpetual economic subjection, involved an inner contradiction; if this desired end was consummated, how could the Germans become sufficiently prosperous to pay for reparations? The French were in a nasty dilemma; they wanted a great deal of money from Germany but at the same time they hoped to keep their eastern neighbor poverty-stricken. No such dilemma confronted the English; they had neither fear nor memory of a German invasion of England, and they were quite willing that Germany become prosperous again, the more so that their own industrial country could not hope to prosper while Central Europe lay prostrate. The English who lived by international trade, could not afford to wait; the French, primarily agricultural in their economy, could do so. In consequence, the Treaty of Versailles was no sooner signed than dissension broke out between the British and French as to the extent of the bill to be levied against Germany, the French advocating that it be raised to a high level, the British favoring a lower amount to revive business as soon as possible.

It proved easier to decide how the receipts should be divided than what the sum total should be. In 1920 it was agreed that fifty-two per cent should go to France, twenty-two per cent to the British Empire, ten per cent to Italy, eight per cent to Belgium, and the remaining eight per cent to be divided among other countries. A year later the total was placed at $56,000,000,000; at which the Germans made a counter offer of $12,500,000,000, contingent on subtraction of $5,000,000,000 which the Germans claimed they had already paid by sequestration of property and goods. They asked also loans to Germany, her retention of Upper Silesia, and the removal of restrictions placed upon German commerce.

The Allies, duly horrified, threatened the occupation of the Ruhr Valley, the heart of industrial Germany, and the Germans made a new offer. Again it was for $12,500,000,000, but without hypothetical deduction of $5,000,000,000 and with the promise of rebuilding by German labor the destroyed villages and towns of France. This, in turn, the Reparations Committee rejected but lowered its own demands to $32,000,000,000, a figure the Germans, after vain protest, reluctantly accepted.

Did the payment of this sum lie within the bounds of possibility? It could only be paid in three ways: (*a*) by the transfer of actual gold from Germany to the Allies; (*b*) by services, the Germans repairing in person the damages they had done and delivering commodities like ships and coal, to the Allies; or (*c*) a revival of international trade whereby the Germans could build up credits throughout the world which might be assigned to the Allies.

Method (*a*) was impossible. Thirty-two billion dollars was more than twice the actual amount of all known gold in the world and but a tiny fraction of the world's gold supply was in Germany. Method (*b*) was unacceptable. The French had no intention of permitting an invasion of German carpenters, masons, and plumbers for the rebuilding of French towns, thus throwing French artisans out of work. The British already had more ships than they could find cargoes for and their own shipyards were deserted. Their coal industry also was paralyzed, injuriously affected already by reparation payments of coal made to Italy and France. There remained then method (*c*). The success of this depended on the willingness of foreign countries to lower their tariff barriers against German goods. The United States was unwilling to do this, as was also France. To the east Poland was erecting and not demolishing tariff walls, and beyond Poland lay Russia in the throes of the Communist Revolution—an old German market now almost ruined.

It is conceivable that given a sufficient length of time the Germans might have paid by method (*c*). To do so, however, meant rigid economy and continuous sacrifice for many years, so many that babies born in the midst of the war would have become old folk before the yoke was lifted from their shoulders. The Germans were not willing to put such a yoke upon themselves. They had been forced to accept responsibility for the war and had so signed on paper; but this they had done because they were strangled by the Allies' economic blockade. In the name of victorious democracy, Woodrow Wilson had made them promises which had not been fulfilled. Why then submit to economic slavery? They had signed the peace treaty rather than starve and they would accept the reparation settlement rather than starve: but they felt no responsibility for either the one or the other.

In less than two years the reparation agreement bogged down. The Germans paid the $250,000,000 due in 1921; but so swift was the decline of their mark in the money markets of the world and so swift was the flight of capital from Germany that in 1922 they asked for and received a partial moratorium. Great Britain now took alarm and Lloyd George,

still prime minister, summoned an international world economic conference at Genoa. Desperately, he hoped that the United States would participate, for if that happened the obtuse Yankees might realize that one
reason for making the Germans pay was to obtain the wherewithal with
which the Allies might pay their war debts to America. Desperately, also,
did he hope that France might rescind her announced intention not to
discuss reparations at this conference. Since both hopes were entirely
imaginary there was no real reason for the conference at all. The Germans
came and again offered to pay in kind but not in money. The Russians
came and struck a treaty with the Germans. Since neither Soviet Russia
nor the German republic had funds, it was comparatively simple for
them mutually to cancel each other's indebtedness. Other results Genoa
had none.

On July 15, 1922, the Germans made their last cash payment; for the
rest of that year they were granted a temporary moratorium. The latter
was inevitable, since German currency was crashing to oblivion. Four
German marks were almost equal to the American dollar in 1914; when
the reparation agreement was signed the ratio was 56 to 1. But by
November, 1922, it stood at 7,000 marks to the dollar, and was gone now
beyond recovery.

The French were very angry. They had sunk huge sums in rebuilding
their own devastated areas, and they believed that the Germans were
wilfully issuing paper money to make reparations impossible. The inflation in Germany had artificially stimulated industry there and German
factories were in full blast. Thereupon the French determined to seize
their foes by the throat and by the hair, and in January, 1923, the forces
of France marched into the Ruhr.

The valley of the Ruhr, east of the Rhine, was neither very wide nor
very long; but it was the heart of industrial Germany. Nine cities with
over 2,000,000 inhabitants lay within its narrow confines, as also eighty
per cent of the coal and eighty per cent of the blast furnaces left to
the Germans. Without the Ruhr, Germany could not exist as an industrial nation. Nevertheless the Germans decided to resist by the only means
that lay within their power—the general strike. German miners refused
to dig coal for the French masters, German puddlers refused to work the
blast furnaces, German engineers would not operate the valley's intricate
transportation system. Nothing lay before Germany but helpless poverty;
but since the mark had already sunk so far, why not print more and more
until the cost of the paper exceeded the value of the numerical digits put
upon it? By the end of 1923 this had happened; the mark was now worth
two and a half trillion to the dollar and milk was priced at 250,000,000
marks per quart.

The Germans thereupon surrendered and agreed to renew reparation
payments if some new basis could be found for so doing. Their middle

class had been virtually wiped out. Houses, life-insurance policies, every-thing that formerly had possessed monetary value was lost to millions of Germans. Almost nobody was employed in industry, practically every one had suffered except peasants and profiteers.

As for the French, their victory was tasteless. Even before the World War, their debt had been colossal and now they staggered under it. They in turn would soon have to devalue their own currency and in the mean-while they had lost the sympathy of the British, and the Germans, putting into effect the Tolstoyan program of "non-resistance to evil by force" had not been unsuccessful in withstanding them.

All things considered, the dark clouds which hung over Europe in 1919 looked even darker in 1924. The Ruhr invasion of 1923 had seem-ingly crushed Germany, but without helping the French exchequer. The French still held the military hegemony of Europe, for what it was worth; they had the largest army and supporting it were the armies of Czechoslovakia and Poland, French-trained. But Russia was an impon-derable factor; suppose Germany should go communist and join with Russia? Mussolini meanwhile had risen to power in Italy and was chal-lenging both the status quo and the League of Nations. France had a permanent seat on the council of that organization and since nothing could be done without the unanimous consent of that council (and perhaps not much even with it), France had nothing to fear from the League. On the other hand, could she depend upon it in time of need? There seemed to the French but one clear line to pursue—by diplomacy and by money to secure as many allies as possible; to keep up the iron ring around Germany; to continue as she had done in the past to follow the traditional rules of power politics. How disastrous a policy this was to prove, we shall see later.

Chapter 8

THE UNION OF SOVIET SOCIALIST REPUBLICS (U.S.S.R.)

PEACE OF a kind dawned on Western Europe in November, 1918, but in Russia there was not even a semblance of peace. The Bolsheviks (the Reds) faced civil war in their own country, large sections of which were either indifferent to the Revolution or actually under control of anti-Bolshevik factions (the Whites), supported everywhere by Allied sympathy and in many cases by Allied money and Allied soldiers.

During the last stages of the war, English and American troops had occupied Murmansk, the Russian seaport on the Arctic Ocean—this to prevent the capture of war matériel by the Germans. The French, after the collapse of Germany, had landed detachments at Odessa on the Black Sea; and at Vladivostok on the Pacific the Americans and the Japanese landed forces, ostensibly to protect supplies and to guard the Trans-Siberian and Chinese Eastern railways. These various Allied interventions greatly encouraged those former adherents of the Czar who were set on reëstablishing the old regime. To their side now hastened many of the Russian Cadets (the former Constitutional Democrats), some of the Mensheviki (minority socialists), and a few of the old Social Revolutionary party. The Reds found themselves hemmed in on all sides. Allied detachments captured Archangel on the White Sea and threatened them on the north. On the west an ex-Czarist general, Yudenich, aided by White Russians and some Estonians, headed toward St. Petersburg (now Petrograd and soon to be called Leningrad). From the south a large White army under General Denikin, outfitted by Allied guns, airplanes, and tanks, was marching toward Moscow. Meanwhile, at Omsk in Siberia, an anti-Bolshevik directorate, with some claim to be the legal successor of Kerensky's deposed administration, seemed strongly entrenched. Backed by the warlike Czechoslovak troops, who had fought viciously with the Bolsheviks on their retreat toward the Pacific, and by numerous ex-Czarist officers, this directorate in western Siberia, soon to fall under the control of Admiral Kolchak, a White, apparently was quite as strong as that of the Reds centering in Moscow.

143

The Bolsheviks in 1919 confronted a situation somewhat parallel to that which the French Jacobins faced in 1793—disaffection from within and intervention from without. Like their radical French predecessors, they met the first with militant terrorism and the second with patriotic zeal. Trotsky, the Red commissar for war, created *de novo* a Red army which made up in morale for what it lacked in equipment. Soon it began to win victories. As in the case of the Austro-Prussian invasion of France in 1792, the Allied intervention was only half-hearted. On the former occasion the approach of the second partition of Poland in 1793 had diverted Allied interests elsewhere. Now, after the terrific strain of four years' fighting, the Allies had no stomach for adventures in Russia. The French, from a financial point of view, were likely to lose most from a Bolshevik victory, since the Russian Reds had repudiated the Czar's debts, and France had loaned more money to Russia than to any other country; but on the other hand no troops in Europe were more war-weary than those of France, and mutinies among French soldiers and sailors at the Black Sea ports made Paris hesitant to support Denikin's advance. The British were in somewhat similar case. They had a huge surplus of unsalable war supplies, speedily depreciating in value, and these they placed readily enough at the disposal of the Whites; but the lives of British soldiers were another matter. A general strike of the British trade unions was imminent if British regiments were ordered to fight the Bolsheviks, and the Lloyd George cabinet shrank back from any such commitments. Both British and French had hoped that the Americans would do something to defeat the Reds, and there had been talk at Paris of General Pershing's leading his relatively fresh forces against Trotsky. But the Americans were not interested; they withdrew their meager detachments from Vladivostok and from Murmansk and declined to participate in the anti-Bolshevik front, except to support the barrier of smaller states backed by the Allies (from Finland to Rumania), that the Bolshevik infection might be kept out of Europe.

Partly owing to these facts, Trotsky's armies proved victorious. They were led in many cases by former officers of the Imperial Russian Army, who preferred to fight for their own Russia, even if revolutionary, rather than for the Whites with their foreign support. The Whites, moreover, had no uniform command. The more they advanced into the heart of Russia, the more they embittered the peasants. Had they been willing boldly to proclaim constitutional and economic reform and formally to recognize peasant ownership of the land it is possible that the result might have been different. But even this partial acceptance of the revolution the Whites were unwilling to concede; they wanted their old rights and their former property restored. And so the peasants, at first more or less indifferent, ultimately sided with the Reds against the Whites; confronted with terrorism as practiced by both factions, they decided that the Reds were the lesser of two evils.

The civil war was over by the end of 1920. For a time it looked as though the Poles, acting on the advice of French officers and equipped with French guns, might overcome the Soviets. The Poles drove south and east from Warsaw, captured Kiev in the heart of the Ukraine; and as they did so Baron Wrangel, heading a new White army in the South, advanced north from the Crimea. Both Wrangel and the Poles, however, were routed. Wrangel followed Denikin into exile at Constantinople, and the hard-pressed Poles were in danger of losing Warsaw and would have done so, had it not been for French military assistance. Peace followed. Russia was still an "outlaw" country in the eyes of Western Europe and none of the Allied powers recognized the Soviet government; but on the other hand they took no further steps to defeat the Russian revolution by force of arms.

Left to themselves, the Bolsheviks were free to put into operation their long-cherished dream of a socialist state. They were without funds; they were inexperienced in the practical details of both government and business; and they had on their hands a backward and poverty-stricken peasantry comprising ninety per cent of the population, quite content with the individual ownership of their land, and to all intents and purposes untouched with Marxian ideas of a state-controlled economic life. So exhausted, indeed, were the Reds at the end of the civil war, that the rest of Europe confidently prophesied that their regime could not last. Trains, it was said, did not run in Russia; telephones did not operate; grass grew in the streets; all business was at a standstill; and in Moscow and Petrograd even the houses were falling to pieces. So thought the enemies of Red Russia.

But one thing they forgot—the energy and enthusiasm engendered by a blind faith in a new ideology and in Nicolai Lenin, the embodiment of it. Lenin, a conspirator for decades, came from the lesser nobility. His brother had been put to death as a university student for conspiring against Alexander III, and Lenin himself had been expelled from a Russian university for political agitation. Watched by the police, he went to St. Petersburg, advocated Marxian doctrines, was arrested and exiled for three years to Siberia. He came back, plunged into socialistic propaganda, spent much time at London, Paris, and Geneva, and was the foremost Russian delegate at the Second Congress (1903) of the Second International at Brussels. Here he led the fight of "the hards," or the Bolsheviks, against the "softs," or the Mensheviki, in other words that of the uncompromising Marxians who opposed any coöperation with bourgeois parties against their more opportunist fellows. The Bolsheviki at first won the day, hence their name, which means *majority*. But the

Mensheviki, meaning *minority,* turned the tables at last, and Lenin's group met defeat.

When the abortive revolution of 1905 broke out in Russia, Lenin slipped back to his own country. Here he again experienced defeat as he had in 1903 at the hands of the Mensheviki, since the revolutionary tempo was slowing down, the Czar winning back power and prestige. The Cadets (liberals) held the spotlight and Lenin hated all Cadets, holding that they were "vermin who take possession of the battlefield when the heroes have been defeated"—the heroes in this instance being the striking workmen of Moscow and St. Petersburg. Lenin's own liberty, if not his life, was in danger, for he was living obscurely on a false passport. There was nothing to do for the time being in Russia, and therefore he quit the country in 1907, not to return for ten years.

This second period of exile was spent for the most part in Switzerland and in secret propaganda work. Lenin remained at the head of the Bolsheviki, but the world knew nothing of them or him. In the first Russian Duma there was little talk of socialism, and what there was came from the handful of Mensheviki in it. The Bolsheviks were not even represented. Consequently, when Lenin, with the kind permission of the Germans, came back to Russia in 1917 in the midst of her new revolution, there were few to note that fact or to realize how shrewd the Germans were in importing this dynamic protagonist of proletariat revolt.

Yet this stocky, middle-aged man within three years was to become a dictator in Russia, the first of the series of twentieth-century dictators. Unlike the others Lenin was a close student of economics, had written extensively, and deservedly ranks with Marx and Engels as one of the founding fathers of communism, his most famous contribution to Communist theory being his analysis of imperialism as the last stage of capitalism. A militant of militants, he put his faith first and foremost on the seizure of power by a thoroughly disciplined and purged Communist party.

The universal acclaim with which Lenin was greeted in Russia was not due primarily to what he wrote. Other reasons help account for it. To some extent it may be credited to luck; to some extent to the complete optimism and self-confidence which made him proclaim the last battle as always the final victory. To some extent also it was due to his character. His revolutionary career had been a long one, and his reputation among revolutionaries for sincerity and determination was of the highest. He knew how to direct the energies and how to incite the loyalties of his fellows. The inflammatory but brilliant Trotsky, generally a lone hawk and a suspicious one, finally became his devoted disciple. The Georgian outlaw and ruffian, Stalin, an exile in Siberia as the revolution of 1917 broke, became another.

But in the last analysis, perhaps the major explanation of Lenin's

NIKOLAI LENIN (1870-1924)

power lay in the fact that he was the high priest of a new and virulent religious faith. Such a theory would have amused him greatly, if such a single-tracked mind could have been capable of amusement. How could anyone be said to be a religious prophet while proclaiming that his followers must be active atheists, and that religion was "the opiate of the people"? Closely examined, however, this statement is no paradox. Lenin, we must remember, had faith in one thing—the Revolution. Capitalism (the world) was at an end; communism (heaven) was at hand. It would come, to be sure, on this earth, but so rapid and so lovely would be its advent that all need for government would disappear miraculously, and justice everywhere would reign triumphant, as class ceased to struggle with class in a society in which class was nonexistent.

Lenin, like a good Communist, would object instantly to the word "miraculously," holding that there was no nexus whatever between such an objective and scientific idea as communism and the miraculous. But the real scientist ever holds his hypothesis tentative, and is constantly re-testing and reverifying not only his observed data but the hypotheses from which they are derived. It was not thus with the Marxians, to whom economic conclusions were axiomatic. As a matter of fact, the theoretical foundations of their belief—and Lenin was a convinced Marxian—rested on assumptions which were sufficiently dogmatic and all-inclusive as to become essentially a religious creed.

That creed, in summary, consisted of the following tenets: (a) all thought of a future life must be abandoned, or else it will be forever impossible to organize society upon a just and satisfactory basis; (b) the individual ownership of private property, the father of capitalism and imperialism, brought on the World War and the nemesis of the old order; (c) the communal ownership of goods and the adoption of the Marxian formula, "from each according to his capacity, to each according to his needs," is a categorical imperative; (d) that ownership can only be obtained by a dictatorship of the proletariat; (e) that in the course of time dictatorship will no longer be needed, for a classless society will not require any government; that the writings of Marx, Engels, and Lenin prove the above propositions up to the hilt and make it unnecessary and even heretical to seek elsewhere for any elucidation of human problems. The Communist explanation is inclusive, complete, final. Nothing need be added; nothing must be subtracted. All who oppose this creed, both within and without Russia, are enemies who should receive no mercy, and their defeat may be sought by utilizing any and every means available.

Such was the Communist creed, a religion held with fanatical zeal by fanatical men.

The acceptance of it, however, was not at first widespread nor was Lenin universally acclaimed as the Revolution started. It must be remembered that when he arrived back in Russia he was the accepted leader of only one of the three socialist parties and that the Mensheviki and the Social Revolutionists also were powerful, to say nothing of the Cadets. Only little by little, from the summer of 1917 to the conclusion of the civil war, did Lenin and his gospel become the accepted creed. Possibly, more than anything else, it was the man's cocksureness that insured his victory. He, almost alone among the leaders, was always utterly and completely confident that he knew exactly what should be done. At a time when the Cadets were still trying to keep Russia in the war, it was Lenin who started the cry for "peace and bread." He denounced the war as an imperialistic one in which Russia's allies were as bad as—though no worse than—the Germans. No annexations, no indemnities, Russia to quit the war and to fight one of her own against the bourgeoisie within her borders. The Cadets were traitors to the Revolution; it was not a *liberal* revolution; it was the *Communist* revolution, the greatest, and the best and the *final* revolution.

Such outspoken ideas, for the time being, meant trouble for Lenin, who was accused of being a German agent conspiring against the provisional government, and it was necessary for him frequently to take to cover. Even after the November Revolution, when the Bolsheviks seized power, the leadership of Lenin was not a certainty. When the elections for the Constituent Assembly which met in January, 1918, were held, it was found that the Social Revolutionaries were in a majority and that the Bolsheviks had only about twenty-five per cent of the membership. That assembly was given short shrift by the soviets; it held one session and then was ended by the fiat of the Petrograd soviet. Lenin's excuse was that of Robespierre or that of Cromwell—the assembly did not represent the will of the people.

What was that will? Patently it was above everything else to stop fighting. The Russian soldiers were brave; but no soldier can endure endless waiting for his comrade to be killed so that he may equip himself with that comrade's rifle. Peace and land, Lenin knew, were what the Russians wanted, and he proposed giving them both, and if necessary, peace at any price. In view of the intentions of the Germans to annex Russian provinces, it was not easy for the soviets to swallow his formula altogether, and at first Lenin was in a minority in the Council of People's Commissars, as the tentative revolutionary government was called. Some of the commissars were for further resistance, and even the realistic Trotsky preferred a Fabian plan by which there would be neither peace nor war, the Russians simply retreating before the Germans. But finally Trotsky changed his vote to Lenin's side and the latter won by a majority of one.

The peace with Germany proved popular, as did also the early legislation which the commissars favored. All non-peasant estates were immediately confiscated and placed in the hands of locally elected committees. So also was it with the homes of the wealthy nobles and bourgeois which were now open to residence for the proletariat of the cities. The banks were taken over and their funds appropriated. All debts of the former government, both national and international, were repudiated. All large factories became government property. And to suppress any objections to these stiff measures, the Cheka, or secret police, was organized and given plenary power. In the summer of 1918 the R.S.F.S.R., the Russian Socialist Federated Soviet Republic, was inaugurated and within two years, with the collapse of the Whites, it was omnipotent in Russia.

Lenin now had a few more years to live (he died in January, 1924), and during them he bent himself heroically to four major tasks: (a) the consolidation of power in the hands of the Communist party, the new name asumed by the Bolsheviks in 1918; (b) the spread of communism throughout the world by the establishment of the Third International; (c) the abolition of individualist business enterprise in Russia and the socialization in that country of all means of production; (d) the transformation of the entire folk psychology of the Russian people, whereby sanctions imposed by the old moralities and the old ethical conceptions shriveled up, to be supplanted by new concepts, strange and bizarre to both Asiatic and Western culture.

Ostensibly, Russia was now a republic, a word which ordinarily in the twentieth century had come to imply a certain quantum of belief in democratic or at least representative institutions. This was not true of the Russian republic; from its inception the R.S.F.S.R. was simply a mechanism through which the Communist party controlled Russia in the name of the proletariat. Therefore, it is far more important to analyze that party and its organization than the theoretical framework of the government. In theory, every Russian adult, except for certain specified social classes, like employers, men working for private gain, clergymen, former employees of the Czar's administration, and so forth, was qualified to take part in the government and to vote. In theory, also, those who voted elected freely, although indirectly through their local soviets or councils, an All-Russian Congress of Soviets, which elected an executive committee, which in turn chose the Council of People's Commissars— seventeen men at the head of the government.

But theory does not always coincide with practice, and since all voting had to be done by show of hands, and since the urban soviets, full of workmen, were heavily overweighted when it came to districting out Russia, it is easy to see how a highly disciplined group within the body of workmen, like the Communist party (it also had a number of peasant members), might readily remain master of the situation as it did.

So also was it when the government was again reorganized in 1923, as the R.S.F.S.R. gave place to the U.S.S.R. (Union of Soviet Socialist

Republics). In theory again this step was intended to demonstrate how liberal the R.S.F.S.R. could be in dealing with the various nationalistic groups remaining in the Russian Empire. The new constitution now recognized no less than nine different republics, bound together in one union, namely, the old R.S.F.S.R., the soviet republics of the Ukraine, the Transcaucasian republics (Azerbaijan, Armenia, Georgia), the White Russian republic, and three smaller ones in the eastern stretches of the empire in Asia. Each of these separate republics had a constitution like that of the original R.S.F.S.R.; each of them sent delegates to an All-Union Congress of Soviets, which again chose a central committee, as in the case of the original constitution described.

Now the idea behind this change from the R.S.F.S.R. to the U.S.S.R. was simple. Since the former constitution was socialistic, it must repudiate imperialism and all of its works. Therefore, the Russian soviet government must not tyrannize over the Ukrainian, Turkoman, and all the other peoples, or other ethnic groups which happened to be within the geographical boundaries of Russia. These other peoples had the right to enjoy their own language, culture, indigenous institutions. Thus the theory ran, and consequently each one was set up as a separate republic. But we must not be deceived by these separate republics which, though republics in name, possessed much less autonomy than the states under the American system. For instance, to the union government fell not only those functions which almost always are attached to a federal government, such as war, peace, currency, and so forth, but also such matters as health, labor laws, and even, to some extent, education.

Constitutions, however, may be one thing and realities another, and especially true was this of both the R.S.F.S.R. and the U.S.S.R. In both of them Lenin took good care to preserve the iron grip of the Communist party. It was the only party which had any legal existence. First through the Cheka and then through the G.P.U., names successively given to the secret police, the party controlled all elections, for it was very dangerous for anyone to vote against the party nominee. There was no such thing under either of these two formal Russian constitutions, it must be remembered, as independent law courts. Judges might be removed at will, and the G.P.U. could arrest and execute at will any individual without his having any recourse to such law courts as were set up. In fact, the G.P.U. was more powerful than the famous Third Section of the Czars; it had more spies; it had more money; it had a private army to enforce its bidding. Quite similar to the dreaded Gestapo (secret police) of Hitler, the G.P.U. was both whip and scorpion in the hands of first Lenin and then Stalin.

The Communist party was composed of city workmen, ex-soldiers, a few poor peasants, and (afterward) of a few professional men. From its inception, all ex-nobles, priests, traders, bankers, and all the middle-class men of every description, together with their relatives, were in theory strictly excluded. One gained admittance only after a probationary period and upon the recommendation of a number of members. Periodically, it was necessary to prove oneself worthy of membership, or else expulsion followed. Unless one was a confessed atheist, one could not join; unless one confessed the pure Marxian faith as laid down by Lenin, one could not join.

The great majority of members continued to be urban workers and soldiers. Highly organized in little groups or cells in the Russian factories, they watched and controlled local elections, reported men they disliked to the G.P.U., criticized or approved factory management, and sternly disciplined one another. Drunkenness, for instance, must never be indulged in by a Communist; he must not pay too much attention to women; he must be ever on the job as a good workman and as a good propagandist; he must not intermarry with the hated bourgeoisie (as much anathema to Communists as Jews to Nazis in Germany); he must bring up his children as good Communists; he must not let them be subject to religious instruction; he must see to it that they joined the "Young Pioneers," a youth organization attached to the Communist party; and above all things in heaven (denied existence) and on earth he must put loyalty to the party and to its principles as laid down by Lenin. For the party and the party alone was Russia's salvation.

Communism, to Lenin, was an international faith, and he set great store by the Third International, the instrumentality through which it was hoped that communism might spread throughout the world. The First International, as organized by Karl Marx, had petered out in the bloodshed at Paris in 1871, following the Franco-Prussian War, and the Second International, in existence at the outbreak of the war, and still more or less alive, was, in Lenin's opinion, hopelessly rightist in tendency, honeycombed with opportunist heresy, and impregnated with national patriotism. He would have none of this agency of Western social democracy, and therefore he promoted the Third International with headquarters at Moscow as a kind of clearinghouse for revolutionary propaganda.

The actual relations of this Third International to the U.S.S.R. have always been a matter of hot dispute. According to official statements of the Soviet authorities, the Third International, or the Comintern, as they called it, was an independent body of world Communists who simply accepted the hospitality of the U.S.S.R., held their meetings or congresses in Moscow, maintained a permanent secretariat there, and functioned independently of the Soviet government. According, however, to the enemies of Soviet Russia, this explanation was a mere blind, and the Third International or Comintern was an agency of the U.S.S.R. which found it convenient to disown the activities of the Comintern in public while supporting and directing them in private. The truth presumably lay between the two statements. There can be no question but that officials of the Comintern held important posts in the Soviet government and thus at least a kind of informal interlocking directorate existed. On the other hand the financing of the Comintern did come from dues collected from Europe, America, and Asia; and the opinions of German, American, and Chinese Communists were vented at the various congresses of the Third International and had influence in determining the policy of that organization.

The Third International was founded in 1919. Its announced aim was "to replace world Capitalism by world Communism, thus abolishing the private ownership of the means of production and with it the selfish lust for profits, exploitation of man by man, all inequalities based on sex, religion, and nationality; devastating crises and still more devastating wars." And this it hoped to do by establishing in every country a Communist party, disciplined, cohesive, and obedient to orders received from the Comintern, pledged to a revolutionary seizure of political power. At least this was true in Lenin's day. In later years the Third International became, until it was abolished in 1943, seemingly less revolutionary in act and willing, apparently, to work in harmony with "leftist" bourgeois interests.

For Lenin was a believer in the apocalyptic version of the Marxian faith. He thought the new heaven and the new earth just around the corner, that capitalism was (everywhere) on its deathbed, and that the universal revolution was imminent.

There was some excuse for this belief in 1919. In Hungary, in Germany, in Armenia, India, and China, Communist revolts either had broken out or were on the point of doing so. Particularly hopeful was Lenin of Germany. He was deceived by the semi-anarchy there into believing that Germany was on the point of going Communist, and he deserves no small amount of blame for the advent of Hitler, since his advice to the German Communists to have nothing to do with the Social Democrats, a policy followed even after his death, weakened the leftist front and made easier the advent of the Nazis.

Only as time passed did Lenin come to conceive of the world revolution as springing up first not in the highly organized capitalistic countries but rather in those regions where capitalism was weak and not yet firmly entrenched. Here, in what were called colonial or semi-colonial countries, it was held, lay the greatest hopes for immediate Communist success.

Largely on account of this theory, there was held in Baku in 1920 a congress of oppressed nationalities whom Russia and the Third International sought to rescue from their oppressors. Nearly 2,000 delegates from no less than 37 different nationalities attended the meetings. Prominent among them were the Turks, who, under Kemal Ataturk (see pp. 252-253), appealed to Russia for help and got it. Lenin surrendered to

Ataturk over 7,000 square miles, formerly part of the Czar's empire, and loaned him money and professional assistance in establishing the Turkish republic. Lenin likewise denounced the special privileges which the Czar's government had obtained at one time or another in Iran, Afghanistan, and China. He deeded land to Afghanistan, proposed that Moscow be linked to Kabul by air, offered to help the Amir in opposing Britain, "the most rapacious imperialistic government on earth." The close hookup of the Chinese Communists with Russia did not come, it is true, until after Lenin's death, but the idea of having one was his. To him Russia's influence in hastening the advent of the New Jerusalem could only come by shunning all contact with the League of Nations, a bourgeois institution controlled by capitalists, and by stirring up everywhere, but particularly in undeveloped and in semi-developed dependent countries, disorder, insurrection, and proletarian dictatorships.

The New Economic Policy

Meanwhile, neither industry nor agriculture was flourishing in Russia. The Communist leaders had no technical knowledge of business. They had been conspirators, publicists, politicians, or, if you will, statesmen. But they did not know how to manage factories, mines, and banks. In consequence, production fell off so alarmingly that in 1920 it was less than forty per cent of what it had been in 1913 and in certain lines of skilled manufacture it was way below that low level.

Nor was this the worst. There was a scarcity of food. The peasants who produced it knew nothing of Marx; they thought that the newly won land of the proprietor, the church, and the state belonged to them outright. They were willing to exchange their surplus wheat and meat for articles which they needed, like spades, and nails, and needles; but they had no intention of giving them away for paper money, rapidly depreciating in value as the articles they sought grew scarcer.

What was to be done? The dictatorship of the proletariat had seemed so simple. Its function was clear; to turn Russia into a socialist state, wherein none should work for his own gain but each for each and for his neighbor. Capitalism was the enemy; it was abolished by fiat. The bourgeoisie were the instruments of capitalism; they were abolished by fiat. "Let him not eat who does not work," was a good Marxian slogan—and also incidentally Christian, since St. Paul said it before Marx. But who was to direct how the work should be done; and how was production to be started again; and how were the people to eat? Lenin's first idea had been simply to appropriate the peasant's surplus; but the peasants saw no occasion for having any surplus. Then followed the creation of food armies, forcibly to collect food from the rural districts. The peasants hid their food, and the armed forces of the proletariat collected it with much bloodshed. Physical hardships, almost unendurable, were now met with in both town and country, and the wise shook their heads and said, "The revolution is over."

But Lenin would not have it so. Like a good soldier he decided on a strategic retreat. This was the *Nep* or new economic policy. In effect it was a partial return to capitalism. The state ownership of all the land of Russia was reaffirmed, but the peasants were no longer to have their surplus expropriated. Instead they were to pay a regular fixed tax and were free to do what they wanted with any surplus remaining. Since the land did not belong to them, they could not sell or mortgage it. But at any rate they had won a respite and were quiescent, particularly the wealthier and more ambitious ones, known as "kulaks," who received permission to rent land from their poorer neighbors.

Small industries, those employing under twenty men, were now, in accordance with the Nep, turned back to private enterprise, as was most retail trading and selling. Men thus engaged were known as "Nepmen" and were not highly regarded by the Communist party. But they were tolerated. The larger industries owned by the state were consolidated into great trusts, and foreign experts were hired at excellent salaries as advisors. These foreign experts and technicians were not desired as Russian citizens; they could not become members of the party, and had no political voice. Neither did the Russian Nepmen. One could not be a Communist and be a Nepman; one could not have the honor of voting and be a Nepman; but if one voluntarily chose to enter this humble class one could make money, always running the risk, of course, that high taxes might take it from you.

In addition to these changes, foreign corporations, as such, were invited to do business in Russia. The country stood in need of fluid capital and the best way to obtain it was to invite the foreigner in—under strict supervision. The proffered concessions promised goodly profits and many foreign capitalists took advantage of Lenin's offers. The economic tide began to turn and production reached its old level. Was this socialism or was it not? People rubbed their eyes; state socialism, or state capitalism, or call it what you will, seemingly existed side by side with individual enterprise. We keep the banks, the big industries, and the taxing power in our own hands, said the Communists, and as long as we do that we have not betrayed Marx. But seemingly they had postponed the millennium.

Yet not for long, in Lenin's opinion. All he had in mind was a brief postponement of that happy day. Very shortly it would dawn, and just as soon as the Russian proletariat could master the secrets of machinery. Motors, dynamos, tractors, electrification, power dams, hydroelectric power, technology—in this direction lay salvation. Lenin particularly was captivated by electricity. His Marxian philosophy, basing all human happiness and well-being on a materialistic accomplishment, led directly to the conviction that the machine, whether composed of flesh and blood or of copper and steel, was the only ultimate reality. He was also a Russian, as well as a Marxian, and he could not escape the tradition of Peter the Great. The great statue of that monarch in Petrograd had been hurled from its base amid the maledictions of the proletariat, for he had built his capital city by the forced labor of sweating peasants; but the tradition which he had set up of adopting Western ways of life still remained. Peter was cursed as the worst of despots, and the name of his city was changed to Leningrad; but he was none the less copied. To England, to America, to Germany, Lenin sent for chemists, agricultural experts, engineers, technicians. They would teach their secrets to his people. Then they could go back home and Russia would be a socialistic state, in fact as well as in theory. And it would not take long!

The Ideological Drive

Meanwhile, there was to be no letup in the ideological drive to use communism as the radical spearhead by which Russian life might become revolutionized. For the revolution was conceived of as something far more fundamental than a mere economic transformation of Russia. Certain ideas and predispositions had to be eradicated from the popular mind and certain others had to take their place. The family, for instance, as the unit of personal loyalty must go, and in place of it loyalty to class must come. Old ideas concerning sex, personal morality, and ethics needed uprooting; and above all it was held essential that man must believe in the ultimate validity and the ultimate victory of a materialistic conception of life.

The family in Russia, as elsewhere, had been based on differentiation of function, man the breadwinner and provider, woman the conserver and dispenser of what man provided. This conception seemed not only out of date but undesirable to the thoroughgoing Communist. Women should work as well as men in factory, field, and workshop. Children should be the wards of the state; in state nursery schools and state primary schools they must be taught that the idea of family loyalty was a selfish, restrictive influence which blinded man to the possibility of social brotherhood.

To break up the family, women were put to work. To break it up still further, free divorce was granted on the application merely of either husband or wife. This did not mean a bacchanalian orgy of sexual licentiousness. Good Communists were expected to refrain from overindulgence in sex exactly the same way as they were to refrain from drunkenness, laziness, or anything else that might lessen their value as party members. From the point of view of the Communist, sex was comparatively an unimportant matter, a question of taste rather than of morality. The

Communist did not advocate a community of women; they insisted on marriage laws and enforced them. But marriage became purely a secular affair. It was necessary to preserve it so that census statistics could be accurate, so that parents could be charged with the cost of supporting the young. If there were no children the state pretty much washed its hands of the whole affair. Even abortion in the early days was openly and legally practised. But afterwards laws were passed forbidding it as a crime against society, since it tended to reduce the birth rate.

Communism meant a complete break with the past in many other ways. Laws concerning murder, for instance, were revolutionized. In accordance with communistic philosophy it was not permitted to kill one's real or fancied enemy; but if such an act was committed as the result of sudden anger it took its place in the category of lesser crimes, as did theft when committed against the personal property of a Russian citizen. For such crimes there were jail sentences; but they were not inordinately long. What was infinitely worse in Communist eyes were offenses against the U.S.S.R. Let a man be proved guilty of petty graft and no mercy need be expected; line him up against a wall and shoot him! One real sin, as such, and one alone was recognized by Communists: the act of being "counter-revolutionary." All privileged persons under the old regime were suspected of this sin, and against them true Communists were expected to harbor bitter hate.

Favorite adjectives among Communist writers were "dialectic," "objective," "scientific," and "materialistic." Since the method of reasoning used by Marx was the dialectic, there could be no other good type of reasoning. Supposedly, Marx was also a great materialistic scientist and good Communists followed the master. Power machinery was materialistic and also something new to the Russians. From Lenin down to the humblest party member, they were fascinated by it. An early Communist poster of what a cathedral should look like represented a great dynamo in place of an altar, and above the altar, where perhaps in a Christian cathedral angels might be carved, the communist artist placed flywheels attached to the dynamo by moving belts. Chicago was hymned in Communist poetry because it was an "electromagnetic city," a true symbol of the Machine Age. All that was essential to the Communist view was to have more and more machinery, owned and operated by the people in common rather than by the individual.

It was difficult to implant such revolutionary ideals in the minds of the old; this was recognized. Consequently, it was all the more the duty of the state to capture the plastic minds of the young. As a result much emphasis was put on education. Young and old were both invited and urged to learn to read and write; but great care was taken with the texts used which centered on the teachings of Marx and explained history almost exclusively in terms of the Revolution of 1917. Competent teachers were lacking and the country was desperately poor, but none the less astonishing headway was made. Enthusiasm took the place of training, and if the pupils were shepherded rigidly into the Marxian fold, they at least learned how to read.

Since materialism and idealism are generally considered antithetical terms, it is always easy to underrate what the Communist party accomplished in the way of social amelioration. Machinery, for instance, devised to protect the workman's life and limb is materialistic, but the use thereof would seem to be idealistic, whether or not the person using it insisted that idealism was a played-out force. The Communists were keen about machinery of this description. They were prepared to do everything for labor, to take the homes of former noblemen and to turn them into sanitaria, to give vacations with pay to pregnant women for a considerable period both before and after childbirth, to provide free medical service, to lighten labor hours, to increase its rewards not merely by more pay but by encouraging cheap literature, cheap music, cheap movies, cheap education—and none of these cheap in the sense of being shoddy.

To be sure, this was all done with an eye toward propaganda, directly or indirectly. There was no freedom in Russia of any kind, except freedom to spread the new faith. The Communists pointed bravely at Pavlov and to his experiments in animal psychology to prove the contrary. But even here the reason they did not molest Pavlov is obvious: if dogs and mice are conditioned in all their acts by external influences, so also by analogy is man, and materialism scores another victory.

Therefore Pavlov the scientist they would leave alone; but not the Christian Church. The latter underwent severe oppression in all of its branches, and although the Roman Catholic Church was a distinct minority in Russia, so successfully did the Roman pontiffs raise the hue and cry against the Communists that Rome seemingly became the principal enemy of the Communist creed.

There can be no doubt that communism was a denial of historic Christianity. For one thing, it insisted that there was neither a God nor a future life; for another it regarded sex as of trifling importance; and finally it denounced as undesirable and as counterrevolutionary all ideas commonly associated with the suffering servant of Jehovah, teaching instead that humility, patience, and long-suffering were base and ignoble thoughts, not worthy ones. No doubt also that the Communists behaved very badly toward priests and monks, killing some, reducing those left alive to beggary, appropriating churches without remuneration for secular purposes, forbidding all charitable work done in the name of Christ, teaching atheism in schools, not permitting Christian schools even to be opened, turning children against their parents, and urging them as a patriotic duty to denounce their own fathers and mothers. Despite these obvious facts it is not without significance that in a curious kind of way there were points of similarity between Christianity and communism. Both religions sought the welfare of the poor. No matter how heartily the Communists might curse the otherworldliness of Christianity, it was evident that the Soviet zealots took a keen interest in social justice; no matter how heartily the Popes might berate the Communists for their materialism, it was evident that Pope Leo XIII himself had stated that the Church was concerned with the material welfare of the poor. That also in theory at least, was Lenin's business.

Trotsky Versus Stalin

In 1924 Lenin died. He had been seriously ill for two years, the result of a lifetime of overwork and constant strain. All Russia paid him honor. His body, embalmed, placed under glass, and guarded day and night by soldiers of the Red Army, was placed in a red granite mausoleum, which became a holy place, a pilgrimage center for the Communist world. More honored than Karl Marx, whose obscure grave in a London cemetery few visit, Lenin and Leninism (as his doctrine came to be known) from now on, were regarded as the ark of the covenant, the foundation of the new moral order of humanity.

For Lenin's mantle there were ultimately two main contestants, Trotsky and Stalin. Of the two, the former was by far the better known outside Russia, and at the time of Lenin's death, within that country. Jewish by birth (Lev Bronstein was his real name), Trotsky had been an intimate collaborator of Lenin's. Twice he had been exiled to Siberia before the War, and in addition he had led a wandering life among the European capitals. Driven out of Paris in 1916, he had gone to New York, whence he came back to Russia and was made commissar for war in the new Bolshevik government. The success of the Red Army in 1919 and 1920 added laurels to his fame. He both wrote and spoke brilliantly and was keenly interested in spreading communism throughout all the world with the utmost speed.

Opposed to Trotsky was Stalin, who, unlike both Lenin and Trotsky, did not hail from the upper and middle classes but from peasant stock. Stalin was a Georgian from the Caucasus, a sturdy, taciturn, and rough apostle of violence. Destined for the priesthood and trained as a boy in a theological seminary, Stalin at eighteen forswore Christianity and accepted the Marxian gospel. He became a conspirator and leader of sanguinary strikes, and very soon was constantly in trouble with the police. Twice, also, he was sent to Siberia. Escaping from there, he was deported all the way to the Arctic Circle, where he was supporting himself by hunting and trapping when the Revolution broke out.

Throughout the summer of 1917, Stalin was one of the most efficient of the Bolshevik conspirators, and with the triumph of the Soviets he became not only commissar for nationalities but also commissar of workers' and peasants' inspection, and as such took a leading rôle in bringing about the ultimate Bolshevik victory. From the very beginning he was a member of the Polit Bureau, or inner steering committee of the party, and in 1922 he became its secretary, a post which became under him the most important in all Russia. First and foremost, Stalin was a party man, and because of his long and intimate knowledge of the party's personnel, he had a certain advantage over the more versatile Trotsky, who, because of his very brilliance, was constantly making enemies.

The two men differed in policy. Trotsky was all for the world revolution, but Stalin considered that for the time being such a revolution was a dream. In his opinion communism should devote itself to perfecting the revolution within Russia. Trotsky had the greater support in the Third International, and the Chinese students at the University of Moscow paraded in his honor; but Stalin commanded the votes in the Congress of the Soviets and Trotsky was forced into exile. It was impossible, however, for Stalin to rid himself completely of Trotsky for several years or for him to entrench himself in power. According to tradition, Lenin himself had regarded Stalin as too brutal and too tough to head the party, and only slowly and by degrees was Stalin able to turn an acknowledged leadership into a dictatorship. It proved impossible permanently to expel Trotsky from the U.S.S.R. before 1929, and from Lenin's death until that year the leftist element of the party, of which Trotsky was the leading spirit, did its best to oust Stalin from the control lever. And even in that year, after Trotsky had set up his residence in Constantinople, Stalin's control was none too sure, for having defeated the left opposition, he was confronted by a new bloc on the right which thought he had gone too far in his ruthless determination to complete the work of socialism in Russia. Since that date, however, there have been few successfully to dispute in Russia with Joseph Stalin, and from 1930 to his death in 1953, to all intent and purpose, his power was absolute.

The Five-Year Plan

Victory over Trotsky once secured, the Russian Revolution entered a new phase. Lenin had driven out the old ruling class and had thoroughly liquidated it; he had socialized big business completely, whether in land, commerce, or manufacturing; and on the ideological front his success in captivating the imagination of his followers both within and without Russia had been phenomenal. But two things he had not done: he had made comparatively little headway in changing the way of living of the Russian peasants, nearly eighty-five per cent of the population; and his dream of a technological revolution in Russia had not yet passed the blueprint stage. "Communism," he had said, "is soviet government plus the electrification of the country." Substitute the word *technology,* or the word *machine* for electrification and Lenin's meaning is clarified. He dreamed of a society in which manual labor would be at a minimum. That goal was far distant when he died. Stalin made it his business to introduce the technological revolution Lenin planned. He did it so thoroughly in the decade before the Second World War that what he accomplished may justly be considered a second revolution.

In 1928 Stalin laid down a revolutionary program. It provided for the scrapping of the Nep and for a five-year plan or blueprint, whereby a tremendous speeding up in the production of capital goods was to go hand in hand with the complete socialization of the land and the substitution of farm coöperatives in place of individual enterprise. During these five years everyone in Russia was supposed to pull in his belt, to consume as little as possible, to work hard and long and scientifically in putting Russia in a place of leadership among the industrial countries of the world. Railroads, hydroelectric plants, steel mills, tractor and automobile factories, more coal, more iron; a total increase of one hundred and thirty per cent was called for in industrial production. And as this was done, agriculture was to be modernized. The state proposed to establish and manage great model farms to serve as an example of what ultimately was to be expected of the peasants. The latter were encouraged to form coöperative groups (*kolkhozes*). If they objected, they were to be forced into these groups. After five years, private enterprise would no longer be found in Russia.

The difficulties which confronted Stalin were enormous. Russia was poor, desperately poor, yet he could not carry out the five-year program without hiring expensive scientists and engineering specialists from Germany, the United States, and elsewhere. At the same time it was necessary to import machinery and tools of precision. All this would take money, and the capitalistic world was chary of granting credit to Russia. It demanded ready money and this could only be had by Russian exports, either of merchandise or gold. Then, too, laborers had to be secured from somewhere and trained as skilled workmen, millions of them. They had to be drafted from the Russian peasantry (there was no other source of supply) and this at a time when the peasants were inevitably irritated by the revolution pending in agriculture whereby they were to be ordered to give up their individual land holdings and forced to join coöperative farm groups. Compulsion would be necessary; the peasants could not be enticed by high wages, for all available money would have to be spent for materials, tools, and foreign exports. Yet economy would be impossible. The expenses of the Red army were increasing, not diminishing. Between the imminent threat of Japanese invasion in the Far East and the enmity of the capitalistic West, Stalin did not dare diminish his army. In Lenin's day there was no danger threatening from Germany; but as

Stalin came to power a wild-eyed agitator, Adolf Hitler, was inflaming his countrymen with bitter hate of Communists. Hitler might well become a serious menace. England, Italy, and the United States were hostile. There was need for haste as well as for money, so Stalin thought.

On the industrial front the principal center of activity was in the Ukraine, in the valley of the Don, in the Caucasus, the Urals, and in Western Siberia. In the Ukraine a great dam providing for the largest hydroelectric plant in Europe had already been projected. This, the Dneprostroi dam, was completed in 1932, making the Dnieper River navigable for 1,500 miles and providing 750,000 horsepower. At Kharkov, also in the Ukraine, a tractor plant was established which in short order was manufacturing 37,000 tractors a year, and near it was a plant for turbine generators and electrical equipment which by 1939 employed 40,000 men. At Rostov on the Don and at Stalingrad on the Volga mammoth steel plants, specializing in tractors and other agricultural machinery were erected.

Still further to the east were the Ural mountains and Siberia. Here lay a land, the Soviet geologists soon proved, rich in minerals and far distant from any invasion, at least 1,500 miles from any European enemy and much further from Japan. On the eastern slopes of the Urals at Magnitogorsk were two mountains so rich in iron as to be one of the principal sources of that mineral in the entire world. Coal also was to be found in the Urals, and straight east from the two mountains some 1,400 miles from Magnitogorsk where the Altai mountains separate western China from Siberia were the Kuznetz coal reserves with over 400 million tons of accessible coal. Here lay the land of Stalin's imagination; here he determined, cost what it might, to develop an industrial region to vie with Pittsburgh, Birmingham, or the Ruhr Valley.

The far northern part of this region already was traversed by the Trans-Siberian railroad. Stalin proposed to double-track it, to drive a new railroad south to Magnitogorsk, to connect that city with the Kuznetz coal, to join these new railroads to the already existing Transcaucasian railroad which linked together the oases of Turkestan, and to make western Siberia a great inland empire.

Magnitogorsk was planned as the industrial center. To create a city, several hundred engineering experts were imported from abroad, some at a salary of $100 a day. Under them was an army of many thousand laborers, most of whom were dispossessed peasants or kulaks. The latter suffered much; food shortages were chronic and such food as could be had was mostly black bread, cabbages, and potatoes. The winters were bitterly cold, the summers unbearably hot and dry. Hastily constructed, ill-heated, and overcrowded barracks housed the men. Confusion reigned. Essential tools were missing, spare parts difficult to obtain, accidents numerous. From the scaffolding "inexperienced riggers fell and untrained

bricklayers laid walls which did not stand." Skilled workmen were con-
tinually deserting. One locomotive working on the mine had thirty-four
engineers in one year. Only one single-track railway led to the city and
soon the workmen "were faced with the necessity of supplying themselves
with hammers, saws, chisels, bits, small castings and other small tools
which could be made in makeshift shops. Many materials, such as copper
wire for rewinding motors, simply could not be had. The workers swore
at the foremen, the foremen complained to the superintendent, the supply
department telegraphed to Moscow. There was no copper wire." [1] But
the city was built and in less than five years was swarming with over
200,000 inhabitants.

The story of Magnitogorsk is the story of a dozen manufacturing cities
with mushroom growth in eastern Russia and in western Siberia during
the nineteen-thirties. The coal deposits at Kuznetz, for instance, soon
proved far in excess of the Magnitogorsk demand, and smelters at Stalinsk
in the Kuznetz area became busily engaged in turning Magnitogorsk ore
into finished steel. Stalinsk by 1939 was a city of 220,000, connected by
rail with the Russian Transcaucasian system on the south, with the Trans-
Siberian system on the north and with Magnitogorsk to the west, and by
1939 the population of the surrounding district had risen to 800,000. Instead of having one Pittsburgh, Russia had two, both safe from European
or Asiatic invader. There could be no doubt, on paper that is, that the
first five-year drive was a success on the industrial front. No matter what
the cost, both in human suffering and in money, the rails were laid, the
factories built, the oil wells dug, the mines opened, the steel, the tractors
(also the tanks) in operation. Officially the drive was declared closed after
four and a half years—and in theory ninety-three per cent complete.

The above percentage was Stalin's estimate. It needs qualification. If
measured in terms of rubles (money) the estimate is correct. But the
ruble was a shifting standard, and since it had depreciated externally in
value during the five years, the real increase in production was far below
93.7 per cent. Furthermore, the increase was one in industrial production
only. It ignored the question of real wages, the amount of goods that
might be had in terms of rubles. The available food supplies did not
increase; in fact they diminished. The great industrial undertakings were
only accomplished by the semistarvation of many million workingmen,
who lived on black bread and cabbage soup.

Difficult as it proved to be to introduce highly specialized industrial
processes among a people who by tradition were primarily agricultural,
it proved even more difficult to turn these same peasants into practising
socialists, willing to give up their privately owned and privately tilled
acres in order to share both work and gains with their neighbors. Never-

[1] John Scott, *Behind the Urals* (Houghton Mifflin Company), p. 76. Reprinted by
permission of the publishers.

theless, Stalin determined to push the agricultural offense as hard as the industrial one. It would not do, in his opinion, to have Russia half capitalist and half socialist, and unless the reluctant peasants were driven into the practice of coöperative farming, such would be the case. The peasants were stupid and the patient state would show them the way by example, by state farms, by lectures on scientific agriculture, by attractive offers and bonuses to those peasants who pooled their resources, by harsh taxes levied on the recalcitrant.

It was soon discovered that there were a great many of the latter, well-to-do peasants, or kulaks, who had prospered, partly by working hard and intelligently, partly by hiring as farm laborers their more shiftless or less fortunate neighbors. These kulaks continued to exist somehow, even though taxed unmercifully, and the soviet authorities determined to "liquidate" them. They did so thoroughly. The kulaks were driven from their homes by the hundreds of thousands; they were forced to work in the lumber-mills of the North, in the gold mines of Siberia, in the new factories. Soon there were hardly any kulaks left. By January, 1934, Stalin was able to announce that there were no less than 224,500 collective farms in Russia which, in the preceding year, sowed some 73.9 per cent of Russia's grain. Since an added ten per cent came from the state farms, the success on the agricultural front as well as on the industrial seemed assured.

Whether that success was worth the price paid for it is open to question. The forced industrial development of the country was put through by compulsory labor. The imagination of the Communists had been captivated by machinery and there can be no doubt that it was a part of their faith to work hard and long with utmost enthusiasm. But while this was true of convinced Communists who organized shock brigades in the factories to hasten production, there were not enough of them for the task in hand. If it was to be accomplished within the time limits set, forced labor was essential and Stalin did not hesitate to use it. For this the kulaks were conveniently available, as well as thousands of political prisoners. Suffering greatly from lack of decent living quarters, and half-starved, these other groups provided much of the human raw material which poured into the industrial undertakings.

Furthermore, although factories were built and filled with machinery, although mines were opened, railroads constructed, iron dug from the hillsides and turned into steel, there were many bitter criticisms of the effectiveness of the result. It was claimed that the railroads broke down continuously, that the machines were so poor in quality as to be in many instances useless, that the tractors were too heavy and too clumsy to operate. To some extent it is necessary to discount these criticisms since most of them came from European and American technicians employed by the Soviet government, and it was only natural that they should compare unfavorably the efficiency and skill of the Russian workmen with that possessed by the highly trained industrial workers of the West to which they had been accustomed. But despite all this, the cumulative evidence would seem to indicate only a partial victory as yet for this industrial revolution in Russia, brought into existence by socialistic practice. Compared with American standards, Russian factories with ten times as many workmen turned out far less per capita. Machines always seemed to be breaking down, burning out, rusting, exploding. The new dynamos, locomotives, and tractors, were there, it is true, but they did not seem to be good tractors, locomotives, and dynamos. Enthusiasm, it was found, could not take the place of mechanical skill; and the latter, it was demonstrated, could not be created overnight by fiat.

The results of the first Five-Year Plan in agriculture were more open to question. In the more advanced agricultural districts, such as the Ukraine and southern Russia, there was bitter opposition on the part of the peasants to Stalin's program. Throughout 1932 and 1933 famine raged in the Ukraine, due in part to unseasonable weather, in part to compulsory grain requisitions, in part to the unwillingness of the peasants to surrender their individual holdings. Some three or four million people lost their lives from starvation, and the country-side was well-nigh deserted. The Soviet authorities were not altogether displeased; the famine proved a convenient instrument for political policy, and after its ravages were over, there was less opposition to collective farming. Statistically, however, the official figures as released by Stalin in 1934 did not seem encouraging as far as the agricultural front went. From 1923 to 1934 the numbers of cattle, horses, sheep, and goats decreased alarmingly, and all that there were in their places were some 200,000 tractors! Theoretically, their presence on the Russian farms meant more acres cultivated and a greater consumption of cereals. Nevertheless, it is doubtful if the per capita consumption of grain at the conclusion of the Five-Year Plan was in excess of that under the Czars. The cost in terms of human suffering unquestionably was very high.

Stalin himself realized that, but like a good politician he did not acknowledge it. He made a statement called "Giddiness from Success," in which he announced certain qualifications in regard to rural coöperatives in which peasants might retain individual ownership of homes, gardens, live stock. Grain was still to be sowed and reaped by the *kolkhozes*, but a certain leeway was now granted to individual enterprise. Stalin likewise, and again merely by implication, toned down the harshness of the drive for industrialization by announcing a second Five-Year Plan, to be completed in 1937. Unlike the first plan, this one stressed consumers' goods. Factories were to be built for textiles, shoes, canning, candies, and no less than 350 of these factories were for food products. Prices of consumers' goods were to be lowered and the supply of them was to be augmented three hundred per cent.

Did Stalin Betray the Revolution?

Meanwhile, in certain respects, both in regard to external and internal policy, Soviet Russia became more and more conservative. As an instrument for stirring up world revolution, the Third International almost ceased to function. Lenin had hated the League of Nations but Stalin consented to enter it. The Communist parties outside of Russia were advised from the Kremlin that they should coöperate with liberal bourgeois groups against fascism, and in countries like the United States, China, France, and Spain the Communists either made common cause with such groups or tried to. Thus, in the United States, the Communists were friendly toward Roosevelt in 1936 and in instances actually supported him, adopting a stand in American politics more conservative than that of the old Social Democratic party hitherto regarded by all honest Reds as lukewarm and yellow. In China the Communists joined forces with their old enemy, Chiang Kai-shek, in opposing the Japanese advance; and in France and Spain Communists took a leading part in the organization of "popular fronts" to oppose reaction.

The same general trend to the right was noticeable also in internal affairs. In 1936 Soviet Russia adopted a new constitution which, on paper at least, seemed to denote that the U.S.S.R. was becoming both democratic and liberal. Freedom of speech and of religion was guaranteed (again on paper), and no longer was the scale weighted in favor of the more radical town and factory as against the more conservative country districts. All Russians were given the vote, even priests and kulaks, and voting was to be by ballot and not by show of hands.

Did Stalin have any real intention of going democratic? That may well be doubted. The control of the country still remained with the Communist party, the only one legally authorized, and that party remained in the hollow of his hands, as we shall note later. But perhaps Stalin did betray the Revolution, if not in whole at least in part, by drawing a line boldly between social classes in Russia, thus preventing instead of creating a classless society. Such was the argument of the exiled Trotsky who, driven out of his own country, out of Constantinople, and out of France, found a haven of refuge in Mexico. Trotsky insisted that the Russian Revolution was passing through its Thermidor, and that in the same way as the Directory, after the death of Robespierre, ended the real revolution in France, likewise was it under Stalin in Russia.

The arguments adduced by the exiled leader to prove this point were various. He pointed out that Stalin, by approving a speeding-up process in Russian factories and mines, really was paying workmen by the piece instead of by the time, the more skilful workingmen getting higher pay and receiving favors from the authorities. He also asserted that the renting of land went merrily on in Russia, some *kolkhozes* renting land at a profit to others, some even renting land to individuals. Russia, said Trotsky, was now ruled by some 400,000 bureaucrats who feathered their own nests very nicely, drew more pay than workmen, had better housing, and rapidly were becoming class-conscious. In the army the old discipline and the old caste system was said to be cropping up again. The Third International, in the interim, had been stifled and a new revolution would be necessary if ever Marxian socialism was to win. And to start this new revolution Trotsky sent out summons for a Fourth International.

The Purges

To what extent Trotsky continued from overseas to influence the course of events in Russia, it is impossible to state. Certainly many of the old Bolsheviks were discontented with Stalin's iron rule; some were of the right who disapproved of the abrupt ending of Lenin's Nep; others were of the left, in sympathy with Trotsky. Both groups plotted against Stalin; both were ruthlessly liquidated by him in thoroughgoing purges.

In 1935-37 the world made note of many curious trials for high treason in Russia. They were not conducted by Western methods, for evidence was not introduced into the court proceedings, unless wholesale confessions of willingness to sell out to the Germans and to betray the revolution be considered as evidence. Not only did almost every one put on trial freely admit guilt; the astonishing thing was that they tried to make this guilt appear as black as possible. The men placed on trial had been very high in governmental places, men like Kamenev, at one time a likely successor to Lenin; Zinoviev, former head of the Third International; a considerable number of high-ranking officers in the Red Army, among them General Tukhatchevsky, second in command; and finally numerous civil executives who were said to have wrecked railroads, trains, bridges, and to have retarded industrial production. Before he was through Stalin had gotten rid of almost every man of note who had participated in the Revolution of 1917.

Was it possible that these men were guilty? The capitalistic West was sceptical; it suspected that secret torture before trial might have caused the confessions, or that by making them the poor wretches hoped to avert the wrath of Stalin from their families. Some even suggested that the confessions were made as absurd as possible in order that the outside world might read between the lines and realize that the trials were a farce and that Stalin's regime was one of stark tyranny.

The total number of those executed by Stalin for treachery, treason,

Trotskyism, and sabotage between 1935 and 1939 is difficult to estimate, but presumably it was well over 10,000. Many were given no public trial at all, a simple announcement of their death alone being given. At the height of the executions there was a veritable reign of terror, when secret arrests were numerous and men simply disappeared. It was not healthy to inquire about their whereabouts, and few did.

Nevertheless the great body of Stalin's countrymen were prepared, it seems, to accept his word without question, and even to worship at his shrine in a way quite similar to the contemporary attitude of Germans and Italians toward Hitler and Mussolini. Stalin, indeed, became so personally identified with communism that he equalled in stature both Lenin and Marx. And this was the more noticeable in that he remained essentially a silent man, neither given to oratory as was Trotsky nor to the written amplification of the Communist scriptures as was Lenin.

Chapter 9

ITALIAN AND GERMAN FASCISM

IT WAS JUST a bundle of sticks tied around an ax, but when it was borne by a lictor the mob gave way in ancient Rome. The Romans called that symbol of authority *fasces,* and from it we derive our modern word *fascism,* the answer of Italy and Germany to Russian communism, and to some extent that of other lands as well.

A strange doctrine is fascism, at once very old and very new. In so far as it concerns the dictatorship of an individual, of a Mussolini or a Hitler rising to well-nigh omnipotent power in times of anarchy, there is nothing new in Fascist doctrine, and one might as well use the term "Cæsarism" to describe it. In so far, on the other hand, as fascism is intimately correlated with capitalism, socialism, and twentieth-century nationalism, it is new, strikingly new, unlike any hitherto existing dictatorship, whether Cromwellian, Frederician, or Napoleonic.

Fascism triumphed in Italy in 1922 with Mussolini's march on Rome, and in Germany in 1933 with Adolf Hitler's appointment as chancellor of the Reich. As might be expected, its character assumed different forms in the two countries. Nevertheless, the points of likeness far exceed those of dissimilarity. What, then, is fascism, and in what respects may it be said that it is alike in all Fascist countries?

Fascism is an all-embracing doctrine which demands a one hundred per cent surrender of the individual will in the name of mystical nationalism—with ends not clearly defined. This nationalism is beyond good and evil, and thus is deified. Therefore, fascism properly should be classed as a kind of religion like communism, the latter based on class-consciousness, the former on nationalism. As such, fascism was compounded of three elements—violence, state socialism, totalitarianism. Direct and clear was its repudiation of the Sermon on the Mount, for the Fascist insists that he only is blessed who smites and smites again. Emphatic was its assertion that the economic life of the people must be controlled by governmental agencies. And furthermore, since the be all and the end all of life is the exaltation of the State, all members of it must act alike, think alike, obey alike. Such, in general outline, is the Spartan-like philosophy of twentieth-century fascism.

How explain its origin? Such an extreme reversal of the main currents of European culture, especially since the Renaissance, could only come about through revolutionary upheavals produced by disillusionment, sharp suffering, social anarchy. This was the case in both Italy and Germany. Both countries felt that they had been cheated by the peace treaties; both suffered enormously from economic maladjustment; both were at the mercy of politicians unable to bring order out of chaos; and, what is more important, in both there were large numbers of ex-soldiers, young but toughened by war, unemployed, bitter, finding after four years in the trenches that back home there was "greed in the saddle, disorder in the street, and poverty on the hearth."

The Rise of Italian Fascism

Since this greed, disorder, and poverty characterized Russia as well as Italy and Germany, the question naturally arises why those two countries did not turn toward communism. Several reasons explain why. In the first place, both in Germany and in Italy the bourgeoisie were too powerful, too numerous, to well-led to be driven to the wall by Communist uprisings. In both countries such revolts occurred; in both they were snuffed out by the enraged bourgeoisie. Secondly, in both countries, but especially in Germany, there was a tradition of discipline and order and of national cohesiveness which militated strongly against the Communist world revolution. And thirdly, one is confronted with that insoluble equation, the personal factor, the adroit cunning of Benito Mussolini in Italy, the mystical appeal to Germans latent in the raucous vocal cords of Adolf Hitler.

Of these two fiery ex-corporals, the Italian is by far the easier to understand. Benito Mussolini, ex-schoolteacher, ex-journalist, ex-laborer, and so forth, was an influential young Italian Socialist when the first World War broke. In his father's smithy he had absorbed *The Prince* of Machiavelli, with its cynical assertion that most men are "ungrateful, fickle, false, cowardly, covetous . . ." governed by fear rather than by affection. Sorel, the French syndicalist, with his philosophy of strikes and violence, had been a favorite author of his youth, and Gustave Le Bon's *Psychology of the Crowd*, with its teaching that the mob is ever unreasoning, moved hither and yon by passionate exaggeration, had left its impression upon him. Indeed, Mussolini never evinced any interest in the more scientific and theoretical aspects of socialism. He was not that kind of socialist; rather, by nature, he was inclined to masterful assertiveness, to stress will rather than reason, to frighten rather than to conciliate, to bluff and to bluster, but always with shrewd finesse and instinctive feeling as to just how far it would be safe for him to do so.

Under ordinary circumstances Mussolini would not have risen to fame;

but circumstances were not ordinary in postwar Italy. That country smarted from a sense of frustration; it had not really distinguished itself in the war; it had been saved from disaster only by Allied help and had won victory in the end only through French and British aid. Having sold herself to the highest bidder in 1915, Italy was now dissatisfied with her bargain. And she had not received all that she had bargained for! The Tyrol, Trieste, a part of the Dalmatian coast, and islands in the Adriatic and the Aegean she did obtain; but when France and England divided the German colonial empire between them, there was for Italy only the suggestion of a rectification of the boundaries of Tripoli (now Libya) and of Italian Somaliland. The Italians felt slighted. True, the German colonies were only being held in trust by France and Britain for civilization and the League of Nations. But why did Italy receive no mandates? Furthermore, in addition to the letter of the bond, the Italians had asked for Fiume at the peace conference; Fiume was not given them.

Then again, economic conditions in Italy were peculiarly distressing. Since Italy was a poor country, she had felt the strain of the war more than had France or England. Her finances after it were in terrible plight, and her currency had depreciated more than a third of its value. The well-intentioned but weak and purposeless men in charge of her government in 1919 had no plan, no program, by which the situation might be bettered. Brigandage broke out in the South, and the homes of landlords were burned; communism raised its head in the industrial North, and workingmen seized factories and announced they would operate them. Their experience was brief and unprofitable, and they gave back the factories to the former owners of their own free will. But anything might happen, apparently, in Italy, and if ever an affirmative voice was called for it was then.

Mussolini provided that voice. After the commencement of the war he had deserted his erstwhile friends, the Social Democrats, who opposed Italy's participation. Wounded, he was discharged from the army and founded in Milan a radical, pro-war newspaper. With the coming of peace he gathered around him a number of former soldiers and organized a small group, the *Fascio di combattimento*. Its program, like the original program of the Nazis, was a hybrid mixture of radical economic theory and extreme nationalism. No one thought it would amount to anything; it nominated two men for election to the Chamber of Deputies in 1919 and both were defeated. Nevertheless, when that neurotic man of letters, the poet Gabriele D'Annunzio, pounced upon Fiume with a few adventurers in the name of Italy and was shortly forced to abandon it by the Italian government, Mussolini began to gather headway by denouncing the puerile and weak-kneed authorities who interfered with Italy's destinies. And later, when the government did nothing to prevent Communist seizures of the factories, his party grew. Under his leadership, antimonarchists, antisocialists, anticlericals and antipacifists gathered, all eager to attack someone. They found the Italian Communists, who were already surrendering the commandeered factories, an easy mark; and they launched their major offensive against them, thereby delighting the wealthy bourgeoisie. Organized into squads with semimilitary discipline, they began attacking all Communists, or men suspected of being Communists, administered castor oil to their victims, and beat them up severely. Money, meanwhile, poured into the Fascist coffers and the ranks of the Black Shirts swelled with recruits.

By the spring of 1921 fascism was becoming popular in Italy with the middle and upper classes. Ostensibly, it stood for public order and the suppression of anarchy, and in the election to Parliament that year the Fascists won thirty-five seats. And along with this increase in popularity went a decrease in radicalism. Mussolini announced that he believed in monarchy, that he hated both communism and socialism, that his Black Shirts would prevent society from disintegrating as it promised to do with warring factions. In 1922 the Fascists held a grand congress in Naples which demanded either a new election or the inclusion of Fascists in the cabinet. Since the government would not listen to either alternative, a "march on Rome" began. The government offered no resistance; instead Mussolini was appointed prime minister by the King.

Parliament voted him dictatorial powers for one year and by its conclusion Mussolini was firmly seated in the saddle. To prevent ousting by subsequent parliaments, he forced through the Chamber of Deputies a law which provided that in any election the party with the biggest vote automatically should receive two-thirds of the seats. The Fascists thereupon won a majority in the election of 1924, obtained their two-thirds of the seats; and from that date on, open and organized opposition to Mussolini's dictatorship withered away. The head of the Socialist party was kidnapped and murdered under suspicious circumstances; Socialists and Liberals fled from Italy; others voluntarily retired from public life; a few, ardent nationalists, entered the Fascist ranks. Mussolini, meanwhile, by law after law, made secure his own hold on Italy; he was made head of the state; he took over several cabinet posts in person; no law could be initiated except by him; and by 1928 all elections in Italy had become a mere farce, there being but one party recognized (the Fascist) and but one list of candidates for whom it was possible to vote (the Fascist list).

In Italy, as in Germany and Russia, the new-style dictators of the twentieth century operated through the instrumentality of a political party over which they held tight rein. Again, as in Germany and Russia, the victorious political party was limited as to membership, Mussolini much preferring a party of one million to one of ten; the one million could be better organized, disciplined, watched. Entrance to the Fascist party came under ordinary circumstances entirely from below, from auxiliary youth organizations. Almost at the cradle fascism began; when eight years old, a youngster might join one of these youth groups, graduate to another at fourteen, to another at eighteen, and finally present himself as a candidate for membership in the Fascist party at twenty-one. Ostensibly, it remained a political party, not the government of Italy. But only Fascists could be elected to Parliament and the law provided that the Grand Council of the Fascist Party (presided over by Mussolini) must be consulted by Parliament on important matters. Also, the Fascist Grand Council had at its disposal a private Fascist militia and there were even special Fascist magistrates appointed. The consequence was that within ten years after the march on Rome only the shell remained of a liberal constitutional monarchy.

Fascist domestic policy, both in Italy and Germany, followed parallel lines in one respect: within both countries it aimed at the complete subordination of the individual to the will of the state. Particularly true was this of all economic activity. In Italy the Fascists took control of economic enterprise by a peculiar invention of their own, the corporative state, which reflected both the origin of Italian fascism and the method by which it had won power. Most of the early Fascists had been socialists of a sort, at least to the extent of believing in state socialism or syndicalism but, we must recall, the Fascists had risen to power by rushing to the defense of private property. They were radicals and conservatives at the same time, pledged to obtain rights for workingmen, pledged to protect private property. The corporative state combined both of these ideas. Under it the economic life of Italy was divided into six main categories: manufacturing, commerce, maritime transportation, inland transportation, agriculture, and banking. In each group there was to be a syndicate of workmen and a syndicate of employers, thus making twelve legalized syndicates; and to them a thirteenth was added, a syndicate of the learned professions. In theory the thirteen syndicates were to be autonomous. All trade unions were forbidden, and employers and employees, as represented by their respective syndicates, were to work together and engage in collective bargaining in accordance with a "Charter of Labor" granted in 1927, whereby certain rules were laid down in respect to rates of pay, old-age insurance, holidays with pay, and so forth. All syndicate members had to be in good standing with the Fascist authorities and the autonomy granted was more superficial than real.

Two years later (1929) the syndicates were fused with parliamentary representation, and Parliament was now said to be functional: in other words, to represent jobs and interests rather than districts or localities. In accordance with the new law, the thirteen syndicates selected 800 names and gave them to the Fascist Grand Council, which body also was presented with 200 additional names from other sources. Out of the

1,000 names the Council selected 400 as a Fascist list for Parliament members. An election was now held, yes or no, to this official list. No other candidate could be voted for and the ayes naturally had it. Such Parliament as Italy now had represented banking, transportation, and other interests, rather than electoral districts.

In this fashion the corporative state became identified with the national state. As an experiment in political theory it was interesting but not conclusive, for always behind the syndicates was the Fascist party and its Grand Council, the master and presiding genius of which was Mussolini. Nevertheless, for the corporative state this is to be said: The number of strikes diminished rapidly; the currency debacle was first halted, then checked, and a semblance of business recovery was noted, that is, if we judge simply from indexes of production. Excellent automobile roads were constructed by Mussolini's orders; large and spacious ocean liners owed their existence to his continued enthusiasm; and the "battle of wheat," namely, the effort to make Italy self-supporting in foodstuffs was waged strenuously and continuously by the energetic Duce, as Mussolini came to be called.

To all of this there was another side. Taxes of extreme severity were levied on the middle class, which groaned silently and paid. More serious was a decline in the standard of living of the poorer classes, already very low. There were no strikes; the workmen did not dare to strike. On the other hand they were conscious that others paid the costs as well as they. Mussolini could hardly be called a modern Robin Hood, robbing the rich to pay the poor. What he did was to exact a tremendous toll from all classes, partly to restore his country's credit, which did improve up to the great economic depression of the thirties; partly to pay for increases in armament made necessary by his determination to gain land by the sword or by threats.

The totalitarian doctrines of the Duce were less clearly defined than those of Hitler, nor did he crush out individual liberties quite as comprehensively as did his fellow dictator in Germany. There was the same talk in both countries of the decadence of liberalism and democracy, the same boasting of national solidarity and racial prowess. But with this difference: the Italians seemed disinclined to carry out their slogans to their logical conclusions. The best illustration of this fact may be found in the field of religion. As a matter of logic, pure and simple, there is no room for any religion in a totalitarian state except the religion of the State. The Germans, being logical almost to the point of the irrational, proceeded relentlessly, as we shall see, to persecute Jew, Protestant and Catholic. In Italy this was not so. The tiny group of Italian Protestants were not molested by Mussolini and with the Roman Catholic Church he made friends.

IL DUCE, WITH HONOR GUARD OF HIS YOUNGEST WARRIORS.

The Lateran treaty of 1929 with the Holy See was proof that Mussolini, the Fascist, knew how to compromise. By it the long-standing political feud between the Roman Curia and the Italian monarchy was settled amicably. The Pope recognized for the first time the legality of the Kingdom of Italy and agreed to support it. Mussolini, on the other hand, paid a handsome price for this recognition. A diminutive state of a hundred or so acres which included St. Peter's and the Vatican was ceded to the Pope, completely independent of Italy from legal code to postage stamp. In this state the Roman Pontiff was to be sole ruler. Nearly $40,000,000 in specie and an even larger sum in Italian bonds was added. The Roman Catholic religion was recognized as the religion of the State, and the canon law of the Church added to the law of Italy, Mussolini thus granting the Church privileges which had long lapsed in regard to education and marriage. Compulsory education in the Catholic faith was now prescribed for all youthful Italians.

The victory of the Church seemed very great, but Mussolini, too, secured advantages. Ecclesiastics were now called upon to support his regime. Only one source of friction between Church and State remained, the possibility of papal interference with what Mussolini considered purely political issues. A society of Catholic laymen, the Catholic Action, caused the Duce some trouble; it criticized his labor policy and he promptly abolished it. The Pope at first stood by the society; but a compromise was effected. In the future the society was to be under the direction of bishops and not of laymen; and Mussolini, on his part, agreed that the incessant drilling of small Italian youngsters in the practice of arms should not interfere, as it had been doing, with religious instruction.

For the Duce's domestic policy there was perhaps this to be said: an Italy confused, baffled, discouraged, torn by factions, and ruled by weak politicians, gave way to an Italy united, ruled by a man who knew what he wanted and knew how to obtain it. To be sure, there was a price, and a heavy one: liberties of the individual were snuffed out; newspapers printed simply what they were told; there was espionage, cruelty, and occasionally assassination of those Italians who opposed Mussolini. No mercy was shown the dissenters. Those who dared use pen or mouth in criticism either fled the country, going to France by thousands, or were rounded up and imprisoned, again by thousands. But the Duce's foreign policy was another matter. To it may be attributed the commencement of the Second World War (unless that honor be granted Japan); for the Duce established the European precedent and set the pace for Hitler to copy. When Mussolini invaded Abyssinia in 1935, fascism showed its real hand and Europe has not been at peace since. So important, indeed, was that invasion and Fascist Italy's foreign policy that its significance is left to another chapter.

The German Scene: Troubles of the Weimar Republic

Far more complicated was the picture presented by Germany after the First World War. In the spring of 1918 German hopes were high; by autumn they were shattered. A year later came Versailles and renewed disaster. That treaty had been no Carthaginian peace; but it was evident that the economic demands of the Allies could not be met without the virtual enslavement of German generations as yet unborn. The Fatherland in 1919 was in the abyss.

Under such circumstances, the constitution of the Weimar Republic was drawn up. It was a liberal, progressive, advanced constitution, and only slightly tinctured by the radicalism of the German Socialists who but one year earlier, as we have seen, administered the final blow to the Kaiser's regime. All Germans over twenty now had the ballot, and the new Reichstag which they were to elect was to govern the country through a chancellor representing a majority group or groups within it. The president of the new republic was supposedly a figurehead. The initiative, referendum, recall, proportional representation, and other up-to-date gadgets of the political scientists were included, and a gesture toward socialism was made by declarations concerning the unearned increment, condemnation of land (with indemnity), and an economic council.

This Weimar Republic was to last little more than a decade, and of its numerous elections and interminable party strife but trifling account shall be given. At no time in its history did any single party have a majority in the Reichstag. The Social Democrats, in the very first election held under the republic (1920), had by far the largest single representation; but even at the beginning they were deserted by left-wing socialists who had formed their own parties. At the extreme left were the Communists, listening to the siren voice of Lenin, confident of a second revolution which would sweep away this bourgeois republic. Other socialists to the left were the Independent Socialists, who abhorred a bloody revolution which was the dream of the Communists, but who demanded the immediate expropriation of private property throughout Germany. Had these three groups of socialists stuck together, they might have had a majority over all and Germany might have been spared Hitler; but owing to the absurd overconfidence of the Soviet authorities, constantly meddling in German affairs, this chance was lost. Meanwhile, on the extreme right, were the Nationalists, the Prussian Junkers, ex-army officers, and other defenders of the old regime. Both Communists and Nationalists, when not at each other's throats, started little civil wars of their own. For several weeks the Communists were able to hold Munich; for a short time the Nationalists were in military possession of Berlin. Both revolts were crushed; but Nationalists and Communists remained in the Reichstag, prepared to knife the republic at the slightest opportunity. Other parties of importance in the early history of the republic were the Centrists (the old Centre party of the Catholic Church); the People's party (the old National Liberal party rechristened), the stronghold of the upper bourgeoisie; and the Democratic party, a renewal of the old Radical party under the empire, drawing its membership largely from the lower bourgeoisie. There were also a few other parties of less importance; that of the National Socialists (the Nazis) did not come into prominence until 1923 and was of no special significance until late in the decade.

Who should control the destinies of the republic? For a long time the answer was an uneasy and constantly changing coalition of the more moderate groups. Sometimes a Social Democrat would be chancellor; sometimes a Centrist would be chancellor, supported in turn by Social Democrats and other factions; occasionally even a Nationalist would find his way into the cabinet. Election followed election for several highly unstable years, and the politically inexperienced Germans fought hard against terrific odds to bring some kind of order out of chaos. They were handicapped in many ways. If the Social Democrats had been somewhat more resolute, it is possible the skies might have cleared. But they had no Oliver Cromwell to lead them, nor any one else of ability, for that matter, who would dare to put through a genuine economic revolution by illegal means. The Social Democrats were democrats first and only secondarily socialists. They did not lift their little fingers against the property rights of the old nobility and the middle class; they did not even confiscate the wealth and the lands of the Hohenzollern family. The hands of the Social Democrats, and of all other parties, for that matter, were tied by proportional representation. Under it each party was represented in proportion to the number of votes which it received, and therefore the minor parties continued to live, although their existence was a continued threat against any consistent policy being carried out. Coalition government is generally weak government; and this was true of the different ministries of the Weimar Republic at the very time when Germany's principal need was for a strong government.

Then, too, from the Allies came no helping hand. They continued to treat Germany as a pariah country, whether republic or empire. She was excluded from the League of Nations; her natural resources were sadly diminished; and within four years of the signing of the peace treaty, the *poilus* were holding the Ruhr Valley by the throat. The utterly discredited Weimar Republic in 1923 suffered both from domestic malice and foreign levy.

Hitler

In that year of German crucifixion (1923) a wild-eyed, unkempt ex-corporal of the Kaiser's armies leaped on the table of the Reich commissar at Munich, fired his pistol in the air, and demanded a march on Berlin. There was no march on Berlin, but there was a parade in Munich. Headed by General Ludendorff, men known as Nazis, carrying a strange banner, forced their way through the streets of this South German city until stopped by the soldiers of the republic. Ludendorff was permitted to pass, but no others. Shots were fired; some Nazis were killed; some saved themselves by quickly dropping to the ground. Among the latter was their leading spokesman and orator, Adolf Hitler, who promptly was thrust into prison.

Before this event he was an unknown man, and for several years afterward this absurd coup d'état was regarded simply as one of the almost innumerable street brawls which desperate men had been starting in Germany ever since the defeat of the Second Marne. That this uneducated and most unprepossessing Austrian nobody should become dictator of the Reich in less than ten years, and in seven years more raise Germany to heights unknown even to Bismarck, no one dreamed.

Napoleon's origin was most respectable compared to his; the Emperor of the French at least started his career as a well-trained army officer. But in the obscurity of Hitler's early days there seemed to be no gleam of promise. The boy Adolf had some slight, very slight, artistic talent which he hoped to develop in Vienna. Poverty-stricken, a physical weakling, he only kept body and soul together in that city by accepting the hospitality of charitable institutions and by standing in bread-lines. He was not strong enough for manual labor; he was not talented enough to win more than a few miserable schillings as a decorator of gift-cards. Living from hand to mouth among the lowest of the Vienna proletariat, lazy and shiftless, he spent much of his time in the casual reading of the obscure pamphlet literature of the Pan-German expansionists and in listening, whenever chance offered, to music. In Vienna Hitler developed a bitter dislike for his companions in misery; he detested workmen, socialists, and above all else, Jews. He hated Vienna, the Hapsburg monarchy, and everything around him; and in his queer, tortured mind he found vicarious satisfaction for his own unhappiness in dreaming of a Germany which knew of no existence outside the imagination, a Germany great and glorious whose men and women, in the grandeur of their bodies, in the nobility of their souls, in the might of their wills, someday would dominate the world. He, Hitler, was a German!

In 1914 he enlisted in the German army and fought throughout the entire war. He was a brave soldier, a dispatch-bearer, who was wounded, gassed, and given the Iron Cross. When the armistice was signed he thought the end of all things had come. Germany, his one love, was broken; all that he hated was victorious—the Allies, international banking, international socialism, and the Jews.

The ex-corporal, wandering aimlessly in Munich, dropped into a beer cellar. He listened to talk of a German Labor party, no Marxian inter-national, bloodless and colorless, but a *pure* German party which would repudiate such vague things as interest slavery, and would fight to the death against such concrete actualities as the Treaty of Versailles and the payment of reparations. Four men around a beer-stained table—and Adolf Hitler! The party was formed, Hitler joined, and discovered that he had a wonderful talent—his voice. The party doubled and trebled its membership rapidly; men came to hear Hitler. Why?

The theme of his speeches was of the simplest: We did not lose the war; the German people always win! We were betrayed, stabbed in the back by Socialist and Jew. We have nothing to be ashamed of; we shall yet conquer. *"Deutschland Erwache,"* Germany, awake! Down with the international bankers, the international socialists, the evil Communists, the "November criminals," those who signed the Treaty of Versailles. We are not bound by that treaty; we will not be enslaved; down with Com-munist Russia; down with the Allies and their false promises! Throw off the shackles. *Deutschland Erwache!*

The German Labor party soon enlarged its scope. It became the N.S.D.A.P., the *National-sozialistische deutsche arbeiterpartei,* soon to be called Nazi, for brevity. The emphasis from the beginning was on the word *National,* and as the years sped on the labor aspect of the party's program grew less and less. The party was given a flag (Hitler was not an artist in vain), red because of its psychological stimulus, white circle on the red background that the flag might be distinguished from the Communist banner, and on the white circle a black, crooked cross—the swastika—symbol of human fertility in India, of anti-Semitism in Russia.

Fortunately for the ultimate success of the Nazis, came the collapse of the 1923 *émeute.* That failure threw Hitler into jail, thus giving him time to formulate his dreams, and to bring to the boiling point the yeasty depths of his subconscious. And now, a captive, he wrote *Mein Kampf!*

This Bible of the Nazi faith, calmly and objectively considered, is a queer mélange of semitruth and unadulterated nonsense, combined with an almost uncanny psychological insight into the mind of the mob. It is wordy, turgid, repetitious, ill-written; but it does throw light on Hitler, his aims, methods, character. It is easier to tell big lies than little ones, the author tells us. The people are always gullible; they will believe any-thing if sufficiently repeated. Hitler is quite on a par with Mussolini in his contempt for democracy. The Jews brought about the ruin of Germany; they must be driven out of the country. France is pictured as the eternal enemy, but communism as Germany's more immediate foe. The Father-land must arouse itself, must repudiate the Versailles *diktat,* must fight, must expand, must seize land in southern and eastern Europe. The Nazi party will do all this.

There is not much more in *Mein Kampf.* Hitler speaks at length of his

early career in Vienna and how he came to detest the Jews; he exults in
the way the Nazis were able to exploit mob psychology by the use of
storm troopers (hired roughnecks) instead of depending on police support. There is anticapitalistic talk of a kind; but Hitler really was not
interested in economics. Where he lets himself go with feeling and
abandon is when he talks about the *Volk* (people). But Volk means far
more than "people" in the English sense; rather it implies an antecedent,
primitive, racial throwback to a mythological German people invented
during the days of the fight waged against Bonaparte by poets and
philosophers and found useful by politicians. *"Blut und Boden,"* blood
and soil—a sacred something in the German blood-stream, an equally
sacred something in the earth on which Germans have lived. Here is
nothing but a pouring forth of disjointed fragments from H. S. Chamberlain, Fichte, and Jahn, with stray bits of the Pan-German gospel picked
up here and there by the casual reading of a tramp-artist in beer-cellar
and public reading-room.

We are also told why Germany lost the war, what kind of government
befits the longed-for volk state and what ought to be the German foreign
policy of the future. The policy of the Hohenzollern regime in international
affairs is adversely criticized and Austria is assailed as partly responsible
for the war; but what really lost the war, according to Hitler, was (*a*) the
inefficient propaganda of Germany in comparison with England; (*b*) the
traitorous character of German socialism; and (*c*) the poisonous infiltration of Jewish influence in the Fatherland.

One thing Hitler instinctively grasped, the art of propaganda.

The great masses' receptive ability [he tells us], is only very limited, their
understanding is small, but their forgetfulness is great. As a consequence of
these facts, all effective propaganda has to limit itself only to a very few points
and to use them like slogans until even the very last man is able to imagine
what is intended by such a word. . . . It was completely wrong to ridicule the
adversary as was done in Austrian and German propaganda in comic papers. It
was basically wrong for the reason that when a man meets the adversary in
reality he was bound to receive an entirely different impression; something that
took its most terrible revenge; for now the German soldier, under the direct impression of the resistance of the enemy, felt himself deceived by those who
were responsible for his enlightenment, and instead of strengthening his fighting spirit or even his firmness, quite the contrary occurred. The man despaired.
Compared with this, the war propaganda of the British and the Americans was
psychologically right. By introducing the German as a barbarian and a Hun
to its own people it thus prepared the individual soldier for the terrors of war
and helped guard him against disappointment . . .[1]

Concerning socialism and Jews, the future dictator of Germany was
grossly partisan. There was, it is true, a socialistic revolution in the Father-

[1] Adolf Hitler, *Mein Kampf*, p. 234, quoted by permission of the Houghton Mifflin
Company, proprietors of the basic copyrights of all American editions.

land as the war officially ended, and there was socialistic propaganda in
favor of peace before that date; but the influence of the latter was very
slight until late in 1918. As for the Jews, their history and their character,
Hitler knew nothing. Page after page of *Mein Kampf* is devoted to their
vilification. Those pages do not need examination if we remember that
the ratio of casualties in the war for the German Jews was approximately
the same as for the German Gentiles; that 35,000 Jews received war
medals; that 23,000 Jewish soldiers were promoted to the rank of officer;
that of less than 600,000 Jewish citizens of Germany, 100,000 bore arms.

The importance of *Mein Kampf* as a book is difficult to estimate.
Certainly, it does not belong in the same category in the field of political
science as Rousseau's *Social Contract* or the essays of John Stuart Mill.
The voice, and not the pen, was the medium through which Hitler rose
to power. On the other hand, it is foolish to dismiss *Mein Kampf* as
simply the wild ravings of a paranoiac. After all, millions read this book,
which possibly will rank in later years as the most famous or infamous
production of the first quarter of the twentieth century.

Why National Socialism Continued to Grow

Hitler, once out of jail (1924), gave all his time to resuscitating the
N.S.D.A.P. Only very slowly did it grow, for Locarno in 1925 (see p.
624) seemingly placed the Weimar Republic on a firmer basis, and not
until as late as 1929 were Nazis much more than a joke among serious-
minded Germans. Nevertheless, grow in numbers they did, and for a
variety of reasons. Among them were: the peculiar appeal of the National
Socialists to the lower half of the middle class, slowly slipping into the
proletariat; the adroit use of propaganda; the financial assistance of
wealthy Germans; and the absurd antics of the German Communists.

The middle class, particularly in the lower strata, felt the shock of
Germany's financial disaster in 1923 more than any other. The peasants
managed to live; they had their cattle and their gardens. The aristocrats
had their rent rolls; and the wealthier bourgeoisie still owned factory
and workshop which they operated as soon as the new currency, the
rentenmark, was established. So also was it with the workmen who had
no capital anyway to disappear with inflation and who could depend
more or less on unemployment insurance. But there was no sun at all
on the horizon of the little man of business, the people with money in
savings banks, those with insurance, the doctors, the dentists, the professional men, and the civil servants who had saved a little for retirement
or for a rainy day. All they had was wiped out overnight. Vaguely, the
N.S.D.A.P. was against big business, the little people liked that; it was
against war profiteers (many of them Jewish), and the little people liked
that. To all baffled and defeated and discouraged men it offered two

scapegoats—the Versailles *diktat* and the Jews. Those who despaired the most and who thought the least were attracted as by a magnet.

The National Socialist propaganda was unique and telling. Hitler explained in his book how meetings held at night were always more effective than those held during the day in arousing the emotions, and most of the Nazi meetings were in the evening. Nothing was omitted that might arouse passion. The Nazis made great use of huge banners borne by their separate units. These flags were consecrated by the Fuehrer by touching them with that most sacred blood-stained banner borne in the tragi-comedy of 1923 in Munich. Singing and neon lights made their appeal. Hitler's advent was frequently delayed until excitement reached the fever pitch. As time wore on the Fuehrer traveled over large stretches of Germany by airplane. Searchlights would pierce the black night for his coming; bands would burst into martial music; and then the ex-corporal with magic voice would scream defiance at his various foes.

Where did the money come from to pay for uniforms, publicity, a Mercedes automobile and airplanes? In part it was derived from the sale of tickets; the Hitler shows were good ones; in part it came from the dues of party members, very considerable in the lump sum. But in addition there were contributions from the big industrialists, who contributed more or less impartially to all the anti-Marxian factions. These industrialists were not Nazis; but many of them thought the Nazis useful, since they beat up Communists in the street and demanded the rearmament of Germany, a pleasant note to the ear of the Ruhr steel men. Even the Nationalists, the Junker crowd, were sufficiently foolish to believe that Hitler, mountebank and charlatan though he might be, could be taken into camp and made a convenient tool for the reëstablishment of the monarchy. The Nationalists could not agree upon a candidate for the vacant imperial throne, some favoring Rupprecht of Bavaria, some the Hohenzollerns; but in the meanwhile a subsidy to the ex-corporal could do no harm.

Then, too, the Communist party in Germany continued through the nineteen-twenties to be a great help to Hitler. The Communists looked to Moscow for their orders and they received them. Nothing detracts more from Lenin's reputation as a statesman than his conviction that a Communist revolution was imminent in Germany, a Russian fantasy that lived long after Lenin died and still, perhaps, is cherished in Moscow. Lenin instructed his disciples in Germany to undermine the Weimar Republic; to hate and to abhor all Social Democrats, those traitors to the Marxian faith, instructions followed after Lenin's death. They fitted nicely into Hitler's hand; he denounced the Communists as base international-ists; he insisted that they went further, that they advocated loose sexual relations, free week-ends without matrimony, and so forth. The Nazis posed as the defenders of the German home. Purists of the pure (in theory), they harkened back to the folkways of the primitive Germans, their sexual cleanliness, their Spartan virtue. How these *Urdeutschers* would have revolted against the social decadence and flaunting vice of the contemporary republic in which the Communists reveled! And there is a good deal of evidence to support the Nazi claim that such conditions existed in Germany after the war, as is true more or less in all countries after the strain of war, and particularly in those where the currency depreciates so rapidly that the wise thing seems to be to spend any money available while it still has purchasing power. But to the Nazi orator the purveyors of this vice were always the Jew and the Communist!

Under such circumstances, the Weimar Republic was fortunate to survive as long as it did. Assailed from both right and left, by Nationalists, Communists, and Nazis, it kept its head well above water until the world economic crisis of 1930-31. One reason why it did so was the tactful foreign policy of Gustav Stresemann, who was Germany's foreign minister in no less than ten different ministries between 1923 and 1929. During the war Stresemann had been a violent Nationalist, and after it he was the spokesman in the Reichstag for the German People's party, the right wing of the bourgeoisie. But these facts did not prevent him from realizing the immediate necessity of placating France and England if the republic was to get on a firm basis. Within one year after the evacuation of the Ruhr by the French, the Dawes Plan for lessening the strain of the reparation problem was accepted by Stresemann, and one year later he negotiated the Treaty of Locarno with the former enemies of Germany on the basis of perfect equality.

Locarno and the Dawes Plan

That treaty guaranteed the western frontier of the Weimar Republic as drawn by the Treaty of Versailles, and the signatories—Belgium, Italy, France, England, and Germany—not only pledged themselves to respect it but also to enforce it. Thus the Germans of their own accord surrendered all claims to Alsace-Lorraine, and the French to further invasions of Germany to enforce treaty rights, such as the invasion of the Ruhr. The Germans likewise agreed to the demilitarization of Germany fifty kilometers east of the Rhine, as provided in the Versailles pact. Locarno was to go into effect with the entry of Germany into the League of Nations, which took place late in this same year, 1926.

Along with this partial settlement of political disputes and the recognition of Germany's political equality with her former enemies, came a very decided economic revival. The Reich after the war had no ruined cities to rebuild, and the very fact of inflation had enabled her to modernize her industrial machinery by borrowing huge sums which were repaid in marks which had no value. Furthermore, since the old mark now was worthless, her war loans, raised from her own citizens (domestic debt), were wiped out. There remained her debt to the Allies (reparations). This now, by the Dawes Plan, was placed upon a more intelligent basis than it had before. The Dawes Plan was still a stop-gap; it was irritating in so far as it called for a certain amount of international control over German finance; it was annoying in so far as it made the amount of the annual total due from Germany depend on an index of prosperity which meant that the more prosperous the Germans became the more they had to pay; and it was discouraging, as it set no final total of indebtedness. On the other hand, it was an improvement which worked as long as foreign loans poured into Germany. The plan called for immediate loans which were granted, and these were followed by many private ones.

Stresemann, indeed, had accomplished much, but he was heavily attacked for not doing more. The fourteen points of Wilson had called for general disarmament; but all the Germans saw was unilateral disarmament as far as they were concerned, and practically nothing accomplished by the other countries in this direction. The Dawes Plan, too, seemingly laid an almost perpetual burden on German backs, even if a slightly lighter one than that already carried. Stresemann realized this and worked hard to ease the burden still further. This he was able to accomplish by the Young Plan, 1929, which was adopted by general consent in place of the Dawes Plan. The new agreement provided a definite limit for German payment, lowering the total indebtedness. But unfortunately the agreement came too late. In this year (1929) Stresemann died and an economic blizzard began to sweep the world which transformed the situation and gave Hitler his great opportunity.

The Great Depression and the Nazis

The storm clouds burst on the New York stock exchange late in 1929 and a first-class panic followed in America. This meant not only no more loans to Germany but also the calling in of short-term credits to that country. Whereupon, in 1930, banks in Germany and Austria began to close their doors and German factories to dismiss their employees. In vain did the German chancellor appeal to the British and the French for help; the former, fearful of their own financial status, were afraid to aid; the latter were not only afraid but unwilling. A moratorium on reparation payments was, indeed, granted; but that came too late to be effective, and international trade was paralyzed.

Under such circumstances came the election of 1930. Both the German right and the German left strengthened their position against the moderate center; the Communists increased their representation at the expense of the Social Democrats, but that of the Nazis went sky-rocketing

upward. Before the election the Nazis, despite their clamor, had but
twelve seats in the Reichstag; after it was over they numbered 107 and
were the second largest party.

The chancellor was Brüning, a Centrist. For support at home he had
to depend on a slight majority made up of many different party groups
and on the backing of the President of the Republic, the octogenarian
Hindenburg. Support outside his country he had none. A customs union
with Austria which might have helped save the day had been vetoed
by the French, a veto upheld on technical grounds by the World Court
at the Hague. Meanwhile, unemployment rose by leaps and bounds, and
starvation threatened. The very liberalism of the Weimar Republic was
telling now against it. For years the Nationalists and the Nazis had been
organizing and drilling informal private armies of their own, the former
the Steel Helmets, the latter the *Sturmabteilung* (Brown Shirts). Even
the peaceful Social Democrats had done likewise with the *Reichsbanner*
corps. Germany was seething with violent disorder. Armed bands were
attacking Jews and Communists, the former not retaliating, the latter
fighting back.

Between the accession of Brüning in March, 1930, and the burning of
the Reichstag building in February, 1933, which threw Germany into
Hitler's power, the utmost confusion reigned. Plot and counterplot followed. There were two presidential and two Reichstag elections; there
were innumerable street riots and many murders; and the political
balance swayed backward and forward between the defenders of Weimar
and the Nationalists, the Nazis, and the Communists who hated the
republic. Much is still obscure concerning these three hectic years during
which the Nazis and the Nationalists, wearing their private uniforms,
marched out of the Reichstag and into it again, during which Brüning, a
confirmed moderate and well-wisher of the republic, was compelled to
rule largely by decree until he lost the support of the President, during
which also the Junker aristocracy played constantly with fire (Adolf
Hitler), only in the end to be badly scorched.

The three years were full of economic misery and semistarvation,
since Brüning's answer to the world depression was economy. But they
were also full of betrayals of one sort or another. Hindenburg, very old
and perhaps not altogether in possession of his faculties, was reëlected
by the Social Democrats, the Centrists, and other moderate groups. Yet
within a few weeks after the election, he seemingly betrayed his constituents by dismissing Brüning, who had at the time a majority behind
him. Von Papen, a Junker, was made chancellor by Hindenburg, but he
in turn was betrayed by General Schleicher and other Nationalists who
intrigued against von Papen. Schleicher, von Papen, and the Nationalists
(Steel Helmets) were afterward betrayed by Hitler, who played cleverly
for power and only obtained it by betraying also his own leftwing

followers who took their socialism seriously. Possibly the "anticapitalistic romanticism" which the coming Fuehrer had advocated hitherto, with its implied attack on land values and big business, had never been of any real significance to him; but it was imbedded in the platform of the Nazi party, and in order to obtain the support of the wealthy, Hitler threw most of it overboard, driving out of his own party many of his oldest and warmest friends.

Finally, in January, 1933, Hindenburg, field marshal, war hero, and President of the republic which he had sworn to defend, appointed ex-corporal Hitler as chancellor. This was done through the connivance of von Papen and other aristocrats, who thought Hitler would play their game. The Nazis, at the last election, had captured only thirty-two per cent of the votes and the Nationalist vote was less than one-third that of the Nazis. There was then no majority for the Nazi-Nationalist combination and another election was called, the third in one year. By the first and earlier election of 1932 the Nazis had captured thirty-seven per cent of the electorate and therefore they seemingly were declining in strength. The decline from thirty-seven to thirty-two per cent was serious; could they hope for a majority now? It looked as though they could not; but luck or treachery now stood them in good stead—the Reichstag fire!

Who destroyed the parliamentary building where the Reichstag met? "The slimy Communists did it!" shouted the Nazis, from a thousand platforms in Germany. "It was to be the signal for a Communist revolt; we and the Nationalists were in power; our General Goering nipped the plot in the bud or else there would have been a Red revolution." But that the Communists engaged in this act of arson there is no evidence, and everything points to the Nazis as having perpetrated this destruction. True, a half-witted young Dutchman, afterward executed, helped set the Reichstag on fire, and at one time he had been associated with Communists in Holland. But this fire was well planned, well executed, and required the help of several men. And there is some evidence, both direct and circumstantial, to indicate that it was done by a number of Brown Shirts, presumably under orders from that fire-eating Nazi, General Goering.

However that may be, it was the Nazis who profited. There were only three Nazis in the cabinet and they were supposedly kept well under control there by the numerical majority of Nationalists; but one of the three was Hitler, the chancellor, and they controlled the police. This latter fact really determined the result of the election in advance; Communist, Socialist, and even Centrist newspapers were suppressed and every possible hysteria was encouraged. The increase in the Nazi vote which followed brought it to forty-three and nine-tenths per cent of the total. If we add to this the eight per cent won by the Nationalists, it is evident that the coalition had fifty-two per cent, a narrow but clear majority.

The Reichstag met and the first thing done was to exclude from its meetings the 81 members elected by the Communists, an act which gave the Nazis, by themselves and for the first time, a majority over all. Followed then rapidly the abolition of the German trade unions, the abolition of the Social Democratic party, and that of all other political groups in the Reichstag except the Nazi. The Reichsbanner of the Socialists was dissolved without a fight and, unkindest cut of all, the Nationalists were forced out of the cabinet and their Stahlhelm abolished. The Centre party meanwhile voluntarily ended its own existence, and political parties, as such, were abolished in Germany with the exception of one, the N.S.D.A.P. All this took place rapidly during the year 1933 and, toward its end, Hitler, in a blaze of patriotic fervor, withdrew Germany from the "unfair" League of Nations. As he did so, he asked for a vote of the German people in approval or disapproval of his various activities. A ballot was to be cast, a curious ballot. There were Nazi names printed on it and no others were permitted. One could simply vote *"Ja"* or *"Nein"*; there was no other choice. Before the election there was to be no propaganda of any kind except Nazi propaganda. To the Nazi belonged the exclusive rights to the press, to the radio, to illuminated night meetings, and brass bands. And the S.A., the storm troopers, Brown Shirts, guarded the polls and watched the voting. The result—ninety-five per cent voted *"Ja."*

Party government now was ended, liberty vanished, democracy dead. Germany was on the verge of being a totalitarian state controlled by the will of one man, except in so far as he delegated that will to his leading subordinates like General Hermann Goering, a former aviator, now President of the Reichstag, and Joseph Paul Goebbels, the most learned of all the Nazis, a doctor of philosophy with a crippled body, whose venomous diatribes against the Jews had endeared him to Hitler. The Reichstag, it is true, continued to exist; but from now on it became merely a sounding board for Hitler's voice. Von Hindenburg still lived; but he was in his last illness and within a year was to die. Hitler did not choose to succeed him as president. That exalted title, he explained, belonged only to Hindenburg; he, Hitler, would be content to be simply *Der Fuehrer,* the man who founded the Third German Reich which would last one thousand years.

Very thoroughly now did Hitler subordinate all things in Germany to the will of the Nazi party—his will. From 1934 to the outbreak of the second World War in 1939, the Nazis proceeded (*a*) to destroy root and branch all traces of a labor party in Germany; (*b*) insanely and abominably to persecute the Jews; (*c*) to attack the Christian Church, both Catholic and Protestant; (*d*) to revolutionize education; (*e*) to cast off one by one the last remnants of the Versailles pact; (*f*) to rearm to the teeth; and (*g*) finally, to plunge Europe into another war. The first four of these seven policies of Hitler will be discussed here; the remaining three belong to the field of international relations and will be taken up later.

The Nazis and Labor

The German labor movement succumbed without a fight, whereas the churches, and the Lutheran Church in particular, seemingly weak and defenseless in the postwar period were able to withstand to some degree the will of the dictator. The German trade unions, which accepted disbandment without a murmur, were strong in numbers but weak in will. Their members were socialists who had looked forward for so long and so confidently to the time when Germany would *hineinwachsen* (grow into) socialism that they were inhibited from realizing that their cause might be lost altogether unless they were willing to meet force with force. Many of their members were led by Nazi propaganda to believe that National Socialism, as advertised, was really socialistic. The Nazis, during their first year in power, certainly succeeded in reducing unemployment. They did so by extreme economic nationalism, by starting public works, by establishing labor camps, by ordaining export subsidies, by commencing the rearmament of Germany.

Then, too, the Nazis announced a labor policy which in theory was favorable to labor. "Full authority downward, full responsibility upward," was their slogan, undemocratic, if you will, but not necessarily injurious to the material welfare of the workingman. If the latter lost his right to collective bargaining, that did not mean free competition in the labor market and the right of the employer to determine wages. Over both employer and employee now were placed fourteen labor trusts, which were to determine wages; and social honor courts with power to deal with labor disputes took the place of the old trade unions. Labor was forbidden to organize, but labor was not left completely helpless, for the Nazi party controlled the honor courts.

The historian, indeed, must walk warily in generalizing about Nazi labor policy. In certain respects it was favorable to labor. A "Strength through Joy" movement was started, whereby free vacations at state expense were provided; six months' labor service (*arbeitsdienst*) was required of all Germans irrespective of social position and rank; German peasants were protected against usury and were assured title to their holdings in perpetuity; and great care was taken to prevent the price of foodstuffs customarily used by the poor, such as potatoes, margarine, and sausages, from rising.

The Nazis did not, to be sure, satisfy their own more radical members who hoped for a genuinely socialistic revolution and the ending of capitalism in Germany. The latter were completely crushed by the bloody purge of 1934, and most of their spokesmen were killed. Just what happened behind the scenes is still obscure. There was talk of a second revolution, and Roehm, commander of the Brown Shirts, aroused the suspicions of Hitler. Just what Roehm was after it is difficult to tell; he wanted more power given the Brown Shirts and was jealous of the S.S. men, the Schutzstaffel, or private police who guarded Hitler and who seemed to the storm troopers a kind of aristocratic organization supplanting them. Roehm had been one of the more radical Nazis and he was thought to have been intriguing with von Schleicher, the ex-Nationalist chancellor and a general in the army, who might conceivably be stirring up a coup d'état against Hitler. It was also said that Roehm for a long time had been a notorious homosexual, a fact hitherto ignored by Hitler.

Suddenly now, in the summer of 1934, Hitler pounced upon Roehm and his more intimate friends and summarily put them to death. Simultaneously, Goering in Berlin slaughtered in cold blood many other Nazis, likewise General von Schleicher, his wife, and a number of other suspects. All told, upward of a thousand Germans were shot down in cold blood. "There was none of the courage of mercy. There was none of the coolness of wisdom." With berserker rage the Nazi chieftains acted, and bullets spat against cement walls as Nazi after Nazi with "Heil Hitler!" on his lips gave up his life. Hitler, in a long, rambling speech to the Reichstag, explained later that the victims of the purge were traitors, that they were dissipated, immoral, and deserved death. The world looked for some proof of the former statement; none was advanced. The immorality was nothing new, nothing hidden; it had not hitherto excited Hitler's rage. But even the sexual abnormality which characterized Roehm and certain other well-known Brown Shirts was not charged against all of those slain. A number of them, like von Schleicher, were not even Nazis. Could it be possible that von Schleicher had proof that Hitler had never received the Iron Cross for valor in the war; was he really intriguing with Roehm to overthrow the dictator; was there any significance in the fact that those Nazis employed in firing the Reichstag now were killed, thus ending any chance of their talking? Robespierre gave Danton a trial in the French Revolution; Hitler behaved otherwise to his old comrades.

The Nazis and the Jews

Possibly the single most extraordinary fact about Hitler and the Nazi victory was the anti-Semitism which characterized it. After the Nazis came to power they excluded Jews from all learned professions in Germany, forbade them to practise law, removed their physicians from state hospitals, drove Jewish judges off the bench and Jewish professors out of the universities. Jews were excluded from all governmental posts, and one by one the various economic enterprises which Jews headed were "Aryanized," placed under non-Jewish management. Jews were compelled to dispose of their large business enterprises for nominal sums, Jewish-owned department stores, banks, printing presses, manufacturing plants, were put under non-Jewish control. And finally Jews were subjected to an ever increasing flood of humiliating insults, aimed apparently at driving all Jews and those of partial Jewish blood outside the country of their birth.

Hitler himself had written "the wretched Jew, enemy of the human race, the Jew, cause of all our miseries," and Goebbels, appointed minister of propaganda by Hitler, constantly referred to Jews as beneath the contempt of all decent men. But more important, perhaps, than the statements of these two Nazi chieftains were the fulminations of Streicher, a popular Nazi propagandist, whose foul sheet *Der Stürmer*, specifically blest by Hitler, was made compulsory reading in the German schools.

Der Stürmer, by cartoon and by story, stressed one major theme—the lascivious desire of the Jewish people to contaminate the German people by sexual intercourse with it. The Jewish religion, *Der Stürmer* said, called for the spreading of the seed of Israel among non-Jews; Jewish physicians could never be trusted because they gave anesthetics in order to rape German girls. Jews must not be spoken to on the street; they must have separate benches in the schools; no German girl was to be permitted to work as a servant in a Jewish home; she must never marry a Jew; the *Protocols of Zion* (an absurd forgery) was dug up to prove that Jews conspired to rule the world; rabbis were accused of drinking Christian blood in foul rituals; and by the Nuremberg laws none could claim to be a German citizen unless he could prove that all of his four grandparents were non-Jewish. Even the non-Aryan Christians, those contaminated by having one or more Jewish grandparents, were forbidden to give the Nazi salute. They were equally guilty of belonging to an inferior race.

The situation grew worse constantly, and when a young Jewish boy assassinated an official in the German embassy at Paris in 1938, it reached its height. Mobs roamed the streets of German cities, burning synagogues, smashing the windows of Jewish stores, stealing their contents, and beating all Jews they encountered. The authorities made no effort to stop them; instead they levied a huge fine on all German Jews, so huge as virtually to wipe out all remaining Jewish wealth. Some Jews escaped from Germany, penniless; but a majority, unable to obtain visas for countries beyond the seas or in Europe, sunk back into the depths of despair as the Nazis prepared to set apart ghettos for Jews, miserable districts in the more squalid parts of German cities in which Jews must live and out of which Jews would emerge at their peril.

Why this persecution of the Jews, the most vicious, the most barbaric in modern times? It was not just the dictatorship; Frederick the Great was a dictator, but he welcomed Jews in Prussia, and Napoleon was well disposed toward them. It has been urged that Germany was always an anti-Semitic country; but the facts do not bear out this interpretation. During the period of the Second German Empire, which lasted from 1871 to the Weimar Republic, there was far more active anti-Semitism in both France and Russia than in Germany. The Germans discriminated against the Jews even then, socially, and governmental and military rank was denied them; but Jewish students were not put on a narrow quota basis in the universities as in Russia, and the learned professions in Germany were full of Jews—Jewish doctors, Jewish lawyers, Jewish professors. Important newspapers, banks, business houses, were Jewish-owned, and mixed marriages were more common in Germany than anywhere else in Europe. The very presence of the numerous non-Aryan Christians refutes this argument. The latter were more than three times as numerous as the professing Jewish people, of whom there were only some 600,000 in the Reich.

It has likewise been suggested that economic competition brought about the Jewish persecution, the Jews being held up to scorn as battening on the ills of Germany—war profiteers and usurers, prosperous while others starved. The economic level of the German Jew was, it is true, relatively high; he did own most of the department stores which took away trade from the small shopkeepers, and there were Jewish usurers. But there was nothing new about this, and all the evidence at our command goes to show that the Jew did not benefit by the war. His income declined, like that of other Germans; and as a matter of cold statistics, there were proportionately fewer Jews among the leading industrialists and bankers of Germany after the war than before.

Even less valid a reason is the assertion that the principles of National Socialism are so foreign to Jewish psychology as to make inevitable the exclusion of all Jews from a Nazi state. Jews, naturally, are opposed to anti-Semitism; but aside from that there was no proposal of the Nazis that Jews as such would automatically oppose. There are international Jews, socialist Jews, nationalist Jews, capitalistic Jews. In fact, there were certain tenets of Nazi philosophy which might be considered as rather attractive to Jews, particularly, the idea of national unity transcending all religious barriers.

What then is the explanation? Possibly the best that can be given is the racial myth that Hitler expounded, the supremacy of Aryan and particularly Teutonic blood over all other racial strains. Some reason had to be given for this superior racial strain losing the war, and the inherent wickedness of Marxian philosophy was a partial one. But Marxism could not be dramatized quite so readily as that biological absurdity of the Nazis—the poisoning of racial purity by Jewish blood. The Jews were a convenient scapegoat. Communists as scapegoats had disadvantages; they were poor and there was no booty to be gleaned from them; they were Germans, and when they transferred themselves into good Nazis, or pretended to, they had no distinguishing marks. But the Jews had money, which might come in handy; they also had distinguishing marks; their names, their physical appearance—they were Jews. As such they offered a shining mark for the attack of the bigoted, and they became the principal scapegoat upon which was loaded all the unhappiness and misery of postwar Germany.

The Nazis and the Christian Churches

The Nazis' attack on Christianity is perhaps easier to understand than their animosity toward the Jews, but the evidence of it is slightly more confusing. Whether in the long run it was more serious than the open atheism of the Russian Communists it is difficult to say, for while the Communist attack was direct and open, that of the Nazis was indirect, insidious, and therefore possibly the more dangerous. The Nazis never repudiated Christianity as a party; rather they tried to corrupt it from within, to twist and to distort its meaning.

Certain of the Nazis, to be sure, repudiated Christianity, lock, stock, and barrel. Seeking openly to reëstablish the pagan rites of their early ancestors, they resurrected Odin, Thor, and the old stone gods. By picturesque ritual and dramatic rites, they glorified bravery, loyalty, and physical force into a trinity of virtues. But these professed pagans were but a minority. What was far more characteristic of the Nazi attitude toward religion was the program of the German Christians. The latter threw out the Old Testament as a Jewish book, and many parts of the New Testament as well. They denied that Christ was Jewish and interpreted him as a kind of warrior who, by his death, had preserved the world from Jewish domination, an act of virtue duplicated by their Fuehrer, in turn a kind of second Christ. These so-called German Christians demanded that the swastika be introduced into the churches as a kind of sacred symbol, and that the church be regarded solely as a kind of adjunct to the government.

All Nazis did not go as far as these German Christians, and many of them were indifferent to the Church, whether Catholic or Protestant, as was the case, apparently, with Hitler. Nevertheless, the latter was determined to put the Lutheran Church of the country under his direct control, and appointed as head of it a reichsbishop with German Christian tendencies. This met with such stiff opposition that Hitler withdrew his appointee and selected another. Many Lutheran pastors objected to taking an oath of loyalty to Hitler which would deprive them of freedom of conscience. In consequence, a number of them were put in concentration camps.

Much to the surprise of the outside world, the Lutheran Church in Germany, hitherto considered more dead than alive as far as spiritual fervor was concerned, took on a new lease of life. Churches began to be filled, many coming, perhaps, not so much to worship the Lord as to show that they would like to voice disapproval of the Nazi tyranny in their own country. Going to church was about the only way they could show it.

The Roman Catholic Church also came in conflict with the government. It had consented to liquidate the Centre party and to retire from politics; but it would not consent to the untiring campaign of the Nazis in trying to break up all church youth organizations and compelling boys to join the Hitler *Jugend*, wherein they were taught that force alone ruled the world and that Christian ethics were better suited for a slave society than for a self-respecting Aryan nation like Germany.

Roman Catholic bishops in both Austria and Germany protested firmly in their pastoral letters against this almost complete assumption of authority by the State over the time and the activities of the young. Whereupon the Nazis fought back; they placed on trial many members of monastic orders on a variety of charges running from accusations of smuggling gold out of Germany to sexual malpractices; they banned the circulation of Catholic literature; they forbade Catholic processions; and they sternly insisted that the Church confine its activities to what the Nazis considered religious matters, education being distinctly not one.

Nazi threats on the one hand and the protest of the Pope and of Protestant pastors on the other, continued down to the commencement of the Second World War in 1939, without any final solution or compromise being reached. To claim that in this general strife the Nazis met their match would be an exaggeration; nevertheless it is evident that the Nazis did not dare go too far in their opposition to the churches. They did not, for instance, close them; they did not forbid Mass being sung. In view of the necessity of unity in foreign affairs, even Hitler refrained from a completely totalitarian policy in church affairs, and the churches retained something more than the semblance of autonomy.

Possibly in this matter the Nazis felt that time was on their side. The older generation would die before long, and boys and girls who had experienced nothing outside the Nazi fold would take its place. The same would occur in Germany as was taking place (so they thought) in Italy— the coming to maturity of youngsters trained in a new faith.

GIRLS OF THE NAZI YOUTH PARTY

Nazi Education

For the Nazis had a faith (of a kind) and they went about its indoctrination in a most thorough manner. Superficially, it copied the Italian model. Boys and girls were expected to join the various Nazi youth organizations appropriate for their age, there to drill, to march, to sing the praises of the new regime, to listen to its glories, to grow accustomed to warlike discipline, to learn in true Spartan fashion that luxury, comfort, individualism, were not for them. But in reality this Nazi faith was much more serious than its Italian counterpart. The Fascist teachings of Mussolini were never taken, one suspects, very seriously by him or by the better-informed Italians. The Duce found these very useful for a clever adventurer, but he never took pains to define them very closely. Not so with the Nazis. Their philosophy was much more definite. To the ardent Nazi the Fuehrer was a man sent by God, and in him were embodied all those racial characteristics which dated from Odin, Thor, and Siegfried. The necessity of obedience, the hatred of Jews, the substitution of the state for the family as the social unit were encouraged and enforced. Studies in the schools which did not serve these ends were either curtailed or abolished. Pseudoscientific racial nonsense was given a most prominent place; strength of body and steadiness of nerve, dangerous and arduous physical exercise were exalted over mental acumen and ability. The German universities became the laughingstock of the Western world. Famous teachers were driven from them for not hewing to the party line, standards were lowered, the course of study narrowed. Almost for the first time in German history, learning became unimportant; the duty of man was to obey, not to think.

That course of study may best be comprehended by an analysis of two books, *The Nazi Primer*, an official handbook for the young, and *The Myth of the Twentieth Century*, by Hitler's favorite philosopher, Dr. Alfred Rosenberg, a German Balt and Hitler's agent extraordinary for the promulgation of official Nazi philosophy.

In two words, *Blut* and *Boden*, blood and land, may be found the essence of Nazi educational theory. According to the primer, about seventy per cent of the German people belong to the Nordic race, which has the purest and finest blood in all the world. Most of the Nordics are in Germany. Their race, the primer assures us, "is uncommonly gifted mentally. It is outstanding for truthfulness and energy. Nordic men possess for the most part, even in regard to themselves, a great power of judgment. They incline to be taciturn and cautious. They feel instantly that too loud talking is undignified. They are persistent and stick to a purpose when once they have set themselves to it. Their energy is displayed not only in warfare but also in technology and in scientific research. They are predisposed to leadership by nature." About twenty per cent of the Germans belong to the Phalic race, second only in virtue to the Nordic. "Differences in the soul qualities of the two races are not very great." The Phalic man is less emotional than the Nordic man. He is said to be better suited for being the driving force under the leadership of Nordic men than for leadership itself. Great patience characterizes his pursuit of an aim. Never could he be as foolhardy, perhaps, as the Nordic man. He is governed by a strong feeling of loyalty toward other men. He is more good natured and more cordial than the Nordic man.

Ten per cent of the Germans belong to the other four European races, the Dinaric, the Eastern, the East Baltic, and the Western. Fortunately only two per cent belong to the Western race, which has little steadiness and is not given to reason. The man of the Western race is excitable, even passionate. The Western race with all its mental agility lacks creative power. This race has produced only a few outstanding men.

"All in all, the contrasts between the Nordic and the Phalic races and the Western race appear to be very great, but chiefly in the realm of mind and soul."

The primer describes the six European races in regard to physical appearance, shape of skull, color of hair, soul qualities, and the like. It laments the fact that great harm has come to the Fatherland by the adulteration of the pure Nordic blood-stream; but it is not too late to mend matters. The laws of heredity are then described in detail and the boys are instructed that the purification of German blood is their first duty.

The Boden, the German land: by this is not meant just the German

Fatherland as entrusted to Adolf Hitler. "By German territory," the primer informs us, "we mean every region of central Europe which is inhabitated by Germans in more or less permanent settlements and has received its cultural imprint from the German people." This region of German language and cultural influence is, indeed, spacious. In area it is about three times as large as the Third Reich and for the most part stretching to the south and east. Concerning it the primer narrates much dubious history. It seems that the Germans brought about the unity of Europe between 100 A.D. and 1000 A.D., and "The Reich of the Middle Ages," we are told, "was about six times as large as it is today." Since the Thirty Years War, it appears, the Germans have been ill-treated, that is before the advent of Hitler. Their land was taken from them. "We are," laments the primer, "volk without space." [2]

What the primer states in simple language Dr. Rosenberg elaborates in sonorous and mystical praise-paeans. The lost continent of Atlantis sunk beneath the ocean the Doctor peoples with Nordic heroes. "These swarms of Atlantis men," he assures us, "went forth in their swan boats and their dragon boats" on conquest bent. They fought like heroes and they were very brave; but they were also very soulful. "Soul," the Doctor pontificates, "means race seen from within . . . ; race is the outer form of the soul." It appears that only races have souls; individuals do not. The race is immortal. A nation is simply the physical embodiment of a race.

First above all comes race! The race must be cherished, guarded, exalted, and also strengthened by the most up-to-date genetic methods, by breeding men like cattle or like plants, and especially by decontaminating the German blood-stream of Jewish blood. It also must find elbow room in crowded Europe.

In order to secure it the new German education aimed straight at preparation for inevitable war. The Nazi overlords did not intend to stop with the reëstablishment of the old frontiers of Germany, or even with inclusion within the new Germany of racial brothers excluded from the old Reich, in Austria, Hungary, or elsewhere. The intimation in *Mein Kampf* is quite clear. "The frontiers of the year 1914," wrote Hitler in that book, "signify nothing at all for the future of the German nation." His people were "penned into an impossible area." They had a right to more land and would take it.

Lebensraum, living space for eighty million cramped Germans, must be found, and preferably to the east and south where the rich soil of the Ukraine stretches down through southern Poland all the way to the Black Sea. Here was superb *Lebensraum*, closely adjacent to Germany, where also there were many settlers of Germanic blood, small islands in a sea of Slavic people. To annex it would be in line with the ancient

[2] All quotations from the Nazi primer are taken from H. L. Childs' translation, courtesy of Harper & Brothers.

tradition of civilized Germany on guard against irruptions of Asiatic barbarians. Furthermore, proposals for its annexation always could be coupled with denunciations of Communists, and so not be altogether displeasing to blind politicians in London and Paris who might congratulate themselves with the thought that they were using Hitler as their cat's-paw in attacking Russia, and her horde of hateful Communists.

The Fuehrer, to be sure, would be glad to extend his boundaries even beyond the Ukraine. "How Germany has to work," he said in 1936, "to wrest a few kilometers from the ocean and from the swamps while others are swimming in a superfluity of land! If I had the Ural Mountains with their incalculable store of treasures in raw materials, Siberia with its vast forests, and the Ukraine with its tremendous wheat fields, Germany and the National Socialist leadership would swim in plenty." [3]

In justice to Hitler it should be stated that the rest of his speech was devoted to the praise of the German worker. Nevertheless the quotation is illuminating, not only as showing the drift of the Fuehrer's mind, but also because it is in close harmony with what the Nazis liked to think was a new science, that of geopolitics.

The term *geopolitics* was invented by a Swedish professor of history and it dates back to 1916, when in the midst of the first World War he defined geopolitics as "the science which conceives the state as a geographical organism or as a phenomenon in space." The state, according to the professor, must either grow or wither, and that, too, in a geographic sense. Geographic space, and plenty of it, is politically essential. This was true, he wrote, of England and is today the position of Japan and Germany. It is clearly a case not of the lust of conquest but of "natural and necessary growth. . . ."

The ideas of the Swedish savant received a setback after the war. When it was over, however, they caught the imagination of Major General Doktor Karl Haushofer, professor of geography and military science at Munich, an intimate friend of Rudolf Hess, in turn an intimate friend of Hitler and his most trusted confidant. After Hitler became chancellor he made Haushofer president of the German Academy and set his approval on the new science of space relationship.

What the latter really amounted to was a new rationalization of an old idea—imperial conquest. The Romans never heard of geopolitics, nor did anyone else, for that matter, before the twentieth century, but they did know what conquest meant. Economics, psychology, anthropology, politics, sociology, all were lumped together by Haushofer and fused in geopolitics as a justification for the seizure of land occupied by non-Germans. Certain new and poetic expressions were coined to give an emotional overtone to these ideas. Thus Europe and Asia became the

[3] Adolf Hitler, *My New Order,* p. 400.

"Island Continent," and the central plains of Eurasia, "the Heartland." It was the destiny of the Island Continent to be dominated by one integrated racial group, presumably the German *Volk*. Once under its control, global supremacy would be within its grasp because the Island Continent, owing to its space, resources, numerous inhabitants, would easily hold the world balance of power. Land power was held more important than sea power, provided there was sufficient land.

Hitler was determined that there would be sufficient for a thousand years of his Third Reich. His early speeches stressed the sacred character of German soil; his later fulminations tended more and more to emphasize the *Lebensraum* motif, space for cheated Germans, always at a grave disadvantage because room was lacking. Thus, Hitler reasoned, "Forty-six million Britishers dominate and govern approximately 16 million square miles of the surface of the earth. Thirty-seven million Frenchmen dominate and govern a combined area of 4 million square miles. Forty-five million Italians possess, taking into consideration only those territories in any way capable of being utilized, an area of scarcely 190,000 miles. That is to say: 85 million Germans own only 232,000 square miles on which they must live their lives and 46 million Britishers possess 16 million square miles." [4]

Here was injustice which Hitler was determined to rectify. He brushed aside the fact that the greater part of Canada was frozen tundra, that the greater part of Australia was a waterless desert, that England was far more thickly populated than his own country, that Englishmen living in England had no control over the property of Englishmen living in New Zealand or South Africa. He did not stop to note that the phenomenal industrial development of the Reich necessitated the importation of Polish and Italian laborers, since there were not enough Germans available; he did not consider that the only way the land area of Germany could be increased would be by annexing lands already thickly occupied, primarily by Slavs whose increase in population per hundred thousand ran well ahead of that in Germany. The only indication of the Fuehrer's pondering upon his statistics is his obvious stacking of the cards in favor of Italy. Note the qualifying clause, "taking into consideration only those territories in any way capable of being utilized." As far as Italy was concerned Hitler was willing to subtract African deserts.

Potsdam had conquered Weimar; the Germany of Goethe and Thomas Mann was now under the heel of Prussian tradition. The Nazis brought Sparta back again; women were encouraged to become brood mares for the strengthening and augmenting of the race; and boys, trained in rough discipline, were to regard obedience to command and the fighting spirit as the culmination of German virtue. From these boys a future

---

[4] Adolf Hitler, *My New Order* (Reynal & Hitchcock, Inc.), p. 874.

Nazi elite was to be selected which would take over in time the work of the founder. To train this elite, a number of castles were set apart in Germany where, in strict seclusion, the rulers of the future Reich were to undergo training. Entrance requirements were strength, bravery, unquestioned and unquestioning obedience to orders, and the course of study in these Nazi nurseries was equally drastic.

Chapter 10

FRANCE AND ENGLAND
BETWEEN TWO WARS

In CONTRADISTINCTION to the three totalitarian powers—Russia, Italy, and Germany—both France and England remained loyal in the postwar period to the democratic, liberal tradition of the nineteenth century. In both countries there was Communist agitation, more noticeable in France than in England; in both there were signs of incipient Fascist revolution, much more noticeable in France than in England; but in neither country did communism or fascism become a really serious threat.

France

The aftermath of the war, in France as elsewhere, was unpleasant. Even before the advent of that struggle the finances of the Republic were in shaky condition; for light taxes, heavy expenditure for armaments, and an unbalanced budget had created a tremendous burden of debt. That situation had caused little worry in the prewar days, for if the government was poor, the national wealth was astonishingly high; and for several decades France had become the leading banker of the Continent. After four years of war, however, there was real cause for worry; France had borrowed to the limit everywhere, both within and without her borders; the huge sums loaned to Imperial Russia had been repudiated by the Soviets; and a tenth of battle-scarred France lay in ruins.

The Republic had pledged itself early in the war to make good all damage done by the Germans in the invaded departments, and this alone was a Herculean task. Northeastern France, occupied by German armies, had been industrial France. Here had been the great textile mills, their machinery now in ruins; here had been the coal mines of France, now flooded by the Germans. Almost all of the small towns and villages in the battle zone had been wiped out by shell fire; thousands of orchards had been cut down, thousands of wells had been filled up or poisoned; the cattle and sheep had been killed or eaten, the houses destroyed.

The Germans, to be sure, in accordance with the Treaty of Versailles, were to pay for this damage; but how was France to extract money from Germany? And while the manner and method of doing it was debated, was rehabilitation to be delayed? The French said, "No!" and immediately they began, in somewhat reckless and extravagant fashion, to rebuild their factories and towns. In theory, the money thus expended was not part of the national budget but was kept in a separate account charged to the Germans. Upwards of $7,000,000,000 was thus spent; and of this sum but trifling part ever was collected from Germany.

Little wonder that the French franc could not withstand the strain. Despite the cleverest devices of clever bankers, the franc started to follow the German mark to the graveyard of repudiated currencies. And as this went on, larger and larger grew the issue of paper francs, thus hastening repudiation. The war alone had raised the national debt of France from 35,000,000,000 francs to 180,000,000,000 francs, and during the first five years of the peace that debt had nearly doubled. It was impossible even to pay interest upon it, and soon the debt was found to be maturing at the rate of 7,500,000,000 francs a month! The result was that the franc sank rapidly. In 1914 it had been quoted at slightly less than five francs to the dollar, but by 1926 forty-eight francs could be bought for that sum, and American tourists in Paris were goading the French to fury by pasting paper francs on their luggage together with hotel stickers.

There was trouble, too, in Alsace and Lorraine. Those two redeemed provinces promptly were incorporated into France proper and turned into three departments, for the Third Republic had a passion for uniformity, and all Frenchmen, it was held, should be subject to the same laws. But Alsace and Lorraine were overwhelmingly Roman Catholic. When they had been annexed by Germany in 1871 the Napoleonic Concordat with the Catholic Church still was the law of France, and the priests in Alsace and Lorraine had been supported by the State and the schools had been Catholic schools. The Germans had not changed the status of the Catholic Church in the two provinces, but when they were returned to France their inhabitants found that the Concordat had been repudiated, that the Republic no longer concerned itself with religion, that the schools were laicized. Furthermore, there was the ever important question of language bobbing up again. Most of the Alsatians used German as a primary language and the Republic changed overnight the primary instruction in the schools from German to French. No wonder, then, that protests were loud and numerous, and that agitation arose for autonomy under the Tricolor, similar to the agitation in the two provinces when ruled as a Reichsland in the German Empire.

And yet another never-ending source of worry to the French was the problem of security. The Germans still outnumbered them at the close of the war, three to two, and if Austria ever came to be included in the Reich, the disparity in numbers would be still more pronounced. The

French had surrendered at the Versailles Congress their desire for the Rhine frontier in return for guarantees from England and America, as well as from the League of Nations, guarantees which they soon discovered worthless or of slight value. The problem of French security more properly belongs to the discussion of international politics in the two postwar chapters. But it never ceased to cause friction within France herself; it was intimately correlated to the financial problem, since it contemplated construction of the expensive Maginot Line to the east, and since it further involved large loans to potential allies, such as Poland, Czechoslovakia, Yugoslavia, and so on; and it also played an important part in the constant swinging back and forth of the political pendulum between the different party groupings or blocs which controlled the government.

Party Politics in Postwar France

The Third Republic never had been blessed or cursed with the two-party system. Instead, a dozen political parties were to be met with, and the art of government, both prewar and postwar, consisted in bringing together a number of these into an alliance or bloc, whereby a majority could be secured in the Chamber of Deputies. In the period between the two World Wars, three different blocs contested political power in France, the "bloc national," the "bloc des gauches," and the "front populaire."

The first of these was generally conservative, consisting of right-wing politicians, middle-of-the-roaders, and a sufficient sprinkling of near-radicals to secure a majority. The leader of this bloc national, in the heyday of its triumph, was Poincaré, the hard-bitten French patriot from Lorraine who had been president during the war. The bloc des gauches, as its name implies, was more radical than the bloc national. It might properly be described as a working alliance of the center with the left-center, or the more conservative radicals. The United Socialists (orthodox Marxians) were wary of this bloc des gauches, and its real nucleus was the Radical-Socialist party, which, as far as tradition went, was more radical than socialistic. Its leading representatives were Herriot, popular mayor of Lyon, and Briand, now an aged radical and a broad-minded statesman who was willing to let bygones be bygones and to come to amicable understanding with the Germans. The front populaire, on the other hand, was a genuine combination of left-wing groups under the leadership of a cultured and wealthy Jewish citizen of the Republic, Léon Blum. The creation of this bloc was something new in French politics. It did not come into existence until 1936, and it brought together for the first time the United Socialists, of whom Blum was the titular head, and the Communists, hitherto strictly shunned as ultra-revolutionary.

The *bloc national* should be given credit for doing two things—appeasing Alsace-Lorraine and saving the franc. The Roman Catholic control of education was not restored in the two provinces, but provision was made for Catholic instruction, and great care was taken to smooth over the injured feelings of the Alsatians so that their demand for autonomy lessened.

More important was the salvaging of the franc. The *bloc national* had been responsible for the invasion of the Ruhr, and after that fiasco it was driven from power, the *bloc des gauches* taking over the government. But the latter did nothing to save the franc, and it was not until Poincaré returned to power in 1926 that financial recovery really set in. Poincaré, following a conservative course, cut expenditures to a minimum, reduced salaries and pensions, heaped on new taxes, and then stabilized the rising franc at about four cents. The instant effect of doing so was to cut down the national debt some eighty per cent in terms of the old franc. Bondholders and all others living on a fixed income suffered heavily, and the creditor classes in general had to bear the burden; but they did not object too loudly, for the franc no longer depreciated, and it was recognized that it was better to lose four-fifths of one's capital than to lose all, as would have happened if the franc had followed the mark. For the first time in many years it was now possible to balance the budget and there was an actual surplus! Promptly, Poincaré took advantage of improved credit to retire bonds paying a high rate of interest by issuing new ones at a low rate, to reduce the floating debt and to restore France's credit throughout the world. Something akin to the old prewar prosperity of the country was noted; the iron of Lorraine, the textile mills of Alsace added to it; and, had it not been for the world economic depression of 1929-33, all might have been well.

That depression, however, raised havoc in France as elsewhere. Poincaré, old and feeble, retired from politics in 1929 and with his going, French politics became very confused. Trade fell off rapidly, tourists to France were few, there was much unemployment, and the franc started to depreciate again. Royalists, Fascists, and Communists paraded in Paris; pictures of Robespierre began to appear, and there were a number of street fights. Premier followed premier in rapid succession, those between 1932 and 1934 all members of the Radical Socialist party, and all speedily thrown out of office by adverse majorities in the Deputies.

France Is Cut in Two

In 1934 a Fascist revolution threatened. Its immediate causes were unsavory revelations linking sundry conspicuous French politicians to what had come to be called "the Stavisky scandals." Stavisky, naturalized son of a Russian dentist and socially charming, had for a long time been mysteriously protected. Moving in high circles he floated worthless securities, forged checks, gambled with marked cards, and entertained lavishly. After he stole some 200,000,000 francs from the municipal pawnshops of Bayonne, legal proceedings were taken against him. He fled to the French Alps and was found dying in a hut. Rumor had it that he was murdered by the police to prevent his talking, a rumor which met with wide credence because of his intimacy with many cabinet members, the Minister for the Colonies having recommended his worthless securities to French savings banks, the Minister of Justice having postponed his trial, and the Premier himself having served at one time as legal adviser for one of Stavisky's accomplices.

"Democracy is another name for political corruption," screamed Léon Daudet, the royalist, and the ministry, under fire from deputies of both right and left, resigned. Daladier, the new premier, was unable to maintain order. The Croix de Feu, a veteran and Fascist organization, marched on the chamber, its partisans smashing windows, overturning buses and beating up a countermob of Communists. In expectation of trouble, Daladier had stationed troops at the Palais Bourbon. Troops and police opened fire, killing seventeen and wounding several hundred. Daladier then resigned and Colonel La Roque, head of the Croix de Feu, announced, "Our first objective is accomplished. Remain on duty and await further instructions."

Paris was in an uproar. The Fascist demonstration of the extreme right was followed at once by a drive toward the left, Radicals, Socialists and Communists flocking to the "Popular Front" for safety from fascism. As a well-known French woman wrote in her diary, "One feels that France is cut in two."

This was indeed the case. Ever since the great French Revolution a unique schism had divided France, the people never wholeheartedly accepting that revolution as a permanent achievement. They were loyal to France, yes; but loyalty to the government (the regime), that was another matter.

For a time it had seemed as though that schism might heal, but the economic distress of the nineteen-thirties led both the wealthy and the poor to distrust political democracy and to lose faith in a regime rooted in the bourgeois ideologies of 1789. The Third Republic had survived serious difficulties in the past, but attacks then had come mainly from perfervid Catholics and royalists, for the most part members of the privileged classes. Now the attack was a cross fire from two directions, from property-owners and men of wealth who found their economic status lowered by drastic depreciation of the franc, and from the workers suffering grievous unemployment. French prosperity depended on luxury trade, and economic shadows over Germany, Britain, and the United States ruined that prosperity, for the export of fine wines and wedding garments became negligible. Discontent grew rife, the gulf between classes opened wider, and from 1934 to the outbreak of the Second World War German Nazis and Russian Communists were only too successful in keeping it open.

The part played therein by the Nazis was the more obvious if not the more fundamental. Their instrument was a young school teacher from Karlsruhe, Otto Abetz, afterwards chosen by Hitler as his ambassador to what was left of the French Republic in 1940. Abetz residing in France became very popular there, posing as a devoted and nonpartisan friend of all young Frenchmen and all young Germans. He got them to meet together in a camp in the Black Forest and taught them to forget their differences. He became the paid agent of Von Ribbentrop, Hitler's choice to head Nazi propaganda and diplomacy outside of Germany, a man whose past career as a salesman of champagne had given him a special entrée among the wealthy and special skill in handling them. Von Ribbentrop kept in the background and entrusted Abetz with what he called "psychological soundings." Abetz had plenty of money and spent freely; he entertained French war veterans sumptuously in Berlin; he flattered French literary men by insisting that there was a large demand for German translations of their works, which he subsidized; he financed French lectures, and he never ceased to proclaim that the Fuehrer had absolutely no demands to make on France. Sensible Frenchmen, he intimated, should be suspicious of England and should hate the Soviets. Germany was their friend; political democracy was dead; Communism threatened a world upheaval which only could be averted by overthrowing corrupt and degenerate republics. The French royalists and the right in general heartily approved the two-timing Abetz, who also won many friends on the left by constantly stressing pacifism. Few suspected that he was a slick wolf in sheep's clothing.

Abetz' adroit campaign was to some degree offset by Communist borings from within; but the Communists were neither so well financed nor so clever, and for two years France drowsed toward fascism. Four premiers in these two years added to general confusion. Of the four, three were nonentities, and the fourth, Pierre Laval, since infamous at Vichy, was so underhanded and so tricky as to arouse the suspicion of all non-Fascists. Laval, posing as a pacifist in the first World War, had unquestionably aided Germany then by defeatist propaganda. Now his continuous postponement of a mutual aid treaty with Stalin, coupled with his comradely admiration for Mussolini, contributed not a little to French ills: internal strife at home and loss of influence and prestige abroad. Meanwhile, Léon Blum, leader of the popular front and of the French Socialist party, was murderously assaulted in public by members of the Action Française, a monarchist and Fascist organization, barely escaping with his life. And as this happened the government was vainly trying to curb semi-military organizations which were springing up, armed, on every hand.

Blum and the Popular Front

Finally came the national election of 1936. Thoroughly frightened by the rampant onsurge of fascism, Radicals, Socialists, and Communists buried their disagreement for once and worked together. This Popular Front was politically successful since the Socialists for the first time in French history won a plurality of seats, and, when combined with the Radicals and Communists, had a slight majority over all. It was not only slight but extraordinarily shaky, since it rested on the support of seventy-one Communists who were too suspicious to enter the cabinet, and on that of so-called radicals, wedded by tradition to property rights. Nevertheless, for the time being the advent of fascism was stayed.

Léon Blum, the new premier, was a highly cultivated and wealthy Frenchman, more at home in art and literature than in the hurly-burly of bloc politics into which he had plunged more from duty than inclination. He was too soft by nature for the crisis which confronted France.

France was economically in the doldrums, and politically torn wide open by contending factions. Blum tried to save her by inaugurating certain reforms parallel in many ways to the American "New Deal" of 1933. He started in bravely enough by establishing a forty-hour week, holidays with pay, and government ownership of munition plants. He followed the precedent of America and of England in depreciating the currency; he even tried to wrest control of the Bank of France from the exclusive group of seventy families which had long controlled it. A wave of sit-down strikes then spread through France and these Blum seemed unable to control. He was a pacifist by conviction and that made it difficult for him to deal effectively with his enemies, whether domestic or foreign. Perhaps this was his blind spot. "We do not believe," he wrote, "as did our forefathers in 1792 and 1848, that there can be any good in war, nor that war can be an instrument for liberty. . . ." The sentiment was nicely phrased but scarcely revealed a man capable of dealing with the venomous Cagoulards, a secret Fascist society engaged in hoarding machine guns and ammunition for the coming revolution of the right.

As the Spanish Republic slowly bled to death at the hands of German and Italian Fascists, and of foreign non-interventionists, Blum hesitated, and then lost prestige both within and without France. Whether England was responsible or not for the supine foreign policy of the Popular Front is extremely difficult to fathom; but even if England had supported a firmer French attitude toward the Spanish war, it is difficult to conceive a man with Blum's pacifist psychology standing up against the fire-snorting bullies of Italy and Germany. In little over a year he resigned in disgust owing to a quarrel with the French Senate over a money bill. The Popular Front lingered on six months and then faded out. To some extent it may justly be blamed for the consequent defeat of France, soon to follow, not for its ineptitude in foreign policy alone but because it fatally slackened the production of military matériel. But on the other hand, it may have saved France from a revolution in 1936, and its leaders, though blind to fascism's menace, were less deserving of censure than those Frenchmen who preferred Hitler and his gangsters to their own radical countrymen.

France now swung to the right again; sit-down strikes and the forty-hour week led to renewed financial trouble; and the gathering of war-clouds in 1938-39 made for conservatism, the majority being of the opinion that this was no time for further social reform. When Hitler occupied Prague in March, 1939, the Chamber of Deputies did not hesitate to endow Daladier, a Radical-Socialist premier, with power to rule by decree. The city of Marseilles was deprived of its autonomy and placed directly under the national government; unemployed workers on relief could now be sent anywhere in France the government chose to send them; the forty-hour week was abandoned, and the sixty-hour week became permissible. Something approaching a government of national defense was formed under Daladier—no new election was held, but the seventy-two Communists were regarded with suspicion, as Blum and his Socialists listened to the call of patriotism and joined Daladier and the more conservative deputies of the right and center in a different kind of a united front, this time against Germany. Unfortunately the unity thus achieved was merely superficial. In 1914 the French stood united against the invaders; in 1939 they did not. During the First World War France had been bled white, losing far more lives in proportion to her population than any other country involved. Frenchmen in 1939 had no stomach for fighting; they felt they could not go through with it again. That fact alone goes far to explain the debacle that was to come in 1940. But it is not the only reason. Abetz had done his work far too well. Large numbers of Frenchmen had lost all faith in Liberty, Equality, and Fraternity, and tended to regard fascism, if not as desirable, then at least as more desir-able, more unifying than communism. As for the Communists, they followed the party line laid down in Moscow. Since Russia was not in the war they considered themselves out of it. France was half conquered before a shot was fired.

Britain

The end of the war found Britain unprepared for peace. A million soldiers came back home to wives and sweethearts, but in all too many cases there were neither homes in which to live nor jobs to work at.

No new houses had been built for years and old jobs had been discontinued or were held by women. Many discharged soldiers were shell-shocked or otherwise impaired, unfit for jobs even if these had been available. To the conservative-minded, all Britain seemed shell-shocked. The psychological rebound from the hardship of war, both civilian and military, led to a mania for dancing, jazz music, and American cocktails. The motor scooter, pogo stick and mah-jong, a complicated Chinese game, became the craze one after another. Journalism went "yellow" and university undergraduates went Bohemian; young women took to lipsticks, to stimulants, and to companionate marriage; the divorce rate doubled; and learned exponents of Freudian philosophy put all the blame for human unhappiness on "inhibitions."

The economic situation was both ominous and dolorous. England's foreign trade had fallen badly during the war and there seemed little likelihood of its recovery, not as long as Germany and Russia, two of her best customers, were too poor to buy. The British coal trade, over-expanded by the war, now came in competition with cheap German coal, turned over to the French and Italians as part payment on reparations. British shipping was surfeited with extra cargo space provided by the surrendered merchant ships of Germany just at a time when exports were falling off. British shipyards consequently became as idle as British coal mines. For a time it looked as though Britain would have to fight a war within after the war without, this time against unemployment. Her finances were in better shape than were those of her sister democracy across the Channel; but whereas France at a pinch could live largely on her agriculture, to Britain foreign trade was a necessity of life.

This explains why the British speedily sought to change those economic clauses of the peace treaty which led to Germany's default on reparation payments and to the French occupation of the Ruhr. Lloyd George, who had been more responsible than any other man for imposing the economic penalties of the peace, promptly tried to reverse himself, and at an international conference at Genoa had believed hopefully that his magnetic eloquence might win the French over to his point of view. Lloyd George failed. His successor in office, Bonar Law, tried to prevent the French from entering the Ruhr. He failed. Bonar Law even offered to remit the French debt to England if the French would cut down correspondingly on Germany's debt to France. Again he failed.

The British were in favor of letting bygones be bygones and of starting up business again. They suggested to the United States that if the latter would cancel the British debt to America of some $4,000,000,000, the British would cancel continental debts due them far greater in amount. But the Americans had the idea that the British could and would pay, and so were adamant ("They hired the money, didn't they?"—Coolidge). Thereupon the British signed a debt agreement with the Americans whereby they agreed to pay the debt in full over a period of sixty-two years but with reduced interest.

Lloyd George, meanwhile, lost his wartime popularity; he had promised to make England a land fit for heroes, and four years after the war that promise remained unfulfilled; with his usual buoyancy he had tackled the Irish problem, only to be smartly rebuffed by Sinn Fein; the French refused to take him seriously in the matter of reparations; the vigorous Turks made mincemeat of his Near Eastern policy; and the enemies within his own Liberal party, numerous and influential, awaited impatiently his downfall. He was Prime Minister of a national coalition the mainstay of which was the Tory party which detested him. His prestige once gone, the Tories inevitably would drive him out. They did so in 1923 and took over the government on a one-party basis, first under Bonar Law, the Canadian-born British statesman who died within the year, and then under Stanley Baldwin.

The First Ministries of Baldwin and MacDonald

Baldwin promptly was defeated for advocating a protective tariff and in the ensuing election he won a plurality of seats but was without a majority. To the surprise of almost everyone the historic Liberal party, torn between the followers of Lloyd George and those of H. H. Asquith, came out third in the race, second place falling to MacDonald and his Laborites.

The Labor party in theory was socialistic. During the election it had advocated the nationalization of railways and mines, and a capital levy on large fortunes. To put it in control of Britain's fortunes seemed a most dangerous procedure. Yet that is what the British Liberals did. The alternative was to support Baldwin, and they considered MacDonald the lesser of two evils; after all, they would hold the whiphand over the Socialists and forestall any danger by voting with the Conservatives! As a matter of fact, there was no trouble. The Labor party had long been committed to the truly British policy of "gradualness." The idea of revolution was repudiated and the Laborites regarded Moscow with almost as much abhorrence as did the Tories themselves.

Once in office Labor took no steps toward a capital levy; instead it contented itself with various odds and ends of amelioration, the building of inexpensive homes on a moderate scale by government subsidies, the removal of taxes on cheap movie tickets and their reduction on sugar and chocolate. The Cabinet seemed quite bent on proving itself British first and Socialist second. MacDonald was an effective worker for international peace; he promoted the inauguration of the Dawes' plans; he tried to gain the good will of the Japanese by suspending work on the great Singapore naval depot; and he even made certain friendly gestures toward Soviet Russia.

The latter brought about his downfall. Lloyd George somewhat earlier had renewed commercial relations with Russia and these MacDonald sought to implement by an Anglo-Russian treaty, a commercial, not a military or political understanding. But Russia to good Britons was still a most dangerous country, and when British Communists, supposedly under orders from the Third International in Moscow, tried to sow discontent among British workers the British Liberals joined with the Tories and voted MacDonald out. A dramatic election followed. Mac-Donald might have been returned to triumph had it not been for a mysterious letter (presumably forged) purporting to have been written by Zinoviev, head of the Third International, urging the revolt of British workers. Middle-class Britain saw red in reverse and middle-class Britain had belonged for the most part to the Liberal party. In fear and anger lest MacDonald win, it surged to the polls and gave Baldwin a majority over all. The Labor party lost only a few seats; but the Liberal party was reduced to a mere thirty-six and no longer held even the balance of power. From this date on it was hardly more than a cypher in British politics.

The Second Baldwin Ministry

Baldwin returned to power in 1924 to be confronted by one of the most serious crises in British history. The British coal miner during the World War had won a decent working day of seven hours and had been granted minimum wages. The wage was not high but it soon proved impossible to pay it and at the same time operate the mines at a profit. The coal trade was in the doldrums everywhere in the world in the nineteen-twenties, owing to the increased use of gasoline, oil, and hydro-electric power, and the coal trade of Britain was in even a more precarious plight than elsewhere, owing to the great depth of the mines, which made their operation expensive, and to substantial royalties paid to ground landlords like the Duke of Northumberland, who held title and merely rented coal lands to operating companies, assuming no responsibility for management.

What should be done? The miners, highly organized, adopted a slogan and clung to it desperately: "Not an hour on the day, not a penny off the pay." The operators said there was nothing to do but close the mines. The government, in desperation, subsidized miners' wages and this kept the mines in operation. They could not do this indefinitely at the expense of the nation and therefore a commission was appointed, to report in 1926 that the only salvation for the coal mining industry lay in closing certain uneconomic mines and in increasing the hours of labor in others.

Baldwin supported his commission, withdrew the subsidy, and the Trade Union Congress voted a general strike throughout Britain, all good union men, whatever their jobs, to lay down tools, certain exceptions being made for lighting, sanitary, and health services.

This was bringing revolutionary pressure to bear on Parliament, since if the Trade Union Congress could compel government to bow to its will in this matter it could do so in others and thus would become the real source of authority in the state.

The strike was badly managed. MacDonald and other leaders of the Labor party supported the miners in theory but had no stomach for a real fight on this issue; nor for that matter did the Trade Union Congress. Not so the British middle class. A vast number of amateur middle-class volunteers hastened to run the railways, to unload cargoes, to deliver food. There was little violence and the Trade Union Congress after only a few days rescinded the general strike orders. The miners, considering themselves betrayed, fought on for several months but ultimately succumbed. Parliament overwhelmingly supported Baldwin, and in 1927 passed an act curbing trade-union activities and making all general strikes illegal.

Aside from this, Baldwin resisted successfully the drive within his own party for a more authoritarian government. If he would not yield to the left, he would not give way to the right, which saw its opportunity at this time to strengthen the powers of the House of Lords. The Prime Minister, indeed, was not ill disposed toward labor; he brought about pensions for widows and he did lower the price of tea. Hopefully, he looked forward to an increase in international trade, of which there was some indication. "Safety First" was his motto; unemployment is bad, but not so bad as it was; all we need is to wait for clearer skies! This philosophy did not appeal to the impoverished electorate, and in 1929 it voted Baldwin out and MacDonald in once more.

The National Government

Again MacDonald had a plurality in the Commons, but again his total Labor strength was less than that of the Conservatives and Liberals combined. In foreign affairs this ministry was a creditable one, particularly in regard to disarmament, but at home his best efforts proved unavailing. His political dependence on the ever diminishing Liberals continued to irk him, and furthermore there was revolt within his own party. The "wild men of the Clyde," as the leftist Laborites were called, demanded a capital levy and party discipline disintegrated. Before, however, an open rupture broke out, the coming of the international trade depression of 1930-33 brought about a financial crisis in England such as that country had not experienced since the black year of 1797, when she faced Revolutionary France without allies and the Bank of England suspended specie payment.

The storm broke in 1931. Unless drastic reductions were made in relief costs, the bankers held, it would be impossible to make the necessary loans to save the pound sterling and the Bank of England. MacDonald reluctantly consented to the economies demanded, but he found it impossible to carry his party with him. Thereupon he resigned and formed a "National Government" supported by Conservatives, Liberals, and those Laborites who stayed loyal to him. Instantly, a ten per cent cut was made in all forms of individual remuneration, from the unemployed on the dole to police, admirals, generals, and cabinet ministers. The government went off the gold standard, thus depreciating the pound; the budget was balanced, the necessary loans made, and financial England weathered the worst storm encountered in over a century.

The price was heavy. MacDonald was still prime minister, at the head of a coalition. But his own Labor party, which had been steadily growing in numbers and experience ever since its creation, received as deadly a blow as the Liberal party in 1886; and in the Parliamentary election of 1931 it sank to 52 members. The Conservatives rose to 470, a signal triumph; and the Liberals, divided into warring factions (one supporting the National Government, the other opposing it), netted 70 seats.

From 1931 to 1935 MacDonald headed this National Government. It was such in name only, since the Tories had a large majority over all. The Tories now pressed for protective tariffs and this time they got them. A ten per cent levy was made on imports and some success attended the government's efforts to make reciprocal trade agreements with the Dominions. Thus unmourned and almost overnight died the free-trade dream of Cobden and of Bright. And it was not only free trade that perished. The National Government repudiated in fact, if not in theory, many other chosen tenets of laissez faire; it compelled agreements to fix prices in many industries; it granted financial aid to agriculture; it guaranteed loans to railways and built motor highways; and it heavily subsidized the building of new homes for the poor.

During this third ministry of the Scottish socialist (really but a continuation of his second), the Liberal party disintegrated rapidly. There were Liberals who supported both the National Government and the tariff; other Liberals supported the government except on the tariff issue; other Liberals kept warm the dying embers of an independent Liberal party; and a tiny group of still other Liberals held aloof under the now scarred banner of that drummer boy of the World War, David Lloyd George. The Labor party was also torn asunder; the rank and file, bitter foes of MacDonald, were bereft now, not only of his leadership, but of any leadership worth the name. MacDonald himself was saddened by the hatred of the many common people who once had trusted him and who now assailed him as a traitor to labor. A sick and disillusioned man, he gladly surrendered the reins of office in 1935 to his erstwhile political enemy, Mr. Baldwin.

The latter still kept up the pretense of a National Government. He took quick advantage of a most critical turn in international relations to hold a new parliamentary election, and the country again underwrote the Conservative control of Britain, although with a reduced majority. This third ministry of Baldwin, like the third one of MacDonald, was of the stop-gap variety. Baldwin, like his predecessor, was old, tired, discouraged. He saw the country through a temporary flurry created in 1936 by the death of George V and the unwillingness of Edward VIII to be crowned without his right to marry an American divorcée being recognized. With the coronation of Edward's younger brother as George VI in 1937, Baldwin resigned.

He was succeeded by Neville Chamberlain, second son of Joseph Chamberlain. The new Prime Minister was considered not as brilliant as his older half-brother Austen, but as one nevertheless well suited to carry on the middle-of-the-road policy of the amiable Baldwin. The Chamberlain ministry was given over largely to foreign affairs, and we shall note later in another chapter how the constant surrender of the Prime Minister to the incessant clamors of Mussolini and Hitler tended to make him unpopular, not only with the Labor opposition but with many of the abler Conservatives.

Economic Recovery

Between 1932 and the outbreak of war in 1939 there was a slow but steady economic recovery in Britain. The proud commercial hegemony of the world which was Britain's in 1914 did not come back; certain of her former leading industries, such as coal mining, shipbuilding and cotton manufacturing, remained in the doldrums; but the country as a whole did become more prosperous than at the height of the depression; unemployment was reduced and the budget was balanced.

The "New Deal" in America somewhat erroneously has been held to have copied British precedents. It did so in part; both countries went off the gold standard and depreciated their currencies; both countries developed social security programs, the British implementing what they had inaugurated before the First World War, the Americans copying British precedents; and both countries adopted complicated controls over industry. But here the general parallel comes to an end. In America the major answer to the economic black-out in the early thirties was found in public works. In Britain, as to some extent in the United States, it took the form of financial coöperation with business, provided management agreed to accept certain directions and controls.

Thus in Britain in 1932 a "Wheat Act" set standard prices for wheat and when the market price fell below that set, a subsidy was paid the wheat grower. In 1933 a "Potato Marketing Scheme" was devised. The national government established a "Milk Marketing Board" and all Britons who sold milk had to contribute to regional pools with provision made for a minimum price. Subsidies were granted for the beet sugar industry, for cattle raising; and by an intricate system of quotas what actually amounted to a protective tariff on agricultural products was enforced.

To encourage new industries a great deal of emphasis was placed upon electric power. A Central Electricity Board known as "The National Grid" was set up which subsidized 135 generating stations, and as a result power became cheaper and very many new industries were developed, particularly in the neighborhood of London.

The problem of housing was also stressed. Subsidies paid builders and home owners for new houses began as early as 1923, and the duty of the government decently to house those on the lower income level has been constantly emphasized since that date. Altogether between the two World Wars over one and a quarter million new homes were constructed in Britain by governmental aid.

It cannot be said that the problem of poverty was solved; in fact, in certain areas, particularly in South Wales, and in sections of Northern England, it continued to be very acute. In 1933 the national government flatly refused to spend money on any larger scale in public works; that method of relieving poverty it considered extravagant and wasteful. In 1934 it did appropriate some £2,000,000 for the "depressed areas," a beggarly sum in view of the distress there. But it followed this in 1935 by a so-called "Means Test," whereby the dole given to unemployed men and women for their support and that of their families was reduced to the lowest possible minimum consistent with bare existence, a direct blow at the physical well-being of the nation.

"It was all very puzzling," wrote the English novelist Priestley in his *English Journey*, published in 1934.

Was Jarrow still in England or not? Had we exiled Lancashire and the Northeast coast? Were we no longer on speaking terms with cotton weavers and miners and platers and riveters? Why had nothing been done about these decaying towns and their workless people? Was everybody waiting for a miracle to happen? I knew that doles had been given out, Means Tests applied, training places opened, socks and shirts and old books distributed by the Personal Service League and the like; but I was not thinking of feeble gestures of that kind, of the sort of charity you might extend to a drunken old ruffian begging at the back door. I meant something constructive and creative. If Germans had been threatening these towns instead of Want, Disease, Hopelessness, Misery, something would have been done quickly enough.[1]

[1] J. B. Priestley, *English Journey* (Harper and Brothers), p. 327. Reprinted by permission of the publishers.

What was the answer? The Labor party, of course, thought it knew. It wanted nationalization of railways, mines, and banking. But the Labor party was powerless, partly because a three-cornered fight in labor circles almost paralyzed that political party. The machinery of the Labor party was in the hands of conservative trade unionists who would have nothing to do with the Independent Labour party, strong in ability but weak in numbers. And neither the I.L.P. (Independent Labour Party) nor the official Labor party would have anything to do with the British Communists. In vain did Sir Stafford Cripps with his Socialist League endeavor to bring these warring elements together. Cripps, a brilliant and wealthy lawyer, was regarded with suspicion by orthodox labor and was expelled from the party. British workmen would not work together in politics. And even if they had been willing to do so, they might not have been able to carry the Parliamentary election of 1935, for the economic skies were brightening somewhat by that date and to the British poor, desiring employment above all else, half a loaf was an encouraging sign.

Pacifism Versus Preparedness

More serious in the long run for Britain was the failure of her statesmen and of her people to realize the peril which confronted her abroad. The former, perhaps, may have been blamed too much for their folly in appeasing the Axis, since for the most part they did but follow the public opinion they should have led. The average Briton was most pacifically inclined; he was fed up with war and war talk; he placed a most curious and blind trust in the League of Nations even after the impotencies of that organization were manifest to all the world; and while he was opposed to Nazi terrorism he refused to consider seriously the Nazi threat to European peace. In all this the worker believed as many of his betters did.

Pacifistic propaganda made headway everywhere. The British masses were only mildly interested in the death struggle of the Spanish Republic. The appeasement of Hitler and Mussolini which is dealt with elsewhere in this book was not cheered, but the government which indulged in it was never in danger of an adverse majority in the House. One of the most popular books of the decade was *Cry Havoc,* published in 1933. It was made compulsory reading in hundreds of schools, and overseas the Department of Education in Toronto, Canada, alone bought 7,000 copies. Pacifists in the pulpit and in the press pledged themselves to participate in no more wars, and over one thousand enthusiastic British men and women agreed to march unarmed between the ranks of future opposing armies, there to die for peace. Even at Oxford the undergraduates voted that never again would they fight for king and country.

There were, of course, countercurrents, one stirred up primarily by

Winston Churchill over air power, the other by British sea dogs concerning the American navy and Singapore. But these countercurrents carried little weight against the tide of "peace in our time."

The Singapore Naval Base

The friction between British and American admirals in regard to the size and number of cruisers made good newspaper copy, but in reality it was of no great import. Far more significant was the long-drawn-out debate over the creation of a great naval base at Singapore. The Washington Conference of 1922 once more focused attention on the Far East; it also brought an end to the Anglo-Japanese Alliance and thereby isolated the Anzac Dominions. Whereupon the British admiralty saw its chance to realize Sir Stamford Raffles' dream of the early nineteenth century—Singapore not only an entrepôt of Asiatic trade but also a naval bastion of empire. The Tory government of Baldwin backed the admiralty and in 1923 preliminary surveys were made.

Since £20,000,000 was about to be spent, an uproar arose in Labor and Liberal circles, where it was pointed out that the money might better be used to clear slums and to educate the young. Furthermore, they said, the fortification of Singapore although not technically a violation of the Washington treaty did violate its spirit and indicated a lack of faith in the League of Nations.

At this juncture MacDonald became prime minister and immediately work on the new base was suspended. And now a new uproar arose, this time in Conservative circles and in the Anzac Dominions, who felt that they were left undefended in case of future trouble with Japan.

MacDonald, as we have seen, was shortly shooed out of office and Baldwin promptly renewed the Singapore project. One main feature of it, the towing of a huge 50,000-ton drydock all the way from Britain to Singapore, was completed in 1928, much to the satisfaction of imperial-minded Britons everywhere, and much to the dissatisfaction of Japanese public opinion, highly inflamed by the jingo press of Nippon.

The British Labor party upon its return to office in 1929 was not pleased with the fortification of Singapore, but since so much money had already been spent on the enterprise they did not propose its abandonment. Work, however, on the base was retarded, so much so that the completion of what was popularly hailed as an impregnable Gibraltar of the Pacific was not attained until 1938. Nor was it then fortified against attack by land.

Churchill Sounds the Alarm

Far more significant than Singapore were the Cassandra prophecies of Winston Churchill, who, like his father before him, ever was a thorn in the side of Tory complacency. Outspoken and bulldoggish, the future war premier had no confidence whatever in disarmament proposals adumbrated in many conferences in the twenties and thirties. What dominated his imagination was the potential strength of the Third Reich and the rapid growth of the Nazi Party. He did *not* believe that *all* the Nazis wanted was equality of status, and he warned the Commons as early as 1932 that "all these bands of sturdy Teutonic youth, marching through the streets and roads of Germany, with the light of desire in their eyes to suffer for their Fatherland, are not looking for status. They are looking for weapons, and when they have weapons, believe me, they will then ask for the return of lost territories and lost colonies."

This speech was delivered in November, 1932, less than three months before Hitler was appointed Chancellor by Hindenburg. But Churchill was regarded as a firebrand who only caused trouble and MacDonald wished to make a pacifistic gesture at the coming Disarmament Conference at Geneva. Therefore, instead of increasing the appropriation for the Royal Air Force (RAF) he diminished it.

Look out, cried Churchill, we are only fifth in potential air power (France, Italy, Japan, and the United States all were rated above Britain); Germany is our nearest neighbor and Germany is rearming. But Churchill, according to Sir Herbert Samuel, Liberal leader in the Commons, used "the language of a Malay running amok," and few heeded his warning.

The skies now darkened rapidly; Germany left the League; Germany announced conscription; Germany rearmed fast. As she did so, Churchill did his best to arouse his lethargic countrymen. "It would be folly," he said in May, 1935, "for us to act as if we were swimming in a halcyon sea, as if nothing but balmy breezes and calm weather were to be expected." The British were increasing their air force at last, but the Nazis were increasing theirs at a faster tempo. Already they had surpassed Britain.

Came 1936, the abandonment of Haile Selassie in Ethiopia, the abandonment of sanctions, and Britain continued to fall farther behind. Midsummer holidays were due, but to Churchill rest and peace were illusions. "Do not forget," said he, "that all the time those remorseless hammers of which General Goering spoke are descending night and day in Germany, and that the most warlike . . . people in Europe are becoming welded into a tremendous fighting machine. . . ." "The army," he said in 1936, "lacks every weapon which is required for the latest form of modern war. Where are anti-tank guns, where are the short distance wireless sets, where are the field anti-aircraft guns. . . . ? Nothing has been done in the years the locust hath eaten, to equip the tank corps with new machines." In quality, British tanks were inferior to those of Germany, Russia, Italy, and the United States. The RAF, Churchill estimated, had 960 first-class planes, the Germans 1,500. "Owing to our past neglect," he affirmed, "in the face of the plainest warnings, we have now entered upon a period of danger greater than has befallen Britain since the U-boat campaign was crushed."

Baldwin's Parliamentary apology for this state of affairs aroused some criticism but few listened to Churchill. Not even in the year of Munich (1938) would they listen to him. "For five years," he said,

I have talked to the House on these matters—not with very great success. I have watched this famous island descending incontinently, fecklessly, the stairway which leads to a dark gulf. It is a fine broad stairway at the beginning, but after a bit the carpet ends. A little farther on there are only flagstones, and a little farther on still these break beneath your feet. Look back over the last five years. It is true that great mistakes were made in the years immediately after the War. But at Locarno we laid the foundation from which a great forward movement could have been made. Look back upon the last five years— since, that is to say, Germany began to rearm in earnest and openly to seek revenge. If we study the history of Rome and Carthage, we can understand what happened and why. It is not difficult to form an intelligent view about the three Punic Wars; but if mortal catastrophe should overtake the British Nation and the British Empire, historians a thousand years hence will still be baffled by the mystery of our affairs. They will never understand how it was that a victorious nation, with everything in hand, suffered themselves to be brought low, and to cast away all that they had gained by measureless sacrifice and absolute victory—gone with the wind!

Now the victors are the vanquished, and those who threw down their arms in the field and sued for an armistice are striding on to world mastery.

Chapter 11

THE BRITISH COMMONWEALTH

THE GREATER Britain overseas was neither commonwealth nor empire; it was both. The four Dominions, Canada, Australia, New Zealand, and the Union of South Africa, comprised the Commonwealth; all other lands over which his Majesty's government held sway, the Empire.

The First World War wrought great changes in the constitutional status of the Dominions. Not only had they raised armies and fought battles; they had been consulted openly, confidently, by Great Britain. Lloyd George's Imperial War Cabinet had been a true Commonwealth Cabinet, the premiers of the Dominions sharing in decisions of moment to the Empire, their influence and position well above that of many members of the ministry who debated on the floor of the House. The peace conference brought the premiers still greater prominence. The Dominions had separate representation, five British premiers, representing five different electorates, participating in the settlement of the war. Even if the Dominion premiers were subordinate in fact as well as in theory to their colleagues from England, their influence was felt in many ways. On the commission which dealt with Greece was Canada's representative; on that which decided Poland's boundary was Smuts of South Africa. Hughes, the Australian, was consulted about Czechoslovakia and reparations. Furthermore, in the projected League of Nations seats were duly provided for each Dominion; and at the grand conclusion of the Congress of the Nations in the Hall of Mirrors, their premiers signed the peace treaty separately on behalf of their own nations.

The Versailles treaty was ratified by all four Dominions, but not without considerable grumbling in three. In Australia, Mr. Hughes announced that his government had not been sufficiently consulted; the Americans had interfered, and German New Guinea, which otherwise would have been annexed by Australia, was now only a mandate. Besides, as a result of the treaty the Japanese were now two thousand miles nearer Australia. In Canada there was criticism of Article X of the League of Nations covenant guaranteeing each signatory its territorial integrity.

Opposition in South Africa was stronger. There were three major political groupings: the South African Party, a union of British immigrants and Dutch farmers (Boers), pledged to reduce friction between the two nationalities; the Nationalist Party, a purely Boer organization bitter against British annexation of the two Dutch republics; and the Unionist Party, purely British in membership and spirit, intent upon opposing Boer or Afrikander nationalism, as it came to be called. The Nationalists desired to repudiate the treaty, since its authors had ignored their claims. At the conclusion of the war they had betaken themselves to Paris to urge before the peace conference the cause of the Boers. This they were not permitted to do, although an audience was granted them by Lloyd George. It was easy for him to argue that, since the Nationalists were in a minority in the Union, they could not well contend that they were deprived of self-determination. He had been their friend during the South African War; but the Union constitution of 1909 had met with their approval; they could not now reverse their position. The Nationalists returned home, angry. They found nothing to praise in the work of the peace conference. "The League of Nations," said one of them in the Union legislature, "was built on a foundation of pillage and hypocrisy." "The treaty," exclaimed another, "breathes the spirit of domination, jealousy and revenge." But they were helpless to prevent its ratification. The South African Party had a plurality of votes in Parliament; when assisted by the Unionists, pro-British to a man, a safe majority was assured. The S.A.P., as it was called, found a clever leader in General Smuts. The latter had no difficulty in maintaining his liaison with the Unionists, and the treaty therefore received the imprimatur of the Union government.

The Dominions and British Foreign Policy

For decades before the War the Dominions had been self-governing except as to foreign policy, which by general consent, although not by statute, had been left to the mother country. In 1919 it became a question whether they were even thus bound. The covenant of the League gave them seats in the Assembly; were their votes there to be considered British votes as such or were the Dominions virtually independent nations, free to determine their own foreign policy? Just what was their status? The situation was anomalous, even to British statesmen not customarily troubled by want of logic in constitutional practice.

Before the War many Britons, both at home and abroad, had argued in favor of imperial federation, closer unity; but after the war there were fewer to favor it. Hughes of Australia was violently opposed. "I think," he said, "the surest way of destroying this mighty empire is to tamper with its constitution. Complete autonomy of the parts is the foundation upon which it rests." In Canada, as though it was the most casual thing in the world, the government announced that a Dominion embassy would be established at Washington. As for South Africa, General Smuts announced in Parliament that the peace conference had been a "formal recognition of the new position of the Dominions, and that in foreign relations they were to take part and speak for themselves, and that they no longer would be bound by the voice and signature of the British Parliament."

General Smuts' political position was delicate. The South African Party which he headed was composed principally of Boers, and a continuous flow of deserters constantly made its way toward Hertzog and the Nationalist tent. The very brilliance of Smuts' speeches and his unrivalled mental acumen brought him under suspicion. This philosopher-statesman, so idealized in Britain, was he true to the Afrikander? The Nationalists intimated that he was not, and as a result turned the election of 1920 against him.

The political divisions in the Assembly, after the election, show some striking changes:

	Number of seats before 1920	After 1920
South African Party	53	41
(mainly Afrikander, but friendly toward the Commonwealth)		
Unionists	38	25
(solidly British)		
Nationalists	27	44
(Boer irreconcilables)		
Labor	6	21
(Socialistic and, for the most part, indifferent toward the Commonwealth)		
Independents	6	3

For the first time in the history of the Union the extreme party of independence had a plurality of votes in the Assembly; and in order to carry on the King's government through the agency of the South African Party, Smuts had to form some kind of coalition. To do this he turned first to the Nationalists, attempting to bring the two Boer factions together. The Nationalists, however, insisted on a republic; the S.A.P. stood staunchly for Dominion nationality within the Empire. On this point there could be no compromise. The General turned now to the Unionists. The latter were willing to do anything to defeat Hertzog, even to the extent of committing political suicide. This, in effect, they did since they agreed to destroy their own political organization and to merge themselves completely in the South African Party. The political atmosphere being thus cleared, Smuts struck home and appealed to the electorate, this time winning the election for the S.A.P.

Dominion Representation

In 1921 an imperial conference between the Dominion premiers and the British ministry convened in London. Winston Churchill, the ubiquitous, was colonial secretary and the conference was ambitiously baptized by him, "Imperial Cabinet." The delegates from overseas, however, did not take to this innovation. Cabinet was synonymous with authority, and they feared centralized authority in London; that word and the word *imperial* was dropped, this meeting of British statesmen preferring the title of "Conference of the Prime Ministers of the Empire."

The program was extensive but the results meagre. The conference supposedly discussed the Pacific problem of the Anglo-Japanese treaty of 1902, and its possible renewal, the division of reparation receipts from Germany, the possibility of placating Indian opinion by alleviating the conditions under which Indians lived in the Dominions, and the possibilities of empire-settlement and migration. But the gravest question of all, that of Dominion partnership in British foreign policy, was left untouched.

Yet the problem of Dominion representation at the forthcoming disarmament conference at Washington showed the need for some common understanding in regard to that partnership. No individual invitation to attend had been given to the Dominions, since the American government thought it discourteous to the British government to issue one; whereupon the Dominions took offense. General Smuts intimated that if not invited in their own right they should ignore the proceedings; Hughes spoke of the American invitation to Great Britain alone as "slamming the door." Here was protocol with a vengeance, and Dominion sensitivity was only partially allayed by drafting an Australian, a New Zealander, and a Canadian on the British Empire delegation, Mr. Balfour signing the Washington treaty twice, once for the Empire and once for South Africa.

The ostensible object of the Washington Conference was the cutting down of naval expenditure; but this could only be obtained by abrogating or fundamentally altering the Anglo-Japanese Alliance. The treaty which inaugurated this pact, as renewed in 1905, guaranteed military aid in case "either contracting power should be involved in war in defense of its territorial rights or interests." That treaty threatened to involve Britain in war with America should the latter country come to blows with Japan. To make this impossible Britain and America had entered into special treaty obligations which provided for mutual arbitration of all difficulties. But the Senate of the United States amended this treaty in certain vital particulars and President Taft refused to accept the amendment. Thereupon the United States and Britain agreed, in 1914, to a treaty which provided for a peace commission to investigate all causes of difference between the two countries. This was not a treaty of arbitration, techni-

cally speaking; but Downing Street gave notice to Tokyo, although not
to Washington, that it should so consider it, and would regard it as
coming under the special clause in the second renewal of the Anglo-
Japanese treaty in 1911 which excluded from the pact any country with
which either signatory had a treaty of arbitration.

The Americans did not hear of this qualification until 1921, and in the
meantime the race for naval supremacy in Pacific waters continued apace.
British statesmen saw nightmares; they did not want to break with
Japan; they did not want to antagonize America; and they must not
antagonize their own Dominions. The Japanese, on the other hand, disliked the qualifications read into the treaty by the British in regard to
America; the United States was ill disposed toward any Anglo-Japanese
alliance; and the British Dominions, like the mother country, desired to
avoid friction with America. The result was highly satisfactory to the
Dominions, even if not to other participants; they at least obtained what
they wanted, the abrogation of the Anglo-Japanese treaty and recognition for themselves as co-partners in the British Commonwealth.

The year of the Washington Conference was also the year of the
Chanak incident, which demonstrated an unsatisfactory state of affairs as
far as the relations of the Dominions to British foreign policy went.
Mustapha Kemal, at the head of the Turkish Nationalists, having driven
the Greeks into the sea, turned his forces against Constantinople. The
porcelain treaty of Sèvres was threatened with destruction; and of the
European signatories Great Britain alone gave proof of a willingness to
defend it. Under Lloyd George's direction a small British force was
landed at Chanak, on the Asiatic side of the Dardanelles, and an ultimatum delivered to Mustapha Kemal. The British pickets again faced
those of Turkey as in 1915; war seemed imminent and the Prime Minister
of England appealed by cable to the Dominions for support.

Except for New Zealand they were not as ready to give it as in 1914.
The Prime Minister of the smallest Dominion cabled instantly: "Government of New Zealand desires to associate themselves with action being
taken and will send contingent." Australia was less eager to offer aid.
Hughes' cabinet was prepared "to associate itself with the British government," and was ready, "if circumstances required," to send an Australian
contingent. Canada was even more reluctant, the Prime Minister stating,
"It is for Parliament (the Canadian Parliament) to decide whether we
should participate in wars in different parts of the world." South Africa
aligned herself with Canada. "When the crisis in the Near East was
raised," said General Smuts, "and this Government was addressed by the
British government on the question of sending some contingents to take
part in the operations that might take place in the Near East the Government replied that in a matter ... of such far-reaching issues they would
not commit themselves unless they consulted Parliament."

The reaction of the Dominions to the Chanak affair was disconcerting; supposing a new and more serious crisis should arise, then what? The Dominions and India had participated in the treaty of Sèvres, which broke up the old Turkey; that of Lausanne, which patched certain portions of it together again, had been negotiated and signed solely by Great Britain. Did or did not Lord Curzon's signature involve the Dominions, logically, legally, or morally, in the support of it?

The answer of the Canadian Prime Minister was an emphatic, "No!" "We take the position," he said, "that not having been invited to the Lausanne Conference, not having been represented there, not having, for the reasons which I have mentioned, signed the treaty, the treaty does not impose obligations on Canada, and those parts of the Empire on which it does impose obligations are the only parts that should be expected to sign and ratify."

Shortly after, came Locarno (see p. 184) and when Britain signed that pact she did so with the express provision that the treaty did not apply to India or to the Dominions, unless they chose to sign. From now on it was evident that a distinction must be made in the future between the foreign policy of Britain and that of the Dominions. To quote article nine of the pact: ". . . the present treaty shall impose no obligation upon any of the British Dominions or upon India, until the Government of such Dominion or of India signifies its acceptance thereof."

This was a distinct constitutional departure. At Paris and at Washington the Dominions and Great Britain had stood together. At Lausanne the Dominions were not represented and Canada had insisted that she was under no obligation to enforce that treaty. At Locarno the objections of Canada were formally recognized as valid, and upon Great Britain and Northern Ireland alone fell the onus of supporting the treaty in the name of the Empire.

In accordance with international law, when Britain was at war so also were the Dominions. But in accordance with this treaty it was evident that they might claim not to be. Suppose any Dominion should issue a declaration of neutrality in a war in which Britain was engaged in defense of this treaty of Locarno. What then would be the status of enemy aliens in Bombay, what that of a British warship at Auckland? On the other hand, why should India and the Dominions pledge themselves to Locarno and an agreement purely European in its guarantees? Were the men of West Australia concerned with the delimitation of the Rhine frontier; could one ask them to fight for it?

Immediately there was talk of yet another conference. But could it accomplish anything? Too often, it was felt, had the Dominion premiers been summoned from their own preserves for a friendly chat with the Prime Minister of Britain. Why bring men from half way round the earth for an exchange of social amenities? All vestiges of British control in

Commonwealth and Empire foreign policy had now disappeared. Such traces of subordination to Great Britain as might still be discovered were purely incidental in character: the British flag, the traditional right of veto of the Crown (as dead in the Dominions as in Britain), and the appeal to the Privy Council. Was it worth while to hold parleys over matters such as these?

Many thought that it was. In Australia and in Canada there had been agitation in favor of the appointment of native-born Australians and Canadians as governors-general. In Queensland the appointment of British-born governors had been resented. The Irish Free State had appointed a minister to Washington; why should there not be a representative of South Africa at the Hague, an Australian emissary at Tokyo? The Empire was confronted with a number of minor issues of this description which made for friction between the Dominions and the Motherland. Perhaps it would be just as well to have the Dominions understand, once and for all, that they were free in every respect to follow their own bent.

Baldwin's government wanted to make this quite clear and so it summoned still another imperial conference to meet in London in 1926.

The Imperial Conference of 1926

For the first time in history the relations of the Dominions to the mother country were now defined. The Dominions are, the conference asserted, "*autonomous Communities within the British Empire, equal in status, in no way subordinate one to another in any aspect of their domestic or external affairs, though united by a common allegiance to the Crown, and freely associated as members of the British Commonwealth of Nations.*"

There was nothing new in this pronunciamento; everybody understood before this that the Dominions were free. None the less this formal acknowledgment of equality cleared the air of any possible suspicion of imperialistic rule, and also paved the way for the construction of a true system of coördination. The committee on inter-imperial relations which drew up the above statement indicated in outline how this might be done. Treaties in the future could be signed by all the Dominions, by a number of them or even by one. All treaties were to be in the name of the King, but none were to be negotiated except by the governments concerned. In the Dominions the governors were no longer to be considered the representatives of the British government. Official communications in the future, therefore, would pass not through the governors, as representatives of the British Crown, but direct, government to government. Between the Dominions and Great Britain there was to be absolute equality.

From now on the only direct connection between Britain and the

Dominions lay through the Crown. The governor-general in each Dominion represented the Crown and had the same function in his Dominion as the King possessed in London. Since the King of England was constitutionally bound to accept the advice of his ministers it followed that the King in Canada (the governor-general) was obligated to do likewise. Theoretically, of course, this meant that the King might approve one course of action in England and a diametrically different one in Canada, where the governor-general, the King's alter ego, was equally bound to accept the opinion of the majority in the Canadian Parliament as expressed through the Canadian cabinet. It might seem illogical that the Crown could be thus split, that the King could have five different personalities, one for each Dominion (governor-general) and another as King of England. Nevertheless such was the British system as defined and practiced since 1926. The colonial office had already ceased to exist as far as the Dominions were concerned and a new cabinet officer, secretary of state for the Dominions, was one of his Majesty's ministers. But this official had no powers except to convey information from one government to another. Even the various governors-general were now selected by the Crown on the nomination of the Dominion Prime Ministers.

This curious system meant that the fiction of the Crown was maintained while the authority of the British Parliament was liquidated. There still remained even after 1926 a few who insisted that since Parliament was the source of all authority the decision of a mere imperial conference could not supersede it. To satisfy those critics Parliament passed in 1931 the Statute of Westminster which stated that no law passed by Parliament in the future had any validity in any Dominion without its express agreement. Thus a formal seal of approval was placed upon what already had become an accepted practice.

Dominion Loyalty to the Commonwealth

First and foremost in devotion to the Commonwealth stood New Zealand. Of all the Dominions it was the smallest,[1] the most isolated, the most purely British in blood, and the most closely linked of all to the mother country by commercial ties. Ninety per cent of New Zealand's exports went to Britain, and despite the efforts of her Labor party to build up home industries the one and a half million inhabitants of that country continued to rely on Britain for manufactured goods.

With Australia and Canada it was otherwise. The five million Australians and the fifteen million Canadians were more independent; their respective countries dwarfed Britain in area; their populations were more

[1] Newfoundland, Britain's oldest colony, had dominion status in 1834. Being bankrupt, she asked to be relieved of the expense of self-government. Newfoundland is now (1956) a province of Canada as the result of a plebiscite.

heterogeneous in blood, and in both instances they were more economically independent, establishing their own industries and protecting them behind tariff walls.

Australia had her own tariffs, her own army, her own navy. Betweeen the two World Wars her attention was focused on her own domestic problems, the building of a new capital in the wilderness, the financing of new railroads, the opening of her northern territory, and currency troubles resulting from overexpansion and the world depression of the early thirties.

Canada was somewhat similarly situated. The population of that Dominion was even more heterogeneous than that of Australia. The French Canadians kept aloof; the western provinces were full of immigrants from Eastern Europe and from the United States. The descendants of the old Empire Loyalists who had fled the United States after the American Revolution were more British than most Britons; but they were in a minority. Commercially and financially Canada was closely tied to Britain, but even more closely tied to the United States, the latter taking a greater volume of her exports than the mother country.

Centrifugal forces in Canada and Australia were powerful, but nonetheless the attachment of those two Dominions to the British connection was beyond cavil. Neither of them, for instance, hesitated to declare war against Germany in 1939. But the same was not true of the Union of South Africa. A change of thirteen votes in the South African legislature and the Union would have declared neutrality in the Second World War. What was the reason? The Boer War had ended in 1902 and the British had done their best to make amends for harsh treatment of the two Boer republics during that conflict by turning over the destinies of all South Africa to their keeping, for those of Boer (Afrikander) blood were in the majority in the Union. Nevertheless, memories of the old conflict stayed green and were the constant talk of the veldt. Smuts' popularity with his own people was great, but so, too, was that of General Hertzog, leader of the bitter-enders, the more intransigent Boers who composed the Nationalist Party. General Smuts had put down a strike among the gold miners and therefore was unpopular with the Labor Party. Here was Hertzog's opportunity. To maintain himself in power Smuts had brought into the fold of the South African Party the British voters. Hertzog now sought by the magic power of old association to draw out from it the Boers. "Come out of the House of the stranger," he said to them. The Boers are one in language, blood, and religion. South Africa is their first concern. The Labor and Nationalist Parties should stand as one against Smuts and his adherents, imperialists and agents of foreign capitalism.

Socialism, to the land-owning Boers, was anathema; and the Labor Party was socialistic. To the miners, on the other hand, largely of British origin, secession from the flag of their youth seemed hateful. Was it possible to make a coalition here?

Hertzog cleverly constructed it, and with Labor the South African Nationalists signed a formal pact. By it the Nationalists pledged themselves, if victorious, not to insist on secession from the Empire; by it, Labor pledged itself not to demand confiscatory legislation.

The alliance once struck moved forward to a victorious outcome. Again an election was held in South Africa and this time, to the dismay of the friends of the Commonwealth, Smuts went down to defeat. The seats held by the South African Party decreased from 72 to 53. Those in the possession of the Nationalists increased from 47 to 63. Labor enlarged its membership from 13 to 18. The alliance was victorious and the implacable Hertzog became Prime Minister.

This was in 1924, and from that date to the opening of the Second World War racial and economic strife was the norm in South Africa. Both Smuts and Hertzog were conservative at heart; both were intent upon suppressing socialist agitation among the miners and any agitation among Negroes, heavily in the majority in South Africa; both were Afrikander generals who at one time had fought against British armies; and both were Afrikander nationalists. The only real difference between them was that Smuts believed heartily in the British Commonwealth, whereas Hertzog, though seemingly appeased by the declaration of the conference of 1926, was innately suspicious of British influence and perhaps secretly hopeful that even the British Commonwealth would disintegrate. In 1932 the discreet and conciliatory Smuts went more than half way and patched up an uneasy truce with Hertzog whereby a new political party emerged, the United Party, avoiding the extremists on both sides, and this party with Hertzog as premier and with Smuts as deputy premier controlled South Africa to 1939. When war broke out then Hertzog resigned in a huff because he could not carry a neutrality resolution and Smuts became premier, supported by a very narrow majority, and then only with a promise that South African troops would not be ordered to serve beyond the confines of Africa.

Ireland or Eire

Whether Ireland or Eire should be included in a discussion of the Commonwealth was a moot question. Disaffection in South Africa was rife but it was nothing compared with that in Ireland. During the First World War there was a rebellion in South Africa, but the rebels once conquered were treated with leniency; after the 1916 Easter revolt in Dublin of Sinn Fein (the Irish Republican Party) there was bloody repression, and death by court martial.

The Irish Republicans then adopted new tactics. They boycotted the Royal Irish Constabulary, and they inaugurated Sinn Fein courts of law. Since the members of the constabulary were Irishmen, the refusal of the community round about them to engage in any form of intercourse was an effective weapon. Farmers refused to sell to the constabulary; women would not sit by the members of it in church; no good Irishman, so said Sinn Fein, should even speak to these upholders of an alien rule. Meanwhile, British judges traveled about on empty circuits and held vacant courts. From fear or preference, or both, the people made use only of the irregular and illegal tribunals set up by Sinn Fein. Within a year these were the only courts functioning over a large part of Ireland.

Came then 1920, a year so black in Irish annals that to find its counterpart one must look to the seventeenth century. And now between Irish and British an actual war arose, none the less war although there were no battles, but only raid and counterraid, murder and countermurder. For a year and a half blood was to flow freely in Ireland. The sworn servants of the Crown vied with the members of the Irish Republican army in a saturnalia of crime and cruelty. The British, to assist the fast thinning ranks of the constabulary, introduced into Ireland an auxiliary police force, clad in the old army khaki, but with black glengarry hats. To wear their uniform anywhere in Ireland soon became foolhardy; to wear it after dark or without friends at hand was to invite death. To belong to Sinn Fein, on the other hand, or to be related by marriage to Sinn Fein politician or soldier was all too often held sufficient warranty for prompt execution. Throughout all Ireland the country districts were dangerous and even in large cities the sound of the curfew bell gave warning to beware of assassins.

Between the responsibility of Sinn Fein on the one hand and Dublin Castle on the other the historian can draw no fine distinction. In the words of Mr. Griffith, Sinn Fein's founder: "The military mind is the same in every country. Our military men are as bad as the British.[2] They were. The Sinn Fein army, commanded by Michael Collins, a youthful agitator, was ill disciplined, widely scattered, and composed largely of young boys. By it many acts of vicious cruelty were perpetrated, such as dragging unarmed British officers from their beds and slaying them in cold blood. The "Black and Tans," on the other hand, well-paid, seasoned veterans in many instances of the Great War and hardened to suffering and misery, did not hesitate to burn and destroy the homes of those held suspect, and to shoot in the back prisoners whom they told to run for safety.

Lloyd George, Prime Minister, denounced the Sinn Feiners to high heaven; but after a year he changed his mind, suggested a conference, offered concessions. For weeks the delegates of Sinn Fein wrangled with

[2] P. S. O'Hegarty, *The Victory of Sinn Fein*, p. 47.

the British in London. Dominion status was offered with safeguards, mainly in regard to military and financial matters. One by one, the safe-guards were surrendered by the British. The question of allegiance proved a stumbling block: The Irish would accept no allegiance to the King, but a majority of the delegates agreed "to be faithful to the King by virtue of their common citizenship" in the British Commonwealth. Even this, however, would not satisfy De Valera, the Sinn Fein president, and when he was voted down by a pro-treaty majority in the Irish Parliament, he started civil war. This came to an end by 1924, and the Irish Free State accepted dominion status.

In 1932 De Valera and his extremists carried the elections and swept into power on an anti-British platform. Promptly, De Valera began cutting such slender links as still joined Ireland to Britain; he got rid of the British governor-general; he repudiated the financial agreement whereby, in return for the cession of two strongly Roman Catholic counties in Ulster to the Free State, the latter assumed responsibility for repaying to the British treasury money advanced in the past for the purchase of Irish homesteads; and what is even more significant, the Irish Parliament passed an act defining Irish citizenship as distinct from British citizenship. Eire, or Ireland, was now regarded by De Valera as a distinct and sep-arate country, and when England declared war on Germany in 1939, Ireland, as everyone expected her to do, proclaimed her neutrality, presumably thereby voiding her Dominion status and withdrawing from the Commonwealth.

Ulster, the northeastern province, remained aloof. The majority there so desired it, since it was Protestant in faith, largely industrial by vocation, and still in good measure descended from Cromwellian soldiers and Scottish business men. On the other hand, a very large minority in Ulster wanted union with Eire and still does. That it may some day become a majority is the lively hope of the rest of Ireland.

Chapter 12

THE LESSER STATES OF EUROPE (1919-39)

THE GROWTH of communism in Russia and of its totalitarian counterpart, fascism, in other countries was symptomatic of a general reaction throughout all Europe to the liberal ideology of the nineteenth century. Only a small part of the continent seemed immune to this general wave of discontent, namely, the four Scandinavian nations—Denmark, Norway, Sweden, and Finland, and the small democratic states of Switzerland, Holland, Belgium, and Czechoslovakia.

From 1815 to 1905 Norway had been linked to Sweden under the House of Bernadotte. For all that time there was a Norwegian Parliament, but foreign affairs were conducted under Swedish auspices. The Norwegians in their unfertile valleys would have been desperately poor, indeed, had it not been for the sea. As it was, they not only became noted fishermen but built up an excellent mercantile marine, having in the early twentieth century the largest in the world in proportion to population. Naturally, therefore, they desired their own consular service, and because King Oscar II tried to keep it in Swedish hands, the Norwegian Parliament voted to separate from Sweden and to have a King of Norway.

A prince of Denmark was selected for this honor and under him Norway became more and more democratic; the Norwegians already had universal manhood suffrage, but in 1913 they extended it to include women, and such slight power as had remained to the King in the way of vetoing legislation was abolished.

Swedish democracy, likewise, grew rapidly in strength in the years before the First World War. Until 1863 Sweden had been ranked as one of the more conservative countries in Europe, retaining a strong monarchy and being governed by a kind of medieval estates-general of four houses —nobility, clergy, burghers, and peasants. From that date onward, however, a steady and constant change in the direction of democracy took place, the result of the impact of the Industrial Revolution, for Sweden was not only rich in timber but in iron ore. Woman suffrage, old-age pensions, progressive legislation gave Sweden the reputation of being one of the most advanced democracies in Europe; and the World War seemed to strengthen rather than to weaken Sweden's devotion to democratic ways, that country becoming noted as one which kept to the "middle way," whereby capitalism was so checked and guarded by consumer co-operatives and state intervention on behalf of the poor that the latter remained content with the security which they had gained. Disparity between rich and poor was reduced to a minimum and Sweden seemingly became a kind of middleclass paradise.

It was not otherwise in Denmark. During the long reign of Christian IX (1863-1906) there was sturdy resistance on the part of the King to democratic innovation, but toward the end of his reign, and during that of his successor, particularly in 1914-15, Denmark went decidedly demo-cratic, both houses of the legislature being elected by universal suffrage, the powers of the King becoming nominal. Even before that time, the growth of coöperative agencies for the standardizing of Danish agri-cultural products had given the Danes good training in democratic practices. About one quarter of all the Danes lived in Copenhagen, one of Europe's most charming capitals, where the extremely modest royal castle of a democratic king is quite obscured by a magnificent city hall redolent with the pride of equalitarian burghers.

The fourth Scandinavian country, Finland, had lain under the heavy yoke of Russian imperialism from 1809 to the Revolution of 1917. Fin-land, soon after, jumped into popular notice as a thriving progressive democracy. The Finns paid their debts, experimented democratically with prohibition only to end it, encouraged modern architecture, turned their capital, Helsinki, into a model city, and desperately prepared to defend their hard-earned freedom from renewed Russian aggression in 1939. True, as far as blood and language are concerned, Finland belongs in a separate category from the other three Scandinavian states; but institu-tionally, as well as geographically, she justly may be considered as linked to Denmark, Norway, and Sweden.

All four of these northern countries were members of the League of Nations, and the Danes in particular took a lively interest in its work, a Dane serving on the commission on the Saar Valley, another on the high court, and Denmark herself being elected to serve a term on the council of the League. All four of these countries also have consulted together from time to time during the intervals between the two World Wars. They organized a Scandinavian bloc; they invited coöperation from other small countries, such as Holland; and within them neither fascism nor com-munism seemed to have gained a foothold.

Switzerland was another democratic country, fortunate in that her annals have been so quiet. The twenty-two states or cantons which com-pose Switzerland were bound together by a federation in 1815 and by a somewhat stronger one in 1847 after a brief civil war of three weeks. In almost all matters apart from national defense the twenty-two cantons preserved their autonomy, and six of these semi-independent cantons in this miniature country are so small that pure, unadulterated democracy is possible, voting being conducted on cantonal business directly in huge mass meetings out of doors. Universal military service holds in Switzerland, but the soldier owns his own rifle and takes it home with him. The Swiss, like the Finns, were ever careful to preserve their liberty and their democracy even if they had to fight for it.

In the Netherlands and in Belgium the picture was not radically different. In both of these lands there was much greater concentration of wealth, in the former in commerce, in the latter in manufacturing and mining. Partly because of this, partly because of surviving religious disputes, the Netherlands and Belgium can hardly be considered fully as democratic in their constitutional practice as the other democracies we have considered, for the former country did not adopt universal suffrage until 1917, and the latter not until after the war. Nevertheless, fascism and communism made relatively little headway in either land. The daughter of the Queen of Holland married a German prince, but the Queen and her country both seemed more concerned in regard to the Prince's personal behavior than for fear lest he import German ideas. A curious form of Roman Catholic fascism developed in Belgium—the Rexist movement—only to be routed at the polls. The Social Democrats still remained a powerful faction in the Belgian Parliament, but by definition they were stanch defenders of democracy; and the same also may be said for the Belgian Catholic party.

There remains the republic of Czechoslovakia. Within the borders of this new, or resurrected, country (depending on the point of view) there seemed to lie great promises for the future of democracy. The Czechs, indeed, appeared not only capable of solving those problems which confronted the other small democracies but able also to settle minority problems by democratic means. Surrounded by Fascist and semi-Fascist states, the Czechs were a beacon of light and reason until overwhelmed by the German inundation of 1938-39.

The Czechoslovak state, as set up by the Allied powers in 1919, was both republican and democratic. The legislature, elected by universal, secret, and compulsory voting, was empowered to choose a president to serve seven years. The Czechs themselves were socially democratic; there was little difference in wealth among them; until only recently the great estates and more important industries had been in German hands; the majority of the Czechs had been workmen or peasants.

There was bound to be some trouble, since one-third of the population was non-Czech. The Slovaks caused friction and so did the minority Poles and Magyars. But most troublesome of all was the German minority that lived, for the most part, toward the German border. These Sudeten Germans (a name derived from the Sudeten Mountains) had just cause for complaint. There were discriminations made against the German language; there were other grievances, mainly economic, and, above all, the sense of injustice at being included in the Czechoslovak nation against their will. But it could not be justly said that these Germans were down-trodden; politically they were on a basis of complete equality with the Czechs; they could and did have their own parties in the parliament at Prague; and, up to 1935 when the crisis came about, there were no less than three German parties—the German Agrarian, the Christian Socialist, and the Social Democratic, the three together polling sixty-five per cent of the German vote.

The Czechoslovak Republic justly can be criticized for overcentralization, and some considered that it would have been wise from the beginning to have federalized the country on the Swiss model. The Czechs were afraid to do this. Not having enjoyed freedom for centuries (it was in 1526 that the Austrian Hapsburgs absorbed the Bohemian Crown), they dared not risk the adoption of Swiss federalism. Meanwhile, secure in their military alliance with France, protected, supposedly, by a friendly Russia, the Czechs occupied what seemed to be a strongly defended bastion in Central Europe, an outpost of democracy between Nazi Germany on the north and semi-fascist Austria on the south.

Poland

Among those countries which were neither totalitarian nor democratic, Poland was the most important. That nation, resurrected from the dead by the peace treaty, full of dreams of former glory, were bent on continuing the war after the war by an aggressive anti-Russian campaign not concluded until the Treaty of Riga in 1921. By that date Pilsudski had carried the frontiers of his country eastward beyond those of 1793. Shortly afterward came the Polish occupation of Vilna, forcibly torn from Lithuania, and by 1923 Poland had become a country of 150,000 square miles, with a population of 28,000,000. In area larger than Italy, in population larger than Spain, Poland could now claim to be the sixth most important European state.

But it was a very weak state. Only on the south might it claim to have any natural boundary, the Carpathian Mountains. To the east, the north, and the west, purely artificial boundary lines were drawn, and as one approached those lines the population was of mixed nationality—Polish-German, Polish-Lithuanian, and Polish-Russian. No country in Europe had so many large minority groups within its borders. There were approximately 5,000,000 Ukrainians (Little Russians), 1,500,000 White Russians, 750,000 to 1,000,000 Germans, an indeterminate number of Lithuanians, and some 3,300,000 Jews within Poland. The country was very, very poor. During the First World War, Russian, German, and Austrian armies fiercely had swept back and forth across the Polish plain, and the subsequent two-year war against Russia had added to the devastation. Live stock had been killed, forests destroyed, towns, villages, railways, and bridges ruined. Furthermore, the Poles were without experience in self-rule. Throughout the ninetenth century they had kept alive their longing for nationality, but actual practice in free government had been denied them.

Nevertheless, in the halcyon days of 1919, with sweet freedom in the air, they did their best. The *Sejm,* or Polish Parliament, which assembled in that year was elected not only by universal suffrage but also in accordance with the principles of proportional representation. It drew up a constitution (1921), and a very liberal one, somewhat on the model of that of the Third Republic, the president possessing very limited power.

Pilsudski, Poland's strong man, considered that feature a direct slap at himself, and so he declined to accept the presidency. With Achilles sulking in his tent, Polish politics degenerated speedily into a series of factional fights which only came to an end with a coup d'état on the part of Pilsudski, who marched on Warsaw in 1926 and overthrew the government. Pilsudski, however, did not make himself dictator or establish a totalitarian regime—at least not at first. Instead, he again refused the presidency, although consenting to act as premier. From 1926 to 1935 Pilsudski's role in Polish history is difficult to disentangle. The General certainly played strong-arm politics, even at times imprisoning hostile deputies of the Sejm. Twice he resigned the premiership, only to continue to manipulate elections and parliamentary blocs; and to all intent and purpose he was about to become dictator at the time of his death in 1935, when a new constitution was adopted, one described as an "authoritarian democracy," whatever that is.

That constitution had one very unusual feature. It made an emphatic denial that a totalitarian government was desirable—did not Article 5 state: "The creative action of the individual is the lever of collective life."? On the other hand, the peculiar method adopted for selecting the president of the Polish Republic pointed in the opposite direction. He was to be chosen by a college of electors composed of high officials and members of the Sejm. If the incumbent in the presidential office approved, no further steps were necessary. If, however, he chose to nominate a candidate not approved by the electoral college then a popular vote should decide between the two nominees. Extensive additional powers were also granted the president. He was authorized to issue ordinances having the authority of law during such times as the Sejm was not in session.

In the few years remaining to the Polish Republic before its annihilation at the hands of Germany and Russia in 1939, the political pendulum swung back and forth, not between right and left but between right and center. The Communist party was forbidden and the only question was:

would Poland swing into the fascist column or continue halfway democratic? Army officers took an active part in this struggle. In the cabinets were a number of generals and colonels, and General Smigly-Rydz, commander-in-chief of the Polish army in the one-month war of 1939, was made a marshal and then officially declared "first person in Poland after the President." The marshal, in the eyes of liberals and socialists, was a suspect; he was said to be committed to a fascist program. But this could not be proved.

Poland, as the year of her doom drew near, was most dangerously balanced between democracy and totalitarianism. Superficially the country seemed strong. A Polish port, Gdynia, was constructed on the sandy wastes of the Baltic and through it flowed considerable commerce; a Polish mercantile marine was in the making; and there were even demands for Polish colonies. Seemingly, the government was in good position financially, with monopolies of alcohol, salt, matches, tobacco, and lotteries to buttress up its treasury. But this was on the surface only; below was a poverty-stricken peasantry, so poor that in eastern Poland matches were divided four ways before being struck. The "colonels," now sitting in the political saddle as well as in the military, did not know how to deal with poverty, were not interested in poverty, nor were they more enlightened in regard to the minorities.

The Germans, the Ukrainians, and the Jews in Poland continued an outcry about the discrimination levied against them. Scattered throughout western Poland, German landlords complained that their leases were illegally defined by Polish law courts, and that, contrary to the Treaty of Versailles, the use of German in schools was frowned upon. The Ukrainians asserted that they were deprived of the cultural autonomy promised them, and that even Ukrainian Boy Scouts were disbanded by Polish orders. The Jews, who comprised some twenty-seven per cent of the city population, were humiliated by "ghetto benches," separate seats assigned to Jews in university lecture halls, a practice encouraged by the government, although not ordered by it. The treatment given minorities in Poland was far less fair and just than that guaranteed by her sister republic, Czechoslovakia. In fact, nowhere else in Europe were minorities more at a disadvantage than in Poland. That country, indeed, was in sorry plight as the German hordes drove over the western borders in September, 1939.

Spain

The only large European state spared the horrors of the First World War was Spain. The King, the court, the army, rumor had it, favored the Germans; but British commercial interests were dominant and, isolated as Spain was from the Central Powers, neutrality had been a necessity. After the war Spain swung violently to the right under a military dictatorship (1923-30), then violently to the left under a radical republican government, greatly influenced by communistic ideas (1930-36), then violently to the right again (1936—?) under a military dictatorship established through the active support of the Italian and German dictators.

Spain in 1919 was a constitutional monarchy, but not a well-governed one. Most of the Spanish people, however, were so long accustomed to misrule that opposition to King Alfonso and to the junta of corrupt politicians who controlled the country was not highly developed. There were, however, danger signals flying in two places—in Catalonia, the northeastern province of Spain, and in Morocco.

Catalonia was at once the most prosperous and the most radical section of the Iberian peninsula. It contained the large manufacturing city of Barcelona; it possessed a language and a literature peculiarly its own—the Catalan—for not until the nineteenth century did Catalonia cease to be at least partially autonomous. During the World War the deputies from Catalonia in the Spanish *Cortes* (parliament) had protested as a body against the weight of taxation borne by their constituents, and at the conclusion of that conflict, Catalonia demanded a revision of the Spanish constitution whereby Spain should become a federated rather than a unitary state, the various provinces having parliaments of their own.

In Spanish Morocco, meanwhile, there was active rebellion. Spanish troops sent to defeat it were badly mauled by the Moors, and King Alfonso lost such little prestige as he had managed to retain by issuing orders which resulted in further defeats, one of which resulted in the death of over 10,000 Spaniards. An investigation of these disasters was promptly suppressed (1922), and loud were the complaints in press and Parliament. Alfonso decided to abdicate, not his throne but his constitutional authority. Having made arrangements with General Primo de Rivera for a coup d'état, he left for France.

The general established himself (1923) as military dictator, brought civil liberties to an end, ruled by court martial. For a while it seemed as though Rivera might be as successful as Mussolini, since in many ways he resembled that condottiere chief. Seemingly, the general was a kind of human dynamo, very conceited, and not without ability. He ended successfully the revolt in Africa; he organized a political party, the Patriotic Union, standing ostensibly for country, religion, and monarchy; and he shared political power with it. Unlike Mussolini, however, he grew less popular with the passing years rather than more so. The Spaniards proved more fractious than the Italians; there were mutinies in the army; there were anti-Rivera demonstrations in the universities; and Rivera himself did not enjoy robust health. Suddenly in 1930 he resigned, and Alfonso immediately restored the constitution suspended in 1923 and announced the election of a new Cortes.

But it was too late to save the monarchy. Most Spaniards considered

THE VICTIM

Spain. "Whichever Wins, My Agony Endures!"

(*Punch,* Aug. 12, 1936. Reprinted by permission of the proprietors
of *Punch.*)

Alfonso responsible for the late dictatorship and they did not hesitate
to demand his abdication. The monarch refused to abdicate, but once
again fled the country; and as he did so in 1931 the republic was proclaimed in Madrid.

The foundations upon which it rested were shaky. Few Spaniards had any use for a King who never did anything but run away from trouble; but aside from that one slender thread of unity, there was no common agreement as to the kind of government best suited to the country. On the right were those who favored a political revolution, but who looked askance upon any social revolution which might undertake a redistribution of land, and an educational program which would take away from the Catholic Church its traditional monopoly of Spanish education. On the left were innumerable grades of revolutionary sentiment, running from that professed by Social Democrats (gradualists in temperament, hoping for the piecemeal establishment of socialism) all the way to the more extreme dogmas of the Communists (some favoring Stalin, some Trotsky, but all for the red flag and immediate revolt), and to the Anarchist-Syndicalists (very strong in Barcelona), believing in no government at all and defiantly hoisting the black flag of anarchy.

Delegates drawn from these divergent groups drew up a constitution calling for a "republic of the workers of all classes," a title indicative of a certain leftist tendency in the constitution which was reflected by provisions that made for exclusively lay education and for the confiscation of large landed estates. The more conservative members of the constitutional assembly were not pleased. The more extreme right, namely, the few followers of the exiled Alfonso and those known as Carlists, who favored the pretender to the Spanish throne, began once more to plot against the republican regime, and the moderate right (much larger in numbers) became disaffected.

Shortly it became more so, as the constituent Cortes drove the Jesuits out of Spain and tried to put through an educational program without religious instruction. Under the circumstances it was perhaps foolish to act thus, for the country was over forty per cent illiterate, and to set up a sufficient number of schools to provide overnight for the 250,000 children educated by the monastic orders was impossible for such a poor country as Spain.

The Spanish republicans, indeed, fell into the same error as did the revolutionary leaders in the French Revolution: being more or less contemptuous of religion and thinking it moribund, they awoke the Catholic Church out of its lethargy. They sequestrated immediately all property of the Church not directly used for religious purposes; religious orders were forbidden to teach; the crucifix was removed from all classrooms; divorce was freely granted; and complete separation between Church and State was guaranteed.

The Pope immediately protested against these anticlerical clauses in the constitution, and many Spaniards promptly renewed their interest in a religion which lay dormant but never dead. They found themselves annoyed by the Republic in many other ways; they were angered by the success of the Catalan radicals, who were soon able to obtain a high degree of autonomy for their own province; they were worried by the confiscation (with little or no compensation) of the great estates, estimated at 50,000,000 acres, which were to be given to the peasants. These factors converging together brought about an uprising in Madrid and Seville in the name of a conservative republican dictatorship.

This revolt of the right was quickly squelched, but no sooner was that done than a rising of the left occurred, this time on the part of Anarchists who wanted no government at all and who fomented strikes to do away with it. Confronted, therefore, with revolt and counter-revolt, the constituent assembly felt far from secure as Spaniards voted in 1933 for their first national Parliament under the new constitution.

The popular vote went to the right, although the center parties in the Cortes, together with the left, could have had a small majority. The center, however, preferred the right to the left, and combining with it made possible a rightist ministry. It proved a weak one. Violence broke out on every hand. In Asturias, a mining district in northern Spain, Communists and Socialists forgot their differences and descended on the town of Oviedo. For nine days they held it, sacking banks and churches, and putting many priests to death. In Catalonia Premier Companys proclaimed Catalonia independent of Madrid. And elsewhere in Spain an organization began to be heard from known as the *Falange Española,* started ostensibly for the purpose of protecting nuns from molestation but soon to become famous as a Spanish Fascist party, bent upon the destruction of radicalism by force. The government did, indeed, succeed in crushing out the revolt in Asturias and in Catalonia, but against the incipient anarchy breaking out, now here, now there, it seemed powerless, and in a new election to the Cortes in 1936 it met with repudiation at the hands of the electorate.

This time Spain swung to the left, as the various radical groups, so frequently at each other's throats, combined in what was known as the *frente popular.* Out of 473 members chosen, the leftists now had 266, the center parties 65, and the right only 142. This was the last general election held in Spain. Civil disorder and mob violence prevailed well-nigh everywhere. The various Marxist and anarchist groups claimed that they simply countered violence by justifiable reprisals. The Falangists (Spanish Fascists), on the other hand, reversed that argument. Where the truth lay, none can tell. The facts are that nerves were frayed and patience exhausted on both sides. The conservatives claimed that the government permitted radical mobs to fire churches and to kill priests and nuns, and only intervened when conservatives tried to prevent such acts. The republican government, not communist nor socialist nor anarchist, but influenced none the less by these three groups, asserted that it had a preponderant voice in the Cortes and represented the will of the Spanish people, that the Falangists violated that will, that they took the law into their own hands, that they compelled magistrates "to sentence their opponents and acquit their members." One thing and only one is demonstrable: "the left did not know how to win, the right did not know how to lose. . . . Blue shirts and red shirts covered breasts in which hatred was hatching the most terrible revenge. The shadow of murder was spreading over Spain."[1] For many a year it was to remain there.

Murder is not too strong a word to use for the civil war which raged through Spain from 1936 to 1939, a vicious, cruel, and bloodthirsty war in which not Spaniards alone but many other Europeans, as well as Americans and also Moors, took active part. It began with a revolt in the army, many officers of which were enemies of the republic. Under the command of General Franco, who had been exiled to the Canaries by the republican government, a part of the army stationed in Morocco revolted and invaded Spain, accompanied by the Moors.

The revolt spread, particularly in western Spain, where a Falangist capital was set up at Burgos. Slowly the rebels in the South and West gathered strength, joined forces, and were at the very gates of Madrid. Associated with the Falangists were the Traditionalists (Carlists), and both groups from the beginning had the active sympathy and coöperation of Hitler and Mussolini. It seemed as though only a miracle could prevent the Fascist occupation of the Spanish capital.

That miracle almost occurred; the republicans matched zeal with zeal, and if they lacked military training they had numbers on their side, and also help from without. Airplanes from Russia speedily engaged in duels with Italian planes over Spain, and volunteers dashed to their assistance —exiled Germans, Italians, and radical youth from a dozen countries.

The war soon took on the aspect of a fight betwen international communism and international fascism. Hitler and Mussolini sent armed help to Franco; the former planes and many technicians, the latter doing likewise, and supplying artillery and infantry as well. The Russians soon withdrew their active support, but from England, France, and the United States several thousand individual Communists and left-wing sympathizers dashed to the rescue, forming an international brigade for the defense of the Spanish Republic. The president of the Spanish Republic was no Communist, and his premier, Caballero, was only a Social Democrat; but so loudly did Hitler and Mussolini proclaim the Holy War, and so strongly did the Holy See proclaim the conflict a crusade of Christianity against communism that a large part of the world somewhat wrongly regarded the war as purely a Communist-Fascist duel.

The Spanish Loyalists, as the republicans were called, managed to stave off the inevitable for over two years. They hung on tenaciously to Madrid, even though the Fascist forces were entrenched in the suburbs; they administered a smashing defeat to the confident Italians advancing

[1] A. Mendizabel, *The Martyrdom of Spain*, pp. 264-265.

from the north on that city. But the war in the air they could not fight. Relentlessly, the Fascists with the help of German and Italian planes swept north and west, conquering the poor Basques, who were at once both good Catholics and stanch republicans. With uncalled-for cruelty, low-flying planes carried death and destruction to innumerable small towns. The Loyalists were compelled to abandon Madrid as a capital, though they still kept military control of that city, and they moved their headquarters to Valencia. Then came Franco's drive to separate Valencia from Catalonia. It succeeded, and the Loyalists moved their capital to Barcelona, prepared to put up their last fight in the radical northeast. Soon all of Spain was lost except Madrid and Catalonia; Barcelona fell to the enemy, and the Loyalists, driven up close to the French border, crossed into France. The war was over, Madrid surrendering shortly after.

It had been fought with the utmost ferocity on both sides. The Moors in Franco's employ had been guilty of particularly abominable practices, but for that matter no mercy had been shown by either faction. Meanwhile, the conflict had important repercussions elsewhere in Europe, hastening the military advance of fascism in Italy and Germany, slowly awakening England and France to the dangers which confronted them. But these international aspects of the Spanish Civil War must be left to another chapter.

Austria

The Austrian Republic was proclaimed in Vienna on November 12, 1918, one day after the armistice. In the beginning it was quite democratic, with a constitution resembling that of the Weimar Republic. Slowly but surely, however, the democratic features gave way under the force of circumstances to a full-fledged dictatorship in 1933 under Engelbert Dollfuss, a dictatorship resembling that of Mussolini in certain respects and strikingly different in others.

From the very day of its birth the Austrian Republic was afflicted by two well-nigh incurable diseases—lack of economic self-sufficiency on the one hand and deep-rooted ideological antagonisms on the other. Austria had a large population within a very small area; worse than that, it contained within its borders a large city which once had been the commercial and banking capital of the Danube valley, and which now, having lost its economic hinterland, was in danger of starvation. The plight of Vienna, terrible beyond belief, was alleviated by the League of Nations. In 1922 Britain, France, Italy, and Czechoslovakia backed an international loan through the League for $135,000,000 and Austria struggled to her economic feet, reorganizing her currency and preserving her economic life, albeit with much difficulty, until the international financial crisis of 1929-30.

There were, however, other troubles. The majority of Austrians called themselves socialists; but between the Social Democrats of Vienna, moderate Marxists, and the Christian Socialists of the rural districts there was profound disagreement. The new constitution was federal in character, and since half the money raised by taxation had to be handed over to the particular province in which it was raised, the Social Democrats of Vienna found that they had more money to spend than had the Christian Socialists of the country districts. Vienna spent this money freely in building very decent homes for the working classes and raised increased sums for other social purposes by virtually confiscating the property of the wealthy by high taxes.

The Christian Socialists, much more conservative, disapproved of this radical procedure; they were also attached to the Roman Catholic Church and they hated the agnosticism of the city socialists. They were somewhat akin to the Centre party in Germany, although more powerful, and like that Centre party were really between two extremes, that of the Social Democrats on the left, and that of the Nationalists on the right.

The Austrian Nationalists were divided into two groups; one, under Prince von Starhemberg, was aristocratic, agrarian, Catholic, and, after the advent of Hitler to power, opposed to the submergence of Austria in Germany; the other group consisted of Pan-Germans, clamoring loudly for "*anschluss*," or union with Germany, before long virtually becoming an Austrian Nazi party taking orders from Berlin. Both sections of the Austrian Nationalists added together were in a minority in Austria; but for that matter, neither the Christian Democrats nor the Social Democrats had a majority, and since these two groups would not work in harmony, a democratic government soon became almost an impossibility. The aristocratic Nationalists founded a private army of their own, the Heimwehr, commanded by von Starhemberg; the Social Democrats countered by another private army, the Schutzbund. That of the Nationalists was not opposed to a restoration of the monarchy; it numbered some 60,000 and was better drilled. In the Schutzbund, on the other hand, there were some 100,000 men devoted to the republic; they knew less about fighting, but they did have arms and they were opposed to reaction.

For several years a rather confused political fight followed, mainly along the lines of city against country. During most of that time the Christian Socialists nominally held the reins of government; but they had little jurisdiction over Vienna; their common ground with Starhemberg was slight, and with the Austrian Nazis they had no common ground whatever.

Soon, as the Nazi propaganda spread in Austria, the Christian Socialists under Dollfuss were confronted with a grave decision. Their control of the country was extremely precarious. Dollfuss, an ardent Roman Catholic, was chancellor, and he kept his post by a temporary and tentative alliance with the Social Democrats. The Chancellor sought and obtained the warm friendship of Mussolini as insurance against Hitler and the Nazis. But for it he had to pay a heavy price. The Duce did not like Social Democrats and, to keep the Duce on his side, Dollfuss broke off his alliance with them, and with the help of von Starhemberg established a Christian Socialist dictatorship.

It was not done without severe fighting. The Social Democrats, warned by the example of what had taken place in Germany one year earlier, in 1933, went on general strike. As they did so, Dollfuss sought to disarm them. The Social Democrats thereupon barricaded themselves in the new apartment houses which they had built for the workmen of Vienna and for several days defended them against machine-gun fire. Forced to capitulate, they were disarmed and disbanded and Dollfuss ruled, a Fascist dictator.

It was a "Christian Corporate State" which Dollfuss set up in this year of 1934 with the cordial approval of Mussolini. The republic vanished and democracy vanished with it. A number of corporations with hand-picked members were organized, and these were to elect a president and to rule the country. A parliament was provided with power of veto over the acts of the corporations but with no power of initiating legislation. The real government was Dollfuss, assisted by Starhemberg.

The new Christian Corporate State, having repulsed an attack from the left (the strike of the Social Democrats), was immediately threatened from the right by the Austrian Nazis. With the backing apparently of Hitler, the Austrian Nazis now tried to destroy the Dollfuss regime. Their coup d'état almost succeeded; desperate Austrian Nazis invaded the chancellory and brutally murdered Dollfuss; the radio was about to announce the new revolution, and Austrian refugees on the border in Bavaria were ready to rush across into Austria.

But the plot failed; Mussolini was furious at the murder of his friend Dollfuss, and Hitler at this time was in no condition to oppose the Duce. Starhemberg remained loyal to his late leader and acted promptly. The ringleaders were executed and this curious Christian Fascist state survived the storm. The new chancellor of Austria was Kurt Schuschnigg, and Starhemberg became vice-chancellor.

The dictatorship continued, but it was very weak. The Social Democrats, who might have defended the country against Nazi aggression from Germany, now were no more, and their leaders were in prison or in exile. The Austrian Nazis for the time being had been dispersed or were in jail. But Schuschnigg himself was in the minority and did not dare hold an election. There had not been one since 1930; and Dollfuss, with all his personal charm, had become chancellor with a majority of only one. Schuschnigg had neither charm nor, as events were to prove, the backing of Mussolini. He might have gone ahead without the former but the latter was essential if this tiny Austria was to survive as an independent state. As soon as it suited the Duce to act in conjunction with Hitler, Austria was lost, as we shall note later.

East of Austria

East of Austria, in Hungary and the Balkan states, the general drift of political life went in the direction of totalitarianism. In Hungary, Yugoslavia, and Greece dictatorship rose in the postwar era, and in Bulgaria and Rumania representative government rested on a very shaky foundation.

The history of Hungary may be briefly noted. Here, as in Austria, a republic was proclaimed at the close of the war. Quickly it was snuffed out by a Communist dictatorship, and for nearly six months the red flag flew in Budapest. Then came a counterrevolution, this time to the right, as Admiral Horthy of the old Hapsburg navy set up a restored monarchy without a king, for Horthy ruled simply as regent in a monarchy limited by a parliament of restricted powers, chosen by a narrow suffrage by voters deprived of the protection of the secret ballot.

Hungary was a country of large estates, great landlords, illiterate peasants. The Magyar nobility, retaining its economic and social privileges, was not discontent with the new status quo, that is, within the country. It would not and could not forget the Treaty of Trianon, whereby Hungary had been so tremendously reduced in area. Irredentist ambitions to recover the lost lands showed no signs of abatement with the passing of the years. On the other hand, the government of Hungary was stable as well as arbitrary. Twice did the Magyars' former king, Charles of Hapsburg, lead an expedition to recover his lost throne; twice was he driven back, and even for a while imprisoned. Some day, the Magyars said, they would choose a king; but they were in no hurry to do so, nor were many of them enthusiastic about the House of Hapsburg.

The League of Nations was kind to Hungary, and through its agency large sums were granted to rehabilitate the country. Had it not been for two things—the economic depression of the thirties and the Nazi regime set up in Germany—domestic politics in Hungary might have remained tranquil. But like all other agricultural lands, Hungary was hard hit by the decline of grain prices which was incidental to the depression; and German Nazis, flushed with victory, lost no time in trying to stir up internal discord in Hungary as they did in Austria.

The Hungarian National Socialists (Nazis) used three arguments to good effect—anti-Semitism, revenge for Magyar territory seized by Yugoslavia, Czechoslovakia, and Rumania, and the semisocialistic plea that the big estates should be subdivided among the peasantry. Needless to say, the third of these arguments had little weight with the Magyar nobles; and furthermore, since most Magyars, poor and rich, were ardent

Catholics, the attitude of German Nazis toward the Church of Rome acted as a brake on the growth of an indigenous Nazi party in Hungary. Nevertheless, the Magyar Nazis increased rapidly in number, particularly in 1938 and 1939, as Germany swallowed up Czechoslovakia, offering as she did so tidbits of that former republic's territory to Hungary.

"The Kingdom of the Serbs, Croats, and Slovenes," or Yugoslavia, was torn by internal dissensions from the very beginning. Serbs and Croats soon found that they could not agree; and the Slovenes, by far the weakest element in this triangular grouping, took sides with the Croats. The Serbs, in the majority, were not content with having their capital, Belgrade, the capital of the new kingdom, and with the acceptance of the Serbian dynasty; they also wanted a unified rather than a federalized constitution. The Croats, proud of their culture and tradition, their use of the Latin rather than Cyrillic alphabet, their religion which was Catholic, not Orthodox, looked down upon the more numerous Serbs and were determined to preserve their own particularism.

What almost at times might be described as undeclared war was waged between Serbs and Croats from 1920 to 1939. In the course of it, King Alexander, taking advantage of the perpetual strife in the Yugoslav Parliament, took the reins in his own hands and ruled for a few years as a despot, pure and undefiled. Finally he relinquished part of his authority to a parliament organized on the model of that of Fascist Italy, in so far that whatever political party won a plurality of seats at an election was guaranteed two-thirds of the final membership. Two political assassinations bespoke the low tone of political life in this Yugoslav kingdom. One was that of the leader of the Croatian Peasant party, the spokesman of regionalism and federation; the other that of Alexander, murdered while visiting France by a member of a secret Croatian society. The Serbs thus had a taste of their own medicine, since a secret pan-Serbian society had been responsible for the murder of the Austrian Archduke in 1914. Alexander's oldest son, eleven years of age, was now proclaimed as Peter II of Yugoslavia, and the government, in the hands of a regency, nominally returned to constitutional methods. The Croats, however, were not content; and as the war clouds gathered once more over Europe in 1939, they were actively engaged in plots to disrupt by internal revolt this South Slav kingdom, so large in area, so desperately poor, so torn by internal strife.

Rumania, as far as statistics went, emerged from the First World War a European state of importance, her area doubled by the annexation of Transylvania, Bukovina, Bessarabia, and a large part of the Banat of Temesvar. She was even larger in size than Italy! But beneath the surface there was discord. Minorities were more troublesome in Rumania than in Czechoslovakia and Yugoslavia; Magyars, Jews, Germans, Ukrainians, Russians, and Bulgarians comprised a good quarter of the population; the peasantry, close to Russia and subjected to Communist propaganda, demanded the splitting up of the great landed estates; and as a further source of constant discord there were scandals in the royal family, well aired and well ventilated. When the old King Ferdinand died in 1927 his son and heir, Carol, was living in Paris with a mistress for whom he had sacrificed the throne. The latter's young son, Michael, was proclaimed king, but before long Carol returned to Bucharest to assume the throne for himself. Unsavory quarrels between the Queen Mother, Marie of Rumania, a granddaughter of Victoria of England; Helen, the queen, daughter of the King of Greece; Magda Lupescu, the mistress; and Carol II of Rumania, crowned in 1930 and a most temperamental sovereign, filled the European press and unsettled Rumania still further. As for the King, he ruled sometimes in accordance with constitutional principles and sometimes not. Between fascism, anti-Semitism (the Jews were very numerous in Rumania), communism, the "Green International," a term very loosely applied to the spasmodic efforts of landless peasants in southeastern Europe to obtain land, and the endless friction of the divergent minorities, the position of Carol was far from pleasant.

In Bulgaria the forms of constitutional government were preserved in the intervals between the two World Wars. But the reality was somewhat different from the theory: bombs were thrown, army officers cashiered, and King Boris was now about to become a dictator and now about to refrain from assuming that dangerous role. What might be called a kind of authoritarian democracy characterized the Bulgarian scene, for there continued to be a parliament and within it there were political parties. The only real authority, however, was a group of army officers who pulled the wires in the parliament, their puppet politicians voting in accordance with suggestions, gentle or forceful as the occasion dictated.

Throughout this period Greece swung backward and forward between monarchy and a reputed republicanism, ending up in 1936 under a military dictatorship with General Metaxas at the helm. King Constantine, driven out by the Allies in 1917, came back in triumph to Athens in 1920, only to lose the throne again in 1922 as the result of a disastrous campaign against the insurgent Turks. His son, George, succeeded him, only to be deposed in turn, as a republic was proclaimed in 1923. For the next twelve years there was nothing but confusion and disorder, the venerable and now aged Venizelos trying in vain to bring back some semblance of stability. Premier followed premier during this black period, when Venizelos generally was in eclipse and when it seemed at times as though he was the only patriotic Greek. Suddenly in 1935 the country swung to monarchy once more, the exiled King George returning. As far, however, as one may peer beneath the cloudy uncertainties of Greek politics, the King was but a figurehead for the very capable and conservative Metaxas, who ruled with an iron hand until his death in January, 1941.

Throughout all the Balkans there was little evidence of any progress, and none at all of stability during the postwar period. Everywhere there seemed to be a regression to some form of despotism and arbitrary rule. So was it also with various other small countries in Europe, too unimportant for detailed analysis, such as Albania, Portugal, and the tiny independent states south of the Baltic—Estonia, Latvia, and Lithuania. Dictatorships, veiled, open, semi-veiled, were the lot of all of them. Indeed, of the new countries brought into being by the peace treaties of 1919, Finland and Czechoslovakia alone showed signs of progress during these distressing times.

Chapter 13

THE MIDDLE EAST DURING TWENTY YEARS ARMISTICE (1919-39)

THE MIDDLE EAST is a blanket term covering Asia Minor, the Arabian peninsula, the Tigris-Euphrates Valley and Egypt, all formerly part of the Ottoman Empire. And probably one should also include in it Persia, directly to the east of Mesopotamia, since it too was a Moslem country, vexed by many of the same problems which confronted its neighbors: economic distress, nationalistic uprisings, xenophobia, and dictatorship.

Turkey

In 1919 the fortunes of the Ottoman Empire seemingly had reached their nadir. Continuously at war since 1911, except for a few months between the second Balkan and the first World Wars, Turkey seemed done for. The victorious Allies were in possession of Constantinople, of the Tigris-Euphrates Valley, of Palestine and Syria. It never occurred to them that they would have trouble in partitioning the Sultan's realm as they saw fit. They determined that the Turks should be excluded entirely from the Arabian peninsula, the French and the British sharing that enormous area, for the most part divided into various mandates under the League of Nations. Then, by the Treaty of Sèvres (1920) which three Turks were dragooned into signing, Greece was extended eastward to include Thrace and Adrianople so that only a tiny strip of Europe was left to the Turks behind Constantinople. Even that ancient capital of the Ottomans was not given to the Turks in full sovereignty, since a wide zone on either side of the Sea of Marmora was to be controlled by an international commission. Greece was accorded the choicest part of the western littoral of Asia Minor around Smyrna, where there were many Greeks. By an Anglo-Franco-Italian agreement, the southern coast (Adalia) was to fall to Italy, and the French were to preëmpt for themselves Cilicia, directly north of Syria. The Turks were to be pushed inland to the upland plateaus and highlands, and not even all of these inferior districts remained to them, since two republics were planned in eastern Asia Minor, Kurdistan, and Armenia, it being hoped that the United States would assume responsibility for the latter as a mandate under the League of Nations.

This Treaty of Sèvres, harsher than that of Versailles, harsher even than that of Brest-Litovsk, was well-named "the porcelain treaty," for like Sèvres china it was easily shattered, and that almost immediately. Turkey, like Prussia in 1807, France in 1871, and Germany in 1919, took on a new lease of life, under the guidance of one of the most remarkable men of the twentieth century.

Mustafa Kemal, the "Ghazi," the Victorious One, or Ataturk, as he chose finally to be known, takes rank with Hitler, Mussolini, Gandhi, and Sun Yat-sen in any summary of twentieth-century nationalism. In a way his accomplishments were more notable than those of these distinguished gentlemen, since starting with nothing he accomplished well-nigh everything, not simply throwing off the yoke of the conqueror but revolutionizing the religion, the language, the very mores of his countrymen.

In 1908, as the Young Turks marched on Constantinople, Kemal was a colonel in the Turkish army. A brusque and silent man, but highly patriotic, he had long been a suspected revolutionary. Under the Young Turks he served as chief of staff against the Bulgars; before that he had fought against the Italians in Tripoli; and after that against the British in the Gallipoli campaign, against the Russians in the Caucasus, and against the British once more in Syria. At the conclusion of the First World War he did his best to persuade the Sultan not to submit to humiliating terms of peace. Failing in this, he left Constantinople to assume command of the gendarmes which the Allies permitted the Turks to maintain in Anatolia.

Mustafa Kemal put himself at the head of a Turkish nationalistic movement which defied both Sultan and Allies. The Sultan tried to break the growing influence of his general by urging the Kurds to attack him, and failed; the Allies, inviting the Turkish nationalists to a conference at Constantinople, arrested and deported many; but they also failed, since the suspicious Kemal refused to attend. Instead, he raised an army of some 25,000 ill-paid and ragged troops.

Whereupon the Allies bethought themselves of the Greeks, and the latter, encouraged by a British loan, drove inland at Kemal from Smyrna with 80,000 soldiers. In 1921, at the Sakkaria River in central Asia Minor, they were met by Kemal, and a fourteen-day battle ended such rosy dreams as King Constantine of Greece might have harbored of a restored Magna Græcia. Almost instantly the wily French saw the writing on the wall and withdrew from Cilicia, and soon afterward the Italians gave up their claims to Adalia.

The Greeks, however, still thought they had the backing of England and continued to fight. Kemal forced them back to the sea. Their retreat became a rout, and early in 1922 they evacuated Smyrna as the Turks swept into that city. England was very angry at both the French and the Turks: at the former because they had given up Cilicia without conferring with the English and because, it was rumored, the thrifty French had sold old uniforms and rifles to Kemal; at the latter because they had humiliated England's friend, Venizelos. England still held the Dardanelles and landed troops on the Asiatic side to bar the way to Kemal so that he might have no chance of pursuing the Greeks into Thrace. But Lloyd George thought better of it; the beating of the war drum in 1922 sounded but dimly in the Dominions, and England refused to enforce the Treaty of Sèvres by unilateral action. She tried to settle the Turkish problem by negotiating with the Turkish Sultan, ignoring the Turkish Nationalists led by Kemal; but the latter deposed the Sultan, who fled Constantinople on a British warship. Then England consented to confer with Kemal and his National Parliament. At Lausanne in 1923 a treaty was struck whereby all Anatolia, as well as Constantinople, Adrianople, and eastern Thrace were recognized as integral parts of an independent Turkey, and whereby, in a separate Græco-Turkish convention, all those Greeks within its borders were to be deported to Greece, in exchange for Kemal's promise to accept in Turkey all Turks still remaining in Greece. This same year Turkey became a republic. Its President was Mustafa Kemal, commander of the Turkish army, creator and master of the one political party recognized by Parliament. Thus, within five years after the great powers forced a negotiated peace, he drove out the conqueror and restored the independence of his country. A military dictatorship could have been his for the asking but he preferred one of a different sort. In the very year of Lausanne (1923) a Turkish republic was proclaimed and a constitution adopted. Under it the Ghazi was a man of unique power. He became president of the republic, president of the council of ministers, president of the assembly, and president of the people's party—the only one which the law recognized. Like Mussolini he did not hesitate to fill many offices at the same time, and like Mussolini again he took great delight in introducing startling innovations.

Only in the case of the Ghazi they were more numerous and more fundamental than those introduced in any postwar country with the possible exception of Russia. For the Ghazi was determined to "Westernize" Turkey from the very roots, not simply in laws, religion, and economics but in language, culture, and even clothes.

The sultanate had already been abolished, but the califate remained, and a relative of the ex-Sultan was calif, still holding, as representative of the Osmanli line, this ecclesiastical primacy honored by a large part of the Moslem world. Mustafa Kemal determined to divorce his country entirely from any theocratic traditions, and therefore he abolished the califate and drove into exile all remaining members of the Osmanli family. The legal code of Turkey was then transformed. All legal sanctions derived from the Koran and Moslem jurisprudence were ended; and the new Turkey took over the Swiss code as the basis of its civil law, its criminal being based on legal prescripts drawn from the Italian and German codes, and its commercial law based on the German. At this wholesale destruction of the religious foundations of Turkey, the principal Moslem state, there were loud outcries, and in the east the Kurds rose in rebellion. Speedily they were crushed by an army of 80,000 and the leader of the rebellion executed in the public square of Angora. Turkey was to be a secular state!

Its capital was placed not at Constantinople, henceforth known as Istanbul, but at Angora, renamed, Ankara. This desolate, windswept town in central Asia Minor forthwith became the center from which the ever restless and ceaselessly active Kemal spread reform after reform among his thirteen million fellow Turks.

Among these the most striking was the persistent and successful effort to change the costume of the Turks. The red fez, customary headgear, was abolished, and Turks were compelled to wear hats. First the Ghazi shocked everyone by appearing in a Panama; then he introduced the képi, or brimmed cap of the soldier, into the army; then all civil servants were ordered to wear European hats with brims; and finally, all who did not voluntarily adopt the new headgear were imprisoned. By the same method the salaam or oriental greeting was made illegal, and so also the wearing of veils by women. The personal appearance of the Turks was thus Westernized.

Turkey went Western all the way in regard to women; they were given the franchise; they were elected to Parliament; they were encouraged to enter business; they were forced out of their Eastern seclusion. And all this was done partly by example, partly by statute. The Ghazi was neither anchorite nor puritan, and was much given to cocktail parties and to dances, always, however, with women present. Those who sought his favor copied his manner. Women found it worthwhile to dress according to the latest Parisian fashion and men found that it helped advance their interests to swing their partners. "Oriental music no longer satisfies the Turkish soul," so said the Ghazi, and promptly Oriental music ceased. Soon in this land, where from time immemorial man and woman never walked together in public but always the man in advance, the woman humbly following, mixed classes of boys and girls were studying the nude of both sexes in art schools.

We must change our language, said the Ghazi, as he set the example by taking the name Kemal Ataturk. Arabic words, Greek words, French words must be exorcised from speech and pen. Turkish must be pure; Turkish must no longer be written from right to left but in the reverse or Western fashion; nor were the old characters to be used, for in the

West Latin characters were customary. There were not many printing presses in the country, and such as Turkey did possess had no Latin type; that made no difference; it must be bought. Not many Turks could read and write, and those who could found it irksome to learn the trick all over again. Nevertheless, it had to be done. First, on the postage stamps appeared the new letters; then they blossomed forth again on the paper currency; then it was announced that beginning in 1929 no printed matter might legally appear in Arabic type. Indefatigable in this reform was Ataturk; he gave lessons in the new script to all and sundry; he would stop in the middle of a state ball and with chalk in hand would explain on a blackboard how good Turks must in the future write their letters. His enthusiasm was contagious; all Turkey went to school; and soon books began to appear in purified Turkish, written with Latin characters.

Ataturk was also interested in everything that concerned economics and the physical well-being of his people. He found a country which still plowed with wooden sticks shod with iron, and harrowed with logs weighed down with stones; a country without banking facilities, or railroads worthy the name; disease-ridden, unsanitary, without irrigation, and without manufacturers. Problems like these were grist to Ataturk's mill. Olives and figs, cotton and tobacco were developed by him as staple crops; medical inspections were held; the ravages of syphilis were reduced; agricultural experts were hired; prize cattle were bought; railroads were laid; and the village of Angora grew into the avenue-lined city of Ankara. Nor was defense neglected; the straits were fortified; armaments were bought in both Germany and England with fine impartiality; and a merchant marine was started.

Ataturk planned wisely but he forgot one thing—nature. He lived not only vividly but too richly. Tobacco, wine, women, endless labor, and endless dissipation took heavy toll, and in 1938 he died in his fifty-eighth year.

Palestine

Stretching south from Turkey for thousands of miles lay Arabia, for the most part a tremendous desert, with oases here and there and certain fertile strips of land, particularly on the Mediterranean littoral and in the east where the Tigris-Euphrates Valley joined Arabia to the Asiatic mainland. Lost to the Ottoman Empire by the First World War, Arabia was in a ferment after it, the scattered nomadic tribesmen who comprised most of its population having in many instances drunk the heady wine of nationalistic aspiration and being quite uncertain what to do next.

Arabian postwar history can scarcely be taken up with the peninsula as a unit, for such a history must inevitably stress growing nationalism;

and since there never was an Arabia in the national sense, it is necessary that we turn to certain sections such as Palestine, Syria, and Iraq, and from them perhaps draw some conclusions as to the drift of affairs in the Arab world.

The history of Palestine during the twenty years' armistice between two European wars was confused, hectic, contradictory. In 1917 it was the happy thought of the British government that this ancient foyer of Jewry might become again a Jewish national home, and to make it such the British government publicly pledged itself. In doing so it forgot two important facts: first, that the Arabs in Palestine outnumbered the Jews eight or nine to one; and second, that those Arabs who had enlisted to help the British drive the Turks and Germans back through Palestine and Syria into Asia Minor during the last half of the war considered, rightly or wrongly, that Britain had promised an independent Arab state which would include Palestine. Britain, however, stuck by her word to the Jews. There had been no such formal pledge to the Arabs as there had been to the Jews; and furthermore such assurances as had been given the former were not to be interpreted, so said the British, as including Palestine. There was plenty of room in the peninsula for an independent Arab state without including Palestine, the British asserted; so they went ahead with their plans for a Jewish national home protected by Britain as a mandate under the League of Nations—Britain thus to be trustee for civilization, and incidentally for Jewish Zionists.

When the plans for this new state were published in 1922, both Jews and Arabs were dissatisfied, the former discovering that Britain, with the necessity of mollifying many million Moslems within her empire, had no intention of creating a purely Jewish state; the latter displeased that there was even the rough semblance of one and angry that Sir Herbert Samuel, an English Jew, should be the first governor.

Samuel tried to hold the balance even between Arab and Jew; to his advisory council he named four Moslems, three Christians and three Jews, a fact which pleased neither Jew nor Arab; he limited to a certain degree Jewish immigration, a fact which angered the Jews but did not satisfy the Arabs, who did not want any immigration at all. Before long the British were at their wits' end. It was not that Palestine was un-prosperous. London made no charge for the imperial troops which garrisoned the mandate and defense therefore cost nothing. Meanwhile, into the country poured much Jewish money which went for power plants on the Jordan River, for building a new university at Jerusalem, for the construction of a Jewish city at Tel-Aviv on the sea coast, for the pur-chase of land from Arabs for Jewish agricultural colonies. What caused increased unhappiness and riots, ultimately bordering on civil war, was the conflict between Jewish and Arab nationalisms. The Jewish Zionists, enthusiastic, and well financed, looked forward to the resurrection of a

Jewish state; the Arabs, both within Palestine and without, awakening, perhaps, for the first time in their history to a sense of national consciousness, considered Palestine theirs, resented the presence of the Jewish interloper, and opposed all British schemes for the division of power between Jew and Arab.

Meanwhile, the immigrants, mainly from Poland and Rumania, increased rapidly, doubling the Jewish population by 1929. The Arabs began to fear for their land, not the wealthy Arabs who sold it to the incomer, but the Arab peasants who found themselves dispossessed by the new owners. These peasants attacked the immigrants and killed many; but the British sent reinforcements to Palestine and preserved order; and as they did so world Jewry continued to pour money into Palestine. That country scarcely felt the depression of the early thirties, so great was the influx of new capital; Haifa was made a modern port, and from it, all the way across the desert a pipe-line was laid to Mosul, thus tapping the oil fields of the upper Euphrates Valley. There was even talk of a railroad to Bagdad.

And still the Jews flocked into Palestine. The advent of Hitler in Germany stimulated their advent greatly, so much so that in 1935 no less then sixty thousand reached the land of promise, and the Jews by that date had increased to almost one-third of the entire population. Thereupon, the next year the Arabs declared a general strike in which a thousand lives were lost.

This resulted in the British sending a Royal Commission to Palestine in 1937 to investigate and to recommend. It produced a report which angered both Jew and Arab. The Commission proposed that Palestine be divided into two independent countries, one Jewish, one Arab. The mandate of the League of Nations, which Britain held, was to be ended, but the cities of Jerusalem and Bethlehem, sacred to both Jew and Arab as well as to Christian, were to continue under British protection and were to belong to neither of the two new countries.

The report was a counsel of despair. The two new states would be too small to be self-sufficient units, for the total area of even the undivided Palestine was only approximately that of Wales or Vermont. The proposed Jewish state, the smaller in area but with the best land, contained some 300,000 Arabs who would have to be uprooted somehow and placed elsewhere. And even into this Jewish state, immigration on any considerable scale was to be forbidden for a number of years, just at a time when Jews throughout all Central and Eastern Europe were desperately seeking a harbor of refuge. The Arab state suggested would be larger and was promised access to the sea; but that was small comfort to Arab nationalists, who pointed to the original promises made to them by the British high commissioner to Egypt as early as 1915, when they plotted in connivance with him to revolt against Turkey. The report of the Commission glossed over these promises and did not even mention certain British guarantees to prominent Arabs in 1918, assuring them that their political and economic rights would be safeguarded in the new Palestine.

The Arabs now rose in arms and the British found it necessary to dispatch several thousand troops to Palestine. Concentration camps were established, Arabs were deported, sporadic attacks on Jews sternly punished. The partition commission, sent out in 1938 to draw up the boundaries of the two new states, gave up its task as hopeless, and a conference of Zionists and Arabs in London in 1939 accomplished just nothing at all. In view of the fast approach of world war in that year, it seemed best to the British to postpone further action, but in the meantime to close all immigration to the land of Canaan for the time being to many thousand Jews who clamored for entrance.

Lebanon and Syria

In 1916 the Russians, French, and British made a secret agreement dividing the Turkish Empire between them. The share allotted to France was generous; it included Lebanon and Syria to the north and east of Palestine, reached deep into Asia Minor still further north, and toward the east even beyond the headwaters of the Tigris. After the war the claims of the French were drastically cut, but they did receive, in the final settlement, Lebanon and Syria as a Class A mandate under the League.

For a time it appeared as though France would prove herself even more unsatisfactory as a mandate power in Lebanon and Syria than England in Palestine. There was no Jewish problem to perplex the French, but the Arab nationalism with which they had to deal was at once more vociferous and better organized than Arab nationalism in Palestine, and the French had the added necessity of stepping warily between a great variety of religious faiths, for there were numerous sects of Christians, like the Maronites, and divergent brands of Mohammedanism, such as that professed by the Druses, a warlike, schismatic Moslem tribe, in Lebanon and Syria.

For a good sixteen years after the establishment of the French mandate in 1920 there was serious trouble. Part of it may be traced to the French demand that the mandate should be in the name of two different countries rather than one, for from the beginning the French favored Lebanon, a narrow stretch of territory facing the Mediterranean, over Syria which lay behind it, although neither geographically nor racially was there good reason for so doing.

But there was a reason of another sort. Lebanon, with its capital at Beirut was for the most part Christian, and French influence there had been strong since time immemorial; Syria, on the other hand, was almost entirely Moslem. Therefore the French favored the former land at the expense of the latter, a policy which was shortsighted in the long run, for by enlarging Lebanon as they did, they brought within its boundaries a large group of hostile Moslems, while at the same time, by shutting off Syria from the sea, they antagonized the Moslems residing there and increased the xenophobia already prevalent among them.

Then, too, the French were too eager to gallicize both Lebanon and Syria. They did not realize that paternal methods which succeeded with barbaric tribes of Africa were inapplicable to this more settled and more highly developed corner of the Arabian peninsula. The French, for instance, were eager to spread their language through the schools, to teach Arab children to sing the "Marseillaise"; and the more they insisted on planting their own culture down upon the Syrians, the more restless the latter became.

Finally, by 1926, there was open rebellion. It began among the Druses in the hill country and then spread widely. There was fierce fighting in Damascus, the capital of Syria. The French bombarded its most crowded quarters both from the air and from the citadel. Thereupon the civilized world was shocked and the French high commissioner was withdrawn. From Paris came orders for a change in policy.

For the next ten years there was constant pressure put upon the French by Arab nationalities to withdraw altogether from Syria, and constant yielding of small points at issue by France. There were arrests, there were strikes, but there was no more open rebellion. Finally, in 1936, the French gave way almost entirely and signed treaties with Lebanon and Syria. In effect these recognized Syria and Lebanon as independent states which were to be admitted to the League of Nations, thus bringing the mandate to an end. The treaties were made for a duration of twenty-five years, and while they were in force France was to be permitted two airplane bases in Syria and the right to station troops in two specified areas; in Lebanon, she retained the right to station troops wherever she saw fit. The final solution, on the whole, was an Arab victory.

Iraq and Saudi Arabia

In 1920, when France received Syria as a mandate, the British obtained another on similar terms—the Tigris-Euphrates Valley with its three important cities, Mosul on the upper Tigris, Bagdad on the middle Tigris, and Basrah sixty miles above the Persian Gulf, at the confluence of the two rivers of ancient Mesopotamia. All indications pointed to a difficult and not too lucrative future for the British in this new outpost of empire. Even as they secured their mandate, a revolt of the native tribesmen kept these trustees of civilization cooped up in the cities. The Arabs had no chance of winning; the British airplanes were a guarantee against that. On the other hand, the pacification of this region, known as Iraq, was very expensive, and the British in 1920 were seeking no further expansion by land or sea. Consequently, a policy of nonintervention with strict economy was adopted.

The boundary of Iraq joined on the west that of the British mandate for Palestine and that of the French for Syria. The eastern part of their Palestine mandate the British early cut off from Palestine proper, renaming it Transjordania—now known as Jordan. No Jews were to be admitted, this a sop to Arab nationalism. Meanwhile Jordan would provide an airplane base on the way to India. Iraq's other western neighbor, Syria, was in the midst of turmoil, for the French were driving out of Damascus, Feisal, a former ally of Britain in the World War who had been chosen King of Syria by local Arabs. Why not then transfer Feisal from Damascus to Bagdad and set up a new kingdom there of Iraq? To do so would relieve the French of further trouble with Feisal, would placate the latter by giving him another throne, would put England in the good graces of the Arab world, and would bring to an end the beastly expense of governing Iraq, for the rebellion there in 1920 had cost Britain £40,000,000.

Feisal, it seemed, was willing to accept an election to the new throne, and was proclaimed king in 1921. His reign lasted twelve years, and fruitful years they turned out to be. It was a desolate region over which he governed and the three million inhabitants of this new kingdom, brutalized by Turkish misrule, occupied a region half desert, half swamp. To imbue them with patriotic spirit for an invented country called for skill, patience, and perseverance. Feisal possessed all three qualities.

Troublesome was the situation in the North, in the neighborhood of Mosul. The population here consisted largely of Kurds, a non-Arab Moslem folk whom Turkey desired to join to their fellow-Kurds in Kurdistan. But it would never do to let go the oil of Mosul, so argued the British admiralty, and Mosul was made an integral part of the new Iraq. But the British had pacified this country very largely by employing as soldiers the Assyrians, supposedly a Christian folk of Nestorian antecedents, and Feisal had both Kurds and Assyrians, unhappy and dissatisfied.

Four different treaties were struck with Britain during Feisal's reign, all of them marking successive stages of devolution on Britain's part, until finally, in 1930, one was drawn up whereby Iraq and Britain became allies in case of future war, the former granting certain facilities in respect to air bases, the latter agreeing to provide officers to train Iraq's army. In 1933 the treaty went into effect, the mandate ended, Iraq became a member of the League of Nations, and Feisal died.

His death was a signal for renewed troubles. The poor Assyrians, having lost their protector, England, crossed the border into Syria looking for new homes. Not finding them, they tried to get back into Iraq and were massacred by the Iraqi. Feisal's young son proved less able than his father, and before long (1936) a military dictator threatened to bring an end to such trifling constitutional guarantees of liberty as Iraq had achieved. He was careful, however, not to interfere with the oil route (Mosul to Haifa via pipe-line), or with the imperial British air route, which went via Jerusalem to Jordan, through Iraq to India, Singapore, and Australia.

The greater part of Arabia lay far to the south of Palestine, Syria, and Iraq. Here stretched the inhospitable desert over which roamed bands of nomadic Bedouins, loosely—very loosely—belonging to five separate Arab kingdoms, with boundaries ill defined and political authority shifting back and forth like the sands of the desert.

Of the five kingdoms, three were particularly important—the Hedjaz to the east of the Red Sea, Nejd in the interior of the peninsula, and Yemen in the southwest corner, bordered by the Red Sea on one side, the Indian Ocean on the other.

Again, of the three kingdoms, that of the Hedjaz seemed the more likely to gain the permanent hegemony over the peninsula; within its borders were the holy places, Mecca and Medina, and over it ruled Husein, father of Feisal of Iraq.

Husein, however, ran into difficulties; he had assumed the califate over the Moslem world without due thought to the susceptibilities of other Arabs; he was blamed for French activities in Syria and for Jewish activities in Palestine; and he refused to sign a treaty with Britain because that country demanded that he acknowledge the British mandate for Palestine. Therefore, when he lost British support, he could not withstand the energetic Ibn Saud, ruler of Nejd and regions adjacent thereto.

The followers of the latter were puritanical as well as fanatical Arabs; they were Wahabis, Moslem fundamentalists who harked back to the primitive rigors of the Moslem code, and they had no use for the wine-bibbers of the Hedjaz. Under Ibn Saud they attacked Husein, captured Mecca, and annexed the entire kingdom of the Hedjaz (1926). Shortly after, Ibn Saud led his Wahabis against the Yemen. That kingdom he did not annex, although he absorbed oases adjacent to it.

Ibn Saud proved himself a decidedly efficient administrator; he obtained from England recognition of his independence; he entered into treaty relations with other states; he established permanent colonies for wandering tribesmen, trying to teach them to live in houses rather than in tents; and best of all he brought law and order to the caravan routes which traversed the desert, ending brigandage, introducing motorcars and the wireless.

Iran

Persia suffered severely during the First World War. The nationalists, annoyed for many years by Anglo-Russian control of their country, favored the Central Powers. Upon receiving encouragement from the Turks to wage a Holy War on behalf of Islam and aided by German gold, they revolted against the puppet government of Teheran and twice defeated the Russians and the British in the field. Later in the war their cause looked even brighter, when the Bolshevik Revolution of 1917 led to the withdrawal of Russian troops. But the British had their eyes not only on Iraq to the west, but on Afghanistan and Baluchistan to the east. They could not suffer a loss of prestige at this critical moment, and also they had in mind Persian oil. Troops were needed, and troops were sent, and the British were able by 1918 to sweep through Persia, all the way to the Caspian.

In 1919 Persia tried to gain admission to the Versailles Congress, but a British veto barred the way, as in the case of Egypt and Ireland. England was "top dog" and was determined to remain so, for both political and economic reasons. This same year she concluded a treaty with the de facto Persian government, whereby in return for a loan of £2,000,000 she gained the power of dictating the economic and political policies of that country to whatever extent she deemed necessary. The idea that Persia should be given to Britain as a mandate under the League was rejected; the Anglo-Persian treaty was a much simpler method of control.

This treaty was highly unpopular in Persia and almost immediately there was civil war. The Nationalists declared a provisional republic, hoping with Communist aid to drive the British out of the country. They made good headway, but their Russian allies demanded that the red flag be hoisted and the Persians refused. Russia withdrew and the revolt collapsed.

Scarcely, however, had it died down before it was renewed, this time by a nationalist coup d'état which captured Teheran and overthrew the government. The rebels lost no time; they instantly repudiated the British treaty, and they drew up a long list of social and political reforms.

Prominent among the rebels was Rheza Khan Pahlavi, commander of the Persian army and soon the most influential man in the country. As minister of war he worked in close harmony with Dr. Millspaugh, recommended by the American State Department as economic adviser. The two men achieved wonders; they unified the country, balanced the budget, opened schools, built roads. Pahlavi acted as a kind of advance agent for Millspaugh, conquering and subduing restless tribesmen, the American following after with plans of economic rehabilitation.

Meanwhile, Pahlavi grew more and more popular; in 1923 he became Prime Minister while still keeping command of the army; in 1926 he deposed the weak and useless Shah and proclaimed himself Shah-in-Shah. Pahlavi's career runs parallel in many ways to that of Ataturk: he abolished the old; he introduced the new. He changed the name of Persia to Iran; modern hats had to be worn; women were sent to schools, and coeducational ones, at that; railroads were ordered and a huge railroad station built in the capital (this before the railroads); the Persian language was purified; the priests were held in check (not to the extent that they were in Turkey, for the Persians were more religiously inclined than the Turks); the capitulations were abolished; foreigners lost all power.

Yet between the dictator of the new Iran and his Turkish counterpart one striking difference was to be noted—Pahlavi was the more Asiatic in temper; he insisted on surrounding himself with a good deal of pomp; he was difficult to meet; he always traveled in style, the roads being kept clear of all traffic when he and his retinue made royal progress in their motor cavalcade. Justice was more Oriental in Iran than in Turkey, and men critical of the Shah-in-Shah simply disappeared. Pahlavi was very sensitive to criticism; his private life was hidden; how many children he had was a matter of guesswork.

But he made Iran independent, very much so. He refused to build railroads where the British wanted them; he would not permit the latter to use Iran for their imperial air communications; and what is more he drove a sharp bargain with the Anglo-Persian Oil Company, almost an adjunct of the royal navy. That company was already paying from £1,000,000 to £2,000,000 a year to the treasury of Iran in royalties; but that was not sufficient for Pahlavi. In 1932 he threatened to close down the company altogether. The British appealed to the League of Nations; but Pahlavi was not to be moved; the company must pay a great deal more. It consented to do so, the royalty was changed from a share of the profits to a base rate per ton, and Iran's share of this new-found wealth increased promptly several hundred per cent.

Egypt

The story of England's relation to Egypt during the interval between the World Wars parallels in some ways her relation to Ireland. In the land of the Pharaohs there was seething discontent; and the rising tide of nationalism noticeable everywhere in the postwar world led to nasty riots in Cairo and other Egyptian cities, directed against the protectorate which England had proclaimed over Egypt during the war. These demonstrations Britain alternately met by stiff opposition and conciliatory concession; with the emphasis on the latter word, for military occupation of the Nile Valley was expensive and the British lion was in a generally pacifistic mood.

Three times did Britain yield to Egyptian pressure. In 1922 she announced that Egypt was "an independent national state," but coupled this declaration with the acceptance by Egypt of reservations in regard to the stationing of British troops there and the acknowledgment that foreign interests in that land were under British protection. The Egyptians, greatly irked by these "safeguards," refused to ratify the treaty which embodied them. Followed then more riots and the assassination of the British governor-general of the Sudan. Thereupon the British levied heavy fines and seized customs houses. Then, when MacDonald became Prime Minister again in 1929, the British held out the olive branch; they offered a treaty whereby their troops would be withdrawn to the canal zone, Egypt to be completely independent but joined in military alliance with Britain. Once again the Egyptian Parliament refused ratification, and a final settlement was not made until 1936. The agreement reached on that date was on the model of the British proposals of 1929. It called for a military alliance, but the Egyptians were under no obligation to fight unless Egypt was invaded. The British agreed to limit their peacetime forces to 10,000 soldiers and to station them only in the canal zone. Naval bases at Alexandria and Port Said were granted to Britain, likewise the right to move troops over Egypt in time of war. The Sudan was to remain under British control, with special rights there reserved for Egypt. In accordance with this treaty Egypt broke off relations with Germany in 1939 but did not declare war on that country.

Here were a congeries of associated problems calling for expert statesmanship. Not only did they involve self-determination for subject nationalities but also the entry of Israel on the diplomatic stage, a tiny enclave of Arabia as far as area went, but a stick of political dynamite thrust into a world of anti-Semitic Arabs who were, themselves, Semites. The results thereof we shall read later.

Chapter 14

INDIA AND THE FAR EAST (1919-39)

India

THE FIRST WORLD WAR gave a tremendous boost to Indian nationalism. The British lost a great deal of prestige when General Townshend surrendered to the Turks in 1916, and the Indians feared their overlords less than before. In addition, the winged words of President Wilson in regard to self-determination had due repercussion in India. Many thousand native Indian troops were serving on the western front, and Indians back home expected England to show her gratitude for Indian support by concessions in the way of political devolution.

They were not altogether disappointed. In 1917 the British government pledged itself to develop in India "self-governing institutions with a view to the progressive realization of responsible government in India as an integral part of the British empire." After the war in 1919 this promise was implemented by what were called the Montague-Chelmsford reforms. They did four things for India: (*a*) they decentralized the government by giving a wider degree of autonomy to the provinces; (*b*) they introduced into the provinces a new constitutional device known as the dyarchy, whereby representative government was permitted in respect to certain limited governmental functions, that is, elected legislative bodies were placed in full control of the administration of forests, sanitation, and so forth, while more important functions, such as those dealing with justice and finance, remained still under the direct supervision of the governor; (*c*) they greatly enlarged the electorate, both for the provincial and the central legislatures; (*d*) they decreased the proportion of nominated members for the upper chamber of the central legislature (the council of state) so that it was slightly under half, and of the lower chamber (the assembly) so that it was about one-third.

These reforms were not ungenerous. The viceroy still held in reserve great power, and the property qualification remained high; but it surely would have been contrary to British precedent to have gone further at this time. What really caused trouble in India was not the paucity of reform but rather the Rowlatt Bills and Mohandas Gandhi.

The Rowlatt Bills, in force during the war, suspended guarantees of individual liberty, such as the right of habeas corpus and trial by jury, and made it legal for the government of India to deport agitators without trial. That these bills continued to be in force after the peace aroused the antagonism of Gandhi, soon to be known as the Mahatma, or Holy One.

That emaciated little Hindu lawyer had distinguished himself many years before the war by leading a strike of Hindu coolies in South Africa to protest against racial discrimination. He was an ardent pleader for Indian nationalism, but believed that it should be won by noncoöperation and nonresistance, not by force. The foolish British forbade him to travel in certain districts of India and put him in jail when he went there. Their doing so led to instant riots, and in view of the dramatic events connected with them, the specific reforms which the British had introduced received little attention.

For Gandhi had captured the imagination of the Hindu peoples. His teachings were summed up in his doctrine of *satyagraha,* or spiritual nonresistance. To practice it, one must (*a*) boycott all government functions, government schools, and law courts; (*b*) one must boycott foreign-made goods and buy only those produced in India. Thus, and thus only, could *swaraj* (self-determination), be secured.

Now between boycott and physical violence there is no necessary connection; none the less, the two are apt to go hand in hand. So it proved in India. The followers of Gandhi were not content to shun cloth made in England; they made bonfires of it. The result was an increase in rioting. Furthermore, it now happened that the more zealous Sikhs, disciples of the Mahatma, attracted the attention of the world by an exhibition of nonviolence. Anxious to recover a certain sacred shrine which the government had decided belonged to certain other Sikhs, they advanced on their temple unarmed. Felled to the ground by the *laithis* (bamboo rods shod with iron) of the police, they continued for six weeks to practise this painful sort of martyrdom. Gandhi, reproaching himself for all acts of violence taking place in India, pleaded guilty of causing them and accepted a jail sentence of six years gratefully.

Meanwhile, the experience of the Indians with popular elections was not altogether happy. The more ardent disciples of the Mahatma boycotted the elections. Other nationalists, however, participated, and were known as Swarajists, standing for independence. For the time being they professed that they would be satisfied with dominion status; but even that was displeasing to the British, who expected a ten-year trial term of the new reforms before further devolution was demanded. The Swarajists, however, were impatient; to annoy the government they threw out the budget, and to carry on administration the viceroy was forced to certify it on his own responsibility.

India, indeed, presented a complicated and anarchic picture during the middle twenties. The Nationalists were divided among themselves as to what should be done. Friction between Hindus and Moslems was rife. The Moslems were poorer than the Hindus and also less well educated. On the other hand, they came from fighting stock; at one time they had conquered India, and they felt competent to do so again. They laughed at many of the sacred tenets of the Hindu faith. Every year they were accustomed to kill a cow to celebrate the anniversary of the sacrifice of Isaac offered by Abraham. But according to the Mahatma the cow "is the poem of pity. . . . She is the mother to millions of Indian mankind." Little wonder there was strife in "Congress," as the annual convocation of Indian nationalists was called.

Even the Hindus in that congress did not agree among themselves. Gandhi was not interested in voting and in contesting the political control of England in Indian legislatures. He put more and more emphasis on the resuscitation of ancient Hindu culture by trying to revive the spinning wheel and by manufacturing *khaddar,* home-woven cloth. The Indian peasant, he argued, was idle for many months in the year, and if he would spend his time with handloom and spinning wheel he would get rid of the moneylender, and India would become economically independent of England. He set the example by spinning virtuously, and soon it became fashionable in nationalistic circles to copy him. One could even pay one's dues to Congress by spinning a certain quantity of thread.

The British decided in 1927 to send a royal commission to India to report on progress and to make recommendations for the future. The trial period of ten years for the reforms promulgated in 1919 would soon be up and it would be well if full discussion preceded any further change. Heading the commission was Sir John Simon, an English Liberal, who with all the other members was immediately boycotted in India. The Nationalists had no grudge against Simon; the shout, "Simon, go back," simply meant that they were indignant that native-born Indians had no representation on the commission. The British were logical; they wanted a unanimous report of some kind and they knew that it would be impossible to get one if conflicting Indian opinions were represented on the board of inquiry. But there are times when tact is more important than logic, and for all the good it did, the commission might just as well never have sailed from England. Nevertheless, that commission did make a report; in guarded terms and with many qualifications, it recommended three things: (*a*) doing away with dyarchy, which it admitted was a failure, and the substitution for it of greater Indian responsibility in actual administration; (*b*) a further enlargement of the suffrage, for there had been only 5,000,000 Indians given the right to vote by the reforms of 1919, whereas there were over 250,000,000 people in British India alone; (*c*) decentralization, to be gained by making the provinces more autonomous and by federalizing the whole peninsula, the native princes to give up their independent status.

This was not at all what the Nationalists wanted; before the Simon Commission reported at all, most of them had approved in some degree or other of the Nehru constitution drawn up by Congress, which called for complete dominion status and universal suffrage. Until they could approximate this constitution, they were determined to make life in India unpleasant for the British; and in this they were greatly aided by the example of Gandhi, who undertook a dramatic march to the sea to make salt without the payment of the salt tax, thus symbolizing his contempt for British law. It was very little salt that Gandhi made; but the whole world watched him make it. Soon thousands refused to pay taxes and the jails overflowed with protesting Hindus. Acts of violence also took place which Gandhi repudiated; strikes were numerous; bombs were thrown; and an incipient Communist movement arose, not interested in Gandhi's *satyagraha*.

Back in England Ramsay MacDonald, former pacifist, was Prime Minister. He still had faith in conferences, and round-table discussion became the order of the day. Let the various Indian groups iron out their own difficulties, was his motto, and three of these roundtables were held in 1930, 1931, and 1932. None of them was successful. The Indian princes came, but they were unwilling to surrender the arbitrary power they still held in their own independent states. The Hindus and the Moslems were unable to agree upon any compromise in regard to the basis of representation. And to add to these dissensions, the Hindus could not agree among themselves, for the outcasts, the "Untouchables," as they were called in India, now became articulate. The Untouchables were the lowest of the low, from the Hindu point of view. They composed the proletariat in the religious and social scale, and very generally in the economic scale as well. But one of their own number had risen in the world, had been well educated at Columbia University, and had become a lawyer at Bombay. This man, Dr. Ambedekar, was now as vociferous as the Moslems in demanding separate representation for the Untouchables; for otherwise, scattered as they were throughout India, they would be at the mercy of the more numerous caste Hindus. Gandhi, recently out of jail as the result of a hunger strike (the British having made the discovery that India was generally more restless with the Mahatma in jail than out of it), came to the second round-table conference. London was intrigued by his loincloth and the fact that he brought his own goats from India; but it speedily discovered that while Indians were willing to worship him as a saint, they were unwilling to follow him as a politician. Neither Gandhi nor anyone else could bring about an agreement by general consent. All three conferences failed, and the British shrugged their shoulders. They always knew it would be so! If the Indians could not settle their own affairs then the British Parliament must decide what the government of India should be like.

Whereupon, in 1935, a new constitution was promulgated, drawn up by the British alone and certainly an advance in the direction of dominion status, but still far short of it. The new instrument of government followed along the lines suggested by the Simon report: It decentralized India; abolished dyarchy, making all the cabinet ministers in the provinces responsible to their legislatures; gave these legislatures more power, and permitted over thirty million men and women to elect their membership; reorganized the all-Indian legislature by providing for a council of state with 150 elected members chosen indirectly by the provincial legislatures, as opposed to 100 to be appointed by the native princes (should they choose to enter the Indian federation) and 10 nominated by the viceroy. The lower house was to have 250 members, 125 chosen by the princes, the balance elected by 6,000,000 electors. In both the provincial and national legislature, electoral districts were to be based partly on communal representation and partly on population, thus compromising the Hindu-Moslem impasse.

The constitution looked fair enough but there were jokers in it. These were termed, by the British, "safeguards." The lieutenant-governors, placed over the provinces, were removable by the viceroy but not by an adverse vote of their legislatures. There were other safeguards in regard to the army, foreign affairs, and finance, the viceroy possessing enormous residual powers in respect to these vital interests should he choose to exercise them.

This, Congress realized; and within that body there was a movement to boycott the new constitution. The radicals who favored this line of action were led by Nehru, a left-wing Indian Nationalist who had become almost, if not quite, as popular as Gandhi. Like the Mahatma, he was a Hindu trained in England in the law, but unlike his famous fellow Indian, he was not interested in religion, and instead of urging a return to the hallowed traditions of Hinduism as did Gandhi, he favored discarding them. Nehru came from a wealthy family on good terms with the British. Not only did he become a radical Nationalist but he persuaded his father to do likewise, and it was the father, not the son, who drew up a Nehru constitution on behalf of Congress. Both father and son suffered imprisonment for the cause. The younger Nehru served almost as many terms in prison as Gandhi himself, for whom he had intense admiration. But the Mahatma was too willing to compromise, so thought the younger Nehru, who became the recognized leader of the left center in the Congress, the extreme left position being occupied by Communists and acknowledged Socialists.

Gandhi, now approaching seventy years of age, might be regarded as the leader of the right center, then somewhat inclined to coöperate with the British. When the new constitution had first been promulgated he had been very indignant because provision had been made in it for separate communal representation of the Untouchables. His reason for so doing was that it was a disgrace for Hindus to admit that there were such people as Untouchables, that separate representation would prevent their merging with other Hindus. So keenly did he feel about this that he began one of his famous fasts. Again the British did not dare permit his death, for they feared the repercussions it might bring. Therefore they compromised once more, and Gandhi ate. Having won this victory the Mahatma was willing to permit his followers to vote, and they did so.

Nationalists won the elections in a majority of the provinces; but the constitution was only partially enforced, for to complete federation, native states containing fifty-one per cent of the population of non-British India must first ratify it. Gandhi, aroused by an act of signal injustice in a native state, began still another fast, this time he said to the death. It was a dramatic way of calling attention to conditions in the native states, for Gandhi was a clever politician as well as religious prophet. As usual the Mahatma judged rightly; this time he had to fast to dangerous lengths, for he was ninety-eight hours without nourishment. And the British gave in; the injustice was remedied by the advice of the viceroy, and all that was left of the shriveled little mystic scored another victory over the greatest empire the world has seen since Rome.

Irritation against the British in India was still profound. Half of the famous Indian Civil Service, well paid, hard-working, efficient, was to be manned by Indians not later than 1940; but Congress did not see why there should be any British on that particular payroll. They pointed to the great powers held in reserve by the British viceroy, to the British control of Indian foreign affairs, to the British control of the Indian army, and to huge sums remitted every year to Britain in return for British capital invested in India, and to high taxes. Indian taxation was very low per capita compared with other Asiatic countries; but it was a heavy burden for a teeming population on the borderline of starvation. From the point of view of the Congress, the money thus raised should go to rid the land of illiteracy rather than to support a big army.

The British had an answer. Without the investment of millions of pounds of British capital in railroads and irrigation projects, famine would be rife in the peninsula, for the railroads had made it possible to move grain to those districts where there is scarcity, and the irrigation engineer made possible a greater grain supply. The army was large; but India paid nothing for the royal navy, and a strong defense force was needed on the northwest against Afghanistan with Soviet Russia in the background. Furthermore, without the presence of British troops in that army, what chance would 250,000,000 meek Hindus have against

70,000,000 Moslems? High as taxes were in British India, they were much higher in the native states. A good deal of Hindu poverty was caused by regarding the cow as a sacred animal which can never be killed and which must be fed when worthless, as a religious duty. For the good of the Hindu *ryot* (peasant), ignorant and illiterate beyond measure, knowing nothing of Congress or of those educated Hindus who claim to represent them, the British argued that they must continue to control, in part at least, the destinies of the subcontinent.

So stood the situation as the Second World War broke. Congress immediately offered to back Britain, provided dominion status be instantly granted. The British said that was impossible during the war.

The Far East

In the Far East, meanwhile, nationalistic fervors and fevers were even more intense than in Central and Western Asia. The essentially disruptive, anarchic, and volcanic qualities of contemporary nationalism were completely unloosed in this part of the world. The xenophobia which aroused the passions of Turks, Arabs, Persians, and Indians was no less noticeable here than elsewhere; but combined with it there arose such a terrific clash between Chinese and Japanese nationalism that there resulted what the Japanese politely called "incidents" but what the historian calls "war."

The outbreak of the World War in 1914 in the West was Japan's golden opportunity in the East. Declaring war on Germany, the men of Nippon promptly captured the German colony of Kiauchow, after which they presented in 1915 an ultimatum to the weak and disorganized government of Yuan Shi-kai.

The Chinese yielded to what they considered were twenty-one Japanese demands but what the Japanese ever since have termed the Treaties of 1915, whereby China placed herself pretty thoroughly under the thumb of her island neighbor, ceding to Japan all German concessions in China proper, as well as Russian concessions in Manchuria, while agreeing to accept military and economic advisers from Japan.

The following year Yuan Shi-kai died and chaos dominated the Chinese scene. China, disgruntled at her inability to get rid of the Japanese stranglehold, refused to sign the Treaty of Versailles. Two years later at the Washington Conference which we shall discuss later, she was more fortunate; her independence was clearly guaranteed by nine different countries; she was granted the right to increase her tariff; and the Japanese agreed to restore to China the German concessions which they had secured in 1915. But these gains did not stop the spread of anarchy in China, continuous and widespread, until the Kuomintang party (southern nationalists) was able to capture Peking in 1929.

Those nationalists were ardent followers of Sun Yat-sen, a capable conspirator but no executive. Before the World War came to a conclusion, he had betaken himself to Canton in the south and had there headed a revolt against the central government. While Dr. Sun lived it met with only local successes, for its leader was more prophet than statesman. In the former role, however, he wrote a book of lasting significance to the historian, for it became the Bible of the Kuomintang, and within a decade the most authoritative written word in China.

Dr. Sun's *Three Principles of the People* tries to lay the foundations for a new Chinese society in "nationalism," "democracy," and "social welfare." Individual and family interests must be subordinated to the welfare of the nation—nationalism. The Chinese should never forget that they invented the compass, gunpowder, and a wonderful indigenous architecture of their own; they were just as strong, as intelligent as the peoples of the West, and they must be proud of their past. From the West they should learn the art of government—democracy. That word, to Dr. Sun, was an all-inclusive one, including such concepts as the separation of powers and universal suffrage, and even certain ancient Chinese practices such as civil service examinations, for the West might well profit from Chinese precedents. Then, too, the Chinese must never forget social welfare, which he defines as resting on a social and political platform evolved about one-third from Marxian socialism, one-third from Henry George's land-value theories, and one-third from economic nationalism in respect to protective tariffs. Of these three principles, which was the most important? "Nationalism," asserted the more conservative right-wing members of the Kuomintang; "social welfare," affirmed the left wing. Seemingly, Dr. Sun sympathized more with the latter, and he entered into negotiations with Soviet Russia, who sent representatives to Canton to drill the Kuomintang army and to capture the Kuomintang mind. They were more successful with the first venture than with the second, for the Kuomintang began to win victories in the field while still torn in regard to ideology.

Dr. Sun died in 1925, honored and revered as the founder of Chinese nationalism, and his mantle descended upon Chiang Kai-shek, a quiet, hard-working, abstemious young soldier, ardent disciple of Sun Yat-sen, and commander of the Kuomintang forces. He led the latter to victory after victory as Hankow, Shanghai, Nanking, and Peking fell before his troops. Peking was abandoned and the capital of China was transferred to Nanking. By the end of 1928 the government of the Kuomintang there had been recognized by all the Great Powers and had been admitted to the League of Nations. At last China's main troubles seemed to have ended, for Chiang Kai-shek was a strong and able man, moderate, liberal, devoted to the three principles which were the platform of his party.

There were, however, two obstacles to overcome before China could present a unified front against the foreign capitalist and could call her house her own: (a) dissensions in the ranks of the Kuomintang, and (b) Japanese ambitions in Manchuria. A part of the Kuomintang, led by its more radical members, among whom Dr. Sun's widow was prominent, was under Soviet influence and rejected Chiang Kai-shek's leadership. At Hankow, well up the Yangtse River it constantly stirred up trouble and virtually threw off its allegiance to Nanking. In Manchuria young Marshal Chang, governor of that province, got in hot water with the Japanese in 1931 so that the latter launched an attack on him which was to prove the beginning of a campaign to conquer a large part of China.

The Japanese were not without legal rights in Manchuria, some of them dating back to the Treaty of Portsmouth, more of them dating to the treaties (or demands?) of 1915. Manchuria had been the original home of the Manchus, who had conquered China, and legally was a part of the Celestial Empire. Nevertheless, within its borders was the Southern Manchurian Railroad, Japanese owned; and Japan had been granted the right to police that railroad and to develop the economic resources of Manchuria in its vicinity, the Chinese being forbidden to build parallel or competing lines. Japanese colonists also had been granted concessions in the country and Japan had received recognition of extra-territorial rights there which, as interpreted by her, carried with them authority not only to try cases involving Japanese citizens but also to protect the latter by Japanese police.

All these special privileges the Japanese had been able to enforce without too much difficulty after the war, because old Marshal Chang, warlord and governor, had been concilitary toward Japan. But the elder Chang died in 1928 and his son, the younger Chang, was not only a Chinese nationalist but an adherent of the Kuomintang and of Chiang Kai-shek. As such, he adopted an anti-Japanese policy, trying to prevent Japan from expanding further, interfering with Japanese colonists, and even defying the Japanese military when their activities became too pronounced.

Therefore it happened that there was an "incident." It took the form of an explosion on the Southern Manchurian Railroad, caused, so claimed the Japanese, by the soldiers of Chang. A section of track supposedly was destroyed—supposedly, because the through express passing there shortly after was only a little late at its destination. But the incident was all that was needed. Immediately, the arsenal at Mukden in which slept the soldiers of Chang was rushed by the Japanese, and the Chinese garrison made prisoners, after which Japan proceeded to flood Manchuria with her own troops.

General Chiang Kai-shek and His Wife

China appealed to the League of Nations, of which both she and Japan were members. That body investigated at length, its committees visiting China, Japan, and Manchuria, interviewing both Chinese and Japanese authorities, passing over their testimony to the opposition for rejoinders and surrejoinders, and making a unanimous report signed by a German, an Englishman, an Italian, a Frenchman, and an American, a report accepted by the League (Siam not voting).

This Lytton Report acknowledged that although China held sovereignty over Manchuria that province could not be administered as a part of China since Japan held legal rights there. On the other hand it accused Japan of violating the Nine-Power Treaty of 1921, of violating the Briand-Kellogg international peace treaty, of violating the covenant of the League of Nations.

Japan already had virtually reduced Manchuria to a Japanese dependency by setting up a puppet ruler, and now in 1932 she renounced the League and all its works, resigning from that body. Manchukuo, she claimed, was an independent country. Did it not have a flag, a capital, even an emperor—no less a person than Mr. Henry Pu-yi, the last Manchu Emperor of China, now restored to a part of his ancient heritage by popular demand? This gentleman had, indeed, been elevated to the peacock throne in Peking at the age of three, only to be driven out in a few years by the Chinese Revolution of 1911. He had lived in exile most of his life, and was a quiet, demure young man about thirty years old when luck and Nippon made him emperor again—a most convenient puppet, so the Japanese thought. Surrounded by Japanese officials and advisers, and by the Japanese army, he was circumspect in behavior.

From 1931 to the present there has not been even the semblance of order in the Far East. Russia, England, and the United States all took a hand to some extent in the devil's brew constantly boiling over in that part of the world. Russia, it must be remembered, came close to circling Manchukuo; her maritime provinces bounded that new country on the east, as did Siberia on the north and northwest. Then, too, the Soviets were deeply interested in Outer Mongolia, the northwestern part of China, due west of Manchukuo. Outer Mongolia had become virtually independent of China and established within its steppes was a semi-Communist government in close military alliance with Moscow. From 1936, the date of that alliance, there had been sporadic "incidents" on Manchukuo's western and eastern borders. To separate rumor from fact in regard to them is impossible; but armed encounters had been numerous between Japanese and Russian patrols, and occasional skirmishes at times assumed the proportion of little battles.

England, too, was concerned, primarily on account of her immense financial interests in the Yangtse Valley radiating out from Shanghai and those centering around Hongkong and Canton, further to the south.

With the United States, trade was less an issue, for American investments in China were small compared with those of Britain. On the other hand, American educational institutions had spread out across a large part of China and a great many of the leading Chinese Nationalists had been educated in the United States—facts which drew the American people much closer to the fray than they otherwise would have been.

But the protagonists have been China and Japan. A relatively weak but ever growing nationalism, that of China, was challenged in one form or another by the most virulent and most concentrated nationalism that the world has ever encountered—that of the chauvinistic Japanese Empire.

In China, Chiang Kai-shek's problem was extremely difficult; at one and the same time he was confronted with an internal Communist civil war and by incessant Japanese nibbling at the frontiers of his country. For a number of years it seemed difficult to discover which of these two dangers he considered the more serious. He was conservative by nature, and by marriage connected with the famous and wealthy Soong family, who, aside from his sister-in-law, the widow of Dr. Sun, believed that Chinese nationalism stood to gain more by accepting loans from capitalistic countries than by relying on hypothetical aid from the Soviets; on the other hand, it was impossible to contend with the Japanese without a united country behind him, and to gain that the Communists must be either conciliated or hunted down and destroyed.

The best Chinese weapon for fighting Japan at first seemed the boycott. Its inauguration in 1931 led to the death of certain Japanese citizens in Shanghai and to the bombardment of that city by the Japanese fleet, followed by a land attack of the Japanese army, said to have involved 50,000 troops. Much to the surprise of the world, the latter were withstood for several weeks by the Chinese Nineteenth Route Army. This army, however, came from South China and received no active assistance from Chiang Kai-shek, who believed it was sympathetic toward communism.

The Japanese were aroused and the militarists apparently gained the upper hand at Tokyo. Their entire country, they realized, could be tucked away in the American state of Montana with room to spare. Much of it was mountainous and could not be tilled. Of mineral wealth, oil, and iron, there was very little. The Industrial Revolution had made such rapid progress in the twentieth century that Japan inevitably would go under without raw materials and without foreign markets. And both were to be found across the narrow seas in China.

The Japanese wasted no time. In 1933 they invaded Jehol, an ancient Chinese province southwest of Manchukuo but beyond the great wall of China; it was a rich province and might open the way later to Outer Mongolia. Again Chiang Kai-shek took no active steps in opposition, and the Soviet Bear only growled.

During the next three years Japan stretched out her hand over the five northern provinces of China proper, which included Hopei, wherein Peking was located. Bit by bit these provinces were detached from Chinese sovereignty and drawn into the Japanese net. Finally, in 1937, came a new "incident." Japanese forces at the Marco Polo Bridge within ten miles of Peking lost a private (he came back the next day) and in revenge 35,000 Japanese troops advanced from the sea coast toward that city.

This time Chiang Kai-shek was ready to fight. He recently had gone through strange adventures. The Chinese Communists (frequently and erroneously held to be by many not really Communists at all, but radical democrats mainly interested in peasant proprietorship and the end of landlordism) had moved in a dangerous and courageous migration all the way across China from the low lands of the southeast to the hilly country of the northwest. Against them Chiang Kai-shek had sent an army commanded by the young Marshal Chang, late ruler of Manchuria. Then rumor had it that Chang, instead of fighting Communists, had adopted a friendly attitude toward them. Chiang Kai-shek went to investigate. No sooner did this happen than he was kidnapped by Chang, who suggested that Chiang Kai-shek treat the Communists as allies instead of enemies and join with them in driving the Japanese to the sea.

Chiang Kai-shek angrily refused. His wife flew in an airplane to his side, and he returned to Nanking with her and the apologetic Chang, having made no promises. But he had seen the light; he would forget communism for the time being and so would the Communists. Both wings of the old Kuomintang now united with one sole aim, the eviction of Japan from Chinese soil. In the summer of 1937 the Generalissimo plucked up courage; he demanded the withdrawal of the Japanese from the vicinity of Peking. The answer was the prompt occupation of that city and of Tientsin by Japan. The war was on.

It raged with unabated fury. Again the Japanese attacked Shanghai, but this time Chiang Kai-Shek's national army, German-trained, dashed to the defense, and a battle of World War dimensions followed. The Japanese ultimately won, and driving inland up the Yangtze Valley they captured Nanking, the Chinese capital, before the year was out.

The Chinese Nationalists, however, abandoned that city in time, and retreating still farther up the river established their capital at Hankow. The next year the Japanese continued the chase; they captured Hankow; they captured Canton, source of munitions for the Nationalists by way of Hongkong. According to their reckoning they had won the war.

But Chiang Kai-shek had no thought of giving over. He moved his capital still farther up the river to Chungking in western China and encouraged guerrilla warfare against the enemy from within their own lines.

SOVIET UNION

Chita

MONGOLIAN
REPUBLIC

MANCHUKUO 1931-33

Harbin

Vladivostok

CHAHAR
1937-39

JEHOL

SUIYUAN
1937-39

Paotow

Mukden

SEA OF
JAPAN

Peiping

Tientsin

Port Arthur
1905

KOREA
1905, 1910

HOPEI
1937-39

HWANG HO

SHANTUNG

Tsingtao

JAPAN

CHINA

YELLOW
SEA

Nanking

Hankow

Shanghai

YANGTZE

Chungking

Wenchow, 1939

RYUKYU ISLANDS

PACIFIC

Foochow, 1939

OCEAN

Amoy
1938

Canton
1939

Swatow
1939)

FORMOSA
1895

JAPAN'S INVASION

Hongkong (BR)

OF CHINA

SOUTH
CHINA
SEA

TO 1939

HAINAN
1939

500 MILES

TRM

The Rise of Japanese Fascism

The speedy victories won by the soldiers of the Mikado did much to speed the rise of fascism in Japan. As in Germany it was semi-socialistic in character, deriving much of its strength from army officers embittered by the hardships of the proletariat from which many of them came. As in Germany it was aided by the discovery that bluff and bluster in foreign policy bore good fruit and brought easy victory; and, as in Germany, it grew from roots deeply embedded in traditions of racial grandeur.

The world economic depression of 1930-1933 brought sharp declines in agricultural prices in Japan as elsewhere but no decline in taxation. Japanese farmers sank deeper and deeper into debt. Those who were small landlords were almost as hard hit as their tenants; they were either forced to sell their tiny estates to mortgage banks or else to raise the rent of the miniature farms which they sublet to peasants. The latter were already living on such a narrow margin as to barely keep alive; now they were driven in many instances to sell their daughters into virtual slavery by apprenticing them to mill owners in the big cities. The introduction of cheap competitive farm labor from Korea added to these troubles, and the ground was well laid for sowing seeds of discontent among the soldiers, quite willing to believe that Japan's woes were due to wealthy shipping, manufacturing and banking interests, pretending that they loved Japan and international peace, but with hearts focused on the pocketbook.

Bluff and bluster in foreign relations worked; that was Japan's experience. The world let her do what she wished in China. One country, and one only, was not easy to deal with—Soviet Russia. But when Japan demanded possession of the Chinese Eastern railroad which crossed Manchuria and was half owned by Russia, she found Stalin willing to sell out at a ridiculously low price. Twice after that she tested Stalin's willingness to fight and twice to her surprise she found him ready to do so. In 1938 the soldiers of the Mikado charged up Changkufing Hill to the south of Vladivostok and just within the borders of Russia's Maritime Province, only to be hurled back with heavy loss. One year later they invaded the Mongolian People's Republic (in military alliance with the Soviets) and after a sharp battle were defeated by the Red army. Russia patently would have to be watched.

But the British and the Americans the Japanese feared not at all; why should they? In 1937 they sunk the small American gunboat, *Panay,* in the Yangtse and shelled the survivors as they sought refuge in the reeds on the river bank. Nothing happened. True, the Japanese government promptly apologized and paid an indemnity, and the Japanese people subscribed some $2,000,000 for the survivors, money paid by us to the Japanese Red Cross. But the Japanese militarists found out what they wanted, namely that we were not greatly exercised by this act of war; and, what is more, we were utterly unwilling to take any joint action with Britain when her gunboat, the *Lady Bird,* was shelled with impunity. Roosevelt was powerless to check the rising power of the Rising Sun. He did refuse to proclaim our neutrality laws as applicable to the Far East, and this he could do since the Japanese had refused to admit that they were waging war in China. But in all other respects he was at the mercy of an isolationist Congress. Japan had violated the Nine-Power Treaty which she signed at Washington in 1922, guaranteeing the status quo in the Orient, and the Kellogg Peace Pact which she signed later, together with almost every country on the globe, outlawing war: but when our state department made the slightest move to implement these international agreements it was accused of complicity with "the international intriguers of Geneva," that is, the League of Nations. The isolationists even tried to go farther; they almost succeeded in gaining the approval of the House of Representatives for the Ludlow amendment which would have deprived Congress of the right to declare war except in case of actual invasion of the United States. This was an oblique way of hitting at the President, and was so understood not only in this country but also in Japan. It was an indirect way of saying to all and sundry that it would be fairly safe for venturesome countries to defy the warnings of our chief executive.

Meanwhile, without the support of the United States, Britain was as powerless as Roosevelt to curb the predatory Japanese, a fact which they gleefully recognized in 1939 when they blockaded and maltreated beyond the bounds of decency British nationals in Tientsin. All in all, strong-armed methods worked abroad.

And they also worked at home. In the period between the two World Wars no less than five statesmen who urged conciliatory and liberal policies were assassinated by patriotic cutthroats, members of secret Fascist societies, the best known of which was the Black Dragon; and prominent business men like Baron Dan of the House of Mitsui were either murdered or else compelled to hire bodyguards and to wear steel vests, even while playing tennis. These societies, gaining more power, were back of an open rebellion in Tokyo which, led by two young army officers, threatened in 1936 in the name of the Emperor to destroy parliamentary government completely. The mutineers surrendered and a few were punished. Nevertheless, this mutiny was only suppressed on the surface; it really won the victory, for parliamentary government (never very strong in Japan) grew steadily weaker.

A kind of fascist militarism now characterized the government of Japan, similar to German fascism in that both countries tremendous emphasis was laid on traditions of racial glory and queer hypotheses of racial purity. The Japanese claimed to be descended from the Sun Goddess who gave birth to the Japanese Islands and to a parent of the first Japanese Emperor. Since all Japanese were considered relatives of the first Emperor, all Japanese were blood brothers, and all Japanese were divine. In both Japan and Germany the sacredness of the blood has been mystically elaborated; but in the former country it has not been so essential to twist and to torture anthropological data to prove the impossible. In Japan it is a matter of faith, not one for laboratory analysis. To some historians, and particularly those who like to indict an entire nation, it has always been a matter of faith in Japan; and in a sense they are correct since the animistic aspects of Japanese tradition did not die out completely when Japan adopted western ideas in the late nineteenth century. If, however, those aspects did not die out, they did die down, so as to be to the better-educated Japanese a mere quaint survival. It suited the Japanese fascists to revive this thing, to pump fresh enthusiasm into it. They were altogether successful.

Chapter 15

FROM THE RUHR TO PRAGUE (1923-39)

FRANCE had Germany by the throat in 1923. The Ruhr was in her hands; the German mark was tumbling to destruction. It would have needed a bold prophet then to have proclaimed the resuscitation of the Reich, the challenging of the conqueror within ten years, the union of Germany and Austria within fifteen—a more powerful empire than that made by Bismarck. Nevertheless, kaleidoscopic changes in international politics brought this about, and in the autumn of 1938 a prime minister of France and a prime minister of England were to plead in vain, with a German Fuehrer that he withhold his heavy hand from a country created and guaranteed by the Versailles pacts. Roles were now quite reversed: it was Germany and not France that held the hegemony of Europe!

The factors which underlay this extraordinary reverse were these: the financial settlements made by the Dawes and Young Plans which, unintentionally and indirectly, strengthened Germany; the impotency of the League of Nations; the procrastination of the Great Powers in implementing the disarmament clauses of the Versailles treaty; American isolationists; repudiation of agreements, first by Japan and then by Italy; the superb timing of German foreign policy by Hitler; the Spanish civil war; the unwillingness of France and England to coöperate with one another until a rearmed Germany virtually had annexed Czechoslovakia, master now of Central Europe; the fact that there were approximately eighty million Germans in Europe, the largest cohesive national group to be found there if we except Russia; and the social tensions of this period, which affected not only the rise and the achievements of the Fascists and Nazis but also the attitude of the capitalistic democracies toward fascism, many leaders of the democracies shaping their policies on the belief that fascism and national socialism were simply uncouth ways of putting down communism.

Finance

The war-weary legions of the French Republic withdrew from the Ruhr Valley in 1924. Seemingly, they had won a victory; they had not been able to operate the industrial plants of Germany but they had forced that country to its knees and to an acceptance of the Dawes Plan, which, in essence, amounted to a kind of international receivership in bankruptcy. The plan and its successor, the Young Plan, have been described already. Both operated successfully for a season, but owing to one reason alone—the lending of fresh money to Germany. The loans were made partly by the English, more largely by the Americans, childishly believing the fairy stories of their bankers, who, in the lush decade of easy money in the twenties, seem to have lost their heads altogether. In addition to several hundred million dollars lent the German government, private investments amounting to some $5,000,000,000 were made in European securities, mainly German, only stopped in 1929 by the orgy of speculation on the New York Stock Market of that year and the subsequent crash. Money began to go round and round in a kind of circle, from England and America to Germany, from Germany to England and France in reparations, from England and France to America in war-debt payments. But always more money stayed in Germany that was paid out! And this money went toward building new German steamships, new German factories, new German machinery, new German homes and public buildings. From the date of the Dawes Plan, 1924, to the Hoover moratorium of 1931, Germany paid handsomely on her reparation account; but in terms of dollars she received more than she spent. Terrible as was the economic disaster which overwhelmed her in 1923, her complete bankruptcy was not without compensation. By wiping out all internal debt, the Reich was able to start afresh with a new currency, owing no money to her own citizens; but both France and England labored under colossal internal debts inherited from the First World War and before it.

The League of Nations

Meanwhile the League of Nations proved an impotent agency for world peace. In dealing with certain weak states it exerted its authority manfully. In a dispute between Turkey and Britain over the oil lands of Mosul there was a League decision in favor of Britain, and Turkey yielded. In a dispute between Sweden and Finland over the Aland Islands there was a decision in favor of Finland, and Sweden gave way. And when Yugoslavia threatened Albania in 1921, talk of sanctions at Geneva stayed the hand of Yugoslavia. The League also kept peace between Greece and Bulgaria, and did useful work in regard to international health, in codifying laws, and bringing about international agreements in regard to opium, the white-slave traffic, and the hours of labor.

But when it came to curbing the will of any Great Power, Geneva failed dismally. Poland seized Vilna in Lithuania, and despite the protests of the League nothing happened. It was not that Poland was a great power, she was not; but Poland was backed by France! Mussolini, as early as 1923, tested the temper of Geneva, and to his own satisfaction. He bombarded the Greek island of Corfu, killing many Greek citizens— this despite the fact that Greece was a member of the League. The Duce refused to acknowledge that Geneva had any right at all to intervene between Italy and Greece, the plain wording of the Covenant to the contrary.

The disabilities under which the League labored were many, but perhaps the two most prominent were that it had no way to enforce its decisions, and unanimous action on the part of the Council of the League was necessary even to obtain decisions. France was a permanent member of that Council and France was always alert lest the peace settle- ments of 1919 be weakened. Therefore, Geneva tended to become an agency for perpetuating those settlements rather than for readjusting them.

For two or three years after the invasion of the Ruhr it seemed possible that the machinery of the League might be so changed as to make that body a real agency to insure real peace. Scarcely had the ink dried upon the bankers' agreement (the Dawes Plan) than the French and British governments tried to fill the gaps in the Covenant and to outlaw war. They did succeed in getting the League to accept what was called the "Geneva Protocol" which gave teeth to the Council of the League, en- abling it to compel arbitration, "to forbid mobilization, or to impose an armistice." This protocol defined the aggressor in specific terms and pro- vided for outlawing him. At last France had what she wanted, security. And England agreed to give it to her.

But before Parliament ratified the protocol, Ramsay MacDonald was out as Prime Minister and Baldwin in. The British Tories would have none of the protocol. Austen Chamberlain, brother of Neville, was British foreign secretary, and he scented commitments which he was unwilling for his country to make. The chief agency for enforcing the future de- cisions of the League would be, in his opinion, the royal navy, for even if the method of enforcement took the mild form of economic sanctions, it would be sea power in the last analysis which would enforce them. England, therefore, decided to keep her fleet to fight her own battles, and consequently the protocol never was ratified.

Despite this drawback, the cause of international peace guaranteed by a league made headway. England, following the policy of Pitt in Napoleonic times, was willing to make local commitments, and so, too, it seems, were France and Germany. In 1925 Stresemann, the German foreign secretary, Austen Chamberlain for England, and Briand for France met at Locarno in Switzerland. From this conference emerged the Locarno treaties by which Belgium, England, France, Italy, and Germany guaranteed the existing frontiers between Belgium and Germany and those between France and Germany. The demilitarization of Germany for fifty kilometers east of the Rhine was agreed to, and a permanent place on the Council of the League of Nations was to be given Germany. That country also agreed to arbitrate any disputes she might have with Poland and Czechoslovakia. She reserved the right to seek peaceful changes in her eastern frontier, but her western one she accepted as permanent. In case there should be a flagrant violation of these sacrosanct boundaries in the West, there was to be immediate action taken by the signatories; in case of doubt the Council of the League was to determine what should be done.

With the signing of the Locarno treaties the world breathed easier. There were, of course, a number of problems yet unsolved; there was as yet no guarantee of Europe's eastern boundaries for although everyone promised not to go to war over them, that was not very specific; there was no assurance that Germany's permanent seat on the Council would carry with it colonial mandates; there was no time limit set for Germany's payments under the Dawes Plan; and, possibly even more important, there was no strengthening of the machinery of the League of Nations, aside from the presence of Germany on that body, and no indication that the pledges given and taken at Versailles in regard to future disarmament would be implemented. A local and regional pact had been drawn up, and an important one. That was all.

Within five years dark clouds settled down again upon Europe. One of them was the disastrous and complete failure of Geneva to function in a Far Eastern dispute, resulting in Japan's resignation from the League. Another was the equally disastrous and equally complete failure to bring about disarmament, resulting in Germany's withdrawing from the League, which, from now on, despite the subsequent adhesion of Russia, grew gradually less and less influential.

The sudden flooding of Manchuria in 1931 by Japanese troops inevitably had serious consequences. Almost instantly China complained to the Council of the League, which called upon both China and Japan to withdraw their soldiers from the disputed area. Japan refused, asserting that negotiations and a settlement must come first. Weeks were spent in argument and finally a suggestion of Japan's was accepted, the sending of a commission of the League to the Far East.

In the interim came the Japanese attack on Shanghai, and immediately China made a new appeal to the Council and, when that body did nothing, to the Assembly. Fifty nations attended the 1932 meeting of the Assembly which appointed a committee of nineteen to deal with the Shanghai incident. Its report called for the withdrawal of the Japanese troops from Shanghai, and Japan complied.

The commission of the League sent to the Far East reported this same year. It disputed some of the Chinese claims but leaned very heavily against those of Japan, called for the recognition of Chinese sovereignty (with limitations) in Manchuria, and for the strict enforcement of three treaties: the Covenant of the League of Nations of which both Japan and China were members, the Nine-Power Treaty of the Washington Conference of 1922, and the Kellogg-Briand Pact of 1928, whereby war was renounced by almost every country in the world as an instrument of national policy.

The Committee of Nineteen now swung into action, asking for a conciliation commission on which both Russia and the United States were to be represented. Japan refused to accept this offer, whereupon the committee reported to the Assembly against the actions of that country in the Far East in no uncertain language, recommending that all nations should refuse to recognize the Japanese puppet state of Manchukuo. The League accepted the report and Japan withdrew from Geneva. Reliance upon the Covenant of the League of Nations had proved useless in a real emergency. In the few years intervening before the Second World War it was to prove so again and again.

Disarmament

Number four of the fourteen points had been specific in regard to disarmament. "Adequate guarantees," it said, "given and taken that national armaments will be reduced to the lowest point consistent with domestic safety." But in regard to Germany alone had any such guarantees been enforced; the German army had been reduced to 100,000 men and the German navy sunk. But how about the other signatories of the Versailles Treaty?

They did do something in regard to naval disarmament in the Washington Conference of 1921-22. Britain, the United States, Japan, France, and Italy agreed there to set a ratio for their capital ships at 5: 5: 3: 1.75: 1.75—the ratio to be set in the order of countries named. There was to be no new construction of battleships for ten years, and after that date Britain and the United States were to be allowed only a total tonnage of 500,000, Japan of 300,000, and France and Italy of 175,000 respectively.

To bring about this modest limitation, all the signatory powers made sacrifices except Italy. That country was so far short of 175,000 tons and so far behind France in naval equipment that to be placed upon an equality with her Latin neighbor was no hardship for the Italians. The French, on the other hand, saw objections, and refused to agree until the conference applied the ratio only to battleships. It was very largely a matter of prestige with the French; they were not building any battleships at the time, and were not likely to exceed the 175,000-ton limit anyway. Submarines, however, were another matter; and for them and other small craft they would not accept the ratio.

For the Japanese it was likewise a matter of prestige. Their pride was hurt at accepting a lower ratio than that for the British and the Americans. On the other hand they secured some concessions. They won the right to complete a new battleship under construction; and the Americans and the British agreed not to build naval bases within striking distance of the Japanese homeland.

It was not easy for the British to yield parity to the Americans. Still, two monster British battleships were nearing completion and Britain was permitted by the treaty to finish them. With these two ships, capable of sinking anything afloat, she was still mistress of the seas. The Americans, meanwhile, offered to scrap battleships which they had commenced to build but which were far short of completion. This was their contribution to world peace.

Less successful were the conferences held at Geneva in 1927 and at London in 1930. The purpose back of the first was to extend the ratios of the Washington Conference to smaller craft, that of the second to accomplish the same end, and also to provide for the continuation of battleship limitation, the earlier treaty running out in 1931. Both conferences were failures. At the first a lively quarrel broke out between American and British admirals as to the size of cruisers. The Americans, having few naval bases, insisted on large cruisers but few in number; the British, well-equipped with naval bases but having a large mercantile marine to protect throughout all the seven seas, wanted small cruisers but many of them. The quarrel was renewed in 1930, this time primarily between France and Italy. The two countries wrangled long and loud, the Italians demanding complete equality with the French in small ships as well as large, the former country unwilling to grant it unless Britain agreed to a Mediterranean Locarno guaranteeing the status quo in that sea. This, Britain would not give unless the United States was willing to commit herself by something more than words to the cause of world peace.

The conference broke up, to meet again in 1930 in London. All that was accomplished then was a highly tentative agreement between the big three naval powers—England, Japan, and the United States—to retain the old ratio (with minor concessions to Japan) for five more years; but even this agreement was contingent upon France and Italy not exceeding their old allotment of tonnage.

Meanwhile, there had been no progress at all in disarmament on land. The League of Nations did nothing in regard to this all-important question until 1926, and then only by the appointment of a commission to consider drafts presented by the British and French governments. The commission could come to no specific agreement. Countries with conscript armies objected to counting their reserves as "effectives"; countries like Germany and England wished to have the reserves included in the total armed force allowed. Some countries, like England and France, were willing enough to reduce expenditures, but countries like the United States where the military budget was high in proportion to the number of enlisted men wanted to reduce the number of soldiers rather than lower the expense of supporting them. The French reverted time and again to the necessity of an international force to compel the observance of such disarmament as should be agreed upon, for the French did not trust the Germans, and above everything else they were concerned about their own security. The "have not" states—such as Italy, Germany, Hungary, and Bulgaria—wished to remake the map of Europe, or at least to modify existing boundaries as part of a scheme for general disarmament. The "haves"—France, Poland, Czechoslovakia, Rumania, and Yugoslavia —preferred to "freeze" European boundaries as they stood, and only to disarm with some assurance that they could retain their wartime gains. In consequence it was not until 1932, fourteen years after the war, that the League finally summoned a world conference on a vital matter which should have been tackled ten years earlier.

Some sixty nations were represented at this conference which, if we include adjournments, lasted for a year and a half. It was a heart-rending affair, since at times it almost seemed as though an agreement could be reached. The Russians professed themselves quite willing to disarm altogether, if the other nations would only do so; the Americans, first under Hoover and then under Roosevelt, withdrew to some extent from their postwar isolationist policy and said that they would be willing to consult as to violations of the Kellogg-Briand Pact, even if they would not bind themselves to enforce it. The British were eager that aerial warfare be placed under the ban, with a caveat in regard to distant and desolate regions like Afghanistan where the possession of planes made much easier their task of maintaining the Pax Britannica. The French even agreed to a German army equal to their own in Europe, with the caveat that additional troops be given to the Tricolor for service in Africa and Asia. Even the Germans finally intimated that they might be willing to wait a few years before insisting on full equality, provided they were permitted to have immediately a limited number of tanks and planes as an indication of good faith and ultimate equality. Now at last it seemed possible to rid the world of at least one nightmare.

When, indeed, the British presented a detailed plan showing how the sum total of men under arms in Europe might be reduced by 450,000, although adding to the armed force of Germany, Austria, Hungary, and Bulgaria 177,000 men, and when the Germans accepted the British plan on principle, hopes ran high.

Suddenly, then, Hitler ordered his representatives back from the conference and withdrew Germany from the League of Nations. He appealed to the German nation for a vote of confidence. He had done his best, he said, to preserve peace, but he would no longer submit to the humiliation of his country. His action was endorsed overwhelmingly at the polls in a burst of patriotic fervor, and in the next year the German budget for armaments was published—an increase of three hundred per cent for aircraft (forbidden altogether by the Versailles Treaty) and an increase of over fifty per cent for the army. Disarmament was dead in Europe!

And why? One answer may be found in a table, prepared by the Carnegie Endowment for International Peace, which shows the following figures in millions of dollars for military and naval purposes:

Country	1914	1931	Percentage
Britain	375	535	+42
France	348	455	+30
Italy	179	258	+44
Japan	95	232	+142
Russia	447	579	+30
Germany	463	170	−60

Geneva had dallied too long with this question, so the Germans thought, and perhaps Geneva really intended to continue the humiliation of Germany by insisting on a far too lengthy trial period. That such presumably was intended would seem to be a fair interpretation placed upon the legalistic phraseology of Sir John Simon, British foreign secretary. Perhaps also Hitler had secret intimation of possible support in the future from Mussolini; perhaps he realized that a quick election on this issue in Germany might endear him so greatly to his German *Volk* that it would be worth while simply from the point of view of domestic politics. At any rate, disarmament was dead; Germany was rearming.

American Isolationists

The rearmament of Germany was a danger signal and so recognized in Europe; but in America Hitler's withdrawal from the League scarcely created a ripple. The reaction against Wilsonian idealism as shown by the 1920 election of Harding grew stronger during the period between the two wars. True, in regard to the Far East we were willing to bring pressure (apart from the boycott and armed force) to preserve the open door in China, and in everything that concerned disarmament, particularly naval, we took a lively interest. We were even willing to have an "observer" present at Geneva to represent the American viewpoint. But throughout this entire period (1920-39) we refused to make any commitments which might involve us in action, and as the war clouds gathered in the late thirties the United States drew more and more within herself, absorbed in her own domestic crisis, confident that nature protected her by a broad ocean on the east and an even broader one on the west.

The indifference of the United States to the growing power of Nazi Germany was due to many causes but prominent among them were two: we felt that we had been generous and kind to our late allies both in the war and in the settlement of their war debts and we thought them ungrateful; we also harbored the naïve belief that future wars could be voted down, prevented, by merely agreeing not to fight, as though war were a kind of disease, like intemperance, and that taking the pledge might ward off its recurrence.

During the First World War and the armistice period, European governments borrowed from that of the United States $10,338,000,000, and concerning repayment there was much dispute. The British, sagacious in matters of finance, proposed a general cancellation all around. They owed us between four and five billion dollars and they offered to cancel a larger sum owed them by France, Germany, and other countries if we would cancel their indebtedness to us. We rejected their proposal. Instead, we signed a contract with the British on the basis of reducing interest from five to three per cent, payments to stretch over a period of sixty-two years, and we signed similar agreements with our other debtors, in all cases cutting the interest charges way below three per cent, but in every instance demanding and receiving (on paper) full repayment of principal.

We thought ourselves very generous; Europe thought us avaricious. There was something to be said for both points of view. Most of the money had been loaned before the armistice and when the loans were originally made they were not thought of as ordinary commercial transactions; they were popularly regarded, even in the United States, as part of our contribution to the war effort. We were at war with Germany, and until our soldiers could be trained and sent into battle the Allies would hold the line, aided by our money. Now we wanted it all back!

The only way our former allies could pay us was by gold, by goods, by services, or by getting the money out of Germany. A large share of the world's gold was already in American banks (soon to be buried in the ground in Kentucky), and it was impossible for our debtors to pay in gold. Our high tariff, raised much higher after the war, made it impossible for them to pay in goods. Payment by services rendered would have been possible had we welcomed British and French workmen in our factories; but that solution would have created unemployment in America. The only possible way remaining was to have our debtors pay over to us what they first must garner from the Germans. But we stoutly insisted that reparations from Germany were none of our affair. We not only did not ask for reparations for ourselves; we considered our former allies greedy, forcing the defeated enemy to pay unjust reparations. Our former allies said, "The money we get from Germany we pay to you. Uncle Sam is the greedy one; he insists on making the Germans sweat."

The Americans refused to acknowledge that this was so; they pointed to the secret treaties made during the War for which they were not responsible, to incessant European broils subsequent to that conflict, to huge sums wasted in rearmament, to their own modest demands made on Germany as evidence of their own moral worth.

These debt settlements made bad blood between Europe and America. Calvin Coolidge put it bluntly when he said, "They hired the money didn't they?" It was not so simple: debt contracts running for generations are apt to be voided, since grandchildren are not concerned about debts incurred by their grandfathers, and currencies are apt to fluctuate in value; thus, when the British pound dropped from $4.86 to $4 the British discovered that although they had paid us several hundred million dollars they owed us more in terms of their own currency than before they paid anything at all. To the significance of these facts we were blind, and then as the years passed and the European countries one by one defaulted (except Finland) the ire of Americans at European bad faith mounted higher and higher until in 1934 Congress passed the Johnson act forbidding American loans to foreign governments already in default on payments due the United States.

Meanwhile we celebrated the "outlawing of war" by the Kellogg-Briand Peace Pact, drawn up during the administration of President Coolidge and signed in 1929 by his successor, President Hoover. The original impetus for this unusual document came from Aristide Briand, Premier of France, who thought a public declaration of eternal peace between the United States and France might be useful. The idea was taken up with enthusiasm in the United States and enlarged so as to include all countries. As amended by us it became a general international agreement whereby the signatories (and practically every country in the world signed it) renounced war as an "instrument of national policy" and agreed that all disputes "of whatever nature and of whatever origin" were to be settled by pacific means.

This Kellogg Pact was our principal contribution to world peace during the hectic years before 1929. As a gesture of friendliness to all the world there was, perhaps, something to be said for it. Since, however, there were no provisos in the pact for its enforcement, the evangelical warmth with which we greeted it was open to question, and herein lay a genuine danger; it led too many Americans to clothe themselves and their country in the righteous garments of peace at far too easy a price.

When the world entered the depression of the thirties President Hoover, like a good business man, proposed a one-year moratorium on all international debts. One year later the Lausanne agreement virtually ended reparations. Our newspapers were delighted at this magnanimity displayed toward Germany; but when they discovered that our allies were only willing to forgive Germany provided we forgave them, they were horrified. Hoover, however, realized that there was a real connection between reparations and war debts and he was willing to reopen the debt question at a world economic conference in London. But before it met, Roosevelt succeeded Hoover, and the former commenced his long presidential career by siding with the economic isolationists, thus torpedoing the London conference in 1933. The President, hypnotized by his theory of the commodity dollar, instructed our representatives to have nothing to do with any program which led to any international stabilization of currency, a bad omen, indeed, for future relations between countries. Without such action there was no sense in holding the conference and it shortly closed its sessions.

Toward the end of his first administration the President, realizing that peace was being rapidly undermined, did his best to align the United States with those powers trying to stay the storm cloud of fascism then rising fast in both Europe and Asia. But he was blocked by an isolationist Congress. Thus, in 1935 the United States Senate refused to ratify the World Court Treaty, a most innocuous treaty whereby under carefully worded reservations the United States agreed to join the Permanent Court of International Justice. Isolationists within Congress and without beat patriotic tom-toms, chanting the Declaration of Independence and George Washington's Farewell Address. The world court, they said, was a child of the League and anything sired at Geneva in their eyes was anathema; the world court was a political, not a judicial body and had so shown itself in the decision against Germany in the matter of an Austro-German customs union (*anschluss*); and people of foreign origin with unpronounceable names (Senator Huey Long's argument) might come to sit in judgment on legal disputes concerning the United States.

An even more striking illustration of isolationist strength was the way in which Congress tied our country up in so tangled a web of neutrality legislation as to deprive the Executive of much needed liberty of action. We not only forbade the export of arms and ammunition to all nations at war, irrespective of who was the aggressor, we also turned our face completely against the historic American doctrine of the freedom of the seas, supplanting it by a new doctrine, "cash and carry." No longer did we propose to protect our American ships, our American goods, or even our American citizens upon the ocean lanes. What we fought for in the First World War we now renounced. In case of war we would sell only for money paid down and for delivery on this side of the Pacific or Atlantic.

The League of Nations was supposed to enforce peace by inaugurating sanctions, penalties laid down, economic or otherwise, against predatory powers. American foreign policy also envisaged peace, for America at least, by a theory quite different. Our position during the second half of the thirties was aptly described by Senator Thomas when he said, "The primary object of sanctions is to stop or prohibit war. The primary object of our neutrality is to keep America out of war. The sanction theory is based upon the acceptance of a moral attitude that war is bad, that it is of universal concern and therefore should be prohibited. The neutrality theory does not consider the moral question nor does it accept the idea of wars being a matter of universal concern. War is not condemned by the law; it is merely assumed to exist. Our neutrality's purpose is one of expediency."

This frank statement in some respects comes close to representing average conviction in the United States. It is somewhat unfair to the isolationist majority. They did not consider "expediency" their watchword; instead what was in their minds was the golden dream of American tradition that this country had been set apart by the Almighty as a haven of refuge from the wickedness of the old world and as a home for the free, the brave, the energetic folk who had cast off forever the effete fetters of Europe. The slogan, "The Yanks are not coming" was not yet posted on American billboards but it was deeply imbedded in the psychology of isolationist America.

Europe seemed far away to most Americans. So thoroughgoing, indeed, was reaction in this country against Woodrow Wilson's idealism that many Americans thought on the flimsiest of evidence that our entry into the First World War had been due to hard-boiled munition manufacturers, crafty bankers. Americans were interested in Europe, but at a distance. We were highly critical of the ineptitude of the League of Nations in the Ethiopian crisis, but we had no intention of doing anything ourselves; we denounced the weak-kneed acquiescence of France and England when confronted by the rape of Austria, but we did not regard that dastardly act as our affair; we were wildly indignant at Chamberlain and Bonnet for selling the Czechs down the river, but that America was in any way responsible for Munich never occurred to us. By the middle thirties most Americans were too engrossed, anyway, with the industrial depression at home, to take more than an academic interest in Europe, a fact not displeasing to those three desperado countries, Germany, Italy, and Japan.

The International Scene (1934-39)

During the next six years (1934-39), the remaining bulwarks of European peace were swept away, one by one. All the major countries of Western Europe played at cross-purposes with one another, and charges of double-dealing and treachery reverberated back and forth between Berlin, London, Rome, and Paris. "*Homo homini lupus*—man is a wolf to his fellow-man," said the cynics, pointing to treaties broken almost before the ink dried on the parchment, and to bold words no sooner spoken by bewildered statesmen than repudiated by fatuous contradictory act. With the single exception of the first year, the tide set steadily against the democratic powers, England and France, and in favor of the fascist countries, Germany and Italy. The cynical observer was prompt with his explanation: British Tories and French bourgeois, fearing above everything else the shadow of the Soviet, were willing to jettison the League of Nations and the cause of international peace in the vain hope of protecting their own pocketbooks by an ultimate war between Nazis and Russians from which they themselves would be delivered. The accusation is questionable. It can only be defended by drawing up an indictment based on a priori hypotheses, by using historical data for the purposes of a lawyer's brief. There is no such clear trail to be found in the diplomatic labyrinth of these perplexing and confused years. In summing them up, about all we may truthfully say is this: Hitler and Mussolini, leaders of the "have-not" bloc of nations, found by 1935 that they could play ball with each other by alternating pressure on the democracies. The latter, wedded to the status quo, suspicious of one another's good faith, began a disorganized and almost panic-stricken retreat before fascist advance, until Adolf Hitler, in March, 1939, entered the Czech city of Prague at the head of his armed forces, there proudly to prophesy the rebirth of the Holy Roman Empire of the German Nation, the ghost of which (supposedly) had been finally buried by Napoleon in 1806.

Only during the first year was there a temporary check to the forward march of the German Cæsar. The Nazis overreached themselves when they tried to gain Austria in 1934 by a blundering coup d'état which succeeded only in killing Dollfuss and in enraging his friend and champion Mussolini. The Duce was not yet willing to have the swastika fly in Vienna, and Hitler did not dare aid those Austrian Nazi cutthroats who broke into the chancellery and slaughtered in cold blood Austria's diminutive Christian Socialist dictator.

It is true that direct evidence is lacking that connects the German Fuehrer with that vile act. But the German Nazis could not well have been uninformed of Austrian Nazis on Bavarian soil, who had used the radio for a year past to foment revolution in Austria. They must have known of plans to invade that country from Germany at the very moment when the state radio in Vienna, which the insurgents in Vienna had captured, proclaimed the downfall of the Dollfuss regime.

In 1935 the German star was in the ascendant. In January came the plebiscite in the Saar which united that valley with the Reich. Within two months followed the proclamation of universal military service in Germany. France and England fumed at this repudiation of Versailles. The former country sounded out Russia for a mutually defensive pact and signed one in May, 1935. The latter tried to make the best of a bad situation by a unilateral bargain with Hitler. The realistic British knew a *fait accompli* when they met one. Germany had built two pocket battle-ships, as she was entitled to by the Versailles Treaty. Now Britain agreed to her repudiation of that treaty in regard to naval construction, pro-vided Hitler would promise not to build a fleet more than thirty-five per cent as strong as Britain's.

The French were not pleased by this act on the part of their sister democracy. If the Germans built to within thirty-five per cent of the British they would have a larger fleet than France, a fact not forgotten by the French when there were intimations a year or two later that France was reluctant in assisting the British to maintain sanctions against Mussolini in Abyssinia.

But Germany's greatest triumph lay ahead. On Saturday, March 7, 1936 (the Fuehrer was said always to choose Saturdays for his thunder-bolts because of the British habit of week-ending), Hitler announced that German troops were crossing the Rhine. "We have no territorial demands to make in Europe," said Hitler, "but the Russian menace is intolerable, and France has broken the Locarno treaty by making a defensive pact with that country."

France had done no such thing. There was nothing in the Locarno Treaty which forbade a defensive pact similar to that made between France and Russia in 1935; and even if there had been room for differ-ences of opinion on that point, the signatories of Locarno had pledged themselves to arbitrate questions which might arise in the future con-cerning that treaty. Locarno had been freely entered into by Germany and had been guaranteed by her as well as by France, England, Italy, and Belgium.

Hitler had no legal justification for violating this treaty, and to do so was an extremely risky act. His army was still small and not well trained; and France could easily without aid from outside have driven his troops, only 90,000 at the end of a week, back fifty kilometers east of the Rhine where the Germans had promised to keep them. Only the year before, in 1935, Italy, France, and England at a meeting at Stresa in Italy had formally rebuked Germany for rearming, and Italy was supposed to be very angry at the German threat against Austrian independence at the time of the Dollfuss murder. No wonder that Schacht, the German finance minister, Neurath, the foreign secretary, and Blomberg, commander of the German army, advised against Hitler's rash adventure.

But the Fuehrer trusted to luck. Had not the British made a bargain with Germany whereby they had insured their naval supremacy? He did not think that they would fight to keep German soldiers away from the Rhine. Italy was already in difficulties over her Abyssinian expedition and there were questions of oil sanctions aired at Geneva; he might be of use to the Duce in regard to these. There remained only France; and with the French alone he was willing to take a chance.

GERMAN JUBILATION IN THE SAAR, JANUARY, 1935
Crowds give "Heil Hitler" at announcement of result of Saar plebiscite.

France hesitated and was lost. The Czechs were in alliance with her and would have hit Germany from the south as she struck from the west. It was her golden oppportunity, and all she did was to explode verbal bombs! This grave infringement of the Locarno pact most certainly would have to be referred to Geneva, so she said, and when the League acted, then France would act. General mobilization was too expensive at this time, in the opinion of the French. Their frugality was ill timed. Needless to say, the Germans remained, and nothing happened except many and violent protests on the part of almost everybody, the Germans being loudest of all, saying that they would be perfectly willing to retire fifty kilometers east of the French boundary if the French would retire fifty kilometers west of it.

Mussolini and Abyssinia

Japan defied Geneva and departed from the League in 1933; Germany did likewise in 1934. It was now the turn of the Duce to defy that august body. He had done so in 1923 without let or hindrance, and he thought it fairly safe to do so again in regard to Abyssinia.

That country, like Italy, was a member of the League, but it was a wild, barbaric land without means of self-defense; and it was flanked besides by two low-lying coastal Italian colonies, Eritrea on the Red Sea and Italian Somaliland on the Indian Ocean. The two colonies were not worth much, but they might serve as pincers between which Abyssinia might be squeezed and conquered, and thus a sizable empire found for Italy.

Mussolini knew that the League (as such) would not be apt to prevent him. It had already been greatly weakened by the successive withdrawals of Japan and Germany, and the only interference with his schemes of conquest that he might encounter would come from Britain and France. The former country depended somewhat on the waters of the Blue Nile for the irrigation of Egypt and a British-constructed dam had been projected for Lake Tana, the headwaters of the Blue Nile, and Tana was in Abyssinia. Furthermore, the mistress of the seas was still mistress of the Mediterranean, and an Italian empire to the east of that sea might tempt the Italians to challenge Britain's control of her route to India.

France, of course, would also object, but he was not afraid of France. The tiny French colony of Obok, or French Somaliland, on the Red Sea, lay between the two Italian colonies, and from Djibouti, its capital, ran the only railway to Addis Ababa, the capital of Abyssinia. The conquest of Abyssinia might threaten the French colony and most certainly would involve readjustments in regard to the railway. Furthermore, there had been friction for many decades between France and Italy over Tunis, and a successful Italian campaign in Abyssinia might make the French fear lest the Italians, on conquest bent, might turn west from Libya as well as east, and take Tunis in their stride.

But France, the Duce knew, had her hands full with a revived Germany. So had Britain, too, for that matter, but Britain's frontier did not run side by side with that of Germany on the Rhine, and Britain had less to fear from hostile Germans in the near future than had France. The German Fuehrer had proclaimed after the return of the Saar Valley that he had no further ambitions in the west, but the French did not believe him. With the French concerned first with Germany, the Duce thought that he was fairly safe in attacking Abyssinia.

In 1934, frontier clashes occurred between the tribesmen of the Negus of Abyssinia, the King of Kings, and Italian soldiers in the hinterland of the Italian colony of Eritrea. Ethiopia (to use the new name coming into vogue for Abyssinia) appealed to the League; but Mussolini sent reinforcements to his troops. The League delayed acting on Ethiopia's complaint. An arbitration commission appointed by Geneva decreed with the wisdom of Solomon that no one was responsible for the frontier incident, since it took place in a region where both contestants believed themselves fighting on their own land. Then France and England offered financial aid to Italy in developing the economic resources of Ethiopia, and they got the ruler of that doomed country to consent to this projected exploitation. But this did not please the Duce; he said that he was going to annex part of Ethiopia and that he was determined to set up a protectorate over the rest of that country.

Committees of the League now tried to bring about a compromise of some sort; but while they talked the Duce acted. In 1935 he began an invasion of Ethiopia both from north and south, and in the autumn captured Adowa, the scene of Italy's debacle in 1896. Geneva now plucked up courage; the council of the League denounced Mussolini as the aggressor and so reported to the Assembly, where by a vote of fifty-one to three, sanctions were invoked—Austria, Hungary, and Albania alone supporting Italy. The fifty-one countries agreed that they would withhold from Italy money, munitions, and necessary raw materials, and they also would not buy from her.

For a short time it seemed as though there would be war between Britain (the foremost country urging sanctions) and Italy. A large British fleet was concentrated off Alexandria in the eastern Mediterranean to close, if necessary, the Suez Canal, thus preventing the Duce from sending any reinforcements to Ethiopia; and England's mightiest battleships lay off Gibraltar, to close the western gates of the inland sea.

But there was neither war nor Italian submission. Instead, the Italians defied the League, advanced on Addis Ababa, and finally captured it in May, 1936. The King of Italy was proclaimed Emperor of Ethiopia and the entire country was annexed to Italy. The conquest had cost that country in the neighborhood of one billion dollars and some thousands of lives. And the League of Nations once again had proved its futility. England, not Italy, had been compelled to eat humble pie. And why? Presumably the historian does not know yet what happened in the British cabinet in the late autumn of 1935. In October Mr. Baldwin was resolute enough and promised "no wavering." No sooner, however, was he safely returned to office than his foreign secretary, Sir Samuel Hoare, made an agreement with Premier Laval of France, by which England and France agreed that the Duce might annex large parts of northern Ethiopia, become entrusted with the economic exploitation of southern Ethiopia, and assume even a kind of veiled protectorate over what was left of Haile Selassie's kingdom, the League of Nations to act as "a kind of consulting specialist, or more probably as a mortician." The implication, to the British Labor party and to the Liberals, was plain: Baldwin had betrayed the cause of collective security; he had permitted himself to be reëlected on a platform supporting the League of Nations and sanctions; once in office again he had shown his real hand, and that of the class-conscious Tories who really admired Mussolini, by offering up Ethiopia as a sacrifice to the Duce and dynamiting the League. Instantly there was hue and cry raised against Baldwin, and this time not by the Laborites and Liberals alone. The Prime Minister, in evil odor with many of his own Tories, yielded before the storm. Sir Samuel Hoare resigned and Anthony Eden, a great advocate of Geneva and of sanctions, succeeded him.

The government intended to continue sanctions; so it said. But it did so half-heartedly, the necessary supply of oil not being cut off. The Duce did not worry; the Germans would soon give the British more serious things to worry about than Ethiopia, and so he pushed his soldiers forward until by the spring of 1936 Addis Ababa was in their hands.

During the interval Hitler occupied the Rhineland and unilaterally tore up Locarno, a menace which struck home to France, which had no intention whatever of risking a war with Italy over Ethiopia. The British knew that they could hold the Mediterranean against the Duce; but how about the North Sea; and the German airplanes as an additional liability if they chose to check the German Fuehrer's forward march?

The Germans were rearming with lightninglike speed. From 1933 to 1936 inclusive it was estimated that they spent some $7,500,000,000 on rearmament, and a large part of that sum on new airplanes. Britain might control the sea but she was well behind in the air race. Winston Churchill instantly sounded the alarm. The facts were that Germany was spending money on rearmament at a much faster rate than Britain, and the Prime Minister's reply to Churchill was not effective. "Supposing," said Mr. Baldwin, "I had gone to the country (1933) and said that Germany was rearming and that we must rearm, does anybody think

SWITZ. AUSTRIA HUNGARY

RUMANIA

YUGO-
SLAVIA

ITALY

Nice
(FR)

CORSICA
(FR)

Rome

SARDINIA

SICILY

PANTELL-
ERIA
(IT.)

MALTA
(BR)

TUNISIA
(FR)

ALGERIA
(FR)

MEDITERRANEAN SEA

BULGARIA

BLACK SEA

SOVIET

UNION

CASPIAN
SEA

ALBANIA

GREECE

TURKEY

DODECANESE IS.
(ITALY)

CYPRUS
(BR)

SYRIA

IRAQ

IRAN

Tripoli

Bengazi

Alexandria

PALESTINE

SUEZ
CANAL

Cairo

TRANS-
JORDAN

LIBYA

EGYPT

Aswan

RED SEA

SAUDI

ARABIA

FRENCH

WEST

AFRICA

FRENCH

EQUATORIAL

AFRICA

NIGERIA
(BR)

NILE

ANGLO-

EGYPTIAN

SUDAN

Khartoum

BLUE NILE

Port
Sudan

Massawa

ERITREA

Adowa

LAKE
TANA

Addis
Ababa

ETHIOPIA

YEMEN

ADEN
PROT.
(BR)

FRENCH
SOMALILAND

BRITISH
SOMALILAND

ITALIAN
SOMALILAND

ITALIAN EMPIRE

1939

BELGIAN
CONGO

UGANDA
(BR)

KENYA
(BR)

LAKE
VICTORIA

TRM

that this pacific democracy would have rallied to that cry at that moment? I cannot think of anything that would have made the loss of the election from my point of view more certain."

Thus spoke Baldwin in November, 1936. Four months earlier Geneva had lifted sanctions and Mussolini's victory was complete.

Spain

No sooner had England and France abandoned Ethiopia to its fate than they became concerned about Spain. In the summer of 1936 General Francisco Franco raised the standard of revolt, as we have seen, and a sanguinary war commenced which was to rage with unabated fury for almost three years.

At times it almost seemed as though this civil war were an international one, or about to become so. The Italians and the Germans supported Franco, both morally and physically. They sent him supplies, munitions, airplanes, and also men—the Italians an expeditionary force, the Germans air pilots and technicians. The Russians, on the other hand, forwarded a number of planes to the hard-pressed Spanish Republicans during the first part of the conflict, and from Britain, France, the United States, and elsewhere many thousand volunteers, for the most part communist sympathizers, dashed to the fray, forming an international brigade which did yeoman service fighting against Franco and his rebels.

The Spanish Republicans (the Loyalists) fought against terrific odds, and had they received half as much assistance from the outside world as did Franco and his Fascists, they would have won. Even as it was, the medley of Spanish leftists who composed the Republican or Loyalist armies put up the only real fight waged in all Europe against triumphant fascism between Hitler's advent to power in 1933 and the Second World War of 1939. Even if the French, British, and Americans had only permitted the Loyalists to buy arms in the open market, they might still have kept the Fascists at bay. But this opportunity was denied them. A strict embargo was maintained against the Republicans, but no such embargo, except on paper, prevented the free flow of arms to Franco and the Fascists.

Why was this so? The French government was leftist under Blum, and why could not the popular front in France support the popular front in Spain? It certainly was not to the interest of any Frenchman to have Italian armies south of the Pyrenees in friendly collaboration with German airmen, nor to have Italian troops in the Balearic Islands menacing the French communication with Algeria. The British foreign policy was directed by Tories; but the latter by tradition were supposedly imperialistic, and the extension of German and Italian influence was scarcely a favorable augury for the British Empire. Presumably, both Italians and

Germans would be paid somehow by Franco. There were the Straits of Gibraltar for the British to consider, to say nothing of Port Mahon in Minorca which might readily fall into Italian hands, a *point d'appui* in the western Mediterranean similar to Malta in the eastern; there were the Spanish copper and iron mines which the British might not care to have under Hitler's control. Why, then, should England and France turn their backs on cries for aid from stricken Spain and give, as they did, a completely free hand to Hitler and to Mussolini?

Two reasons would seem to have motivated France—fear of Germany and advice from England. Blum, the premier, had just taken office. He knew that his country was far from united, that there were discordant elements in his Popular Front threatening its dissolution any moment, that his country was in no mood for challenging both Germany and Italy, that those two countries were already collaborating with each other in Spain, that France could not possibly survive another war with Germany without the active assistance of Britain, and that in this emergency it was necessary to let England take the lead. The British motivations were somewhat different. The Conservatives in control of Downing Street disliked all radicals in general and communists in particular. They considered the Spanish Civil War an ideological struggle in which there was so much to be said on both sides that there was nothing to be said for intervening on behalf of either. They wanted a stable government in Spain with which they could do business, and the various leftist alliances which formed the Loyalist majority they suspected would prove unstable. The Loyalists might claim to be merely Republicans, but the British Tories saw communists and anarchists of every stripe and description allied with them, and the fact that the Pope had publicly blessed Franco's cause made them perhaps unduly suspicious of his Spanish enemies. Then, too, Russia was supporting the Loyalists, and the British tradition, with the exception of 1907-17, had been Russophobe for over a century. Lenin and Stalin had been bitter in their jibes against British imperialism, and Russian policy had been orientated too long against the British Empire for British Tories to regard the friends of Soviet Russia with a friendly eye. Neither Hitler nor Mussolini had gone so far as the Russians in abolishing the very foundations of bourgeois society, namely, private property, and possibly they were less dangerous in the long run than Moscow. The British Tories were not prepared to sacrifice the national interests of Britain for their own class interests, but they did tend to identify their class interests with those of the nation. They longed for appeasement, the end of war, the lowering of taxes, and the unity of western Europe against the Soviets—if such were only possible. Whether they went so far as to tell Blum that England would not support him if he got in trouble with Hitler over the Spanish situation is a matter of conjecture. The facts are that Blum visited London, made a favorable impression there, returned to France, and then put on a strict embargo on all arms exported to either side in Spain.

To do so was scarcely to preserve neutrality. By international law the Loyalists, as the official government of Spain, had a right to buy arms in foreign countries, whereas Franco's regime was legally only a rebellion and was not entitled to buy arms. Consequently, the British, the French, and the Americans who placed an interdict on the sale of all arms must be said actually to have taken sides with the Spanish Fascists, no matter how far their sympathies lay with the other side.

Italy and Germany, meanwhile, recognized Franco's government as the legal government of Spain and sent him arms and men. They did, it is true, preserve a semblance of neutrality, since they agreed to join with twenty-five other nations in adopting a policy of nonintervention. All twenty-seven countries prohibited volunteering for the Spanish war, and an international committee meeting in London supported an international blockade of Spain to be carried out by the British, French, Italian, and German navies.

The blockade was a farce; neither Germany nor Italy paid any attention to it. A number of British and Russian freighters were sunk by submarines, supposedly of Italian origin, and for a brief period the international horizon looked very dark. There were threats from England and the submarining ceased. But not so the flooding of Spain by Italian volunteers. England and France tried to get Italy to withdraw her nationals, but Italy hedged, claiming that she could not enter any conference in regard to Spain without the inclusion of Germany, and that belligerent rights should first be extended to Franco. Later in the year 1937, when Franco's victories in northwestern Spain seemed indicative of ultimate conquest, Italy and Germany said they would be willing to consider "token withdrawals," provided they were made by both sides.

The fatal year 1938 dawned with democracy in retreat everywhere before advancing fascism. Baldwin had been succeeded in 1937 as prime minister by Neville Chamberlain, as prone even as his predecessor to make concessions. Chamberlain was determined to appease both Hitler and Mussolini, and this meant the sacrifice of his foreign secretary, Anthony Eden. The latter had acted reluctantly at Geneva as England's agent in removing sanctions against Italy; but he was determined that he would not give way in regard to Italian soldiers in Spain. Chamberlain thought otherwise and took Italian negotiations in his own hand. Eden resigned, a hero to Liberals and Laborites, and to many of the Tories as well, although party discipline kept them from going into the lobby with the opposition. The Duce was delighted and promptly signed an agreement with England on April 16, pledging the withdrawal of Italian troops from Spain *after* the termination of the war. One day earlier Franco reached the sea, thus cutting Loyalist Spain in two halves. That the war could continue in the Iberian peninsula for another year seemed beyond belief.

Austria

The downfall of Eden synchronized with the end of Austrian independence. Hitler's timing had been perfect. He had supported Mussolini tacitly in Ethiopia and openly in Spain; it was now his turn, and the pay and the prey was Austria. The English and the French had not been without intimation of the Fuehrer's dash to the Danube. Rapprochement between the two dictators of Central Europe had become more and more pronounced during the preceding autumn. The Duce was welcomed with pomp at Berlin. Shortly afterward he proclaimed his adherence to an anti-Comintern pact between Germany and Japan, which seemed to prophesy a political alliance between the three Fascist states. And as the year closed, Rumania seemed on the verge of joining the Fascist parade with a pro-Fascist premier. Early in 1938, Hitler announced that Germany would not forget her racial comrades who were persecuted in other lands. He mentioned 10,000,000 of them—and nearly 7,000,000 were in Austria. He then reorganized the German high command, dismissing certain conservative generals and appointing in their place officers said to be more amenable. Nazi agitation increased visibly in Austria, and a Nazi plot was unearthed whereby a legion of exiled Nazi agitators was to march on Austria from nearby Germany to save their country from the Red menace. Schuschnigg, successor to the martyred Dollfuss, feared the worst and fled to Rome to beseech the Duce to protect Austria as he had done four years earlier.

Then Schuschnigg received an invitation from Hitler to attend him at Berchtesgaden, the favorite residence of the Fuehrer, in Bavaria. Here he was berated for many hours by an angry Hitler and presented with an ultimatum. He must release all Nazi prisoners in Austria; he must give Austrian Nazis full political rights; and he must appoint two Nazis to his cabinet. These were Germany's minimum demands.

Schuschnigg hurried back to Vienna and made another desperate attempt to talk to Mussolini. The latter could not be located. The Chancellor then capitulated. With the streets full of recently imprisoned Nazis and with a Nazi in the cabinet in command of the police, it was the beginning of the end. The Chancellor made belated overtures to the Socialists shot down by Dollfuss, but it was too late. There was no help to be had from without in this month of March, 1938. France was in the midst of a ministerial crisis and had no government; in London the German ambassador, Ribbentrop, was supposedly laying the foundations for an Anglo-German entente; and in Italy the Duce had gone skiing.

EXPANSION OF NAZI
GERMANY
1935-39

100 MILES

MEMEL
ANNEXED
1939

BOHEMIA AND
MORAVIA ANNEXED
MARCH, 1939

POLISH AND HUNGARIAN
GAINS FROM
CZECHOSLOVAK PARTITION

SLOVAKIA BECOMES
GERMAN PROTECTORATE
MARCH, 1939

AUSTRIA
ANNEXED
MARCH, 1938

SAAR BASIN
ANNEXED
MARCH, 1935

RHINELAND
REOCCUPIED
MARCH, 1936

SUDETEN AREAS
ANNEXED
OCTOBER, 1938

LITHUANIA

Vilna

Memel

EAST
PRUSSIA

Danzig

POLAND

Warsaw

VISTULA

BALTIC SEA

NORTH SEA

DENMARK

GERMANY

Hamburg

Bremen

Berlin

ELBE

Dresden

Breslau

ODER

SILESIA

Prague

BOHEMIA

CZECHOSLOVAKIA

MORAVIA

Vienna

Slovakia

SUBCARPATHIAN
RUTHENIA

RUMANIA

HUNGARY

AUSTRIA

Munich

DANUBE

Stuttgart

Cologne

RHINE

NETHERLANDS

BELGIUM

FRANCE

Geneva

ITALY

TRM

Schuschnigg resigned, as per order, but that did not stop the Germans. The new Austrian Chancellor requested Hitler to march in and restore order. The Fuehrer generously acceded. His triumph in the land of his forefathers was complete. After April, Austria no longer existed as a state, 99.75 per cent of its inhabitants approving by a popular plebiscite its incorporation into the Third Reich as the *Ostmark*.

Thus there came to an end another of the provisos of the Versailles pact—Austrian independence. And the Fuehrer had broken his word once again. In 1934 he had promised to respect Austrian independence, and in 1938 he had promised Schuschnigg that if the latter yielded to the German ultimatum he would reaffirm his promise. Both promises were broken. France and England pretended to be deeply shocked. Chamberlain said he was shocked. There were even whispers of what the half-buried League might do. In Czechoslovakia, now surrounded on three sides by Nazi Germany, there were those who recalled Hitler's words of the previous January in regard to ten million racial comrades. Seven of the ten millions had been redeemed by Austria's annexation, including those unfortunate Austrians who happened to be Jews, Slavs, and Magyars. Roughly speaking, there were three and a quarter million Germans in Czechoslovakia; could it be that they were the remaining racial comrades in captivity?

Czechoslovakia

The Czechs had watched with anxious eye, as well they might, the submergence of their southern neighbor in the German Reich. Not only did they have Nazis to the north of them and Nazis to the south of them, but within their own border was a clamorous German minority. It had received more consideration than that given to any other minority in the postwar world. It had full parliamentary representation and equal educational opportunities—in fact, there were more German secondary schools in Czechoslovakia in proportion to the population than there were schools for Czechs. On the other hand, that German minority had just cause for complaint: Public officials were generally Czechs; and minor officials, such as postmen and ticket agents, were apt to pretend that they could not understand German. The great estates in Czechoslovakia before the war had been owned by German landlords who were dissatisfied with the compensation paid them when the lands were subdivided after the war among the peasants. More important yet, the condition of the German workingmen in the industrial districts was deplorable. The Czechs were not responsible for the world economic depression of the nineteen-thirties, but they might have been more generous in the relief given to the stricken areas. At one time there were nearly a million unemployed in this little country, and over half were Germans!

Until 1935 most of the Germans in Czechoslovakia coöperated with the Czechs in carrying on parliamentary government, but in that year Konrad Henlein's *Sudetendeutsch Partei,* intransigent and disaffected, captured sixty per cent of the German vote. This party, the S.d.P., was not originally allied with the German Nazis. It did, however, stress certain German principles: hatred of democracy, devout obedience to a Fuehrer—Henlein—and racial particularism. The S.d.P.'s demands now increased, one of them being "full liberty for Germans to proclaim their Germanism and their adhesion to the ideology of Germans," and another a demand that Czechoslovakia should renounce its treaties with France and Russia, the former calling for the military support of the Third Republic should Germany threaten invasion, the latter promising Russian aid, provided France aided the threatened state first. Neither of these demands could safely be granted by the Czech majority; to accede to the first would invite open propaganda against democracy in a democratic state; to accede to the second would make Czechoslovakia defenseless in case of attack.

War was narrowly averted in the month of May, 1938. A frontier incident resulted in the death of two Germans; Hitler promptly cut off negotiations with the Czechs and hastened troops to the border. Czechoslovakia as promptly mobilized and rushed 400,000 men to the German frontier. France affirmed her support of Czechoslovakia and that meant that Russia must follow suit. Britain agreed to support France, and Hitler withdrew his troops.

But he did not change his intentions, nor did the Czechs their resolution to fight for their country. What did take place during the four succeeding months was the betrayal of Czechoslovakia by France, aided and abetted to no little degree by England.

It is very difficult to fathom what lay behind French and British policy in the crisis of September, 1938. Mile by mile the two governments gave way to Hitler's threats and bombast, until finally there was nothing left of Czechoslovakia except a completely disillusioned and discouraged little rump of a country, which could not fight if it wanted to, and which was occupied without a shot by the Fuehrer the following spring.

Czechoslovakia was by no means defenseless in the summer of 1938. She had a good army, a mountainous frontier, defended by a Maginot line reputed stronger than even the famous line of that name in France. Near Prague were the strategic Skoda munitions works, the largest in all Europe, owned by a resolute people, protected not simply by their natural frontiers but by the pledged word of France. In addition, Czechoslovakia was a member of the Little Entente, and both Yugoslavia and Rumania were sworn to aid her. True, Yugoslavia might stand aside for fear of Mussolini, and Rumania was not a dependable ally. But the Rumanians presumably would at least permit the passage of Soviet troops through their territory to aid the Czechs if they were attacked. With France, England, and Russia behind them it seemed improbable that Mussolini would give any active aid to Hitler in order that the latter might occupy Prague.

Nevertheless, the British and the French between them opened the mountain passes to the Bohemian plain, permitted Nazi troops to pass through unopposed, and thus made sure of a war in which they would not have Czechoslovakia as their ally, and Hitler would have Skoda.

The feeble and inept behavior of Britain and France during the last six months of 1938 is incredible. It began when the British sent Lord Runciman to Prague as a kind of unofficial adviser to the Czechs. The Czechs did not ask for him; they did not want him; but they were afraid that if they did not accept him Britain would wash her hands altogether and persuade France to do likewise. Chamberlain had blown neither hot nor cold. He had refused a definite guarantee of Czech independence, but at the same time he had intimated that British policy was not to be interpreted as one of non-intervention under all circumstances. Plainly, they had better accept Runciman.

The Czechs, urged on by his lordship, now offered generous concessions to the S.d.P. and Henlein. They agreed to a cantonal division of Czechoslovakia on the Swiss model. "All nationalities should share proportionately in all state offices and in state enterprises, monopolies, institutions and other organizations." Autonomy in all local matters was assured the Sudetendeutsch, and a large sum of money was to be granted for their economic relief.

This was fair enough, but not sufficiently fair for the London *Times*. It proposed that Czechoslovakia cede its border districts to Germany. The *Times*, of course, was not an official organ of the British government, but the Nazis had good reason to believe that it flew the Chamberlain kite. Hitler took the cue. A few days later, September 12, he addressed a huge meeting of Nazis and said that he intended to come instantly to the relief of his oppressed racial comrades in Czechoslovakia and announced simultaneously that the most impregnable defenses ever built by man were being rushed to completion on the western frontier of Germany.

On September 13 there were uprisings among the Sudeten Germans (acknowledged later by Runciman to have been stirred up by Nazi agitators) and the instant reply of Beneš, President of Czechoslovakia, was to proclaim martial law. One day later Chamberlain announced that he would go by airplane to consult with Hitler.

This was to be the first of three trips by air to Canossa which the Prime Minister of England was to take—successive steps, all of them, in humiliating subservience to the will of the German dictator. The first flight was to Berchtesgaden, where he was told by Hitler that Germany insisted on the instant inclusion of the Sudeten Germans in the Third Reich, even at the cost of a general war. Time would be given Chamberlain to consult with his ministers; no other concession was offered.

What was to be done? The British cabinet was divided; so was the French. The Premier of France and his foreign secretary flew to London and a decision was reached without consulting Prague. Czechoslovakia was told by England and France that she must deliver "the districts mainly inhabited by the Sudeten Germans" to Germany. If this was done there would be guarantees of her future independence.

This was selling the pass, for the districts to be ceded lay along the frontier where the Czechs had their fortifications. England and France were now offering Hitler all that he demanded. Beneš and his cabinet begged for reconsideration. Czechoslovakia had, they said, a treaty of arbitration with Germany. Why not invoke it?

Runciman, meanwhile, made his formal report. It proposed not only to give Germany all that Hitler had demanded but a little more, for he suggested not only that parts of Czechoslovakia be ceded Germany but also that the rump which remained should renounce all treaties of defense with other countries, suppress all anti-German agitation, and enter into close economic relations with the Reich.

The Runciman report was followed by sharp insistence at Prague on the part of the French and British ambassadors that Beneš agree to the Anglo-French proposals. Beneš asked that the demands be given him in writing; he was refused. Would the Czechs yield or not? If France fought on their side they had a good chance, but even so there were German divisions to the south of them in Austria and their own Maginot line was in the north. They would, in any case, be subject to a severe bombardment from the air. But France had now repudiated her word, and without France, Russia was under no obligation. Beneš and his colleagues decided to yield—with the understanding, they said, that Britain and France would guarantee the future independence of what was left of their country, and that the land transferred to Germany would not be occupied by German troops until the new frontiers had been delimited.

Whereupon followed Chamberlain's second flight to Canossa, this time to the little German town of Godesberg. To his surprise he found Hitler in a towering rage. The German army was going to march on October first, roared the Fuehrer, and nothing could stop it. There might be "subsequent corrections" in the boundaries suggested, and perhaps plebiscites. But Germany was going to take by force what was hers by right and would listen to no one. Hitler presented Chamberlain with a map showing what districts Germany was going to annex immediately, and Chamberlain received it, agreed to present it to the Czechs without recommendation, and flew back to London.

The Czechs indignantly rejected the Godesberg ultimatum, the British mobilized their fleet, the French their army. It looked like war. Trenches were dug in London streets, tanks and trucks rolled through Berlin on their way south, and gas masks were distributed in Paris. The British foreign office gave categorical assurance to France that Britain would come to her assistance if she took military action against Germany in the event of that country's invading Czechoslovakia—a much stronger guarantee than Britain gave France on August 2, 1914. Seemingly, Hitler must give way or the Second World War would break.

The Fuehrer gave no indication of yielding. Within five days his Germans were to march. He had no claims, he said, against Poland or France. "After the Sudeten German question is regulated," he asserted, "we have no further territorial claims to make in Europe." But October 1 was the deadline, and to prove that he meant business, German divisions were concentrated on the Czech frontier, and German workmen labored day and night on the "Westwall." To frighten the democracies he even took another step: "German action" (whatever that meant), he told the British ambassador, would commence the next day at 2 P.M., namely, on September 28.

The democracies, on the other hand, did give signs of yielding. The French newspapers deliberately minimized as unofficial the British guarantee of standing by France; and Chamberlain, in a most ambiguous speech, showed that he was of two minds—he spoke of Czechoslovakia as a "far-away country" for whom it seemed almost impossible that England would be fighting, the general tenor of his remarks in the House of Commons sounding more like Hamlet than Pitt or Palmerston. Then, just as the last sands were running out of the hourglass, the Fuehrer, at the request of Mussolini, postponed mobilization twenty-four hours and invited Daladier and Chamberlain to a conference with the Duce and himself at Munich.

Chamberlain accepted, and for the third time made a journey to Canossa. This Munich Conference was still another victory for the dictators. Czechoslovakia was an uninvited onlooker as the four statesmen carved up that unhappy country in accordance with the Godesberg ultimatum. Minute concessions of no importance were made by which England and France might save face. Four zones were to be occupied by the Germans "in four rapid bites instead of one." A fifth zone was created in which there were supposed to be plebiscites. "But the final result was worse for the Czechs than Godesberg would have been." The international commission supposedly in control of plebiscites was a farce. The Germans took what they wanted, marched to within forty miles of

Prague, and absorbed about 750,000 Czechs in the new Germany. As they did so the Poles invaded Teschen, annexing about 80,000 Poles and 120,000 Czechs. Hungary then advanced on the helpless Czechs from the south, crossed the Danube, took Bratislava, and would have divided Ruthenia and perhaps Slovakia with Poland had she been permitted to by the all-powerful Germans. The latter, together with the Italians, decided everything. All French and British guarantees vanished into thin air.

"I return from Germany," said Chamberlain to cheering thousands, "bringing peace with honor." He brought back neither.

Why did the British give way all along the line? Several explanations have been offered. A number of journalists asserted that the British Tories were bluffing from the beginning, that the mobilization of the fleet was a blind and a fake, carried on to deceive the simple, the real intent of the Tories being to support Hitler so that he might become strong enough to be ultimately victorious over Soviet Russia, or at least strong enough to act as their agent in staving off the Red menace. This is pure assumption and a rather silly one, for it lays too much emphasis on economic determinism and suggests an altogether too complicated and subtle a plot. The Tories, after all, were British citizens, and to impugn their patriotism and common sense without evidence is, to say the least, not being historically minded.

Another conjecture was that Britain was profoundly pacifistic, unwilling to fight in any cause which did not directly concern land over which flew the Union Jack. In this there was probably an element of truth, but not a great deal. Pacifistic or otherwise, the sons of John Bull presumably had not been transformed in less than a generation into gentle Quakers.

Two other reasons for Chamberlain's stand come closer to the truth. He knew that, arrogant and boastful though Hitler might be, he had a good talking point in demanding the inclusion of Sudeten Germans in the Reich on the grounds of self-determination. Bohemia had been a part of the old Austria, not a part of the old Germany, but that could not offset altogether the argument for self-determination. Might not Hitler be content with just annexing Germans? Perhaps there was a possibility that he would be! And finally, and perhaps most important of all, was the military argument. Russia was an uncertain factor. The Soviets were said to have promised 200 airplanes for the defense of Czechoslovakia, but on the border of that country were 1,000 German planes that probably would sweep over it before France, England, and Russia could do anything. Stalin had but recently put to death so many generals that Chamberlain might well have questioned the importance of any help Russia might provide, even if she honored her treaty with France. The French were well prepared with their Maginot line for defense, but how could they reach Czechoslovakia to rescue that country from Hitler's maw? And if the French could not, how about England? His first duty was to secure the safety of his own country. He knew that Germany was better prepared for air battles than Britain, and it is possible that he had reliable information that the Reich had a two-to-one superiority in the air. Could he afford to risk a war under such circumstances? Possibly Hitler was bluffing; but on the other hand, possibly he was not. Chamberlain's role in this affair certainly was not brilliant, but that does not necessarily mean that it was absurd. Perhaps he had some right to feel that Baldwin and MacDonald were more responsible in the long run than himself, for it was they who neglected for so many years to make ready against the day when no argument could prevail against Hitler's lawless will unless backed by superior force.

The triumphant Germans, meanwhile, had won two astonishing diplomatic victories in less than six months, since without any fighting at all not only Austria but also the mountain bastions of Bohemia lay in their hands. Hitler had solemnly pledged himself to go no farther, but he had not the slightest intention of keeping his word. Having swallowed somewhat more than one-third of the area of Czechoslovakia, and somewhat less than one-third of the population, he was still greedy for more. What was left of the Republic of Czechoslovakia soon found that it was independent in name only and that it must look to Berlin for guidance. The Germans demanded and obtained a corridor across the country for a military highway; they demanded and obtained the right to decide on the destinies of Slovakia and Ruthenia, not only in respect to government but also in respect to how much land should be ceded to Poland and Hungary. And when Hacha, the last president of the republic, protested against Germany's highhanded interference, he, like Schuschnigg, was summoned to Hitler's presence.

His going to Germany was a formality. Even before he reached Berlin, the German army had started south again. Hacha, berated and browbeaten by Hitler, signed away the independence of his country, and almost simultaneously with his so doing, the Germans entered Prague, none resisting. A few snowballs were thrown at the Teutonic invader; that was all. Czechoslovakia was made a German protectorate, and Hitler could boast of adding still more military booty, to say nothing of much needed gold, to Germany's store.

In characteristic vein, he boasted also of the first German Reich which had been born again. That German Reich had been the Holy Roman Empire, reaching far across the Rhine into France and across the Alps into the heart of Italy.

And he spoke of other things as well, this fateful month of March, 1939. It was not self-determination that Hitler emphasized now, but rather the idea of a German *Lebensraum,* a living space, which he was now in process of gaining for the Third Reich. How large was that living space to be, and where beyond Czechoslovakia was it to be extended? Always until March, 1939, there had been explanations of Nazi diplomacy based upon the iniquity of Versailles and of the violations by the Allies of the sacred right of self-determination. But the demise of Czechoslovakia could not thus be explained. Quite evident it now seemed to thoughtful men that, unless Hitler was stopped, a large part of eastern Europe would fall speedily under his control. And after that, what about Alsace-Lorraine, and French, Belgian, Dutch, and British colonies?

Chapter 16

THE SECOND WORLD WAR

THE OCCUPATION of Prague made war well nigh inevitable. Up to that event there was always a chance that Hitler would be content with his many victories; from now on it was evident that the Nazis were bent on further conquest. Always hitherto they had been able to argue that their successive victories had simply united to the Reich good Germans who longed for a common fatherland. That argument no longer held. The Czechs were not Germans, and the brutal attack on their country in March, 1939, seemed conclusive evidence that Hitler would not stop until the entire continent lay under his thumb—and perhaps not then! Presumably Poland might well be his next victim, but after Poland, what country? It might be Russia; but there were those in London fully aware that Britain administered former German colonies; and there were those in Paris who remembered the ominous words in *Mein Kampf*, "The German people's irreconcilable and mortal enemy is and remains France."

In the spring of 1939, France and England increased their military preparations, drew closer political ties, sought allies. They struck alliances with Poland and Turkey; they guaranteed to march to the aid of the former if she were invaded by Germany; they joined the latter in a mutual defense pact to preserve the status quo in the eastern Mediterranean; they promised unilateral protection to Greece and Rumania; and they invited the Soviets to join them in a defense pact against German aggression.

Joseph Stalin pondered deeply. He hated and distrusted Hitler; he also hated and distrusted Chamberlain. If the Germans drove through Poland or across the Baltic states and attacked Russia, guarantees were needed of armed support from France and Britain. But suppose those two countries failed him at the last hour; suppose they consented to a second Munich whereby Poland fell a prey to Germany and the Wehrmacht stood on the borders of the Ukraine? France and England had ignored Russia in 1938; Stalin had not been invited to Munich; the protests of his representative, Litvinoff, had been ignored at Geneva; the two western powers had abandoned, apparently, the whole idea of collective

313

security. There seemed to be more than an even chance, so Stalin thought, that they would not be displeased at a German-Russian war from which they would stand aloof.

The inept and temporizing character of Franco-British diplomacy did much to heighten his suspicions. Chamberlain three times had flown to Germany to placate Hitler, and Chamberlain, accompanied by Lord Halifax, secretary of state for foreign affairs, had visited Mussolini; but to Moscow at the height of the crisis the British had accredited as their special envoy an under-official of the foreign office, without prestige, without authority.

Nevertheless, Stalin stood ready to make a hard-and-fast military alliance with France and Britain, provided that it included not only guarantees for Poland but for all six small countries on the western Russian frontier, Finland, Estonia, Latvia, Lithuania, Poland and Rumania; guarantees not only against external but also against internal aggression. What this latter meant was clear enough to Stalin. He proposed to ward off and to prevent Fascist propaganda and revolt from within, such as had given Hitler his excuse for invading Czechoslovakia.

These guarantees the British and French were unwilling to give. They feared, and perhaps justly, a Soviet advance in the region of the Baltic, and they argued that the Baltic countries did not want a Soviet guarantee. They would guarantee Poland and Rumania alone; but Stalin thought an attack by the Germans on Russia might readily be staged through the Baltic countries, and he held out for their inclusion in any pact.

Germany, meanwhile, claiming that she was being encircled, and flushed with her bloodless victory of March pounced upon the tiny area of Memel on her northeastern border, hitherto administered by Lithuania in the name of the League of Nations, and made demands on Poland for the return of Danzig to the Reich, together with a strip of land across the Polish Corridor. As she did so Hitler renounced his ten-year peace pact with Poland, proclaiming that the treaties just made by that country with the western democracies had broken friendly relations between Germany and Poland. Likewise for good measure he renounced Germany's naval treaty with Great Britain.

At the other end of the Axis the Duce, not to be outdone, let forth a tremendous blast against the follies of democracy and peace, invaded Albania, and annexed that country to Italy.

The spring of 1939 had been hectic, the summer more so. None could tell just what was happening in Moscow.

Then in late July the French and British sent a military commission to Moscow. Despite many clear warnings from a number of authoritative sources that Stalin might bargain with Hitler, it did not go by airplane; it took a slow steamer and did not reach Moscow until August 10th. Immediately it encountered a snag. The Russians were willing to fight the Germans in Poland provided the Red army was permitted to defend Poland's western boundary. But neither the Poles nor the western allies would accept this qualification. If the Russians were once in Poland, who could or would evict them? On the other hand, from the Russian viewpoint, if the Red army was to fight the Nazis it did not intend to wait until the latter swallowed Poland and were on the Russian border.

Stalin, in the meanwhile, determined not to be caught napping. If the anti-Nazi powers would not do business with him, he would do business with the Nazis. It would be a risky thing to do, but to wait longer was also risky. So it came about that on August 23rd the Nazi foreign minister, Von Ribbentrop, was welcomed in Moscow, and one day later a Soviet-German non-aggression pact was signed, the two contracting powers agreeing that for a period of ten years they would "refrain from any violence, from any aggressive action, and any attack against each other, individually or jointly with other powers."

The Brief Polish Campaign

This act gave the green light to the Nazis in Poland, and in Germany the government-controlled press unleashed a slashing attack on that country, accusing her not only of refusing all concessions but of maltreating Germans within her borders. The Polish question must be settled immediately, said Hitler. He would be content with the return of Danzig to the Reich and the ownership of a super-corridor across the Polish Corridor, in other words with a strip of territory one kilometer wide, sufficient for four railways or motor roads; but that strip must be German. Polish lines of communication north and south must go over or under this strip.

In the summer the skies darkened over Poland. Poles were persecuted in Germany, according to the Polish newspapers; Germans were brutalized in Poland, if the German press was to be believed. Hitler outdid himself in truculence; he would negotiate no longer with the Polish ambassador; the Poles must send a plenipotentiary to Berlin, presumably their prime minister, to accept a German ultimatum, else Germany would act.

In vain did the French and British ambassadors at Berlin assure the Fuehrer that they would investigate carefully German charges made against the Poles. Hitler would not listen, asserting that he had no quarrel with Western Europe, that England and France had no right to intervene in Polish-German controversies. German troops were concentrated on the Polish border and south of it in Slovakia, supposedly an independent country. Then, to frighten the Western democracies still further, Hitler published in triumph a ten-year non-aggression pact with Soviet Russia.

his old enemy. Germany was secure now on the east; let the two democracies to the west beware!

The Germans, set on forcing the issue, on August 31 presented the British ambassador with a peace proposal in sixteen points which considerably enlarged their demands on Poland. Not only were Danzig and the extraterritorial traffic zone to be annexed, but also there were to be plebiscites whereby the Germans hoped to add the entire Polish Corridor to the Reich. The Poles, unwilling to sign on the dotted line, were not unwilling to negotiate. But Hitler refused to wait longer. On September 1, without declaration of war, the German armies invaded Poland, Hitler asserting that he had waited two days for the Poles to submit, that Germans were being mutilated by Polish mobs, and that the preceding night Polish troops had fired across the border.

Within one month Poland was conquered. England and France declared war on Germany on September 3, but did nothing to stave off annihilation of their ally. The first day of September saw Warsaw bombed three times and German armies advancing on doomed Poland from four different points. So swift was the German onrush by motorized divisions on land and by squadrons of planes in the air that the Poles never had a chance. While optimistic prophets in London and Paris predicted that French and British planes would soon be shuttling back and forth across Germany to Polish airfields to refuel and return, those very airfields were wrecked by German bombs, and Polish planes were destroyed on the ground. The famous Polish cavalry was helpless against the German *panzer* (armored) divisions. Brilliant sunshine baked the Polish plain, and the rain upon which the Poles depended to make their fields a sea of mud failed to materialize. By the middle of the month all of Poland's important cities (except Warsaw) were in German hands and the Polish government had begun its flight toward the Rumanian frontier.

The Poles fought bravely; they simply were not equipped for modern war. Here and there, scattered Polish divisions thrust vigorously at the encircling Germans. The civilian population of Warsaw turned out en masse to dig trenches around their capital, and the Warsaw radio alternated martial music, defiance of the enemy, and appeals to the world for succor as German planes droned overhead, reducing the proud city to a mass of ruins.

Then, on September 17, came an invasion of Poland by the Soviet army. The Polish government, so the Russians said, no longer existed, and Soviet forces were needed to restore order and to rescue peasants from oppression. Caught between the Germans and the Russians, Poland collapsed. Warsaw, that shell of a city, bombed and burning in a dozen places, held out until the end of the month. On October 1 the Germans occupied what was left. Russian and German armies met as Russia and Germany divided Poland between them, the lion's share of the booty in

HITLER ADDRESSING THE REICHSTAG JUST AFTER THE OUTBREAK OF WAR.

economic resources going to the Reich, the eastern marshes and the Polish Ukraine falling to Russia. Thus within one month perished Poland, a country of 50,000 square miles and 35,000,000 people.

Nazi Germany and Soviet Russia were in accord. Their non-aggression pact now was supplemented by another agreement, the opening paragraph of which struck an ominous note. "In the case of the war's being continued," it read, "joint consultations will take place between the German and Soviet governments on the subject of necessary measures." Just what did that mean? The rest of this pact simply provided for lines of demarcation in Poland and for economic coöperation between the two signatories, Russia agreeing to supply Germany with raw materials in exchange for manufactured goods. From the German point of view this economic accord by itself seemed sufficient guarantee of victory; if the Germans could depend on the Soviets for oil and food, what more was necessary!

Meanwhile, on the western front the French and British were almost immobile. The former wrested a few square miles from the enemy in the region of the Saar and the Moselle; the latter contented themselves with the worldwide seizure of German shipping and with setting up again the blockade of Germany as in 1914. During the autumn, the German submarines sank a number of British merchant vessels, also one airplane carrier and a large battleship, the *Royal Oak*. These victories were offset in December in the South Atlantic when the German pocket-battleship *Graf Spee* crept into Montevideo after an eighteen-hour engagement with three British cruisers, later to be sunk by her own crew rather than fall into British hands.

For the first six months the war in the West was remarkably quiet. The bulk of the British regular army, upward of a quarter of a million men, was transported to France without mishap and went into winter quarters. In both France and England the idea seemed to hold that the war could be won by simply exhausting the economic life of the enemy. It would not be necessary to fight; all one had to do was to wait! The Germans in turn seemed perfectly willing to wait. There were occasional flights of German planes over France and Britain, and of British and French planes over Germany; but these, primarily were for observation purposes. British children evacuated from London gradually slipped back again. Life was uncomfortable during the long, record-breaking cold winter of 1939-40, but as the months passed with little happening, the war almost seemed unreal.

Russia Attacks Finland

All but in one country—Finland. No sooner did Stalin occupy eastern Poland and agree with the Germans in regard to the Polish loot than he stretched out his hands to the Baltic states. Three of them, Estonia,

Latvia, and Lithuania, were too feeble to offer resistance and almost immediately agreed to cede land to the Soviets for naval and air bases. Not so with Finland. The Finns had fought hard for their independence and had won it in 1920 from Red Russia. Now when Stalin sought to whittle it down by demands for Finnish territory the little republic refused to accede. To fight Russia might be madness, but even that was better than surrender.

The Russians pressed the Finns hard. They asked for a rectification of their frontier at Petsamo, a port on the Arctic Ocean belonging to Finland, for six islands commanding the approaches to Leningrad, for a naval station at Hangö, and for a considerable stretch of Finnish territory on the southeastern frontier where Finland's boundary was only twenty miles away from Leningrad. That distance, so the Russians said, made it possible for the Finns to bomb a large Russian city from their own forts, an intolerable situation. If the Finns would yield to these demands, then the Soviets would be conciliatory and offer territorial compensation.

The Finns would not yield. Thereupon the Russians, asserting that they were in danger of Finnish attack (they outnumbered the Finns 50 to 1), commenced an undeclared war, dropping bombs on Helsinki, Finland's capital, on November 30.

The world expected that Finland speedily would be overrun by the Russian steamroller; but the world was mistaken. From December 1, 1939, to March 12, 1940, the Finns put up an astonishing resistance, only to capitulate when their vastly outnumbered soldiers, without ammunition and without sleep, could fight no more.

History has on record no braver epic than this. The Russians swept into Finland along several different routes. They tried to conquer north Finland near Petsamo; they tried to cut across the narrow central section or waist of that underpopulated country, thus severing the north from the south; and they advanced on both sides of huge Lake Ladoga on the southeast, endeavoring to storm the main Finnish defenses, the Mannerheim line, which stretched across the Karelian peninsula from Lake Ladoga to the Gulf of Finland.

In every direction the Finns beat them off. There was only a handful of Finns; but their country was two-thirds the size of France and was said to contain 65,000 lakes, while the land between was covered for the most part with dense forests where roads were few and poor. The athletic Finns, skilful on their skis and well-nigh invisible in their white clothing against the background of their frozen countryside, mowed down the invaders from numerous ambushes; they dug traps for Russian tanks; they set off dynamite under the ice; they broke the Russian lines of communication and captured thousands of the enemy.

Aside from the Karelian peninsula, immediately in front of Leningrad, the Russians had only one approach to Finland, a railway 800 miles long which stretched from Leningrad all the way north to the Murmansk coast and at no great distance from the Finnish frontier. This railway was easy to raid. The Finnish air force, as might have been expected, was unable to cope with the air armada let loose by the Russians; but on the other hand a number of planes were sent to Finland by France, England, Sweden, and even Italy, and the Finns were not helpless in the air. Furthermore, Finland was almost exclusively an agricultural country, and outside of Helsinki and Viborg there were few towns worth bombing.

The Soviet army during the early stages of the war was most inefficient. The army purge of 1937 had resulted in the execution of three out of five field-marshals; and all of the eight general officers who court-martialed them had since been shot. The morale of the Russian troops was poor. So also was the equipment; the soldiers were clad in flimsy cotton uniforms and thin boots; the fighting was in subzero weather; they never had seen skis; their tanks, huge and cumbersome, broke down in swamps, were surrounded, isolated, captured. Not until Russia threw the best of her fighting men into the war in 1940 was she able to make headway.

The Finns got a great deal of sympathy from the outside world, but little else. It was impossible to reach Finland except either through the arctic wastes south of Petsamo or across Norway and Sweden; and the Germans made it abundantly clear to the Scandinavian countries that they would not permit French and British expeditionary forces to cross Scandinavia. The Germans were not sympathetic toward Russia; but the major source of iron ore for Germany came from northern Sweden and they were determined not to risk having that region overrun by Allied troops. The British had sent the Finns considerable supplies of munitions, and the volunteers also made their way thither in civilian clothes, and that was all.

Then came a final massed assault by the Russians. Throughout February an incessant rain of steel blasted away concrete forts and wave after wave of Russian tanks drove at the defenses. The number of fresh Russian troops was inexhaustible, but for the Finnish regiments no more men were available. Finland, therefore, with inevitable collapse staring her in the face, yielded to all of Russia's demands, made peace in the middle of March, and commenced evacuating the choicest part of what had been Finnish soil, the Karelian peninsula. From it some 400,000 Finns, more than one-tenth of Finland's population, packed their scanty possessions and moved westward into what was left of their country.

Thus far there had been two victors, Russia and Nazi Germany. England and France seemed semiparalyzed with inaction. In the former country Neville Chamberlain, firm in declared purpose but sluggish in act, was still prime minister. That the situation was highly critical and that his own country was well-nigh unprepared for "total war" he never

Gibraltar, Britain's "Western Key to the Mediterranean"

seemed to realize. At the very commencement of the war the Germans began strict rationing of not only food but clothing; not so in England. The British enforced a strict blackout in their cities and called to their colors their young men. But the necessity of operating their factories day and night and of throwing all they had into military preparation for total war, while there was yet time, did not dawn upon the government. Only Winston Churchill, pugnacious head of the royal navy, had sufficient imagination and foresight to know that the Germans were implacable and ferocious foes who had not yet begun to fight.

So likewise was it in France. General Gamelin, generalissimo of the Allied armies, was reputedly Europe's ablest soldier, and the French army reputedly was the best in Europe. The Maginot line, from Switzerland to the Belgian frontier, was regarded as impregnable. The Belgians, supposedly, were much better prepared for war than in 1914, and the Belgian army was mobilized and on guard. Military experts spoke of the day of offensive war being over, and the French were determined not to sacrifice their diminishing manpower by a useless and costly offense. There was the living example of what happened to Poland; but the Poles had been caught napping, so thought the French, and they were not regarded as scientific fighters anyway. And so in Paris there were even less precautions taken than in London. The French made scarcely a pretense of rationing either food or clothing. They stamped down rigorously on the Communists, established a strict censorship of the press, and increased the hours of labor. But they were as confident of ultimate victory as the British—a victory to be won without shedding much blood!

There was, of course, danger of Italian intervention on the side of Germany; but this the Allies discounted. Mussolini was constantly proclaiming that his alliance with Hitler held; but the Italians certainly hated the Russians and feared their possible advance in the Balkans. After all, Mussolini's threats might be nothing more than blackmail, a bid for concessions in return for neutrality. Italy was for many months no major problem. With the Suez Canal and Gibraltar in British hands, the Franco-British naval control of the Mediterranean secure, there was nothing Italy could do. She would scarcely risk an invasion of the Lombardy plain which might easily be launched from the French Alps. To be sure her nuisance value to Germany was considerable, since her warlike gestures made it necessary that the French keep a large army on the Franco-Italian frontier; but that was all.

The Germans Conquer Denmark, Norway, Holland, and Belgium

Of all the small states, the one which had suffered the most from the war had been Norway. Ship after ship of the Norwegian mercantile marine had been destroyed by Nazi mine and submarine while plying between British and Norwegian ports. There was nothing the Norwegians could do about it except put their shipping under the protection of the British convoy system, which the Germans claimed would be unneutral. Norway, indeed, had legitimate complaint against both Germans and British. A British destroyer boldly entered Norwegian territorial waters to rescue British seamen from a Nazi prison ship, and the British constantly interfered with German shipping threading its way down the coast of Norway with the much-prized iron ore of Sweden which, when the Baltic was frozen in winter, reached Germany via the Norwegian port of Narvik, far north within the Arctic Circle.

Then, with the coming of the spring, war came to Norway with sudden fury. On April 8 the British announced that they had mined the approaches to Narvik, despite the fact that these were within Norwegian territorial waters. One day later Germany invaded Norway.

To reach that country the Nazis were compelled to occupy Denmark, which they did in one day, the Danes offering no resistance. Less than one year earlier the Nazis had signed a nonaggression pact with Denmark. But they did not hesitate to violate it. They were eager to swallow two countries in one bite—Denmark and Norway—and they did.

The very day the Germans swept across the Danish plain, small picked detachments of the German army seized Oslo, Norway's capital, and her only important ports—Stavanger, Bergen, Trondhjem, and Narvik. Only a few thousand men proved necessary, 1,500 being sufficient to secure Oslo. By various routes the Germans came—some by sea, some by transport planes, some disembarking from German merchant ships anchored innocently alongside Norwegian wharfs, while some were already within the country in disguise.

The Norwegians, taken by complete surprise, honeycombed by Nazi propaganda, and ill equipped for war, were not able to put up much resistance. Here and there, Norwegian detachments fought bravely, and effectively. A Norwegian mine-sweeper sank a German cruiser and so did a land battery, and in the mountains hastily assembled militia (the Norwegian army was scarcely more than militia) retarded the German advance.

But there was treachery in Norway. Some Norwegians, dubbed "fifth columnists," welcomed the invaders, and among them were officers in the army. The German plans had been prepared in great detail, long before the British mine-laying at Narvik, and everything ran like clockwork. On the very first day all the Norwegian airfields were occupied by Germans and the tiny air force of Norway was useless. So completely taken by surprise were the Norwegians that their king, pursued by Nazi troopers in four autobuses, barely escaped capture.

Nevertheless, for two weeks or so it looked as though the Allies might successfully come to Norway's rescue. With Britain in command of the seas it should have been easier to land larger bodies of Allied troops in Norway than of Nazi soldiers. To many commentators Hitler's coup seemed a rash adventure, even more rash than the great Napoleon's invasion of Spain.

But the facts were that the Germans commanded the air if not the sea, that they did not need many troops, that at the start they had secured all the available ports at which any large number of troops could be disembarked easily. The British navy did score a minor success in sinking some German ships in the Skagerrak; but it proved difficult for the British to operate successfully in those nearby waters, with the German submarine beneath and the German airplane overhead, and after all it was not necessary for the Nazis to transport many men by water. Speed counted far more than numbers, and needed reinforcements were sent by passenger airplanes.

It was a difficult task to dislodge the German invader, and one beyond the none too brilliant British war office. At Narvik the British had their greatest success when their battleship *Warspite*, veteran of Jutland, did break into Narvik fiord, there to sink seven German destroyers. And this most northern port of Norway, far away from German reinforcements, ultimately was captured by the Allied besieging army, only to be evacuated in early summer, as the German advance in the Low Countries and in France made it necessary for Britain to recall all soldiers available for the defense of their island home.

The Allies could not well fight the Germans from Narvik; too many miles of well-nigh trackless forest intervened between that arctic port and the more inhabited parts of Norway. Therefore an expedition against Trondhjem was decided upon. This Norwegian port, at the head of a long and winding fiord northeast of Scotland, could not well be approached directly because of fear of German mines, even though there were only a handful of German soldiers within the city. The plan was to assault the port from the land, and for that purpose the British landed 12,000 men in two divisions, one to the north and one to the south.

These two expeditionary forces had to disembark on open beaches and were ill supported by light artillery and anti-aircraft guns. What was more serious, they were practically without planes, for the Germans had the landing fields in their possession. Nevertheless, the British advanced boldly, seeking to join their forces and encircle Trondhjem. As they did so the Germans moved swiftly to succor their detachments in that city. Scattered Norwegian units attempted to hinder the swift moving German motorized detachments, but German speed and German efficiency were at their best. On April 30 the German advance units had made contact with the German garrison of Trondhjem. Three days later the British took to their boats which lay north and south of the city.

To conquer Poland took five weeks; now within less than a month Denmark and Norway (aside from the half-frozen Narvik) followed Austria, Czechoslovakia, and Poland down the Nazi maw. With Denmark gone, the British lost an important source of food; with Norway gone, the British lost not only supplies of fish and timber but were confronted by German airmen within striking distance of northern England and Scotland; and in addition the coastline of Scandinavia, indented with deep fiords, provided ideal lurking places for the submarine. A consolation prize for Britain was the Norwegian mercantile marine, the larger part at sea.

For a few days the Nazis rested. There were ominous troop concentrations on the borders of Holland, Belgium, and Switzerland, but none knew where the next blow would fall. In Parliament there was angry debate. Men asserted that the Norwegian fiasco might have been prevented, that a bold assault on Trondhjem fiord by the navy would have captured the city, that Chamberlain was inept, supine. A vote to censure his government failed, but so heavy was the cut in its usual majority and so many were the abstentions that Chamberlain resigned.

Instantly he was succeeded by Winston Churchill, First Lord of the Admiralty. A short time before it seemed impossible that Churchill ever would become Prime Minister. For many decades a stormy petrel in Parliament, he had numerous enemies. He had been a Tory, a Liberal and a Tory again without qualm or misgiving; he had served in many cabinets, holding the home office, the treasury, and twice the naval portfolio. Trenchant in speech and with pen, he was thought somewhat too brilliant and too erratic to head a cabinet; he had been responsible for the Dardanelles expedition in the First World War, and that had failed. Churchill's continuing prophecies of approaching disaster in the years immediately preceding the Second World War had made him persona non grata to those Tories who like Chamberlain believed in appeasement. Now Britain applauded him.

As England changed her Prime Minister, the Nazis struck again, this time at the Netherlands and Belgium, claiming that they did so only to forestall an Allied invasion. Simultaneously, they came by air and by land. Within five days the Netherlands, always at their mercy, was completely conquered. The Dutch resisted as well as they could; but their airplanes were few, their country flat and tiny, and many Netherlanders were fifth columnists, National Socialists, and Dutch Fascists who aided the seizure of vital points by the Germans. The latter dropped down from the skies by parachutes; they came by the thousand in transport planes; they crossed flooded areas in rubber boats; they bombed the airports and almost captured Queen Wilhelmina. Futile resistance soon ceased, but not until a large part of the city of Rotterdam had been reduced to smoldering ruin by aerial bombardment.

Belgium also was able to withstand the Nazis only a few days longer. The first line of Belgian defense went down almost without a fight, but the second line, following the course of the Meuse River and the Albert Canal from the French frontier to Antwerp on the Scheldt, was stoutly defended, with the hope that the oncoming French and British reinforcements might enable the Belgian armies stationed there to withstand the German attack.

On the second day of the invasion that hope died, as the Germans captured the bridgeheads of the Albert Canal, stormed the great fortress of Eben Emael, outflanked the Belgians, and drove at Brussels. Within one week they had not only occupied that city but, pushing south, had pierced the French defenses in the Ardennes forest (the little Maginot line), opening up a sixty-mile gap in northeastern France between Montmédy, the northern end of the Maginot line proper, and the French fortress of Maubeuge to the west.

The Fall of France (1940)

Neither in 1870 nor in 1914 had the Germans advanced with such speed. And now for six weeks there was fighting all the time, continuous correlated movement of troops, airplanes, tanks, a continuous, unremitting slicing forward of irresistible Nazi power, a continuous retreat of baffled, broken-up, and out-maneuvered Allied armies.

What sometimes is called the battle of Flanders, began with the German breakthrough of the little Maginot line and ended on June 2 with the miraculous escape from the beaches of Dunkirk of four-fifths of the British expeditionary force. Sometimes it is spoken of as the Battle of the Pockets, due to the way in which the onrushing Germans segregated by flanking movements large sections of the Allied forces.

What took place was this: The Germans dashed through the gap they had made at Sedan in the little Maginot line, pressed forward with all speed until they reached Soissons on the Aisne. Then, instead of keeping on toward Paris as in 1914, they wheeled toward the right in the direction of the English Channel, their idea in so doing being to cut off the Allied armies—French, British, and Belgian, upward of a million men, which were retreating slowly down the seacoast in western Belgium—from the French armies to the south.

Seemingly it was impossible to stop this destructive process. At the apex was the tank and airplane, and not until they opened the way did the artillery and the infantry follow. The weather was dry and clear, and so rapidly did the German tanks push forward that frequently they became isolated from supporting columns. But the French artillery was too light to destroy the huge German tanks, few of which fell into French hands and the roads were cluttered with fleeing civilians, Belgian and

French, a fact which impeded Allied resistance but aided the German advance, since the German *stukas,* low-flying dive-bombing planes, struck mercilessly at civilians and soldiers alike.

Speedily the German scythes swept on down the valley of the Somme toward Amiens; then cut through to Abbeville, only a few miles from the Channel, and sweeping toward the north reached Boulogne. The exultant Germans, not stopping, kept on to Calais and, finding that town stoutly defended, swept around it, almost reaching Dunkirk. A million Allied soldiers apparently had been surrounded.

There were for the latter two alternatives: to cut through the German lines of communication, not as yet very wide or strongly held; or to escape by sea to England.

On paper the first possibility seemed feasible. In less than a week the German lines had been so distended by the great, huge arc which they formed that a simultaneous thrust by the Allies on the Channel and by the main French armies before Paris might have pierced it, thus creating a pocket or pitfall whereby the German armies, which had passed the point of piercing and which had reached the Channel at Abbeville, would be severed from the main German forces and in turn be in danger of segregation and forced to surrender.

Why was this not done? Gamelin had been removed as Allied Generalissimo and Weygand, pupil of Foch and hero of the First World War, now in command, was expected any moment to commence this counterattack. Instead of doing so, he began hastily to dig trenches and to form a new line of defense. Possibly he considered that essential to protect Paris; possibly, and more likely, owing to the confusion created by the sheer audacity of the German thrust, and by the activity of German fifth columnists in France, he was unable to concentrate his troops. Yet every hour this counterattack failed to materialize saw the German lines of communication strengthened by German artillery and German infantry.

Then, whatever chance the Belgian, French, and British armies at the Channel had of piercing the German lines and joining forces with the French armies to their south went begging when the Belgian king surrendered. His army, upward of a half-million men, was in sorry plight, its ammunition spent, its food supply gone. King Leopold's men held the left wing of the Allied forces, and if they were out of the combat apparently there was nothing to prevent the Germans in Belgium from pushing on until they joined hands with the German army advancing eastward along the Channel. The French and British had come to Belgium's succor at the request of the Belgian King and he was under deep obligation to them. On the other hand, could he fight longer? To do so, he thought, would simply result in sacrifice of life.

The Belgian lines covered a distance of thirty miles which instantly had to be covered by the hard-pressed British. The result was that the latter lost contact for the time being with parts of the French army, several divisions of which were cut off by advancing German columns. What was left of the French army joined with the British, and these Allies, closing their ranks, pressed close together along the sea coast at Dunkirk, where it seemed improbable that more than a few thousand could be conveyed across the Channel.

Then out of the jaws of death and gates of hell over 335,000 French and British soldiers were rescued. From the end of May to the fourth of June the Royal Navy and the Royal Air Force, aided and abetted by all kinds of miscellaneous seafaring folk, worked at this task. The skies were darkened by planes as the RAF and German planes engaged in one unceasing duel; German artillery sprayed the beaches with its shells; German submarines and motor-launches, equipped with torpedo tubes and rapid-firing guns, swarmed out for the kill; and the German infantry threw itself "on the ever narrowing and contracting appendix within which the British and French armies fought."

The British would not use their battleships in these too-narrow waters, but every available light cruiser and destroyer was commandeered, as well as innumerable other craft. Over 200 naval warships took part, and three times as many other vessels. No one will perhaps ever know just how many, since with complete unanimity the owners of yachts, tugs, fishing smacks, motorboats, river steamers, and barges aided in it. Anything afloat that could carry men was used. Only one narrow pier at Dunkirk, constantly bombed by the Germans, was available, and over this poured a steady stream of men. Soldiers by the thousand waded into the shallow waters off the beaches and stood up to their armpits waiting for a friendly hand. Old men past sixty and young boys of fifteen worked together in hauling them into lifeboats. Almost everyone in southeastern England connected in any way with boats and shipping took part.

Day and night the work continued; back and forth the impromptu ferries plied; and on one day alone over 60,000 half-starved Soldiers of the King reached home in safety.

The evacuation was unparalleled in military annals, and the total loss to the British army was but 30,000, but little over ten per cent. Nevertheless, the very fact that there had to be evacuation made it a disastrous British defeat. Left behind in France and in the hands of the Germans were over 1,000 heavy pieces of artillery, vast stores of munitions, food, gasoline. For the time being, Britain's scarcity of war matériel was appalling, and a militant foe, flushed with victory, held Scandinavia, Holland, Belgium, and the Straits of Dover.

Not since the days of Bonaparte had Britain been in such evil case. Churchill, while praising his fighters, did not minimize the issue. Said the Prime Minister in the House of Commons: "We shall defend our island whatever the cost may be; we shall fight on the beaches, landing grounds, in fields, in streets, and on the hills. We shall never surrender, and even if, which I do not for a moment believe, this island or a large part of it were subjugated and starving then, our Empire beyond the seas, armed and guarded by the British fleet, will carry on the struggle until in God's good time the New World, with all its power and might, sets forth to the liberation of the Old."

Dark as the Allied cause was, it speedily grew darker. The Germans did not hesitate a minute. While the world wondered whether they would instantly "sail for England" or try to destroy France first, the Nazi legions embarked on the latter course. On June 5, the superbly mechanized armies of the Third Reich attacked the French in an offensive that stretched from the northern end of the Maginot line all the way to the mouth of the Somme at Abbeville—the Battle of France had begun.

Everywhere they met with victory. For a brief moment it looked as though they might be foiled by the new tactics of Weygand. That general, copying German precedents in 1918, made no attempt at holding a rigid line but let the German tanks through the first French defenses and tried to lead them into carefully concealed traps. But all that Weygand did was to retard the enemy slightly. The Germans now were using 1,500,000 men, nearly 100 divisions, and the French were outnumbered in the field two to one, since large numbers of their best troops were either isolated in the Maginot line or guarding the Italian frontier. The line of battle extended over 200 miles and so swiftly drove the Germans that the breaking French had no time to gather their forces to counter-attack.

Soon it was all over. As the German armies drew close to Paris for their final battle, Italy declared war on France and England. The Duce said the time had come to break the Mediterranean prison in which Italy was confined, to strike a blow at the "pluto-democracies." On the Franco-Italian frontier were 400,000 Italian troops ready to attack France from a new quarter. Italy was to be in at the death.

The latter was not unduly prolonged. The Germans marched into an undefended Paris and three days later Marshal Pétain, at the head of the French government which was now at Bordeaux, asked for an armistice. On June 22 it was granted, and the French armies surrendered, the Germans occupying France to the Loire, the Italians having advanced a few miles in the French Alps and along the Riviera.

The Battle of France had ended. Like that of Flanders it was a quick, decisive victory for the invader. The French had been no more successful than the Poles in defending their country; and why?

Certainly one important reason was the subversive activity of the Nazi fifth column. France was betrayed as well as defeated. It had long been flooded with Nazi agents pretending to be tourists or salesmen or sometimes refugees from Nazi oppression. Now, during the war, wearing the uniform of the French staff, they gave contradictory orders, signaled German planes, aided German parachutists, spread rumors of defeat and disaster, demoralized the civilian population and paralyzed military action.

The French generals were old men, veterans of the First World War, deluded in the belief that wars of maneuvre were things of the past. They were Maginot-minded, placing all their bets on skillful defense. They laughed at young De Gaulle, a tank expert, and regarded his enthusiasm for tank divisions as fantastic dreaming. The French had tanks, good ones: but here again came the defense delusion. Tanks according to the French high command were moveable forts, serviceable for guarding bridges and fords, of auxiliary value only.

But most important of all; the French had no stomach for fighting. Their casualties in the First World War had been proportionately much higher than those of any other country. They just could not bring themselves to go through it all again.

The armistice paralleled in many ways that earlier armistice of November 11, 1918 (see p. 120). It was signed in the same railway carriage at the same spot where the Germans surrendered in the First World War. Its terms were equally harsh, and in one important respect even more so. Not only were the French to give up all their military supplies and equipment and to pay for the cost of occupation, but more than half of France was to be occupied by the triumphant Germans, including the entire Atlantic sea coast from the Belgian border to that of Spain. Concerning the ultimate disposal of this occupied territory nothing was stipulated. Even the Italians, who signed a separate armistice with France a day later, were content to wait until the war was over before receiving the jackal's share of booty.

The Germans had reason to think that the war was over. To be sure, the British had retrieved most of their troops, but the greater part of their war matériel had been left behind in France. A few days before the armistice Churchill had begged the French government to flee to North Africa, promising political union with the British Empire and a joint fight for victory. The offer had nearly been accepted; it failed by but one vote in the French cabinet. But the French, like the Germans, thought the war at an end, and the aged Marshal Pétain, who had assumed control of the government with dictatorial powers in the midst of the crisis, believed it his duty to come to such terms as he could with the enemy.

Fortunately for Britain, the Germans were in no condition to start an immediate invasion of that hated island. The disarmament of France had to be completed and vast military preparations made at the Channel ports before that happy event could be announced. Consequently there came a lull in hostilities which, apart from various intermittent air attacks on British ports and British shipping, was to last the greater part of the summer.

Britain Fights On

England was not only stunned; she was bitterly disappointed at her ally's withdrawal from the war. If Pétain had only transferred his government to Morocco it would have been safe from the Germans except for a possible air attack, so the British thought. Furthermore, the large French army in Syria would also be safe, and with the French army in Tunis threatening Italian Libya on one flank and with the British in Egypt on the other, any Italian offense in North Africa could be checked. Churchill had promised to carry on the war from Canada if England should be subjugated; why should the French be less determined?

What disturbed the British more than anything else was the future of the French fleet. The armistice terms provided that it should be interned, and the Germans promised not to make use of the French navy against France's ally. But suppose they did not keep their word? In that case German, French, and Italian navies might readily cripple British sea power, and in that eventuality the war would indeed be lost.

Thereupon the British decided they must act. The French fleet was scattered; part of it was in British harbors, part in home ports, part at Alexandria in Egypt, with the British squadron stationed there, part in the Pacific and in the West Indies. But the larger part lay off the French North African port of Oran, and to it steamed three of Britain's largest warships. Their commander delivered an ultimatum to the French admiral; he must either join forces with him against the Germans or sail to British ports or cross the Atlantic to dismantle his ships there, or else the British would use force to prevent the French ships from falling into German or Italian hands. The French elected to fight rather than yield; the British opened fire and sank or disabled three French battleships, a seaplane carrier, and two destroyers. One battleship, badly crippled, escaped, together with some lighter craft, to Toulon. The French squadron at Alexandria, meanwhile, agreed to dismantle and the French ships in British ports surrendered without much fuss, some of the sailors agreeing to continue the fight on the British side. One great French battleship stationed at Dakar was put out of action by a surprise attack, and here and overseas some French naval vessels were seized. Of the very considerable French navy, only a few scattered units remained and the British breathed easier.

This naval activity ushered in the month of July. Otherwise it was to prove a comparatively quiet month. Despite the fact that the entire coast of France was in German hands, the British managed to send their merchant ships through the Channel. There was a great increase in the number sunk, and the British lost several destroyers of which they had all too few, but they were able to keep the Channel open. What is more, they could claim by the end of the month that despite all losses since the commencement of the war the total tonnage of their mercantile marine had increased, since large numbers of Norwegian, Danish, Dutch, and Belgian ships were now under their control.

The only marked successes of July, curiously enough, were won without bloodshed by Stalin. That wily Russian seized this moment to annex to the Soviet state Lithuania, Estonia, and Latvia, the three little Baltic states which he had already cowed into granting naval bases to the Soviet. Bessarabia also was demanded from Rumania and obtained without a fight, and together with it the Russians took part of Bukovina for good measure.

Meanwhile, England girded herself for battle on her own soil. At last the British were fully awake to their own danger. They made an armed camp of their island. To its strength were added certain Polish detachments, many French soldiers under General De Gaulle, recognized by the British as the head of "Free Frenchmen" who would continue the fight, and over 100,000 soldiers as well from Canada, New Zealand, and Australia.

There were men enough, over 1,000,000 under arms, but the immediate danger lay in civilian coördination and in war matériel. Almost overnight England was transformed. Parliament placed every man and every shilling at the disposal of the government. Arrests were made of all suspects; possible landing fields for enemy planes were blocked by concrete pillars and trenches; home guards were organized to watch for parachutists; and factories worked day and night turning out planes, guns, shells.

Fortunately for the British, the Germans were so occupied in coalescing their continental gains that it was a good six weeks after the fall of France before they were able to strike at England with force. Intermittent air raids continued during that time on British seaports, and the RAF struck back as far as it was able on Nazi-controlled French air bases, but it was September before the Nazi power really showed itself.

The Nazis then struck straight at London, their bombers swooping across from Calais and swarming up the Thames Valley. Their planes came in squadrons of 100 or more at a time, first by day and then by night, and kept on doing so for weeks at a time. Occasionally there would be a lull, a day or two with scarcely an alarm. Then would follow renewed raiding. In September it was directed mainly at London, but as the autumn wore on it extended elsewhere—to Bristol, Southampton, Liverpool, and other shipping centers, to the Midland cities of Coventry, Birmingham, and Manchester.

Early in the air war the RAF was able to strike down a great many of the invading planes, for the latter flew mainly then by daylight, seeking definite targets such as docks, railway yards, manufacturing plants. But when the Germans switched to night attacks it was not so easy for the RAF or the anti-aircraft gunners to locate the foe. In the summer the British had looked forward to the short winter days as partial protection against the *Luftwaffe* (air force) of General Goering. But now with night attacks the autumn and winter season made it all the harder for the harassed islanders.

The damage done by the Luftwaffe was extensive. First would come a squadron of planes to unload incendiary bombs to start fires which would serve as beacons; and then successive waves of bombers would follow. Thousands of houses were destroyed, in many cases their inhabitants buried beneath the debris. Docks, churches, hospitals, factories, whole city blocks were left in ruins.

The Germans could report great material success, but one thing they had not been able to accomplish: they had not "softened" the fighting spirit of the British. Rather they heightened it. Crowded into congested and unsanitary bombproof shelters and in the London subway, snatching a few hours' sleep here and there, the citizens of London responded superbly to the German challenge. The killed and seriously wounded numbered several thousand a week while the raids were at their worst, but after all, this was only a very slight proportion of London's many millions of inhabitants, and the latter, regarding themselves as real soldiers (as they were), kept their thumbs up, working like beavers to clear their streets of debris and to "carry on."

As a matter of fact, serious as were the air raids over British cities, they were far less serious than the ever increased activities of the German submarine. Bad as the situation had been in 1917, it threatened to become worse in 1941. In the former year the U-boat bases were confined to the narrow shore line of Germany and of Belgium. In 1941 the sea coast of Norway, Denmark, Germany, the Netherlands, Belgium and France was now at Germany's disposal. Forth from their innumerable lairs now crept the Nazi submarines, not one at a time as formerly but hunting in packs like wolves and assisted by planes of wide cruising area, serving as eyes for the submarines.

The sinking of vessels flying the Union Jack jumped up to dangerous proportions and early optimism gave way to genuine alarm. More civilians thus far had lost their lives than had British soldiers, in England; but after all civilians could, if they must, adjust themselves to sleeping underground. But the war would be lost if cargoes could not be delivered, cargoes of food as well as of munitions. And what made the British worry more than anything else was that the Royal Navy, gravely deficient in destroyer strength at the war's commencement, had suffered severely in this category of ships, many destroyers having been sunk and many more laid up for repairs because of damage from the air.

Fortunately for the British, they had a warm friend in President Roosevelt, who did not hesitate by a stroke of the pen to deliver to the British Admiralty in September fifty over-age American destroyers in return for naval bases in the Atlantic and Caribbean.

The agreement was as follows: Great Britain presented two of the eight bases, those in Newfoundland and Bermuda, as a free gift. The other six, those in Jamaica, St. Lucia, the Bahamas, Trinidad, Antigua and British Guiana, were in payment for the destroyers. All eight bases were to be leased to the United States for a period of ninety-nine years, free from rent.

Congress was in session at the time but the President did not consult that body. Arming himself with an opinion handed down by his attorney general as to the validity of the transaction, he acted with speed and secrecy, and certain of the destroyers were already on their way to a Canadian port before America knew of their transfer to the British flag. Nevertheless, there was only scattered criticism in the United States, partly because the "destroyer deal" was an extraordinarily good bargain for the United States, partly because American public opinion was whole-heartedly on Britain's side.

The destroyers helped; but by the end of the year Britain stood in need of even more naval assistance, and particularly in need of more cargo vessels. Over 3,000,000 tons of shipping was sunk by Germany during the first fourteen months of the war, if we are to include Belgian, Dutch, and Norwegian shipping flying the Union Jack. With British yards producing less than 1,500,000 tons a year, and with small likelihood of speeding up that production, the gravity of the situation became more and more apparent.

Japan Joins the Axis (1940)

On September 27 an important victory on the diplomatic front was won for the Axis when Japan joined Germany and Italy in a triple alliance whereby Japan recognized the leadership of Germany and Italy in establishing a "new order" in Europe, in return for which Germany and Italy recognized Japan's leadership in establishing a "new order" in "Greater East Asia." In accordance with the treaty: "if one of the three contracting powers is attacked by a power at present not involved in the European war or in the Chinese-Japanese conflict" then the other two powers must assist "with all political, economic and military means."

Ostensibly this was a thrust against the United States, since that country and Russia were the only nations which could well be called powers not already engaged in the conflict, and since Article 5 in the treaty expressly stated that its terms "do not in any way affect the political status which exists at present between each of the three contracting parties and Soviet Russia."

Why this treaty? The reasons motivating Japan are easy to fathom. Angered by the Russo-German neutrality pact on the eve of the war, Japan had stood warily to one side during the first year of the conflict, waiting to see who would win. Now she felt she could wait no longer. The Japanese longed for French Indo-China; their mouths also watered at the thought of the Dutch East Indies, so ripe and so rich a prize almost within their grasp. Victorious Germany was now willing to concede to Japan the leading part in organizing a "new order in the East" in return for hypothetical aid against the United States. If the Japanese did not accept now and if Germany won the war without their aid, they might not find the Nazis quite so generous in the future. If, on the other hand, Britain won the war there would be no Indo-China and the Netherland East Indies for the Japanese Empire.

Just what Germany and Italy hoped to gain is not quite so evident. Clearly the alliance meant that Germany was now granting Japan the hegemony if not ownership of lucrative colonial pickings which the Nazis had hoped to secure for themselves in Asiatic seas. Probably it meant an insurance policy taken out against the United States, a policy which Germany might hope to cash in on later by causing the United States to keep her fleet in Pacific waters. Also, and very probably, it was a bait to the Soviet. Let the latter join the new triple alliance and there would be "new orders" and *Lebensraumen* for all the allies: the Far East for Japan; India, Afghanistan, and Iran for Russia; the Mediterranean for Italy; western Europe, central Africa, and perhaps South America for the Nazis!

If this latter was the main Nazi motive, it failed of accomplishment. The Russian foreign secretary, Molotov, came to Berlin and engaged in long conversations. But nothing apparently eventuated except protestations of neutrality and good will. The Russians were said to have advanced claims too extensive for the three allies to accept, claims which involved territorial concessions in eastern Asia at Japan's expense. What actually took place was a closely guarded secret. But Russia did not sign the pact and the three allies had to be content with the adherence, as we shall note later, of Rumania, Hungary, and that pygmy creation of Nazi Germany, Slovakia.

For the time being, the diplomatic adherence of Japan to the Axis accomplished little. It gave the Japanese an easy entrance into northern Indo-China, which they occupied with very faint protests from the defeated French government of Pétain—located at Vichy in unoccupied France, supposedly independent, but entirely at the mercy of the Nazis who had incarcerated in Germany over 1,000,000 French soldiers. But it also led to action on the part of the United States which took the form of an embargo on certain highly desired war matériel and an official warning to all Americans to withdraw from Japanese-controlled China. The United States even went further: she extended financial aid to the embattled Chinese Republic and encouraged Britain to reopen the Burma Road in order that war supplies might be rushed to Chungking and Chiang Kai-shek. The Japanese did not take these rebuffs kindly. On the other hand, there was little they could do about it. The American fleet stationed at Hawaii was superior to their own, and presumably the great British naval depôt at Singapore would be open to it in case of emergency. The Japanese army had bogged down in China, and certainly no help was immediately available from Germany and Italy. Therefore the Japanese government did nothing; but the Japanese press boasted loudly of Japan's Monroe Doctrine for eastern Asia and that the dawn of Nippon's greatness would soon come.

The Near East

Meanwhile, in 1940 the war spread to the Near East. The Balkan states had no desire to be drawn into the conflict. Nevertheless it was almost impossible for them to avoid it, partly because within their borders were raw materials much sought after by the Germans, like oil and foodstuffs, partly because they lay between the triumphant Axis and lands subject to British and French overlordship, such as Syria, Lebanon, Palestine, Egypt, and countries still farther distant, such as Iraq and Iran.

Of the five Balkan countries, three leaned toward the Allies, one might be said to be at first almost completely neutral, and one leaned somewhat toward the Axis. The Turks were both anti-German and anti-Italian. They were not, however, anti-Russian, and the defense pact which they had signed with the Allies before the war and which they had strengthened after its advent specifically excluded action against Russia. Yugoslavia and Greece also were pro-Ally in sympathy, not so much because of fair liberty as for fear of Hitler. The Yugoslavs had neither forgotten nor forgiven the unwillingness of the Italians to aid Serbia during the First World War, nor Italian determination to control the Adriatic. The same held true of Grecian memories of Mussolini's earlier bombardment of the island Corfu. To both of these Balkan countries the Italian annexation of Albania in 1939 was an ominous warning. Rumania was more or less equally poised between the conflicting powers. She asked nothing of her neighbors but she feared them all; feared Hungary lest she demand the return of Transylvania; feared Bulgaria, from whom she had taken Dobruja after the second Balkan War. She also feared Soviet Russia lest that country should invade Bessarabia, a czarist possession in 1914. What Rumania wanted was to be left alone, and therefore she played Germany and the Allies against each other, hoping for the best. Bulgaria alone somewhat favored the Axis, for the status quo displeased her mightily and she held grudges against all her neighbors.

Meanwhile, in the Near East one other country, theoretically independent, hoped against hope to stay out of the war. Egypt was an ally (as far as the law went) of England. But the alliance had been part of the bargain whereby Egypt had won recognition of her independence, and since British troops were in Egypt to guard the Suez Canal, the independent status of Egypt seemed only a nominal affair to many Egyptians.

To act as a counterweight against an Axis offensive in the Near East, and possibly to organize a thrust of their own, directed against Germany's back door, the Allies had stationed relatively large armies in that region, the British components of which were located in Egypt and Palestine, the French in Syria and French Somaliland. Before the fall of France this seemed good strategy. If the Italians should strike east from Libya against Egypt and the Suez Canal, they would be caught between two fires— between the French in Tunis and the British in Egypt. Should the Italians in Ethiopia move against the Nile Valley or the Suez, they would be exposed to a flank attack from French Somaliland. But with France out of the picture the situation was reversed. The British in Egypt now were in danger of being caught between the Italians in Ethiopia on their east and the Italians in Libya on their west.

Even before Italy was in the war she proceeded to augment her already large forces in Libya and to prepare an offensive against Egypt. During the summer of 1940 the Italians started their march against Egypt from Libya, and invaded British Somaliland from Ethiopia, easily conquering that sandy waste south of the Red Sea. And as they did so, they pushed westward from Ethiopia into the northern Sudan and southward into the outlying districts of Kenya. The hard-pressed British were indeed in danger and had, for the time at least, but one ally upon which to depend—the weather, since campaigning in Egypt and in the Egyptian Sudan is extremely difficult in the summer.

Then, as the Italians struck at the southern sections of the Near East, the Germans laid their heavy hands upon Rumania. The Russian occupation of Bessarabia and Bukovina almost instantly reverberated in Bulgaria, which threatened now to seize the Dobruja, and in Hungary, which mobilized for a thrust at Transylvania. Whereupon Germany acted, compelled the Rumanians to give up the northern half of Transylvania to Hungary and to cede the southern third of the Dobruja to Bulgaria.

This dismemberment infuriated the Rumanians who considered King Carol responsible for their calamities. That unfortunate monarch fled from his country. Young Michael, his son, became a puppet ruler, doing the bidding of the Iron Guard, a Rumanian Fascist organization. The

Germans, under pretext of preserving order and preventing the British from blowing up Rumanian oil wells, sent larger and larger bodies of troops to Rumania and finally forced that Balkan state, together with Hungary and Slovakia, to join the all-Fascist alliance of which Japan, Italy, and Germany were the charter members.

Rumania now was lost to the democracies, and with the coming of autumn Egypt was invaded by the Italians from Libya, who reached Sidi Barrani on the Mediterranean littoral without serious opposition. For some reason, perhaps the water supply, this offense bogged down, but as it did so the Italians on October 28, struck at Greece through Albania.

To the surprise of almost everyone the Greeks flew to arms with apparently all the spirit of ancient Hellas; they drove the Italians out of northern Greece; they followed after them, forced them into precipitate retreat, and by December a large part of southern Albania was in Greek hands. Throughout that month and January, 1941, Greek victories continued. The snow lay heavy on Albanian hills but the dogged Greeks continued slowly but persistently to carry hill after hill at the point of the bayonet until, by February 1, 1941, they had not only reached the Adriatic but were within seven miles of Valona, Italy's strongly fortified prized port on the Albanian coast.

The British, meanwhile, rendered the Greeks valuable assistance by air and by sea; they attacked the Italian fleet at anchor at Taranto; they steamed into the Adriatic and bombarded Albanian seaports; and they established themselves snugly on the island of Crete. Nor did this aid to the Hellenes interfere with a most dashing offense against the Italian land forces in Africa. In December the British army in Egypt, strongly reinforced by Australians and supported by "Free French" troops, swept across the desert and ferociously attacked the Italians at Sidi Barrani. That town capitulated and some 30,000 Italians surrendered. The British offense continued without letup, this time in Libya. Bardia, the Italians' strongly fortified port in eastern Libya, bombarded by land and by sea, capitulated in early January, 1941, and the British, having bagged some 40,000 additional prisoners, swooped down on Tobruk, another Libyan port still farther to the west, running up their total number of prisoners to approximately 100,000. Nor did they stop. Striking across the desert, they soon were before Derna, which they stormed as the month drew to a close. They now were no less than 145 miles west of the Egyptian frontier. Some 100 miles beyond lay Bengazi, next to Tripoli, Libya's most important city. A long way to go; but in modern warfare, tanks and planes travel fast, and fortunately for the British there was at Derna a superb water supply. If they could only capture Bengazi, all of Eastern Libya (ancient Cyrenaica) would be lost to Mussolini.

As 1941 opened, the Italian dreams of turning the Mediterranean into a *mare nostrum* seemed faint, very faint indeed, since the British kept on rolling westward, not only taking Bengazi in early February but advancing far beyond it to El Agheila, well along the sea-coast road to Tripoli. It was evident to all that Britain would soundly thrash the Italians in Libya and perhaps elsewhere unless Germany took prompt action. This Hitler realized, and soon German airmen came pouring into Italy. In January the famous *stukas* began striking at Malta and at the British convoys in the Middle Sea, doing more damage in one day than Italian planes in six months of war.

The United States on the Brink of War

The Greeks and the British had defeated the Italians, but the latter had never been anything more than the tail of the Nazi wolf. The German armies still dominated the land mass of Western Europe. Nothing could prevent their occupation of that part of France still ostensibly "free." Their legions might continue southward through the Iberian Peninsula to besiege Gibraltar or to plunge west into Portugal. Sweden and Switzerland lay at their mercy; and, if the Nazis chose to risk the enmity of Stalin, Bulgaria, Greece, and Yugoslavia might be conquered with comparative ease. Until the German armies were defeated there was scant likelihood that the Nazi grip upon conquered territory would relax. Here and there a daring Dane, Norwegian, Netherlander, Belgian, Pole, Frenchman, or Czech might try as an individual to sabotage the Nazi regime or escape to the British flag; but so long as Rumanian and Russian oil flowed to Germany, so long as Swedish and French mines produced iron ore for German smelters, and so long as the conquered peoples were compelled to share their food supply, as well as everything else, with the victors, there was no chance for revolt succeeding, within the Reich or without.

This the British fully realized. They could not by themselves defeat the Germans; their only hope of ultimate victory depended upon America. To that country Britain looked for food, munitions, planes, and shipping, since without them Britain could not survive.

And so, with the coming of 1941, it became evident to the clearsighted on both sides of the Atlantic that the United States, and the United States alone, could stave off German triumph. The Americans with their tremendous resources could, in conjunction with British efforts, surpass the German plane production by 1943—if they tried hard enough! The American mercantile marine (9,000,000 tons), plus those European vessels interned in American ports which flew the Dutch, Belgian, Norwegian, French, German, and Italian flags (158 in number), should offset submarine sinkings. Some or all of these ships Britain urgently needed. And if the Americans should be willing to turn over to the Royal Navy another fifty destroyers to guard the sea-lanes, so much the better.

What would America do? That country was closer to war in January, 1941, than most Americans realized. Informal war against Germany to all intent and purpose had seemed assured early in the contest when Congress authorized the sale of munitions; but to active armed conflict Americans were averse. The presidential election (1940) gave relatively little clue as to American opinion in this matter. Both the major candidates favored aid to Britain without stint; but both also promised that American boys would not fight in Europe. A formula, "all aid short of war," seemed to represent average American opinion.

It is, however, always easier to invent a formula than to implement it. Billions of dollars had been voted by Congress in 1940 for national defense; conscription had been adopted; and a "two-ocean navy," presumably invincible in both the Atlantic and the Pacific, had received Congressional approval. Suppose the British said their need called for every available American plane; in what situation would that leave the armed forces of the United States? This single difficulty was met by the President in assigning fifty per cent of all new government planes to Britain, thereby presumably inserting the adjective "reasonable" between the words "all" and "aid." But who was to decide on what was "reasonable," the President or Congress; and did such aid involve unlimited credit? The Johnson Act forbade loans to nations defaulting on previous loans, and Britain had defaulted. Would it be necessary to repeal the Johnson Act; was Britain's financial need really pressing; was it desirable that more naval vessels be given to Britain, with or without a quid pro quo; could the United States open its ports to British warships, take over German shipping in American ports, release these ships to Britain, and at the same time avoid war with Germany?

There was no doubt where the President stood. In December, 1940, at a press conference he suggested the possibility of a lease-lend program whereby help to Britain could be instantly granted. This he followed up by a radio address in which he suggested that in case of fire one lends one's garden hose to one's neighbor, expecting that it be returned, but not trying to sell the hose first. Satisfied with the reaction of public opinion, Roosevelt went further and in his annual message to Congress on January 6, 1941, did not hesitate to speak as follows:

Let us say to the democracies: "We Americans are vitally concerned in your defense of freedom. We are putting forth our energies, our resources and our organizing powers to give you the strength to regain and maintain a free world. We shall send you in ever-increasing numbers, ships, planes, tanks, guns. That is our purpose and our pledge."

Followed then a bill in Congress to grant to him almost unlimited, as well as unprecedented, powers in placing the material resources of the country in the scale against Germany. The bill was fought stubbornly by

noninterveners, who insisted that America had little to fear from a victorious Germany; that if the Germans could not invade England across
the Channel it was absurd to be alarmed at the specter of Germany invading the United States; that democracy and all that went with it would
perish in this country if it became involved in the war; and finally that
opening American ports for the repair of British naval vessels, the seizure
of foreign shipping in American ports in order to supply British needs,
and the convoying of American ships to England by the United States
navy were, in fact, acts of war.

These arguments were variously met. The more intelligent interven-
tionists did not stress the likelihood of a Nazi invasion of the United
States but sketched a situation wherein South America fell under Nazi
influence, thus leaving the United States isolated in a hostile world, confronted by totalitarian states across both oceans, and subjected to subversive propaganda from all sides. Democracy here, they held, stood or
fell with democracy elsewhere: the Fascist-molded states had won
hitherto because the democracies had failed to support one another. As
to whether such support as they proposed to give Britain was an act of
war or not, that was an academic matter. The Nazis, in the President's
words, "did not wait for Norway or Belgium or the Netherlands to
commit an act of war. Their only interest is in a new one-way international law which lacks mutuality in its observance and therefore becomes an instrument of oppression." The United States, by implication,
then, was under no obligation to regard "international law" as binding in
dealing with an outlaw nation such as Hitler's Germany. The case for
intervention was tersely put by Roosevelt in one sentence: "Those who
would give up essential liberty to purchase a little temporary safety
deserve neither liberty nor safety."

The bill, introduced into Congress on January 10, 1941, became law
on March 11. To many it meant a last desperate effort to keep America
out of the conflict by turning that country into an arsenal for Great
Britain; to others it meant that the full military and naval strength of
the United States would inevitably be used to destroy the armed strength
of Germany; and that, as in 1918, America would arrive like Blücher at
Waterloo before the coming of the night.

Chapter 17

FROM LEND-LEASE TO TUNISIA

In 1941 the long shadow of Nazi enslavement darkened Balkan skies, and by midsummer a series of German victories carried the swastika to the Aegean and came close to driving Britain out of the Mediterranean.

The Germans cared nothing for the Italians; but it did not suit their purpose to let them be exterminated by British and Greek armies in Libya and Albania. A blitzkrieg in the Balkans against the Greeks not only would rescue the Italians but also might pay good dividends, both economic and psychological. Perhaps the threat of war, combined with economic and diplomatic pressure, might enclose the entire Balkan Peninsula in the Nazi net. If Britain chose to jeopardize her army by assisting Greeks, so much the worse for her; a British expeditionary force in the Balkans would drain England's strength in Libya and in Egypt, and if this happened it might prove possible to drive the British not only out of Greece but also out of Africa.

For months past, Nazi troops had poured into Rumania. On March 1, 1941, they crossed from it into Bulgaria and within one day clicked their heels in the streets of Sofia. Thus two out of five Balkan states went down without a fight. Beyond Bulgaria lay Turkey and Greece. Both countries threatened to resist, but British troops already had landed in Greece and the Germans decided to leave Turkey alone for the time being. How to get at the Greeks? The frontier between Greece and Bulgaria was mountainous and the Germans hesitated. They could hit at Greece more readily through Turkey in Europe but they did not want to put the Turk to the test, not yet. Better to engulf Yugoslavia first, and then to flow through the Vardar Valley to inundate both Greeks and Britons from the north.

Yugoslavia, that triune kingdom of Croats, Serbs, and Slovenes, was in a serious dilemma. Prince Paul, the regent, signed a pact with Germany which admitted German technicians to Yugoslavia and gave to Hitler the right of transit across his country to munition and hospital trains. But now the Yugoslavian army under Serbian officers revolted, overturned the government of the regent, raised young King Peter, not yet eighteen, to the throne, and defied the Germans. The latter did not hesitate: they invaded both Yugoslavia and Greece.

The Balkan Campaign of 1941

The campaign thus initiated was to last less than a month. A German arc of 1,000 miles stretching from Austria through Hungary, Rumania, and Bulgaria ran parallel with two-thirds of the Yugoslav frontier. All the Nazis had to do was to keep the Greeks and British occupied on the Bulgar-Greek frontier while they launched several convergent attacks on Yugoslavia. The most important struck like lightning at the Vardar Valley from Bulgaria, thus cutting off the greater part of Yugoslavia from her allies. The German wedge now fanned out north and south, while units of it going west joined hands with the harassed Italians in Albania. Meanwhile, Belgrade fell before a German rush from the north. The oncoming Germans, with new light-built tanks for mountain warfare, with trained parachute troops supported by two of Germany's six air fleets and some 3,000 planes, were irresistible. At Sarajevo the Yugoslav army made its last stand. Here it was trapped, in part by aid given the enemy by treacherous Croats. On April 16th, it laid down its arms. There was nothing left of Yugoslavia now unless scattered bands of guerilla fighters in remote valleys could be said to represent her.

The Greeks were next on the German slaughter list. Although they held the Wehrmacht back on the Bulgarian frontier by furious fighting, they could do nothing to stem the Nazi offensive down the valley of the Vardar. Germans, streaming down that spacious valley, captured Salonika, where the Vardar flows into the sea, and thus the Greeks in the east were isolated from their main army. As this happened, the 57,000 British troops sent to their assistance, for the most part Australian and New Zealand Anzacs, retreated across the flat Thessalian plain, harassed by a murderous assault from the Luftwaffe which the feeble squadrons of the RAF could do little to check. The Anzacs kept their ranks intact and managed for three days to hold the pass at Thermopylae against six German divisions. But this they did, not so much to help the Greeks, who had already told them that nothing more could be done, as to make possible their own debarkation. Again, the Royal Navy did its part, and from tiny ports and scattered beaches it managed to rescue 44,000 exhausted British soldiers. A second Dunkirk.

By May 1st all was over. The Greeks who had fought to the last ounce of endurance lay prostrate under German and Italian rule, for Mussolini, Hitler's lackey, claiming his share of victory, was permitted to police Athens. Yugoslavia was hung, drawn, and quartered. Croatia fell to Italy, the Banat to Hungary, and that part of Macedonia formerly in Yugoslavia was thrown to the Bulgars. The Germans took what was left.

A German army rested on its laurels in Belgrade. As for Britain, this was just one more disaster.

Crete and Libya

There were others to follow in this spring of 1941. Both in Libya and in Crete the British were to undergo defeat, and at home to stave off starvation and destruction by the narrowest of margins.

The Nazis had their eye on Africa as well as on the Balkans. For a long time they had been training men in Germany for desert warfare, conditioning them to excessive heat, preparing them with Teutonic thoroughness for what they must contend against in Africa. This German Afrika Korps, commanded by General Rommel, they despatched to Tripoli. With its armored tanks it became the spearhead of the Axis army, the Italians under Rommel's orders being left the minor function of consolidating land won by the more warlike Nazis.

Rommel struck out at El Agheila in March; and then and there began the retreat of Wavell's Britishers all along the weary, dusty coastline of Cyrenaica over which they had so recently driven the Italians. The British had advanced rapidly; their retreat was even more rapid; past Benghazi, past Derna, all the way to Tobruk. They clung so doggedly to that wretched seaport that the Afrika Korps was not able to dislodge them. Leaving it besieged, Rommel drove the British further east, past Bardia and into Egypt. He then halted to capture Tobruk, for he did not dare leave his flank exposed. In vain, however, did the Germans roll their tanks forward against the British lines. Reinforced constantly by sea, the tenacious Britons retained their toehold on the African coast, and Rommel, far now from his base, was compelled to give over further advance.

The greater part of the British expeditionary force rescued from the Grecian fiasco fled to Crete. That island protected both Palestine and the Suez; it threatened Italian communication with the Dodecanese Islands. It should and could be defended; so thought the British.

But once again they underestimated Hitler's men. Before they knew it, German paratroopers began dropping from the skies all over Crete, thousands of them. They came by air, in transport planes, in gliders towed by transport planes, ten or twelve men to a glider, equipped with radio sets and machine guns. The Nazi air superiority was marked; the British had no fighter planes competent to drive off the Nazis; bombers flying at low levels raked the British with machine guns and soon rendered untenable their hold on Crete. Within ten days, evacuation became inevitable. It was a third Dunkirk. Nearly half the British troops were killed or taken prisoner. Four cruisers and six destroyers were sunk, a battleship crippled. It was a sad day for Britain. What now could stop victorious Nazidom from spreading further east, to Syria, to Palestine, to Iraq?

Iraq and Syria

As the Nazis drove the British out of Grecian valleys and pried loose their grip on Crete, they noted with great glee events in Baghdad. Rashid Ali Beg Gailani, former premier of Iraq, a disgruntled Anglophobe, deposed by force the pro-British regent who acted for the six-year-old king. Britain had secured the admission of Iraq in 1930 to the League of Nations and Britain had recognized the independence of Iraq; nevertheless by treaty she was authorized to maintain troops in Iraq, to guard imperial communications, and more especially the precious oil fields. And now, as Britain reinforced her slender garrison at Basra at the head of the Persian gulf, Rashid Ali besieged a large British airport at Habbaniah. That airport was unfortified, and to defend it the British had to fly both men and artillery in from Basra. If the Iraqi won, if they once succeeded in cutting the pipeline to Haifa in Palestine, the plight of the royal navy and of the RAF in the eastern Mediterranean would be serious. Fortunately the Germans were so heavily engaged this month in Crete that they were unable to help Rashid Ali except by flying in a few planes from Syria; fortunately, also, many Arabs revolted against Rashid Ali. By the end of the month his inglorious rule was over and the former regent was back on the throne.

The planes which the Germans sent to Iraq had been flown from French bases in Syria, and the excuses offered by the French governor there, who had been appointed by Vichy, were very flimsy. The British felt they could take no chances; a German occupation of Syria was by no means impossible, and once nested there the Nazis could put pressure on Turkey from the south, on Palestine from the north, and on Iraq from the west. Only part of the oil from Mosul went to Haifa; the pipeline bifurcated and a great part of it flowed to the sea at Tripoli in Syria, an invaluable source for the Luftwaffe. The British decided to strike. Conjointly with the Free French troops of General De Gaulle they crossed from Palestine into Syria. By June 28th, Damascus fell and immediate danger was over.

The Threat Nearer Home

Clearly it had been an Axis spring; and not in the Near East alone. The Luftwaffe had been turned loose once more on Britain, this time to focus primarily on British ports. Eight raids on Plymouth left that city a smoldering mass of ruins, more battered in 1941 than Coventry in 1940. Eight nights in succession the Nazis blasted at Liverpool's docks. Hull, Newcastle, Bristol, Portsmouth, and even Belfast were visited by Nazi airmen who also were not forgetful of London, giving that city the most savage pounding it received during the entire war.

Upon the high seas the U-boats took heavier and heavier toll of British shipping. In April 589,273 tons were sunk, this the peak month since the war commenced. Ships were lost at three times the rate of construction in British and American shipyards; and food and war matériel piled higher and higher on American and Australian docks. The food ration was cut in Britain and her margin of safety grew appreciably less. The German subs were prowling further and further afield, far south of the equator and up and down the coast lines of the Americas and Africa.

The picture was not altogether one-sided. In the Mediterranean the Italians felt the weight of British armor when three of their heavy cruisers and presumably a battleship were sunk. Moreover throughout the spring their Ethiopian empire faded into dust when Addis Ababa fell. Also German victories of April and May were marred somewhat by the sinking of their finest battleship, the *Bismarck*, after a long and exciting chase by the most powerful units of the British fleet. Nonetheless, the over-all picture was highly favorable to the Axis. The Balkan Peninsula was under their thumb, to do with as they wished. The southeastern door to Europe was shut and bolted. There would be no second front there to worry about for months or years to come.

Hitler Invades Russia

When German armies invaded France in 1940 Russia saw her chance and took it; she ordered Rumania to cede to her Bessarabia and northern Bukovina. The former province had been Russian territory before the First World War and Russia had never acquiesced in its loss. Bukovina had been part of the old Austrian empire and never had been Russian. Its population, however, was predominantly Ukrainian and Stalin thought there was no time like the present for uniting all Ukrainians under the Soviets. In 1940 he gauged the situation correctly: the Nazis were not consulted about this enlargement of the Russian frontiers and the Nazis were sulky; but the Nazis did not interfere.

A month or two later, after France had fallen and England seemed about to fall, the Nazis were not so conciliatory toward Soviet ambitions in the southeast. So Stalin discovered when he put renewed pressure on Rumania. This time the Nazis took action in a supposedly Russian sphere of influence without consulting him. They carved Rumania according to their own plans, presenting part of Transylvania to Hungary, the Dobrudja (formerly Bulgarian territory) to Bulgaria, granting what was left a guarantee of territorial integrity backed by the immediate presence of German troops.

FROM LEND-LEASE TO TUNISIA   347

It was now Stalin's turn to be conciliatory; he had miscalculated German strength and had neither wished nor expected such a speedy and overwhelming German triumph in the west. With Germany supplying the Finns with numerous planes and fresh ammunition in the autumn of 1940, the Russians decided to be circumspect; they scrupulously delivered to Germany the goods called for by their trade agreement of 1939; they sent Premier Molotov to Berlin late in 1940. It was not a pleasant visit for the Russian, since he discovered that his country was expected to join the Axis, as had Rumania and Slovakia. This Stalin would not do; he had no intention of duplicating Mussolini's fateful career and playing second fiddle to Hitler.

Stalin knew Russia was ill prepared for war; he also knew that Hitler distrusted him as much as he did Hitler. And so he made his preparations. He signed a peace pact with Japan, thus insuring Russia against war on two fronts; he lengthened the work-day from seven to eight hours; he made it a crime against the state to be more than twenty minutes tardy at the factories; he shunted nearly a million boys and girls into trade schools for special training in mechanical pursuits; he speeded production in war matériel; and he gave orders that many vital war industries in Moscow, Leningrad, and elsewhere should dismantle their machinery and reassemble it east of the Urals.

Meantime the Soviet chieftain tried by diplomacy to stave off Nazi attack. To curry favor with the Germans he refused recognition any longer to the Belgian and Norwegian embassies and he gave it to the pro-German rebels in Baghdad. And finally in May, 1941, he dismissed the ministers of Greece and Yugoslavia.

All this to no avail. By June Hitler had determined to smite the Russians, if troop concentrations have any meaning. The Rumanians mobilized on the Russian border; Nazi storm troopers who had conquered Greece were ordered to the Polish frontier; to Finland the Nazis dispatched German units; and the Luftwaffe, withdrawn largely from the West, was concentrated in the East, its squadrons flying over Russian territory on reconnaissance flights.

Then without warning on June 22 the Nazi legions crossed the border and there was war with Russia! The most gigantic duel in recorded history now had opened. Never before had so many million men been hurled so savagely at one another; never before had there been a battle line of 1,800 miles across which so many armies lunged. Tanks ripped holes in opposing lines and syphoned through to widen salients. And then, the pincer movements; planes droning overhead and dropping death amid the ack, ack of the anti-aircraft guns; pockets of resistance, now large, now small, contracting, expanding; encirclements, escapes, the trapper sometimes trapped; a constant fluid war of movement; a ruinous scene of hell on earth which Lucifer himself could not surpass.

The Germans had a plan of campaign, brilliant in design, brilliant in execution, which suited well their temperament and their superb military skill. The "Blitzkrieg" tactics so successfully applied two years earlier in Flanders were repeated. The Nazis aimed at Moscow, but it was neither this river nor that town that was their main objective. The Russian armies were their quarry, and these they proposed to run down and to exterminate before cold weather came, by wide open maneuvres across wide, level plains. Dive bombers and tanks, speed and force would encircle the Slav, enfold him in unexpected pockets, and then crush and slay the ponderous red giant. And this the Germans almost did in 1941, but not quite; and once again in 1942, but not quite.

For the Russians, too, had a plan, one suited to their temperament, their tradition, their climate. It was very simple; to keep their armies intact no matter how much ground they yielded. A hundred thousand square miles was less important to them than their armies. Space, time, and winter weather, Russia's ancient allies, had served her well against the Swedes in the eighteenth century, against the French in the nineteenth. The Russian defense was one in depth, not ordinary depth but Russian depth. Stalin proposed to contest the frontier lightly, to lure on the enemy, to depend on guerilla action to harass his communications, to hammer away at his flanks, and above all to be patient under defeat, conscious that new Russian armies, and still more new Russian armies, given time, would hurl themselves at the Hitlerites, expel them from Sovietland.

As might have been predicted, 1941 was a year of German victory. In little more than three weeks the Luftwaffe destroyed a considerable part of the Russian planes before they even left the ground, the German tanks penetrated the Stalin line of frontier defense, and the German infantry was in Smolensk with Moscow only two hundred miles away. To have covered two-thirds of the distance to the Russian capital in twenty-six days was good going. Nevertheless, the war was still young and the road to Moscow was no open highway.

It was now midsummer and the Nazis looked forward hopefully to the conquest of Moscow. But the Russians had just begun to fight. Already they had ruined by fire and by dynamite their bridges, railways, power houses, water mains, dwellings; and now they counterattacked all along the line, warily, intermittently, avoiding encirclement. The series of sanguine battles which followed one another in quick succession in central Russia are known collectively as the Battle of Smolensk, although for the most part they took place to the east of that strategic rail center and at some distance from it. The spearhead of the German advance reached Vyazma, northeast of Smolensk and only one hundred miles from Moscow; it penetrated to Bryansk to the southeast, athwart the Moscow-

Kiev-Odessa railroad. But the Russian lines were elastic; they bent but did not break.

Long before German pressure on the central front slowed down it was felt in the Ukraine in southern Russia and at Leningrad in the north. The black earth of the Ukraine, the mineral wealth of the Donets basin, and the rich oil-fields of the Caucasus lured on the Nazis. From early August to late November they kept advancing. Bypassing Kiev, they raced for the Black Sea coast and reached it; they then dived at Kiev from the east, and that capital of the Ukraine fell into their hands. All through October Teutonic victory-waves flowed east and south. They swept to the Sea of Azov; they submerged Stalino on the Don and Kharkov, the Ukraine's second largest city. Then they abated somewhat, finally seeping into Rostov at the mouth of the Don, a good eight hundred miles from the old Russian frontier. The Ukraine, Russia's granary and main center of heavy industry was now entirely in German hands. The blow was heavy but the Red armies remained intact.

Almost simultaneously came a dash for Leningrad. That city once captured, the Nazis would touch hands around the eastern shores of the Baltic with the Finns, who had renewed their war with Russia. Victorious to the far north of Moscow as well as to the far south, the Nazis could then initiate a gigantic pincer movement, which closing in on the Soviet capital could choke and end the Bolshevik menace.

Leningrad the Germans failed to capture. No matter how hard they tried; no matter how heavy and sustained their air bombardment; no matter how powerful their siege guns, the Russians still withstood them. A great part of the city was pulverized from the air, and so close did the Germans come that the noise of battle echoed in the streets. The civilian population worked day and night upon the fortifications which ringed their city. And since the Nazis could not break them they settled down on November 1 to a long siege.

Meanwhile the hard-hitting Germans decided to wait no longer in subduing Moscow. On October 2 Hitler told his troops, "To-day begins the last great decisive battle of this year"—a true statement, but not in the sense intended. This time the swastika came close to floating over the Kremlin. The German tanks tore vicious gaps in the Russian lines and in less than three weeks Moscow was nearly encircled. On came the Germans, from north and west and south. The fall of Moscow seemed inevitable. But fate and weather ruled it otherwise. In November came welcome snow and ice. The Nazi tide had reached its perigee but could not rise above it. Then on December 6, eve of Pearl Harbor, the Red armies launched a counterattack against the half-frozen German tank formations. The surprised Nazis were forced back; two days later they announced the suspension of major activities on the eastern front, due to the weather.

The United States Closer to the Brink

"Give us the tools and we will finish the job," thus spoke Churchill in 1941 as the American public debated the pros and cons of lend-lease. But did "give us the tools" mean give them to us in America, or deliver them to us in England?

The majority of Americans would avoid "a shooting war," yet that same majority was determined that the Nazis must not win. To find an intermediate way between lend-lease and war was difficult, but the President found it. To order the American navy to convoy transatlantic cargoes meant "shooting"; but how about patrols instead of convoys? To use the President's analogy, a patrol on the high seas had the same function as a scout on the western plains: not to fight but warily to watch, and instantly to report the presence of hostile Indians. Warships on patrol would do the same, would look for submarines, those "rattlesnakes of the ocean," and send word by wireless of their whereabouts. If British naval units picked up said messages and acted thereon, that did not mean war, or did it?

By April 11 our navy was on patrol duty and on April 25 the President said that patrol would be extended, if necessary, to "all the Seven Seas." Two days after, the day the Germans entered Athens, Churchill addressed his faithful House of Commons. "When you come to think of it," he said, "the United States are very closely bound up with us now.... When I said ten weeks ago: give us the tools and we will finish the job, I meant, *give* them to us: put them within our reach—and that is what it now seems the Americans are going to do." The situation in the Near East is perilous but what of it? "Nothing that can happen in the east is comparable with what is happening in the west." And Churchill ended, quoting Clough:

> And not by eastern windows only,
> When daylight comes, comes in the light;
> In front the sun climbs slow; how slowly!
> But westward, look, the land is bright.

Through the spring we drifted toward war with Nazi Germany; we occupied Greenland to forestall Hitler; British warships limped into our drydocks to have their war wounds treated, unquestionably an unneutral act on our part; and, May 21, the *Robin Moor*, an American ship far from the prescribed war zone, was sunk in the South Atlantic, unquestionably an act of war on the part of the Reich. Technically we were still at peace, but more thoughtful isolationists, realizing the inevitable, were resigning from America First Committees, and more did so when President Roosevelt announced July 7th that our troops had landed in Iceland.

The Atlantic Charter

On August 16, the President of the United States and the Prime Minister of England made rendezvous off Newfoundland. While their naval and military staffs took common council the two chief magistrates signed the Atlantic Charter, a document reminiscent of Wilson's fourteen points. Both statesmen proclaimed that they opposed "aggression, territorial or otherwise"; that "they desired to see no territorial changes that do not accord with the expressed wishes of the people concerned"; that "they respect the right of all peoples to choose the form of government under which they will live"; that they favored "access on equal terms to the trade and to the raw materials of the world"; that they wished to secure for all nations "improved labor standards, economic advancement and social security"; that "after the destruction of Nazi tyranny" a peace should be established which would guarantee "to all men, in all lands" the chance to live "in freedom from want and fear"; that the high seas be free for all; that the use of force be abandoned; and that "a permanent system of general security is essential."

This charter was not binding; it was not an alliance; it stated the ideal goal toward which both countries meant to strive. British public opinion was disappointed that the Atlantic Charter did not go farther. But would an alliance have been ratified by the United States Senate? Roosevelt and Churchill were practical and experienced politicians; and both were confident that time, tide, and Nazi Germany would soon bring such hopes to happy fruition.

Nor were they disappointed. On September 4th the United States destroyer *Greer* was fired on by a German submarine. The *Greer* escaped, but promptly the President stated that henceforth the navy "would shoot on sight." On October 17 the U.S. destroyer *Kearney* was badly mauled in fighting a German submarine, and shortly after, the destroyer *Reuben James* was sunk. These acts of war brought congressional repeal of neutrality legislation which had forbidden the arming of merchant vessels and their entry into combatant harbors. But the vote in the House of Representatives was only 212 to 194 in favor of such repeal, and this was on November 13, less than a month before Pearl Harbor. Pacifists and noninterventionists were still numerous in America. Yet to many it seemed that we had been at war since the sinking of the *Robin Moor*, or at least since the "shoot on sight" order.

The United States Enters the War

December 7, 1941. All doubts were removed; America was in the war.

Relations between the United States and Japan had been increasingly strained since 1931. Our refusal to recognize the Japanese puppet state of Manchukuo and our steadfast sympathy with China led the militarist statesmen of Japan to conclude that they must either abandon their ambition to rule East Asia or fight the United States.

In July, 1939, the United States gave the requisite six months' notice that it intended to denounce its commercial treaty with Japan, due to expire in January, 1940. The Japanese were furious, also somewhat alarmed. The United States was their best customer and from us they imported much war material, particularly scrap iron and high octane gas. Why should America act thus? Our ambassador at Tokyo, Mr. Grew, told them the blunt truth. "The people of the United States," he said, "resent the methods which the Japanese armed forces employ in China today and what appears to be their objective."

Meanwhile we advanced loans and credits to the Chinese whereby they could purchase tools of war. But how could these be imported? There were only two feasible routes—one by rail through French Indo-China; the other by the Burma Road, a steep and twisting motor high-way from railhead in Burma to Chungking in far western China, a road handmade by Chiang Kai-shek's people with pick-axe, crow bar and wheelbarrow. The first route the French promptly sealed, for impotent Vichy dared not defy a Japanese ultimatum to do so. Britain in 1940 knew she had no chance to defend Hongkong without aid from America, and very little with it. Therefore she, too, gave way, and that summer agreed to close the Burma Road for three months.

The British held no cards and could not do otherwise; but this was not true for the Americans. We could stop shipment of vital war matériel to Japan, and this we gingerly began to do by restricting export of scrap iron and gasoline. In September, Japan joined the Axis and shortly after the United States advised her citizens in Japan to return home. Whether this act of ours stayed Japan's hand, or whether the cautious Nipponese were waiting the results of German air assault on Britain one cannot say.

For some months Japanese policy remained uncertain. Japan might sail south and seize the Dutch East Indies, taking French Indo-China, Hongkong, Malaya, Singapore, and the Philippines en route. But Japan was not sure of Russia; and with that traditional foe on friendly terms with Germany and snugly dug in at Vladivostok, perhaps it was as well to see what diplomacy might win.

And so Matsuoka, secretary for foreign affairs, visited first Berlin, then Moscow, signing a nonaggression pact with Stalin. The absorption of French Indo-China followed, the French, in June, 1941, granting military bases and the right to troop transit. Thereupon soldiers of Japan were rushed to the Thai border, thus putting pressure on Thailand to accept Japanese domination, or else! As Churchill broadcast in August, "They stretch their grasping hand into the southern seas of China. They snatch Indo-China from the wretched Vichy French. They menace by their

movements Siam. They menace Singapore, the British link with Austral-
asia, and they menace the Philippine Islands under the protection of the
United States. It is certain that this has got to stop."

Who was to stop it, and when? Both Britain and the United States
froze Japanese credits this fateful summer of 1941, thus ending trade
relations with Nippon; the Dutch East Indies, absorbing courage from
the two democracies, grew recalcitrant about selling Tokyo more oil; and
there was talk of the A.B.C.D. powers (America, Britain, China, and the
Dutch East Indies) acting in unison: but China was otherwise engaged
and so was Britain; only a handful of Netherlanders were in the East
Indies; the native peoples were not organized for defense; and that left
the United States as the solitary lion in the path of aggressive Japan.

The American public had been so engrossed with the European drama
that it had not paid much attention to the Far East, and President Roosevelt had been careful since the outbreak of the war scarcely to mention
Japan in his public addresses. With one war menacing us in the Atlantic
we preferred avoiding another in the Pacific, and the state department
did its best to delay an outbreak there. But our government remained
adamant in helping China; it extended lend-lease to that country; it
permitted an American officer to organize a Chinese air service; it dispatched a military mission to Chungking; and it continued to protest the
boa-constrictor engorgement of Indo-China.

Few dreamed the Japanese might attack us. After three years invasion
of China and with a million soldiers stationed there, it surely would be
the height of folly for Japan to engage America. We little realized the
bitter hate and scorn with which we were regarded in Tokyo, or how
the war lords had hypnotized their people in regard to the divine mission
of Japan. What we thought was that Tokyo probably intended to absorb
Thailand; and few Americans cared much about that remote nation. Once
secure in Thailand Japan might then invade Burma to close the Burma
Road. But why cross that bridge until we came to it; it was not nearly
as exciting a topic as Mr. Roosevelt's Atlantic patrols.

And so when the Konoye cabinet fell in October, 1941, and militarist
General Tojo became premier, Americans were not much concerned. On
November 5 Tojo announced that he was sending Kurusu as a special
envoy to the United States. His *peace* mission was but a screen behind
which Japan made ready her lightning stroke of December 7, and so
Churchill saw it when he warned Tokyo on November 12 that if war
came between Japan and the United States, Britain would be at war with
Japan "within the hour." Americans, however, were more optimistic.
Kurusu doubtless would tempt us to abandon the Chinese, and this we
would not do; but possibly he had some compromise to offer.

Kurusu suggested a modus vivendi, with the United States acting as
mediator in the Sino-Japanese War. The President agreed under certain

conditions to act as "introducer" but not as "mediator"—a subtle distinction to avoid offending China. Kurusu then proposed on November 20
to evacuate southern Indo-China as soon as an agreement was signed with
the United States, and all of Indo-China on the conclusion of general
peace in the Far East. We were to cease our aid to China and withdraw
our economic sanctions against Japan.

We countered with a note withdrawing the President's offer to act as
introducer, reaffirming continued aid to China and proposing that Japan
withdraw from China and resign from the Axis. If Japan would do this
we would remove all restrictions on exports to Japan and help that country stabilize its currency. The Japanese reply was handed to Mr. Hull on
the afternoon of December 7. All this was superfluous; torpedo planes
and fighter escorts blazoned with the Rising Sun of Japan were already
dropping bombs on our naval base at Pearl Harbor.

Japanese Victories

Our carelessness in Hawaii was inexcusable. More than ten days before, our commanders there had been advised that war might break at
any instant, yet few precautions were taken. The navy took it for granted
that the aircraft warning system operated by the army was functioning
all the time, and would give adequate advance notice of the approach of
enemy planes; but the army only operated this system three hours a day.
The army took it for granted that the navy kept constant watch by long-
distance reconnaissance flights; but the navy patrolled to the south only,
and the Japanese came from the north. The army had one chance to
save the day and muffed it; a soldier experimenting after hours with the
aircraft detector heard the approaching Japanese planes only to be told
by his superior that they were American flying fortresses. The navy also
had its chance; a full hour before the attack it sank an enemy submarine just off Pearl Harbor but gave no general alarm.

Down swooped Japanese planes upon motionless aircraft, lined up in
close formation, wing to wing. Having destroyed at one blow most of our
planes the Japanese airmen made for our warships and caught them at
anchor. The crews did what they could with their anti-aircraft batteries,
but a battleship at anchor, unsupported by planes, is helpless, and in a
few minutes five battle-wagons were either sunk or badly crippled.

Three days later the *Prince of Wales* and the *Repulse,* two of the royal
navy's best and biggest ships, were sent to the bottom off the coast of
Malaya. The British admiral in command took a chance, and lost. Without air escort he steamed north to intercept a Japanese convoy, trusting
to murky weather to screen him from air attack. The weather suddenly
cleared and down upon the huge ships swept the Japanese planes. The

JAPANESE EXPANSION
IN ASIA AND THE PACIFIC

GREATEST JAPANESE EXPANSION

JAPANESE EXPANSION, 1895-1941

U. S. S. R.

TANNU TUVA

MONGOLIAN PEOPLES REPUBLIC

MANCHUKUO

Vladivostok

KAMCHATKA

SAKHALIN I.

KARAFUTO

KURILE IS.

JAPAN

Tokyo
Kobe Yokohama
Kyojun KOREA

Shanghai

C H I N A

Chungking
Kunming

Canton
Macao (PORT.)
Hong Kong (BR.)
HAINAN

FRENCH INDO-CHINA

Saigon

THAI-LAND

BURMA
Rangoon

NEPAL

INDIA

BAY OF BENGAL

Penang
MALAY STATES (BR.)
Singapore (BR.)

SUMATRA

Barabok

SARAWAK (BR.)

BORNEO

NETHERLANDS EAST INDIES

CELEBES

Surabaya

TIMOR (PORT.)

Darwin

I N D I A N   O C E A N

AUSTRALIA

OKINAWA

FORMOSA

Manila

Cavite

PHILIPPINE IS.

Amboina

NEW GUINEA

Port Moresby

GUADAL CANAL

SOLOMON IS.

BONIN

MARIANAS
SAIPAN
ROTA

GUAM (U.S.)

YAP

PELEW

CAROLINE IS.

(JAPANESE MANDATE)

PONAPE

NAURU

WAKE (U.S.)

MARSHALL IS.
WOTJE
JALUIT

GILBERT IS.

ELLICE IS.

SANTA CRUZ

NEW HEBRIDES

P A C I F I C   O C E A N

ALASKA

Dutch Harbor

ALEUTIAN IS.

ATTU
AGATTU

KURE MIDWAY

HAWAIIAN (U.S.) ISLANDS
Honolulu HAWAII
JOHNSTON

KINGMAN REEF

PALMYRA

HOWLAND (U.S.)
BAKER (U.S.)

CANTON
PHOENIX IS.

TUTUILA (U.S.)

TRM

British put up a stiff fight for three hours; but the Japanese got their quarry.

These two naval disasters were catastrophic. The Japanese army was well trained, needing little food, fanatically patriotic, hardened by years of war in China; but without command of the sea even that army could not approach the Philippines or the Dutch East Indies, much less Singapore. United, the Anglo-American fleets would have controlled the seas off Asia; but now the Rising Sun of Japan shone far and wide across those waters.

Almost simultaneously the enemy struck at Singapore, Hongkong, Guam, Wake Island, and Philippines. We had recently sent to Manila many new planes. Parked in rows, wing to wing, precisely as at Pearl Harbor, most of them were caught on the ground before dropping a bomb. Guam, located in a veritable nest of Japanese islands and (thanks to Congress) still unfortified, succumbed after four days. The 378 marines on Wake held out heroically until December 23, sinking with their light shore batteries two destroyers and a cruiser. Two days later Hongkong, battered by artillery and dive bombing, surrendered to Japan. Within one week after Pearl Harbor the Japanese army had landed in force in Luzon. Our army retreated with its Philippine allies into the wild and mountainous peninsula of Bataan, to fight on for months, hoping for succor that could not come.

If the Japanese had struck only at the Philippines we would, of course, have gone to war, for we had pledged the independence of those islands. But the voices of isolationist and pacifist would have risen high in lamentations for the death of our soldiers, sailors, and marines in lands far away. Now all such internal wrangling ceased. The Americans were angry; all of them. And as the casualty list lengthened they became more so.

The United States declared war on Japan; Germany and Italy declared war on us; Churchill flew the Atlantic to consult with Roosevelt. The world-wide issue now was joined. The United Nations (in 1917 it had been the Allies) signed on January 1, 1942, a military alliance. The Chinese Republic, Britain, and the United States, in addition governments in exile Luxemburg, Holland, Belgium, Norway, Greece, and Yugoslavia, as also the Central American and Caribbean republics and India, made up the original list. Russia remained at peace with Japan. But the "phoney war" of 1939 was global war in 1942.

The Swarming Japanese: Bataan

The American garrison in the Philippines was well situated for defense. Corregidor in Manila Bay was strongly fortified; it could be approached only by sea or air, and deep within its bowels was a huge tunnel the length of a city block, sufficiently wide to permit two ambulances to pass abreast, and with lateral tunnels on either side. Corregidor seemed a safe refuge from Japanese bombing and artillery fire. So long as our flag flew over it the enemy was not safe in Manila; and so long as our artillery could fire from it we could protect to some extent our troops on Bataan, only four miles away. Bataan was a natural fortress; its precipitous hills and deep ravines, covered by jungle growth, and its relatively narrow neck made penetration difficult.

Equally important was the loyal support of our Filipino allies. The Filipino Scouts, hardy, agile, well disciplined, proved themselves as good as any soldiers; and the regular Filipino army, largely without training, acquitted itself with distinction. Even the aboriginal Negritos joined in lustily, capturing Japanese stragglers and bringing them into the American lines in bamboo cages. The wise policy of Philippine independence bore good fruit; had it not been for these allies we could have done little to stave off the enemy.

In mid-January, 1942, the Japanese made a major assault on the American lines, and again in early February. And on both occasions they were driven back. None could gainsay their reckless courage: they charged into nests of machine guns without faltering; they hurled themselves on barbed wire, electrically charged, and stuck there, making of themselves a living bridge over which poured their reserves; they dangled like monkeys from tree tops; they fought by night and day. Death had no terrors for the men of Nippon.

Even so, Bataan's 40,000 defenders, mostly Filipinos, could have held out had it not been for lack of air support, food, and matériel. After January 1, MacArthur never had more than five military planes, all old models, continuously damaged and repaired with great difficulty. Four antique civilian planes, called "the bamboo fleet," because held together by splicing them with bamboo and bits of wire, were his service of supply, and the Bamboo Fleet could do little to replenish drugs, spare parts, and food, even if Corregidor could have spared them its stores. The defense grew weaker from malnutrition, malaria, dysentery, beriberi, and hookworm. Soon our outnumbered men could get no sleep. There was no intermission, no relief, for there were not soldiers enough to spell the half-starved malaria-stricken men in the front-line fox holes. Driven back to the sea some few were evacuated to Corregidor by motor torpedo boats, and some, challenging the sharks, swam four miles to the island where the flag still flew. What remained of the ammunition was destroyed and the flag of Nippon flew over the peninsula of Bataan.

General MacArthur, complying with the command of the President, had left by motor boat and submarine to renew the war as commander-in-chief of the United Nations in Australia. General Wainwright, his successor, continued American resistance on Corregidor until May. His men were sick, half-starved, cooped up underground, their island refuge shaken day in and day out by Japanese bombs. Before long the enemy made good a landing. Resistance futile, Wainwright surrendered.

Malaya and Singapore

The British had over 70,000 troops to defend Malaya and Singapore, but their naval strength was puny, their air force utterly inadequate. Even so, if their troops had been trained for jungle fighting (which was not the case) and if the Malays had been given Commonwealth citizenship (or even the promise of it) and trained to fight, the story of Singapore might have been different.

At Singapore there were British regiments famous for tropical warfare of the nineteenth-century variety celebrated by Kipling, the hollow square beating off the Fuzzy-Wuzzies. In all the Far East the British had nothing comparable to our Filipino Scouts. The Malays were not treacherous, nor had they been ill treated by the British raj, which had left them under their native sultans. But the Malays simply did not consider it their war.

The Japanese fought this brief, incisive, and completely victorious campaign with astonishing skill and foresight. Their shock troops, carefully selected and better paid than the average soldier, were snipers. Especially trained in tree climbing, in remaining motionless for hours, in camouflaging themselves to look like leaves, the snipers dropped hand grenades on the British by day and, to give the illusion of attack, set off firecrackers by night. Japanese troops were everywhere; they were lightly clad and carried no heavy equipment; they lived on hard rice cake impregnated with meat; they needed no fire; they were prepared for every emergency, with rubber sneakers in place of shoes, with bicycles for jungle paths, with collapsible boats for jungle streams, with chemicals to purify muddy water.

The British army was a land force; that of the Japanese was amphibious, traveling by boat and barge, sometimes by river, sometimes by sea, forcing its way along roads or through rubber plantations, forever getting in the rear of the baffled British and cutting off detachments. The Japanese tanks were light but far superior to the British armored cars, some of which dated from 1918. Excellent, too, were the Japanese paratroopers, skilled in signaling with the radio, adept at ambush. And so the British land army never had a chance. Defeated in skirmish after skirmish, in foray after foray, it staggered back to the tip of Malaya, crossed the causeway to Singapore, blew up the bridge behind it, and thought to hold Singapore until help came.

The Americans still held Corregidor; the British still held Malta; but Singapore was too big; there were forty miles of coastline and the Straits of Johore were easy to cross, particularly in the west where the water

was shallow and where reedy swamps and shallow streams on the Singapore side invited Japanese infiltration. There were no underground
caverns as on Malta or man-made tunnels as on Corregidor. Fighting
was in the open, and from the pitiless skies poured down the Japanese
bombs. The British did their best to send reinforcements, even endanger-
ing their Eighth Army in Egypt by so doing. Planes arrived, but too late,
for the Japanese had already infiltrated through the marshy shorelands of
the west and had repaired the dynamited causeway. With the enemy in
command of both sea and air a Dunkirk was impossible. After a thirty-
day siege came the surrender—the most humiliating in British army
annals and, historically speaking, the most significant since Saratoga.

Burma

Burma in many ways repeated Malaya and Singapore, the soldiers of
the Rising Sun bobbing up where least expected; the Imperials baffled
and confused, fighting back blindly, strafed from the air, losing contact
with their own detachments, cut off from retreat, poorly led by officers
whose ingrained contempt for "natives" was costly.

The Burma campaign synchronized with Malaya and Singapore and
lasted longer, but only because Burma was of large area and it was
impossible to push all the British to the sea. Nevertheless, the outcome
was soon a foregone conclusion.

For a long time Burma had been a neglected ward of the Empire, the
Burmese complaining that they had no land communication with India,
owing to the pull of shipping interests, and that their pleas for self-
government were without effect. The Japanese took full advantage of
this disaffection; their spy system in Burma was well organized, their
promises of independence for Burma loud and emphatic. British propaganda could hardly have been worse; it promised nothing apart from
protection; it did not even try to enlist the Burmese to defend their own
country. Keep cool and trust us, was the British slogan; and in consequence as fast as the Japanese won victories just so rapidly did the
Burmese lose their respect for British arms.

The main Japanese objective was Rangoon at the mouth of the Irrawaddy. Once Rangoon fell the Burma Road would be bottled up, the
Chinese lifeline severed, and the Japanese could attack the oil fields far
up the Irrawaddy.

January 15 the invasion started, and it took the Japanese over two
weeks to cut through the tangled jungles on the Thailand border, to
capture Moulmein opposite Rangoon on the Gulf of Martaban. Once
there they fanned out, crossed the broad and shallow Salween (three
miles wide at its mouth), and circled around to the north of Rangoon.
Meanwhile, detachments slipped across the Gulf in small boats to strike

at Rangoon from the south and west. The city became impossible to hold and its evacuation in early March was a military necessity.

During the next two months the Japanese swarmed north up the Irrawaddy, the Sittang, and the Salween, driving before them the British and the Chinese, who had finally been welcomed as allies. Numerous and isolated engagements took place between invaders and defenders; the former, wary in frontal attack but swift in movement, appeared with monotonous regularity from nowhere to block roads, to bomb tanks, and to worry and harass the exhausted soldiers of Britain and China; the latter kept on retreating toward the borders of India, the foothills of the Himalayas, and to the far southeastern corner of China, dynamiting oil wells and burning lend-lease matériel as opportunity offered.

The retreat became a rout. The British, burdened with mechanized equipment utterly unsuitable for a terrain of interlaced swamps and forest, abandoned their tanks and scurried on toward India. Most of them made it. The Chinese under the American General Stilwell came near being caught. They had stayed, perhaps, too long in central Burma and the Japanese had already cut off their retreat over the Burma Road by penetrating northeast from Thailand. The problem which confronted this fifty-nine-year-old American general was to press north faster than the Japanese could outflank him. Radio communication with Chungking was interrupted, and the Chinese forces in Burma widely scattered. Stilwell succeeded in extricating some Chinese and British soldiers and miscellaneous civilians by a march of wild adventure and diversified hardship which deserves well the attention of future historians.

For months to come refugees straggled into India. Fed from the skies by British planes, with swamps under their feet as often as dry land, plunging blindly where trails were not even blazed, many lost their way and perished; how many died will be forever unknown.

Java and Australia

"The fall of Singapore opened the battle for Australia," thus spoke the Prime Minister of Australia in the middle of February, 1942. But the battle for Java had first to be fought. Java was the key island of the East Indies. Although not the largest, it was, owing to its tea and coffee, rice, quinine, manganese, and oil, the most prosperous. To defend it the Dutch had a hastily drilled army of 100,000 natives, not too reliable, some 400 planes, mostly obsolete, a few cruisers, none very large, and a number of destroyers and submarines. Add to this our own Asiatic squadron (which had left the Philippines in the nick of time) of one heavy cruiser together with a number of destroyers and submarines, a British cruiser, an Australian cruiser, and some lesser British craft, all under the command of a Dutch admiral.

The Japanese took few chances; their game was to isolate prey before devouring it. In December, 1941, British North Borneo with its oil fields fell to their attack, and in January the eastern coast of Borneo and the island of Celebes. Delayed by continued British resistance at Singapore, the Japanese spread further east, taking the northern coastline of New Guinea in their stride and landing a force at Rabaul in New Britain, thus planting the flag of the Rising Sun well to the northeast of Australia. Then came direct action toward Java down through the Macassar Straits. This time the Japanese were driven back, American and Dutch submarines dealing heavy damage to their destroyers and transports.

The check was momentary; no sooner did Singapore fall than the Japanese made good their conquest of Sumatra, thus closing off Java to the west; and as they did so they occupied Portuguese Timor to the east, and after that Bali on Java's eastern tip. It was now late in February, and as the invaders prepared their armada for Java the United Nations' motley fleet boldly challenged the navy of Japan.

The ensuing naval Battle of Macassar Straits sealed the fate of Java. Only a few Allied ships survived this two-day sea fight, and when these tried later to escape almost all were sunk.

On now came the Japanese hitting at Java from east, west, and center. Their transports drew close to shore, and then, just above the water line great doors opened and out came motored barges. On reaching shore these barges dropped gangways, and dashing pell-mell over them came the little yellow men with bicycles, motorcycles, the lightest of tommy-guns and artillery. It was Bataan, Singapore, and Burma over again, with one difference. In Java were many well-paved roads over which the Japanese scooted so rapidly that their conquest made record time. They landed on February 28 and by March 9, aside from isolated fighting in the mountains, it was all over.

Then began the battle for Australia, an island-continent in area approaching the United States and with population centered in the far south and southeast. There were Australian air bases on the southeastern shores of New Guinea (Papua) at Port Moresby, and also at Darwin in north Australia. In 1940 the Australians had rushed a railroad to Darwin, and that city and Port Moresby, with the help of the Americans, they determined to hold.

The Japanese though persistent were cautious. Before trying invasion they tried to soften Port Moresby and Darwin by air raids. Perhaps they were not even certain whether to keep on to the southeast or to advance westward. During April they attacked Ceylon and sank British ships in the Indian Ocean. Possibly the course of empire ran that way; and having Vichy under the yoke they might try the same manoeuvre in Madagascar. While they were making up their minds, the British landed in Madagascar and American planes bombed Tokyo from carriers. This challenge to their homeland may have decided the Japanese to veer to the southeast against both Australia and America, for the Americans were now rushing to help their allies "down under."

So it happened that during the first week in May a great concentration of Japanese shipping was seen in the Coral Sea, which separated Australia from the Solomon Islands. The Japanese objective was plain: abandonment of the invasion of North Australia and a bold bid toward Sydney and Melbourne, heartland of the continent. Could the Japanese land near those cities in force and hold their lines of communication, Australia would be lost. And not Australia alone. Going further east they could pounce upon New Caledonia where we had a base, and this meant severing the American-Australian life lines. South of New Caledonia was New Zealand. The prospects for Japan were truly imperial.

But now Japan met her first reverse in six months of war. A task force of the United States navy met the oncoming Japanese in the Battle of the Coral Sea. It was a fight unparalleled in naval history, a battle not only at huge distances but also by planes. No battleship, apparently, was engaged by either side: but Japan did lose two airplane carriers to one of ours, and her loss in cruisers and destroyers was heavier. For the time being the Japanese would have to be content with their enormous and swiftly won conquests of millions of square miles, millions of people across 3,000 miles of ocean.

Rommel Routs the British

The Allies fared no better amid the sand dunes of Libya than in the archipelagoes of the South Seas. Their African prospects in December, 1941, were bright; but so alarming was the tale of disaster from the Far East that few rejoiced over British advance in Africa. Nevertheless the Eighth Army was repeating in late 1941 its victories of 1940, covering the old ground once more, bypassing thousands of Axis troops in Halfaya Pass and compelling them to surrender, hoisting the Union Jack again over Bengazi, driving back the Axis forces even farther than the Italians in the earlier year, this time one hundred miles beyond Bengazi, all the way to El Agheila, where Rommel, protected by the sea on one flank and by salt marshes on the other, stayed his retreat. But 1942 reversed all this; and disaster so serious overtook the overconfident Britons that as fast as their sun of empire sunk in the Far East almost as rapidly did it sink in North Africa.

January, 1942, and thousands of fresh troops were added to the Italo-German army in Libya under that wolf of desert warfare, General Rommel, also many new high-powered field guns, self-propelling, which could outshoot the light British field artillery, and many new tanks of the Mark IV model, a better tank than any thus far shipped to Egypt from America or England.

Rommel struck so hard, and so skilfully, at the end of January, that he threw the British back 360 miles to the Egyptian border and, breaking through, kept on halfway to Alexandria.

His campaign was superb; he not only had better tanks but knew how to concentrate them to best advantage; he caught the British off center by feints to the wasteland in the south as he kept on with his main offense along the seacoast; he outflanked and outwitted his enemy so fast that over and over again their food, their oil, their ammunition, their tanks fell into his hands; and in odd moments he delivered lectures on desert strategy and tactics to captured British officers.

The British, exhausted by their rush from east to west, now had no time to rest as they were rushed back faster than they had come. For a brief season in May it looked as though Rommel might be held; he was far from his supply line and every week that passed the British came closer to their own. Thanks to American and British matériel rushed around to Egypt through the Red Sea they were now nearly equal to the Germans in tanks and probably superior in the air: but Rommel was a genius in the art of war and he led the overconfident British into ambush. Out of 300 tanks, 230 were lost. And without tanks one does not win desert battles.

Tobruk had been reinforced and had withstood one long siege. So long as the Union Jack flew above its low ramparts Rommel's advance would be endangered. But now before the garrison could sow mines properly the German panzer divisions were upon them. In some ways what followed was even worse than Dunkirk, Crete, Greece, or Singapore. A very few managed to escape by sea; the remainder died or were made prisoners; and the piled-up war matériel came in very handy for Rommel.

That master of war gave his enemy no breathing space; by the end of June he was deep in Egypt. If he once reached Alexandria, then Cairo and the Suez were at his mercy. Once at Suez, the shadow of the swastika would darken the entire Middle East. At this very moment the Wehrmacht was striking across the Ukraine toward the Caucasus. Rommel's army was the southern prong of a gigantic pincer, the northern prong of which was approaching the Volga and the Caspian. The two prongs might close in northern Persia.

To throw Rommel back the British put in everything they had: soldiers from Iraq, Palestine, and Syria, green troops from England, and equally green Americans handling a few American lend-lease tanks. The RAF flew to the rescue, aided and abetted by American airmen. It was nip and go: but much Nazi matériel en route to Rommel was reported sabotaged in the Balkans, and he was held at El Alamein, seventy miles west of Alexandria. El Alamein was on the sea and forty miles inland was the

Quattara Depression of sand so soft as to make tank warfare impossible. But forty miles left ample room to manoeuvre, and on July 1 a panzer spearhead broke through the British lines. It was driven back by almost superhuman counterattack, and Rommel stopped. The Nazi tide in the Near East had reached its perigee; but who could then be sure of that?

Russia: The Second Nazi Offensive, 1942

Throughout the winter of 1941-42 the Nazis went defensive in Russia, depending on strategic fortresses to hold the furious Russians back. Out around these fortresses were fortified villages like the quills of the hedgehog, and to strike through to the center of a hedgehog or to encircle it point by point and compel surrender was costly business. All winter long that was the main Soviet endeavor.

The Red army fought through long winter months with abandon; its soldiers endured subzero weather better than did the enemy; they were better clad; and the Russian inferiority in tanks, noticeable in the summer of 1941, was now ended. From their factories beyond the Urals came new tanks, "white mammoths," as they were called by the Germans, huge brutes of fifty tons, which the Red tankmen drove at the Germans with ferocious skill through great snowbanks, across frozen lakes and rivers. The ice groaned and bent beneath their weight but the winter-wise Red soldiers put down timbers, covered them with water so they froze, and made precarious roadways like frozen pontoons. Time and again they surprised startled Nazis, cut deep behind German lines, and looked forward hopefully to a major German defeat. It never came. "Hedgehogs" might be surrounded, but their garrisons were supplied with food by plane. There were not enough of the white mammoths, not enough of their "little brothers," English tanks sent to Russia and manned by Russians. The Red cavalry performed prodigies of valor; so did the Red ski troops; so did the Red paratroopers. The Nazis suffered horribly, as Hitler acknowledged. But reinforced in February they held most of their hedgehogs. Staraya Russia, Vyazma, Bryansk, Orel, Kursk, Kharkov were still in their hands by the spring of 1942. The Russians at most had retaken but 20 per cent of the invaded lands, and the invaders were in good shape to try again.

This time the Nazis must not fail. They had now been at war two years and a half, and now with the United States a foe, with the RAF hampering their production, it was essential that 1942 see all Europe under their yoke. They had underestimated Red armies once; they would not do so again.

Very carefully they made ready a concentrated drive south and east, a surge to carry the swastika to the Black Sea, the Caucasus, and to the Volga. If Germany held Stalingrad on the Volga, lend-lease matériel

500 MILES

RUSSIAN FRONT
1941 - 42

RUSSIAN AREAS
HELD BY AXIS,
NOV., 1942

OTHER
AXIS-DOMINATED
AREAS

ARCTIC OCEAN

NORTH CAPE

ALLIED SUPPLY LINES

NORWAY

Murmansk

WHITE SEA

SWEDEN   FINLAND

Archangel

LAKE LADOGA

BALTIC SEA

ESTONIA

Leningrad

SOVIET

LATVIA

VOLGA

LITHUANIA

Rzhev   Moscow   Gorki

EAST PRUSSIA

Smolensk

"GREATER" GERMANY

BYELO-RUSSIA

Orel

DEC., 1941
FARTHEST AXIS
ADVANCE
NOV., 1942

POLAND

Kuibyshev

SLOVAKIA

Kiev

UKRAINE

Voronezh   Saratov

UNION

Kharkov

Stalingrad

HUNGARY

BESSARABIA

VOLGA

DON

SERBIA

Odessa

Rostov

RUMANIA

Kerch

Maikop

Astrakhan

SEVASTOPOL

BULGARIA

Sevastopol   Yalta

CASPIAN SEA

Mozdok

BLACK SEA

Grozny

ALLIED SUPPLY LINE

Istanbul

TRANSCAUCASIA

Batum   Tiflis   Baku

DARDANELLES

Ankara

GREECE

TURKEY

Izmir

Tabriz

IRAN

SYRIA   IRAQ

T·R·M

which was seeping into Russia via Persia and the Caspian would be blocked. If once she dominated the Black Sea she would have the Turks at her mercy. With Bulgar-German forces close to Istanbul, and with a victorious German army on their eastern frontier, the Turks could be persuaded (or compelled) to open the gates of Anatolia. What chance then of Syria or Palestine remaining under British occupation?

For many months, beginning in May, 1942, German victories came in such quick succession that almost every day fresh disaster overwhelmed the Red armies. Within two weeks the Wehrmacht penetrated 150 miles further east than in 1941. Sebastopol, under siege all winter, resisted stubbornly. But the Germans were not to be denied. They could not use their tanks effectively among the jagged hills which ringed that seaport but their artillery and their Luftwaffe blasted the city into ruins. It took three weeks of hand-to-hand fighting before they forced their way into the town, and even after that the Russians did not give over. They fought from street to street, from house to house, retreating to their few ships gathered in the harbor. It was a kind of Russian Dunkirk.

Meanwhile in the eastern Crimea the Kerch peninsula had already fallen to the Nazis and just beyond the narrow straits lay the Caucasus. The Nazis were not quite ready for adventure there; an army of several hundred thousand needs room in which to operate, and to secure it the German steamroller moved steadily and relentlessly in June across the eastern Ukraine, pushing the Russians back beyond the Donetz River.

Then at the end of June, 1942, came the final rush for oil and glory. Behind the Donetz lay the Don, sweeping in a majestic arc far to the east before flowing into the sea at Rostov. To force a crossing of the Don, to seep through the rich lands of the Don basin, to conquer Rostov at the river's mouth, to cross the Kerch Straits and invade the Caucasus took the greater part of the summer.

Early in July the Germans were across the Don; by the middle of the month they had cut the railroad from between Stalingrad and the Donetz, thus severing the northern from the southern Russian armies; and by the end of the month they were attacking Rostov at the Don's mouth from the east. Early in August the Maikop oil fields which produced seven per cent of Russia's oil fell to the invader, whose rate of advance in the Caucasus was rapidly accelerated as the Russians withdrew their tanks and depended for defense on cavalry. Meanwhile by the middle of August the entire Don Bend was in German hands and by the 31st a Nazi panzer division shoved into the outskirts of Stalingrad.

Unlike Bataan or Sebastopol, Stalingrad had no natural defenses. It stretched north and south along the west bank of the Volga for twenty straggling miles, and between it and the victorious Germans was open steppe with a few low-lying hills. The Nazis had superiority in numbers, in tanks, and especially in the air, assailing the city with a thousand planes. They held the west bank of the Volga both north and south of Stalingrad; they had cut all rail communications; no reinforcements could reach the Russians except by water; and German planes hovered over the river. The prospects of making Mother Volga the eastern boundary of Hitler's Thousand Year Reich seemed excellent.

Nevertheless, as week followed week and the war swung into its fourth year the Nazis failed to nail their conquest down. They drove their tanks again and again into the heart of the city; they blasted tall new factories and turned residential quarters into shambles; they took house after house, street after street, and even reached the Volga. But always the Red army fought back. Houses and factories became debris; but behind crumbling walls and shattered cement crawled Red army men with machine guns, bayonets and knives, careless of death. The very destruction the Germans wrought helped the defense against them, for the streets of Stalingrad choked with collapsed buildings stopped the ingress of German tanks. Sometimes the Nazis would clear an entire city block, but always was there danger of losing it next day. Yet the Germans dared not lift the siege. So long as the Soviets held here on the western bank of Russia's greatest river any further drive to the Caspian would fail by a Soviet flank attack.

As for the Russians, their Stalingrad was the sign and symbol of the 1917 revolution. Stalin had ordered it defended to the death and so long as their flotilla on the Volga could shell Nazi outposts, so long as fresh troops could seep into their city across Mother Volga under friendly shelter of the night, the cursed Nazis were deprived of their prey and Red Russia lived.

Midway, the Aleutians, and Guadalcanal

In the summer of 1942 the outlook for the United Nations would have been bleak indeed but for the Pacific. There, in the far North among the fogbound Aleutians, in the central Pacific at Midway, as also at Guadalcanal in the Solomon Islands in the South Pacific, the Americans took the war to their foes.

The most important of these engagements was the Midway battle. As in that of the Coral Sea opposing warships never sighted one another and offensive fighting was entirely by plane. Early in June some eighty vessels under the Rising Sun ensign—battleships, carriers, cruisers, destroyers, transports—converged on American-held Midway. This was no reconnaissance in force. Clearly the Japanese intended, if victorious here, to attack Hawaii. But the Mikado's soldiers never landed on Midway. Land-based bombers of the army, navy planes from carriers, navy flying boats intercepted the Japanese fleet and it sought safety in flight. Action continued for four days. The loss of American planes was heavy, five out of six in one sortie, eight out of sixteen in another, and fifteen out of fifteen in a third. The Japanese also sank our carrier, the *Yorktown*. But their own losses were far more serious, four carriers, two battleships, two heavy cruisers, three destroyers and transports. Midway was a happy augury for the future, particularly heartening in the destruction of carriers, a type of craft in which the enemy's navy hitherto had been predominant.

Along with the raid on Midway came a Japanese thrust at Dutch Harbor in the eastern Aleutians. Planes based there could easily raid Alaska, make possible an invasion of continental America.

Sixty miles west of Dutch Harbor lies Umnak Island, and upon it two months earlier had been laid steel landing mats for planes. From this secret base in the fog our army Warhawks swooped down upon the foe—and from west of them. Confused by this attack, the invaders fled. They stopped in retreat to capture Kiska, 672 miles from Dutch Harbor, and Attu, still further distant at the Aleutians' western tip. Hence our North Pacific victory was incomplete. But for the time being Alaska, Canada, and our northwestern states were clear of enemy bombers. Conversely, as long as Kiska and Attu remained in their hands, Nippon was similarly protected.

Despite the Battle of the Coral Sea the Japanese were still set upon the conquest of Australia. They strove persistently to capture Port Moresby on the southeastern side of New Guinea; their forces fanned out steadily from the northern Solomons southeastward along the thousand-mile length of that archipelago and built an airfield on the large island of Guadalcanal in the southern Solomons. Their objective was evident—cutting the American lifeline to Australia. And this we had to protect by an offensive-defensive at Guadalcanal.

On August 7 American marines, protected by a naval air task force, landed on Guadalcanal and on the nearby islands of Tulagi and Gavutu. They surprised the enemy on Guadalcanal, captured the airfield, re-naming it Henderson Field. On Gavutu they ran into a hornet's nest, the Japanese defending their caves with reckless courage, dying to a man. On Guadalcanal the surprised Nipponese rallied to the attack. So did the Japanese navy. Smashing into our task force on August 8, it sank three heavy American cruisers and one Australian. Our transports, how-ever, escaped destruction, and our marines, heavily reinforced, beat off the Japanese on land.

Throughout August and September the enemy did its best to dislodge the marines, strafing from the air and shelling from the sea the narrow and confined area which they had won, only about seven miles along the coast by four or five in depth. On the island there was endless fight-ing. Japanese troops, continuously reinforced at night by fast destroyers, proved worthy antagonists. Few were captured; many died. So also was it with the marines, who found the hot miasmic air, the malaria, and insect life of Guadalcanal quite as unpleasant as the soldiers of the Mikado. Time after time the latter returned to the fray, supported by naval carriers, destroyers, and battleships; time after time they were repulsed. The flag still flew over Henderson Field, and from it rose American bombers to harry Japanese ships and bomb Japanese installations. The yellow tide of conquest still lapped these shores, but whether it had passed its peak and was now receding was anybody's guess.

Air Raids and Submarines

In 1942 the war in the air encouraged the United Nations. There was no proof as yet that the Luftwaffe was outclassed in Europe, since a large part of Goering's fleet was heavily engaged on the eastern front; but German assaults on Britain did peter out, while British attacks on Germany, and upon armament factories, docks, and railroads in the German occupied lands began to tell heavily against the Nazis.

There were more allied raids than before; there were many more planes to each raid; and the bombers were much heavier, huge Stirlings, great four-motored Lancasters, and 300 planes often in a single raid. The British focussed on the Ruhr and on industrial Germany; they lambasted Cologne in one night with 3,000 tons of bombs carried by over 1,000 planes; they spread afield; they flew to Augsburg in southern Germany and destroyed Diesel engines being fabricated for submarines; they flew to the distant Baltic ports of Rostock and Lübeck, wiped out docks, shipbuilding yards, aircraft factories, doing more damage to those ancient cities than the Germans ever did to Coventry. And they found time to smash as well at French factories.

Autumn, 1942

The war swung into its fourth year, and almost everywhere the Axis still was winning. The Hitlerites had one foot in Stalingrad and looked hopefully to sweeping up the Volga valley to roll in on Moscow from the east. They were already deep within the Caucasus, the Maikop oilfields had been won, and Nazi advance units were progressing steadily along the western shoreline of the Black Sea toward Batum. On the east the Axis' chances of forcing its way through Daghestan to Baku were slight, but the Nazis might slip around the snow-clad mountains of that wild and sparsely settled province and following the shoreline of the Caspian penetrate to Baku, there to quench the thirst of their war machines with endless Soviet oil. Over the Caspian, then, soon would fly the Nazi banner, and the southern supply line from the United States to Russia would be severed. If necessary, northern Persia could be taken, and Turkestan. Perhaps a junction could be effected with Japan in Afghanistan or in the Pamirs. The prospects were enticing.

In Egypt, Rommel was halted at El Alamein. But Alexandria was only sixty miles away, a glittering prize. Nothing favored the British except terrain, and their badly battered Eighth Army only recently had been outwitted and outflanked by military wizardry which might well outwit and outflank them again. One more deceptive infiltration, one more successful ruse, and the entire delta of the Nile with Cairo at its apex was at Rommel's mercy.

India, meanwhile, seethed with rebellious unrest and the victorious Japanese, engorged with Burma, were at her borders. The leaders of the Indian National Congress, exasperated by the evident unwillingness of British authority to implement promises of self-government after the war by trusting Congress with any important share in the prosecution of it, actively engaged in fermenting "non-violent resistance," that is, promoting strikes, discouraging enlistment, spreading defeatism. Gandhi, whether prophet, saint, or politician, implied that he was not unwilling to negotiate with Japan. And communication between China and India was now ended except for a trickle by transport plane over high mountains.

The entire East Indies lay quiescent under Japanese authority. The northern coastline of New Guinea was in Japanese hands and Port Moresby on the southern shore in grave danger. Everywhere north of Australia the Japanese swarmed. The Americans, it is true, had won a great mid-Pacific victory at Midway and had driven back an armada aimed at Hawaii and Alaska, had won a toehold on Guadalcanal. But this was most precarious, a single airfield only, surrounded by a jungle infested with Japanese soldiers, constantly under attack from their land-based planes in the northern Solomons and at Rabaul, still further north in New Britain Island. The southward expansion of Japan toward Australia and New Zealand was blocked for the time being, and that was all.

In Western Europe, meanwhile, there was no second front, nor any near prospect of one. In August a reconnaissance in force met with bloody rebuff at Dieppe on the French coast. After this, it seemed obvious that no second front could be established in 1942. Yet Stalin kept on insisting that there must be one. Churchill flew to Moscow to pacify him. The British are sea animals, he explained, the Russians land animals. The latter must be patient. But still the Russian chieftain was dissatisfied; he did not think the British and Americans were doing their fair share to win the war.

The United Nations fought for time as well as victory; time to convert America into the arsenal of democracy promised by Roosevelt; time to make the tools with which to make the ships, the planes, the tanks that would beat Hitler down; time to build factories, and homes for men and

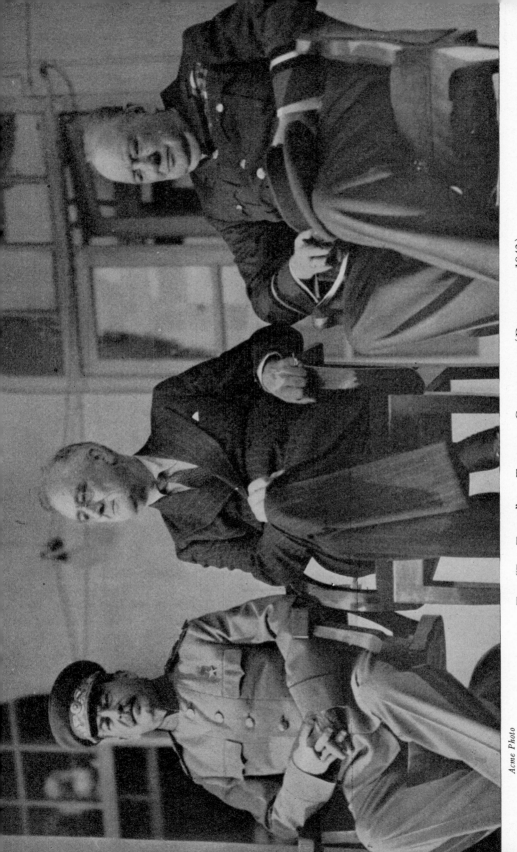

The "Big Three" at Teheran Conference (December, 1943)

women to work in them; time to assemble raw materials, to train crafts-
men, chemists, soldiers, technicians; time to transport overseas millions
of men from Canada and the United States with arms and food; time to
equip and drill these forces, and to pile up in Britain vast reservoirs of
all things necessary for offensive war.

If America was the arsenal of democracy, Britain was its warehouse.
The average Englishman ate less now than formerly, but his health
was better; his house, if he had one, was damp and cold, but his spirits
were high. He knew it was not so bad as in 1940 when England faced
the Nazi storm alone; his island now was an armed camp, and with every
passing month became more crowded with fighting men. The worst, he
sensed, was over. Sometime, somewhere, somehow, the measure of the
Axis would be taken.

The Axis, on the other hand, was not so confident as in 1940. The
English were still in the war, and now there were Russians and Americans in as well! The conquered countries would not support the new
order. The name of Hitler's Norwegian viceroy, Major Quisling, was a
hissing and a byword to all the world. Norwegians refused to enlist for
the crusade against bolshevism; they turned their backs on German
soldiers, put poison in fish canned for the German army, stood by their
bishops, ministers, and teachers who refused to follow Quisling's orders,
and escaped when possible to England.

So likewise was it in Denmark, the Netherlands, Belgium, Luxemburg,
France, Czechoslovakia, Poland. Fines, exactions, court-martials, starvation, death—they made no difference. The terrorism of the gestapo met
with sullen bitterness, secret sabotage, sporadic assassination. When
"Hitler's hangman," Heydrich, was killed in Czechoslovakia and the
Nazis slew every male adult in Lidice, the wrath of the Czechs but
mounted higher. In Yugoslavia's mountains the breath of freedom never
died, and every outlying German garrison knew it must keep constant
watch or else, perchance, be slaughtered. In London, General de Gaulle
still kept the Tricolor flying, and by ones and twos and threes his Free
French forces were augmented, as young lads slipped through the
German lines to join him. There were many accidents in French factories;
trains were derailed, bridges mysteriously blew up, cars were set afire,
and German soldiers died. The French respected old Marshal Pétain,
who had signed the armistice with Hitler, but Pierre Laval, the Nazi
stooge, was anathema in France as was Quisling in Norway. A scattering
few were found to fight bolshevism, and Frenchmen agreed to work in
Germany that French prisoners of war might be delivered from German
concentration camps; but the great majority watched dumbly as their
goods and chattels, machinery, horses, cattle, even grain were passed over
the border into Germany. They were helpless and knew it; but collaborate
with Hitler they would not.

Three years of war had not turned Nazi victims into Nazi slaves, nor had it convinced Chinese that Japan was sincere in her grandiloquent proclamation of the "Great East Asia Co-Prosperity Sphere." In this, and in their fast accumulating stores of war matériel, lay the major hope of the United Nations.

November Victories

The autumn of 1942 was to bring sweet revenge for 1940, for 1941, for 1942. In Africa, Europe, and in the South Seas the United Nations could list these victories: Rommel routed in Egypt and in Cyrenaica; French Morocco and Algeria occupied by British and American troops; the collapse of the German offense in Russia; and a new defeat of the Japanese navy in the South Seas, together with the drowning of thousands of soldiers headed for the reconquest of Guadalcanal.

General Montgomery and his British Eighth Army struck at El Alamein at the end of October, with superb superiority of artillery, tanks, planes. Most of his new matériel had reached Egypt via the long sea route around Africa, much of it American. Montgomery's army was mixed, pure British units, New Zealanders, men of Australia, long accustomed to desert war, men of South Africa, Punjabis, Sikhs, and other Indian warriors, a few Americans, most of them tankmen or airmen. It was a clear-cut British victory.

The Afrika Korps withdrew swiftly but with skill. Past all the old landmarks flowed the retreating German tide, past Tobruk, Derna, Bengazi with its useful harbor, around the bend of Cyrenaica, back to the salt marshes of El Agheila. For the first time since the war began the church bells pealed in England. As Churchill told his public: "We have now 100 Italian generals and 300,000 of his (Mussolini's) soldiers in our hands as prisoners of war."

As Montgomery's artillery barked at El Alamein an Anglo-American expeditionary force bound for Northwest Africa was on the high seas. It was hoped that the French garrisons there, upwards of 100,000 men, would welcome our arrival. For the most part they did so. At Algiers only a few shots were fired. At Oran, 130 miles west, there was more serious resistance. And at Casablanca on the Atlantic coast of Morocco there was, for a time, stiff fighting. It was necessary to land tanks both east and west of that city and begin siege operations. Fortunately the mysterious Admiral Darlan in Algiers, the North African representative of Marshal Pétain, gave orders to end resistance.

The American general, Eisenhower, commander-in-chief of the expeditionary force, immediately recognized Darlan as head of the civil administration and for this was violently criticized. Darlan's previous career had been that of a bitter Anglophobe, and since he had yielded from time to time to Nazi pressure most Englishmen and many Americans considered it undesirable that we should have any dealings with him. But Darlan, as our enemy, could cause us no end of trouble; and as our friend he could, and did, render possible our occupation of a great empire in record-making time.

His collaboration gave Hitler an excuse for occupying all France and for seizing the French ships at Toulon. The French army did not resist but Hitler lost the fleet. As the Nazis reached Toulon, their planes filling the skies, the French blew up their vessels! Meanwhile the British First Army, along with American detachments raced for Bizerte and Tunis. These two seaports in the French Protectorate of Tunisia were five hundred miles from Algiers and less than a hundred from Sicily, too great a handicap. The Germans got there first by air and sea, and in superior numbers. The Allies, within twelve miles of their goal, were driven back.

The redoubtable Russians also took the offensive this month of November, all the way from Leningrad to Stalingrad. Instead of capturing Stalingrad before snowfall, as Hitler had promised his people, 300,000 desperate Germans and Rumanians before and within that ruined city found Russian forces slowly closing in around them from north and south. Besiegers became the besieged. Farther south in the Caucasus trapped and widely scattered divisions of the mighty German host now sought safety in retreat. Back in Germany dreams of the gushing oil from Baku faded fast; instead came memory of last year's trials on Russian steppes and forebodings lest another and a worse year be in store.

Nor was this all! The Japanese suffered a double setback in the South Seas. Just as Hitler prophesied the fall of Stalingrad to his own men and the capture of Port Moresby in Papua by his yellow allies, the nimble Nipponese infiltrating through the jungle and over the Owen Stanley range of mountains were driven back by MacArthur's Australian-American fighters. And better yet, the American Admiral, Halsey, won in mid-November a victory at Guadalcanal, sinking many Japanese transports heavily loaded with troops.

Winter, 1942-43

In all three major theatres of war, in the Asiatic and Pacific area, in Africa, and in Russia the United Nations kept on winning. The Japanese made little headway in China and were subject there to continuous and effective, if somewhat meagre, air raiding; a Japanese army in Papua (eastern New Guinea) was exterminated and Papua cleansed of the invader; in Africa the British Eighth Army, still in pursuit of Rommel, this time went beyond El Agheila, captured Tripoli, cleared the Axis entirely out of Libya, penetrated southern Tunisia; and in Russia the greatest victory thus far of the United Nations was won at Stalingrad.

The major fighting in the Southwest Pacific took place in Papua, where some 1,500 Japanese troops tried to force their way across high mountains to attack Port Moresby. Soon they were in full retreat as a somewhat larger force of Americans and Australians drove them back to their base at Buna on the northern shore of Papua. Absence of roads and the necessity of transporting all food, ammunition, and supplies by hand or by airplane made progress slow; and the further our soldiers dipped north over the Owen Stanley mountains and the closer they got to Buna the slower the drive became. Slowly we closed in on the trapped Japanese. Reinforcements were sent them from their island bases farther north; but these were wiped out by our airmen. The fighting was carried on by every ruse known to the jungle. Thick undergrowth made visibility only possible a few feet ahead, and underneath was soggy ground in which fox-holes filled with water. We inched forward; we drove wedges in between Japanese detachments; we isolated them in pockets; and these one by one we exterminated. To do this was the work of weeks. Not until January 3rd did Buna fall.

The North African winter campaign would have ended in stalemate had it not been for General Montgomery and his British Eighth Army. Early in the winter it was at El Agheila, still in pursuit of Italians and Germans. The closer the latter got to their main base at Tripoli the shorter became their lines of communications; conversely the further the British shoved ahead the more difficult became theirs. Nevertheless, the British were not held up long at El Agheila. By the time their artillery was ready to clear a passage, and their engineers had exploded mines and booby traps, the Afrika Korps was in full retreat. Montgomery pushed on. Beyond lay Tripoli, capital of Libya, a good seaport, well defended from encircling hills. But the Germans did not choose to hold it, and Italians could not. A brief skirmish and Italy's African empire had fallen. In thirteen weeks the Eighth Army had chased the enemy 1,300 miles, the longest drive in history. On went Montgomery. The retreating Germans panted after the security of the Mareth line in French Tunisia, and Montgomery followed them there. To breach these strong fortifications was a first-class military action as Montgomery well knew, and the Eighth Army halted.

Elsewhere in North Africa the situation was more complicated. There was the problem of logistics, how to supply an army of approximately 200,000 with food and guns, tanks and planes, from bases as far distant as England and the United States, with submarines lurking in the ocean pathways; how after the matériel once reached Africa to distribute it to fighting men often hundreds of miles from the port of debarkation. Railways in North Africa were few and in disrepair; in some instances they had to be rebuilt and locomotives and freight cars imported from America.

Then, too, there was the political problem; who was to govern the restless, seething population, part French, part Arab. It had been solved temporarily by putting Darlan in authority; but Darlan was promptly assassinated. The men under him had been of Vichy and in consequence were anti-British. Though not pro-German they were undemocratic, loyal to Pétain alone. They hated de Gaulle and his "Free French" who had done so much to keep alive the fires of French resistance; and the Free French replied in kind.

The only common denominator available seemed to be General Giraud, an officer reputed as patriotic as de Gaulle himself. Giraud had not been a party to the fall of France. Imprisoned by the Germans in 1940, he had escaped from Germany and been taken to North Africa by a British submarine. Giraud succeeded Darlan as the head of French administration in North Africa; but the Free French would not acknowledge his leadership and bitter feud continued.

And finally there was the military problem. Germans and Italians had entrenched at Bizerte and Tunis and behind these two cities were fortifying a range of hills from which it would be difficult to oust them. They had already forced back the British First Army, and American and French contingents. If we were not careful we might be caught between Axis troops rolling down from Tunis and the Afrika Korps, rolling up from the Mareth line.

Meanwhile Hitler insisted that his bridgehead in Africa be held, and Axis reinforcements flowed into Tunis and Bizerte. All over Tunisia the weather was atrociously bad and for a large part of the winter the war was reduced to patrol action. Then it flared up suddenly and with startling reverses for the Americans.

On February 11 the Nazi army poured through Faid Pass at the eastern end of the American sector. Tanks and dive bombers seemed to come from everywhere, and all at once. We took quite a beating, retreating to Kasserine Pass, surrendering some 4,000 square miles of territory. We were even driven out of the Kasserine, and that meant serious business, for if the Germans gained control of the plateau region beyond, they might encircle the British First Army to the north and drive the United Nations back into Algeria. This was our baptism of fire, and apparently we were caught with equipment too light, with poor air support, and inferior tactics. We tried to rescue detachments which could not be rescued; we fell into traps and got what was coming to us.

Then the very next week we held and defeated the Wehrmacht. That drubbing had served us well. Our army functioned like a well-oiled machine. Stuka bombers were something to laugh at; our artillery fire was excellent; and the hitherto triumphant Nazis retreated through the

Kasserine Pass with their tails between their legs. Eisenhower was quoted after our initial defeat as saying, "Our boys will fight better now they are mad."

Stalingrad

The Fuehrer's New Year's message to his folk was not cheerful. The best he could say about the eastern front was that the winter there could not be worse than the preceding one. He erred. In January and February, Stalin's armies hurled themselves with such terrific and unrelenting force upon the discouraged Nazis as to free Leningrad from its besiegers, draw tighter and tighter the noose around twenty German divisions trapped at Stalingrad, and on February 2nd to compel the half-starved and abandoned soldiers left there to surrender.

There had been time enough to withdraw these divisions and sufficient warning during the autumn that fatal consequences would follow if they were not withdrawn. Only the conceit of a paranoiac would have abandoned them to their fate. Early in January they were cut off completely by a ring of Red armies, and beyond that ring a second was in process of formation, and beyond that a third. And now as the Red soldiers closed in for the kill it was the turn of the Nazis to dig for shelter in the ruined cellars of Stalingrad and to feed as the Russians had on horse meat, when and if it could be found. Their only contact with the outside world was by plane, and that too intermittent to provide sufficient food and ammunition, much less reinforcements. Nevertheless they stuck it out, and did so until over half had been exterminated.

Germany was thrown into consternation. "Europe is in mortal peril," cried Goebbels. "Only Germany can save Europe now. The onrush of the steppes against our venerable continent has broken out this winter with a violence overshadowing all human imagination." European civilization would be defended in total war which the Nazis would wage. If they were to do the fighting the least the rest of Europe could do was to labor in the common cause. His words speak volumes.

The Axis Expelled from Africa

Autumn victories over the Axis had cautiously been hailed by Churchill as "the end of the beginning." And now as winter turned to spring one could somewhat confidently write of "the beginning of the end." The tide had been slow in turning but by the middle of May it had run out a good six months, and there was rejoicing in the camp of the United Nations.

A second front clearly was impossible until Tunisia was won, and as winter ended that task seemed formidable. In northern Tunisia the Germans and Italians were safe behind a range of jagged hills and in the south they held the Mareth line against Montgomery. Their weakest point was the elongated corridor which led to the Mareth line, but it was protected by the sea on one side and by deep gorges and ravines on the other. Both French and Americans had tried to break through here in the neighborhood of Faid Pass and had been rolled back. Could they have done so they would have split the Axis forces in two. Conversely, so long as Montgomery's Eighth Army was on the other side of the Mareth line the United Nations' armies remained split.

Montgomery tried to crack the Mareth line, failed, then deployed his New Zealanders and the Free French who had crossed the Sahara to join him, into the desert at his left. These sturdy warriors circled around the Mareth line way to the northeast thus compelling the outflanked Afrika Korps to abandon their fortifications and to follow the coastal plain toward Tunis. Montgomery lunged after them as fast as his engineers could dig up land mines left by the capable Germans, who now had steadily retreated some 1,600 miles from El Alamein.

By these manoeuvres the Axis armies were forced back into northern Tunisia in an area somewhat smaller than Connecticut. They could not adopt defense in depth, for they were held too close to the Mediterranean; yet they had a long line to defend, well over one hundred miles. Their front wound like a snake around mountainous crags which their artillery commanded, and it was thought they might hold out many weeks, perhaps longer, if reinforcements could be gotten in from Sicily.

In less than a fortnight, however, the Italians and Germans were surrendering in tens of thousands. What took place was roughly as follows. As Montgomery swept north along the seacoast the British First Army, the Americans, and the French closed in on the now shrinking Axis lines. As formed now the Allied line ran from northwest to southeast thus: French Moroccan troops faced Bizerte on the Mediterranean, then came the Americans, the British First Army, the main body of the French, and the British Eighth Army.

The American assignment was to pry open the mountain gateway at Mateur, leading to Bizerte. To do this it was necessary to storm three hills, the key one, Hill 609, defended by as good troops as Germany had, and in a region so rough that mules were used for trucks. In the face of heavy machine-gun fire the Americans stormed this hill with hand grenades and at the point of the bayonet. Beyond they could see Mateur, now defenseless, and farther beyond shimmering in the sunshine the white houses of Bizerte and the blue Mediterranean Sea.

Our men streamed down toward Bizerte, cut the road to Tunis, captured Bizerte without further fighting. An hour or two later the British First Army was in Tunis, likewise meeting no resistance. In almost every direction German and Italian detachments threw down their arms. Some took refuge on Cape Bon but soon surrendered. Part of the famous

Afrika Korps, bypassed by the quick dash of the Allies, fought for a few days in the hills. By May 8 victory was assured; by May 15, 1943, the African resistance ended everywhere.

This Tunisian campaign cost the Axis dear. It lost over 300,000 men, among whom were 266,000 prisoners; it also lost its last outpost in Africa. More than that: it proved that the U-boat campaign, however successful, had not prevented the enemy conveying and supplying large armies overseas; it proved that air supremacy had at last shifted from the Luftwaffe to the United Nations; that Axis naval supremacy in the Mediterranean was a dream, that the soft under-belly of the continent was now open to invasion.

Italians became jittery and talked alternately of peace and of fighting to the bitter end. The Nazis belittled what had occurred and explained to their people that they had fought in Tunisia merely to gain time to make invincible their Europa fortress. The Maginot line psychology of defensive warfare which bedeviled the French in 1940 had in turn infected the Nazis, an augury of good fortune for the United Nations.

Was this battle for Bizerte and Tunis to be *the* turning point of the second World War? Churchill at once flew to Washington, where final plans were in process for insuring and for speeding campaigns to follow. The Prime Minister's address in Congress late in May compared Bizerte-Tunis of 1943 to Gettysburg of 1863, but warned that though the grey tide of the Confederate army never rose so high again, two years passed and thousands died before the victors came to Appomattox.

Chapter 18

STORMING FORTRESS EUROPA

SUMMER, 1943, and Fortress Europa seemingly was as strong as ever. The central keep was Germany; the outer bulwarks, Norway, Denmark, Holland, Belgium, the Channel and Biscayan ports, Spain, Italy, the Balkans, Crete, the Crimea, and bristling Nazi hedgehogs firmly planted in the heart of western Russia, from the Baltic south to the Black Sea.

There were many countries, but there was one sole command, not only military but also economic. Manufacturing centered in the greater Germany. Other areas supplied raw materials: wheat from France; iron ore, timber, and fish from Norway and Sweden; butter, eggs, and bacon from Denmark; fruits, copper, minerals from Spain and Italy; cereals, meat, bauxite, and oil from the Balkans. Such a fortress could not be starved into submission nor could the siege safely be delayed, since every month that passed without assault the Nazi screws on Europe's economy tightened and hope of succor for many millions under the Nazi yoke grew dim.

Since these things were so, it was the better part of wisdom to give *priority* to the European war, to defeat first the major enemy, Germany, and to regard Japan the lesser foe. Stalin called loudly for an invasion of the French coast. To launch one in 1943 was impossible. But there were two other ways whereby the Anglo-Americans might strike at Germany—by air and by way of Italy, and both were tried.

Air Blitz in Reverse

Some Allied experts were certain of knocking out Germany from the air alone, but Churchill was as ever conservative. "The experiment," he prudently told Congress in May, "is well worth trying so long as other methods are not excluded." The plane did not knock out Germany, but it did severely weaken military power there. The RAF, numerically stronger in 1943 than the American air arm in Europe, concentrated on the Ruhr, pounding congested areas in that industrial valley over and over again, blowing up houses, railroads and dams, flooding towns, pulverizing factories, killing unknown numbers of persons, reducing German steel production perhaps thirty per cent.

Hamburg in particular took heavy punishment, more severe than that inflicted on London. Night after night British bombers blasted docks, shipping, and factories. Their raids were costly, the defense desperate; but there was precious little left of Hamburg, second city of the Reich.

Far and wide through occupied France and Belgium scoured the Allied planes, ripping up airfields, smashing railroad trains, destroying coastal installations, and focusing on German submarine bases at Lorient and St. Nazaire. The damage done the submarine pens, those cement caverns reinforced with steel of which one at Lorient was spacious enough to stable thirty U-boats, was disappointing; but the ruin inflicted on shipyards, repair depots, and transportation facilities which the U-boats used, was held worth the sacrifice of Allied planes and airmen.

For this harassing from the west the Germans had small answers—the U-boat and the Luftwaffe. In 1943 the Reich navy concentrated exclusively on the U-boat, and for awhile sinkings rose rapidly. But there were Allied answers for the new U-boats. One of them was the frigate, easily constructed in great numbers, somewhat smaller than a destroyer, but capable of convoy duty; another smaller ship was the destroyer escort, and finally there was the patrol plane, weighed down with gas rather than with armament, good for long-distance aërial convoy work. There were ups and downs this year in the U-boat war but gradually its menace faded, particularly in the North Atlantic where the Canadian navy specialized in convoy duty, with some five hundred ships flying the Canadian flag by 1944.

The Luftwaffe also failed as signally as did the U-boat. It was not that German science fell behind; it was German production and German manpower that failed to keep pace. The Germans simply did not have the trained pilots, the trained mechanics, factory facilities, aluminum, and oil necessary in 1943 to meet what was thrown at the Reich by Allied air raiders. Top priorities went to fighter planes so that German bombing of Britain dwindled. Goering's organization for air mastery had planned too small and could not catch up.

Meanwhile production in the United States was swelling into incredible torrents of matériel. The Americans and Britons lost 335 heavy bombers in June alone, but British plane production had quadrupled and that of the United States had doubled, and redoubled and redoubled again. The new type planes carried four-ton bombs, later to be six- and even eight-ton "block busters." Over Coventry the Germans had strewed 450 tons of small stuff; now in 1943, many a German city was plastered four times that heavily.

The Sicilian and Italian Campaign, 1943

On July 9, 1943, two allied armies landed on the Sicilian coast, the American Seventh and the British Eighth, some thirteen divisions in all.

To conquer Sicily took thirty-nine days. The fighting, comparatively light in the earlier stages, became heavy and bitter, Allied casualties in dead and wounded going over the 20,000 mark, the Axis somewhat more.

The American Seventh Army encircled the western shore; its tanks rolled overland to Palermo, capital of Sicily on the Tyrrhenian Sea; the greater part of the island's 9,000-odd square miles was overrun; Italian garrisons surrendered after token resistance; and villagers with smiling faces offered fruit and flowers.

The British Eighth Army had a harder task. The eastern shore up which it slowly pried its way was precipitous, and close to the sea in the northeast towered Mount Etna, 10,000 feet in elevation. To its protecting security the Germans withdrew their three and one-half divisions; their temper was excellent; their courage beyond question; their defense position superb.

The terrain was so rugged and the ravines cut by swift streams so deep that any breakthrough by tanks was impossible. Tanks were used for brief snorting charges but the battles, or rather the incessant series of little local battles, were for the artillery and infantry. Slowly the British and Canadians won through the foothills to the west of Mount Etna, where they linked up with the Americans. From one strategic height after another the united Allies pressed the foe. Ferociously fighting and with great skill, the Germans withdrew by August 16. Almost all their troops were ferried over the narrow straits by plane or in small craft. There was no big bag of German prisoners as in Tunis; this time the booty consisted of Italians and German tanks. The underbelly of the Axis thus far was not so soft.

Then on September 3 the British Eighth crossed the straits to romp over the toe and heel of Italy, Italian garrisons surrendering with abandon. The more forehanded and more treacherous of the Fascist leaders, among whom Dino Grandi, the obsolete Marshal Badoglio, and Count Ciano, the Duce's infamous son-in-law, were notorious, having determined that the ship of state was sinking, decided to desert it. At a ten-hour session of the Fascist Grand Council at which Mussolini presided they somewhat disclosed their hand. A motion was made and carried calling upon the king to take the leadership of the nation. Mussolini sped to Victor Emmanuel, was arrested and sneaked away to prison, and Badoglio was asked by the king to form a "new" government.

Ruin came over Italy like some great pestilential fog; Italian armies were in full retreat; the civil population was semi-starved; the lynx-eyed Gestapo watched Badoglio; and the German forces in Italy were enlarged.

Victor Emmanuel and Badoglio played their cards with treacherous cunning. They were between three fires, the jittery mobs in Italian cities, the coldly suspicious Germans, and the overwhelming Allies. Crookedly

WORLD WAR II
IN WESTERN EUROPE
1942-45

S. S. R.

ENGLAND

London

AXIS STATES

AXIS-OCCUPIED STATES

ALLIED INVASION, JUNE 6, 1944

Brussels
NETH.
BELG. LUX.

GERMANY

Berlin

Warsaw
GOVT GEN. OF POLAND

SLOVAKIA
BOH.-MOR.
Prague
Vienna
Budapest
HUNGARY

RUMANIA
Bucharest

BULGARIA
Sofia

Belgrade
YUGOSLAVIA

ALBANIA
Tirana

GREECE
Athens

BLACK SEA

TURKEY

CRETE (GR.)

GERMAN CAPITULATION AT REIMS, MAY 7, 1945

Reims
Paris
SWITZ.
Berne

FRANCE

Nice
Marseilles

CORSICA (FR.)

FALL OF PARIS, AUG., 1944

ALLIED LANDINGS, AUG., 1944

ITALY
Rome
Naples

FALL OF ROME, JUNE, 1944

CAPTURE OF NAPLES, OCT., 1943

ADRIATIC SEA

CONQUEST OF SICILY, AUG., 1943

SICILY

MALTA (BR.)

SARDINIA (IT.)

BALEARIC IS.

PORTUGAL
Lisbon

SPAIN
Madrid

TANGIER
SPANISH MOROCCO
GIBRALTAR (BR.)

Oran
Algiers

ALGERIA

TUNISIA
Tunis
Bizerte

Tripoli

CONQUEST OF TUNISIA, MAY, 1943

MEDITERRANEAN SEA

LIBYA
Bengazi

EGYPT

Alexandria
Tobruk

ALLIED INVASION, NOV., 1942

FRENCH MOROCCO
Fez
Casablanca

willing to double-cross anyone or everybody, they played possum. The Allies gave Badoglio a brief thinking spell, suspected that he still fancied the Hitlerites, then enforced on him a rough reminder of their power by renewed air raids. The effect was instant and salutary. Through devious channels Badoglio intimated that he wished to join the Allies.

The terms offered were harsh, or would have been had Italy had anything to lose, unconditional surrender, demobilization of the Italian forces, surrender of the fleet—what was left of it. Badoglio agreed, begging that negotiations be kept secret lest his German friends and masters get wind of his spoor.

With one tremendous military stroke the Allies now planned to bring the fighting in southern Italy to a quick conclusion. Their strategy called for a landing in force on the beaches of Salerno just south of the Bay of Naples and Mount Vesuvius; for the withholding of the news of Italy's surrender until just before disembarking; for a rapid and more or less unimpeded march inland to join forces with British troops advancing north from the heel of Italy. They would then be in position to strike for Naples and Rome, cities which they thought would fall like apples ready for the plucking.

But the Germans were not caught napping. Two days before General Clark led his men ashore on September 9, approximately half from the British Eighth Army and half from the American Fifth, the Germans had cleared the beaches of Italians, armed the hills with Germans, and were at the ready. The Battle of the Beaches swung first this way, then that, for several days. The Germans held high ground north, south, and east of the dried mud flats and pebbly shores on which the landing barges grated. They strafed the barges, the beaches, and the thin line of soldiers in their foxholes, by artillery and from the air; they came so close to driving them into the sea that the German radio blared "another Dunkirk."

It almost was one. What saved the day was Allied fire power. Salerno was the outside limit for land-based planes operating from captured Sicilian airfields. Fighter aircraft, as it was, could not stay more than fifteen minutes over the front without running short of gas. But there were thousands of them, and frequently they made two trips a day. It was no longer necessary to give any thought to Italian warships, for they had surrendered, and the British brought up their largest battlewagons to pour withering fire on German batteries. Meanwhile on the beaches the LCTs (landing craft tanks) were close-packed together like monster whales. And out of them came tanks to crash incessantly into the enemy's lines.

The British Eighth Army was 150 miles to the south when Clark landed at Salerno, but it came on with astonishing speed, leap-frogging forward by the use of planes and parachutists. Within ten days the Allied forces joined, and the Germans, in danger of being outflanked, retired to Naples.

That Italian seaport they thoroughly wrecked. Out of what seems pure malice, and aimless vengeance they burned libraries, plundered art treasures, dynamited the water system as well as gas and electrical services, and set time bombs in hotels and post offices which exploded later and brought death to civilians. After this joint work of coverage and sadism they retired north to strong entrenchments beyond the Volturno River.

From Naples two historic highways led north toward Rome, the Via Appia, across Pontine marshes near the sea, and the Via Latina, often known as the Via Casalina, which wound its way around craggy little mountains through the town of Cassino. By this route the Allies hoped to force their way into Rome before 1943 came to an end.

They were doomed to disappointment. The Germans held savagely all along the Volturno, scene of Garibaldi's victory over the Neapolitans in 1860, and when driven back entrenched themselves anew on the Liri River flowing by Cassino. As the year ended the British Eighth Army on the Adriatic was still short of reaching Pescara, east of Rome and the terminal of the only decent route from the Adriatic to that city. And the American Fifth Army under Clark, to which were attached British, New Zealand, French, and Indian troops, had only begun to claw its way through the tangled mountain heights around Cassino.

Russian Victories of 1943

From every side the storm clouds of 1943 converged on Fortress Europa. From the south, so far distant were their thunders echoing in the Apennines that they scarce were heard north of the Alps. Blockbusters on German cities were devastating proof of very present foul weather, but, after all, such bomb smashes were intermittent, and though black nimbus clouds in westward Britain piled higher with every convoy and transport from America, the continent still seemed immune from invasion out of the west. Not so on the east! There through all this ghastly year raged a war storm, more widespread, more violent than any on record in German history.

It bore some resemblance to that of 1941 and 1942, but this time the all-conquering Germans were in retreat. From river to river, from city to city they were crushed back toward their Fatherland. The gains of two superhuman years were erased, the brags of Hitler and Goebbels now proved a mockery by German dead, the flower of the Wehrmacht scorched beneath the smoldering ruins of a dozen Russian cities, drowned in swamps, strewn carelessly by indifferent death in forests or on wind-swept steppes.

Rostov, on the Sea of Azov, was in Soviet hands by February 14, and German threats to Soviet oil ended. Equal success crowned Red army campaigns in the Donetz and the Ukraine, and all the way north to Leningrad. Kharkov was taken and the Russians pressed beyond it toward Poltava, where Charles XII of Sweden had had his greatness crushed in the seventeenth century. The battle line in three months had been pushed four hundred miles west of Stalingrad.

As shadows deepened over the Reich, Hitler spoke less frequently and in different strain. No longer did he boast of coming conquests but dwelt rather on how long Germany could withstand her enemies. All that was necessary was for her to hold out staunchly and her foes would tire. Had this not happened in the Seven Years War? Was it not obvious that the great Frederick had emerged triumphant even after the Russians had stormed Berlin? That, too, was Goebbels' theme. But he had others; bombed out civilians would have no chance to get their property restored if the Allies won the war; an American book had urged that Germans be made eunuchs; the "grey wolves" (U-boats) were being steadily improved and would yet starve England; new secret weapons in the blueprint stage would revolutionize the art of war.

The approaching winter found Germany jittery. There was plenty of money but nothing to buy with it. Shops were closing all over the Reich and general trade was reduced to barter, a baby carriage for a frying pan, shoes for furniture. Everything was scarce. In May, 1943, some 30,000,000 persons were employed in field, factory, and workshop, a larger number than in time of peace; but of these 12,000,000 were foreigners and of the Germans more than half were women and children. The output of the foreigners was estimated at only 65 per cent by prewar standards and that of the German workers at only 80 per cent, facts which indicated a lowered war potential at a time when the demand for war matériel was at its peak.

Without setting enemies and foreigners to work, outnumbered Germany could not survive; on the other hand, their presence caused uneasiness. A few came more or less willingly to the Reich and relative freedom of movement was granted them. But the great majority were either prisoners of war or deportees from the conquered areas. These had to be watched, confined in barracks. Armed guards and machine guns could and did prevent their rioting, but sloppy work is not easily proved, prevented, or punished.

On the surface, discipline in the Reich was excellent. The only approach to disorder was at the University of Munich where some students were executed for advocating Hitler's overthrow. But there was much grumbling and latent fear, as was shown by party members ducking for safety.

What kept all this rebelliousness from organizing and breaking out into the open was the appointment of Heinrich Himmler, on August 25, as home secretary. Most criminal in act and in nature of all the Nazis was this Gestapo chieftain, a specialist in low cunning and sadistic cruelty, as well as in devilish insight and mastery of police work. His elevation to dictatorial authority over civilians, and the favors showered on his instrument, the SS forces, were proof that Hitler would stop at nothing to hold Germany to the war. If love of Fuehrer and Fatherland could not do it, then fear and tyranny would. The SS numbered in the summer of 1943 some 1,000,000 men. Himmler enlarged it. Its functions were military and political; it had its own uniform and its own officers, answerable not to German generals but to Himmler; its purpose was terrorism; its political agencies the headsman's axe, the torture chamber, and the concentration camp. The SS received higher pay than the Wehrmacht; promotion was more rapid; its picked divisions fought to the last man, stiffening resistance on every front; and to its sponsor, Heinrich Himmler, now master of German destiny, it gave unswerving obedience.

And so approached the fifth winter of the war. From Narvik in Norway to Bordeaux, France; from Finland to Odessa still flew the Nazi flag. There was as yet no second front, and the Atlantic Wall, reinforced by heavy guns dragged from the Maginot line, seemed an insuperable obstacle to Anglo-American armies beyond the Channel moat; German armies held Rome and the war-worthy part of Italy. Except for a few guerrilla partisans in Yugoslavia, the entire Balkan Peninsula was under German domination, as well as Crete and the islands of the Aegean Sea.

Seen from without, the *Festung Europa* was impressive in its massive strength.

Prospects of 1944

Nineteen forty-four, and at long last the Russians, the British, and the Americans had the men, the weapons, the will, and the skill to blast Germany back into the homeland. Now coördinated strategy toward that end could be and was perfected. This meant the Second Front, attack from the west and south, for which Stalin had long clamored; it meant threefold hammer blows upon the German anvil for the first time in this war; it meant grimly crashing through to victory. Most of all, it meant that for the first time in history the superlative technology and exhaustless resources of the twentieth-century United States were to be hurled against the newest of empire imperialisms.

The United States had close to 4,000,000 men overseas, and Britain was rapidly turning into our armed camp against Hitler, soon to have more GIs than British Tommies stationed there. There was less and less to fear from U-boats. The last German battleship available to threaten sea lanes, the *Scharnhorst*, had been sunk by the Royal Navy the day after Christmas. That great battlewagon *Tirpitz*, sister ship of the *Bismarck,* lay bottled up, in a Norwegian fiord. The Red armies, driving hard on a winter offensive, were already west of Kiev and in January had planted the hammer and sickle flag within ten miles of the Polish-Latvian border. In Yugoslavia, Marshal Tito and his slashing partisans had tied up several more divisions which the Germans needed in Italy. Rome was only seventy miles from the American Fifth and the British Eighth Armies. Few Italians had any notion of fighting further. Finland, Rumania, and even Hungary showed no interest in anti-Bolshevism but a great deal in their own safety. German civilians and German industry were being smashed and destroyed by the merciless downpouring of bombs. The conquest of the Hitler lands might be delayed but it could not be stopped.

The Eastern Front Before D-Day

By the first week in January the Red army had crossed the Polish border of 1939 and was threatening Sarny on the main north-south route from the Baltic states to southern Poland. The Russian steamroller was grinding westward on the road to conquest, hoisting a red warning to the Polish "government" in London, acutely conscious as these exiles were that Stalin's announcement spoke of "Poland" as still 200 miles to the west, and therefore that much west of the 1939 line between Poles and Russians!

That same month Red armies hit the German forces elsewhere; across the frozen Pripet marshes toward Pinsk in what had once been eastern Poland; south and southeast of Kiev in the Ukraine, thus continuing the vast encircling movement earlier begun to cut off Hitler's divisions in the deep bend of the Dnieper north and east of Odessa.

The eastern battles raged with mounting fury. Whenever, it was noted, the Nazis suffered reverses anywhere, whether the *Scharnhorst* was sunk or a defeat inflicted in the Ukraine, they speeded up shelling Leningrad, under siege now two and one-half years. That city was not in as dire peril as formerly, for rail connection of a kind had been opened with Moscow. It was no longer necessary to fend off scurvy with a brew of pine needles, nor for women and young girls to shovel earth into their aprons and carry it to desperately driven earthworks. Yet Germans pumped shells into the city, and some thirty German divisions were still involved in what looked like a lunar landscape but was called the Leningrad front.

They could not retreat, partly because it would isolate their ally Finland, partly because of pride in their huge, ingenious "Leningrad Padlock," an inferno of mine fields, booby traps, and underground pill boxes or "wells" strung on deep trenches. But the Russians whanged away at the Germans with artillery and dropped hand grenades down into the German wells. By the end of January the padlock was broken.

It was in the milder Ukraine, however, not in the bleak far north that the startling victory march was staged. Here in midwinter (January 24-February 3, 1944) the First and Second Red Ukrainian Armies encircled and all but annihilated some ten German divisions in the Upper Dnieper Bend southeast of Kiev where the Eighth German Army held a front of fifty miles. The Russians threw round their motorized divisions in two great sweeping arcs, forming the aptly named "Russian rat trap." The area, at first broad and spacious, was soon squeezed tight as Don Cossacks and Russian tankmen pared it down into small and smaller pockets, until the last was but a few kilometers across.

The cornered Germans, told by radio that help was near, and fed by parachutes, milled round in these battle pens, stacking their dead like cordwood, as they fought off Russian blows. A few escaped, more were taken prisoner, most died, and ten divisions were lost to the Reich.

Wiped out on the Upper Dnieper, the Germans soon were hard pressed near its estuary. The Germans backed up steadily westward all through March. To the west of the Dnieper and somewhat parallel with it flows the Bug River, a strong defensive barrier. The Russians forced passage March 15. Another and a greater river, the Dniester, was sixty miles farther west. In four days the Red army was on the east bank and Stalin's men surged over to invade Bessarabia, from 1919 to 1939 a province of Rumania but not by any means Russia's frontier as now seen by Stalin. Not until the Red flag waved along the east bank of the Pruth, some seventy miles farther west on March 26, had Soviet forces reached what the Kremlin promptly called "The Soviet State frontier." The Germans were back where they started from in 1941. In 1,009 days, to be exact, they had made the round trip of 1,700 miles from the Pruth to the Volga and return—tidal waves of war unique in history.

Odessa, Russia's largest port on the Black Sea and the only bit of Ukraine left in the Nazi grip, fell on April 10. Five days later Red soldiers overran the Crimea to rebesiege Sebastopol. Nature had made that town of more strength than Gibraltar, as French and British found in 1854 and Germans in 1942, when they were kept at bay a good six months. The fighting ended this time in four weeks, as the garrison was mainly Rumanian. The Black Sea was once more a Soviet lake.

All southern Russia and more, too, had been "redeemed." Russian armies marched into Bukovina, another long disputed and lately Rumanian province northeast of the Carpathians. Here they were within rifle shot of the old Mongol conquerors' Tatar Pass leading into Czechoslovakia. They could turn at will north to Poland or south to the Balkans, and the Germans could only reinforce their Balkan forces through Hungary.

Italy Before D-Day

Nineteen forty-four opened with French, Polish, Brazilian, Indian, Dominion, British, and American troops slowly hacking and edging their way to Rome. From Ortona on the Adriatic to just south of Gaeta on the Mediterranean, the Gustav line wound its way in and out among the mountains; and behind it was the pick of the German Army, SS troops and paratroopers, amply supplied with the best of artillery.

To reach Rome one must either breach the Gustav line at the town of Cassino through which ran Route VI, the Via Casalina, the only adequate highway leading north to the goal, or else make amphibious landings on the seacoast nearer the Eternal City, thus outflanking the Germans behind the Gustav line and compelling their withdrawal. Ultimately the Allies were successful in doing both, but it took all they had, and nearly five months hard hand fighting.

The Liri Valley, in which Cassino nestled, was flanked by commanding hills on either side, and through the town ran not only the Via Casalina but also the Rapido River, in winter a raging torrent. We tried to wipe out Cassino from the air and apparently did so, as far as reconnaissance photographs showed. But the more the ruins, the harder the fighting, as Spanish Alcazar and Russian Stalingrad had proved. New Zealanders did pry open doors with bayonets, killed Germans, and in turn were killed by them; Indian Gurkhas did gain the summit of Hangman's Hill; and Germans did surrender in what had once been the Hotel Continental. But fresh waves of German paratroopers recovered much the New Zealanders had won; the Gurkhas on their hill were isolated and had to be fed by parachute; the hotel filled up again with German warriors as though by magic, and German tanks dashed in and out the ruined lobby. By April, after three months' attack, Cassino was only cellar holes and roofless houses, but in there with machine guns the Germans held fast, and their artillery on nearby hills still commanded the Via Casalina.

If the Gustav line could not be breached, why not outflank it? This, the Fifth Army, under our General Mark Clark, tried to do in January by a surprise landing above and below the shore village of Anzio on the Mediterranean, some thirty miles south of Rome.

The beachhead was relatively long, fourteen miles, and much too shallow, only eight miles. The land Clark's men squatted on was low and marshy, cut up by numerous drainage ditches in many of which our infantry stood waist-deep. Down from the high ground of the hinterland the enemy soon poured a murderous fire on Anglo-Americans closely packed together, the British to the north, the Americans to the south. Ten days later the rosy prospects of a quick breakthrough had faded into lurking fear lest another Dunkirk loom ahead.

UNITED STATES TROOPS LANDING ON THE NORMANDY BEACHHEAD

Meanwhile, sixty miles to the south lay Cassino. A breakthrough there would save the beachhead; conversely a successfully widened beachhead would disrupt the enemy's communications, cut the Via Casalina north of Cassino, compel its evacuation. But could the Yanks and Tommies do either?

From January 22, through the whole infernal winter until well into spring, day followed day and week followed week at Anzio, a few yards gained, a few yards lost. The Anglo-Americans by day were hammered by German tanks, at night bombed by German planes, soaked by blinding rain, and stuck fast in bogs and mud. Only by the narrowest margin did the Fifth Army stick it out. After a month it was stalemate both at Anzio and at Cassino. In London Churchill sounded his usual cheery note, and American war correspondents praised the grim humorous staying quality of the Yanks. But facts are facts: the casualty lists were much too long, and "half a year had gone by since the Salerno landing and the Allies had pushed forward less than a hundred miles."

April wore by, and then with May our air-blasting of the Reich began to tell on its war power, so that a strong thrust forward opened the road to Rome. Although formally under over-all command of a British general, it truly was an international fracas in which roles were played by Free French under General Juin and even by Poles fighting under their own flag. The French contingent opened the attack by storming Mt. Faito to the south of Cassino; the British, Canadians, and Indians swept forward across the Rapido River and circled toward a junction with the Polish detachment; the Americans, posted between the French and the sea, scored the largest gains in mileage but over easier terrain; on the Adriatic the Eighth Army made good headway, while at Anzio both British and Americans at last secured needed headroom, pressed close on German communications between Rome and Cassino.

May 11 the Allied offensive began and within a week the Germans were in retreat, neatly and quickly abandoning also the Hitler line which lay behind the Gustav barrier. June 4, 1944, and Rome fell. Barring slight skirmishes in the suburbs, the Allied occupation of their first Axis capital was bloodless. Taking such small loot as they had a fancy to, the invaders made their way north to the hills surrounding Florence.

D-Day

In 1915 a younger Churchill had fathered an impromptu and risky invasion of the Dardanelles; it failed and stunted his career for twenty years. Now an older Churchill was Prime Minister of England, a Churchill stubbornly refusing to take chances. It might have been possible to gain a beachhead on the French coast in 1943, but the cost seemed too frightful, and the question then would have arisen how to enlarge it. The Russians had been indignant because the hazard was not put to the test, also some Americans. But Churchill preferred the slow and sure, an African landing and flank attack on Fortress Europe from the south. He had to wait while Germany was softened up as much as possible from the air before making the grand attack through France, a truly Allied enterprise, though one in fact in which the Americans, as much the greater power, must, of necessity, play the larger role.

The Americans had certainly been speeded fast to the battle lines. June 1, 1944, Secretary Stimson stated that there were 5,223,000 Americans in our armed forces overseas, 3,300,000 of them soldiers, the great bulk in Britain. Many had only recently been inducted and these reserves must undergo severe training before action or else incur ghastly losses. In the initial stages it was planned to deploy in approximately equal numbers Americans and British Imperial troops.

And behind all these fighting men, both Yanks and Tommies, were the factories, workshops, shipyards, and spacious farmlands of the entire Allied world. There were in Britain 33,000,000 men and women between fourteen and sixty-four, and of these no less than 23,000,000 were in war work of all sorts. To Britain fell the major task of conveying and convoying the Yanks to Europe. The British had to house them, for the most part to feed them, and also to build new port facilities for their landings in England. All this in addition to piling up munitions and to expanding the tonnage of bombs dropped on Germany (48,200 tons, for instance, for the first quarter of 1944 as opposed to 34,075 for the entire year 1943). And as they did this, it must be remembered that during the one month of May, 1944, British and American ships moved almost 4,000,000 tons of cargo from American ports to Britain. Into one gigantic pool the industrial products of the whole English-speaking world and their allies were poured to feed the flaming maw of war. A magnificent testimony to the loyal sweat of men and women in overalls making possible the deeds of those obedient in khaki.

June came. Behind their Atlantic Wall the Germans prepared more sites for the rocket bomb. Shabby and half-starved French of all ages and both sexes drilled in secret for guerrilla war. And in millions of homes all over the earth there were high-strung nerves and anxious worry, for all knew D-Day was near.

Tuesday, June 6, and D-Day. From six minutes past midnight paratroopers in long trains of gliders hopped the Channel to drop down in Normandy before daybreak behind the German lines. And as they did so, landing craft drew near the hostile shore. All night they had worked twisting passage through the choppy seas, keeping lookout for the well-marked buoys, close-convoyed by destroyer watchdogs and corvettes, the GIs and the Bors (British other ranks, the British equivalent for GI) channel-sick, half-frozen, conscious that for many life was a matter of hours or minutes.

The landing was hard. Barely beneath the surface of the water the Germans had driven down six-pronged iron spikes upon which many a landing craft was impaled; and in the same deadly fashion anchored logs lay hidden to which mines were attached. As stumbling soldiers and lumbering tanks hit their beach, the Germans shot into them with en-filading fire from machine-gun nests and from heavy artillery deep-sunk in concrete emplacements up on banks which must be stormed, and that right speedily, lest the successive waves of ground troops find no stand-ing room on the crowded beaches. No time to dig foxholes. Up the narrow ravines toward the cliffs they charged, ravines and gullies filled with murderous booby traps, barbed wire, the German fire-storm and death.

Four landings came on in one great drive, two British, two American. They were spaced widely over sixty miles of the northern shore line of Normandy. The British Second Army, soon to have Rommel's tanks launched against it, had a relatively easy time at the start. So likewise was it with the Canadian First Army, the men of Canada penetrating seven miles in one day to Bayeux. Lady Luck also smiled on those Yanks who landed farthest west, for swamp rather than frowning cliff con-fronted them, and they were able to drive inland and make speedy con-tact with the airborne forces.

But it was nip and tuck for those Americans who stormed ashore east of the Vire River. All D-Day the GIs there clung desperately to shallow beachheads, suffering most grievous casualties, and not until late after-noon were they out of deadly peril. On D-Day plus one came reinforce-ments and with them America's beloved correspondent, Ernie Pyle, who described the scene: "Submerged tanks and overturned boats and burned trucks and shell-shattered jeeps and sad little personal belongings were strewn all over those bitter sands ... bodies of soldiers lying in rows covered with blankets, the toes of their shoes sticking up in a line as though on drill." [1]

Victory in Normandy

Six weeks' grueling battle came and went before the northwestern corner of France was wrested from the foe. The Allies were held back by execrable weather, high seas, and the lack of harbor facilities; by the deep-ditched Norman hedgerows, dense thickets lining roadsides, "horse-high, bull-strong, hog-tight"; by the counterattack of German rocket guns on London and by German panzer divisions in France. Had it not been for their overlordship of the air, our forces would have had a far tougher time of it. As it was, British and American planes rode high, wide, and handsome over northern France, demolishing rocket gun em-

[1] Ernie Pyle, *Brave Men* (New York, Henry Holt and Company, Inc., 1944), p. 360.

placements, smashing bridges as far south as the Loire, strafing locomotives, stations, railway lines, and motor roads so that the Germans had to move troops by night or else detour them long distances.

A united front once achieved, the first task of the Americans was to push on to Cherbourg. Elements of four German divisions within put up one of the hottest defenses of the war; they knew how imperative it was for the Allies to have a harbor; and if there was no chance of holding Cherbourg for the Reich, time might be won in which to ruin it for the Allies. And so for five days the Stalingrad and Cassino scene was reënacted, fighting through house by house, cellar by cellar, street by street, tanks versus tanks, tanks versus pill boxes, tight little pill boxes of reinforced concrete with wicked slits through which machine guns spit, while the heavens were dark with our droning planes. Caveman war worsened by all modern science.

A ding-dong fight for Caen followed, the Tommies driving hard at that Norman city time after time from different angles, the German panzers strongly beating them back and for two weeks with considerable success. But the British finally took Caen. Plunging forward through a sea of mud, they even got four miles beyond. Here they were held down by anti-tank fire and heavy German artillery (July 19).

The Americans, after taking Cherbourg, wheeled south heading for the rail junction of St. Lô which, if taken, would serve to seal off German forces in Brittany and on the Atlantic seaboard from potential reinforcement from those major German armies based elsewhere in France.

The approaches to St. Lô had to be fought for inch by inch, almost every farmhouse (and they were all made of stone) had been converted into a fortress; and in the omnipresent hedgerows, lining all roads, dividing all fields, the Germans had their machine guns. Out of these hedges they had to be driven, flushed like so many human partridges, by tanks equipped with side-cutters which split the path open for the advancing Yanks. St. Lô was one of the nastiest fights of the entire war. It took us a good month to take the place, a month of heavy casualties, 7,944 American boys being killed and 39,549 wounded. It was worse than D-Day itself.

But by late July, the Americans, the British, and the Canadians between them had accounted for 156,000 Germans, of whom 60,000 were prisoners. And, what is more, the Allies held half of Normandy and, out from ruined Caen and blasted St. Lô, were in position to strike hard.

The Rush for Paris

General Patton in command, driving incessantly full speed ahead, sent probing thrusts of Sherman tanks both north and south as he sped toward the French metropolis. His dirty, sweating, sleep-short tankmen were soon in the streets of Orléans, cutting off German forces in the south of France; almost simultaneously they appeared north of the Seine; one day later the Eiffel Tower was in view of Patton's outposts twenty miles away.

And as this happened the Canadians sweeping eastward toward Rouen, another ancient capital of Normandy, cut off the Germans at Le Havre on the coast; the British Second Army also crossed the Seine and pushed on to the Somme, thirty-four miles distant; and on August 15 an entirely new American army, the Seventh, broke in on the coast of the Riviera.

This new menace to the Germans was made up of troops withdrawn from Italy, some American, some French. Aided by British paratroopers and with strong naval backing, it struck at the Riviera coast. The Seventh was soon in position to roll back on Italy from the northwest, or to plunge toward Toulon and Marseilles, or to hit north up the valley of the Rhône. And wherever it was ordered to go, it was sure of the assistance of the FFIs (French Forces of the Interior), the Maquis, guerrilla bands of young Frenchmen, poorly armed but knowing well the countryside, enraged by subjection, spoiling for a fight, eager to trap and to kill.

In three short weeks the outlook in the west was revolutionized. In what had been a bare two months earlier a prostrate France, everywhere the Germans were on the way out, their convoys, tanks, and ground troops constantly strafed from the air, escaping over bridgeless rivers as best they might. On August 19 some 50,000 FFIs revolted in the invader-emptied Paris. A remnant garrison resisted until advance units of Patton's army dashed into that city, then surrendered on August 25. In Paris there had been much loose looting, but of dynamite and destruction there was none, of real damage very little. These were surrender times for invaders.

In Paris the American GIs were kissed freely but their effective pursuit of the Germans never let up. From twenty to fifty miles a day it raced along in a dozen different sectors. The Canadians took Rouen and went past it to the Channel to sew up the German garrison at Dieppe. The British, somewhat farther to the south, recovered Amiens, their headquarters in World War I, continued eastward, eager to seize the launching platforms of rocket guns if they could find them; the American First Army kept rolling along without meeting a foe, past Château Thierry, Soissons, and Rheims of the old war, all the way to an older Sedan. Patton's Third Army, farther south, surged on through Châlons, Verdun, St. Mihiel, and approached Metz; while the American Seventh, advancing up the Rhône, took Grenoble and was fast nearing Alsace, ready for its part on the southern flank of the vast Allied drive for the Rhine. As the crow flies, our tanks were now 350 miles from Cherbourg and close to the German frontier, less than forty days after pouring through the St. Lô funnel, less than three months after "D" Day itself. As for the enemy, his overall picture September 1 was summarized by General Eisenhower: "The equivalent of five panzer divisions have been destroyed and a further six badly mauled. . . . The equivalent of twenty infantry divisions have been eliminated and a further twelve very badly cut up. . . . Total enemy casualties amount to more than 400,000 killed, wounded and prisoners." The war seemed certain to end in Europe before Christmas.

Italian Front of 1944

Allied invaders were weaker in Italy than elsewhere. Soon after Rome was taken they had reason to feel that they were the forgotten front. Black death was just as hard to meet in Italy as in Normandy, and the foe confronting us was relatively stronger in numbers and morale, his dislodgement in some ways more difficult. Nevertheless all summer the American Fifth Army and the British Eighth plugged away at the German defenses in Italy, the Americans to the west, mainly along the Tyrrhenian coast, the British at the center and along the Adriatic side. For a short time after passing Rome the pursuit of fleeing German forces was relatively rapid, as the foe was retreating fast to newer and even stronger positions than the Gustav line; once there, it was a different story. The Apennines in northern Italy run south and east of the Po, and that valley the Germans tried to hold to the bitter end, and did. Its fields are one of Europe's major granaries and, with the swastika waving there, Nazi rule could endure in Bavaria, Czechoslovakia, Austria, and north Italy, though all the rest of the Reich surrendered. The Po Valley was vital to this citadel of the inner Fortress-Germania, sometimes called "The National Redoubt," and the Gothic line which defended it on the south was defense in depth from Pisa on the Tyrrhenian Sea to Rimini on the Adriatic. At all hazards it must remain German.

The American Fifth had a tough time of it; the British Eighth had one even tougher. The little mountains fringing Florence vied with those around Cassino in height and number, and the confusedly protracted siege-battling in and around Florence sadly battered Italy's loveliest city. British troops forced an entry there August 4, the Germans clinging still to strong points within and just north of Florence until August 10. Meanwhile other elements of the Eighth Army, some Polish, some Indian, and in 1945 some Greek, paralleled the American advance on the Tyrrhenian flank by taking Pesaro on the Adriatic Sea, and finally Rimini, baffled this time not by mountains but by swamps, canals, and drainage ditches. The Gothic line bent back a little at both ends, but held in the middle. Whenever the Allies made gains fierce counterattacks threw them back. Owing to the Anglo-American rush past Paris in the west and the vast Russian tornado roaring down on Berlin from the East, the world paid little attention to Italy during the second half of 1944. The black eagles of the Teutonic North had been her curse a good fifteen hundred years, and their talon clutch still dug deep in her fairest provinces.

The Red Russian Storm

As the western Allies swarmed into Normandy, the Russians were making good their grasp on the Karelian Peninsula, forcing Finland out of the war. Then, with the opening of the summer offensives, the Red armies struck first and hardest against the Baltic states and East Prussia; for so long as the Wehrmacht held on there in strength it was impregnably placed for outflanking any direct Soviet drive on Warsaw and Berlin.

Soon, then, the whole eastern front was ablaze. The First, Second, and Third Baltic Armies were out to trap and to destroy thirty German divisions in Lithuania, Latvia, and Estonia. Consummation of this project took months but the shadow of coming Baltic events was clear when Soviet forces reached that sea on August 4. Meanwhile, three other Russian armies hurtled at the Germans farther west, the First and Second White Russian Armies rushing on into Poland, the Third plunging for East Prussia, cradle of the Teutonic knights of old. Inside of six weeks eastern Poland was taken, the fortress of Brest-Litovsk fell once more, the Reds reached the Vistula both north and south of Warsaw, and its suburbs could be bombed from Russian lines. The Third White Army struck harder going, but it made headway, and pressed now against the East Prussian defenses.

As the Baltic lines bent back and German Poland caved in, the omnipresent Russians opened yet another offensive, this time in the south. All the way from the Carpathians to the Black Sea, the Ukrainian Red armies rolled into action. It was Rumania's turn. By August 29 the Russians were at the Danube's mouth. In two more days they pierced the Galati Gap, pounced on the Ploesti oil fields, broke into Bucharest, the second Axis capital to capitulate. There a palace coup d'état "headed" by boy-king Michael drove the pro-German premier, Antonescu, from office and the bewildered Rumanian army, what was left of it, got orders to turn and fight, not Russians but Germans and Hungarians.

With Rumania reversing sides, fifteen German divisions were stuck in the Balkans in ever worse plight than those foundered in Finland. Before long all Balkan Nazis were cut off from the Reich except for circuitous routes through Yugoslavia where pro-Russian Marshal Tito was rapidly gaining the upper hand. On September 6 the Red Army hit the Yugoslav border and two days later broke into Bulgaria. Politically-minded Bulgar colonels rapidly followed Rumanian precedents, and Bulgaria was at war against Germany by September 9. Lost now to the Reich's power was the entire Near East, apart from various garrisons stranded on cut-off Greek islands, elsewhere in Greece, and in isolated German enclaves of Yugoslavia. Of all the satellites, Hungary alone stood faithful as conquering Russia kicked in the gates of Fortress Europa from north, east, and south.

Why the Germans Kept On Fighting

In September the front caved in on every side, and from the air augmenting death came showering down on German cities, factories, and airfields. Plainly the Reich must yield. But she would not; and why? Three reasons tell the story; hope, not altogether fanciful, of secret weapons; hope, more illusory, that Allied dissensions might split and unbalance their enemies, lead perhaps to German victory in the field, and win some sort of compromise peace; and finally not hope but fear; fear of Allied vengeance and extermination, particularly Russian, and what the Cossack East might do when once within the Reich; fear at home of Heinrich Himmler's gestapo, prison camps, and Nazi superthugs.

Rumors of secret weapons were now running wild in Naziland. "Within six months," said an SS propagandist, "all Germans will know something which for the time being must be kept secret. You will wake from the dark depressive night. Tomorrow will be very calm and clear. Everything that threatened and terrified you will have vanished."

The Allied press sneered at these rumors of secret weapons, but the British and American governments, knowing full well what their own scientists hard at work were developing in new techniques, were fairly certain that the Germans were doing likewise. As early as April, 1943, the British secret service heard of strange events taking place on a tiny island in the Baltic, and the RAF promptly photographed that island. It was well for Britain that they did so, for the Germans were experimenting with Hitler's *Vergeltungswaffe*, vengeance weapon, the rocket bomb.

That same month the RAF heavily attacked that island, but a month later British reconnaissance planes discovered a whole series of launching platforms or ramps similar to the Baltic specimen. All pointed toward London, and all that were visible the RAF and the AAF bombed, an action which cost the Allies 450 planes and nearly 3,000 aviators. That attack slowed up the German program which was to start New Year's Day, 1944, with 1,000 rocket bombs, but had to be postponed until June 15 when the first "buzz" shells were launched on the British capital. They came fast and furiously at five to seven miles per minute.

Through June and July some two hundred a day came hurtling down the war-torn air. In some ways it was worse than Goering's great 1940 blitz. Then, at any rate, there was siren warning, bombs came mostly at night with comparative immunity in daytime. Now no one could tell what second of day or night the robot death might strike, or where, for these lethal missives could be aimed only in the general direction of London. Only a few planes had speed enough to overtake the rockets, the new Tempests, Spitfires, and Mustangs. Had it not been for radar and innumerable anti-aircraft guns, both British and American, lined thick along the coasts, London would have been pulverized.

There was still hope of a super-robot launched from farther away and flying at greater speed and higher altitude, a promise actually fulfilled by autumn with the V-2, launched out of occupied Holland. But Germany then was being so rapidly submerged that the V-2, looking for all the world like a flying telegraph pole, did not get any real testing. The sites were taken too soon.

Always there was a chance for a rift between the Allies, and the Nazis looked for one in Yugoslavia and Poland. In Yugoslavia, any dreams of Allied discord that the Germans might fancy vanished into thin mist as Anglo-American aid shifted from General Mihailovich, Commander-in-chief of the Yugoslav Army under the direction of the exiled Yugoslav government in London, to Marshal Tito, victorious Communist-sponsored patriot and partisan. Tito might be a deep, dark Red but he fought Germans with vim, vigor, and velocity, which no one could say for the royalist Mihailovich.

The Polish problem was more complicated. The exiled Polish government in London was recognized by Britain and America; Polish soldiers fought in Italy. But Stalin condemned that Polish government as a clique of landlords and loan sharks. He knew what he wanted and would take nothing else, the Polish frontier of 1921 and the establishment of a Communist Polish government in which Communist influence would be dominant.

Stalin had early broken relations with that exiled Polish regime in London, and as his armies scorched Warsaw he set up in Lublin a committee of Polish Communists to whom he proposed to turn over a liberated Poland, which distressed his democratic allies, Britain and the United States.

Then in midsummer, 1944, as the Russians reached the Vistula, General Bor of the Warsaw underground revolted and defended part of that city for weeks. Fighting the Germans, he clamored for Russian aid. It was not given. The Russians said the rising had been premature; it had been done without Russian approval or knowledge; the Red army for the time being had other objectives than the taking of Warsaw. And so, although it pushed both north and south of Warsaw, it did nothing to relieve General Bor.

Britain was particularly upset. The London Poles had urged Bor to fight on; they had sent Poles to fight for Britain in Italy, and the British in turn sent Bor supplies all the way by air from the Mediterranean.

The Germans let Poles out of German prisons; they urged Poles to enlist in the Wehrmacht to save Poland from Bolshevism.

Between the intransigent Polish government in exile and the stubborn Stalin, Britain was on the horns of a dilemma and was to stay so. The best Churchill could do was to ask Stalin to receive Mikolajczyk, their Polish premier, in Moscow and persuade the London Poles to despatch their premier to Stalin. Mikolajczyk made the trip twice without result, except that the Polish question was left on ice. It remained a thorny one, and Churchill pleaded with the House of Commons "not to engage in language which would make our task harder." That task was to let Russia have her way and to save face if possible. There was still a war to win and we were winning it, so the Germans gained little from these Polish quarrels.

Last but not least, fear gripped the German heart, sheer terror of what might be if they lay their weapons down. It was not now so much the shrill voice of Goebbels but the black deeds of Himmler which sent shivers down the German spine. A mighty weapon his SS troopers and his gestapo, but a mightier one yet in Germany after July 20, 1944, the day on which the army plot to kill the Fuehrer failed. From that date forward the world heard little that was authentic of Adolf Hitler, for in his name Himmler now ruled the Reich. "The blueblooded swine," the Prussian aristocrats who had tried to save something of Germany by a revolution from within, not only lost their lives, as did those remotely associated with them, but, as matters worsened, a fresh twist was given to the strangler's noose which tightened around the neck of every German who gave voice to doubts about the war or who even was caught with a Swiss or Swedish newspaper.

This terror from within transcended the terror from without. With the foes' forces on all German frontiers, children were ordered out of school, the old out of their armchairs, marched, drilled, put in uniform. The *Volksturm* of Napoleonic days was revived to include all Germans from sixteen to sixty. The last man and boy were rallied that ditches might be dug, mines laid, cities and towns fortified for street-to-street and house-to-house defense. *Festung Europa* was out. The ungrateful continent could look out for itself. Germany would defend her own. If the flat plains of northern Germany were foe-engulfed, then retreat to the stark citadel of Nazidom, the Bavarian Alps! Here, flanked on every side by close-linked mountains, ringed by set defenses, would come the last fight of those to whom death was infinitely better than defeat.

Hitler's Last Stand

The Nazi Inner Fortress was shrinking day by day, must be weakening, must be bleeding from every vein of war-power, yet in the northern mists and from out of the chemical fogs of airborne ruin it loomed grim, grey, and evil as some great, gaunt timber wolf, cornered for the kill in the last of his granite holds, death in its fangs still.

That autumn German resistance hardened—east, south, and west. In the far northeast the Russians did not cross East Prussian frontiers until October 18, and then in that lake-studded land of swamp and forest they made but slow headway. Red armies had forced the Vistula barrier but Warsaw was German still, as was Cracow in southern Poland, and as long as the latter city held out the approaches to industrial Silesia were relatively safe. Once having cracked the Carpathian defenses, it would seem as though nothing could withstand the sweep of Red armor across flat Hungarian plains, but though Szeged, Hungary's second largest city, fell October 11 it proved impossible in 1944 to capture Budapest, no great distance away.

From Italy, that forgotten front, came word that the Gothic line was being pierced, that Americans soon would reach Bologna, that the British were rounding the foe's eastern flank at Rimini. But prophecies are not facts, and the truth was that the Gothic line stymied the Allies; their victories were rather patrol actions, so minor as hardly to be noted on an ordinary map.

So, too, was it in the west. The German frontier once passed, the Canadians, British, and Americans found the going much rougher. The British captured Antwerp September 4, but since German forces still blocked the exits from the Scheldt, the occupation of Belgium's great seaport was not much help. Almost everything the Allied armies used had to be carried by motor or be flown from a few congested ports hundreds of miles west, and even after British engineers sank a gasoline pipeline across and under Channel waters the fuel still was far from thirsty tanks. Hitler's Westwall was far more a defense to the Reich than the Maginot line ever could have been to France. It might be, and was, bent in spots by tank rushes, but a defense in depth cannot readily be broken or surmounted.

The Allies were too confident too long of having the Germans on the run; they underestimated the foe's resiliency; the war, they thought, might be forced to a swift finish by outflanking the Westwall far to the north, where the Rhine River flows sluggishly across Holland through several branches. To strike the enemy in this supposedly weak sector the British First Airborne Division parachuted to earth beyond the Lek River, a tributary of the Rhine. Instantly it was encircled by Nazi forces swarming in like angry wasps. For over a week the Tommies, reinforced constantly by air, put up a heartrending fight. The British Second Army did its best to rescue them and almost succeeded. But only some 1,800 British paratroopers fought their way back across the Lek.

This was discouraging, but the steady though costly Allied gains of the autumn might well restore the balance by December. The Canadians, clearing the Channel ports, had conquered Nazi garrisons at Boulogne and Calais, as had the Americans at Brest. British marines, His Majesty's Jollies, had forced a landing on Walcheren Island at the mouth of the Scheldt in a daring exploit. The British Second made good its hold on Belgium, and had swept on into Holland. The American First Army, bypassing Aachen, capital of Charlemagne, was well over the frontier, pressing toward Cologne. Patton's Third, retarded by a distinguished defense of an old French fort at Metz by German military cadets, had edged toward the Saar. And the American Seventh, together with a fully equipped French army, had got within striking distance of Belfort near the Swiss corner.

November passed. Still the German lines bent backward. The Tricolor flew again over Strasbourg and the upper Rhine was tapped. Patch's Seventh was forcing its way through Alsace. Patton's Third was at the Saar, one bridge across it, with German blast furnaces under American fire. Hodges' First U. S. Army surged forward to the west bank of the Rohr, the only sizable stream between it and Cologne, less than thirty miles away. Farther north Simpson's Ninth U. S. Army and the British Second clawed their way into German areas, and to the far north the Canadians swung up forward ready for a second shot at outflanking the Siegfried line.

Winter was now at hand and the war would not end in 1944. The Allies had moved forward; but the most successful of their armies, the American First, had taken four weeks to go twelve miles. Some months earlier Churchill had prophesied that the war would be won by the early spring or early summer of 1945. He now suggested eliminating the adjective "early."

Battle of the Bulge

Then, December 16, to the amazement of all and to the consternation of many, the Wehrmacht lashed out at the Americans in one great burst of flame and fury. Behind German lines, unseen by Allied intelligence, the German commander, Von Rundstedt, had gathered his strength, fused a mass of his best fighters, concentrated motorized divisions with new tanks better for this last battle than any of the British or American armies had.

Out from their Westwall leaped the Germans on a sixty-mile front from south of Aachen into northern Luxembourg, and on they plunged into the Ardennes Forest, the old, old bloody trail which led toward Liége in Belgium, Sedan in France.

The Battle of the Bulge was on, and it raged for weeks, Von Rundstedt caught the Americans off balance. The Allies were hammering hard on a 450-mile front; he hammered harder and hammered through on one of sixty. Once reach Liége on the Meuse, he might strike at Antwerp, drive a wedge between British and Americans, roll back our forces, and fuel his thirsty Tiger tanks with American oil, so tantalizingly near at hand.

As it was, he unhinged the American line, isolated and pulverized American regiments, destroyed thousands of our men in the thick, snow-covered forestland of the Argonne; and his armor forced its way fifty miles in, rushing to probe either side of the deep bulge thus created to mark a further breakthrough.

At Christmas the German flood reached its crest, and soon thereafter subsided. Many German tanks stalled for lack of gas. Time was lost trying to wipe out American enclaves of resistance enclosed by the greater German pocket. Of these, Bastogne has a place in American history. Completely circled by the surging German tide, our men fought round the whole front and held out as aid and munitions reached them by air, and finally paratroopers, without whom they would have died.

From the south Patton dashed with his armor to the rescue of this pocket, as from the north Montgomery came on with the Second British Army. Placed by Eisenhower in command of American troops on the northern side of the bulge, Montgomery hooked up Yanks and Tommies to press on against the German area from that side, as did Patton from the south, and between them they narrowed the base slightly, but enough to be dangerous for the Germans within. An old rule of warfare decrees that a penetration must not exceed one-half the base from which it starts. That base in early January was only the same as the farthest depth, around fifty-five miles. The danger point for Von Rundstedt clearly had been reached. There was even talk of the hunter being hunted, of trapping the Germans, forcing their surrender. The wary Von Rundstedt was not to be caught thus. He extricated both men and armor and by January's end the British and American forces were back pretty much where they had been in early December.

Once again we had underestimated the adversary. GIs cursed loud and long when they found our vaunted General Sherman no match for the German King Tiger tank of sixty-seven tons and eight-inch armor. Having learned their lesson, our generals went more cautiously with their march on Rhine.

Ebb Tide Speeds Up

That the Germans hung on thereafter for three months and more was little short of a miracle. Fortress Germania was shrinking now as fast as Fortress Europa had six months before. Finland took her peace from Russia, pledged to intern German divisions left within her lines. The Red armies drove across Finland to attack Germans in northern Norway; they captured Riga and were cutting up the Wehrmacht isolated in the northeast; they commenced the invasion of East Prussia after long probing the frontiers of that iron homeland of iron men; they rolled into Warsaw and were well on the way to Berlin across western Poland; and reaching the banks of the Oder opposite Frankfort they came at long last within striking distance of the Nazi capital. Farther south, after bypassing beleaguered Budapest, Soviet armor drew near Vienna.

Only in Italy did Germans really withstand the adversary. Northern Italy, all but the tip of Norway, Denmark, parts of Finland, Holland, and a few French ports still were held by German soldiers needed for that last-ditch fight at home, if there was to be one. No hope gleamed on any horizon. But many were yet to die before Russians joined hands with Yanks across the Oder.

Futile though further war was, the Nazis kept on with it all through February, March, April, and into May. At ever accelerated pace the Allies closed and drove in on the doomed Reich. In February closely co-ordinated blows struck at its heart from both west and east. The Allies had long been stalled by the little Rohr River flowing parallel to the Rhine. They were on its banks, but dared not force a crossing since they knew there were huge dams on its upper reaches still in enemy hands, and these, once dynamited, would flood the lower Rohr to a good 1,000 yards in width. The Germans clung desperately to their dams, their single ace in hole, and the greater part of February was consumed in mastering the Rohr Valley. Once done, progress became rapid, German resistance spotty. Hodges' First Army took Cologne March 6; the American Ninth, arriving at the Rhine a few days earlier, turned north to meet Canadians coming south, both armies now behind the Westwall, and by their junction cutting off the retreat of thousands of Germans. And meanwhile the British Second, storming into Cleves in the lower Rhineland, headed toward Westphalia.

The west bank of the Rhine was now taken from Cologne north through Holland, but the Allies had yet to cross the river. The American First then got a toehold on its eastern shore north of Cologne March 8, by a rapid dash up the Rhine for the Ludendorff bridge at Remagen. Patton with the American Third now swept down the Moselle Valley and, whirling round to his right, drove in behind German forces which had held him at bay in the Saar. Patton going south met the advancing U. S. Seventh coming from that direction and the Germans thus cut off surrendered in droves; the Saar was lost; so, too, the Palatinate west of the Rhine; the Westwall ceased to exist and became mere history.

Far north the British fought their way out of Holland onto the Westphalian plain; in the south the French redeemed all Alsace; and now along the whole Rhine River's length British, Americans, Canadians, and French threw new bridgeheads over, to cross the swift and beautiful Rhine in almost every conceivable way, using parachutes, pontoons,

Bailey bridges, ferrying over in barges, motor boats, "buffaloes," "ducks," and other special craft, many manned by U. S. naval forces. Before March turned to April, Germany collapsed in the west.

So also in the east, and in the south. By early February the Russians were at Frankfort-on-Oder, a city they had taken twice before, once in Frederick the Great's time, once toward the close of Napoleonic days in 1813. The battered rubble of Hitler's capital was fifty miles away. Berliners saw the flares by night and heard by day the clamor of the guns. But the Red army paused. In its rapid leap from Warsaw to the Oder, it left behind strong enemy pockets; like Von Rundstedt's bulge, the base of Russia's holding in Germany was too narrow for the depth of penetration. Fifty miles to go, but these fierce with German fortifications. The Russians wanted no Stalingrad in reverse, took no chances. And so, through February and March they widened their base, struck north in East Prussia against Königsberg, hit against Danzig and Stettin, overran Pomerania, drove south to Breslau, and even farther south in Hungary and Austria. Budapest, with more than half its buildings wrecked, surrendered February 13, the third Axis capital to succumb; Vienna, the fourth, held out until April 13.

That same month the end came in Italy. American Mountain Infantry (ski troops long trained in Colorado) at last accomplished what American armor and the Brazilians had been unable to do. By a brilliant demonstration of highly specialized mountain warfare our ski fighters drove out the Germans from their fortified nests on 3,760-foot Mt. Belvedere where they outflanked the only good road from Florence north to Bologna. The British Eighth, meanwhile, came circling in from the Adriatic. The Gothic line was erased, the Germans beaten down, a signal for partisans in Genoa, Venice, Turin, Milan, to rise and throw out the Germans. All German troops in Italy and in southwest Austria as well surrendered. One day earlier Mussolini was taken near the Swiss frontier, shot, his body and that of a woman hung up by the heels in Milan.

Curtain Falls

'Everywhere the twilight of the end was dusking down on Europe's tragedy. The German armies in the west were gone, British and American armies driving at will over Adolf Hitler's super-highways, the British to the north, Americans to the center, and in the south Americans and French. Over half a million war captives were locked in prison pens during the first two weeks of April, and on the 24th Himmler tried to surrender exclusively to the British and Americans. His offer was refused.

May, and in one week more it was over. American armies near Berlin were halted by Eisenhower's orders. It would have been easy for us to have marched straight into the Nazi capital, for our arrival would have been greeted with joy by defenders who dreaded Red devastation. But Hodges' First rested on Elbe bank, leaving, as was right, the war's major honors to the men of the Soviets, who had done most to merit those dread laurels.

Why the German High Command strove still for another week is hard to fathom; the last chance of a last stand had faded with Italian surrender as the American First struck fast across central Germany and two southern American armies and the French forces drove ahead toward Bavaria and Czechoslovakia. No union of last-ditch fighters was possible. All plans were useless, even "planned chaos" was now impossible for the Nazis. Adolf Hitler was perhaps somewhere in Berlin. Power was gone and leadership also.

Berlin was a city dying. Their air ministry, the opera house, the vast chancellery of the thousand-year-old Reich-to-be, a blasted shambles. Riots at soup kitchens. Huddled civilians in cellars. The streets a terror by night. The city plastered with Russian shells, British and American bombs. The probing, implacable Red army crept north and south around the city. Russian tanks crashed through barricaded streets. From subways SS men dashed out at them from the rear, the death gasp of men already dead.

May 2 the Russians had Berlin, all of it; and farther south where a bridge spanned the Elbe Red army men and Yanks on April 26 shook hands, drank together. The European war was at an end. The Hitler Empire, Europe's most terrific adventure in militarism, in twelve years had run its course.

Chapter 19

JAPAN OVERWHELMED

THE SURRENDER OF Germany in 1945 set free the British and the Americans to complete the conquest of Japan, clearly foreshadowed in the not too distant future by British victories in Burma and American victories on the High Seas.

As 1943 opened all of Burma, except the northern tip, lay quiescent under the flag of the Rising Sun, and an invasion of India impended. In less than two years such detachments of the Japanese army as remained in Burma were in full flight. In January, 1943, the long march of the American navy across the Pacific had not yet begun, and the land approach of MacArthur along the northern coastline of New Guinea toward the Philippines was still in the blueprint stage. By the time the Yanks were swinging over the Rhine in 1945, all this had changed. The Japanese inner defense line had been breached: the marines held Iwo Jima in the Bonins and leathernecks and G.I.'s in Okinawa were driving Hirohito's men to cover. Meanwhile MacArthur was on shore at Leyte, back in the Philippines.

These American victories were slow in starting, had to be since the European war held precedence over that in the Pacific. But the date of their commencement stands out clearly, the Battle of Midway, June 4–5, 1942, only seven months less two days since Pearl Harbor. Fought and won by carrier planes against carrier planes, "it permanently crippled Japan's naval power by reducing her carrier strength to so low a level that she never was able to catch up with American production." [1] First and foremost factor in the Pacific war was the carrier plane.

Tough fighting lay ahead for the Americans. Japan's geographical isolation was superb. North and east of her homeland were the Kuriles, island wardens along the inner moat of Hirohito's hidden country. And to the south and southeast was the farflung shield of the Ryukyu and Bonin islands. Beyond the Ryukyus was Taiwan (Formosa) and far beyond Taiwan were Hainan, the Philippines, Borneo, Sumatra, Java, the Malay states, and French Indo-China, to enclose the whole China Sea with the arrayed imperial outposts of Japan. And still farther, barrier be-

[1] Major General J. F. C. Fuller, *The Second World War*, p. 152.

yond barrier, the mandated islands in the Marianas, the Carolines, the Marshalls. Here were stationary aircraft carriers past which, if unconquered, it would not be safe for us to venture. Nor was this all. South and east of the Marshalls our foe's talons clutched the once British-owned Gilberts, a threat to Fiji and to the Australian-American life-line, clutched also at the northern coastline of New Guinea, New Britain, and all the Solomons except for one airstrip on Guadalcanal fiercely held by too few American marines.

To break through these barriers was America's business. These Japanese islands must be conquered or immunized. It was a large order. To the north it meant dislodging the enemy from the American-owned Aleutians; in the mid-Pacific it meant driving out the Japanese from their strongly fortified mandated islands, the Marshall Islands, the Caroline Islands, and the Marianas; and to the south and southwest it meant the recovery of the British Gilberts and the Solomon Islands, occupied by Japan after Pearl Harbor, and the approach to the Philippines by way of New Guinea.

American action in the Pacific theatre in 1943-44 falls under two general heads, mopping up operations in regard to these islands, and MacArthur's slower but none the less dramatic approach to the quarry from Australian waters.

The Aleutians

First, then, the Aleutians in the spring of 1943. The main Japanese base there was Kiska, halfway between Kamchatka and Alaska. The American command decided to crack down on fog-shrouded Kiska by encirclement. Some 170 miles west of Kiska was Attu, upon which we landed in force during mid-May.

Our landings both to the north and to the south were unopposed; but when it came to pushing inland through the deep ravines and being ambushed by snipers hidden on the mountain slopes, then death took a hand. Five days passed before the two American expeditions met, only to find their hardest work still ahead. The soldiers of Nippon were most excellently screened in their base at Chichagov Harbor. Between them and the Americans were mountains 2,000 feet high, swept by snowstorms and thick fogs, and between the mountains were precipitous winding passes of over 800-foot elevation. The Japanese had dug in skilfully; their final defenses could only be reached along a ridge so narrow that two men could not walk abreast thereon, a treacherous ridge, half the time from fog and with a sheer drop 200 feet down on both sides. Manpower lugged up the ammunition in this campaign; soldiers fought, ate, and slept in wet snow, or on stones, or on soggy, treacherous tundra; Japs and Yanks stumbled into each other's mist-hidden fox holes; and a hundred miniature mêlées between half-seen combatants scattered by fog and wind made up the summary of the Attu adventure. May 30, and that island, not good for much but still American terrain, had been gripped and firmly held by our forces.

The wind-up of the Aleutian campaign came quickly. The Attu conquest had enabled us to dig in well to the west of the chief enemy base at Kiska; we had that island at our mercy; all that remained necessary was to soften it by intense bombardment from the air and from the sea, and then move in on foot as before. But to our surprise and even to our annoyance, Kiska proved to be quite empty. Some 10,000 Mikado soldiers had slipped through our fog-bedeviled blockade and had betaken themselves elsewhere.

Tarawa

The American occupation of Kiska sealed off Alaska from any would-be conquerors. The Aleutians gave us a springboard from whence to bomb the Kuriles and we did so (intermittently); but the game was scarcely worth the candle. Distances, even for our new planes, were phenomenally long; williwaws, terrific and sudden storms characteristic of the North Pacific, were frequent; and the Kuriles were far distant from Hokkaido, northernmost of the Japanese home islands, mountainous, underpopulated, far from the heart of the enemy's empire. Not by attack from the north could the foe's lifeblood be drained.

The major American offensive thus far had been directed against the Solomons and the great enemy base at Rabaul on New Britain to the north. But the way thither was long, some 7,200 miles of circuitous steaming from Hawaii to Port Moresby. The route lay almost due south from Honolulu to Samoa, then curved westward to Fiji and New Caledonia, then north by west to the Solomons, and the Japanese-held Gilberts lay athwart any direct approach. The task of wresting them from Japan fell mainly to the navy and marines. Sixteen island groupings comprise the archipelago, about equal in area to one-half of New York City. None were as mountainous as the Carolines, and granted East Pacific naval supremacy, which was ours by November, 1943, their conquest seemingly should have been easier than that of Attu.

But it did not prove so, our four-day fight for Tarawa, keystone of the Gilbert area, being the most costly thus far experienced in the war against Japan. Tarawa was a typical atoll, a cluster of some twenty-five islands grouped in a ragged circle around a lagoon, the islands only a few feet in elevation, most of them joined together at low water by a coral barrier reef. On one, Betio, less than one square mile of land was a Japanese garrison, the American objective.

As the U. S. marines set out in their landing barges it seemed as though most of the island's defenders must be dead, for hour after hour our battlewagons, cruisers, and destroyers had been lobbing shells on Betio;

hour after hour American planes had filled the sky, dropping thousands of their smashing eggs on this narrowly constricted target; hour after hour dense smoke had risen from Betio. But our landing barges could not get near shore. A reef far from land obstructed the way and the marines had to be transferred from barges to amphtracks, amphibious contrivances capable of carrying a few men on either land or water. This led to much confusion; the defending garrison, far from dead, strafed both barges and amphtracks; of the latter there were an insufficient number, and our men got ashore as best they could, many of them wading two or three hundred yards waist-high in water, carrying full equipment, many of them dying without touching land.

After one day of fighting they held only a few yards of narrow beachhead. On Betio the enemy had constructed some 500 pill boxes, most of them made of a double section of palmetto logs, filled with sand, covered with sand, almost impossible to destroy by shell fire, impossible to locate with precision from the air or the sea. Here, dug in and armed to the teeth, the Imperial Japanese marines fought to the last man, taking their own lives by hugging exploding hand grenades to their chests rather than surrender. Of our first men ashore almost all died, and in many of the pill boxes were found later two or three dead marines, six or seven dead Japanese. The American dead had given a good account of themselves; they had to die so that their comrades might conquer, for we were in haste to take Tarawa.

Betio once won, and Abemama and Makin, also atolls, the two former by marines, the latter by the army, and the Gilberts by the end of November were ours. The long process of leap-frogging across the far Pacific waters had really begun. And the annals of the United States Marine Corps had another name, Tarawa, as illustrious in their history as Tripoli in North Africa, Fisher's Island, North Carolina, or Château Thierry in 1918, or Guadalcanal of the Solomons.

The story of Tarawa was to be repeated over and over again with variations for the next year and a half. Northwest of the Gilberts were the Marshalls, another and larger archipelago, Japanese mandated-island areas, *terra incognita,* and forbidden to foreigners for many years. There were thirty-two islands in the Marshalls, spaced out over hundreds of ocean miles, most of them enclosing spacious lagoons. The Marshalls lay across the direct line between the Gilberts and Japan, and were much closer to the all-important Carolines, northeast of New Guinea, than the Gilberts. Quite evidently the Americans had to nail down a few of the Marshalls. And this the American navy did, capturing Kwajalein, a Marshall Island atoll, and shortly after Eniwetok, some 340 miles beyond it.

Victory followed victory. The navy swept on westward, bypassed the eastern Carolines and by the middle of the month was close enough to

Truk, the vaunted secret Gibraltar of Japan in the mandated South Pacific, to attack it and the Japanese ships there from American plane carriers. Our planes sank twenty-three hostile vessels and wiped out 201 planes. We had hoped for more, since Truk was reputed to be the rendezvous of Tokyo's main fleet. But the cruisers, destroyers, and auxiliary craft we did sink made up in part for Pearl Harbor and gave a sad shock to Japan's pride, as shown by the immediate dismissal of her naval chief of staff. This fortress, Truk, was no ordinary atoll. Within its spacious lagoon were several volcanic islands and many airfields, and from its supposedly impregnable isolation the Japanese had sent reinforcements to New Britain, New Guinea, and the Solomons.

Saipan and Guam

The American navy meanwhile roamed the East Pacific, seeking a battered foe not any too anxious to do battle, launching attacks from carrier planes at Palau in the Western Carolines, less than 600 miles from the Philippines and over 2,200 miles from the Marshalls, paying reconnaissance calls in force on the Marianas, Guam, Tinian, and Saipan. Whether we were headed straight west via Palau to the Philippines, or northwest from New Guinea to the same goal, or straight toward Tokyo by the Marianas route, was anybody's guess.

The last proved the choice of our strategists, and of the three largest islands in the Marianas they selected the most northern, Saipan, in distance 3,800 miles west of Pearl Harbor, about 1,500 miles from either the Philippines or Japan, 110 miles north of Guam, still in hostile hands.

American strategy was on the scale of our strength. Simultaneously it planned to feint south from the Aleutians with bombers and cruisers against the Kuriles, to assail the Japanese homeland with the new B-29 superforts now based on Chinese airfields, to strike north from New Guinea at Yap, Palau, and the Philippines, to bomb Truk, Nauru, and Ponape in the Carolines, as well as to land on Saipan. Coördination was not perfect but it was pretty good, and though the Japanese got wind of our main objective before our marines were ashore another victory was won, both by land and by sea.

The fight for Saipan was more deadly than that at Tarawa, far more protracted than that at Kwajalein, for the island was long and tapering with a curving mountainous spine well suited for defense. In, under, and behind every possible barrier the hostile snipers were located and their fire was deadly. The center of the battle line was reported as safe as anywhere else. First a hundred yards here and a hundred yards there, until finally the foe were forced back into a narrow pocket at the north. Here they re-formed and at last dashed out to destruction in a frenetic banzai charge. Some 22,000 dead soldiers of Nippon lay upon the ground.

Shortly after came the reconquest of Guam. Once more there was a stiff workout against mountain terrain, resistance to the death. Early in August it was all over and the Marianas, all three, were added to the American string of Pacific islands. In Tokyo the loss of Saipan had forced the resignation of Premier Tojo. In his own oblique way he stated the facts of disaster. "Japan," he said, "has come to face an unprecedentedly great national crisis. . . . The situation now approaches when the opportunity will occur to crack the enemy and to win the victory." Alarm in Tokyo was well founded. Between that city and our men lay only the Bonin and Volcanic Islands; between them and the Chinese coast but one island, Formosa.

These quick-paced American victories were won by a type of amphibious warfare hitherto unknown to history. Admiral Nimitz needed no base west of Honolulu to range over the vast Pacific because he carried his base with him. "Each class of warship—battleship, cruiser, destroyer, aircraft carrier and submarine—had a special type of supply and repair ship. . . ." It was not necessary to send disabled ships back to America to be repaired. In almost every instance the work was done by floating workshops. And no sooner was an island atoll wrested from the Japanese than in moved the Seabees (U. S. Naval Construction Battalions) who, with utmost speed, built hospitals, roads, docks, redeemed ripped-up jungles and made them useful for further advance.

Then, too, the landing barges, many thousands of them. They ranged from the LCRS (landing craft, rubber, small) holding half a dozen men, to the LSD (landing ship dock) a dry dock over 450 feet in length crammed with power vehicles and manned by a crew of more than two hundred. In between was every conceivable type the ingenuity of man could devise. There was the "buffalo," an amphibious tank mounting several guns. There was the LCVP (landing craft, vehicles and personnel); the LCM (landing craft medium), to take either sixty soldiers or thirty tons of supplies; the LCT (landing craft, tanks); the LST (landing ship, tanks) with a complement of 132 men and officers, a cavernous vessel so large that it tucked away in its bowels several smaller type of landing craft filled with still other devices; and the LCIL (landing craft, infantry, large) each capable of putting on shore more than two hundred troops and equipped with machinery to pull itself from a beach back to the open sea. These were the principal American types. The British had still others, as for instance, the LBK (landing barge, kitchen) and the LBF (landing barge, flak). These ships, if they may be called such, were to play as important a role in the war as even the submarine or the destroyer. Thanks to our resources, our workers, and our vast experience in mass production of machinery, autos, and so forth, the American navy really had the tools to do the job.

By 1945 our sea power, in this ultra-modern guise, had grown to such colossal proportions that it was ready to clear the ocean paths all across the Pacific. Never in all history could there possibly have been any enterprise remotely resembling this, a giant-size transoceanic offense over waterways three times any Atlantic distances, involving conquest en route of desperately defended enemy islands; and all the complexities of it concurrent with an even vaster amphibious task in conjunction with Britain, off Normandy beaches, at the opposite end of the world.

Yanks and Aussies, 1943

February, 1943, and the half-starved Japanese garrison on Guadalcanal withdrew. Thus ended the fight for the southern Solomons. The Japanese had need for all the ships, the planes, and men they could muster to defend the northern Solomons and to reinforce their troops in northern Papua at Lae. On March 3–4 came the Battle of the Bismarck Sea in which an entire Japanese division bound for Lae was annihilated by American air power.

With the coming of the spring in 1943 the tempo of the South Pacific campaign rose rapidly. Tokyo's strategists concentrated troops and shipping at their great base of Truk in the Carolines, so far north of Rabaul that it could not be reached effectively. From there they could and did add constantly to their garrisons in New Guinea and the Solomons. The Yanks and Aussies, however, under command of MacArthur took the offensive and were not to lose it again in this war; they skirted along the coast of New Guinea to lay siege to Lae and Salamaua; they repeated all over again their experiences in the swamps of Papua; and as this happened the Americans made it their particular business to rout enemy elements out of the central Solomons.

It was mid-September before Lae and Salamaua fell. The Japanese there strove desperately to hang on to their airfields, to reinforce their garrisons. They had the manpower to do so, but not the transportation. Meanwhile, by landing craft and by parachute the Allies drove in for the kill. With Aussies pressing from one side and Yanks from another, the Japanese were caught. A few escaped to the jungle, the rest died. The Aussies kept right on. In October they took Finschhafen, in November, Satelburg, and were advancing overland toward Madang on the north coast. By the end of 1943 the tedious process of digging out the Japanese from their nests in New Guinea was well under way.

Thus also in the Solomons. At Munda in New Georgia the enemy had an air base much closer to Guadalcanal than Rabaul in New Britain, and Munda we decided to take. The operation proved long and costly. Before New Georgia could be invaded outlying islands must first be occupied, the Russells, Rendova, and Woodlark. Even after we landed on New Georgia, the advance was yard by yard. Despite bulldozers, tanks, and flame throwers, the defenders stuck to their posts until late in August, large numbers escaping then by air. We were now halfway "up the ladder" from the southern Solomons. Still further north lay Bougainville, bigger than New Georgia. Our marines rolled ashore at Empress Augusta Bay in November but the Japanese took to the hills and we did not follow them; instead we isolated their airfields by the seizure of key islands farther north. By the end of 1943 the Solomons were no longer a menace to our march ahead.

The tempo and the tension of the Pacific war tended to heighten. September to September, 1943-1944, MacArthur's campaign in New Guinea slogged out a glorious conclusion. Seven enemy-held airfields were strewn out at irregular intervals along the malarial lowlands of that infernal island, and to have taken them one by one would have involved incommensurate sacrifice. Better to smash steadily at the airfields until the Japanese air force was pulverized there and then leapfrog westward along the coast. For that purpose the American general had at his command sixteen divisions, eight U. S. army, two U. S. marines, five Australian, one New Zealand. By the end of April, 1944, MacArthur had jumped 500 miles to the west to Hollandia in Dutch New Guinea. Two landings here, a pincer-closing movement, a march inland through crocodile-infested swamps, U. S. Hellcats, Avengers, Douglas dive-bombers in the air; buffalos, half-tracks, jeeps, bulldozers vomited out of a U. S. LSD (landing ship dock) on land, and very shortly Hollandia was ours. June 20, and Biak Island off the northwestern tip of New Guinea was taken; another month and we had gone one hundred miles farther to the west. Within three hours thanks to our paratroopers Numfor Island was occupied, and the Philippines were now but 800 miles away.

On went MacArthur, all the way to Sansapor at the furthest northwestern tip of New Guinea. He had reached it by his famous leapfrogging tactics, having bypassed the headquarters of the Second Japanese Army, now 120 miles eastward. Between him and the Philippines there was now but 600 miles. He did not stop. The Halmahera islands were between him and his goal. Leapfrogging once more, he landed on the most northern of that group, Molotai, the Philippines 300 miles away.

"Thus," as General Fuller states, "in a little over twelve months, the Allies had advanced one thousand, three hundred miles and cut off no less than 135,000 Japanese beyond all hope of rescue." [2]

And the very day MacArthur landed on Molotai, September 15, 1944, saw the U. S. Third Amphibious Force (marines) ashore on Peleliu Island on MacArthur's right flank.

[2] Fuller, *op. cit.*, p. 202.

Reconquest of the Philippines

The war with Japan was still two months short of three years, and American planes were soaring again over the Philippines, knocking out of the skies in one day more enemy aircraft than we lost in the Bataan fighting, and sinking in Manila Bay no less than forty Japanese ships. We were coming back.

The Yanks arrived October 20 in the central Philippines on the eastern side of Leyte Island. It had been generally assumed that MacArthur would first invade Mindanao in the south, since to bypass that large island with its excellent airstrips would be risky. But the American armed forces had long since proved that leapfrogging was the best of tactics; and so the Americans jumped clear to the heart of the Philippines, 600 ships convoying and transporting some 250,000 men, a sea invasion of tremendous magnitude, more dangerous than the Anglo-American invasion of North Africa nearly two years earlier.

The total enemy forces in the Philippines were about equal to our own but widely scattered, while ours were concentrated. On the other hand, the enemy's navy, though somewhat battered and deficient in light craft and carriers, had a major advantage. It could menace our fleet of transports by any one of three different routes: across the Sulu Sea, south of Leyte; from the direction of Singapore; across the China Sea through the San Bernardino Straits north of Leyte; and from farther north, skirting the eastern shores of Luzon and Samar, to hit our transports from the east. It was now or never for Japan, and she must strike quickly before our shore footing was secure. She did her best to do so, and from all three directions. Those were anxious days late in October as we divided our naval strength to face this triple threat, for none could tell which one of the three enemy task forces packed the greater punch. We met all three and drove them back. At one time the defenseless transports were stripped of naval coverage and severe, even catastrophic, damage might have overtaken them had it not been for the audacity, courage, and skill of motor torpedo boats, destroyers, light craft, and airmen. But the final results were more than satisfactory. In three crucial engagements the enemy naval power was crippled, three of their battleships and six heavy cruisers being sunk, also one large carrier and several small ones, to say nothing of lighter craft and not far short of 700 planes. Out of a total of some sixty hostile ships, only a few destroyers escaped undamaged. Thus by "Navy Day," T. R.'s birthday, October 27, 1944, the sea power of Tokyo was, as Admiral Halsey reported, "beaten, routed and broken." It was our own American Trafalgar.

The American navy reported the loss of the carrier *Princeton* and that of a few destroyers and escort carriers. "The ghastly annihilation of Allied naval units," said the Tokyo radio, "resulted in forty-five ships sunk"—a cryptic statement in view of the fact that there were left only remnants of their three fleets, and that these were never again to trouble us in Philippine waters during this war.

The Mikado's army, however, could dig in on land and so put up much more of a fight; it constantly brought fresh forces into Leyte from the neighboring islands; it slipped them in by night as on Guadalcanal; it contested every swamp and hilltop. Incessant rain, knee-deep mud, last-ditch warriors in multitudinous caves—it was the old, hard story of a dozen islands. An invasion of Leyte's west coast, paralleling the main attack on the east, finally cut the Japanese forces into segments as our planes time and time again flattened down their dwindling air strength throughout all the Philippines. On the third anniversary of Pearl Harbor the red and white flag of the Sun Goddess still waved over a corner of Leyte, but with the United States navy master of the sea and our planes darkening the skies, our ultimate recapture of the Philippines was assured. By January 1, 1945, no less than 50,000 Japanese dead had been counted on Leyte and resistance there reduced to patrol action. But enemy forces numbering some 50,000 more still remained in Luzon, and no one knew how many more menaced Mindanao, Panay, and the other islands of the archipelago. Our Philippine campaign had just begun.

It had for its next phase the retaking of Luzon. Most fortunately for the United States, enemy air power based there had dwindled steadily, for the Japanese had played it all out and for keeps during the Leyte campaign, with swarms of Manila-based planes hurtling south to dash at reckless odds and in vain against Liberators, Warhawks, Black Widows, navy Hellcats, and marine Corsairs. Luzon was strongly held, and should General Yamashita, Singapore's conqueror, hold out in Luzon in 1945 as MacArthur and Wainwright did in Bataan in 1942, a year or more might pass before the mainland of Japan felt the tread of Yank leather.

Since the Rising Sun flag flew over Corregidor, frontal attack on Manila was out. We had the choice of driving from the south—best as far as distance went and best, too, for air coverage; or, on the other hand, we could strike in at the Lingayen Gulf and assault Manila from the north—at greater distance but mostly along a broad, flat valley with excellent motor roads. We chose the Gulf, conveyed thither seven convoys without the loss of a transport, clear proof that Japanese air power and Japanese sea power fast were waning.

Yamashita did not set up battle on the open beaches nor in the broad valley; presumably he had neither planes, nor tanks, nor enough matériel to do so. Only when we probed inland to the hills on either side did we meet stiff resistance. On February 4, with little loss of life, we were back in the capital of the Philippines.

Burma in 1943

In 1943 the Japanese surging across Burma were at the gates of India. They expected easy entrance, perhaps a junction with victorious Nazis in Persia.

India, seething with rebellion, was but lightly garrisoned. Wavell, the viceroy, however, did not hesitate. He clapped Gandhi, Nehru, and all leading members of the Indian National Congress in jail, reorganized his Anglo-Indian forces, prepared to take the offensive. It was on a limited scale but won its objectives, largely because of the ability and courage of Major Charles Wingate, an outstanding hero of this war.

Wingate's career paralleled in many ways that of Chinese Gordon, England's roving soldier of the later nineteenth century. Both were masters of the unexpected, scornful of brass hats, distinguished for exploits in frontier warfare, famous for winning the friendship of rough tribesmen, and assiduous in their study of the Old Testament. As a young officer in Palestine, Wingate had won his spurs by capturing Arab guerrillas; as a major in the British army his exploits in Ethiopia with a rickety plane, camels, and native warriors had become legendary; and now Wavell gave him a free hand in Burma.

He introduced something new in warfare. The long protracted hardening of average raw recruits into tough, resilient units was not new, nor was the painstakingly minute drill in geographic lore upon which Wingate insisted: what he did that was novel was to plan a campaign in all its details and involving several thousand men, in which commissariat and munitions were to be transported entirely by plane. Food had been dropped from the air to succor the fleeing remnants of British troops in Burma. Now Wingate proposed to articulate the plane so closely to his projected offense that it would replace railroads, motor trucks, bullock trains, and make possible a victorious rapidity of movement despite rain, forest, and jungle.

Early in February, 1943, Major, now General Wingate, led his troops over the Indian border. He called them "Chindits," a name derived from the curious carvings, part lion, part griffin, which protected Burmese temples from the devil. For over two months the Chindits were to emulate on Asiatic land what Elizabeth's sea dogs did to Spain on oceanic waters, to harass and wear down an enemy too potent to challenge face to face.

The immediate task was to sever hostile communication lines. These ran north and south following the valley of the Chindwin, the Irrawaddy, and the Salween rivers. Most important of all was the north-south railway line from Mandalay to Myitkyina. To get there, the Chindits must drive east-west over high mountains, chain after chain of jumbled ranges, down through deep valleys, roughing it over bridle paths or no paths at all.

By the time Wingate's roughies won back to India they had raided on foot over 1,000 miles, penetrated to the east of the Irrawaddy River, disrupted communications over a strategic area of 10,000 square miles in North Burma, killed several thousand foemen, proved that a small army could be fed, clothed, and armed, even in the tropics, by air.

Britain, however, had little to spare for such costly fighting in Burma. Until new airfields in great number were built and equipped in India, both for the RAF and the United States Tenth Air Force, no large-scale offense could be launched against our implacable enemy in that humid-hot malarial jungle of a dysentery-ridden land.

China in 1943 and 1944

After endless years of anarchy and grueling war, China was played out and bogged down. Financial inflation was rampant; lend-lease aid came dribbling in but slowly, all of it borne by air from India; a dubiously pro-Japanese government, presided over by a Chinese carpetbagger, functioned after the fashion of such rascals at Nanking; in North China Communists had their own regime, bitterly oppressed by and opposed to the landlords and loan sharks of the Kuomintang party who ruled what it could reach of China from air-battered Chungking; and Chiang Kai-shek, the generalissimo, rapidly aging, always supersensitive, surrounded by politicians of Asiatic craft and greed, did not take kindly to relentless pressure applied by our own high-octane general, Joseph Stilwell (Vinegar Joe), chief-of-staff for the Burma theater.

In China there were wars within wars, in particular that between the Chinese Communists and the Kuomintang, occasionally breaking out in open strife, soldier against soldier, gun against gun, more often smouldering under cover, a feud of factions contending for the loyalty of starving men and for the lordship of wasted lands.

This internecine strife had long been far from new, and the quarrels it engendered dated back to the twenties. In 1937 the breach was partially healed; but old sores festered, to break out with renewed fury by the forties, and in 1944 there were two distinct regimes in China, united only by hatred of Tokyo, in all other ways mutually distrustful and hostile.

The Chinese Communists, said to number around 80,000,000, were located mainly in the northwest provinces with their capital at Yenan. Here they had a government of their own, with separate currency, separate taxes, and a separate army which they said existed to fight Japan, which the Kuomintang said was for the purpose of spreading Communism. Several of Chiang Kai-shek's advisers, if not the generalissimo himself, were so inclined to this view that many of his Chinese troops, which should have been used against invading Japan, were deployed north to ride herd on the Communists and to keep their power from spreading further.

Meanwhile, the military situation worsened. Beginning in the spring of 1944 and continuing at rapid and accelerating tempo, the Japanese made good their project to cut and to control a wide swathe through all China from Peiping in the north to Canton and Nan-ning in the south, thus bringing their conquests in overland contact with French Indochina, a *fait accompli* which made it possible not simply to sever the coastal plains of East China from Chungking but also to reinforce Japanese troops in Thailand and Burma by land.

Week by week and month by month the somber news of Chinese defeat kept leaking out. The foe long since had controlled the Yangtze Valley beyond Hankow. They now pressed north from Hankow and south from Peiping across the wheat belt of Hanoi to capture Chengchow and Loyang farther west; they drove south from Hankow and north from Canton, taking en route the important city of Chang-sha, making good their rail connections from Korea to Canton; they forced the hasty abandonment of many of the Fourteenth American Air Force bases; and as this happened they occupied one after another Chinese coastal ports between Canton and Shanghai, thus sealing off potential landing sites for an American army invading China by sea.

Burma and India in 1944

Farther to the west in Burma and in one small pocket of northeastern India, the Japanese were defeated. In this remote and pestilential corner, Chinese, Americans, Britons, East Africans, and Indians, together with sundry local hill tribes, reconquered about one-fifth of all Burma and made possible the linking up of the Ledo Road with the Burma Road in order to reopen a back door into China. This was a truly international achievement but credit primarily should go to the Chinese and to the Indians, the former serving under General Stilwell, the latter under British high command. Aside from American aviators, engineers, and a handful of picked raiders and machine gunners, few Americans took part in the obscure campaign which by the end of 1944 had carried Allied arms as far south as Bhamo, eighty miles beyond Myitkyina.

Divergencies of viewpoint, logistical problems, the truly infernal terrain, and the down-streaming monsoon combined to complicate military problems in Burma-India. The Allied commander-in-chief in Southeast Asia, Lieutenant General Mountbatten, was more interested in Central and Southern Burma than in various inaccessible upper valleys; more concerned about the recovery of Rangoon, Mandalay, and ultimately Singapore for the British Empire than about what many considered so hair-brained a scheme as building an impossible highway across impassable mountains. Deputy commander under Mountbatten was our own Vinegar Joe, whose pet project was the Ledo Road. Stilwell did not get on well with either Mountbatten or with Chiang Kai-shek, upon whom he had to depend for ninety per cent or more of his soldiers. But what Stilwell lacked in tact he much more than made up in brains and energy. Furthermore, until the end of the year, he had the backing of Washington.

Many thought Ledo a fantastic idea. It would be necessary to transport bulldozers, trucks, workmen, and all their impedimenta hundreds of miles from Calcutta over a twisting narrow gauge railway to the extreme upper corner of Northeast India before even a yard could be constructed. After that, one was confronted with engineering problems more difficult by far than those encountered in the Alaska highway, dense forests to be felled, zigzagging corkscrew curves to be constructed down precipitous mountain slopes and up steep ridges, and this in the face of determined enemy resistance and the worst climate in the world, with a monsoon arriving in May to terminate operations if not to wash out with torrential floods everything thus far accomplished. But Stilwell clung to his plans; he had the money, the equipment, the engineers, the manpower, and the soldiers to clear the path; and he was going to do just that.

The Sino-British-American objective (for Mountbatten did finally and generously assist his hard-bitten American deputy) was Myitkyina, railhead of Japanese communications in north Burma. That town and its airfield once occupied, hostile detachments on the north could be cut off and the Ledo enterprise once reaching Myitkyina could be continued eastward, despite very bad terrain, so as ultimately to link up with the Burma Road in the Chinese province of Yün-nan. The British said it would be "impossible" to take Myitkyina before 1945; Stilwell arrived there, aided greatly by the British, and did so by converging attacks on the eve of the 1944 monsoon season. His Chinese troops, whom he had trained and equipped, and whom he considered second to none, headed for Myitkyina from northeast and southeast. From the southwest came Wingate's raiders, soon to have over them another commander, owing to the untimely death of General Wingate who was killed before he could know how well Americans could carry out the methods he improved and often originated. And from the northwest, like scouts searching out the ways for the Ledo engineers, came Merrill's marauders, the Yankee counterpart to Wingate's men. And now for the first time in Asiatic jungle war gliders were used to convey troops. The commando fighters of Merrill were joined by Indian troops, coming in glider transports, towed off the ground by planes and landing in the jungle. British and American airplane power was making victory possible in North Burma even as it was doing in western Europe and at Saipan.

The Japanese this spring of 1944 meanwhile launched an offense of their own, and in two directions; one, the lesser, in the Arakan region of the Burma-Indian frontier east of the Bay of Bengal, aimed at the conquest of Chittagong, an important seaport and British air base; the other, more important, directed at Imphal, capital of the little Indian state of Manipur, tucked away amid the Naga Hills on the borders of North Burma and India. North of Imphal for some 174 miles a highway led to Dimapur on the Calcutta-Ledo railway. Once the Rising Sun reached Dimapur, Stilwell's way to China would revert to the jungle and the Sino-American-British forces in North Burma would be isolated. All that would be necessary then would be a holding action while Japanese troops, assisted, it was hoped, by revolting Indians, swung down the Brahmaputra Valley into Bengal, perhaps to stage another Singapore at Calcutta.

This was the Japanese plan. Thanks to General Slim and his Fourteenth British Army, it was thwarted, the Japanese soundly thrashed, all that they gained lost, and by the third anniversary of Pearl Harbor the foundations laid for the reconquest of Burma in 1945.

"The march on Delhi has begun, the Fourteenth British Army is destroyed," thus the Tokyo radio in the first week of February, 1944, as General Tenashi trapped the Fifteenth Corps of that army in the Arakan area. The general's plans were excellent but he had forgotten that Britain, not Japan, had air supremacy over Burma and that the British now were operating on Wingate's advice, "Have no lines of communication on the jungle floor. Bring the goods like Father Christmas down the chimney." The airmen came to the rescue, flew 400 sorties, fed food and munitions to the trapped Imperials, even brought them beer and mail. The foe had rations for ten days only. They stayed too long. Counterattacks sent them reeling eastward, leaving in the jungle 7,000 dead.

The real march on Delhi, however, was by way of Imphal. Against that fourth-rate Indian town the Japanese hurled 80,000 picked troops, besieged it for over two months, surged on north, surrounded for eighteen days another British force at Kohima which if they had only by-passed might have brought them to the strategic railroad. But the Jap orders were: "First take Kohima, then the railroad"; and Japanese soldiers always obey orders, which is not always the way to win.

Time now pressed; the monsoon was not far distant; the Japanese made one final try for Manipur. "You will take Manipur," said their commander, "or the division will be annihilated." The second part of his statement time verified. It was now Slim's turn. Like thistledown before the wind the Imperials drove the adversary south, counting more than 50,000 Japanese dead. How many more of the original 80,000 perished in the jungle of sickness or by knives of irate hillmen there is no record.

The Fourteenth Army, too, had suffered heavily; but Slim was back at Kalewa on the frontier where he had buried his guns on his retreat in 1942. Now he could, and did, dig them up again. From now on it was the British Empire, not Japan, that took the offensive in Burma.

Burma Won Back

The Japanese were already on their way out of Burma. The colossal and catastrophic defeat in 1942 of the British Empire there had been well advertised; but the return in triumph of Imperial forces in 1944 and 1945 attracted little notice. The American press, as was natural, laid such emphasis as it gave to the Allied campaign in Burma on the dramatic achievements of our own General Stilwell and his Chinese troops in taking Myitkyina, in effect minimizing rather unduly the assistance rendered by British penetration forces, and underestimating, very decidedly, the stress and strain imposed upon the British Fourteenth Army which had to drive back the main Japanese invaders. That army, during the first half of 1944, not only suffered over 40,000 casualties, but, according to Churchill, "sustained no fewer than 237,000 cases of sickness which had to be evacuated to the rear over the long, difficult communications, and tended in hospitals."

That army, nevertheless, during the first five months of 1945 "liberated" Burma, retook Mandalay, chased the enemy from Rangoon, killed them by the thousands, drove the rest in full retreat toward the Siamese border. And Burma, it is worth remembering, was as large as Germany, with a fighting front in 1945 of 700 miles, and exceeded in World War II only by the Russian. Here was a country with two enemies to fight— Japan and the climate. Sodden wet, choking dust, malaria, jaundice, dysentery, mud, ticks, a humidity of 95 per cent, and Hirohito's desperate soldiers—a bad land to win.

The American contribution to this Southern Pacific victory of 1945 was relatively small. Our concern, and quite rightly, had been with northern Burma, to open there communication lines with China. Lend-lease had helped make possible the British comeback of 1945; but planning the final campaign, and the execution of it, was a British Imperial achievement. Statistics tell the tale. Of the ground troops in Burma in 1945, about 250,000 came from Britain, some 470,000 were Indian, 30,000 were from British East Africa, 30,000 from British West Africa. Chinese forces engaged were approximately 125,000, and American troops, 25,000. A total of 900,000, possibly more.

Kipling's Mandalay was Japan's main base in Burma, and the attack on it had priority for the 1945 campaign which burst forth with speed and fury late in February. General Slim, commander of the Fourteenth British Army, drove at Mandalay from the north and simultaneously rushed a mechanized force south and east for a surprise assault on Meiktila, eighty miles south of Mandalay. While a Sino-American force assisted by British troops drove down from Lashio in the northeast to assist in the siege of Fort Dufferin, an additional brigade was flown intact to support the troops who had won through to Meiktila. Thus it was that when Fort Dufferin fell, May 8, and the Japanese were forced to evacuate the capital city, they found themselves outflanked in the south and overwhelmed in the north. The most severe fighting in Burma ensued, as the Mikado's men tried fanatically to break through to the south. But the line held, and in little over a week Slim's men had killed over ten thousand of the best Japanese troops in Burma, acquired six airstrips in the arid zone about Meiktila, far from mud and monsoons, tons of Japanese war matériel, the top of the railroad corridor, and Burma's main auto routes, and most important of all, a springboard from which to drive south to the sea.

There was still Rangoon to capture, 700 miles down the pestilent valley of the Irrawaddy. Time was precious, for unless Slim took Rangoon before the middle of May the monsoon would block land operations, write finis to war work in the skies. He therefore took the long chance and disregarded his flanks to speed his truck-bearing infantry and tanks on south. All April the adversary did his best to stay that onward rush, but so fast did it crash through that frequently Japanese headquarters only heard of British victories days after they had occurred, and in one instance Slim's tanks "ran down Jap policemen directing traffic at the crossroads."

The terrain now was flat and open, well suited for rapid movement. May 1, and Rangoon was close at hand. From the sea amphibious British landings drove ashore, and British paratroopers dropped down on the lowlands of the Irrawaddy delta. Rangoon was surrounded, north, south, and west. The foe had had enough and too much; May 3 he fled. "Slim had beaten the enemy and the monsoon."

China Revived

Even before Rangoon's fall and the taking of Okinawa, the resilient and tough Chinese were turning past defeat into present victory. Chinese morale was on the upgrade throughout 1945. There had been a noticeable increase in airborne freight from India, and soon American trucks began to squirm their way through north Burma hills over the Ledo-Burma highway, rechristened "Stilwell Road" in honor of the man whose imagination, grit, and perseverance had made it possible. "Welcome Honorable Truck Convoy," the banners said, as this new stream of matériel-in-aid trickled in over the thirsty desert of a half-starved land.

Also instrumental in reviving China's strength was the reorganization of her army, to a considerable degree "U. S. trained, U. S. supplied, U. S. supported." General Stilwell and the Generalissimo did not see eye to eye; both were touchy men and coöperation lagged. Stilwell's dual job as commander of U. S. troops in China and as chief of staff of Chiang Kai-shek was taken by General Wedemeyer, who made himself *persona grata* to that Chinese chief of state, so that Chinese soldiers were now better fed, better clothed, better disciplined, and consequently better fighters.

The Chinese took the offensive in the late spring and summer of 1945. One by one the American airfields in China were won back and the conqueror's corridor to Indochina, Thailand, and Malaya, for which he had fought so long, was so narrowed by mid-June that he withdrew from it to avoid capture.

Iwo Jima

Nineteen forty-five and Japan's brief day of glory ended. As Slim's Fourteenth British Army drove the foe out of Burma, the American army and navy were delivering a frontal attack that could not be withstood.

The American bases in the Marianas—Saipan, Tinian, and Guam—were a good thirteen hundred miles from Tokyo. Round trips to the targets took sixteen hours in good weather, leaving for emergencies less than one hour's margin on gas supply. If the weather was bad, the superfortress was out of luck and out of the war; and even if the weather was fair, there was always danger of attack by Japanese bombers based on Iwo Jima, 600 miles from Tokyo, 700 from Saipan, and on a direct line between them.

Once the United States had Iwo Jima the picture would shift radically; the Americans then would have a fueling depot for returning B-29s; and, what is more, American fighter planes based on Iwo could escort our superforts to the Japanese mainland and thus enable them to fly at low altitudes, engage in precision bombing. Clearly this miserable excrescence of volcanic rock, Iwo Jima, was an American must, "a good rock to have on our side."

Iwo was bare of vegetation, was crusted and heaped with volcanic ash along the beaches, soft, miry, and treacherous. At the southern end rose 556 feet of rocky Mt. Suribachi, an extinct volcano; at its northern end were cliffs and caves, many of the latter steaming sulphurously from latent subterranean fires; and upon this island battlefield of only eight square miles 23,000 Japanese soldiers held three airfields that meant much both to Nippon and to America. It was a nasty little place for even marines to tackle and, as one remarked, "It ain't like Brooklyn."

The barrage the navy threw up on Iwo was thick enough and black enough to screen the landing. None the less our landing losses were heavy, some twenty per cent, and worse to follow.

To reach the base of Suribachi and scale it took the leathernecks four days. And even then Iwo was far from won. The Japs still held two of the three airfields. Pillboxes and blockhouses of steel-reinforced concrete covered deep with volcanic ash and sand had to be reduced one after another. The foe made full use of his innumerable underground passages; the nasty weather grew nastier; the surf ran high; reinforcements of both men and matériel were hard to get ashore. And even after all three airfields were won, there were thousands of enemy soldiers holed up in the northern cliffs of Iwo. They died in the last ditch and almost to the last man. There were some suicides and but few prisoners. General H. M. Smith, our marine commander on Iwo, said grimly, "This is the toughest fight we've run across in 168 years." In the American cemetery 4,300 marines are buried.

Okinawa

On the last lap of his long outward voyage to Japan in 1853, Commodore Perry, U. S. N., paid an extensive visit to the Lew Chew islands (the Ryukyus of the present day), staying several weeks on Great Lew Chew, the Okinawa of our Pacific war.

Unlike Iwo, Okinawa is a large island, sixty miles long and varying in width from two to twenty miles. It lies half again as close to the two southern islands of Japan as Iwo Jima, and has the further advantage of being only 400 miles from China. Formosa is even nearer to the latter country than Okinawa, but 365 miles south of the Ryukyus. If our strategy called first for an invasion of China and subsequently that of Japan, then Formosa would be our best bet. Reverse this, however, and invade Japan first, then Okinawa, quite evidently would be the prize capture. Planes based on it were within easy range of Shanghai in China, Kyushu, and southern Honshu in Japan. And furthermore, the B-29, if based on Okinawa, could skim the Yellow Sea and the Straits of Shimonoseki and return in safety with fuel to spare.

Easter morning, 1945, and the newly formed Tenth American Army, convoyed and protected by some 1,400 ships and commanded by General Simon Bolivar Buckner III, landed on Okinawa. It looked easy. We had 100,000 men, and we spread across the island to bisect it, scarce hearing a hostile shot. Few suspected then what was to happen, the bloodiest campaign of the whole Pacific war. Eighty-two furious days were consumed to complete it, total American casualties, army and navy together, running to no less than 45,029; while on the other side 90,000 soldiers of Hirohito were killed, 4,000 taken prisoner.

The Japanese had no illusions as to the significance of Okinawa. If they lost that island they lost the war. It was bad enough to lose Iwo Jima; but that infernal pinpoint in the ocean had only three airfields, and was much too small to be made our major base. This was not true of Okinawa, much closer to Japan, upon which endless airfields might be built to harbor thousands of the dreaded B-29s. Okinawa was built by nature for rugged defense; the southern half was rough and mountainous land, and cut in through its hills wound fortifications with interlocking and inter-communicating tunnels, caves, and pillboxes. So now it was share and share alike for GIs and Leathernecks, who faced daily withering fire whenever and wherever they tried to gain a few yards. And there were many more yards to cover than on Iwo.

This time, too, the American navy felt the death-sting of Nippon's wasp-men. The Japanese had a dangerous threat in reserve, the *Kamikaze,* which translated means "divine wind."

Centuries before, Japan, as tradition holds, had been kept inviolate by a divine wind or kamikaze sent by the Sun Goddess, a wind which wrecked the navies of the Mongol conqueror, and now there would be a divine wind, man-contrived, thousands of suicide planes launched at the great American fleet spaced out for miles off Okinawa, an armada in-evitably huge in view of the multifarious need of 100,000 men and all the cumbrous implements of our modern war. The Kamikaze planes were of minimum construction, each pilot locked in his cockpit, no armor for the plane, no parachute for the pilot, only brief specific training. Neither pilot nor plane was expected to survive.

The Kamikaze concept fitted well that older medieval psychology which the Japanese inherit—also their more modern theology. For them, as for Moslems of the earlier centuries, paradise was close at hand; before setting one's course of death, a wonderful party, many drinks, pre-Lethean honors. Kamikaze tactics were an improvement on the banzai charge, for the suicide planes did reach their mark on over 200 of our vessels, sank many a destroyer and small craft, and crippled badly two of our biggest carriers, killing so many bluejackets that in some weeks navy casualties exceeded both those of marines and army.

"One hundred million countrymen: the enemy now stands at our front gate. It is the gravest moment in our country's history." Thus Koiso, Japan's premier, on the eve of Okinawa. But he could do nothing to shake off the black hand of fate that smote Nippon's fighting men. As they lost ground yard by yard, a ministerial crisis ensued at Tokyo and Koiso resigned. His desperate successors ordered the remnants of Japan's navy to Okinawa. Let the Kamikaze attack once more with all it had, and in the midst of hoped-for confusion there might be one last chance for Hirohito's war-craft. But the ships of Japan never got to Okinawa. Our fighter bombers shot out from their flattops to the kill, sank two light cruisers, three destroyers, and the battleship *Yamato* of 45,000 tons, Japan's finest. Meanwhile, Russia denounced her ten-year neutrality pact with Japan, ominous indication that the Soviets would attack in Manchuria as soon as they considered it to their interests so to do.

The European war ended in May but on Okinawa war continued well into June. Through May the dwindling beleaguered garrison fought grimly as our Tenth Army and the marines edged it back to Shuri Castle, pivotal point in the last defense line. Slowly we were winning because we were killing foes who could not be replaced, some 80,000 of the original 90,000 now being dead. We ruled sea and air. On this island they could only die.

On the Eve of Hiroshima

Summer, 1945, and Japan was mortally stricken. Her death throes were those of Germany in February, March, and April, but with this difference: no hostile armies had as yet set foot upon her homeland.

Yet she was done for: her continental conquests were shrinking fast; her scattered garrisons over widespread Oceania were completely useless; the Australians were depriving her of the oil of Borneo; the converging aircraft of the United States were destroying her cities; the American navy conjointly with the planes of the American army were cutting the lifelines to Korea and Manchuria, without which she could not live; and the most imposing armada ever seen on any ocean, mostly American, but joined now by a powerful British squadron, paraded up and down, and down and up her now defenseless coasts, pouring floods of shells on helpless targets.

Invaded Nippon had more to die of and less to fight with than invaded Germany six months earlier. Even before Pearl Harbor, Japan's industrial potential was insufficient for large-scale war; now it was almost nonexistent. Unlike Germany, her domestic resources were few. Much of the food she ate came from out the sea. It now was death to her, the fishing boats sunk or driven to hiding.

Even more than Britain, Japan's life depended on ships, and where were they now? Tiny craft still stole stealthily at night Korea-bound, slunk along the China coast, slid slyly into Singapore, or rusted at the wharves of Shanghai and Batavia; but the navy which so proudly shattered Imperial Russia's fleet in 1905 was to all intents and purposes erased from this war.

During the nine months before Hiroshima our B-29s alone flew over 30,000 sorties, dropped over 169,000 crushing tons on shipyards, airfields, factories, cities. And this does not count the planes catapulted from our carriers against the enemy, or the four-engined bombers based on Iwo and Okinawa. Now, as resistance dwindled, our bombers flew at low levels, used jellied petroleum to start quenchless fires, and sent scurrying to rural hideouts the remnant millions of homeless Japan. And even so, we had not reached the peak of this cosmic destruction, for redeploy-

Ewing Galloway

The Japanese Surrender Aboard the U.S.S. Missouri

ment of the European air forces had scarce begun, and Okinawa airfields still under construction would launch a thousand more planes per day.

This air assault was deadlier on Japan than on Germany, for the former's economic arteries were more exposed, her far flimsier cities more congested. Almost to the war's end, the German radar and German áck-áck kept functioning. Not so with Japan. She did not have the mechanics, the laboratories, the reserve of technological skill, nor the space that the Nazis could command; her citizens had neither the material nor the skill to make artificial gasoline and synthetic rubber.

In August the end was near. Japan turned to Russia, besought her aid to approach Britain and the United States. But Stalin, secretly committed to join in Japan's destruction, refused. The United States and Britain dictated unconditional surrender, and to this the Japanese were not willing to subscribe. And so they husbanded their dwindling planes, hid them as best they might, refused combat in the air to the swarming air fleets of the United States, which now struck at rail communications, bridges, and ferries rather than at burnt-out factories and slain cities. Bracing themselves against our infantry, soon to storm Nippon's shores, they planned then to bring out their last planes, to renew Kamikaze tactics, to kill many thousand Yankees. And they hoped that time soon would come.

Invasion in force had been set for November. It was not necessary, for Hiroshima came first.

Hiroshima

On July 16, some 300 picked scientists assembled in the New Mexico desert. An experiment was up for testing, the fruit of many years of research, and at a cost of $2,000,000,000.

And this is what the scientists, huddled at safe distance, saw: a great green light, changing color, now purple, now orange, instantaneously expanding, shooting upward in a fifth of a second, higher than Mt. Everest. Then came unbearable thunder. Here at long last was total power, total war, which man himself could wield—"the first cry of the newborn world."

This was the atomic bomb, man-made but of the very stuff of the suns, a bomb equal to 20,000 tons of TNT and with the fullest destructive power of 2,000 B-29s. Prometheus in Greek legend had stolen for us fire from the gods, and for that and other presumptions had been chained to a rock by Father Zeus. Man now, for weal or woe, Prometheus-like, was chained to his own full knowledge of this central secret of the universe.

On August 6 an American plane dropped a single atomic bomb on Hiroshima, a Japanese city and army base with a population upwards of

350,000. Sixty per cent of Hiroshima immediately was no more, dead instantly all those in the doomed area, dying those on the perimeter, "a death no men ever died before."

Two days later Russia declared war on Japan. Stalin had previously agreed to do so. And promptly Russian armies now crossed Manchurian borders.

Three days later a second and deadlier bomb was dropped, this time on the port of Nagasaki, and over an area even larger than at Hiroshima.

On the fourth day of this new world, August 10, Japan offered to surrender and accepted terms four days later.

Before our synthetic Sun-Fire destroyed Hiroshima and Nagasaki so utterly, Soviet entrance on the Far East's last act of world tragedy would have been news of great moment, and Japan's acknowledged defeat would have roused joy entire all through the United Nations. But epoch-making though these facts were, the ghost-shadow of Hiroshima and of Nagasaki eclipsed the Soviet act, damped our joy.

It was not that most' men opposed the bomb's use; no doubt it shortened the war, saved many lives. Nor was it horror at what we had done to men that tempered rejoicing among those still capable of thought. There had been too much horror during ten years past for numbed nerves to respond in shock to any new ghastliness. Rather it was a profound sense of awe and fear. Against the energy released by split atoms, how piffling now inventions like gunpowder, the compass, the steam engine! Out of the laboratory of the chemist-physicist had come this miracled genie, his birth hurried by the clash of arms, the mad roar of battle. His future, what? And our own?

Chapter 20

THE POSTWAR WORLD

WORLD WAR II was over, and victors as well as vanquished licked their wounds. Millions had died, millions were in prison, millions were homeless, millions were hungry, and many millions more were numbed by toil, fagged out by nervous strain. To revive and to arouse them to thought and act, to beat swords into ploughshares, to rebuild cities, to restore trade and commerce, to blueprint peace treaties, would have been a staggering task even had the victors stood shoulder to shoulder in peace as in war. But such was not to be, and in five short years a third World War loomed on the horizon.

United Nations Charter

Permanent peace on earth had been one of the ideals of the United Nations. But swaddling clothes bound that infant very tightly as Britain, the United States, and Soviet Russia carefully guarded the cradle, admitting later as subordinate and part-time nurses Chungking China and the Free France of De Gaulle. Not, indeed, until the San Francisco Conference of April, 1945, was that organization much more than window dressing.

Not that history's pages were blank between 1942 and 1945 in the matter of conferences. There were many—Casablanca, Cairo, Moscow, Teheran, Yalta in the Crimea, and two at Quebec; conferences at Hot Springs, Virginia (food and agriculture), at Bretton Woods, New Hampshire (international finance), at Chicago (aviation), at Philadelphia (ILO—International Labor Office), at Atlantic City, New Jersey (UNRRA —United Nations Relief and Rehabilitation Administration), and at Dumbarton Oaks, Washington (preparatory for the San Francisco meeting). Many of these conferences were but consultations of two or three larger states on how to win the war. This was true of Casablanca (January, 1943), a meeting held between Roosevelt and Churchill with their military and naval staffs, in which mention was made of Stalin's inability to attend and assurances given that he had been fully informed of military proposals. It was also true of the first Quebec Conference

(August, 1943), which was concerned primarily with matters of military strategy in Europe and Asia. In the Cairo Conference (November, 1943), Chiang Kai-shek joined Roosevelt and Churchill, and the agenda was confined to war against Japan and how that country was to be stripped after its conclusion, not only of conquests made in the twentieth century but also of those made in the nineteenth. There was nothing here, certainly, of any United Nations machinery for governing the postwar world. So likewise was it with the second Quebec Conference (September, 1944), exclusively devoted to considering Anglo-American political and military interests in eastern Asia.

More important was the conference at Teheran, Iran (December, 1943) at which Roosevelt, Stalin, and Churchill signed a declaration calling for a "world family of democratic nations." So much for press release. What was not made public was a blueprint for Russian expansion (indirect of course) in eastern and southeastern Europe. Greece was exempted from it, and recognition was made of preponderant Russian influence in eastern Asia—a predated check which Russia was to cash a year and a half later at Yalta.

Much more important was the Yalta Conference on the Russian coast of the Black Sea, held in February, 1945. At it Stalin, Roosevelt, and Churchill agreed on joint military action to win the war and ways in which the world might be reconstructed after it was over. The victor was Stalin. Practically everything he wanted he obtained: Soviet control of Manchurian ports and railroads; Communist preponderance in Poland, Yugoslavia, Bulgaria, Rumania, and Hungary; the greater share of German reparations from Germany yet to be conquered; and membership in the projected United Nations not only for Russia but also for Byelorussia and the Ukraine, thus guaranteeing three votes to the Soviet Union. In return for these concessions Stalin promised an early entry by Russia into the war against Japan.

Why did Roosevelt and Churchill concede so much? One reason was that they considered Russian help against Japan highly desirable. Yalta preceded Hiroshima and the mainland of Japan had not yet been invaded. In Manchuria there was a large Japanese army which Russia could immobilize. Furthermore, Roosevelt and Churchill were powerless to stay Stalin's hand in eastern Europe anyway, and they thought it better to obtain certain Soviet pledges for decency and democracy in that part of Europe, flimsy though they might be, rather than do nothing at all to check unbridled Soviet aggression. As for the additional seats in the United Nations for Byelorussia and the Ukraine, Stalin had an argument: from his point of view granting seats to the Commonwealth countries, such as Canada and Australia, added to Britain's prestige, and the bloc of Central American countries he considered added to American influence.

Publicly the three signatories at Yalta agreed to set countries free from the German yoke, to institute democratic regimes, and to hold free elections. Secretly, although indirectly, however, Roosevelt and Churchill suborned if not betrayed a Poland they had fought to save, while at the same time handing over to Stalin an integral part of China, their ally in the war against Japan. The *quid pro quo* looked good, a Russian declaration of war against Japan and relinquishment on Stalin's part of Soviet interference in Italy and Greece. But however Yalta may be regarded, the decisions taken there were unquestionably in Stalin's favor and later were to embarrass both Britain and the United States in dealing with the Russian dictator.

We come now to Dumbarton Oaks at Washington, where for seven weeks ending October 7, 1944, the representatives of the Big Three, plus China, threshed out a specific program in accordance with the Teheran pledge.

What emerged bore striking resemblance to the 1919 League of Nations, a General Assembly in which each state admitted to the privileges of the United Nations should have one vote and a Security Council of eleven members, the Big Three, enlarged to the "Big Five" by the inclusion of China and France with permanent membership, and six other members to be chosen by the Assembly.

Born in San Francisco, April, 1945, the infant United Nations came close to dying. Molotov of Russia and Evatt of Australia, the two protagonists at this full-dress gala event, clashed again and again, the former generally winning, holding better cards, playing them relentlessly; the latter generally losing, but putting up a dogged fight on behalf of real democracy and the lesser nations.

The Russian got what he wanted; he lost two or three minor contests which he could well afford, since he was the victor in major ones, although not because a majority—or anything like it—of the smaller countries favored the Russian demand, but because Britain and the United States yielded their influence to Molotov's side and persuaded many to vote against their real desire, if not against their convictions. For Britain and America were determined at all cost that their ideological baby, the United Nations, must not perish.

Minor combats were over Poland and the Argentine Republic. Molotov asked admittance for the Moscow-trained Lublin Poles as representatives of Poland. To have acceded would have broken the Yalta agreement so barefacedly that the request was refused. He then tried to have the Argentine excluded, on the logical ground that she was a Fascist state. Once more he lost, not because his argument was poor, but because Britain was concerned about her meat deliveries and the United States supported the Argentine to placate our string of South American republics.

The Russian victories, however, were outstanding. That country got three votes in the Assembly instead of one, by insisting on and obtaining additional seats for the Ukraine and for Byelorussia. And, much more important yet, by the Constitution of the United Nations as finally adopted, each one of the five permanent members of the Security Council was acknowledged as having a right of absolute veto, not simply in regard to economic sanctions and the use of troops to coerce warlike nations, but even in regard to the peaceful settlement of international disputes.

Potsdam

Two months later in July came still another meeting of the Big Three in Prussian Potsdam—the three big states, that is, not the three big men of whom the world had long been so aware.

Roosevelt was dead. Organizer and architect of victory, F.D.R. would be sadly missed, his dauntless smile no longer seen, his adroit, uncanny political perception no longer discovering a way out of every conceivable impasse, no longer able to turn enemies into fellow workers if not always into friends. His place was taken by our new President, Harry Truman of Missouri, living embodiment of that commonwealth as popularly conceived in these United States.

And before Potsdam was over Winston Churchill, supreme orator of the Anglo-Americas, also departed, victim of a parliamentary revolution, his place taken by Clement Attlee, quiet-spoken chieftain of the British Labour party.

The Potsdam agreement was as follows: it provided for an interim government of Germany until peace treaties were drawn; it divided that country into four zones for administrative purposes (the largest, if we include that part of the Reich temporarily assigned to Poland, to be occupied by Russian troops, the smallest by the French); it subdivided the city of Berlin administratively among the four allies and provided for joint consultations there; it recognized Russian rights to Königsberg and the region around it and Polish administration of eastern Germany as far west as the rivers Oder and Neisse, but subject to later ratification; it promised Russia immediate reparations, giving her the right to dismantle German factories in her own zone, and in addition a goodly share of such reparations as might be extracted from the rest of Germany; it agreed to the forcible removal of German nationals from the Baltic states, the enlarged Poland, and from Czechoslovakia, and their lodgement in the truncated Reich; and it provided for the trial of German warmongers.

Berlin, meanwhile, lay far within the Russian zone, and by inexcusable oversight there was no proviso made at Potsdam for free access to that city for British, French, and American troops needed to garrison their respective zones in the German capital. Those zones were little islands in a Soviet sea and could only be reached by crossing Soviet-held lands. What if Stalin should withhold permission? Like Yalta, Potsdam was a Soviet victory.

In September, 1945, the representatives of Russia, Britain, and America met in London. It was a disappointing conference. At Potsdam the Russians had agreed to enlarge the Big Three—Russia, Britain, and the United States—by the inclusion of France and China. Now they insisted that the two latter countries be excluded from voting on the terms of peace. Britain and the United States stood out for their inclusion. Neither side would yield and the conference adjourned to meet again in December, 1945, at Moscow. This time the Russians were more tractable; they no longer insisted that the Big Three alone determine the peace. The United States also made concessions. MacArthur's rule in Japan was subjected to distant control by a board sitting in Washington on which Russia was to be represented, and in Tokyo an Allied council was set up to advise the American general. It was likewise determined that there would be an atomic energy commission, responsible to the council of the United Nations, and by the month of May, 1946, all preliminaries were to be completed and the peace treaties made ready for general acceptance.

The Allies Drift Apart

In January, 1946, the United Nations was to make its first official debut in London. Would that infant organization grow in strength and power, develop into a genuine agency for world government, or would it slowly atrophy into impotence as was the fate of the League of Nations? That was the open question of the New Year.

The omens were none too propitious since within a year there was evidence of ill-feeling between Britain and America, and much more serious, a rift between Soviet Russia and the West, soon to result in what became known as "the cold war."

Britain, more than any other country in the world, lived by international trade. For her it literally was necessary to export or die. Yet in January, 1946, her trade was but one-third of its prewar level; her foreign investments were for the most part liquidated; her mercantile marine was shattered; and her factories, machine shops, and general economy had been geared for war production rather than for peace. For the winning of the war she had made every sacrifice and during the last stages of it had relied heavily on lend-lease. The conclusion of the war in the Pacific brought that to an abrupt end. No longer was it possible for the British to obtain even powdered eggs from the United States, and they soon found that their food supply instead of becoming more plentiful tended to become less.

AN EARLY SESSION OF THE UNITED NATIONS

Left to Right: Gromyko, Cadogan, Stettinius, Byrnes

Under these circumstances they turned to us, asking for a loan of $4,000,000,000. They were reluctant to do so, for they were a proud people. But there was no other feasible alternative. The Americans, on occasions, generous to a fault, prided themselves on their acumen. What security had Britain to offer; what interest would she pay; what economic concessions would she make?

In regard to these and other questions there was protracted debate and unfortunately some display of temper on both sides. The British reluctantly agreed to pay two per cent interest beginning in 1951, to end certain economic practices which gave them trade advantages in a number of countries tied to the pound sterling, known as the sterling bloc, and to let the loan be reduced to $3,750,000,000. Nevertheless Congress hung fire, could not make up its collective mind, and delayed action on this essential gesture of friendship to our best customer and most important potential ally for many months, deferring ratification of the loan until July, 1946.

Why? One reason was the lurking suspicion, endemic in certain quarters, that our foreign policy was too closely linked with Britain's, that the latter country was far more concerned with oil concessions and her imperial lifeline in the Near East than with problems of world peace, and that as long as we continued to line up with Britain against Russia in international conferences so long would it be impossible to establish friendly relations with the latter.

Another factor operating against the loan was the political turnover in Britain of August, 1945, that brought the British Labor party to power. There had been no Parliamentary election for ten years and one was overdue. Churchill would have postponed it until after Japan was crushed, but with Berlin's occupation the Labor party seceded from the coalition government which had won the war, and Churchill agreed to an early election, expecting, as did most people, that he would be returned to office.

The British electorate, however, reversed its precedent of 1919 and voted so heavily in favor of the Labor party that for the first time in its history it not only had a majority but a very substantial one, returning to the House of Commons 390 out of a total membership of 640. The victorious Laborites, it must be remembered, were pledged to socialism. They proposed to nationalize the Bank of England, mining, transportation, steel, and other industries, a very decidedly leftward swing from the point of view of American public opinion, which looked askance at the use of American capital to buttress even mild socialism abroad.

Palestine, also, was a source of friction between the two great branches of the English-speaking world. Millions of Jews had been slaughtered in Europe during the war, but there still remained approximately 1,500,000, most of whom were homeless and stateless, barely kept alive by British and American aid. Desperately anxious to leave Europe forever, the majority cast a wistful eye on Palestine as a potential Jewish state as well as a Jewish homeland.

The British Labor party, out of office, had been bitterly critical of the policy of the British government whereby immigration to Palestine had been reduced to a mere trickle, but once in office it found itself enmeshed in traditional British foreign policy: to admit more Jews to Palestine would not only antagonize the indigenous Arabs, still a considerable majority there, but also the Arab League, a loose federation of five Moslem states hitherto well disposed toward Britain. There were anti-Jewish riots in Palestine; Jews were killed and Jews began to arm themselves, many of them already having been armed by the British. Most of these armed Jews became embittered by the unwillingness of the British to admit the refugee Jews, and a few of them, active terrorists, slew a prominent British official. The British began to disarm the Palestinian Jews, an act widely protested in the United States where anti-British mass meetings demanded the free entry of dispossessed Jews into the Holy Land.

A joint Anglo-American commission recommended the admission of 100,000 immigrants and at the same time the continuation of the British mandate, a solution satisfactory to neither Jew nor Arab, the former insisting on free immigration and the setting up of a Jewish state, the latter proclaiming resistance by force to those two proposals.

President Truman urged the prompt admission of the 100,000 in the name of humanity, promising financial aid in transporting them to their new home; but Britain insisted that the United States should join with her in offering them protection once there, an implication of American military action which found no favor in Congress.

Meanwhile tension increased in Palestine. The Jews refused to give up their arms and a few considered that they were at war with Britain, fighting for their independence. Bridges were dynamited, British officers kidnapped, concentration camps established for Jewish agitators and for several thousand Jews smuggled into the country. In Congress violent anti-British speeches were delivered and threats made to defeat the British loan.

Much more alarming, however, than any friction between Britain and America was the rift gradually widening between the Soviet Union on the one hand and the Western democracies on the other. To the West it looked as though Russian imperialism was on the march. The unilateral Russian annexations of the Baltic states and the extension of Poland deep into Germany, with new boundaries far to the west of those she had enjoyed at the height of her power in the Middle Ages, aroused the fears of the West. In Poland, Rumania, Bulgaria, and Yugoslavia the Russians had promised free elections, promises they ignored. Despite the fact that China had suffered grievously at the hands of Japan, and Russia not at all, the Big Three ceded the Soviets economic and strategic rights in Manchuria such as Russia had not enjoyed since the Russo-Japanese war of 1904-5. Russia likewise annexed the Kuriles and the southern half of Sakhalin; she demanded and obtained control over the northern half of Korea; and she stripped Manchurian factories of machinery under the guise of reparations from Japan, machinery which rightfully should have gone to China. Nor was this all; she invaded an oil-rich province of Iran, despite promises to the contrary; she set up claims to the Dodecanese Islands, the population of which was Greek; she demanded of Turkey territorial concessions in eastern Asia Minor; she asked for control of one of the Italian colonies; she cruelly and abruptly drove into Germany German nationals forced out of Poland, the Baltic states, and Czechoslovakia, in violation of her agreement that such compulsory migrations be conducted in an orderly manner; she forcibly compelled German Social Democrats in her half of occupied Germany to amalgamate with German Communists by methods quite comparable to those used by the Gestapo; and, as Churchill was to assert later, she drew an iron curtain from Stettin on the Baltic to the head of the Adriatic Sea behind which the correspondents of the Western world were forbidden entry. Because of these facts suspicion of future Russian aims was inevitable.

Seen from the Soviet angle, of course, the world of the capitalistic West would stand watching. Americans were seemingly determined to control Japan entirely as they saw fit; they supported the Kuomintang in its perennial strife with the Chinese Communists; they were as deeply involved in oil concessions, so the Russians thought, in Southern Arabia as was Russia in Northern Iran; and what is more, the American President by his very presence on the same platform with Churchill in March, 1946, at Fulton, Missouri, was held to have endorsed that Briton's plea for Anglo-American unity to confront the menace of Russian ideology. As for the British, how could they legitimately complain of Russian garrisons in the Balkans while they kept an army in Greece, ruled Palestine with an iron hand, and, it was darkly hinted, retained Polish forces in Italy in British uniforms, potential mercenary troops for future wars?

Nearly a year after Hiroshima and no action taken in regard to the Danube Valley, the Russians refusing all overtures opening it to world trade. No action yet in regard to Austria, that country still occupied by British, American, and Russian armies. No action yet in regard to Europe's major problem—Germany. As long as that country remained divided into four distinct zones with four distinct administrations, Russian, British, French, and American, its political future was unsettled, its economic life stifled. The Russians accused the British of keeping intact large units of the former Wehrmacht under the guise of labor battalions but really for the purpose of using them at some future day against Moscow. The British accused the Russians of dumping down in the British zone thousands of Germans who would have to be fed by Britain. The French accused the British of utilizing the slowly recovering Ruhr mines for the rehabilitation of German industry rather than for supplying France with needed coal. The Americans in their southern zone, like the British to the north, were confronted with well-nigh insuperable problems, among which bulked large the feeding of huge numbers of dispossessed persons flocking in from Russian-occupied Germany and Poland.

And as for the atomic bomb, no action yet! The Americans were prepared to share its secrets, provided that ironclad agreements were first ratified providing for international inspection and control. To this Russia would be no means agree. She demanded first that all atomic bombs be destroyed and after that an international treaty be drawn, guaranteeing that no more bombs be manufactured. The fulfillment of the treaty would depend on the word of the signatory alone.

Only on relatively minor issues did international agreement prove possible. In July, 1946, an international peace conference, to which twenty-one nations were invited, was held in Paris, and it did, after months of labor, hammer out five peace treaties: with Bulgaria, Rumania, Hungary, Finland, and Italy. Bulgaria, owing to Russian friendship, got off very lightly, being assessed but a few million dollars payable to Yugoslavia and Greece. Rumania formally ceded Bukovina and Bessarabia to Russia and agreed to pay that country $300,000,000 in reparations. Hungary ceded minor regions to Rumania and Czechoslovakia and agreed to pay $300,000,000, mostly to Russia. Harsher treatment was accorded Finland. Not only did Russia extract $300,000,000 from that small country but received in addition the northern province of Petsamo (thus making the Russian and the Norwegian boundaries coterminous), and most of the Karelian peninsula in southern Finland with its large population, including the city of Viborg.

Of the five treaties that with Italy was the only one of much importance. The terms were these: Russia yielded all claims to the Dodecanese and to the Italian colonies; she agreed to limit her reparation bill from Italy to $100,000,000, an estimate of one-twentieth the damage done in invaded Russia by Italian soldiers; France won certain minor rectifications along the Franco-Italian frontier; Italy retained South Tyrol, to which she was not entitled, and almost lost Trieste, which should have gone to her—this owing to Russian insistence that Trieste at the head of the Adriatic go to Yugoslavia. Britain and the United States resisted that Russian demand; and Trieste was placed under international control, a compromise agreeable to no one, unless possibly France who proposed it. Final settlement of colonial questions in Africa was postponed.

The Star of Israel

Despite these treaties, shadows of approaching doom gathered headway almost everywhere in Asia and in Europe. Never perhaps in recorded history had there been at any one single time such a widespread area of social and political upheaval. Italy, France, and to a lesser degree Britain faced economic hardships of the first magnitude; Germany, bisected by the Russian iron curtain, lived from hand to mouth, the western half dependent in large measure on food imported from America; Czechoslovakia, Poland, Hungary, and the Balkan countries, succumbing in various degrees and at various rates of speed to communist pressure, were full of turmoil and dissension; the Arab lands of western Asia could not unite even for the purpose of knifing Israel during its birth pangs; India, freed from the British raj, was split in twain by religious fanaticism and intermittent bloodletting; unhappy Chinese Nationalists and Communists were at each other's throats; and in the islands of the South Seas the feeble Republic of Indonesia strove to become viable in a world semiparalyzed with torpor, hunger, and despair.

About the only ray of sunshine in the storm-tossed Eastern Hemisphere shone from the star of Israel in Vermont-sized, sterile Palestine, where in a short time indomitable courage, pertinacity, and vigor made clear what human brain and brawn might do.

In 1947, the United Nations decreed that Palestine be partitioned. Their decision was ignored by Jew and Arab, and Britain, weary of her thankless task, renounced her mandate and withdrew her garrison the following spring. Forthwith the Jews, in quick defiance of the United Nations, proclaimed the new state of Israel.

That act looked like madness. The Jews were outnumbered two to one in Palestine by the Arabs, and on the borders of that land to the north, east, and south were the armies of the Arab League, Lebanon, Syria, Iraq, Transjordan, and Egypt. The Jews were widely scattered. The majority were huddled on the long and pitifully narrow coastal plain, while the hill towns to the east were held by the Arabs. A large minority dwelt in isolated colonies surrounded by a sea of Arabs—north near Lake Galilee, far south in the windswept Negeb, and in the Jewish quarter of Jerusalem. What chance Israel? Little wonder "it was predicted that when King Farouk's Egyptian army marched the 650,000 Jews who occupied the coastal plain would be hurled into the sea." [1]

The Jews, however, with their backs to the sea, fought like wildcats. The Arabs only pretended to fight. Speedily the Israelis, as they choose to be called, were in possession of all Galilee. They soon opened a wide corridor from Tel Aviv to Jerusalem, occupying the greater part of that city; they drove the boastful Egyptians far to the south, and they struck

[1] K. W. Bilby, *New Star in the Near East*, p. 8.

The Inauguration of Chaim Weizmann as First President of Israel through the Negeb all the way to the Red Sea, thus making possible a new port for Israel and cutting off Jordan from Egypt.

Hailed as a miracle, it was not exactly one. Bad blood among the members of the Arab League accounted in part for the Israeli triumph. The Hasamite (heretical) kingdom of Jordan east of the Dead Sea and the Jordan River had a wily ruler, Abdullah, suspected by the other Arab lands of treachery and of being willing to sell out his fellow league members to further his ambition to become King of Palestine. Then, too, the Israeli were the better armed; from America came money to buy arms and from Czechoslovakia came most of the war matériel which it bought.

Nevertheless the Israeli victory was astonishing evidence that men fresh from the ghettos and concentration camps of Europe, who had never held a gun in their hands, could fight—and women too, for the Israeli forces of from 25,000 to 40,000 contained women in large numbers.

But it was not the victory in the field that made the birth of Israel (admitted to the United Nations as the fifty-ninth member in May, 1949) so noteworthy as it was the ordered discipline and self-sacrificing cohesiveness of the Israeli people under their Prime Minister, Ben-Gurion. Pipe lines were laid for irrigation across the desert Negeb, bedraggled Arab villages turned almost overnight into prosperous communities, orange groves sprung up in place of sand dunes. The hearty welcome given to Jews of every age, nationality, class, and degree of infirmity from all over the known world (many of them too weak and too old ever to be capable of earning their own sustenance) and the vigorous give-and-take of parliamentary debate in the Knesset, Israeli's Parliament: these were encouraging proofs of what democracy, energy, and good will can accomplish.

Good will, unfortunately, for Jews but not for Arabs, some 800,000 in number, exiles from their old home, without hope and for the most part without shelter or sufficient food, eking out a miserable existence on the borders of Israel. Yet in that country, it must be remembered, in three short years the population had shot up from 650,000 to over 1,000,000, and the immigrants were still arriving at the rate of from 15,000 to 16,000 a month. The resources of the Israeli were stretched to the limit. That is one reason why they refuse to accept more than 100,000 of the displaced Arabs.

The Peoples Democracies

Slowly but with ever increasing momentum the greater part of the world gravitated into two antagonistic camps, one under the somewhat hesitant leadership of the United States, the other under the domination of Soviet Russia. Well within the Russian camp were those countries called, in the well-known upside-down logic of Soviet semantics, "Peoples

Democracies." They were: Albania, Yugoslavia, Bulgaria, Rumania, Poland, Czechoslovakia, Hungary, North Korea, and somewhat later China.

These Peoples Democracies, or Russian satellites, were not fully developed communist states like Russia, nor were their political and economic systems completely uniform. The one common denominator which they all had with one another and with Russia was that they were all police states in which minority groups of disciplined communists seized power by force and violence, intimidating, imprisoning, and sometimes torturing all whom they suspected of opposing their tyrannical will.

The process by which this was brought about was fourfold: first came infiltration, communists posing as simply desirous of forming Popular Front governments; second, the securing of certain key posts in the government, such as minister of justice, and minister of the interior, to whom generally was entrusted the police power; third, an election in which there would be but one ticket, that of the Popular Front; and finally, the expelling from office of all non-communist officials, thus creating a monolithic communist regime.

Of these Peoples Democracies in Eastern Europe four deserve special mention: Poland, to show how expediency triumphed over justice at Yalta; Czechoslovakia, because the brutal communist coup d'état by which she lost her freedom should have demonstrated long before the Korean War that Communists would stop at nothing to gain their objective; Hungary, as an illustration of how communism can vary from place to place in choice of methods; and Yugoslavia, as proof that Russian threats sometimes backfire.

At its onset the Second World War was fought by the West on behalf of Polish independence. The Polish government in exile was recognized by Britain and the United States as an ally, and a Polish army assembled by it, and under its orders, fought bravely in North Africa and in Italy. Nevertheless both Roosevelt and Churchill turned their back on the London Poles. Victorious Russia placed in authority in Poland a committee of Communist Poles and Russian stooges. Russia, Britain, and the United States then agreed at Yalta that Poland was to be governed by a provisional government composed of the Russian-backed Lublin Poles, with the addition of a number of democratic and non-Communist Poles, thus broadening the provisional government so that all parties would be represented in it until democratic elections could be held.

Soon it happened that Russia vetoed the appointment of men from the government-in-exile in London, even that of Mikolajczyk, Prime Minister. Followed then the mysterious disappearance in Sovietland of sixteen prominent non-Communist Poles invited to Moscow to talk over plans for the enlarged provisional government.

At Yalta it was also promised that there would be free elections. To guarantee their freedom some supervision was essential. None was permitted. At Yalta, Molotov assured Roosevelt and Churchill that the elections would be held in a few months. They were postponed a year and a half by the new Polish government, the time set being midwinter, 1947, when, owing to inclement weather and impassable roads, thousands of peasants could not vote. The elections were a farce. Mikolajczyk, head of the Peasant's Party, largest in prewar Poland, was pressured to join the so-called Popular Front set up by the Communists but refused. The pro-Communist provisional government then saw to it that his followers were refused UNRRA relief, that they were dismissed from all government jobs, that they were imprisoned on absurd charges, that neither radio time nor newspaper space was afforded them, that government agents alone corrected the ballots.

Thus the Popular Front won the election, and almost instantly shed its sheep's clothing and transformed itself into a purely Communist regime, recognized now as the government of Poland by Britain and the United States. The latter, against the earnest solicitation of the American ambassador, granted a $70,000,000 credit to the Communist Poles.

In Czechoslovakia the story was somewhat different. The Czechs, the only truly democratic people in Eastern Europe, believed Russia their friend. It was not Russia but England and France that sold them down the river at Munich and there had been no instance in the past of bad faith on the part of the Russians. Then, too, it was the Red army that liberated Prague in 1945 from the hated Germans. True, General Patton with his tank-men could have done it sooner had his army not been halted, a fact which we may well regret now.

Czechoslovakia was a democracy from its birth after World War I until February, 1948, when within one month it became a Moscow satellite. The story runs as follows: in Czechoslovakia there were several political parties, that of the Communists in 1947 being the largest. The government was a coalition and Beneš had appointed a Communist to head the police. The cabinet voted to reprimand that latter official for filling his ranks with Communists. He refused to heed their warning. Several members of the cabinet resigned in protest. Instantly armed Communists seized the party headquarters of the resigning ministers, purged the parliament of non-Communist deputies, purged the press, purged the university, purged even the numerous athletic associations of anti-Communist critics. Czechoslovakia became a police state and a Peoples Democracy at one and the same time that unhappy spring of 1948, as a new constitution based on that of Russia was adopted and an election was held in which the Czechs were presented with a list of hand-picked delegates to their parliament, the only ones for whom they could vote.

In Hungary, again, procedure differed. In that country a radical agrarian party, that of the Small Landowners, had carried the elections in

1945, Communists gaining but seventeen per cent of the votes. From the Communist point of view peasant proprietorship was anathema and it would never do to have socialistic reforms carried out by democratic parliament. To get rid of Nagy, Prime Minister, was their first aim, and this they succeeded in doing by economic threats in regard to reparations and by military threats from the occupying Red army. Nagy in Switzerland hesitated to return to Budapest. At the same time he also feared for the safety of his small son in that city. A bargain was struck: the boy was delivered to the father and the latter resigned.

The Communists now persuaded parliament to expel some twenty members. The purged parliament quietly submitted, and another Peoples Republic was born. It ran head on into a fight with the Roman Catholic Church. The head of the Catholic hierarchy in Hungary, Cardinal Mindszenty, fought vigorously for the retention of religious education and the property rights of monastic orders. He was arrested and tried for high treason in 1949 with the results quite typical of such trials behind the iron curtain—in other words, the Cardinal pleaded guilty and confessed that he had plotted against the state. There can be little doubt but that his confession was forced from him by torture of one kind or another. He was sentenced to life imprisonment. Not quite so fortunate was Rajk, Nagy's successor as prime minister. Although a Communist he indulged in that dangerous pastime of having ideas of his own. Rajk, tried as an agent of Western imperialism, was promptly executed the same year.

One Peoples Republic, that of Yugoslavia, revolted against the rule of the Kremlin. For a good two years after Potsdam, Yugoslavia was at one with the Soviet Union in both ideology and practice. Mammoth portraits of Stalin the Great hung side by side with those of Tito, the Yugoslav dictator, and the harsh and brutal treatment accorded to all nonconformists in the Peoples Democracies was as pronounced in Yugoslavia as elsewhere behind the iron curtain. The Yugoslavs, however, were a proud people. From their point of view Bulgars, Rumanians, Albanians, and Poles might feel they owed their liberation to the Red army if they wanted to. Not so the Yugoslavs! Never throughout the war had they bent their knee to the German invader, who already was in swift retreat by the time the Russians came. Yugoslavs regarded Stalin with awe as head of the Soviet family; but Tito was quite on a par with the Russian in their esteem and far closer to their hearts as their own Yugoslav deliverer. Therefore, although willing to join the Cominform and to uphold the doctrines of Marx-Leninism, the Yugoslavs would do so as Russia's ally, not as a Russian satellite.

There was no open break with Moscow until 1948, for Marshal Tito needed Russian help in his demands for Trieste and Carinthia which he hoped to detach from Austria, but he had nevertheless been irritated by increasing Soviet pressure similar to that used in Bulgaria and Rumania.

This took the form primarily of Russian interference with Tito's control of his own army, and a demand that Yugoslavia submit her economy to Russian supervision and provide raw materials in return for manufactured goods to be delivered from behind the iron curtain.

Tito balked: he drove out of his country Russian officers who dared interfere with his army; he would brook no interruption of his own five-year plan to make Yugoslavia economically independent. The result was a complete break with Moscow and her satellites. Anti-Tito Soviet agents swarmed into Yugoslavia and were arrested and imprisoned by the proud Tito. Poland and Czechoslovakia now cancelled their commercial treaties with Yugoslavia. Hungarian, Rumanian, Bulgarian, and Albanian armies gathered on her borders. Tito vied now with British and American imperialism as a favorite object of Pravda's vituperation, and Titoism became a deep, dark heresy.

Tito breathed defiance. He built up his army half a million strong; purged it of all disaffected pro-Soviet officers; proclaimed that he, not Stalin, wore the true Marx-Lenin mantle; held Stalin a Russian nationalist, intent on conquering her small neighbor. Tito's military chances seemed none too good, and his likelihood of economic survival slim. His country, about the size of Oregon, had mineral wealth in abundance, but with trade behind the iron curtain prohibited and with no credits with the capitalistic West how was he to survive? Furthermore, fierce and protracted guerrilla war waged against the German invader had ruined cities, bridges, railways.

And so Marshal Tito, still a convinced Communist, turned west for aid. He showed his *bona fides* by evicting Greek Communist bands from his country and so gained commercial credits from England and America; he supported the United Nations in the Korean war as far as he dared, and so American money, earmarked for Marshall aid, was diverted toward Yugoslavia. It came just in time. A crop failure in Yugoslavia of mammoth proportions in 1950 threatened. But as this happened at the very end of that year the American Congress voted a free gift of $37,500,000. If war broke between Russia and the United States, Tito at least might be depended on to immobilize many a Russian division.

Shortly after the conclusion of the war it looked as though two other countries in Eastern Europe might become Peoples Democracies, Greece and Turkey. In Greece, civil war followed in the wake of the retreating Germans. The National Liberation Front (EAM), Greek irregulars, detested the absentee King and refused to surrender their arms to the small British army in Greece representing him. The EAM, radical from the outset, became more and more communist as time passed, and between it, the British army, and those Greeks loyal to the King a sporadic war followed. Greek politics, at no time easy to follow, were in this instance extraordinarily complicated. Unsavory scandals had brought the prestige of the official Greek government, never at a high level, to one even lower. The British, exhausted nervously and financially from the long bitter war, now found themselves embroiled in a nasty minute one, extremely unpopular in England. In 1946, an Allied commission of French, American, and British observers supervised a Greek election. It gave a clear conservative majority; but the EAM, boycotting the election, claimed that it did not represent a majority of the Greek people, a claim disavowed by the neutral observers who asserted that not more than fifteen per cent of the registered voters kept away from the polls. Another plebiscite taken shortly afterwards invited the King to return to Greece. He was an unpopular ruler but still a symbol of anti-Communism. The EAM refused to acknowledge his authority, took to the hills, and continued to fight.

In March, 1947, a bankrupt and shaky Greek government appealed to President Truman for succor. The British, tired of the weary Titan role, intimated they were going to withdraw from Greece altogether. Action on the part of the United Nations proved impossible because of the Russian veto. Whereupon the United States proved to all the world that it had no intention of following the precedent of 1920 and withdrawing into its own shell. By what became known as the Truman Doctrine, Congress voted $400,000,000 for Greek rehabilitation and included Turkey as well as a recipient of American aid.

Most of the money went to Greece. It was spent in building up and equipping the Greek army, bolstering the feeble Greek economy, repairing roads and bridges, digging canals, making war-racked Greece viable. A handful of American officers advised the Greek soldiers on how best to fight the Communist guerrillas; a handful of American civilians, by keeping a tight grip on the expenditure of funds and by threats of withdrawing them altogether, reduced corruption in the Greek government and compelled it to lay heavier taxes on wealthy Greek civilians.

For two years it proved well-nigh impossible to keep Greeks away from one another's throats. Guerrillas burned villages, destroyed crops, terrorized the countryside, kidnapped young boys and took them to neighboring Yugoslavia for indoctrination into Communism. The Greek government rounded up groups of Communists, or suspected Communists, and slew them more or less off hand with but slight attention to judicial decorum. Ultimately, however, when Tito closed his borders to hunted guerrilla bands, it proved possible to wipe them out and by 1950 the semblance of order was restored.

Turkey needed less money and got less, since she had preserved an uneasy neutrality during the war to the last possible moment before declaring for the Allies. But Turkish economy had been rudely undermined during the long conflict, and Russia, once Potsdam was over, made threatening demands for a share in policing the Straits. Therefore, in accordance with the Truman Doctrine of fending off Russian aggression in the Middle East, military and naval equipment was sent by the United States, together with a military commission to help organize Turkish defense.

Western Europe

Of the three major powers in Western Europe—Britain, France, and Italy—only the first managed to avoid internal schism and to keep clear of Communist infiltration. Parliamentary elections in 1945 had put the Labor party firmly in the saddle; but that party had had many a bitter experience with Communists during the period between the two World Wars, and although committed to democratic socialism the right-wing socialists in the British cabinet held a firm grip on governmental policies. The Labor party, busily engaged in nationalizing banks, mines, and railways, regarded with disdain any suggestion that capitalism must be overthrown with force. They were already doing this by sheer weight of votes. Communists in Britain there were; but they buzzed around the fringe of the Labor party and presented no imminent threat.

The British government, to be sure, was confronted with economic problems almost unsolvable. Three and a half million houses had been damaged or destroyed by German bombs, half of Britain's mercantile marine had been sunk by German submarines, export trade had declined nearly a third, and the war debt exceeded £22,000,000,000. Under circumstances such as these how could Britain extend her social services at home, lengthen the age for leaving school, provide free medical care for every citizen, and continue to play an important role in international affairs, supported by an army and a navy?

Nevertheless these things were accomplished, primarily by the highest taxes levied anywhere in the world, and by retaining strict controls over food, clothes, and housing, reducing the standard of living of the upper and middle class, raising that of working folk; and also by the timely assistance of the United States not only by the loan of $2,750,000,000 granted in 1946 but by a large share of the Marshall aid money (known as the ERP, the European Relief Program). For five years after the war everything was in short supply in Britain, more so in fact than during the war years. Nevertheless in the Parliamentary elections of 1950, which the Labor party won by the narrowest of margins, not a single Communist was elected to the House of Commons, even Battersea and the Red Clyde turning their back on Moscow propaganda.

In comparison with Britain, confusion, disillusionment, and despair were widespread in both France and Italy after the war, and to a certain extent still are, despite American intervention (Marshall aid) bringing with it a real degree of economic recovery, and assurance of future military assistance.

The aftermath of the war left France not simply wrecked economically but thoroughly confused, discouraged, and disunited. France, indeed, seemed split three ways, as during the period between the two World Wars: a Communist France, a Social Democratic France, and a relatively conservative France, the latter group attracting more votes than either of the other two but lacking in leadership, unless of course De Gaulle be considered its leader.

That patriotic, Catholic, authoritarian general, accused by his critics as semifascist, was not content with any of the three parties above mentioned. He wanted to stand above party and to that end launched his *Reassemblement du Peuple Français* (Reunion of the French People), calling for a strong France under a strong leader—De Gaulle by implication, since its principal slogan was "De Gaulle to power."

It was difficult to say just where France stood. Cabinets rose and fell with even more than usual French rapidity. Prime ministers shifted back and forth, and in general what was known as "The Third Force," a rather loose combination of Socialist groups in collaboration with the MRP, (*Mouvement Republicain Populaire*), a Roman Catholic party, mildly liberal and opposed to both De Gaulle and to the Communists, retained an uneasy balance of power. Inflation, meanwhile, ran ragged through France; expenditures continued to exceed income; strikes, not all Communist inspired, were numerous; and not until Marshall aid money began pouring into France, 1948-51, was there any indication of economic and industrial recovery.

In Italy the picture was somewhat clearer despite the fact that Italy had suffered far more from the ravages of war than had France. This was due to three factors; the able leadership of De Gasperi, most adroit of all postwar statesmen; the active intervention of the Catholic Church on his behalf; and the vigorous and sustained economic aid reaching Italy from the United States.

The election to the Constituent Assembly to provide a constitution for the new Italian republic showed the Christian Democrats under the Catholic-inspired De Gasperi well in the lead with 207 deputies elected. Communist and Socialist united however, slightly overtopped them in number, and Italian Socialists were decidedly less vigorously opposed to communism than their Social Democratic counterparts in France and Britain.

In 1948 came the first election under the new constitution. It was contested with great bitterness and accompanied by riots which, after the Italian fashion, were more noisy than bloodthirsty. The Catholic Church now entered the fray, threatening excommunication to all who professed communism. The United States having already paid for the greater part of UNRRA relief given Italy, some $450,000,000 for food, now promised further assistance. Italian-born citizens in America were asked to write relatives in Italy counselling against Communists. The U.S. government presented Italy with twenty-nine ships as a token of regard, and both the United States and Britain placed themselves on record as favoring the return of Trieste to Italy.

On the surface the results of the election were a blow to communism. De Gasperi and his Christian Democrats now had a majority over all though a slight one. Nevertheless the Communists polled within a fraction of as many votes as they did in 1946, and were now with 132 seats in parliament the second largest party. It was the Socialists who lost this election rather than the Communists, their deputies being reduced to 82 and badly split at that between right- and left-wing factions. De Gasperi had need for all possible wisdom and acuteness. In his parliament the Communist minority staged nerve-wracking demonstrations; in the countryside the splitting up of the big estates, promised the peasantry, proceeded but at a snail's pace. Italy was a far poorer country than her neighbor, but unlike France had a rapidly increasing population.

Germany

Germany after Potsdam lay prostrate. Four powers—Britain, France, the United States, and Russia—were in complete control. They could agree upon but one thing: prominent Nazi leaders should be tried for crimes against humanity and for plotting war. Twenty-two were brought to trial; three were acquitted; four were sentenced to prison for terms ranging from ten years to life; and twelve received the death penalty. The defendants did plot war; they also were responsible for revolting acts of inhuman cruelty. But did the victors act wisely in this *ex post facto* procedure of defining crimes after and not before the acts perpetrated had been committed? To many a good lawyer it seemed a dubious procedure to invoke the hazy Kellogg-Briand peace pacts as a precedent. Furthermore, one of the judges was a Russian, and it was a known fact that the Russians had murdered some 1,500 Polish officers and men in 1943. The court sternly refused to permit any evidence of this mass murder to be introduced into court—quite naturally, since a Russian judge sat on the bench.

Concerning practically all other matters it proved impossible to agree. The Russians demanded harsher treatment of the enemy than the British and Americans would permit. The Americans brought more Nazis to trial than did the British and objected vigorously to Britain employing Nazis in operating the Ruhr mines. In fact we were so enthusiastic about our denazification program that we jailed little Nazis in droves and so well-nigh crippled German elementary education, for practically all German teachers had been compelled, at least outwardly, to public support of Nazi ideology. Meanwhile the Russians ripped from their zones almost everything moveable, demanded the delivery of more and more machinery from West Germany as reparations due Russia under the Potsdam agreement. They refused admittance of their former allies to their zone, refused to make any audit of reparations they had taken from it, refused to give any accounting of the German prisoners of war, and so maltreated the civilian population in their zone and in the Baltic states that a steady stream of exiles from the east added so to the overcrowded western zones that West Germany had as large a population as all of Germany before the war.

Slowly the four former allies drifted into two camps: France, Britain, and America more or less in harmony in one; unyielding and suspicious Russia in the other, objecting to any German peace treaty except on its own terms, equally recalcitrant as regards the revival of German trade and industry.

In the west by 1946, free elections were held to provide for local self-government, and in them the Communist vote averaged about 10 per cent. By the same year elections were held in East Germany, but there Social Democrats were forced to amalgamate with the Communists forming the S.E.D. (Social Unity Party) thus making a farce of political freedom. The Allied Control Council sitting in Berlin was completely stymied by Russian obstruction in all that concerned economic reorganization. Whereupon it happened that the Americans and the British joined their two zones into one in matters economic (Bizonia), a union which the French later joined.

Economic unity necessitated a common currency, and since Russia would not coöperate in any agreement regulating paper money in circulation, the three Western powers printed their own paper money, which speedily became worth far more than that printed by the Russians. As a result of this currency debate the Russians started a blockade of all trains and trucks entering Berlin from the west. But air at least was free, and in 1948 for month after month the citizens of West Berlin, and the French, British, and American troops stationed there, received by air lift not simply the food they ate but also the coal essential for heating and lighting. It proved enormously expensive but it was a boon to the airplane industry in both Britain and America. Possibly that was the reason why Russia dropped her blockade as speedily as she began it.

The split between East and West Germany widened. In 1949 in the west the Länder (the local governments) sent representatives to Bonn to draw up a constitution for a Federal German Republic, so constituted that the Eastern German Länder might later adhere to it. As they did this a Russian-sponsored German state was set up in East Germany.

Elections were now in order, both west and east. In the Bonn elections the Christian Democrats headed the polls with a slight lead over the Social Democrats and were able to organize a majority government by combining their strength with a few minority groups. Out of 432 deputies in the Bonn parliament the Communists elected but 15. The East German elections ran true to form. One voted S.E.D. or else. Many did not vote at all.

Austria meanwhile like Germany was divided into four zones. The course of events, however, ran in smoother channels than in Germany. Time after time it seemed possible that Austria might be confirmed in her independence and that all occupation troops might be withdrawn. Always, however, there stood in the way Russian insistence that Austrian property appropriated by the Nazis should be regarded as reparations due from Germany. Compromise on this point proved impossible.

Western Upswing

Beginning in the summer of 1947 the international skies lightened in one respect—economic recovery. The impetus for this came from the United States where Secretary of State Marshall suggested extensive American assistance for all Europe, both east and west. In one respect this was nothing new. UNRRA, mostly American financed, had already fed millions on both sides of the iron curtain, but UNRRA had at best been but an emergency measure. This time it was suggested that America would grant money on a very large scale, not just for food but to purchase machinery, set up power plants, build factories, and reinvigorate the economic life of the entire continent.

The proposal was scornfully rejected by Russia and her satellites, despite many a wistful glance westward on the part of industrial Czechoslovakia. But the other countries went ahead with implementing the plan with the exception of Franco Spain which was not invited to participate. A bill of particulars was drawn up by sixteen nations at Paris. Their total needs for four years they estimated at $22,440,000,000, a figure reduced by President Truman in presenting the plan to Congress to $17,000,000,000. The latter accepted the plan in principle but did not commit this country to any final figure. Congress said the money should be voted in allotments and a preliminary appropriation for fifteen months of $6,800,000,000 was voted, the spending to be under the directions of an American administrator, Europe coöperating by lowering tariffs between European states and by currency stabilization. This Marshall Plan proved unquestionably a success to all countries participating in it, the United States included. Everywhere it was in operation the standard of living was higher in 1950 than in 1947. The Russians called the plan American imperialism. That it reduced Communist influence in France and Italy and western Germany cannot be doubted.

As in economics so too in political coöperation the West began to draw together. In consequence of a widespread demand a "Council of Europe" opened its doors at Strasbourg. Ten countries participated, Italy, France, and Britain having 18 delegates each in the descending scale to Luxembourg with 3. The powers of the Council were strictly limited, the delegates for the most part but puppets of their home governments.

Italy and a few other countries sought vigorously to enlarge the scope of this pan-European council but without much success.

More important by far than the Council of Europe was the signing at Washington in 1949 of an Atlantic Defense Pact. It was in the nature of an enlarged Western Union, since in addition to the members of that Union now were added Iceland, Denmark, Norway, Canada, Italy, Portugal, and the United States, all pledged to go to war should their forces be attacked in Europe, North Africa, or on the Atlantic. How they would fight, however, and whether they would combine their forces under a joint commander or not were questions left for future negotiation.

Asiatic Problems

As far as all surface indications went the entire structure of Japanese society, political, economic, educational, and cultural, was revolutionized during the five years subsequent to Japan's surrender. In theory Japan was put under a Far Eastern Commission meeting in Washington, consisting of representatives of the eleven countries which declared war on Japan; in practice her destiny was determined by SCAP, another name for Supreme Commander Allied Powers, otherwise our own General of the Army, Douglas MacArthur. Most Japanese seemingly were greatly pleased with the reforms dictated by that American officer. The country was said to have gone democratic almost overnight, Hirohito merely retaining his title of Emperor as titular head of a people who, under a brand-new democratic constitution, were supposed to govern themselves. This meant they followed rather closely MacArthur's advice. Big business in Japan as represented by financial magnates of the old regime was dissolved, land reform inaugurated, the great estates broken up, peasant proprietorship established, shintoism discouraged in religion, education made over so that children might be indoctrinated with democratic theories of life.

Elsewhere in Asia the very ease with which the Japanese during World War II flung down the flimsy structure of Dutch rule in the East Indies made it forever impossible to restore it; in Burma and India the prestige of the British had been so jolted by years of war that even final victory could not bring it back; and in China, Chiang Kai-shek's regime, honeycombed with corruption, accused of capitalism and Western orientation, fell with a thud heard throughout all Asia as Chinese Communists crashed through to victory in 1949.

World War II commenced with India heavily in debt to Britain; it concluded with Britain heavily in debt to India, for the cost of defending India had not been paid by that country but by the British treasury. The British possessed neither the will nor the power to govern India any more. Nothing stood in the way of complete independence except the problem of finding some agency to which the government of India could be entrusted. And so, in 1946, the British sought desperately for some kind of compromise between Moslem and Hindu factions so that a stable government might succeed them.

Ever fertile in political expedients the British proposed a curious three-tiered constitution. The idea was as follows: tier A would be a central government for all of India with very limited powers; tier B would consist of such regional groupings as the various provinces might choose to make; tier C would be the individual provinces and the native states. Little was done to implement this proposed compromise. A constitutional convention was elected but the Moslems boycotted it; they stood out for Pakistan—entire separation from India of the Moslem peoples. Britain decided she could do no more, and in 1947 announced that by June 1, 1948, she would quit India altogether, no matter what the situation might be by that date.

Reaction in India to this announcement was immediate. Rather than risk war, the Indian Congress (Hindu-controlled) agreed to Pakistan, a separate Moslem state, but located in two different regions where there was a Moslem majority, one in the northwest, the other in the northeast. Before the year closed two new dominions were added to the Commonwealth (the adjective British being deleted from it). Pakistan established its capital at Karachi; India, its capital at New Delhi.

Misery and bloodshed followed as Hindus migrated from Pakistan to India and as Moslems migrated from India to Pakistan. Some 4,000,000 people lost their old homes and journeyed to strange lands where no new homes were to be had; very bloody communal riots took heavy toll of human life, and rival armed forces knifed one another in Kashmir, a province claimed both by India and Pakistan. None could dispute but that the population of Kashmir as a whole was Moslem. On the other hand certain sections had a Hindu majority, and over all Kashmir ruled an hereditary Hindu prince. It did not prove easy to enforce an effective cease-fire among hillsmen. Pakistan offered to let the impasse be settled by the collective action of the Commonwealth premiers, an offer rejected by Prime Minister Nehru in January, 1951.

Burma, meanwhile, abandoning all ties with Britain, preferred to go it alone and declared its independence. Ceylon chose dominion status. And so it happened that by the middle of the twentieth century nothing remained of British imperial rule in central and eastern Asia except a tenuous hold on the Federated Malay States and Singapore, and the equally tenuous hold on Hong Kong off the Chinese coast.

Even more complete than the ending of British imperialism in Asia was the death of Dutch imperialism in the East Indies. After the defeat of Japan in 1945 sporadic and indecisive fighting took place there between the Dutch and the native Indonesians on the one hand, and between pro-Communist Indonesians and those opposed to communism on the other. The Dutch did not surrender their control without a token fight and

Jawaharlal Nehru
Disciple of Gandhi and Prime Minister
of the Dominion of India

three times the Council of the United Nations tried to secure a cease-fire agreement between the Dutch and Indonesian republicans. Finally in 1950 Indonesia was recognized as an independent country.

The withdrawal of the Japanese from China marked the commencement of civil war there in deadly earnest. For three years, 1946-48, it raged fiercely, first Nationalist China (Chiang and the Kuomintang), then Communist China having the upper hand. Beneath the surface, however, a steady deterioration of the morale of the Chinese Nationalist party was taking place while that of Mao and his Communists grew stronger.

The United States government, with the best of intentions, intervened between the contestants and lost the good will of both. We tried to force the Nationalists to coöperate with the Communists and to inaugurate reforms—a policy which angered the Nationalists. We gave arms and ammunition to the Nationalists—a policy which angered the Communists, who asserted that our frequent ultimatums to Chiang were meaningless. Corruption, incompetence, wildcat inflation, and ruinous taxation sapped the will of the Nationalists to resist. Nineteen-hundred and forty-nine, and the collapse came. The Communists crossed the Yangtse and Chiang changed his capital from Nanking to Canton; the Communists advanced south and Chiang changed to Chungking; the Communists drove west and Chiang flew to Taiwan (Formosa) where such few troops as remained loyal to him had already gathered. October, 1949, at Peking the Peoples Republic of China was founded, with Mao at its head—as Chairman of the Peoples Revolutionary Committee, the same Mao who had led the long march of the Chinese Communists in the early thirties from southeast China to the semi-barren northwest, Chiang's armies in close pursuit. Now the tables were reversed.

Mao's victory gave rise to a host of new problems. China, together with England, France, Russia, and the United States, was one of the permanent members of the Council of the United Nations. Somewhat over forty vetoes of Soviet Russia had already done much to retard the usefulness of the UN, and if the vote of Communist China were added to that of the Soviets, it is evident that Stalin's power to hold up the pressing demand for world government would be strengthened. Nevertheless Mao's government was the *de facto* government of China, and in accordance with international practice, American as well as European, it should receive recognition. Logically it followed then that Nationalist China should lose her seat in the Council and that Communist China should inherit it.

Almost immediately England, India, and a number of other countries recognized Mao's China. American recognition of Mao's government hung fire. What should we do? The answer came on June 26, 1950, when the Communist government of North Korea flung its troops across the 38th parallel.

Chapter 21

KOREAN WAR AND AFTERMATH

KOREA, AN INDEPENDENT country before the Russo-Japanese War of 1904-5, fell under Japanese control, and a few years later was officially annexed to Japan. At Potsdam, Korea was bisected at the 38th parallel, to be occupied north of that line by the Russian army, to the south by the American, until such time as Korea might become a self-governing democratic country.

Within a year it was painfully evident that there could be no agreement as to how this was to be done. In the north the Russians promptly set up a Peoples Democracy on the customary lines, armed the Koreans in their zone heavily, closed the frontier to all non-Communist visitors. In the south the Americans encouraged free democratic elections, and as a result there sprang up a plethora of political parties which called for a convention of all Korean factions to establish a constitution for the whole of Korea. North Korea sent no delegates but the South Koreans went ahead and inaugurated a government of their own. A committee of the United Nations authorized to investigate the situation was refused admission to North Korea, and in the meantime the United States Army evacuated South Korea, leaving behind a few score of military personnel to assist the South Koreans in organizing their own army.

The invasion of South Korea by the armies of the North Korean Peoples Republic, reactivated the semi-paralysed United Nations. The Council (Russia being absent) authorized armed aid for the South Koreans. General MacArthur, our proconsul in Japan, on the order of President Truman, immediately sent such few American troops as were available. On came the North Koreans, amply supplied with tanks but with few planes. Seoul fell before their onslaught, and by midsummer the Americans and their South Korean allies were driven to the southeast corner of the peninsula with its excellent port of Pusan within easy reach of Japan.

Russia now hurried back to the Council of the UN. It was too late for her to veto the action of the Council; but she could and did denounce the United States for what the Russians termed the American invasion of Korea and Formosa. The South Koreans were about to attack the North

Koreans, so said the Russians, and the latter were but defending their homeland. At best it was only a civil war which was no concern of the United States. As for Formosa, there was no invasion; but it was true that President Truman had ordered the immunization of that island for the time being by the Seventh Fleet to prevent the war from spreading. Meanwhile American reinforcements poured into Korea.

In the autumn the UN forces struck back. An American army transported by sea landed at Inchon on the west coast near Seoul. Thanks to superb naval coöperation and brilliant tactics Seoul was recaptured and the North Korean Army outflanked, caught now between two fires, one from the south from the Pusan area, the other from the north and east from that of Seoul.

The North Korean forces surrendered in droves and melted away into the hills. MacArthur in hot pursuit did not stop at the 38th parallel, but, armed with a UN mandate to restore order in Korea, speeded his men north so rapidly that in a few weeks some of his detachments had reached the Yalu River, boundary between Korea and Manchuria. Quickly then the wheels of fate reversed. Out from their lairs in Manchuria poured Chinese Communist troops outnumbering the UN forces ten to one. MacArthur ordered retreat. Skilfully it was conducted. The victorious Chinese soon were in the capital of North Korea; they crossed the 38th parallel; they entered Seoul; they drove south from that ruined city, boasting that their enemy soon would be back at Pusan, ultimately forced to evacuate all Korean soil.

Then, in this seesaw conflict the fortunes of war suddenly were reversed. United Nations troops, heavily reinforced, drove north again. In March, 1951, they recaptured Seoul for the second time. In April, they were surging over the 38th parallel once more.

As this happened General MacArthur, demanding that the war be pushed to a victorious conclusion and that the invading Chinese be driven out of Korea, was removed from his command by President Truman. The presidential reasons as given were that the General disobeyed orders and criticized his commander-in-chief by corresponding with hostile politicians. But in the background, and supporting the President, were the chiefs of staff, inclined to agree with General Bradley that this was the wrong war and in the wrong place, and might lead to a third World War with a large American army tied down in a mountainous Asiatic country.

This also was the opinion of our allies in the United Nations. MacArthur was an American general, but he commanded United Nations troops. Serving under him in 1951 were British, Australian, New Zealand, South African, Canadian, Ethiopian, French, Turkish, Greek, and Filipino detachments, with Denmark, Italy, Sweden, and India providing

UNITED NATIONS TROOPS IN KOREA

hospital facilities. The brunt of the fighting was done by South Koreans and Americans, their total casualties running over ninety-five per cent of the United Nations total. Even so it was a United Nations army, and to continue the war without the backing of that organization would have had a deleterious effect on its power to preserve peace and to combat communism, not only in Asia but throughout the world.

"There is no substitute for victory," said MacArthur. We have attained victory, said his critics in the United States and in Europe. A Communist coup d'état has failed. The Communist world has learned a lesson. Aggression does not pay.

And so Washington agreed to negotiate an armistice with the North Koreans and the Chinese invaders. It took two years, from July, 1951, to July, 1953, to do so, while by mutual understanding military operations came almost to a standstill. When finally signed, the armistice established a boundary line between North and South Korea, roughly along the 38th parallel, thus bringing back the *status quo ante* of 1950. Neither side was to reinforce its troops, no new airfields were to be built, prisoners were to be repatriated, or if they refused to return whence they had come, they were to be set free, and an international committee was to see to it that the armistice was observed. The future status of Korea was to be determined by an international conference to be held in Geneva in 1954.

It met that year and promptly deadlocked. The North Koreans proposed elections in which they, with twenty-five per cent of the population, were to have equal weight with South Koreans with seventy-five per cent. In this they were supported by the Chinese, and the Russians who had been invited to attend. The sixteen nations which had repelled aggression supported a settlement which called for elections under UN supervision to elect an assembly chosen by equal electoral districts throughout all Korea. To this the Communist bloc would not agree.

The Chinese Nationalists in Formosa also came into the picture. They continued to hold China's seat in the council of the United Nations, and the Seventh U.S. fleet continued to protect them against attack from the Communist mainland. The Americans were publicly committed to defend Formosa and the Pescadores Islands close to Formosa. But what if the Chinese Communists should try to conquer off-shore islands close to the mainland, held by the Nationalists; would America fight to protect them? No one knew what would happen in such a contingency, since Washington simply reserved freedom of action.

In Korea, meanwhile, the South Koreans complained justly that the Chinese and the North Koreans did not adhere to the armistice but kept on preparing for another round. Only by the United States imposing strict limitations on the gasoline and munitions available were the South Koreans restrained from hurling themselves on the foe.

Indochina

As these events took place another civil war in Eastern Asia, intermittently raging for seven years, approached a climax. After the Second World War French Indochina had been reorganized into three states, Laos, Cambodia, and Vietnam. The ·last was the largest and most populous. And here an anti-French, pro-nationalist and pro-communist revolt had broken out as early as 1942.

It was led by Ho Chi Minh and was fought, ostensibly to make Vietnam independent of France. The French made concession after concession, but unfortunately the puppet emperor they set up in Vietnam, Bao-Dai, was more playboy than statesman, and what at first was considered a minor rebellion drifted into full-fledged civil war, Vietminh (the nationalist rebels) against Vietnam (pro-French loyalists), supported by a French army of 100,000 and by war material supplied by the United States.

As fighting died down in Korea it became accentuated in Indochina. United States rifles, lend-leased to Chiang Kai-shek before he was driven from the Chinese mainland, were used by the Vietminh rebels, and Mao,

Communist ruler of China, proclaimed the Indochina war another evidence of United States plotting against Asiatic freedom. By 1954 it was evident that Vietminh was winning. In May of that year Dien Bien Phu, a strong fortress in North Vietnam, capitulated after a long siege, and the Red River delta, including the important port of Hanoi, fell to the rebels.

Again, as in Korea, peace of a kind was patched up between two contending factions. Once more a country was bisected, in this instance by a line drawn at the 17th parallel. North of it Ho Chi Minh set up a Communist government. To the South there was to be a democratic regime, France assenting to its independence. Finally, in 1956, elections were to be held in both North and South to determine the future of Vietnam.

Nato, Seato, and Bandung

The Chinese revolution which put communism in the saddle, and the subsequent events in Korea and Indochina were striking proof of the effectiveness of Communist propaganda. Repercussion in the West was immediate. The democratic countries had no time to waste. They must unite in fact as well as in spirit if they were to withstand communism. Temporarily they had stopped it seeping westward. But now all Asia was in danger.

Preliminary steps toward Western unity had been taken in 1947 by the formation of a North Atlantic Treaty Organization (NATO). But thus far it had been a gesture, a statement of policy, no muscle or sinew to it.

The Korean War changed all that. In 1950 the United States voted $3,500,000,000 to supply NATO with arms. Eisenhower was appointed supreme commander, and SHAPE (Staff Headquarters Allied Powers in Europe) became a physical fact. Some 28 divisions were immediately available on the continent with more to follow. This was not much against 100 Russian divisions; but NATO was armed with atomic artillery, and it was felt that this army, small as it was, could prevent any sudden engulfment of Western Europe by the Soviets. Meanwhile a semicircle of NATO airfields stretching from England through North Africa to Iraq threatened instant retaliation—if Russia started war. With Greece and Turkey joining NATO some fourteen countries were thus united in a grand alliance.

Germany was the unknown factor. Unless and until German support was assured NATO could not long withstand a Soviet march to the Atlantic. But to admit the German Federal Republic (West Germany)

ASIA
1954

SEA OF OKHOTSK   KAMCHATKA

ARCTIC CIRCLE   LENA R.

SIBERIA

SOCIALIST REPUBLICS

SAKHALIN I. (USSR)

KURILE IS. (USSR)

40°N

LAKE BAIKAL

AMUR R.

Irkutsk   Chita

Khabarovsk

GREAT KHINGAN

MANCHURIA

Harbin

Vladivostok

JAPAN

NORTH PACIFIC OCEAN

ULAN BATOR

MONGOLIAN PEOPLE'S REPUBLIC

Mukden

PEOPLE'S REP. OF NORTH KOREA

SEA OF JAPAN

Tokyo

ALTAI MTS.

GOBI DESERT

REP. OF SOUTH KOREA

Osaka   Yokohama

BONIN IS.

Peking

Dairen

Seoul

HWANG R.

Tientsin

YELLOW SEA

Nagasaki

IWO JIMA

CHINESE

Lanchow

Nanking

Shanghai

EAST CHINA SEA

20°N

PEOPLE'S REP.

Hankow

Changsha

Foochow

Taipei

RYUKYU ISLANDS

OKINAWA

MARIANAS

SAIPAN

MTS.

Chungking

YANGTSE R.

Amoy

FORMOSA (NAT. CHINA)

GUAM (USA)

Lhasa

MTS.

Canton

BHUTAN

BRAHMAPUTRA R.

Macao (PORT.)

Hong Kong (BR.)

CAROLINE IS.

PAK.

BURMA

Kwangchowan (FR.)

Hanoi

MEKONG R.

HAINAN

LUZON

PHILIPPINE REPUBLIC

Mandalay

VIET

Manila

IRRAWADDY R.

SALWEEN R.

LAOS

Hué

FRENCH INDO-CHINA

PALAU I.

Rangoon

THAILAND

Bangkok

ZAMBEZI

SOUTH CHINA SEA

Iloilo

LEYTE

SOUTH PACIFIC OCEAN

BENGAL

CAMBODIA

MINDANAO

ANDAMAN IS.

GULF OF THAILAND

Saigon

Zamboanga

MOROTAI

Hollandia

SPRATLEY I.

Sandakan

NICOBAR IS.

Brunei

DUTCH NEW GUINEA

EQUATOR

MALAYA

SARAWAK (BR.)

MOLUCCAS

CERAM

STR. OF MALACCA

Singapore (BR.)

BORNEO

CELEBES

SUMATRA

INDONESIA

(PORT.)

AUSTRALIA

Jogjakarta

JAVA

TIMOR

Darwin

100°E   120°E   140°E

to NATO meant a German army, and it seemed incongruous that a war to disarm Germans should be followed by rearming them. The French opposed doing so. There were 50,000,000 Germans in West Germany and France feared them quite as much as Communist armies. On the other hand, if the Germans were rebuffed by the democracies'there was always a chance that they might be cajoled by the Russians to join their side; and that would make matters even worse.

Followed then the compromise plan of Premier Faure of France. This was the EDC (European Defense Community), an army organized on a purely international basis but subject to orders from NATO. Conscripts from West Germany, France, Italy, Belgium and the Netherlands would compose this international army which would wear its own uniform. In its divisions the various nationalities would be mixed. This scheme, it was thought, would prevent the recrudescence of a German national army, as such, with German divisions taking orders from a German general staff.

The French National Assembly, however, voted down the EDC, and hope for the alignment of the German republic with the West diminished. Whereupon a new French premier, Mendès-France, with the help of Britain secured membership for Germany in NATO. A principal objection to EDC was that Britain had refused to join. Now, to save the day for European unity, she pledged herself not to withdraw her forces from Germany without the consent of the Western Union (see p. 455). This promise led France to consent to a German army of 500,000 and to Germany joining NATO. And by doing so the German Federal Republic won recognition at last as an independent national state, the only limitation on her sovereignty being the right of Britain, France, and the United States to retain troops in Germany until a final peace treaty was signed, together with certain restrictions on the type of weapons Germans might manufacture.

The German people were far from enthusiastic about this new army. To most of them it was only the lesser of two evils. What they wanted first of all was the unity of all Germany, and since Soviet Russia was adamant against having this brought about by free elections there seemed no way of obtaining their heart's desire except to join NATO and so bring pressure against Russia. Very slowly and cautiously they set about creating this new army. It must be a democratic army and as unlike the late Wehrmacht as possible. By 1956 but a mere handful of recruits had been sworn in.

NATO might offer protection to the West against Communist aggression; but how about Southeast Asia? The Indochina settlement had been a Communist victory. In northern Vietnam was the rich rice-producing valley of the Red River, the important city of Hanoi, and

Eastfoto

PREMIER CHOU EN-LAI DELIVERS A SPEECH AT THE BANDUNG CONFERENCE (APRIL, 1955) far more than half the population of Vietnam was now securely within the Communist orbit. Furthermore, France was utterly discredited as a colonial power in Asia, and the United States, supplier of arms to the French, apparently was unable to stem the Communist tide.

Communism was on the march, south and east. To build a bulwark against its further spreading, a meeting of anti-communist states was held at Manila. Thus was born SEATO (Southeast Asia Security Organization) intended as a kind of NATO for the Far East. Australia, New Zealand, Britain, France, and the United States were the non-Asiatic countries. Pakistan, Thailand and the Philippines represented the non-communist nations in Asia. India, Burma, and Ceylon were all invited. All three refused to join, the first two because they preferred to remain neutral in the cold war, Ceylon on the plea that her primary interest lay in the Colombo Plan which proposed to set up on a very modest scale, a kind of Marshall Plan for Asia.

Whether SEATO was more than a gesture remains to be seen. Its program for holding back communism expressly excluded Formosa, and there was no proviso, as with NATO, for a SEATO army with a commander-in-chief. In 1956 it did give a demonstration as to how it might aid Thailand in case of attack. Manoeuvres of a kind were held there. They were not impressive. Pakistan refused to join them on the ground that she had not been properly notified. A task force of American marines and Filipino troops paraded in Thailand, supported by British and American warships. That was all.

Meanwhile an Afro-Asiatic conference was held at Bandung, Indonesia, presumably inspired by Communists although that was not openly stated. Bandung was attended by Chou En-lai, foreign minister of Communist China, Nehru of India, Nu of Burma, Nasser, prime minister of Egypt, the President of Liberia, and a few other Africans, mainly Arabs. The keynotes struck were anti-imperialism, anti-colonialism, and Asiatic and African nationalism. Bandung did not formally organize for future activity as did SEATO. It refused to take any direct stand in a world conflict arising over communism. But it did serve as a platform for Chinese Communists to denounce American imperialism and for Nehru to put India in the category of neutralist states along with Burma and Indonesia. Israel, although an Asiatic country, was not invited. To have asked her would have angered the Arab world.

African Nationalism

The end of French rule in Indochina was not simply a Communist victory; it also was one for Asiatic nationalism. And the latter in turn was symbolic of worldwide antagonism to white domination over all colored races and in all continents.

This was as true of Africa as of Asia, the main difference being that African nationalism was a more recent phenomenon and seemingly immune to communist ideology until the middle of this century.

With the crushing defeat of France in Indochina Arab nationalism in Morocco, long simmering, broke out in menacing riots, bloodshed, and petty war.

Hitherto it had been relatively easy to suppress. In the ancient practice of *divide et impera* the French had been greatly aided by El Glaoui, a mighty feudal lord with a private army of his own of Berber tribesmen who hated the Arab folk in Moroccan cities. The Istaqulil, party of independence, had been driven to cover. The Sultan, said to favor it, had been exiled to Madagascar, and a Moroccan stooge exalted to the Peacock's Throne. Furthermore, the French Foreign Legion, composed largely of former German soldiers, hitherto had made physical revolt hazardous.

But that same legion had been defeated in Indochina and its prestige was shattered. Mendès-France, engineer of French withdrawal from Asia, now had a new problem—how was the French Empire to be rescued in Morocco?

Mendès-France was conciliatory. He promised reform and ultimate freedom for Morocco. But he had no intention of repealing the laws against the Istaqulil or of recalling the exiled Sultan. Whereupon violence erupted into the open. The Nationalists took to the sword, slaying many French *coloni*, Frenchmen who had settled permanently in Morocco, of whom there were a half million. The Foreign Legion tried to protect them and many died on both sides. To prevent this petty war from spreading, the old Sultan was brought back and reinstated. The prestige of El Glaoui was destroyed. He crawled on his hands and knees before the Sultan he had driven out of Morocco, but received no forgiveness. In 1956 he died just as an important election was held in France that left no man and no party to deal firmly with a crisis which threatened not merely Morocco but Algeria and Tunisia.

Algeria by law was Metropolitan France, an integral part of France itself, sending representatives to the National Assembly at Paris. But in the critical years 1955-56, elections were postponed owing to anarchy and bloodshed in Algeria. Formidable Arab revolts and the murder of the French coloni brought about a situation far beyond the control of the Foreign Legion, and many thousand French troops had to be flown in from France.

The Arab world, stirred up by the Cairo radio, took up the hue and cry of anti-colonialism, and temporarily the Arab delegates at the United Nations won a majority to put Algeria on the agenda. The French in high dudgeon left the UN but decided to return.

In Tunisia the situation was roughly parallel. Here nationalistic demonstrations had been suppressed, the Neo-Destour Party sponsoring them declared illegal, its founder exiled. Tunisia was not pacified. The slaying of French coloni continued. Mendès-France flew to Tunis. Complete autonomy was promised, the ban on Neo-Destour removed, its founder returned in triumph as premier.

Everywhere in North Africa the story was the same. The victorious Nationalists were Arab Moslems, not Communists, and their revolt was as much religious and racist as economic. But in the background lay great poverty and the fact that a few thousand French coloni owned most of the land that was fertile.

Within a year everything drifted from bad to worse. France was unable to withdraw with dignity and prestige from North Africa as had Britain from India. The weak coalition government of Mendès-France gave way to one still weaker under Faure, and that to one weaker yet under Mollet.

The parliamentary election of 1956 brought despair to all friends of France. Now there was not only no majority for any party but seemingly no possible coalition. The old Radical party, which hitherto had served as a rallying ground for men of moderate opinion, was split in two, to the advantage of the Communists, who won the greatest number of seats. A new party in this land of splinter groups appeared on the extreme right composed of reactionary shopkeepers called Poujadists. The Socialists came in second. But they hated Communists and were hated by them. And even if these two parties had united they would have been short of a majority.

Only by adding together Communists, Socialists, and the Radicals who swore by Mendès-France would it be possible to form a government. But Mendès-France had little use for Socialists and hated all Communists. If the men who followed him had been willing to join forces with those Radicals under Faure they might have formed a government with the help of the moderate MRP and certain splinter groups. But Mendès-France and Faure were at swords' points, and both were antagonistic to the MRP.

There was thus almost a complete deadlock. Temporarily it was solved by electing Mollet, a Socialist, premier. At any moment the Communists had it in their power to oust him; so also could Mendès-France with his assorted Radicals, who chose for the time being only to back Mollet.

France no longer, except by courtesy, could be called a first-class power. With Indochina lost, Morocco and Tunis declared independent, and an insurrection in Algeria rapidly assuming the gravity of civil war she was in sorry plight.

Desperately France tried to hold Algeria. Some 1,000,000 Europeans had their homes there, most of them Frenchmen, confronted by 9,000,000 restive Arabs inflamed by the heady wine of Arab Nationalism. Mollet offered olive branches, suggested partial autonomy; all in vain, the insurrection became more ominous. To defeat it 100,000 French troops were detached from French NATO forces sent to Algeria. They proved insufficient. Another 100,000 reservists were summoned to the colors. And as this happened a sharp Parliamentary battle followed between Mendès-France, demanding fresh concessions to the rebels, and Mollet, asserting that the preservation of order must have precedence. All this Moscow noted without disfavor, knowing full well that a telegram sent to Paris would spell Mollet's downfall.

Vigorous demonstrations on behalf of African nationalism were not confined to northwest Africa. To a greater or less degree nationalistic tomtoms reverberated throughout the entire dark continent.

Particularly true was this in Egypt and in the Sudan. Its more recent development in Egypt may be dated to a revolt of Egyptian army officers in 1952 against a corrupt and most noisome Khedive, Farouk, which drove him into exile and proceeded to govern Egypt with an iron hand. One of these officers, Nasser, became Prime Minister. He was a staunch nationalist and as such demanded that Britain abandon the Suez Canal zone and withdraw from the Anglo-Egyptian Sudan.

The British had occupied the Suez Canal zone since 1882, and by their treaty recognizing Egyptian independence (1926) they were authorized to retain a garrison there. Sporadic attacks by inflamed Egyptian nationalists took place and the garrison had been increased to 80,000 men.

Historically the Suez Canal had been a place of great strategic importance, but the advent of the atom bomb changed all that. To remain had become merely a matter of prestige, not worth fighting about. And so Britain yielded to Nasser, began the withdrawal of her troops, promising to have them all out by 1956.

Egyptian nationalists, meanwhile, sought to annex the Sudan, claiming that it was imperative to do so since Egypt was dependent for its existence on Nile water, and was justly concerned about its sources. The British preferred the status quo of joint ownership with Egypt, since much British capital was invested in Sudanese cotton, and since they considered it unwise to turn over the 9,000,000 inhabitants of mixed Arab and Negro blood that inhabited the Sudan to politicians at Cairo.

Followed then an Anglo-Egyptian agreement in 1953 that elections be held in the Sudan so that the Sudanese might determine their own future. A long and confused campaign followed with the upshot that a Sudanese parliament meeting at Khartum in 1956 declared the Sudan an independent country, and applied for admission to the United Nations —a triumph for African nationalism.

The cry of Africa for the Africans resounded in other parts of Africa. Particularly was this true of Nigeria, largest dependency under the British Crown, and in the Gold Coast, north of the Gulf of Guinea.

Nigeria was a federated state, its three component parts known as East, West, and Northern Nigeria, the two former well advanced toward self-government, with the last more backward, more illiterate, still governed by native chiefs under the guidance of the British.

A legislature with limited powers represented all Nigeria, and as successive changes were made in the constitution more and more power was given to it. A further revision is promised for 1956, and in this year Nigerians are to decide for themselves whether they opt for three separate autonomous parliaments for the three states in question, or for a more unified country with a greater concentration of power. The two southern states already are equipped with legislatures and are largely self-governing. In them the clamor for Nigerian independence is loud and persistent. The main trouble is what can be done with the more backward North.

Further along the road to complete autonomy within the Commonwealth, or to independence without it, was the Gold Coast. Here African nationalism had won a great victory with the approval of local British officials, who appear quite willing to turn over the Gold Coast completely to its prosperous cocoa-growing Negro population.

In the Gold Coast there is a popularly elected legislature with an all Negro cabinet—the first in any British dependency—and a Negro premier, Dr. Nkrumah.

The latter was first educated by Roman Catholic missionaries, then graduated from Lincoln University in the United States, and as a graduate student in London much befriended by British Communists.

The doctor describes himself as a Marxian Christian, and has been for many years the leader of a party pledged to secure independence for the Gold Coast. Jailed by the governor for left-wing agitation, he was set free after his party won a decisive victory at the polls in 1951. Ever since then, Nkrumah has been a national hero. Opposed by Communists in the legislature, he acted promptly and expelled them from his party. The British look forward not only to the Gold Coast as becoming her Majesty's first Negro dominion but also as the nucleus around which may develop a larger Negro dominion, including Nigeria.

Uganda and Kenya

Meanwhile, south of the Sudan and athwart the great lakes lay Britain's model African colony, Uganda. Prosperous and well-governed by its local chiefs, with a modicum of authority exercised over them by the colonial office, Uganda was slow to catch the contemporary fever of nationalism. Suddenly it became mildly infected. The most important of the chiefs was the Kabarka of Buganda, a Cambridge university graduate and very popular in high British society. In 1953 the Kabarka opposed the British governor of Uganda who favored uniting Kenya, Tanganyika, and Uganda into a North African federation. The Kabarka refused his consent. The governor exiled him. The Kabarka appealed to Parliament, which upheld the governor. Violent was the wave of protest which swept Buganda. For three years it continued to rise. Britain yielded. The Kabarka returned to his throne in triumph in 1956.

East of Uganda lay Kenya, Britain's worst trouble spot in all Africa. Approximately one quarter of its total acreage, some 16,000 square miles, was known as the Highlands. Within it gathered most of Kenya's 40,000 Whites, for the land was very fertile and the climate salubrious. All land in the Highlands was owned by the Whites, who depended on Negro labor for the cultivation of their coffee plantations. The tribe which provided most of it was the Kikuyu.

Now it happened that a young Kikuyu boy, Jomo Kenyatta, educated by Scottish missionaries, went to London, studied at the London School of Economics, became an anthropologist, spent some time at the university of Moscow, returned to his people, became an agitator among them for self-government. He it was who was arrested in 1952 as responsible for abetting the Mau Mau rebellion of certain Kikuyus.

Mau Mau was a secret terrorist society. A most bloodthirsty and obscene oath was required of all members. Mau Mau was organized to rid Kenya of all Whites and to frighten all Kikuyus into joining it. Murders were perpetrated in an orgiastic ritual. The Mau Mau terror spread rapidly. The Whites were infuriated, the Kikuyus panic-stricken. Mau Mau spared neither age nor sex, killing secretly, slashing its victims until they died, defiling their bodies. It slew relatively few Whites, about sixty, since the latter all carried arms. Among the Kikuyus, death stalked everywhere, Mau Mau slaying thousands, either for betraying the oath or for refusing to take it.

Paratroopers were flown in from Britain and the manhunt began. Thousands of Kikuyus were rounded up, stuck in stockades, screened. Jomo Kenyatta was sentenced to serve a prison term of seven years after a trial scarcely in accordance with the fine record of British law courts. Order was restored, Mau Mau stamped out. To the displeasure of the white settlers the British government revised the constitution of Kenya and insisted that some Negroes be elected to the legislature. Educational and other requirements were high and the number chosen but a handful. White settlers were angry, their country bankrupt, their future uncertain.

The Gold Coast and Kenya are in stark contrast. In the former there is no color bar, and the British regard with approval the approach there to dominion status. In the latter Whites and Blacks do not associate with one another and demonstrations in favor of self-government are sternly suppressed. In the Gold Coast the number of Whites is exiguous. The opposite is true of Kenya where Whites are relatively numerous. For many decades they have been entrenched in the Highlands, accustomed to governing themselves through their own legislature, and therefore largely free from the Colonial Office in London with its long and distinguished record of protecting black folk.

Nationalism is far less an acute problem in Africa than it is in Asia. Negroes are as yet too ignorant, too conditioned by long habit and custom to submissiveness, to be profoundly stirred by it. The Afrikander Whites in the saddle in the Union of South Africa are a powerful and determined people, and Negro nationalism in their midst is nipped in the bud. In the new British federation of the two Rhodesias and Nyassaland the color bar is as strictly enforced as in the Union of South Africa. Negroes may apply for British citizenship, and so have the right to vote for a very few selected men of their own race in the legislature. But the qualifications of becoming a British citizen in this almost wholly illiterate land are high, and to retain the status of "protected person" provides a certain security.

Hitherto Communist propaganda in Africa south of the equator has been slight. It may spread rapidly, however, where people are miserable and have a sense of injustice. There is in Moscow no color bar, a fact that gives Communism an entering wedge.

The Meeting at the Summit (Geneva, 1955)

March, 1953, Stalin died. Taking his place as premier was Malenkov, presumably a stooge for others, since he resigned within a year. Bulganin and Khrushchev took over, the first as premier, the second as secretary of the Communist party. In the interim, Beria, all-powerful head of the secret police, was executed as a traitor. The West looked forward with some hope to what might happen next.

Early omens were propitious. The British, the French, the Americans, and the Russians signed a treaty restoring independence to Austria, a boon which that country had not enjoyed since Hitler's invasion seventeen years earlier. Austria gladly accepted the status of Switzerland, that of a country pledged to perpetual neutrality.

Followed then what was known as a meeting at the summit, not of foreign secretaries but of chiefs of state. It was held in Geneva in 1955. Present were President Eisenhower, Sir Anthony Eden, the new British Prime Minister, Faure of France, and the two new joint rulers of Russia.

Upon the surface there was little wrangling. In the open meetings everyone was smiling; everyone agreed on the necessity of universal peace, the necessity of world disarmament. No tempers were lost. The three men who represented the West asked that the problem of Germany be first on the agenda. They were willing, they said, to give guarantees to Russia if that country would consent to free elections in Eastern Ger-

many, and Eden for Britain suggested a demilitarized buffer state between Russia and a united Germany if Russia would agree to those free
elections. But the Russians asserted that the Germans were not yet ready
for unification and that there was but one way to achieve it, namely, for
the West Germans and the East Germans to negotiate on a basis of complete equality, despite the fact that the West Germans outnumbered the
East German Communists by a good three to one.

As for disarmament Russia said she had already reduced her army
by 640,000 men and the West should do likewise. But how large was that
army before the reduction? Russia would not say, and as a matter of
statistics the Americans had reduced their army twice since the armistice
in Korea. The two Russians once again pleaded for the destruction of
all nuclear weapons but remained adamant on international inspection.
Eisenhower offered free aerial inspection in the United States to the
Russian air force if Bulganin and Khrushchev would permit UN aerial
inspection of Russian plants and military installations. This they would
not concede. So the meeting at the summit amounted to little, except
that both sides agreed that their conversations had been productive of
an excellent spirit of friendliness, and that another meeting should be held
later in the year of the foreign ministers of the four countries concerned
to hammer out something specific whereby world tensions might be lessened. This very small mouse was termed, "the spirit of Geneva."

When the four lesser statesmen met, that spirit completely evaporated.
In the interval the Russians had exploded a hydrogen bomb, and this
proof that both sides now had it within their power to wipe civilization
off this terrestrial globe apparently hardened the Soviet heart. Once again
the conference was completely blocked. In the middle of it Molotov
went back to Russia. He returned saying he had brought something nice
in his baggage. What he brought was a bitter denunciation of the West
and a refusal to yield an inch.

Middle East, 1955-56

In 1948, as we have seen, the state of Israel unexpectedly emerged.
Attacked north, east, and south by her Arab neighbors, Israel emerged
triumphant. There was, however, no peace treaty, only an armistice, and
that none too well observed.

Between 1948 and 1955 an intermittent, informal kind of war continued
between Arabs and Israelis. There were only 1,500,000 Israelis as opposed
to 40,000,000 Arabs. But the Israelis were united and their enemies,
jealous of one another, were without common purpose or leadership, ill
prepared for war.

Bitterness grew steadily in intensity, border raids in number, some
1,200 reported during these seven years. Syria and Jordan clashed with

Israel over the diversion of the waters of the Jordan River for irrigation purposes, Egypt and Jordan over the right of some 900,000 Arab refugees driven from their home in Palestine in 1948, barely kept alive by UNRRA waiting to return to their former homes in Palestine. The frontiers drawn by the uneasy truce of 1948 stretched far beyond those proposed by the United Nations partition plan. And the Arabs made much of this, asserting that the Israelis plotted a greater Israel, all the way to the Suez Canal and to the Tigris River. But, according to the Israelis, the Egyptians, spurred on by Nasser's nationalists, plotted a joint Arab attack that would wipe Israel from the map.

Then suddenly, in September, 1955, the Russians and the Czechoslovaks promised to supply Egypt with heavy armament, jet planes, tanks, and submarines, and some ten ships conveying them shortly after landed at Alexandria.

This presented the Israelis with a serious problem. Their tiny country, only some 8,000 square miles, had a frontier 591 miles in length fronting on four Arab states, Lebanon, Syria, Jordan, and Egypt. Tel Aviv, their principal city, was but a few miles from the Gaza strip and the Egyptians. The average distance from the Mediterranean to the Jordan frontier was only twelve miles. In this narrow space there was no opportunity for manoeuvre should war occur. Israel had no submarines; she also had no heavy armament with which to ward off Arab attack. Therefore she appealed to the United States to sell her arms to offset those sold her potential enemies by the Communist states.

The United States, England, and France had promised action to prevent the status quo from being upset by war. But in case of quick Arab action would these friendly countries have time to implement their promise, and would they really do it?

The United States, Britain, France, all three, were caught in a network of conflicting interests. For Washington to sell the Israelis the arms they desired would have resulted in Czechoslovakia, Moscow's cat's-paw, selling the Arabs more, and an arms race would follow, bringing war closer. To refuse to sell to Israel might result in its destruction, and to prevent this America had pledged its word. Furthermore, the United States at this very time was dickering with the Egyptians over the construction of a great dam over the Nile; and certainly it was to our interest to avoid angering Saudi Arabia from whence came much of our oil.

Britain was even more worried. She had just completed a defensive alliance, the Bagdad Pact, with Turkey, Iran, Iraq, and Pakistan. Jordan, an Arab state, was expected to join. That state owed its birth to British diplomacy, had been and still is (1956), subsidized by the British treasury with an army trained by a British general. But Jordan refused to join the Bagdad Pact and dismissed Glubb Pasha, the general. The

NORTHERN AFRICA
AND THE
MIDDLE EAST
1957

INDEPENDENT STATES
OF NORTHERN AFRICA

500 MILES

reason was fairly obvious. Ibn Saud, luxury-enveloped and enormously wealthy ruler of Saudi Arabia, showered his American dollars and British pounds on Jordan mobs to stage anti-British riots. Without oil Britain could not live. Most of it came from Saudi Arabia, South Arabia, Iran and Iraq.

France, too, needed oil from Arab lands. And with civil war on her hands with Algerian Arabs she must necessarily step cautiously, lest Nasser of Egypt put himself at the head of a belligerent pan-Arab and pan-Moslem group whose influence would extend throughout all the Moslem world from Casablanca on the Atlantic to the gates of India.

It looked like war, so much so that the United Nations sent its secretary to the Middle East to plead with Israelis and Arabs alike to abstain from incessant frontier raids. As he did so the Russians shifted their ground from a pro-Arab position to one of professed neutrality, agreeing that no arms should be sent to either side, pledging Russia to the support of a United Nations program which would prevent any outbreak of war in the disturbed Middle East.

The Dethronement of Stalin

In 1956 the inexplicable Russians seemingly made a complete ideological somersault. At the conference of the Russian Communist Congress Khrushchev announced that Russia and her allies, the Peoples Democracies, had suffered long from one-man rule. Stalin's self-glorification had resulted in spreading a *cult of personality*. This was a grievous error. Leadership must be collective. Furthermore the coming world victory of communism did not necessarily have to be accompanied by force and bloodshed. Under certain circumstances it might be won by democratic majorities secured by peaceful means.

Followed then a secret speech made by Khrushchev in the congress, in which he accused Stalin of gross neglect of duty in not readying Russia against Hitler's attack, of cowardice during the war, of absurd boasting, and of heinous crimes: the murder of old Bolshevik heroes in the amazing and phoney treason trials of 1917, and the appalling slaughter of 5,000 Red army officers.

This philippic was not released either in full or at once to the public, as though it was first necessary to test the reception it would meet with in the Communist world. For a moment the latter was stunned at this denegation of the accepted hero. It recovered very quickly; was not this pronunciamento official, and from the head of the party? And soon, not only in Russia but in all satellite countries, profuse were the apologies for past errors and loud the lamentations for the death by Stalin's orders of good Communists whose only blame was to incur Stalin's displeasure.

Even thus did communism about-face, making Stalin the scapegoat for all tyrannical and brutish acts, "a blundering paranoid murderer whose stupidity and obstinacy almost destroyed the Soviet Union."

Why this speech of Khrushchev? It is possible that he, Bulganin, and their associates suspected a new purge that might include themselves, and so, to save their necks, murdered Stalin. It is possible that they sensed such deep hatred of Stalin in Russia that an internal revolution threatened the downfall of the party unless they took action first. Another explanation might be that they hoped to cozen the European Socialists into the old united-front trap into which Czechoslovak Socialists had fallen, and by so doing destroy the unity of the West.

The significance of Stalin's repudiation is difficult to gauge. The conspirators who had brought it about had been obedient henchmen of the dead tyrant. They had shared in his crimes; could they now repudiate him without self-incrimination? Did their *volte-face* imply fundamental changes in Soviet policy; or was it simply the result of a cutthroat squabble among gangsters, motivated by hate, fear, and cupidity, to substitute the rule of several for that of one, because no one was sufficiently powerful as yet to impose his single will upon all?

However that may be a certain easement in Soviet propaganda occurred. The iron curtain was raised slightly. It became easier to secure Russian passports; newspaper men were given more freedom; Russian officials became more friendly. The advantages of trade were stressed rather than military might. There was less emphasis on Marxian theories concerning the inner contradictions of capitalism, that doomed it to destruction, and more on the beauties of coöperation.

The Russians even proposed to adopt a kind of Marshall Plan of their own for economic aid and technological assistance to impoverished folk in Asia and Africa, with yellow, brown, and black skins. War was still war; but an economic one with the West was more desirable than one waged with guns.

To further this new approach Bulganin and Khrushchev embarked on a pilgrimage to India, Burma, and Afghanistan, traveling troubadours of sweetness and light, praising fulsomely the lands they visited, promising the friendship of Big Brother Russia, commenting freely on Asiatic struggles for freedom from British, French, and even Portuguese imperialism, covertly supported by capitalistic America. Peace, nationalism, and coexistence was the burden of their song.

Just what, specifically, did coexistence mean? Were the traveling Russians sincere in implying that the cold war was over? Would they really do anything comparable to what the West had done to make the depressed areas of the world more viable by economic aid? Was this a Communist subterfuge beneath which the Soviets intended to plant further seeds of discord among those nations endeavoring to maintain a common front against world communism? Did the Russians really intend to do anything at all to solve Europe's major problems—German unification and world disarmament?

In the great international chess game it was now the West's turn to play. It was ill prepared to do so. It had trusted too much to NATO. That organization was perceptibly weakening. The reasons were numerous. Among them were: the withdrawal of more than half of the French NATO divisions from Europe to Africa; the collapse of NATO's Eastern defense line, since Greece and Turkey, admitted to defend it, were now at cross-purposes over Cyprus, the Greeks intent on integrating that island into Greece, the Turks and the British determined that this should not be done; the weakening of the British Commonwealth by the deflection of Ceylon from a pro-Western orientation to neutralism; the failure of France and Germany to compound their differences over the Saar; and finally, lessened support in Germany for aged Chancellor Adenauer and NATO which he had done so much to create.

Prospects for world peace were dark. Both sides now had the hydrogen bomb. Eleven years had passed since the atom bomb had been dropped on Hiroshima with its equivalent of 20,000 tons of TNT. The hydrogen bomb packed an explosive power of 2,000,000 tons. The testing of the first one at Bikini atoll in 1954 led Field Marshal Montgomery to say one year later: "win or lose is no longer applicable to contests between nations which have nuclear power of any magnitude . . . Man will have it in his power in the future to destroy himself and every living thing upon this planet."

Suddenly, in the summer of 1956, came a new international crisis, possibly worse in its implications than the Berlin airlift of 1948 and the Korean War of 1950.

Nasser of Egypt, piqued by American and British withdrawal of aid in the building of the High Aswan Dam, declared the Suez Canal nationalized, under the exclusive control of Egypt. Through this waterway passed the tankers which carried the oil of Arabian lands and Iran upon which the economic life of Western Europe depended. Clearly it was intolerable that the power to open or to shut it should depend on the ruler of Egypt. In consequence, Britain and France began to concentrate air, naval, and military strength in the Eastern Mediterranean.

An international conference in London proved disappointing. Egypt refused to attend, but Soviet Russia went and spoke in approval of Nasser's coup. Three other nations also supported the Egyptian—Indonesia, India, and Ceylon—the last two being members of the Commonwealth. They and Soviet Russia were in agreement; the canal was Egyptian property over which no international control was warranted.

Eighteen of the twenty-two nations attending adhered to the principle that world peace depended on at least a modicum of international administration of the canal. They appointed a committee of five, headed by

...f Australia, to confer with Nasser. He received them ...mpromise the main issue—Egyptian not international

...tes now proposed an Association of Canal Users to ...pt to refuse passage to its ships, free passage to all ...nteed by the treaty of 1888. A second conference was ...the eighteen nations who did approve of international ...presented with the American proposal. A few nations ...he proposed Users Association. Others were lukewarm, ...iginal proposal was watered down. Whereupon Britain ...ealed to the United Nations, where their resolution to ...was promptly vetoed by Russia.

...nto autumn. Nasser remained master of the Suez. Along ...raeli-Jordan frontier bloody forays were increasingly ...n was Britain's ally, and a British subsidy paid for ...But a parliamentary election in that country favored ...britain, and Jordan put an Egyptian general in command of ...y. This made no sense to Englishmen who paid for it, and who ...t an expensive garrison in Cyprus to ride herd over Nasser and the Near East.

And now, from behind the iron curtain, came explosions. In Poland half-starved and frantic Poles demonstrated so vigorously against Moscow that war threatened. For the nonce it was stayed by Soviet concessions that implied that Poland was semi-independent.

This Polish explosion set off another and a greater one in Hungary. In that unhappy land desperate Magyars rose in arms against their own Communist government. The latter called in the Russian army. Soon Russian tanks were roaming the streets of Budapest and blood flowed freely. The Peoples Democracies of Eastern Europe and the countries of the Near East boiled with eruptive violence.

As this happened, the Israeli army stabbed southward into the Sinai peninsula and swung westward toward the Suez Canal. As they did so, France and Britain demanded from Nasser the right to protect the Canal. This demand being instantly rebuffed by Nasser, their bombers attacked Egyptian airfields, their parachutists capturing Port Said at the Canal's northern end.

At this act of war the world stood aghast. The world was angry; and a majority in the Security Council of the United Nations, including the United States and Russia (for once in agreement), censured the Franco-British action, referred the matter to the Assembly of the United Nations. That body with practical unanimity called for the withdrawal of French, British, and Israeli troops from Egyptian territory.

Gone was western unity; NATO became a joke; Nasser and his Russian backers were triumphant.

But the Russians played their cards badly. About to withdraw from Hungary and to leave that land free from Communist dominance, the Russians promised free elections to the Magyars. Suddenly they changed their minds. Fearing an anti-Soviet Magyar regime they brought back their armor. For a few days the Magyars fought the Russian tanks and their own security police. With ammunition spent and gone they had no chance. By November 11, the armistice day of the First World War, thousands of Magyars lay dead.

The United Nations was now as indignant against Russia as against Israel, France, and Britain. Just as its Assembly unanimously condemned Russian aggression in Hungary, from Moscow came word of intervention in Egypt. These acts, together with the knowledge they could expect no support from the United States or the United Nations, led Israel, France, and Britain to sign a cease-fire agreement and to consent to a conditional withdrawal of their forces from Egyptian soil, provided that detachments of United Nations forces were to stand guard in Egypt. Several of the smaller nations, among them Denmark, Norway, Sweden, Finland, Colombia, and Canada, agreed to send them.

What chance now, peace? The free world was bitter at Russia for the barbarous behavior of her troops in Hungary: but so was most of it at France, Britain, and Israel for flouting the charter of the United Nations. A kind of international checkmate resulted. The free world, its unity disrupted by the Suez crisis, could do nothing to aid the Hungarian revolution; the Russians, fearful lest that revolution spread to Poland, were too busily engaged in placating that country to do more than make threatening gestures elsewhere. Only Nasser emerged triumphant—the invading Israelis forced out of Egypt by international pressure, the Suez Canal now completely under his dominance.

Except in Algeria, where the revolt of the Arabs against the French grew steadily in magnitude, an uneasy, undeclared truce settled down on a troubled world, as that world contemplated the new and ever newer horrors of nuclear war.

READING LIST

The purpose of this reading list is to offer suggestions for students desiring to read more widely in the history of recent Europe. For this reason, the suggestions are restricted to books in the English language, and an effort has been made to indicate those volumes which are most suitable for undergraduate reading. While the bibliography follows the general arrangement of the material in the text, the books are listed by topic rather than by chapter.

I. GENERAL WORKS

BIBLIOGRAPHIES AND ENCYCLOPEDIAS: The most useful general bibliographies are W. H. Allison and others, eds., *A Guide to Historical Literature* (1931), which provides a convenient starting point for any historical investigation; L. J. Ragatz, *A Bibliography for the Study of European History, 1815-1939* (1942), with two supplements (1943 and 1945); W. L. Langer and H. F. Armstrong, *Foreign Affairs Bibliography, 1919-1932* (1933); R. G. Woolbert, *Foreign Affairs Bibliography, 1932-1942* (1945); and A. Bullock and A. J. P. Taylor, *Select List of Books on European History, 1815-1914* (1944). For current publications, these guides may be supplemented by the bibliographies in the *American Historical Review* and the *Journal of Modern History*. Biographical sketches and special articles on a wide variety of subjects will be found in the *Encyclopoedia Britannica* and the *Encyclopedia of the Social Sciences*. W. L. Langer, ed., *An Encyclopedia of World History* (1940) offers a compact factual survey. For maps, see W. R. Shepherd, *Historical Atlas* (7th ed., 1929); I. Bowman, *The New World: Problems in Political Geography* (1928); J. F. Horrabin, *An Atlas of Current Affairs* (6th ed., 1939); *Hammond's Historical Atlas* (1953); and H. L. Roberts, assisted by J. Gunther and J. A. Kreslins, *Foreign Affairs Bibliography* (1955).

SOURCE COLLECTIONS: For the consultation of the original texts of treaties, speeches, and other documents in English translation, the following collections may be recommended: A. Oakes and R. B. Mowat, *Great European Treaties of the Nineteenth Century* (1918), which deals with the period from 1815 to 1878; W. P. Hall and E. A. Beller, *Historical Readings in Nineteenth-Century Thought* (1928), and D. O. Wagner, *Social Reformers* (1934), for intellectual documents; J. H. Robinson and C. A. Beard, *Readings in Modern European History* (2 vols., 1908-09), Vol. II; J. F. Scott and A. Baltzly, *Readings in* ii READING LIST

European History Since 1814 (1934); A. N. Cook, *Readings in Modern and Contemporary History* (1937); W. C. Langsam, *Documents and Readings in the History of Europe Since 1918* (1939); Columbia University, *Introduction to Contemporary Civilization in the West* (2 vols., 1954); G. H. Knoles and R. K. Snyder, *Readings in Western Civilization* (1954).

II. EUROPE FROM 1900 TO 1914

ENGLAND: General surveys of this period are R. H. Gretton, *A Modern History of the English People, 1880-1922* (1930); J. A. R. Marriott, *Modern England, 1885-1932* (1934); R. C. K. Ensor, *England, 1870-1914* (1936); and D. C. Somervell, *Modern Britain, 1870-1939* (1941). Many of the best treatments of this period are to be found in such biographies as G. Cecil, *Life of Robert, Marquis of Salisbury* (4 vols., 1921-1932); J. L. Garvin, *Life of Joseph Chamberlain* (3 vols., 1932-1934); S. Lee, *King Edward VII* (2 vols., 1925-1927); J. Spender and C. Asquith, *The Life of Herbert Henry Asquith, Lord Oxford and Asquith* (2 vols., 1932); Lord Haldane, *Autobiography* (1929); Earl Grey, *Twenty-five Years* (2 vols., 1925), and G. M. Trevelyan, *Grey of Fallodon* (1937); and, for one of the best general surveys of British prewar diplomacy, H. Nicolson, *Portrait of a Diplomatist* (1930).

FRANCE: The outstanding history of France since 1870 is D. W. Brogan, *The Development of Modern France (1870-1939)* (1940); a briefer account is R. Recouly, *The Third Republic* (1928). Other studies in this period are: C. W. Porter, *The Career of Théophile Delcassé* (1936); H. R. Weinstein, *Jean Jaurès, a Study of Patriotism in the French Socialist Movement* (1936); E. M. Sait, *Government and Politics in France* (1921); R. H. Soltau, *French Parties and Politics, 1871-1921* (rev. ed., 1930); W. L. Middleton, *The French Political System* (1932); S. Bernstein, *The Beginnings of Marxian Socialism in France* (1933); F. L. Schuman, *War and Diplomacy in the French Republic* (1931); E. M. Carroll, *French Public Opinion and Foreign Affairs, 1870-1914* (1931); T. F. Power, Jr., *Jules Ferry and the Renaissance of French Imperialism* (1944); and W. Williams, *The Tiger of France* (1949).

GERMANY: Good general accounts of Germany during this period are: R. H. Fife, *The German Empire Between Two Wars* (1916); W. H. Dawson, *The German Empire, 1867-1914* (2 vols., 1919); G. P. Gooch, *Germany* (1925). The story of Germany's rapid economic development is told in: W. F. Bruck, *Social and Economic History of Germany from William II to Hitler, 1888-1938* (1938); G. Stolper, *German Economy, 1870-1940* (1940); W. H. Dawson, *Protection in Germany; a History of German Fiscal Policy During the Nineteenth Century* (1904); E. D. Howard, *The Cause and Extent of the Recent Industrial Progress of Germany* (1907); and T. Veblen, *Imperial Germany and the Industrial Revolution* (1915). The best survey of foreign policy is E. Brandenburg, *From Bismarck to the World War, 1890-1914* (1927), and various aspects of it are discussed in M. E. Townsend, *The Rise and Fall of Germany's Colonial Empire, 1884-1918* (1930); R. J. Sontag, *Germany and England: Background of Conflict, 1848-1894* (1938); E. M. Carroll, *Germany and the Great Powers, 1866-1914: A Study in Public Opinion and Foreign Policy* (1938); and W. L. Langer, *European Alliances and Alignments* (1950).

AUSTRIA-HUNGARY: The best analysis of Hapsburg problems is to be found in O. Jaszi, *The Dissolution of the Hapsburg Monarchy* (1929), which may be supplemented by R. W. Seton-Watson, *Racial Problems in Hungary* (1908), and *The Southern Slav Question and the Hapsburg Monarchy* (1911). Foreign affairs are discussed in A. F. Pribram, *Austrian Foreign Policy, 1908-1918* (1923).

RUSSIA: While there is no general history of Russia dealing with this particular period, there are a number of valuable volumes dealing with various aspects of it. An interesting light is thrown on the last emperor in *The Letters of Tsar Nicholas and Empress Marie* (1937); and E. J. Bing, ed., *The Secret Letters of the Last Tsar* (1938). Further biographical material includes: S. Witte, *The Memoirs of Count Witte* (1921); V. N. Kokovtsev, *Out of My Past* (1933); and V. I. Gurko, *Features and Figures of the Past* (1939). A full picture of Russian life is presented in D. M. Wallace, *Russia* (2 vols., 1905) and B. Pares, *Russia and Reform* (1905).

III. INTERNATIONAL RELATIONS TO 1914

Of the many accounts dealing with European diplomacy since 1870, the following may be cited: W. S. Davis, *The Roots of the War* (1919); H. E. Barnes, *The Genesis of the World War* (1926), one of the first attempts to present a balanced view; S. B. Fay, *The Origins of the World War* (2 vols. in 1, 2nd ed., 1931), the standard account; R. B. Mowat, *The Concert of Europe* (1931). In briefer scope N. Mansergh, *The Coming of the First World War: a Study of the European Balance, 1878-1914* (1949); R. J. Sontag, *European Diplomatic History, 1871-1932* (1933); and G. P. Gooch, *Before the War; Studies in Diplomacy* (2 vols., 1936-38). Limited periods and special topics are discussed, for the earlier period, in W. L. Langer, *European Alliances and Alignments, 1871-1890* (1931), and *The Diplomacy of Imperialism, 1890-1902* (2 vols., 1935); the period of the formation of the alliances is discussed in G. L. Dickinson, *The International Anarchy, 1904-1914* (1926); E. N. Anderson, *The First Moroccan Crisis, 1904-1906* (1930); O. J. Hale, *Germany and the Diplomatic Revolution: a Study in the Diplomacy of the Press, 1904-1906* (1931); B. E. Schmitt, *Triple Alliance and Triple Entente* (1934), a brief survey, and *The Annexation of Bosnia, 1908-1909* (1937); R. P. Churchill, *The Anglo-Russian Convention of 1907* (1939); W. C. Askew, *Europe and Italy's Acquisition of Libya, 1911-1912* (1942); and E. C. Helmreich, *The Diplomacy of the Balkan Wars, 1912-1913* (1938). A number of important volumes have also been devoted to the diplomatic maneuvers during the last year of peace: P. Renouvin, *The Immediate Origins of the War* (1928); B. E. Schmitt, *The Coming of the War: 1914* (2 vols., 1930); A. von Wegerer, *A Refutation of the Versailles War Guilt Thesis* (1930); and T. Wolff, *The Eve of 1914* (1935). For other aspects of the problem, see: A. F. Pribram, *England and the International Policy of the European Great Powers, 1871-1914* (1931); R. J. Sontag, *Germany and England: Back-*

ground of Conflict, 1848-1894 (1938); E. M. Carroll, *French Public Opinion and Foreign Affairs, 1870-1914* (1930), and *Germany and the Great Powers, 1866-1914: a Study in Public Opinion and Foreign Policy* (1938); O. J. Hale, *Publicity and Diplomacy, With Special Reference to England and Germany, 1890-1914* (1940); and L. Albertini, *The Origins of the War of 1914* (2 vols. in translation, 1952-53).

IV. IMPERIALISM TO 1914

The problem of European imperialism during this period is one of the most important aspects of international relations; in addition to the general histories of diplomacy cited above, the following books deal more specifically with this problem: L. Woolf, *Economic Imperialism* (1921), and *Imperialism and Civilization* (1928); P. T. Moon, *Imperialism and World Politics* (1926), a general text; N. Lenin, *Imperialism, the Last Stage of Capitalism* (1937), representing the Marxist viewpoint; G. Clark, *A Place in the Sun* (1936), and *The Balance Sheets of Imperialism* (1936); and J. A. Hobson, *Imperialism, A Study* (3rd ed., 1938); L. C. Robbins, *The Economic Causes of War* (1939); E. M. Winslow, *The Pattern of Imperialism: a Study in the Theories of Power* (1948); R. Maunier, *The Sociology of Colonies: an Introduction to the Study of Race Conduct* (2 vols., 1949); and J. A. Schumpter, *Imperialism and Social Classes* (1955).

For imperialism in Asia, see: N. D. Harris, *Europe and the East* (1926); G. W. Keeton, *The Development of Extraterritoriality in China* (2 vols., 1928); H. B. Morse and H. F. MacNair, *Far Eastern International Relations* (1928); G. H. Blakeslee, *The Pacific Area* (1929); D. E. Owen, *Imperialism and Nationalism in the Far East* (1929); G. Bienstock, *The Struggle for the Pacific* (1937); and E. R. Hughes, *The Invasion of China by the Western World* (1938). Special aspects of Far Eastern imperialism are treated in E. S. Tai, *Treaty Ports in China* (1918); T. W. Overlach, *Foreign Financial Control in China* (1919); A. Vandenbosch, *Dutch East Indies* (1934); D. E. Owen, *British Opium Policy in China and India* (1934); W. C. Costin, Great Britain and China, *1833-1860* (1937); J. Pratt, *The Expansion of Europe in the Far East* (1947); B. H. Sumner, *Tsardom and Imperialism in the Far East and the Middle East* (1944); J. F. Cady, *The Roots of French Imperialism in Eastern Asia* (1954).

For imperialism in Africa, see: C. P. Lucas, *The Partition and Colonization of Africa* (1922); N. D. Harris, *Europe and Africa* (1927); H. L. Hoskins, *European Imperialism in Africa* (1930); L. A. C. Raphael, *The Cape to Cairo Dream: a Study in British Imperialism* (1936); and Lord Hailey, *An African Survey* (1938). Special studies in African imperialism are: E. B. Cromer, *Modern Egypt* (2 vols., 1908); L. Mitchell, *The Life of the Rt. Hon. Cecil John Rhodes, 1853-1902* (2 vols., 1910); L. S. Woolf, *Empire and Commerce in Africa* (1919); A. Schweitzer, *On the Edge of the Primeval Forest* (1922); W. P. Livingstone, *Mary Slessor of Calabar* (1925); R. L. Buell, *The Native Problems in Africa* (2 vols., 1928); R. Coupland, *The Exploitation of East Africa, 1856-1890* (1939); J. A. Noon, *Labor Problems of Africa* (1944); R. Rudin, *Germans in the Cameroons, 1884-1914; a Study in Modern*

Imperialism (1938); and M. M. Knight, *Morocco as a French Economic Venture: a Study of Open-Door Imperialism* (1937).

V. WORLD WAR I

THE FIRST WORLD WAR: The best volume on the war is C. R. M. F. Cruttwell, *History of the Great War* (1934); B. H. L. Hart, *A History of the World War, 1914-1918* (1934), and *The War in Outline, 1914-1918* (1936) are somewhat narrower in scope. Some of the most valuable accounts of the war are to be found in the memoirs. For the British: J. French (1919); J. R. Jellicoe (1919); I. Hamilton (2 vols., 1920); W. Churchill (5 vols., 1923-29); and T. E. Lawrence (1927). For the Germans: E. Ludendorff (2 vols., 1919); A. P. F. von Tirpitz (2 vols., 1919); E. von Falkenhayn (1920); A. H. R. von Kluck (1920); R. Scheer (1920); P. von Hindenburg (2 vols., 1921); and L. von Sanders (1927). For the French: H. P. Petain (1929); F. Foch (1931); and J. J. C. Joffre (2 vols., 1932). There are also a number of interesting biographies, of which the following may be noted: C. R. Ballard, *Kitchener* (1930); B. H. L. Hart, *Foch* (1931); R. Recouly, *Joffre* (1931); and K. Tschuppik, *Ludendorff* (1932). See also: Abbott, G. F., *Greece and the Allies, 1914-1922* (1922); A. Emin, *Turkey in the World War* (1930); R. Graves, *Lawrence and the Arabian Adventure* (1928); E. Ironside, *Tannenberg: the First Thirty Days in East Prussia* (1935); J. C. Adams, *Flight in Winter* (1942), a fine account of the martyrdom of Serbia; S. Tyng, *The Campaign of the Marne, 1914* (1935); L. Villari, *The War on the Italian Front* (1932); C. Domville, *Submarines and Sea Power* (1919); J. R. Jellicoe, *The Grand Fleet, 1914-1916* (1922); and A. Moorehead, *Gallipoli* (1956).

ENGLAND: Perhaps the best general account of England at war is W. S. Churchill, *The World Crisis* (5 vols., 1923-29; 1 vol. condensed ed., 1931); *The War Memoirs of David Lloyd George* (5 vols., 1933-36) is of similar scope. Special topics are discussed in H. L. Gray, *War Time Control of Industry: the Experience of England* (1918); and C. R. M. F. Cruttwell, *The Role of British Strategy in the Great War* (1936).

FRANCE AND BELGIUM: H. M. Hyndman, *The Man and His Time* (1919); G. Clemenceau, *Grandeur and Misery of Victory* (1930); G. G. Aston, *The Biography of the Late Marshal Foch* (1929); F. Foch, *Memoirs* (1931); R. Recouly, *Joffre* (1931); E. J. Galet, *Albert, King of the Belgians in the Great War* (1931); and *Cardinal Mercier's Own Story* (1920).

UNITED STATES: N. D. Baker, *Why We Went to War* (1936); B. J. Hendrick, *Life and Letters of Walter H. Page* (1922); W. Millis, *The Road to War: America, 1914-1917* (1935); C. Seymour, *Woodrow Wilson and the World War* (1922); and J. G. Harbord, *The American Army in France* (1936).

GERMANY: E. Bevan, *German Social Democracy During the War* (1919); R. H. Lutz, *The Causes of the German Collapse in 1919* (1934); A. Rosenberg, *The Birth of the German Republic* (1931); and M. Baumont, *The Fall of the Kaiser* (1931).

AUSTRIA-HUNGARY: E. Glaise Von Hostenau, *The Collapse of the Austro-Hungarian Empire* (1930); Nowak, K. F., *The Collapse of Central Europe* (1924); T. G. Masaryk, *The Making of a State* (1921); S. Burian, *Austria in Dissolution* (1925); Jas. O. Jaszi, *The Dissolution of the Hapsburg Monarchy* (1929); and J. Pilsudski, *The Memories of a Polish Revolutionary and Soldier* (1931).

RUSSIA: W. H. Chamberlin, *The Russian Revolution, 1917-1918* (2 vols., 1934); V. Chernov, *The Great Russian Revolution* (1936); M. T. Florinsky, *The End of the Russian Empire* (1931); R. Fulop-Miller, *Rasputin: the Holy Devil* (1928); E. H. Carr, *The Bolshevik Revolution, 1917-1923* (3 vols., 1951-1953); P. Kirby, *The Russian Revolution* (1940); P. Miliukov, *History of the Second Russian Revolution* (1920); N. Lenin, *Preparing for Revolt* (1929); N. Lenin, *Toward the Seizure of Power* (2 vols., 1932); D. Shub, *Lenin, a Biography* (1948); L. Trotsky, *The History of the Russian Revolution* (1934), and *My Life* (1940); J. W. Wheeler-Bennett, *Brest-litovsk: the Forgotten Peace*, March 1918 (1939); and G. F. Kennan, *Russia Leaves the War* (1956).

PEACE TREATIES: The most useful accounts of the Paris Peace Conference are: H. W. V. Temperley, *A History of the Peace Conferences of Paris* (6 vols., 1920-1924); H. Nicholson, *Peacemaking, 1919* (1933); P. Birdsal, *Versailles Twenty Years Afterward* (1941); J. M. Keynes, *Economic Consequences of the Peace* (1921); and J. M. Keynes, *A Revision of the Treaty* (1922). For a reply see: E. Mantoux, *The Carthaginian Peace, or the Economic Consequences of Mr. Keynes* (1946); H. R. Rudin, *Armistice, 1918;* G. B. Noble, *Policies and Opinions at Paris, 1919* (1935); and A. Cobben, *National Self-determination* (1944).

VI. TWENTY YEARS' TRUCE

1919 TO 1939

ENGLAND: C. F. G. Masterman, *England After the War* (1923); A. Siegfried, *Post-War Britain* (1924); W. Dibelius, *England* (1930); D. C. Somervell, *The Reign of George V* (1935); and R. Graves and A. Hodge, *The Long Week-End; A Social History of Great Britain, 1918-1939* (1941). J. Buchan, *The People's King* (1935); H. Bolitho, *King George VI* (1938); and M. Thomson, *David Lloyd George, The Official Biography* (1948), are interesting biographies. The economic crisis is dicussed in H. Heaton, *The British Way to Recovery* (1934); and the problems of post-war diplomacy are treated in: H. Nicolson, *Curzon: the Last Phase, 1919-1925: a Study in Post-War Diplomacy* (1934); R. W. Seton-Watson, *Britain and the Dictators, a Survey of Post-War British Policy* (1938), and *From Munich to Danzig* (1939); W. S. Churchill, *While England Slept; a Survey of World Affairs, 1932-1938* (1938), and *Step by Step, 1936-1939* (1939); N. Chamberlain, *The Struggle for Peace* (1939); N. Henderson, *Failure of a Mission* (1940); A. Wolfers, *Britain and France Between Two Wars* (1940); C. F. Brand, *British Labour's Rise to Power* (1941); H. Dalton, *Practical Socialism in England* (1935); G. A. Greenwood, *England Today: a Social History of Our Own Time* (1926); J. A. R.

Marriott, *A History of My Own Time* (1943); J. B. Priestley, *An English Journey* (1934); and K. Feiling, *The Life of Neville Chamberlain* (1946).

FRANCE: The best general account is D. W. Brogan, *The Development of Modern France, 1870-1939* (1940). P. Vaucher, *Post-War France* (1934); A. Werth, *France in Ferment* (1935), and *Which Way France?* (1937); M. Thorez, *France To-Day and the People's Front* (1936); G. Bruun, *Clemenceau* (1943); G. Wright, *Raymond Poincaré and the French Presidency* (1942); S. Huddleston, *Poincaré: a Biographical Portrait* (1924); and V. Thompson, *Briand, Man of Peace* (1930). For internal affairs: R. L. Buell, *Contemporary French Politics* (1920); W. Macdonald, *Reconstruction in France* (1922); J. Barthelemy, *Government of France* (1924); W. F. Ogburn, *The Economic Development of Post-War France* (1929); and D. J. Saposs, *The Labor Movement in Post-War France* (1931). And for foreign affairs: H. I. Priestley, *France Overseas: A Study of Modern Imperialism* (1938); and A. Wolfers, *Britain and France Between Two Wars* (1940); R. W. Fox, *France Faces the Future* (1936); C. J. H. Hayes, *France: a Nation of Patriots* (1930); G. Peel, *The Economic Policy of France* (1937); A. Siegfried, *France: a Study in Nationality* (1930); J. J. Spengler, *France Faces Depopulation* (1938); R. L. Stokes, *Leon Blum: Poet to Premier* (1937); and A. Werth, *France in Ferment* (1935).

BELGIUM AND THE NETHERLANDS: L. Pierard, *Belgian Problems Since the War* (1929); A. J. Barnouw, *The Making of Modern Holland* (1944); B. Landleer, ed., *The Netherlands* (1944); and H. Riemus, *The Netherlands* (1944).

GERMANY: Of the numerous discussions of post-war Germany, the following may be cited: H. Quigley and R. T. Clark, *Republican Germany* (1928); E. Luehr, *The New German Republic* (1929); R. T. Clark, *The Fall of the German Republic* (1935); A. Rosenberg, *A History of the German Republic* (1936); and, in briefer summary, F. L. Schuman, *Germany Since 1918* (1937). Special aspects of the period are treated in: R. H. Lutz, *The German Revolution, 1918-1919* (1922); R. von Kühlmann, *Thoughts on Germany* (1932); H. Kraus, *The Crisis of German Democracy* (1932); C. B. Hoover, *Germany Enters the Third Reich* (1933); J. W. Angell, *The Recovery of Germany* (2nd. ed., 1932); and A. Mendelssohn-Bartholdy, *The War and German Society* (1937). Memoirs: M. von Baden, *Memoirs* (2 vols., 1928); P. Scheidemann, *Memoirs: the Making of New Germany* (2 vols., 1929); and E. Sutton, ed., *Gustav Stresemann: His Diaries, Letters, and Papers* (3 vols., 1935-40). And biographies: R. Olden, *Stresemann* (1930); J. W. Wheeler-Bennet, *Wooden Titan* (1936), for the career of Hindenburg; R. Olden, *Hitler* (1936); and K. Heiden, *Hitler: a Biography* (1936).

The emergence of National Socialism has given rise to a great flood of controversial literature. The German views are presented in A. Hitler, *Mein Kampf* (American ed., 1939); H. Goering, *Germany Reborn* (1934); and J. Goebbels, *My Part in Germany's Fight* (1935). For critical studies of the Nazi regime, see: K. Heiden, *A History of National Socialism* (1935); F. L. Schuman, *The Nazi Dictatorship* (1935); S. H. Roberts, *The House That Hitler Built* (1937); P. F. Drucker, *The End of Economic Man: a Study of the New Totalitarianism*

(1939); H. Rauschning, *The Revolution of Nihilism* (1939), and *Hitler Speaks* (1939); O. Strasser, *Hitler and I* (1940); O. D. Tolischus, *They Wanted War* (1940); and G. Stolper, *German Economy, 1870-1940* (1940). Of the volumes published more recently, W. M. McGovern, *From Luther to Hitler* (1941); S. D. Stirk, *The Prussian Spirit, 1914-1940* (1941); and R. D'O. Butler, *The Roots of National Socialism* (1941), deal with the ideological aspects of Nazism; K. Loewenstein, *Hitler's Germany: the Nazi Background to War* (1940); and F. Neumann, *Behemoth: the Structure and Practice of National Socialism* (1942). W. E., Jr., and M. Dodd, eds., *Ambassador Dodd's Diary* (1941), by an American liberal; H. zu Lowenstein, *The Germans in History* (1945), by a German Catholic; G. Eisler and others, *The Lesson of Germany: a Guide to her History* (1945); H. Rothfels, *The German Opposition to Hitler* (1948); F. Brennecke, *The Nazi Primer*, read by all Hitler youth (1945); A. Frey, *Cross and Swastika; the Ordeal of the German Church* (1938); E. Winkler, *Four Years of Nazi Torture* (1942); and A. Wolf, *Higher Education in Nazi Germany* (1944).

ITALY, SPAIN, AND PORTUGAL: Mussolini's Fascist regime is sympathetically described in: E. W. Hulinger, *The New Fascist State* (1928); B. Mussolini, *My Autobiography* (1928); L. Villari, *The Expansion of Italy* (1930); M. I. Currey, *Italian Foreign Policy, 1918-1932* (1932); and C. Pellizzi, *Italy* (1939). Critical accounts from the democratic point of view are: G. Salvemini, *The Fascist Dictatorship in Italy* (1927), and *Under the Axe of Fascism* (1936); H. Finer, *Mussolini's Italy* (1935); G. A. Borgese, *Goliath; the March of Fascism* (1937); G. Megaro, *Italy in the Making* (1938); M. H. H. Macartney and P. Cremona, *Italy's Foreign and Colonial Policy, 1914-1937* (1938); G. T. Garratt, *Mussolini's Roman Empire* (1938); I. Silone, *The School for Dictators* (1938); and M. W. Rader, *No Compromise* (1939). Recent studies of Mussolini's Italy are: A. Rossi, *The Rise of Italian Fascism* (1938); M. Hentze, *Pre-Fascist Italy: the Rise and Fall of the Parliamentary Regime* (1939); S. W. Halperin, *Italy and the Vatican at War* (1939); and R. and E. Packard, *Balcony Empire: Italy Under Mussolini* (1942).

On Spain: E. A. Peers, *The Spanish Tragedy, 1930-1936* (1936); H. Gannes and T. Repard, *Spain in Revolt* (1936); J. Castillejo, *Wars of Ideas in Spain* (1937); F. E. Manuel, *The Politics of Modern Spain* (1938); R. Sencourt (R. E. G. George), *Spain's Ordeal* (1940); R. M. Smith, *The Day of the Liberals in Spain* (1938); E. A. Peers, *Spain in Eclipse, 1937-1943* (1943); F. J. Hamilton, *Appeasement's Child: the Franco Regime in Spain* (1943); S. de Madariaga, *Spain* (1943).

On Portugal: G. de Reynold, *Portugal* (1936); V. de Bragança-Cunha, *Revolutionary Portugal, 1910-1936* (1938); A. Ferro, *Salazar; Portugal and Her Leader* (1939); M. Derrick, *The Portugal of Salazar* (1939); and F. C. Egerton, *Salazar, Rebuilder of Portugal* (1943).

CENTRAL EUROPE: C. A. Macartney, *The Social Revolution in Austria* (1926); D. F. Strong, *Austria, October 1918-March 1919: Transition From Empire to Republic* (1939). The general problems of the heirs of the Hapsburgs are presented in: L. Pasvolsky, *Economic Nationalism in the Danubian States* (1926); R. Machray, *The Little Entente* (1929), and *The Struggle for the Danube and the Little Entente, 1929-1938* (1938); J. O. Crane, *The Little Entente* (1931); and G. E. R. Gedye, *Betrayal in Central Europe* (1939), a journalistic account. The tragic story of Austria after the war is told in: V. W. Germains, *Austria of To-Day* (1932); C. Hamilton, *Modern Austria* (1935); J. D. Gregory, *Dollfuss and His Times* (1935); J. Messner, *Dollfuss, an Austrian Patriot* (1935); M. Bullock, *Austria, 1918-1938: A Study in Failure* (1939); K. Schuschnigg, *My Austria* (1938); O. Dutch, *Thus Died Austria* (1938); and M. Fuchs, *Showdown in Vienna: The Death of Austria* (1939); K. Schuschnigg, *Austrian Requiem* (1946); R. K. Sheridan, *Kurt Von Schuschnigg* (1942).

On Hungary: P. Teleki, *The Evolution of Hungary and Its Place in European Politics* (1923), dealing with the period since 1867; O. Jászi, *Revolution and Counter-Revolution in Hungary* (1924); A. Apponyi, and others, *Justice for Hungary* (1928); *The Memoirs of Count Apponyi* (1935); C. A. Macartney, *Hungary and Her Successors: the Treaty of Trianon and Its Consequences, 1919-1937* (1937); M. A. Kobr, *Hungary's War* (1943); T. Mende, *Hungary* (1944); and G. Pálóczy-Horváth, *In Darkest Hungary* (1945).

On Czechoslovakia: F. von Lützow and H. A. Piehler, *Bohemia, an Historical Sketch* (1939), for the historical background; E. Wiskemann, *Czechs and Germans* (1938); T. G. Masaryk, *The Making of a State* (1927); A. Werner, *T. G. Masaryk* (1934); P. Crabitès, *Beneš* (1934); K. Krofta, *A Short History of Czechoslovakia* (1934); F. J. Vondracek, *The Foreign Policy of Czechoslovakia, 1918-1935* (1937); D. A. Lowrie, *Masaryk of Czechoslovakia* (1938); E. B. Hitchcock, *"I Built a Temple for Peace." The Life of Eduard Beneš* (1940); R. Freund, *Watch Czechoslovakia!* (1938). Recent books on Czechoslovakia are: E. P. Young, *Czechoslovakia: Keystone of Peace and Democracy* (1938); R. J. Kerner, ed., *Czechoslovakia* (1940), an important collection of essays; W. P. Warren, *Masaryk's Democracy* (1941); R. W. Seton-Watson, *A History of the Czechs and Slovaks* (1943); S. H. Thomson, *Czechoslovakia in European History* (1943); and E. Tabórsky, *Czechoslovak Democracy at Work* (1945).

On Poland: G. Slocombe, *History of Poland* (rev. ed., 1940); J. Pilsudski, *The Memories of a Polish Revolutionary and Soldier* (1931); E. J. Patterson, *Poland* (1934), and *Pilsudski* (1935); R. Machray, *The Poland of Pilsudski* (1937); G. Humphrey, *Pilsudski: Builder of Poland* (1936); R. Gorecki, *Poland and Her Economic Development* (1935); R. L. Buell, *Poland: Key to Europe* (1939); W. J. Rose, *Poland* (1939); and P. Super, *The Polish Tradition* (1939). The following are more recent books: W. F. Reddaway, ed., *The Cambridge History of Poland, 1697-1935* (1941); S. Segal, *The New Order in Poland* (1942); B. E. Schmitt, ed., *Poland* (1945); and K. Symonolewicz, *Studies in Nationality and Nationalism in Poland Between the Two Wars* (1944).

NORTHERN EUROPE: For the Scandinavian countries as a group, see: R. N. Bain, *Scandinavia: a Political History of Denmark, Norway and Sweden from 1513 to 1900* (1905); J. Stefansson, *Denmark and Sweden, with Iceland and Finland* (1917); B. A. Arneson, *The Democratic Monarchies of Scandinavia* (1939); K. Singer, *Duel for the Northland* (1943); and also G. Bach, *A History of Scandinavian Literature* (1932). On Sweden: C. Hallendorff and A. Schück, *History of Sweden* (1929); R. Svanström and C. Palmstierna, *A Short History of Sweden* (1934); C. Grimberg, *A History of Sweden* (1935); N. Herlitz,

Sweden: a Modern Democracy on Ancient Foundations (1939); B. Braatoy, *The New Sweden* (1939); M. M. Cole and C. Smith, eds., *Democratic Sweden* (1939); and A. Myrdal, *Nation and Family: the Swedish Experiment in Democratic Family and Population Policy* (1941).

On Norway: G. M. Gathorne-Hardy, *Norway* (1925); A. Rothery, *Norway: Changing and Changeless* (1939); and G. R. Harris, *Progressive Norway* (1939).

On Denmark: A. Rothery, *Denmark, Kingdom of Reason* (1937); J. H. S. Birch, *Denmark in History* (1938); and P. Manniche, *Denmark, a Social Laboratory* (1939).

On Finland: T. W. Atchley, *Finland* (1931); J. H. Wuorinen, *Nationalism in Modern Finland* (1931); A. E. Rothery, *Finland, the New Nation* (1936); J. H. Jackson, *Finland* (1938); H. B. Elliston, *Finland Fights* (1940); J. Langdon-Davies, *Finland: the First Total War* (1940). *The Finnish Blue Book* (1940) and *Finland Reveals Her Secret Documents* (1941) give the Finnish point of view, while the Soviet position is presented in A. Brody and others, eds., *War and Peace in Finland* (1940); and W. P. and Z. Coates, *The Soviet-Finnish Campaign: Military and Political, 1939-1940* (1942).

On Iceland: K. Gjerset, *History of Iceland* (1924); H. Lindroth, *Iceland: a Land of Contrasts* (1937); and V. Stefansson, *Iceland, the First American Republic* (1939).

RUSSIA: The controversial history of the Soviet regime is treated from different points of view in: C. B. Hoover, *The Economic Life of Soviet Russia* (1931); L. Lawton, *An Economic History of Soviet Russia* (2 vols., 1932); W. H. Chamberlin, *Soviet Russia* (1931), and *Russia's Iron Age* (1934); S. and B. Webb, *Soviet Communism: a New Civilization?* (2 vols., 1936); V. M. Dean, *Soviet Russia: 1917-1936* (1936); M. T. Florinsky, *Toward an Understanding of the U. S. S. R.* (1939); L. Fischer, *The Soviets in World Affairs* (2 vols., 1930); T. A. Taracouzio, *War and Peace in Soviet Diplomacy* (1940); F. L. Schuman, *Soviet Politics at Home and Abroad* (1946); B. Pares, *Russia and the Peace* (1944); K. Gibberd, *Soviet Russia: an Interpretation* (1943); W. Duranty, *USSR: the Story of Soviet Russia* (1944); and R. E. Lauterbach, *These Are the Russians* (1945). In a more critical tone are L. Fischer, *Men and Politics* (1941), D. J. Dallin, *Soviet Russia's Foreign Policy* (1942), *Russia and Postwar Europe* (1943), and *The Real Soviet Russia* (1944); W. H. Chamberlin, *The Russian Enigma* (1943); W. L. White, *Report on the Russians* (1945); and L. Trotsky, *Stalin* (1946). The Soviet viewpoint is presented in S. and B. Webb, *The Truth About Russia* (1942); A. L. Strong, *Peoples of the USSR* (1944); and N. Mikhailov, *The Russian Story* (1945). See also: S. N. Harper, *The Government of the Soviet Union* (1949); A. Rosenberg, *A History of Bolshevism from Marx to the First Five-Year Plan* (1934); B. Moore, Jr., *Soviet Politics: the Dilemma of Power* (1950); M. Fainsod, *How Russia Is Ruled* (1953); H. Schwartz, *Russia's Soviet Economy* (1954); N. Jasny, *The Socialized Agriculture of the U. S. S. R.* (1949); A. Arakelian, *Industrial Management in the U. S. S. R.* (1949); P. F. Anderson, *People, Church and State in Modern Russia* (1944); J. Somerville, *Soviet Philosophy: a Study of Theory and Practice* (1946); G. S. V. Counts and N. Lodge, *The Country of the Blind: the Soviet*

System of Mind Control (1949); F. Borkenau, *The Communist International* (1938); and F. Borkenau, *European Communism* (1953). On Lenin: V. Marcu, *Lenin: Thirty Years of Russia* (1928); D. S. Mirsky, *Lenin* (1931); D. Shub, *Lenin: a Biography* (1948); H. Barbusse, *Stalin: a New World Seen Through One Man* (1935); and B. Souvarine, *Stalin, a Critical Survey of Bolshevism* (1939).

SOUTHEASTERN EUROPE AND THE EASTERN QUESTION: Many aspects of the recent history of this area have been studied: H. F. Armstrong, *The New Balkans* (1926), and *Where the East Begins* (1929); H. Kohn, *Nationalism and Imperialism in the Hither East* (1932); G. Antonious, *The Arab Awakening* (1939); D. Mitrany, *The Effect of the War in Southeastern Europe* (1936); N. J. Padelford, *Peace in the Balkans* (1935); R. J. Kerner and H. N. Howard, *The Balkan Conferences and the Balkan Entente, 1930-1935* (1936); J. S. Roucek, *Politics of the Balkans* (1939); Royal Institute of International Affairs, *South-Eastern Europe: a Political and Economic Survey* (1939); and T. I. Geshkoff, *Balkan Union: a Road to Peace in Southeastern Europe* (1940). And, more recently, H. G. Wanklyn, *The Eastern Marchlands of Europe* (1941); C. A. Macartney, *Problems of the Danubian Basin* (1942); L. S. Stavrianos, *Balkan Federation* (1944); B. Newman, *Balkan Background* (1945); and, most important of all, H. Seton-Watson, *Eastern Europe Between the Wars, 1918-1941* (1945).

On Turkey: G. F. Abbott, *Turkey, Greece, and the Great Powers* (1917); A. J. Toynbee, *The Western Question in Greece and Turkey* (1922); S. P. Ladas, *The Exchange of Minorities—Bulgaria, Greece and Turkey* (1932); G. F. Hudson, *Turkey, Greece and the Eastern Mediterranean* (1939); H. N. Howard, *The Partition of Turkey: a Diplomatic History, 1913-1923* (1931); A. J. Toynbee and K. P. Kirkwood, *Turkey* (1927); T. L. Jarman, *Turkey* (1935); H. E. Allen, *The Turkish Transformation* (1935); H. Luke, *The Making of Modern Turkey* (1936); D. von Mikusch, *Mustapha Kemal* (1931); D. E. Webster, *The Turkey of Ataturk* (1939); and J. Parker and C. Smith, *Modern Turkey* (1940).

On Greece: G. F. Abbott, *Greece and the Allies, 1914-1922* (1923); P. Hibben, *Constantine I and the Greek People* (1920); H. A. Gibbons, *Venizelos* (2nd ed., 1923); S. P. P. Cosmetatos, *The Tragedy of Greece* (1928); E. G. Mears, *Greece Today* (1929); A. A. Pallis, *Greece's Anatolian Adventure and After* (1937); E. S. Forster, *A Short History of Modern Greece, 1821-1940* (1941); D. Alastos, *Venizelos* (1942); and D. Caclamanos, *Greece: the Whole Story* (1946).

On Yugoslavia: H. Baerlein, *The Birth of Yugoslavia* (2 vols., 1922); W. H. C. Price, *Serbia's Part in the War* (1918); J. Buchan, ed., *Yugoslavia* (1923); C. A. Beard and G. Radin, *Balkan Pivot: Yugoslavia* (1929); R. G. D. Laffan, *Yugoslavia Since 1918* (1929); E. J. Patterson, *Yugoslavia* (1936); and S. Graham, *Alexander of Yugoslavia* (1939); R. West, *Black Lamb and Grey Falcon* (1941); H. D. Harrison, *The Soul of Yugoslavia* (1941); L. Adamic, *My Native Land* (1943).

On Rumania: C. U. Clark, *United Roumania* (1932); J. S. Roucek, *Contemporary Roumania and Her Problems* (1932); D. Mitrany, *The Land and Peasant in Roumania* (1930); Marie, Queen of Roumania, *The Story of My Life* (1934), and *Ordeal: the Story of My Life* (1935); A. L. Easterman, *King Carol, Hitler and Lupescu* (1942); C. Kormos, *Rumania* (1944); and P. Pavel, *Why Rumania Failed* (1944).

On Bulgaria: L. Pasvolsky, *Bulgaria's Economic Position* (1930); R. H. Markham, *Meet Bulgaria* (1931); G. C. Logio, *Bulgaria, Past and Present* (1936); J. Swire, *Bulgarian Conspiracy* (1939); M. Padev, *Escape From the Balkans* (1943); and K. Todorov, *Balkan Firebrand* (1943).

On Albania: E. P. Stickney, *Southern Albania or Northern Epirus in European International Affairs, 1912-1923* (1926); J. Swire, *Albania: the Rise of a Kingdom* (1929), and *King Zog's Albania* (1937); and V. Robinson, *Albania's Road to Freedom* (1942).

THE FAR EAST: P. J. Treat, *The Far East* (1934); H. M. Vinacke, *History of the Far East in Modern Times* (2nd ed., 1936); G. N. Steiger, *A History of the Far East* (1936); P. H. Clyde, *A History of the Modern and Contemporary Far East* (1937); W. W. Willoughby, *The Sino-Japanese Controversy and the League of Nations* (1935); S. King-Hall, *Western Civilization in the Far East* (1924); E. Snow, *The Battle for Asia* (1941); H. S. Quigley, *Far Eastern War, 1937-1941* (1942); O. Lattimore, *Solution in Asia* (1945); and P. Jaffe, *New Frontiers in Asia* (1945).

On China: K. S. Latourette, *The Chinese, Their History and Culture* (2 vols., 1934), and *Development of China* (5th ed., 1937); H. M. Vinacke, *Modern Constitutional Development in China* (1920); T. T. C. Woo, *The Kuomintang and the Future of the Chinese Revolution* (1928); H. A. Van Dorn, *Twenty Years of the Chinese Republic* (1932); O. Lattimore, *Manchuria, Cradle of Conflict* (1932); T. E. LaFargue, *China and the World War* (1937); L. Sharman, *Sun Yat-Sen* (1934); P. M. Anthony, *The Political Doctrines of Sun Yat-Sen* (1937); R. Berkov, *Strong Man of China: the Story of Chiang Kai-Shek* (1938); H. K. Tong, *Chiang Kai-Shek: Soldier and Statesman* (2 vols., 1938); E. Snow, *Red Star over China* (1938); and R. T. Pollard, *China's Foreign Relations, 1917-1931* (1933). Recent books on China are: A. Clegg, *The Birth of New China, 1842-1942* (1943); G. W. Keeton, *China, the Far East and the Future* (1943); O. Lattimore, *The Making of Modern China* (1944); D. N. Rowe, *China Among the Powers* (1945); and L. K. Rosinger, *China's Crisis* (1945).

On Japan: H. Kara, *Introduction to the History of Japan* (1920); H. H. Gowen, *An Outline History of Japan* (1927); J. I. Bryan, *The Civilization of Japan* (1927); G. C. Allen, *Modern Japan and Its Problems* (1928); A. J. Brown, *Japan in the World of Today* (1928); J. E. Orchard, *Japan's Economic Position* (1930); R. H. Akazi, *Japan's Foreign Relations* (1936); A. E. Hindmarch, *The Basis of Japanese Policy* (1936); A. M. Young, *Imperial Japan, 1926-1938* (1938); H. Borton, *Japan Since 1931* (1940); and J. C. Grew, *Ten Years in Japan, 1932-1942* (1944).

INTERNATIONAL RELATIONS: The inter-war period is discussed in F. H. Simonds and B. Emeny, *The Great Powers in World Politics* (1937); W. A. Orton, *Twenty Years' Armistice, 1918-1938* (1938); R. S. Kain, *Europe: Versailles to*

Warsaw (1939); G. M. Gathorne-Hardy, *A Short History of International Affairs, 1920-1938* (1939); E. H. Carr, *The Twenty Years' Crisis, 1919-1939* (1939); R. M. Rayner, *The Twenty Years' Truce, 1919-1939* (1943); A. F. Sturmthal, *The Tragedy of European Labor, 1918-1939* (1943); and, in a somewhat lighter vein, D. Low, *Europe Since Versailles: a History in One Hundred Cartoons* (1940). The immediate background of the war is treated in F. L. Schuman, *Europe on the Eve: the Crisis of Diplomacy, 1933-1939* (1939), and *Night over Europe; the Diplomacy of Nemesis, 1939-1940* (1941); D. E. Lee, *Ten Years: the World on the Way to War, 1930-1940* (1942); and C. G. Haines and R. J. S. Hoffman, *The Origins and Background of the Second World War* (1943). The attempt to establish a permanent system of international peace is described in A. E. Zimmern, *The League of Nations and the Rule of Law, 1918-1935* (1936); J. I. Knudson, *A History of the League of Nations* (1938); M. O. Hudson, *The World Court, 1921-1938* (1938); and W. E. Rappard, *The Quest for Peace Since the World War* (1940).

The problems involved in establishing a new international system are discussed in: E. H. Carr, *Conditions of Peace* (1942); L. W. Holborn, *War and Peace Aims of the United Nations, 1939-1942* (1943); *The United Nations in the Making: Basic Documents* (1945); L. M. Goodrich and E. Hambro, *Charter of the United Nations: Commentary and Documents* (1946); and V. M. Dean, *The Four Cornerstones of Peace* (1946).

The attempt to establish a permanent system of international peace is described in: A. E. Zimmern, *The League of Nations and the Rule of Law, 1918-1935* (1936); J. I. Knudson, *A History of the League of Nations* (1938); M. O. Hudson, *The World Court, 1921-1938* (1938); W. E. Rappard, *The Quest for Peace Since the World War* (1940). Special aspects of the problem are treated in: F. W. Foster, *Europe and the German Question* (1940); A. Wolfers, *Britain and France Between Two Wars* (1940); P. Birdsall, *Versailles Twenty Years After* (1941); I. Silone, *The School for Dictators* (1938); C. K. Streit, *Union Now* (1939); M. M. Rader, *No Compromise* (1939); C. B. Hoover, *Dictators and Democracies* (1937); H. Kohn, *Revolutions and Dictatorships* (1939); E. Beneš, *Democracy Today and Tomorrow* (1939); R. B. Perry, *Shall Not Perish From the Earth* (1940); and G. A. Craig, *The Politics of the Prussian Army 1640-1945* (1955).

VII. WORLD WAR II.

GENERAL: W. S. Churchill, *The Gathering Storm, Their Finest Hour, The Grand Alliance, Closing the Ring,* and *Triumph Through Tragedy* (1948-1953). See also, W. P. Hall, *Iron Out of Calvary, an Interpretative History of the Second World War* (1950); H. C. O'Neill, *A Short History of the Second World War* (1951); C. Wilmot, *The Struggle for Europe* (1952); and A. Van Sinderen, *The Story of Six Years of Global Conflict* (1946).

EARLY STAGES OF THE WAR: W. Anders, *An Army in Exile: the Story of the Second Polish Corps* (1949); J. Bryan, *Siege of Warsaw* (1940); K. Wierzynski, *The Forgotten Battlefield; the Story of Finland* (1944); C. J. Hambro, *I Saw It Happen in Norway* (1940); A. Johnson, *Norway, Her Invasion and Occupation*

(1948); *Belgian-American Educational Foundation: the Belgian Campaign and the Surrender of the Belgian Army* (1940).

FRANCE: H. F. Armstrong, *Chronology of Failure: the Last Days of the French Republic* (1940); P. J. Philip, *France in Defeat* (1941); A. Werth, *The Twilight of France* (1942); A. Géraud (Pertinax), *The Gravediggers of France* (1944); *For All Mankind* (1946), a socialist explains France's defeat; P. Cot, *Triumph of Treason* (1944); A. Maurois, *Why France Fell* (1941); M. Weygand, *Recalled to Service* (1952); J. Flanner, *Petain: the Old Man of France* (1944); S. Huddleston, *Petain: Patriot or Traitor* (1951); C. de Gaulle, *War Memoirs, Vol. 1, 1940-1942* (1955); J. Lorraine, *Behind the Battle of France* (1943); and R. Aglion, *The Fighting French* (1943).

BRITAIN: Defense by air and by sea: P. Fleming, *Operation Sea Lion* (1957); K. Ayling, *The Story of a British Pilot Fighter* (1941); A. A. Michie and W. Graebner, *Their Finest Hour* (1941); W. Churchill, *The War Speeches of the Rt. Hon. Winston Churchill* (1953); R. Carse, *Lifeline: the Ships and Men of Our Merchant Marine at War* (1944); R. Grenfell, *The Bismarck Episode* (1949); N. Monsanirat, *Corvette Command* (1944); I. Halstead, *Heroes of the Atlantic* (1942); and F. Herman, *Dynamite Cargo* (1943).

WAR IN AFRICA AND THE BALKANS: R. Aglion, *War in the Desert: the Battle for Africa* (1941); A. G. Clifford, *The Conquest of North Africa, 1940-1943* (1943); R. Hill, *Desert Conquest* (1943); B. H. Liddell Hart, *The Rommel Papers* (1953); Viscount Montgomery, *El Alamein to the River Sangro* (1949); D. Young, *Rommel, the Desert Fox* (1950); L. White, *The Long Balkan Night* (1943); R. Mitchel, *The Serbs Chose War* (1943); B. Wason, *Miracle in Hellas: the Greeks Fight On* (1943); E. L. Easterman, *King Carol, Hitler and Lupescu* (1942); J. Hetherington, *Airborne Invasion* (1943); and T. H. Wisdom, *Wings Over Olympus: the Story of the Royal Air Force in Libya and Greece* (1942).

WAR IN THE WEST AND IN ITALY: L. E. O. Charlton, *The Royal Air Force and the U. S. A. A. F. from July 1943 to September 1945* (2 vols., 1946-1947); W. F. Craven and J. L. Cates, eds., *The Army Air Forces in World War II* (4 vols., 1948-1951); A. O. Pollard, *Bombers over the Reich* (1941); C. C. Wertenbaker, *Invasion* (1944); J. D'Arcy-Dawson, *European Victory* (1945); D. D. Eisenhower, *Crusade in Europe* (1948); J. Gunther, *D-Day: What Preceded It; What Followed It* (1944); Viscount Montgomery, *Normandy to the Baltic* (1947); G. S. Patton, Jr., *War as I Knew It* (1947); E. Pyle, *Brave Men* (1944); H. Speidel, *Rommel and the Normandy Campaign* (1950); P. Badoglio, *Italy in the Second World War* (1948); E. Linklater, *The Campaign in Italy* (1951); and R. Tregaskis, *Invasion Dairy* (1944).

WAR AND AMERICA: C. Hull, *The Memoirs of Cordell Hull* (2 vols., 1948); W. Johnson, *The Battle Against Isolation* (1944); W. S. Cole, *America First: the Battle Against Intervention, 1940-1941* (1953); T. Sherwood, *Roosevelt and Hopkins* (1951); D. M. Nelson, *Arsenal of Democracy* (1946); H. V. Morton,

Atlantic Meeting (1943); E. R. Stettinius, *Lend Lease: Weapons for Victory* (1944); S. Wells, *Seven Decisions That Shaped History* (1951); and E. L. Stimson, *On Active Service in Peace and War* (1948).

WAR IN EASTERN EUROPE: I. Ehrenburg, *The Tempering of Russia* (1944); W. E. D. Allen and P. Muratoff, *The Russian Campaigns of 1944-1945* (1946); A. Fadeev, *Leningrad in the Days of the Blockade* (1946); S. A. Kovpak, *Our Partisan Course* (1947); L. Lesueur, *Twelve Months That Changed the World* (1943); T. Plievier, *Stalingrad* (1948); A. Poliakov, *White Mammoths: the Dramatic Story of Russian Tanks in Action* (1943); B. Voyetekhov, *The Last Days of Sevastopol* (1953); and W. Anders, *Hitler's Defeat in Russia* (1953).

NAZI GERMANY AND OCCUPIED EUROPE: M. Berg, *Warsaw Ghetto* (1945); S. Christensen, *Norway Is My Country* (1943); J. A. Goris, *Belgium in Bondage* (1944); S. Gudme, *Denmark, Hitler's Model Protectorate* (1942); R. Lemkin, *Axis Rule in Occupied Europe* (1945); B. Shub, *Starvation over Europe: Made in Germany* (1943); J. Karski, *Story of a Secret State* (1943); B. Hoye and T. M. Ager, *The Fight of the Norwegian Church Against Nazism* (1943); W. Jones, *Twelve Months with Tito's Partisans* (1946); A. J. Liebling, *The Republic of Silence* (1947); and R. B. Nyquist, *Sons of the Vikings* (1943).

WAR IN THE PACIFIC: H. Abend, *Chaos in Asia* (1940); K. Matsuo, *How Japan Plans to Win* (1942); H. S. Quigley, *Far Eastern War, 1937-1941* (1942); T. A. Bisson, *America's Far Eastern Policy* (1942); H. Feis, *The Road to Pearl Harbor: the Coming of the War Between Japan and the United States* (1950); W. Millis, *This is Pearl! The United States and Japan, 1941* (1947); G. Morganstern, *Pearl Harbor: the Story of the Secret War* (1947); W. L. J. Bayler, *Last Man off Wake Island* (1943); J. Hersey, *Men on Bataan* (1942); E. B. Miller, *Bataan Uncensored* (1949); E. M. Glover, *In 70 Days: the Story of the Japanese Campaign in British Malaya* (1944); C. P. Romulo, *I Saw the Fall of the Philippines* (1943); J. Stilwell, *The Stilwell Papers* (1948); J. Wainwright, *General Wainwright's Story* (1946); J. Iseley and P. J. Crowl, *The United States Marines and the Amphibious War* (1951); R. L. Eichelberger, *Our Jungle Road to Tokio* (1950); S. Morrison, *History of United States Naval Operations in World War II* (7 vols., 1948-1953); R. Sherrod, *Tarawa: the Story of a Battle* (1944); R. Tregaskis, *Guadalcanal Diary* (1943); C. V. Woodward, *The Battle for Leyte Gulf* (1947); J. Belden, *Retreat with Stilwell* (1943); F. Owen, *The Campaign in Burma* (1946); and J. Hersey, *Hiroshima* (1946).

VIII. POST WORLD WAR II

PROBLEMS OF WORLD PEACE: A. Vanderbosch and W. N. Hogan, *The United Nations: Background, Organization, Functions, Activities* (1952); L. Holborn, *War and Peace Aims of the United Nations* (2 vols., 1934-1948); F. W. Pick, *Peacemaking in Perspective* (1950); S. E. Harris, *The European Recovery Program* (1948); C. P. Kindleberger, *The Dollar Shortage* (1951); I. Burnham, *The Struggle for the World* (1947); E. H. Carr, *The Soviet Impact on the Rest of the World* (1947); G. Stopler, *German Realities* (1948); S. Glueck, *The Nuremberg Trial and Aggressive War* (1946); R. H. Jackson, *The Case Against the Nazi War Criminals* (1946); C. Bowles, *The New Dimensions of Peace* (1955); L. B. Pearson, *Democracy in World Politics* (1955); G. L. Arnold, *The Pattern of World Conflict* (1955); A. and V. Toynbee, *The Realignment of Europe* (1955); and T. Huddleston, *Naught for Your Comfort* (1956).

POSTWAR WESTERN EUROPE: C. P. O. Clarke, *Britain Today: a Review of Current Political and Social Trends* (1951); H. Morrison, *The Peaceful Revolution* (1949); V. Cowles, *Winston Churchill: the Era and the Man* (1953); E. Watkins, *The Cautious Revolution: Britain Today and Tomorrow* (1950); F. Goguel, *France under the Fourth Republic* (1952); D. Pickles, *French Politics: the First Years of the Fourth Republic* (1953); M. Einaudi, *Christian Democracy in Italy and France* (1952); H. S. Hughes, *The United States and Italy* (1953); M. Grinbod, *The Rebuilding of Italy* (1955); and A. Werth, *France, 1940-1955* (1956).

POSTWAR CENTRAL EUROPE: W. Byford-Jones, *Berlin Twilight* (1947); F. Howley, *Berlin Command* (1950); M. Klemme, *The Inside Story of U.N.R.R.A.: an Experiment in Internationalism* (1949); D. Middleton, *The Struggle for Germany* (1949); N. Muhlen, *The Return of Germany: a Tale of Two Countries (Federal and Communist Germany)* (1953); U. S. Department of State, *East Germany under Soviet Control* (1952); K. Gruber, *Between Liberation and Liberty* (1955); and G. Bolton, *Czech Tragedy* (1955).

POSTWAR COMMUNIST LANDS: G. Counts and N. Lodge, *The Country of the Blind: the Soviet System of Mind Control* (1949); E. Crankshaw, *Cracks in the Kremlin Wall* (1951); A. K. Herling, *The Soviet Slave Empire* (1951); G. Schueller, *The Politburo* (1951); F. Rounds, Jr., *A Window on Red Square* (1953); S. M. Schwartz, *Labor in the Soviet Union* (1951); J. S. Curtiss, *The Russian Church and the Soviet State, 1917-1950* (1953); M. Fainsod, *How Russia Is Ruled* (1953); W. O. Douglas, *Russian Journey* (1956); D. D. Dallin, *The Changing World of Soviet Russia* (1956); V. Bartlett, *East of the Iron Curtain* (1950); L. Stowe, *Conquest by Terror* (1952); H. Tennyson, *Tito Lifts the Curtain* (1955); E. Hunter, *Brainwashing* (1956); and B. D. Wolfe, *Khrushchev and Stalin's Ghost* (1956).

CONTEMPORARY AFRICA: J. Gunther, *Inside Africa* (1955); S. Cloete, *African Giant* (1955); M. Slater, *The Trial of Jomo Kenyatta* (1955); A. Campbell, *The Heart of Africa* (1955); C. Dundas, *African Crossroads* (1955); A. Paton, *Cry the Beloved Country* (1950); L. Van Der Post, *Dark Eye in Africa* (1955); J. H. Oldham, *New Hope in Africa* (1955); J. Seymour, *One Man's Africa* (1955); J. F. Macdonald, *Zambesi River* (1955); H. Tingsten, *The Problem of South Africa* (1955); and T. Hodgkin, *Nationalism in Colonial Africa* (1956).

CONTEMPORARY ASIA: K. W. Bilby, *New Star in the East* (1951); G. Hoffman, *The Land and People of Israel* (1950); U. Heyd, *Foundations of Turkish Na-*

tional (1950); J. Nehru, *Independence and After* (1950); J. B. Schechtman. *Population Transfers in Asia* (1949); V. Sheean, *Lead, Kindly Light* (1949); S Hsiung, *The Life of Chiang Kai-shek* (1948); D. Wehe, *The Birth of Indonesia* (1948); P. Spear, *India, Pakistan and the West* (1949); J. F. Muehl, *Interview with India* (1950); F. Moraes, *Jawaharlal Nehru* (1956); G. F. Eliot, *Hate, Hope and High Explosives: a Report on the Middle East* (1948); G. Moorad, *Lost Peace in China* (1948); O. Lattimore, *Pivot in Asia* (1950), and *The Situation in Asia* (1949); D. Warriner, *Land and Poverty in the Middle East* (1948); E. Hunter, *Brainwashing: the Story of the Men Who Defied It* (1956); F. Hunt, *The Untold Story of General MacArthur* (1954); C. Turner, *How Communists Negotiate* (1956); K. M. Pannikar, *In Two Chinas* (1955); F. W. Fernan, *Moslems on the March* (1955); L. P. Elwell-Sutten, *Persian Oil* (1955); D. G. E. Hall, *A History of Southeast Asia* (1955); D. Woodman, *The Republic of Indonesia* (1955); J. Cameron, *Mandarin Red* (1955); M. Lindsay, *China and the Cold War* (1955); R. T. Oliver, *Syngman Rhee* (1955); and R. L. Walker, *China Under Communism* (1956).

GENERAL READING: E. H. Carr, *Studies in Revolution* (1950); G. C. D. Cole, *Meaning of Marxism* (1948); G. Hoover, *Twentieth-Century Economic Thought* (1950); and A. J. Toynbee, *War and Civilization* (1950).

Current events may best be studied in *The Annual Register, The Survey of International Affairs* (annual), *Foreign Affairs* (quarterly), and the weekly edition of *The Manchester Guardian.*

INDEX

Abetz, Otto, 226
Abdul-Aziz, 60
Abdul-Hamid II, 10, 48
Abdullah, King of Jordan, 444
Abyssinia. *See* Ethiopia
Action Française, 226
Addis Ababa, Italian interests in, 296
Adenauer, Chancellor, 480
Afghanistan, 35; Russian interests in, 58
Africa, as market, 12; European imperialism in, 27 *et seq.*, 32 *et seq.*; partition of, 32 *et seq.*; missionaries in, 46; Union of South Africa, 220; position in 1940, 336; German drives in, 362; Axis expelled from, 377; nationalism in, 468-474
Afrika Korps, 344
Afrikander nationalism, 220, 228
Air raids, in World War II, 369, 380
Airplanes, in World War I, 76
Albania, 10; uprisings in, 65; after World War I, 249; dispute with Yugoslavia, 282; Italian annexation of, 336; Russian satellite, 445
Aleutians, battle of, 367, 409
Alexander, King of Yugoslavia, 247
Alfonso, King of Spain, 238
Algeciras conference, 56
Algeria, nationalism in, 469, 470
Allies. *See specific countries*
Alsace-Lorraine, 19 *et seq.*; French interests in, 51, 53; French troubles with, 202, 204
Ambedekar, of India, 267
America. *See* United States
Amiens, battle of, 114
Angell, Norman, 2
Angora, as capital of Turkey, 253
Ankara, as capital of Turkey, 253
Anschluss, 291
Antigua, in lend-lease agreement, 334
Antisemitism, of Nazis, 190; in Palestine, 255
Antonescu, driven from office, 398

Anzac Dominions, isolation of, 217
Anzio, battle of, 390
Arab League, 439, 442
Arabi Bey, 28
Arabia, after World War I, 254
Arabs, in the Ottoman Empire, 10; in Palestine, 439, 442, 444
Arbitration, of international disputes, 2-3
Argentine, dispute over, at San Francisco Conference, 434
Argonne, battle of, 116
Armaments, conference to limit, 3
Armenia, Russian seizure of, 91; communism in, 153
Asia, as market, 12; pre-World War I European imperialism in, 27 *et seq.*, 35 *et seq.*; map of, in 1914, 42-43; after World War II, 460 *et seq.*
Asquith, Herbert, 210
Ataturk, Kemal, 153, 251
Atlantic Charter, 351
Atlantic City Conference, 432
Atlantic Defense Pact, 455; army for Western Europe, 455, 463
Atomic bomb, 430; arguments concerning, 441; hydrogen bomb, 475, 480
Atomic Energy Commission, 436
Attlee, Clement, succeeding Churchill, 435
Attu, battle of, 409
Australia, as English dominion, 220, 228; in World War II, 360; fighting in New Britain, 414; demands at San Francisco Conference, 434
Austria, 2, 17, 19; in League of Three Emperors, 48; relations with Germany, 49; in Dual Alliance, 49; in Triple Alliance, 51; war with Serbia, 67; position in 1914, 75; war with Italy, 84, 90; moves for peace in 1917, 106; surrender in World War I, 119; St. Germain treaty, 135; after World War I, 243; end of independence, 303; occupation of, 440, 454